Time Out

Amsterdam

Penguin Books

PENGUIN BOOKS

Published by the Penguin Group
Penguin Books Ltd, 27 Wrights Lane, London W8 5TZ, England
Penguin Books USA Inc., 375 Hudson Street, New York, New York 10014, USA
Penguin Books Australia Ltd, Ringwood, Victoria, Australia
Penguin Books Canada Ltd, 10 Alcorn Avenue, Toronto, Ontario, Canada M4V 3B2
Penguin Books (NZ) Ltd, 182-190 Wairau Road, Auckland 10, New Zealand

Penguin Books Ltd, Registered Offices: Harmondsworth, Middlesex, England

First published 1991
Second edition 1993
Third edition 1995
Fourth edition 1996
Fifth edition 1998
Sixth edition 2000
10 9 8 7 6 5 4 3 2 1

Colour reprographics by Westside Digital Media, 9 Bridle Lane, London W1
and Precise Litho, 34-35 Great Sutton Street, London EC1
Printed and bound by Cayfosa-Quebecor, Ctra. de Caldes, Km 3 08 130 Sta, Perpètua de Mogoda, Barcelona, Spain

Edited and designed by
Time Out Guides Limited
Universal House
251 Tottenham Court Road
London W1P 0AB
Tel + 44 (0) 20 7813 3000
Fax + 44 (0) 20 7813 6001
guides@timeout.com
www.timeout.com

Editorial

Editor Will Fulford-Jones
Deputy Editor Lily Dunn
Consultant Editor Steve Korver
Listings Editor Laura Martz
Researchers Harriet Conniff, Pip Farquharson, Rebekah McVitie, Becky Wootton
Proofreader Tamsin Shelton
Indexer Selena Cox

Editorial Director Peter Fiennes

Series Editor Ruth Jarvis
Deputy Series Editor Jonathan Cox
Editorial Assistant Jenny Noden

Design

Art Director John Oakey
Art Editor Mandy Martin
Senior Designer Scott Moore
Designers Benjamin de Lotz, Lucy Grant
Picture Editor Kerri Miles
Deputy Picture Editor Olivia Duncan-Jones
Picture Admin Kit Burnet
Scanning & Imaging Dan Conway
Ad make-up Glen Impey

Advertising

Group Advertisement Director Lesley Gill
Sales Director Mark Phillips
International Sales Manager Mary L Rega
Advertisement Sales (Amsterdam) Boom Chicago
Advertising Assistant Catherine Shepherd

Administration

Publisher Tony Elliott
Managing Director Mike Hardwick
Financial Director Kevin Ellis
Marketing Director Gillian Auld
Marketing Executive Jo Tomlin
General Manager Nichola Coulthard
Production Manager Mark Lamond
Production Controller Samantha Furniss
Accountant Bridget Carter

Features in this guide were written and researched by: Introduction Will Fulford-Jones. **History** Will Fulford-Jones, Mark Fuller, Sophie Marshall, Kees Neefjes (*Art for art's sake* Lily Dunn; *You don't know squat* Steve Korver). **Amsterdam Today** Willem de Blaauw. **Architecture** Rodney Bolt, Steve Korver (*Island life* Tim Muentzer). **Sightseeing** Steve Korver; *Museums reviewed by* Laura Martz (*Olympic Glory* Tim Muentzer). **Accommodation** Charlotte Vaudrey. **Restaurants** Steve Korver. **Bars & Cafés** Pip Farquharson, Will Fulford-Jones, Steve Korver, Laura Martz, Charlotte Vaudrey (*Use your head, Tasting room only* Steve Korver). **Coffeeshops** Pip Farquharson (*A growth industry* Steve Korver). **Shops & Services** Kate Holder (*Designs for life* Tim Muentzer; *Never say Neder again* Steve Korver). **Amsterdam by Season** Steve Korver. **Children** Tim Muentzer. **Clubs** Erin Tasmania. **Film** Willem de Blaauw. **Galleries** Steve Korver. **Gay & Lesbian** Willem de Blaauw, Pip Farquharson. **Music** Steve Korver. **Sport & Fitness** Tim Muentzer (*Blade runners* Charlotte Vaudrey). **Theatre & Dance** Maj Green, Marina Peuranen. **Trips Out of Town** Will Fulford-Jones, Laura Martz, Charlotte Vaudrey. **Directory** Willem de Blaauw, Sue Cowell, Lily Dunn, Pip Farquharson, Will Fulford-Jones, Laura Martz.

The Editor would like to thank the following: Sophie Blacksell, Isaac Davis, Paul de Lara, Lily Dunn, Pip Farquharson, Sarah Guy, Tamsin Howe, Kevin Hudson, Ruth Jarvis, Ida Jongsma and all at the Hotel de Filosoof, Steve Korver, Lesley McCave, Rebekah McVitie, Hans Olykan, Nicholas Royle.

Maps by Mapworld, 71 Blandy Road, Henley-on-Thames, Oxon RG9 1QB; Amsterdam Transport map by Studio Olykan.

Photography by Hugo Potharst except: pages 4, 5, 8, 13 (top right), 14 and 15 AKG London; page 12 Rijksmuseum Amsterdam; page 13 (left and bottom right) Bridgeman Art Library; pages 17, 18, 19, 22 and 173 Associated Press; pages 40, 55, 66 and 263 Telegraph Colour Library; pages 79, 247 and 269 Neil Setchfield; page 171 Algemeen Nederlands Persbureau; page 216 Redferns; page 223 Francesca Patella/Boosey & Hawkes.

The following photos were supplied by the featured establishments: pages 77, 85, 241, 249, 253, 256, 259, 260 and 267.

Contents

Introduction

It's no New York; nor is it even a city on the scale of Paris. With a city centre that's easily negotiable by foot, an almost complete lack of city centre traffic with more than two wheels and a population that doesn't even top three-quarters of a million, it's a long way from your traditional, run-of-the-mill buzzing urban metropolis. But even leaving aside matters of population and acreage (though despite its scaled-down size, space is short in town), Amsterdam is incomparable, implausible, a total one-off.

Youthful funseekers and ageing hippies invariably rejoice in the widespread availability of soft drugs, just as haggard-looking men in raincoats, compulsive voyeurs and bachelor partiers always finger the liberal prostitution laws and prevailing culture of naughtiness as the reason for the city's unique character. Art-lovers turn to the extraordinary concentration of great museums packed with painted treasures. Shoppers speak highly of – and spend small fortunes in – the terrific variety of markets in the city. In between mouthfuls, foodies holler about the abundance of marvellous (and marvellously cheap) eateries. Meanwhile, those just after an escape from cities where you can't see the sky for buildings nor breathe the air for pollution will swear blind that the magnificent architecture (rarely topping four storeys) and scenic, peaceful canals that ring the centre of town are what makes the city great.

The truth, of course, is that it's all of these factors and more that make Amsterdam what it is today: in a nutshell, one of the most consistently surprising, thrilling, intriguing, bloody-minded, compelling cities on earth. The sex and drugs grab the headlines, but don't make the mistake of thinking this is just one rabid Sin City. The culture will fascinate the connoisseur, but try not to leave having spent your entire visit in the sheltered confines of the Museum Quarter. The scenery and lack of traffic might delight, until you get knocked over by a fevered Dutchman speeding through town on a bicycle. It won't just be your pride that's wounded.

Contradictions abound, sure, but that's the whole damn point. If variety is the spice of life, then Amsterdam is liable to burn your mouth out. Breathe deeply...

ABOUT TIME OUT GUIDES

The sixth edition of the *Time Out Amsterdam Guide* is one of an expanding series of *Time Out* City Guides produced by the people behind London and New York's successful listings magazines. Our guides are all written and updated by resident experts who have striven to provide you with all the most up-to-date information you'll need to explore the city, whether you're a local or a first-time visitor.

THE LOWDOWN ON THE LISTINGS

Above all, we've tried to make this book as useful as possible. Addresses, telephone numbers, transport information, opening times, admission prices and credit card details are included in our listings. And, as far as possible, we've given details of facilities, services and events, all checked and correct at the time we went to press. However, owners and managers can change their arrangements at any time. Before you go out of your way, we'd advise you to telephone and check opening times, dates of exhibitions and other particulars. While every effort has been made to ensure the accuracy of the information in this guide, the publishers cannot accept responsibility for any errors it may contain.

PRICES & PAYMENT

We have noted whether venues such as shops, hotels and restaurants accept credit cards or not, but have only listed the major cards: American Express (AmEx), Diners Club (DC), MasterCard (MC) and Visa (V). Many businesses will also accept other cards, including JCB, Discover or Carte Blanche, and virtually all shops, restaurants and attractions will accept dollar or sterling travellers' cheques issued by a major financial institution such as American Express.

We have listed prices throughout this book in Dutch guilders. However, in January 2002, the single European currency will come into full effect in the Netherlands, and the guilder will be no more. In 2000, many hotels had already started listing their rates in euros, though we have decided, for the sake of consistency, to list guilder prices throughout.

> There is an online version of this guide, as well as weekly events listings for over 30 international cities, at www.timeout.com.

The prices we've supplied should be treated as guidelines, not gospel. Quite aside from a change in the national currency, fluctuating exchange rates and inflation can cause charges, in shops and restaurants particularly, to change rapidly. If prices vary wildly from those we've quoted, ask whether there's a good reason. If not, go elsewhere. Then please write and let us know. We aim to give the best and most up-to-date advice, so we always want to know if you've been badly treated or overcharged.

THE LIE OF THE LAND

While compact, the layout of Amsterdam can be a little complicated for the newcomer. In line with local practices, throughout this book, the street name has been listed first, then the house number. We've also included postcodes for any venue you might want to write to, as well as website or email addresses where possible.

TELEPHONE NUMBERS

The area code for Amsterdam is 020. All telephone numbers printed in this guide take this code, unless otherwise stated. Numbers preceded by 0800 can be called free of charge from within the Netherlands, but none can be called from outside the country. We have stipulated where phone numbers are charged at non-standard rates. For more details of phone codes and charges, *see page 288*.

ESSENTIAL INFORMATION

For all the practical information you might need for visiting the city – including visa and customs information, disabled access, emergency telephone numbers, a list of useful websites and the lowdown on the local transport network – turn to the Directory chapter at the back of this guide. It starts on page 270.

MAPS

We've included a series of fully indexed colour maps to the city at the back of this guide, as well as a map of the tram system and one of the surrounding area; they start on page 300. We've also printed a grid reference against all venues in this book that appear on the maps.

LET US KNOW WHAT YOU THINK

We hope you enjoy the *Time Out Amsterdam Guide*, and we'd like to know what you think of it. We welcome tips for places that you consider we should include in future editions and take notice of your criticism of our choices. There's a reader's reply card at the back of this book, and you can also email us at amsterdamguide@timeout.com.

Sponsors & advertisers

We would like to stress that no establishment has been included in this guide because it has advertised in any of our publications and no payment of any kind has influenced any review. The opinions given in this book are those of *Time Out* writers and entirely independent.

In Context

History

Always Europe's naughtiest town, Amsterdam's past is dotted with tales of intrigue, war, rebellion and outrage.

According to legend, Amsterdam was founded by two fishermen and a seasick dog, which ran ashore and threw up on the site of the city when their ship ran aground. The reality, sadly, is probably rather more mundane.

Though the Romans occupied other parts of Holland, they didn't reach the north. Waterlogged swampland was not the stuff empires were built on, so the legions headed elsewhere in northern Europe. Archaeologists have found no evidence of settlement at Amsterdam before AD 1000, though there are prehistoric remains further east in **Drenthe**. Amsterdam's site, in fact, was partially under water for years, and the River Amstel had no fixed course until enterprising farmers from around Utrecht began to build dykes during the 11th century. Once the peasants had done the work, the nobility took over.

During the 13th century, the most important place in the newly reclaimed area was Oudekerk aan de Amstel. In 1204, the Lord of

Amstel built a castle near this tiny hamlet on what is now the outskirts of Amsterdam. After the Amstel was dammed in about 1270, a village grew up on the site of what is now Dam Square, acquiring the name Aemstelledamme.

The Lord of Amstel at this time was Gijsbrecht, a pugnacious man continually in trouble with his liege lord, the Bishop of Utrecht, and with his nearest neighbour, Count Floris V of Holland. Tension increased in this power struggle when Floris bestowed toll rights – and some independence – on the young town in 1275. Events culminated in Floris's murder by Gijsbrecht at Muiden (where Floris's castle, **Muiderslot**, can still be seen; *see page 254*). Gijsbrecht's estates were confiscated by the Bishop of Utrecht and given to the Counts of Holland. Amsterdam has remained part of the province of North Holland ever since.

The saying goes that Amsterdam's prosperity was launched in a beer barrel. This story is based on the commercial prosperity the city enjoyed courtesy of a later Count of Holland, Floris VI, who in 1323 made Amsterdam one of only two toll points in the province for the import of brews. This was no trivial matter at a time when most people drank beer; drinking the local water, in fact, was practically suicidal. Hamburg had the largest brewing capacity in northern Europe, and within 50 years a third of that city's production was flowing through Amsterdam. Thanks to its position between the Atlantic and Hanseatic ports, the city increased its trade in an assortment of essential goods.

Though it was a major trading post, Amsterdam remained little more than a village until well into the 15th century. As late as 1425, the 'city' consisted only of a few blocks of houses with kitchen gardens and two churches, compactly arranged along the final 1,000-metre stretch of the River Amstel and bordered by what are now known as Geldersekade, Kloveniersburgwal and Singel. Virtually all these old buildings – like the Houtenhuis, still standing in the **Begijnhof** (*see page 49*) – were wooden, so fire was a constant threat; in the great fire of May 1452, three-quarters of the town was razed. Structures built after the fire had to be faced with stone and roofed with tiles or slates. These new architectural developments coincided with urban expansion, as – most notably – foreign commerce led to developments in shipbuilding.

WAR & REFORMATION

None of the wealth and glory of Amsterdam's Golden Age would have been possible without the turbulent events that preceded it. During the 16th century, Amsterdam's population increased fivefold, from about 10,000 (a low level even by medieval standards) to 50,000 by 1600. Its first major urban expansion accommodated the growth, but people flocked to the booming city only to find poverty, disease and squalor in the hastily built working-class quarters. Amsterdam's merchants, however, weren't complaining: during the 1500s, the city started to emerge as one of the world's major trading powers.

Amsterdam may have been almost autonomous as a chartered city, but on paper it was still subject to absentee rulers. Through the intricate and exclusive marriage bureau known as the European aristocracy, the Low Countries (the Netherlands and Belgium) had passed into the hands of the Catholic Austro-Spanish House of Habsburg. The Habsburgs were the mightiest monarchs in Europe and Amsterdam was a comparative backwater among their European possessions, but events in the 16th century soon gave the city a new prominence.

Amsterdam's burgeoning status as a trade centre led to the import of all kinds of radical religious ideas that were flourishing throughout northern Europe at the time, encouraged by Martin Luther's audacious condemnation of the all-powerful Catholic Church in 1517. The German princelings sided firmly with Luther, but the Habsburgs gathered all the resources of their enormous empire and set about putting the protesters back in the Catholic Church.

Though Luther's beliefs failed to catch on with locals, many people were drawn to the austere creeds of the Anabaptists and, later, Calvin. Advocating a revolutionary Christian equality, the Anabaptists insisted on adult baptism. When they first arrived from Germany in about 1530, the Catholic city fathers tolerated the new movement. But when they seized the Town Hall in 1534 during an attempt to establish a 'New Jerusalem' on the River Amstel, the authorities clamped down. The leaders were arrested and executed, signalling a period of religious repression unparalleled in the city's history. Protesters of every persuasion had to keep a low profile: 'heretics' were burned at the stake on the Dam.

After the Anabaptists were culled, Calvinist preachers came to the city from Geneva, where the movement started, and via France (the Principality of Orange, in the south of France, had links with Holland and was one of the few pockets of Protestantism outside Switzerland and parts of Germany). The arrival of the

Rebel leader **William of Orange**. *See p6.*

Calvinists, with their principles of sober, upright citizenship, caused a transformation in Amsterdam. In 1566, religious discontent erupted into what became known as the Iconoclastic Fury, the most severe of several such outbreaks in European history. In the space of two months, a spontaneous uprising led to the sacking of many churches and monasteries. As a result, Amsterdam's Zuiderkerk was allocated to the Calvinists, and Philip II of Spain decided to send an army to suppress the heresy.

ALTERED STATES

The Eighty Years' War (1568-1648) between the Habsburgs and the Dutch is often seen as a struggle for religious freedom, but there was rather more to it than that: the Dutch were, after all, looking for political autonomy from an absentee king who represented little more than a continual drain on their coffers. By the last quarter of the 16th century, Philip II of Spain was fighting wars against England (to which he sent his Armada) and France, in the East against the Ottoman Turks, and in the New World, for control of his colonies. The last thing he needed was a revolt in the Low Countries.

During the revolt, Amsterdam toed the Catholic line, ostensibly supporting Philip II until it became clear that he was losing. Only in 1578 did the city patricians side with the rebels, who were led by the first William of Orange. The city and William then combined to expel the Catholics and dismantle their institutions in

Key events

EARLY HISTORY
1204 Gijsbrecht van Amstel builds a castle in the coastal settlement that is eventually to become Amsterdam.
1270 The River Amstel is dammed at Dam Square.
1275 Count Floris V grants Aemstelledamme a toll privilege charter, the first historical record of Amsterdam.
1300 Amsterdam is granted city rights by the Bishop of Utrecht.
1306 Work begins on the Oude Kerk.
1313 The Bishop of Utrecht grants Aemstelledamme full municipal rights and leaves it to William III of Holland.
1342 The city walls (*burgwallen*) are built.
1421 The St Elizabeth's Day Flood occurs, as does Amsterdam's first great fire.
1452 Fire destroys most of the city's wooden houses. Building with slate and stone becomes obligatory.
1489 Maximilian grants Amsterdam the right to add the imperial crown to its coat of arms.

WAR & REFORMATION
1534 Anabaptists try to seize City Hall but fail. A period of anti-Protestant repression begins.
1562 Amsterdam has 5,728 houses and 30,000 inhabitants.
1565 A crop failure causes famine among Calvinist workers; William the Silent organises a Protestant revolt against Spanish rule.
1566 The Beeldenstorm (Iconoclastic Fury) is unleashed. Protestant worship is authorised in public for the first time.

1568 The Eighty Years' War with Spain begins.
1577 The Prince of Orange annexes the city.
1578 Catholic Burgomasters and officials are replaced with Protestants in a coup known as 'The Alteration'.
1579 The Union of Utrecht is signed, allowing freedom of religious belief but not of worship.
1585 Antwerp falls to Spain; there is a mass exodus to the north.

THE GOLDEN AGE
1602 Inauguration of Verenigde Oost Indische Compagnie (VOC).
1606 Rembrandt van Rijn is born.
1609 Amsterdam Exchange Bank is established.
1611 Zuiderkerk is completed.
1613 Construction of the western stretches of Herengracht, Keizersgracht and Prinsengracht begins.
1621 The West Indische Compagnie (WIC) is inaugurated.
1623 WIC colonises Manhattan Island; Peter Stuyvesant founds New Amsterdam in 1625.
1642 Rembrandt finishes the *Night Watch*.
1648 The Treaty of Münster is signed, ending war with Spain. Jacob van Campen starts to build the City Hall on Dam.
1654 England declares war on the United Provinces.
1667 England and the Netherlands sign the Peace of Breda.

DECLINE & FALL
1672 England and the Netherlands go to war; Louis XIV of France invades the Netherlands.

what came to be called the Alteration. A year later, too, the Protestant states of the Low Countries united in opposition to Philip when the first modern-day European Republic was born at the Union of Utrecht. The Republic of Seven United Provinces was made up of Friesland, Gelderland, Groningen, Overijssel, Utrecht, Zeeland and Holland. Though lauded as the start of the modern Netherlands, it wasn't the unitary state that William of Orange had wanted, but rather a loose federation with an impotent States General assembly.

Each province appointed a Stadhouder (or 'viceroy'), who commanded the Republic's armed forces and had the right to appoint some of the cities' regents or governors. The Stadhouder of each province sent delegates to the assembly,

held at the **Binnenhof** in The Hague (*see page 258*). The treaty enshrined freedom of conscience and religion, apart from for Catholics (at least until the Republic's end in 1795).

CALVIN & NOBS

From its earliest beginnings, Amsterdam had been governed by four Burgomasters – mayors, basically – and a city council representing citizens' interests. By 1500, though, city government had become an incestuous business: the city council's 36 members were appointed for life, and themselves 'elected' the mayors from among their own ranks. Selective intermarriage meant that the city was, in effect, governed by a handful of families. When Amsterdam joined the rebels in 1578, the only

1674 West Indies Company is dismantled.
1675 The Portuguese Synagogue is completed.
1685 French Protestants take refuge after the revocation of the Edict of Nantes.
1689 William of Orange becomes King William III of England.
1696 Undertakers riot against wedding and funeral tax.
1787 Frederick William II, King of Prussia, occupies Amsterdam in support of his brother-in-law.
1795 French Revolutionary armies are welcomed to Amsterdam by the Patriots. The Batavian Republic is set up and administered from Amsterdam.
1806 Napoleon's brother is made King of the Netherlands.
1811 King Louis is removed from the Dutch throne.
1813 Unification of the Netherlands. Amsterdam is no longer a self-governing city.
1815 Amsterdam becomes capital of Holland.

BETWEEN THE OCCUPATIONS

1824 The Great North Holland Canal is completed.
1848 The city's ramparts are pulled down.
1876 Noordzee Kanaal links Amsterdam with the North Sea.
1877 Gemeentelijk Universiteit (later UvA) is set up, followed in 1880 by the Vrije Universiteit Amsterdam.
1880s Oil is discovered on the east coast of Sumatra. The Royal Dutch Company (Shell Oil) is founded.
1883 Amsterdam holds the World Exhibition.

1887 The Rijksmuseum is completed.
1889 Centraal Station opens.
1922 Women are granted the vote.
1928 The Olympics are held in Amsterdam.
1934 Amsterdam has a population of 800,000.

WORLD WAR II

1940 German troops invade Amsterdam.
1941 The February Strike ensues, in protest against the deportation of Jews.
1944-5 Over 2,000 people die in the Hunger Winter.
1945 Canadian soldiers free Amsterdam.
1947 Anne Frank's diary is published.

THE POST-WAR ERA

1966 The marriage of Princess Beatrix and Prince Claus ends in riots.
1968 The IJ Tunnel opens.
1973 Amsterdam's football team, Ajax, win the European Cup for the third successive year.
1975 Cannabis is decriminalised.
1978 First Metrolijn (underground) opens.
1980 Riots on Queen Beatrix's Coronation Day (30 April) in Nieuwe Kerk. This day becomes National Squatters' Day.
1986 The Stopera is built amid much controversy.
1992 Boeing 747 crashes into a block of flats in Bijlmermeer.
1997 The Euro is approved as the single European currency in the Treaty of Amsterdam.
1999 Prostitution is finally made legal after years of mere decriminalisation; the newly revamped Museumplein opens.

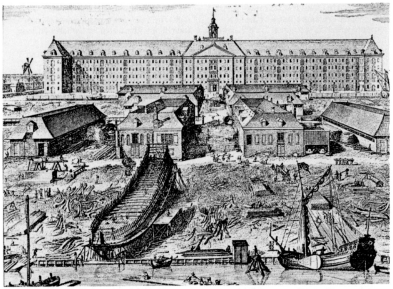

Joseph Mulder's 1694 copper engraving of the **East India Company Shipyard**.

change in civic administration was that the Catholic elite was replaced by a Calvinist faction comprising equally wealthy families.

> **'The Regents would not tolerate any kind of excess: crime, drunkenness and immorality were all punishable by a spell in a house of correction.'**

However, social welfare was transformed. Formerly the concern of the Catholic Church, welfare under the Calvinists was incorporated into government. The Regents, as the Calvinist elite became known, took over the convents and monasteries, starting charitable organisations such as orphanages. But the Regents' work ethic and abstemious way of life would not tolerate any kind of excess: crime, drunkenness and immorality were all condemned and punishable by a spell in a house of correction.

During the two centuries before the Eighty Years' War, Amsterdam had developed a powerful maritime force, expanding its fleet and broadening its trading horizons to include Russia, Scandinavia and the Baltic States. Even so, it remained overshadowed by Antwerp until 1589, when that city fell to the Spanish.

The Habsburg Spanish, rather than engaging in pitched battles, adopted siege tactics, primarily in what is now Belgium. Amsterdam, therefore, was unaffected by the hostilities, and benefited from the crippling blockades suffered by rival commercial ports. Thousands of refugees fled north, including Antwerp's most prosperous Protestant and Jewish merchants. These refugees brought with them the skills, the gold and, most famously, the diamond industry that would set Amsterdam on course to becoming the greatest trading city in the world and herald the beginning of what came to be known as the Golden Age.

THE GOLDEN AGE

European history seems to be littered with Golden Ages, but in Amsterdam's case, the first six decades of the 17th century truly deserve the title. The small city on the Amstel came to dominate world trade and establish important colonies, resulting in a population explosion and a frenzy of urban expansion in Amsterdam: the elegant girdle of canals around the city centre was one of the great engineering feats of that century. This all happened while the country was at war with Spain, the century's ailing superpower, while the country was presided over not by kings, but by businessmen.

The East India Company doesn't have much of a ring to it, but the name of the mighty Verenigde Oost Indische Compagnie (VOC), the world's first ever transnational company, definitely loses something in translation. The VOC was initially created by a States General charter in 1602 to finance the wildly expensive and hellishly dangerous voyages to the East. Drawn by the potential fortunes to be made out of trade in spices and silk, the shrewd Dutch saw sense in sending out merchant fleets, but they also knew that one disaster could leave an individual investor penniless. As a result, the main cities set up trading 'chambers', which evaluated the feasibility (and profitability) of ventures, then sent ships eastwards. The power of the VOC was far-reaching: it had the capacity to found colonies, establish its own army, declare war and sign treaties. The VOC's history is well charted in the **Nederlands Scheepvaart Museum** (*see page 76*).

The story of Isaac Lemaire, whose name was to become immortalised in atlases, is a good illustration of just how powerful the VOC became. Lemaire fled to Amsterdam from Antwerp in 1589 and became a founder member of the VOC, initially investing *f*90,000 in the company (over *f*90 million in today's money). Later, after being accused of embezzlement, he was forced to quit the company, and cast around for ways to set up on his own. However, the VOC had a monopoly on trade with the East via the Cape of Good Hope, and, at that time, there was no alternative route.

Lemaire was not so easily beaten, and heard Portuguese seamen claiming the Cape route was not the only passage to the East: they believed the fabulous spice islands of Java, the Moluccas and Malaya could also be reached by sailing to the tip of South America, where a strait would lead into the Pacific. In 1615, Lemaire financed a voyage, led by one of his sons, that discovered the strait that still bears his name.

While the VOC concentrated on the spice trade, a new company received its charter from the Dutch Republic in 1621. The Dutch West India Company (West Indische Compagnie, or WIC), though not as successful as its sister, dominated trade with Spanish and Portuguese territories in Africa and America, and in 1623 began to colonise Manhattan Island. The settlement was laid out on a grid system similar to Amsterdam's, and adopted the Dutch city's name. New Amsterdam flourished, and areas were named after other enterprising towns with a stake in the colony: the New York boroughs of Harlem and Brooklyn are named after Haarlem and Breukelen, while Staten Island took its moniker in honour of the States General, the 'national' council of the Republic.

However, the name didn't last. After the Duke of York's invasion in 1664, the peace treaty between England and the Netherlands determined that New Amsterdam would change its name to New York and come under British control. The Dutch got Surinam as a feeble consolation prize.

Though commerce with the Indies became extensive, it never surpassed Amsterdam's European business: the city had soon become the major European centre for distribution and trade. Grain from Russia, Poland and Prussia, salt and wine from France, cloth from Leiden and tiles from Delft all passed through the port. Whales were hunted by Amsterdam's fleets, generating a flourishing soap trade, and sugar and spices from Dutch colonies were distributed to ports throughout Scandinavia and the north of Europe. All this activity was financed by the Bank of Amsterdam, which had been set up in the cellars of the City Hall by the municipal council as early as 1609. It was a unique initiative and led to the city being considered the money vault of Europe, its notes readily exchangeable throughout the trading world. Single European Currency, eat your heart out…

WHERE THERE'S A WILL

The political structure of the young Dutch Republic was complex. When the Treaty of Utrecht was signed in 1579, no suitable monarch or head of state was found, so the existing system was adapted to fit new needs. The seven provinces were represented by a 'national' council, the States General. In addition, the provinces appointed a Stadhouder.

The most popular and obvious choice for Stadhouder after the treaty was William of Orange, the wealthy Dutchman who had led the rebellion against Philip II of Spain. William was then succeeded by his son, Maurits of Nassau, who was as militarily successful against the Spanish as his father had been, eventually securing the Twelve Years' Truce (1609-21). Though each province could, in theory, elect a different Stadhouder, in practice they usually chose the same person. After William's popularity, it soon became something of a tradition to elect an Orange as Stadhouder, and by 1641 the family had become sufficiently powerful for William II to marry a British princess, Mary Stuart. It was their son, William III, who, backed by Amsterdam money, set sail in 1688 to accept the throne of England in the so-called Glorious Revolution.

But the Oranges weren't popular with everyone. The provinces' representatives at the States General were known as regents, and Holland's – and therefore Amsterdam's – regent was in a powerful enough position to challenge the authority and decisions of the Stadhouder. This power was eventually exercised in 1650, in a crisis precipitated by Holland's decision to disband its militia after the end of the Eighty Years' War with Spain. Stadhouder William II wanted the militia maintained – and, importantly, paid for – by Holland, and in response to the disbandment, he got a kinsman, William Frederick, to launch a surprise attack on Amsterdam.

'Anyone who made enough money could become a member of Amsterdam's ruling assembly.'

After William II died three months later, the leaders of the States of Holland called a Great Assembly of the provinces. Even though there was no outward resistance to the Williams' earlier attack on the city, the provinces – with the exception of Friesland and Groningen, which remained loyal to William Frederick – decided that there should be no Stadhouders, and Johan de Witt, Holland's powerful regent, swore no prince of Orange would ever become Stadhouder again. This became law in the Act of Seclusion of 1653.

During this era, Amsterdam's ruling assembly, the Heren XLVIII (a sheriff, four mayors, a 36-member council and seven jurists), kept a firm grip on all that went on both within and without the city walls. Though this system was self-perpetuating, these people were merchants rather than aristocrats, and anyone who made enough money could, in theory, become a member. The mayors and the council usually came from a handful of prominent families, the most powerful being the Witsen, Bicker, Six and Trip families; all are still commemorated with Amsterdam street names.

The less elevated folk – the craftsmen, artisans and shopkeepers – were equally active in maintaining their position. A system of guilds had developed in earlier centuries, linked to the Catholic Church, but under the new order, guilds were independent organisations run by their members. The original Amsterdammers – known as *poorters* from the Dutch for 'gate', as they originally lived within the gated walls of the city – began to see their livelihoods threatened by an influx of newcomers who were prepared to work for lower wages.

Things came to a head when the shipwrights began to lose their trade to less expensive competitors in the nearby Zaan region and protested vigorously to the powers that be. The shipwrights' lobby was so strong that the city regents decreed that Amsterdam ships had to be repaired in Amsterdam yards. This kind of protectionism extended to almost all industrial

sectors in the city and effectively meant most crafts became closed shops. Only poorters, or those who had married poorters' daughters, were allowed to join a guild, thereby protecting Amsterdammers' livelihoods and, essentially, barring outsiders from joining their trades.

GROWING PAINS

Though Amsterdam's population had grown to 50,000 by 1600, this was nothing compared with the next 50 years, when it ballooned fourfold. Naturally, the city was obliged to expand to fit its new residents. The most elegant of the major canals circling the city centre was Herengracht (Lords' Canal): begun in 1613, this was where many of the Heren XLVIII had their homes. So there would be no misunderstanding about who was most important, Herengracht was followed further out by Keizersgracht (Emperors' Canal) and Prinsengracht (Princes' Canal). Immigrants were housed more modestly in the Jordaan.

Despite the city's wealth, and the reputation of its people as masters of transport – they could, in theory, have food supplies shipped in – famine hit Amsterdam with dreary regularity in the 17th century. Guilds had benevolent funds set aside for their members in times of need, but social welfare was primarily in the hands of the ruling merchant class. Amsterdam's elite was noted for its philanthropy, but only poorters were eligible for assistance: even they had to fall into a specific category, described as 'deserving poor'. Those seen as undeserving were sent to a house of correction. The initial philosophy behind these places had been rather idealistic, and they were run on the premise that hard work would ultimately produce reformed, useful citizens. But soon, the institutions became little more than prisons.

Religious freedom was still not what it might have been, either. As a result of the Alteration of 1578, Roman Catholic worship was banned in the city during the 17th century, and Catholics were left to practise their faith in secret, if they dared practise at all. Some Catholics started attic churches, which are exactly what their name suggests they might be: of the several set up in the city during the 1600s, the **Museum Amstelkring** has preserved Amsterdam's only surviving example – Our Lord in the Attic – in its entirety (*see page 46*).

DECLINE & FALL

Though Amsterdam remained one of the wealthiest cities in Europe until the early 19th century, its dominant trading position was lost to England and France after 1660. The United Provinces then spent a couple of centuries bickering about trade and politics with Britain and the other main powers. Wars were frequent:

major sea conflicts included battles against the Swedes and no fewer than four Anglo-Dutch wars, from which the Dutch came off worse. It wasn't that they didn't win any wars; more that the small country ran out of men and money.

Despite – or perhaps because of – its history with the Orange family, Amsterdam became the most vocal opponent to the family's attempt to acquire kingdoms, though it supported William III when this Orange crossed the sea to become King of England in 1688. The city fathers believed a Dutchman on their rival's throne could only be an advantage, and for a while they were proved right. However, William was soon back in Amsterdam looking for more money to fight even more wars, this time against France.

The admirals who led the wars against Britain are Dutch heroes, and the **Nieuwe Kerk** (*see page 40*) has monuments to admirals Van Kinsbergen (1735-1819), Bentinck (1745-1831) and, most celebrated of all, Michiel de Ruyter (1607-76). The most famous incident, though not prominent in British history books, was during the Second English War (1664-7), when de Ruyter sailed up the Thames to Chatham, stormed the dockyards and burnt the *Royal Charles*, the British flagship, as it lay at anchor. The *Royal Charles*' coat of arms was stolen, and is now displayed in the **Rijksmuseum** (*see page 67*).

Despite diminished maritime prowess, Amsterdam retained the highest standard of living of all Europe until well into the 18th century. The Plantage district was a direct result of the city's prosperity, and tradesmen and artisans flourished: their role in society can still be gauged by the intricate shapes and carvings on gablestones.

The Dutch Republic also began to lag behind the major European powers in the 18th century. The Agricultural and Industrial Revolutions didn't get off the ground in the Netherlands until later: Amsterdam was nudged out of the shipbuilding market by England, and its lucrative textile industry was lost to other provinces. However, the city managed to exploit its position as the financial centre of the world until the final, devastating Anglo-Dutch War (1780-84). The British hammered the Dutch merchant and naval fleets, crippling the profitable trade with their Far Eastern colonies.

The closest the Dutch came to the Republican movements of France and the United States was with the Patriots. During the 1780s, the Patriots managed to shake off the influence of the Stadhouders in many smaller towns, but in 1787 they were foiled in Amsterdam by the intervention of the Prince of Orange and his brother-in-law, Frederick William II, King of Prussia. Hundreds of Patriots then fled to exile

in France, where their welcome convinced them that Napoleon's intentions towards the Dutch Republic were benign. In 1795, they returned, backed by a French army of 'advisers'. With massive support from Amsterdam, they celebrated the new Batavian Republic.

It sounded too good to be true, and it was. According to one contemporary, 'The French moved over the land like locusts.' Over f100 million (about f1 billion today) was extracted from the Dutch, and the French also sent a standing army, all 25,000 of whom had to be fed, equipped and billeted by their Dutch 'hosts'. Republican ideals seemed hollow when Napoleon installed one of his brothers, Louis, as King of the Netherlands in 1806, and the symbol of Amsterdam's mercantile ascendancy and civic pride, the City Hall of the Dam, was requisitioned as the royal palace. Even Louis was disturbed by the impoverishment of a nation that had been Europe's most prosperous. However, after Louis had allowed Dutch smugglers to break Napoleon's blockade of Britain, he was forced to abdicate in 1810 and the Low Countries were absorbed into the French Empire.

> **'By the late 19th century, the city had begun to modernise production of the luxury goods for which it would become famous.'**

Even so, government by the French wasn't an unmitigated disaster for the Dutch. The foundations of the modern Dutch state were laid in the Napoleonic period, a civil code was introduced and education improved. Conversely, though, trade with Britain ceased, and the growing price of Napoleon's wars prompted the Dutch to join the revolt against France. After Napoleon's defeat, Amsterdam became the capital of a constitutional monarchy, incorporating what is now Belgium; William VI of Orange was crowned King William I in 1815. But though the Oranges still reign in the northern provinces, the United Kingdom of the Netherlands, as it then existed, was to last only until 1830.

BETWEEN THE OCCUPATIONS

When the French were finally defeated and left Dutch soil in 1813, Amsterdam emerged as the capital of the new kingdom of the Netherlands but very little else: extraordinarily, the city wasn't even the seat of government. With its coffers almost totally depleted and its colonies occupied by the British, Amsterdam would have to fight hard for recovery.

The fight was made tougher by two huge obstacles. For a start, Dutch colonial assets had been reduced to present-day Indonesia (then the Dutch East Indies), Surinam and the odd island in the Caribbean. Just as important, though, was the fact that the Dutch were slow to join the Industrial Revolution. The Netherlands had – indeed, still has – few natural resources to exploit and Dutch business preferred to keep its hands clean by relying on the power of sail. Add to all this the inconvenient fact that Amsterdam's opening to the sea, the Zuider Zee, was too shallow to accommodate the new, larger, steamships, and it's easy to see how the Dutch were forced to struggle.

In an attempt to link the city to the North Sea port of Den Helder, the circuitous Great North Holland Canal was dug in 1824. But because it had so many bridges and locks, it was slow and expensive, both to construct and to use. Rotterdam took over the capital's position as the most progressive industrial centre.

Prosperity, though, returned to Amsterdam after the 1860s. The city readjusted its economy to meet modern demands, and its trading position was greatly improved by the building of two canals. The opening of the Suez Canal in 1869 sped up the passage to the Orient, producing a giant increase in commerce. But what the city needed most was easy access to the major shipping lanes of northern Europe. When it was opened in 1876, the North Sea Canal enabled Amsterdam to take advantage of German industrial trade and to become the Netherlands' greatest shipbuilding port again, at least temporarily. Industrial machinery was introduced late to Amsterdam. However, by the late 19th century, the city had begun to

Art for art's sake

During the late 19th century, Amsterdam became one of Europe's most prosperous cities. Commerce was on the up, thanks to the opening of the North Sea Canal. In addition, the city got two new museums, the **Rijksmuseum** (completed 1887; see page 67) and the **Stedelijk Museum** (completed 1895; see page 68). Both were popular from the off, and helped cement Amsterdam's reputation as a city thriving culturally and commercially.

The reputation has stuck. The Rijks and the Stedelijk were joined by the **Van Gogh Museum** (see page 68), and together have made Museumplein one of the city's most popular spots. Here's our pick of some highlights…

The Rijksmuseum is where to go to see Dutch traditions and history in visual form. It holds Holland's biggest collection of artefacts and fine art, including an array of Rembrandt prints and paintings along with a number of works by **Johannes Vermeer** (1632-1675), the king of the honest representation of 17th-century domestic Dutch life. *The Kitchen Maid* (pictured left; 1658-60) is a classic Vermeer: a working woman is depicted in a strong and direct fashion, drawing the viewer into her everyday mundanities and thus raising the status of domesticity. The subdued colouring is typical of Dutch painting of this period, a tradition that was later explored in Vincent Van Gogh's early work before he moved to France where, influenced by the brighter and clearer light, his painting developed into the more expressionist art for which he became famous.

During a spate in Arles in the late 1880s, **Vincent Van Gogh** (1853-1890) painted a series of sunflower paintings to decorate the room where his friend **Paul Gauguin** was to stay on a prospective visit. He completed only four of a planned 12, only two of which he felt were good enough to hang in Gauguin's bedroom. He later painted three copies of these paintings; *Sunflowers* (pictured above modernise production of the luxury goods for which it would become famous: chocolates, cigars, beer and cut diamonds.

Of course, not all of Amsterdam's trade was conducted on water. Though there had been a local railway track between Haarlem and Amsterdam since 1839, the city finally got a major rail link and a new landmark in 1889. **Centraal Station** was designed by influential architect PJH Cuypers in 1876, and was initially intended to be in the Pijp. When it was decided that the track should run along the Zuider Zee, shutting the city off from its seafront, much objection ensued. There was also controversy when the **Rijksmuseum** (*see page 67*) was situated at what was then the fringe of the city, and about the selection of Cuypers as its architect. The result was, like Centraal Station, uniquely eclectic and led to the museum being

ridiculed as a 'cathedral of the arts' – a not entirely inappropriate label, given the contemporary boom in culture.

The city's powers decided to consolidate Amsterdam's position at the forefront of Europe, both commercially and culturally, with the building of a number of landmark structures. In 1877, the Carré Theatre opened, followed in 1894 by the **Stadsschouwburg** (*see page 239*), in 1895 by the **Stedelijk Museum** (*see page 68*) and, in 1926, the Tropen Institute (now the **Tropenmuseum**; *see page 54*). The city's international standing had soon improved to such a point that in 1928, it hosted the Olympics.

The story of diamonds in Amsterdam, meanwhile, acts as the history of social change in the city. The first records of diamond-working in Amsterdam date back to 1586, and, latterly, fabulous stones such as the Koh-i-Noor

left; 1889), now hanging in the Van Gogh Museum, being one of them.

Gauguin loved Van Gogh's sunflowers, and depicted Van Gogh in a moment he thought typical of his friend. *Vincent van Gogh Painting Sunflowers* (pictured above right; 1888) is a wonderful painting for its significant subject matter, but also in its stunning composition and use of colour: the sunflowers dance with a life of their own, just as they do in Van Gogh's famous paintings of the same subject.

Fans of abstract art will love the Stedelijk, whose displays concentrate on the last half of the 20th century. Here you'll see works by the likes of De Kooning, Lichtenstein and Warhol as well as an excellent collection by Russian artist **Kazimir Malevich** (1875-1935). Hailed as one of the most

important pioneers of geometric abstract art, Malevich strove to produce cerebral, unobjective compositions, to achieve 'the supremacy of pure feeling' through his art. And so was formed Suprematism, of which *Suprematist Composition* (pictured below; 1915) is a prime example.

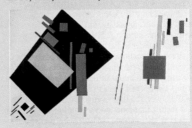

National Socialist Party propaganda from 1942. *See p15.*

(Mountain of Light), one of the British crown jewels, were cut by an Amsterdammer. But as the industry was dependent upon the discovery of rare stones, it was in a constant state of flux. In the early 1870s, diamond cutters could light cigars with ƒ10 notes (the average weekly wage for the rest of the workforce was ƒ8). A decade later, the city prohibited diamond workers from begging naked in the streets. Thankfully for the impoverished diamond workers, however, the working classes had become more politicised in the intervening years, and the ideas behind the old guild system took on a new resonance. Funds were established to protect diamond workers during slumps, a movement that led to the formation of the first Dutch trade union.

In the early days of the union movement, socialists and the upper classes co-existed relatively harmoniously, but by the 1880s things were changing. The movement found an articulate leader in Ferdinand Domela Nieuwenhuis, who set up a political party, the Social Democratic Union. The SDU faded into obscurity after a split in 1894, but a splinter group, the Social Democratic Labour Party (SDAP), won the first ever socialist city-council seat for the diamond workers' union chief, Henri Polak, in 1901. The SDAP went on to introduce the welfare state after World War II.

NEW DEVELOPMENTS

Amsterdam's population had stagnated at around 250,000 for two centuries after the Golden Age, but between 1850 and 1900 it more than doubled. The increased labour force was desperately needed to meet the demands of a revitalised economy, but the major problem was how to house the new workers. Today, the old inner city quarters are desirable addresses, but they used to be the homes of Amsterdam's poor. The picturesque Jordaan, where riots broke out with increasing regularity in the 1930s, was occupied primarily by the lowest-paid workers, canals were used as cesspits, and the mortality rate was high. Oddly, the Jordaan was the first area in the city to have tarmac streets. The decision wasn't philanthropic, however: it came after Queen Wilhelmina had been pelted by Jordaan cobblestones.

Around the old centre, new neighbourhoods were constructed. The new housing developments – the Pijp, Dapper and Staatslieden quarters – weren't luxurious by any means, and most were cheaply built by speculators, but at least they had simple lavatory facilities (though no bathrooms). Wealthier city-dwellers, meanwhile, found elegance and space in homes built around Vondelpark and in the south of the city.

The city didn't fare badly in the first two decades of the 20th century, but Dutch neutrality during World War I brought problems. While the elite lined their pockets selling arms, the poor were confronted with continual food shortages. In 1917, with food riots erupting, especially in the Jordaan, the city had to open soup kitchens and introduce rationing. The army was called in to suppress another outbreak of civil unrest in the Jordaan in 1934. This time the cause was unemployment, endemic throughout the industrialised world after the Wall Street Crash of 1929: historians estimate that in 1936, 19 per cent of the workforce was unemployed.

Unfortunately, the humiliation of means testing for unemployment benefit meant that many families suffered in hungry silence. Many Dutch workers even moved to Germany where National Socialism was creating new jobs. At home, Amsterdam initiated extensive public works under the 1934 General Extension Plan, whereby the city's southern outskirts were developed for public housing. The city was just emerging from the Depression by the time the Nazis invaded in May 1940.

WORLD WAR II

Amsterdam endured World War II without being flattened by bombs, but its buildings, infrastructure and inhabitants were reduced to a terrible state by Nazi occupation. The Holocaust also left an indelible scar on a city whose population in 1940 was ten per cent Jewish.

Early in the morning of 10 May 1940, German bombers mounted a surprise attack on Dutch airfields and military barracks in order to destroy the Dutch Air Force. The government and people had hoped that the Netherlands could remain neutral, as they had in World War I, so the armed forces were unprepared for war. Even when it became apparent that this would not be so, the Dutch aimed to hold off the Germans until the British and French could come to their assistance. Their hope was in vain, though, and Queen Wilhelmina and the government fled to London to form a government in exile, leaving Supreme Commander Winkelman in charge of state authority.

Rotterdam, too, was destroyed by bombing, and when the Germans threatened other cities with the same treatment, Winkelman gave up the ghost on 14 May 1940. The Dutch colonies of Indonesia and New Guinea were then invaded by the Japanese in January 1942. After their capitulation on 8 March, Dutch colonials were imprisoned in Japanese concentration camps.

During the war, Hitler appointed Austrian Nazi Arthur Seyss-Inquart as Rijkskommissaris (State Commissioner) of the Netherlands, and asked him to tie the Dutch economy to the German one and to Nazify Dutch society. Though it won less than five per cent of the votes in the 1939 elections, the National Socialist Movement (NSB) was the largest and most important fascist political party in the Netherlands, and was the only Dutch party not prohibited during the occupation. Its doctrine greatly resembled German Nazism, but the NSB wanted to maintain Dutch autonomy under the direction of Germany.

> ## 'The most shocking institutional collaboration was by the police, who dragged Jews out of their houses for deportation.'

During the first years of the war, the Nazis allowed most people to live relatively undisturbed. Rationing, however, made the Dutch vulnerable to the black market, while cinemas and theatres eventually closed because of curfews and censorship. When the Nazis' soft approach failed to have the desired effect on locals, the Germans adopted more aggressive measures: Dutch men were soon forced to work

Amsterdam Jews faced deportation.

In Context

in German industry, and economic exploitation assumed appalling forms. In April 1943, all Dutch soldiers, who'd been captured during the invasion and then released in the summer of 1940, were ordered to give themselves up as prisoners of war. In an atmosphere of deep shock and outrage, strikes broke out during April and May, but were violently suppressed.

To begin with, ordinary people, as well as the political and economic elite, had no real reason to make a choice between collaboration and resistance. But as Nazi policies became more virulent, opposition to them swelled, and a growing minority of people were confronted with the difficult choice of whether to obey German measures or to resist. There were several patterns of collaboration. Some people joined the NSB, while others intimidated Jews, got involved in economic collaboration or betrayed people in hiding or members of the Resistance. Amazingly, a small number even signed up for German military service.

In Amsterdam, several social institutions gave information about Jews to the Germans, but the most shocking institutional collaboration was by the police, who dragged Jews out of their houses for deportation. The Dutch Railways also assisted the Nazis by transporting Jews to their deaths and received money for doing so. After the war, between 120,000 and 150,000 people were arrested for collaborating. Mitigating circumstances – as in the case of NSB members who helped the Resistance – made judgments very complicated, but, eventually, no fewer than 60,000 people were brought to justice.

The Resistance was made up chiefly of Calvinists and Communists. Though the latter movement gained public support, the Calvinist elite ensured that there was no Communist takeover after liberation. Anti-Nazi activities took several forms, with illegal newspapers – the only alternative to what was then a heavily censored press – keeping the population properly informed and urging them to resist the Nazi dictators.

Underground groups took many shapes, sizes and forms. Some spied for the Allies; others fought an armed struggle against the Germans through assassination and sabotage; and others still falsified identity cards and food vouchers. A national organisation took care of people who wanted to hide, and helped the railway strikers, Dutch soldiers and illegal workers being sought by the Germans, with other groups helping Jews into hiding. By 1945, more than 300,000 people had gone underground in the Netherlands.

Worse was to follow towards the end of the war, when, in 1944, the Netherlands was plunged into the 'Hunger Winter'. Supplies of

Captain Kerk

In early medieval society, the Catholic Church permeated every aspect of life throughout Europe, and Amsterdam was no exception. Contemporary chronicles show that the city became an independent parish before 1334. Documents dating from this period also contain the first recorded references to the **Oude Kerk** (see pages 28 and 45).

As Amsterdam expanded, more and more cloisters cropped up around the city: at one point, 18 were dotted around the tiny urban enclave, though the only remaining example is the **Begijnhof**, just off Spui (see page 49). The proliferation of the cloisters is thought, in part, to be down to the 'miracle' of 1345, when a dying man was given the last sacrament, which he then vomited up into a fire; the host emerged unscathed from the fire, though, and the man remarkably recovered. The cloisters became the main source of social welfare, providing hospital treatment and orphanages, at least until the Protestant elite – which took over the city after the Reformation – obliterated every trace of popery. The Heiligeweg (Holy Way) was the road within the city that led to the chapel on Rokin, close to where the miracle took place. Its length – roughly 70 metres – is an indication of just how small Amsterdam then was.

coal vanished after the liberation of the south and a railway strike, called by the Dutch government in exile to hasten German defeat, was disastrous for the supply of food. In retaliation for the strike, the Germans damaged Schiphol Airport and the harbours of Rotterdam and Amsterdam – foiling any attempts to bring in supplies – and appropriated everything they could. Walking became the only means of transport, domestic refuse was no longer collected, sewers overflowed, and the population, suffering from malnutrition and illnesses brought on by the cold, became vulnerable to disease.

To survive, people stole fuel: more than 20,000 trees were cut down and 4,600 buildings were demolished. Floors, staircases, joists and rafters were plundered, causing the collapse of many houses, particularly those left by deported Jews. Supplies were scarce and many people couldn't even afford to buy their rationing allowance, let alone the expensive produce on the black market. By the end of the winter, 20,000 people had died of starvation and disease, and much of the city was seriously damaged.

Hope, though, was just around the corner. The Allies finally liberated the south of the Netherlands on 5 September 1944, Dolle Dinsdag (Mad Tuesday), and complete liberation came after the Hunger Winter on 5 May 1945, when it became apparent that the Netherlands was the worst hit country in western Europe. In spite of the chaos, destruction, hunger and the loss of so many lives, there were effusive celebrations. But tragedy struck in Amsterdam on 7 May, when German soldiers opened fire on a crowd who had gathered on Dam Square to welcome their Canadian liberators. Twenty-two people were killed.

THE HOLOCAUST
'I see how the world is slowly becoming a desert, I hear more and more clearly the approaching thunder that will kill us,' wrote **Anne Frank** in her diary on 15 July 1944. Though her words obviously applied to the Jews, they were also relevant to the Gypsies, the homosexuals, the mentally handicapped and the Nazis' political opponents, who were all severely persecuted during the war. Granted, anti-Semitism in Holland had not been as virulent as in Germany, France or Austria. But even so, most – though not all – of the Dutch population closed its eyes to the persecution, and there's still a profound feeling of national guilt as a result.

The Holocaust arrived in three stages. First came measures to enforce the isolation of the Jews: the ritual slaughter of animals was prohibited, Jewish government employees were dismissed, Jews were banned from public places such as restaurants, cinemas and libraries and, eventually, all Jews were forced to wear a yellow Star of David. (Some non-Jewish Dutch courageously wore the badge as a demonstration of solidarity.) Concentration was the second stage. From early 1942, all Dutch Jews were obliged to move to three areas in Amsterdam, isolated by signs, drawbridges and barbed wire. The final stage was deportation. Between July 1942 and September 1943, most of the 140,000 Dutch Jews were deported, via Kamp Westerbork. Public outrage at the first deportations provoked the most dramatic protests against the anti-Semitic terror, the impressive February Strike.

The Nazis had also wanted to eliminate Dutch Gypsies: more than 200,000 European Gypsies, about 200 of them Dutch, were exterminated in concentration camps.

Homosexuals were also threatened with extermination, but their persecution was less systematic: public morality acts prohibited homosexual behaviour, and gay pressure groups ceased their activities. In addition, men arrested for other activities were punished more severely if they were found to be gay. In Dutch educational history books, the extermination of Gypsies and homosexuals is still often omitted, but Amsterdam has the world's first memorial to persecuted gays: the **Homomonument** (*see page 201*), which incorporates pink triangles in its design, turning the Nazi badge of persecution into a symbol of pride.

THE POST-WAR ERA
The Netherlands was deeply scarred by the German occupation, losing about ten per cent of all its housing, 30 per cent of its industry and 40 per cent of its total production capacity. The transport system, too, had been immobilised, and some of the country's dykes had been blown up, leaving large areas flooded. Though Amsterdam had escaped the bombing raids that devastated Rotterdam, it had borne the brunt of the deportations: only 5,000 Jews, out of a pre-war total Jewish population of 80,000, remained in the city.

Despite intense poverty and drastic shortages of food, fuel and building materials, the Dutch tackled the massive task of post-war recovery

The Provos disrupt the 1966 wedding of Queen Beatrix and ex-Nazi Claus van Amsberg with a smoke bomb. *See p19.*

Police face down striking construction workers in 1966. *See p19.*

and restoration with the spirit of the Resistance. There was a strong sense of optimism and unity, which was sustained until the end of the '40s. In 1948, people threw street parties, firstly to celebrate the inauguration of Queen Juliana, and, later, the four gold medals won by Amsterdam athlete Fanny Blankers-Koen at the London Olympics.

Some Dutch flirted briefly with communism directly after the war, but in 1948, a compromise was struck between the Catholic party, KVP, and the newly created Labour party, PvdA, and the two proceeded to govern in successive coalitions until 1958. Led by Prime Minister Willem Drees, the government resuscitated pre-war social programmes and laid the basis for the country's lavish welfare state. The Dutch reverted to the virtues of a conservative, provincial society: decency, hard work and thrift.

The country's first priority after the war was economic recovery. The Amsterdam city council concentrated on reviving the two motors of its economy: Schiphol Airport and the port of Amsterdam, the latter of which was soon boosted by the opening of the Amsterdam–Rhine Canal in 1952. Joining Belgium and Luxembourg in the Benelux also brought the country trade benefits, and the Netherlands was the first to repay its Marshall Plan loans. The authorities then proceeded to dust off their pre-war development plans and embarked on rapid urban expansion. Garden cities such as Slotervaart, Geuzenveld and Osdorp were created in the west; the architecture was sober, the setting spacious. But as people moved out to the new suburbs, businesses moved into the centre, worsening congestion on the already cramped roads. Traffic casualties soared.

After the war, the Dutch colonies of Indonesia and New Guinea were liberated from the Japanese and were soon pushing for independence. With Indonesia accounting for 20 per cent of their pre-war economy, the Dutch launched military interventions on 20 July 1947 and 18 December 1948. However, the interventions could not prevent the transfer of sovereignty to Indonesia on 27 December 1949, while the dispute with New Guinea dragged on until 1962 and did much to damage the Netherlands' international reputation. Colonial immigrants to the Netherlands, including the later arrival of Surinamese, and Turkish and Moroccan 'guest workers', now comprise 16 per cent of the population. Though poorer jobs and housing have usually been their lot, racial tensions were relatively low until the mid-'90s, with the rise of neo-fascism in the shape of the CD party. But the CD's gains in previous elections were all but wiped out in 1998, as Dutch voters sent a message that they'd had enough of extremist politics.

Though the economy revived in the '50s, and the welfare state was back to its best, there was still civil unrest. Strikes flared at the port and council workers defied a ban on industrial action. In 1951, protesters clashed with police outside the Concertgebouw, angered by the appointment of a pro-Nazi as conductor. In 1956, demonstrators besieged the Felix Meritis Building, the base of the Dutch Communist Party from 1946 until the late '70s, hurling stones in furious outrage at the Soviet invasion of Hungary.

In the late '40s and '50s, Amsterdammers returned to pre-war pursuits: fashion and celebrity interviews filled the newspapers and cultural events mushroomed. In 1947, the city launched the prestigious **Holland Festival**, while the elite held their own annual event called the Boekenbal, where writers met royalty and other dignitaries. New avant-garde artistic movements emerged, notably the **CoBrA** art group (*see page 70* **Museums further out**), whose 1949 exhibition at the **Stedelijk Museum of Modern Art** (*see page 68*) caused an uproar, and the vijftigers, a group of experimental poets led by Lucebert. Many of these artists met in brown cafés around Leidseplein.

A tokin' gesture in favour of soft drugs.

FAREWELL TO WELFARE

The '60s were one of the most colourful decades in Amsterdam's history. There were genuine official attempts to improve society and make it more prosperous. The IJ Tunnel eased communications to North Amsterdam and the national economy took off. There were high hopes for vast rehousing developments like the Bijlmermeer (now Bijlmer), and influential new architecture from the likes of Aldo van Eyck and Herman Herzberger sprang up around the city.

'The Provos influenced the anti-Vietnam demos in the US, and set the tone for Amsterdam's love of liberal politics and absurdist theatre.'

Yet the generous hand of the welfare state was being bitten; 'welfare is not well-being' went one popular slogan. Discontent began on a variety of issues, among them the nuclear threat, rampant urban expansion and industrialisation, the consumer society and authority in general. Popular movements similar to those in other west European cities were formed, but with a zaniness all of their own. Because protest and dissent have always been a vital part of the Netherlands' democratic process, and because the Dutch have a habit of keeping things in proportion, many popular demonstrations took a playful form.

The discontent gained focus in 1964, when pranks around 't Lieverdje statue, highlighting political or social problems, became the springboard for a new radical subculture, the Provos. Founded by anarchist philosophy student Roel van Duyn and 'anti-smoke magician' Robert Jasper Grootveld, the Provos numbered only about two dozen, but were enormously influential in the late '60s. Call them the flashiest of street scene-makers or call them proto-Yippies, but the Provos had a style that influenced the anti-Vietnam demos in the US, and set the tone for Amsterdam's love of liberal politics and absurdist theatre. Their 'finest' hour came in March 1966, when protests about Princess Beatrix's wedding to ex-Nazi Claus van Amsberg turned nasty after the Provos let off a smoke bomb on the carriage route; a riot ensued, though not quite on the scale of that begun by striking construction workers three months later.

Meanwhile, foreign hippies flocked to the city, attracted by its tolerant attitude to soft drugs. Though the possession of up to 30 grams (one ounce) of hash wasn't decriminalised until 1978, the authorities turned a blind eye to its use, preferring to prosecute dealers who also pushed hard drugs. The city subsequently suffered a heroin (and AIDS) epidemic, but has since developed a well-defined drugs policy. However, a drugs rethink was made necessary in the early 1970s, after the country became swamped with heroin brought in by Chinese triads and the fight against wimpy drugs came to be regarded as a waste of time and money.

In 1976, a vaguely worded law defined a difference between hard and soft drugs – effectively separating these markets from each other's influence – and allowed the use and sale of small amounts of soft drugs. The 'front door' of the then-embryonic 'coffeeshop' was now legal, but the 'back door', where produce arrived by the kilo, was still a gateway to an illegal distribution system. Still, it worked: time passed without the increase of drug use that doomsayers predicted, while the coffeeshop became a permanent part of the Amsterdam streetscape. Meanwhile, concerted efforts against hard drugs have eventually resulted in one of the lowest junkie populations in the world.

The focal points of hippie culture in the 1960s, though, were the **Melkweg** and **Paradiso**, both of which even then emitted such a pungent aroma of marijuana that tokers could be smelt hundreds of metres away in Leidseplein. The city soon became a haven for dropouts and hippies from all over Europe until the end of the decade, when the Dam and Vondelpark turned into unruly campsites and public tolerance of the hippies waned. In the '70s, Amsterdam's popular culture shifted towards a tougher expression of disaffected urban youth. Yet Vondelpark, the Melkweg and the Dam remain a mecca for both ageing and new age hippies, even into the '90s.

Perhaps the most significant catalyst for discontent in the '70s – which exploded into civil conflict by the '80s – was housing. Amsterdam's compact size and historic city centre had always been a nightmare for city planners. There was a dire housing shortage and many inner city homes were in need of drastic renovation. The population increased during the '60s, reaching its peak (nearly 870,000) by 1964. The numbers

You don't know squat

Once upon a time, this city thrived with squats that not only provided affordable housing and studio space, but that served as a focal point where alternative culture could thrive. Even 'straighter' citizens were generally supportive of these inspired grassroot hives built up from abandoned buildings. Unfortunately, in the last decade or so, with Amsterdam obsessed with re-inventing itself as a 'City of Inspiration' for high-dollar investors, the scene has diminished signifigantly. However it remains a city-defining movement, one more that worthy for an overview – albeit fleeting – of some of the many events that help shape it...

The alternative 'zine *Shark* does a good job of keeping track of squat events; as well as being distributed in bars in the city, it's online at www.underwateramsterdam.com). Also online, everything you ever wanted to know about squatting but were afraid to ask can be accessed at www.squat.net.

1000 First inhabitants (fishing squatters, homo squatus) come to the boggy mouth of the Amstel to settle what is to become the city of Amsterdam.
1275 By granting toll privileges to the hamlet, Count Floris V establishes a viable business climate.

1342 With the building of the first city walls, the economically challenged are forced to squat outside the wall's perimeter. This establishes the trend of the poor moving ever outwards as the city expands.
1613 With the Golden Age in full effect, the canal girdle is dug and built to house the prosperous. Squatters are, again, pushed outward.
1965 The first squatting (in the modern sense) occurs when a young family moves into an empty living space on Generaal Vetterstraat. The general populace – unsympathetic to the way speculators held on to their (empty) properties to drive up rents and property values – begin to regard it as a more than viable way of dealing with the housing shortage.
1966 The Provos introduce the 'White Housing Plan'.
1969 *Handbook for Squatters* becomes a national bestseller.
1970 The first National Squatters' Day is held on 5 May.
1971 The High Council determines that squatting does not conflict with the law: ie entering an empty house is not trespassing on private property. However, property owners now start doing the evicting themselves, with the aid of *knokploegen* ('fighting groups').

were swelled by immigrants from the Netherlands' last major colony, Surinam, many of whom were dumped in the Bijlmermeer housing project. It quickly degenerated into a ghetto, and when an aeroplane crashed there in October 1992, the number of fatalities was impossible to ascertain: many victims were illegal residents and not registered.

The Metro link to the Bijlmermeer is itself a landmark to some of the most violent protests in Amsterdam's history. Passionate opposition erupted against the proposed clearance in February 1975 of the Jewish quarter of the Nieuwmarkt, a particularly sensitive site. Civil unrest culminated in 'Blue Monday', 24 March 1975, when heavy-handed police tactics once again sparked off violent clashes with residents and over 1,000 supporters. Police fired tear gas into the homes of those who had refused to move out and battered down doors with armoured cars. Despite further clashes just weeks later, the plans went ahead and the Metro was opened in 1980, though only one of the four lines planned for the city was completed.

City planners were shocked by the fervent opposition to their schemes for large, airy suburbs. It was simply not what people wanted: they cherished the narrow streets, the small squares and cosy corner cafés. The shortage of residential space in the city centre made it a target for property speculators, and the public felt that the council was selling out to big business, complaining that the city centre was becoming unaffordable for ordinary people. In 1978, the council decided to improve housing through small-scale development, renovating houses street by street. But with an estimated 90,000 people (13 per cent of the city's population) still on Amsterdam's housing list in 1980, public concern grew about the shortages.

Speculators who left property empty caused justifiable, acute resentment, which was soon mobilised into direct action: vacant buildings were occupied illegally by squatters. In March 1980, police turned against them for the first time and used tanks to evict them from a former office building in Vondelstraat. Riots ensued, but the squatters eventually came away victorious.

1975 Ruigoord is squatted as an artists' village of eco-hippies. In October 2001, it will become submerged as part of the new Africa Haven, making the future of its 100 or so residents a little uncertain.
1978 Groote Keizer (Keizersgracht 242-52) is established, and becomes the focal point for the city's 10,000 squatters.
1979 Radio de Vrije Keyser is established (indeed, it's still broadcasting at 96.3 FM, and is on the web at www.xs4all.nl/~keyser).
1980 The most violent year in the Netherlands since World War II. In February, hundreds of by-now highly organised squatters retake Vondelstraat 72 by constructing barricades, until tanks deal with the situation in unsubtle fashion. On 30 April, the date of Queen Beatrix's inauguration, huge riots break out, until tear gas is pumped into the crowds. Squatting then becomes yet more politicised, and, as a result, separate squatting factions emerge and infighting occurs. It's the beginning of the end for squatting as a national pastime.
1981 A bailiff who had regularly tipped off squatters with the 'removal' dates of squats (so they could be ready and barricaded) receives a gilded crowbar as a thank-you.
1986 The heyday of hardcore squatting, which began in 1979, is considered to be over.

1997 The continuing decline in the prior decade of the political wing of squatting gets a shot in the arm with the establishment of Groennord, an eco-protest camp using the tactics of Earth First!. A cycle begins whereby tunnels and tree forts are emptied, destroyed and then rebuilt.
1998 Two mega-squats that represented more the cultural/artistic side of squatting are emptied. After ten years, De Graansilo, which held a bakery, a café-restaurant, dozens of resident artists and 100,000 visitors per year is emptied and reclaimed for high-rent housing. The 1994-established Vrieshuis Amerika, home to regular parties, the largest indoor skateboard park in the country and 75 artists and businesses, is emptied and destroyed in the name of the Sydney-fication of the harbourfront.
1999, 2000 The former Film Academy is squatted and may yet be granted a sense of permanence, as the city has belatedly realised that there are no affordable inner city spaces left for artists. The concept of establishing broedplaatsen ('breeding grounds') for the arts enters local politics, and tax money is found to rebuild what had, until the clampdown, basically already existed. The future, then, looks a tad brighter. For now...

The wreckage of the El Al 747 that crashed in the **Bijlmermeer** in 1992. *See p21.*

In 1982, as Amsterdam's squatting movement reached its peak with an estimated 10,000 members, clashes with police escalated: a state of emergency was called after one eviction battle. Soon, though, the city – led by new mayor Ed van Thijn – had taken control over the movement, and one of the last of the city's important squats, Wyers, fell amid tear gas in February 1984 and was pulled down to make way for a Holiday Inn. The squatters were no longer a force to be reckoned with, though their ideas of small-scale regeneration have since been absorbed into official planning.

BACK TO BASICS

Born and bred in Amsterdam, Ed van Thijn embodied a new strand in Dutch politics. Though a socialist, he took tough action against 'unsavoury elements' – hard drug traders, petty criminals, squatters – and upgraded facilities to attract new businesses and tourists. A new national political era also emerged, with the election in 1982 of Rotterdam millionaire Ruud Lubbers as leader of the then centre-right coalition government of Christian Democrats and right-wing Liberals (VVD). He saw to it that the welfare system and government subsidies were trimmed to ease the country's large budget deficit, and aimed to revitalise the economy with more businesslike policies. In February 1984, though, Van Thijn resigned to become Home Affairs Minister.

The price of Amsterdam's new affluence (among most groups, except the poorest) has been a swing towards commercialism. Van Thijn has found it hard to live down a clumsy remark he made about turning Amsterdam into a 'pleasure park'. Yet the evidence of his intentions can be seen in the casino, luxury apartments and shopping complex at the Leidseplein and the massive redevelopment of its docklands. Van Thijn also pushed through plans to build the **Stadhuis-Muziektheater** (City Hall-Opera House) complex, dubbed 'Stopera!' by its opponents (*see pages 52, 222 and 245*).

But the hordes of squatters were largely supplanted by well-groomed yuppies. Flashy cafés, galleries and nouvelle cuisine restaurants replaced the alternative scene and a mood of calm settled on the city. S till, a classic example of Dutch free expression was provoked by the city's mid-'80s campaign to host the 1992 Olympics. Amsterdam became the first city ever to send an (ultimately successful) official anti-Olympics delegation. It seems the city isn't yet ready to relinquish its rebel status.

► For more on **Anne Frank**, see page 63.

► For more on **art museums**, see page 67.

► For more on **Amsterdam's drugs laws**, see pages 134 and 140.

Amsterdam Today

Will the council's clean-up operation affect Amsterdam's reputation as the liberal capital of the world?

After having heard all about the Dutch capital's liberal attitudes towards near enough everything, you arrive for a short break. You are open to sample everything: from a relaxing smoke in a coffeeshop to a gig by a Polish punk band in a squat venue, from a culturally educational visit to the Rijksmuseum to a boat tour along a beautiful canal, from a pub crawl around the town's most notorious bars to a night out at a hip lounge. You will leave having seen Amsterdam at its best. But there are two sides to this city. Stay here a little longer, mingle with the inhabitants and experience day-to-day life, and soon you'll find that cracks begin to appear on the town's beautiful and laid-back façade.

The reason? Amsterdam's reputation as a city where anything goes is as much of a hindrance as a help. Over the last few years, vice and violence have dominated as never before, and even the most liberal-minded locals admitted that their beloved city was going to

the dogs. But despite this, when Schelto Patijn became mayor some years ago, he was frowned upon when he introduced a more formal vision: the city had to clean up, and its inhabitants needed to re-embrace old-fashioned standards. One of Patijn's first actions was to put a hold on the opening of new coffeeshops while ensuring that existing establishments complied to stricter rules, a dictum he followed by banning of the display of explicit material in shop windows outside the Red Light District. Regulations for festivities such as Queen's Day – which were once virtually non-existent – have been tightened almost every year. But after at first opposing Patijn's clean-up bills, Amsterdammers have begun to admit that his actions were changing things for the better.

Another Patijn initiative has been the *afkoeluurtje*, an extra 'cool down' opening hour for the bars and clubs around Rembrandtplein and Leidseplein during which time they can only sell non-alcoholic drinks and coffee. The 1990s saw an increase in fights between partygoers on Leidseplein and Rembrandtplein in the wee hours: during the weekends, riot police vans had to be on standby. According to bar and club owners, the fights were a direct result of legislation that forced all bars to keep the same hours, a law that resulted in crowds of alcohol- and drug-fuelled merrymakers spilling on to the streets at the same time. While the *afkoeluurtje* has proved a success, there are still a few incidents. However, these are most often caused by visitors from out of town, still drawn by Amsterdam's reputation as a city where everything is tolerated.

'Amsterdam's desire to smarten up has not been limited to back-to-basics standards and morals.'

Around the same time as the *afkoeluurtje* was introduced, the Amsterdam police force launched two new campaigns: Zero Tolerance and Streetwise. People who, for instance, urinate against walls – not an unfamiliar sight in the city at night – or who cycle through red traffic lights or on the pavement now have to pay a hefty fine on the spot. And during 2000, the government plans to invest ƒ130 million to battle against crime and violence in Amsterdam, as a recent survey showed that a quarter of all Amsterdammers older than 16 have been subjected to violence in the last few years.

TRANSPORT TRICKS...

In 1999, the Amsterdam Transport Board, the GVB, found itself in the news for all the wrong reasons. Stories about fraudulent employees became commonplace in the dailies: the GVB has lost an estimated ƒ3 million over the last few years, and yet some possibly criminal cases weren't even reported to the police. Add in the frequent assaults against drivers and passengers on buses and trams and the groups of pickpockets that were making a nice living on the system – particularly on tram routes 1, 2 and 5 running from Centraal Station to the area around Museumplein – and it hardly comes as a great surprise that citizens found it hard to say anything positive about the GVB. Even its employees lost faith and went on strike for a day, as they felt they couldn't guarantee a safe ride either for the passengers or, just as damningly, for themselves.

Aware that this bad reputation was losing it both customers and cash, the GVB announced plans to invest millions of guilders into fitting video cameras on trams and buses, and adding

special booths at the backs of trams for ticket inspectors. The underground system is getting a long-overdue facelift, too, in a project snazzily christened 'Metromorphosis'. During the last decade, precious little maintenance has been performed on the majority of underground stations, with the result that walls became covered in graffiti, platforms began to resemble garbage dumping grounds and dark corners became homes from home for local junkies.

The estimated cost of transforming the stations into bright and safe places is an estimated ƒ2 billion. It's a huge investment, but eminently understandable given the fact that the council wants to turn the GVB into a limited company within the next five years. As the council itself will be the largest shareholder, it has to make sure that public transport in Amsterdam is made safe and, thus, more popular, especially with the new Noord/Zuidlijn Metro line on its way.

The Noord/Zuidlijn, a controversial 9.5-kilometre (5.9-mile) line scheduled to open around 2006, will link the north of Amsterdam with the city centre and the World Trade Centre station in the south. Major companies are eager to relocate to the WTC – indeed, the ABN-Amro bank has done so already – while the financial investments in this district should prove economically beneficial for the city. Moreover, the new Metro line will supply jobs for around 10,000 people. Still, many citizens are against the Metro extension. Some simply see it as unnecessary, while others are concerned that small shopkeepers will go broke as large areas of the city, such as those around the Albert Cuypmarkt, will be unreachable during construction.

... AND TAXI TANTRUMS

It's not just the GVB, either: Amsterdam's taxis have been in the news for the wrong reasons, too. The year 2000 started with a bang, but not the kind made by celebratory millennial fireworks. For several years, there was talk about introducing more taxi companies in Amsterdam in a bid to make cabs more widely available and, thanks to increased competition, cheaper. Obviously, the city's only taxi company, Taxi Centrale Amsterdam, was not especially keen on this idea. Its driver's permits, priced at around ƒ30,000, had always been regarded as a safe pension plan. But with the introduction of TaxiDirekt, a new taxi company whose drivers didn't have to buy themselves in, the value of these permits suddenly became negligible.

Early 2000 saw the situation get way out of hand, as a mini-war developed between the two firms. Taxi drivers from TCA attacked their

Only now is safety on the tram system being made a priority. *See p24.*

competitors from TaxiDirekt on an almost daily basis, and riot police vans had to patrol the city at night to protect employees of the new cab company. The image of taxi drivers – already bad enough, given their reputation for racism and ignorance – became even more damaged. Though the government came up with a plan to compensate the TCA drivers for their loss of future income, hardly any made use of it amid whisperings that many of them had used black money to buy their permits.

So far, the introduction of TaxiDirekt has only made for good copy as opposed to good transport, as passengers in need of a cheap, fast and safe transport solution late at night are still out in the cold. TaxiDirekt's fares are just as expensive as those charged by TCA, and by Easter 2000, they'd only introduced about 100 new vehicles on to the streets. Hope, though, lies in the introduction of a third taxi company in 2000, which says it will specialise in short journeys and cheap fares. But given the wild-west scenarios of the recent past, Amsterdam isn't holding its breath.

BUILT TO LAST

Amsterdam's desire to smarten up its image has not been limited to back-to-basics standards and morals: efforts are also being made to

smarten up some of its less attractive thoroughfares. Zeedijk, for example, once a street littered with junkies and lowlife, has successfully morphed into a considerably smarter street thanks to co-operation between the council and local shopkeepers. After the tidying-up of the Spui and the controversial overhaul of Museumplein, Nieuwendijk and Dam Square are next on the agenda for the renovators.

At a cost of ƒ19 million, Dam Square is to be transformed from a drab open space to an Italian/Spanish-style plaza. And not before time, too. Sadly, the plan for a fountain in the middle of the square – surely a must for that authentic-ish Mediterranean look – was swiftly outvoted by Queen Beatrix on the grounds that she wanted to be able to walk in a straight line from her Royal Palace to the World War II Monument on Remembrance Day (4 May). Making Dam Square more attractive tunes right in to the council's clean-up of Rokin, Damrak and Nieuwendijk, three streets that had turned into tacky tourist areas filled with dubious pizza palaces and souvenir shops advertising their gruesome goods on nasty, neon-lit signboards. When prestigious auction house Sotheby's moved away from Rokin, alarm bells sounded at the council, and plans were swiftly drawn up. The 650-year-old Nieuwendijk, for example, will be getting a new pavement, more lights and cleaner façades. By upgrading the street, the city council hopes to attract more high-status shops.

OFFSHORE INVESTMENT

It seems that the efforts to bring Amsterdam back on the right track are paying off in more ways than one. The current economic boost, new job schemes and a more individualistic approach by job centres saw the total number of unemployed Amsterdammers in 1999 drop to just under 60,000 from its longtime range of between 80,000 and 100,000. In addition, 40 per cent of Amsterdammers working in low-paid, council-subsidised jobs have managed to find themselves regular posts. Even ethnic minorities, who still face prejudice on the job market despite policies designed to put a cap on discrimination, have profited from the economic boost, finding jobs more quickly than ever before.

> **'Many see it as ironic that the council makes a song and dance about creating space for young artists, but changes its mind when real estate developers propose building yuppie flats.'**

As with most major cities, there is a huge shortage of housing in Amsterdam. Unlike most major cities, though, Amsterdam has decided to do something about it. New suburbs are currently being developed in the city, with IJburg – a couple of islands near the IJ – the most controversial. After a long debate and a referendum, the ƒ500-million development was finally given the go-ahead. However, only 30 per cent of the 6,240 properties to be built on the island will be council houses, with the rest owner-occupied luxury residences.

Apart from creating new houses, Amsterdam is investing millions in renovating houses in old parts of town. The Mercatorplein area in the west of Amsterdam, for instance, has been completely revamped: once a grim area where drug-related crimes were the order of the day, it's now been smartened up with comfortable apartments, a striking square and a string of shops. However, there is a flipside, for projects such as this often mean that only the well-to-do can afford to rent or buy the rent-increased renovated houses. Large families with small incomes usually miss out, which only makes it harder for them to find somewhere affordable in which to live. Even couples with double incomes find it difficult to get a mortgage to

buy a flat or apartment, as the prices of houses have skyrocketed in the last five years and are now comparable to those of London and Paris.

SQUAT SCENE

Another downside of redeveloping is that old buildings, such as Graansilo and Vrieshuis Amerika, have been demolished. Resourceful squatters had turned many of these once-empty buildings into restaurants, concert venues and artists' residences. One of the few remaining such buildings, Kalenderpanden on Entrepotdok, is also facing the wrecking ball. Many see it as ironic that while the council makes a great song and dance about creating working and living space for young artists – exactly what the squatters are doing – it quickly changes its mind when real estate developers propose building yuppie flats.

It's not only the squatters who want to see the Kalenderpanden untouched, either. Local residents, writers, artists and even some politicians recognise the importance of these artistic breeding grounds and have spoken out in favour of them. But it looks like the council has made up its mind, and the days of the Kalenderpanden are numbered. However, another building, the old Film Academy on Overtoom (on the border of Vondelpark), might have a longer life. Squatters, who have taken over the old academy and turned it into a restaurant, cinema and live/work space, were told they could stay for a while longer.

Though Amsterdam is trying to get used to its cleaned-up image, the sex, drugs and 'anything goes' label is still alive, especially abroad. Since the '60s, foreigners have known the city as the liberal capital of the world, a global infamy that makes it hard to determine whether or not the city's new image will go beyond the surface. The Amsterdam Tourist Board hopes it will, as it tries to draw in more moneyed visitors who'll spend freely in shops and restaurants as opposed to the backpackers whose holidays – and money – are spent wandering between coffeeshops in a drugged-up haze.

But with corporate companies moving to Amsterdam, the squat scene almost erased and young couples returning to the city limits, one thing remains certain. For everyone else – despite the council and the Amsterdam Tourist Board's attempts to give Amsterdam a clean-cut image – the party isn't over just yet.

► For more on **travel in Amsterdam**, see page 270.

► For more on **Amsterdam's squat scene**, see page 20.

From city gate to weighhouse to **In de Waag**. See p29.

Architecture

You won't find many palaces and castles in Amsterdam, just domesticity and functionality at their most beautiful.

'The colours are strong and sad, the forms symmetric, the façades kept new,' wrote Eugene Fromentin, the 19th-century art critic, of Amsterdam. 'We feel that it belongs to a people eager to take possession of the conquered mud.' The treacherously soft soil upon which the merchants' town of Amsterdam is built put strictures on most attempts at monumental display. Thanks to the make-up of the land – combined with the Protestant restraint that characterised the city's early developments – it's not palaces and castles that make up the architectural high points but, rather, warehouses, domestic architecture, the stock exchange and the City Hall.

It doesn't take an expert to see that Amsterdam's architectural epochs have closely followed the pulse of the city's prosperity. The decorative façades of wealthy 17th- and 18th-century merchants' houses still line the canals. A splurge of public spending in the affluent 1880s gave the city two of its most notable landmarks in **Centraal Station** and the **Rijksmuseum**.

Conversely, social housing projects in the early 20th century stimulated the innovative work of the Amsterdam School, while Amsterdam's late-1980s resurgence as a financial centre and transport hub led both to an economic upturn and to thickets of bravura modern architecture sprouting on the city outskirts.

Prime viewing time for Amsterdam architecture is late on a summer's afternoon, as the sun gently picks out the varying colours and patterns of the brickwork. Then, as twilight falls, the canal houses – most of them more window than wall – light up like strings of lanterns, and you get a glimpse of the beautifully preserved, frequently opulent interiors that lie behind the façades.

MUD, GLORIOUS MUD

Amsterdam is built on reclaimed marshland, with a thick, soft layer of clay and peat beneath the topsoil. About 12 metres (39 feet) down is a hard band of sand, deposited 10,000 years ago during the Little Ice Age, and below that, after about five metres (16 feet) of fine sand, there is another firm layer, this one left by melting glacial ice after the Great Ice Age. A further 25 metres (82 feet) down, through shell-filled clay and past the bones of mammoths, is a third hard layer, deposited by glaciers over 180,000 years ago.

'Amsterdam is full of buildings that teeter over the street, tilt lopsidedly or prop each other up in higgledy-piggledy rows.'

The first Amsterdammers built their homes on muddy mounds, making the foundations from tightly packed peat. Later, they dug trenches, filled them with fascines (thin, upright alder trunks) and built on those. But still the fruits of their labours sank slowly into the swamp. By the 17th century, builders were using longer underground posts and were rewarded with more stable structures, but it wasn't until around 1700 that piles were driven deep enough to hit the first hard sand layer.

The method of constructing foundations that subsequently developed has remained essentially the same ever since, though nowadays most piles reach the second sand level and some even make the full 50-metre (164-foot) journey to the third hard layer. To begin, a double row of piles is sunk along the line of a proposed wall (since World War II, concrete has been used instead of wood). Then, a crossbeam is laid across each pair of posts, planks are fastened longitudinally on to the beams, and the wall is built on top. From time to time, of course, piles break or rot, which explains why Amsterdam is full of buildings that teeter precariously over the street, tilt lopsidedly or prop each other up in higgledy-piggledy rows.

STICKS AND STONES

Early constructions in Amsterdam were timber-framed, built mainly from oak with roofs of rushes or straw. Wooden houses were relatively light and so less likely to sink into the mire, but after two devastating fires (in 1421 and 1452), the authorities began stipulating that outer walls be built of brick, though wooden front gables were still permitted. In a bid to blend in, the first brick gables were shaped in imitation of their spout-shaped wooden predecessors.

Amsterdammers took to brick with relish. Granted, some grander 17th-century buildings were built of sandstone, while plastered façades made an appearance a hundred years later and

reinforced concrete made its inevitable inroad in the 20th century. But Amsterdam is still essentially a city of brick: red brick from Leiden, yellow from Utrecht and grey from Gouda, all laid in curious formations and arranged in complicated patterns. Local architects' attachment to – and flair with – brick reached a zenith in the fantastical, billowing façades designed by the Amsterdam School early this century.

TOUCH WOOD

Only two wooden buildings remain in central Amsterdam: one (built in 1460) in the quiet square of **Begijnhof** (No.34), and the other on Zeedijk. The latter, **In't Aepjen** (Zeedijk 1; *see also pages 42 and 123*), was built in the 16th century as a lodging house, getting its name from the monkeys that impecunious sailors used to leave behind in payment. Though the ground floor dates from the 19th century, the upper floors provide a clear example of how, in medieval times, each wooden storey protruded a little beyond the one below it, allowing rainwater to drip on to the street rather than run back into the body of the building. Early brick gables had to be built at an angle over the street for the same reason, though it also allowed objects to be winched to the top floors without crashing against the windows of the lower ones. Wonky by design, in other words.

Amsterdam's oldest building, though, is the **Oude Kerk** ('Old Church', Oude Kerksplein 23; *see page 45*), which was begun in 1300, though only the base of the tower actually dates from then. Over the ensuing 300 years, the church developed a barnacle crust of additional buildings, mostly in a Renaissance style though with a few Gothic additions. Surprisingly, nearly all the buildings retain their original medieval roofs, making the church unique in the Netherlands. The only full Gothic building in town – in the style of towering French and German churches – is the **Nieuwe Kerk** (at Dam and Nieuwezijds Voorburgwal; *see page 40*), which is still called the 'New Church' even though building work on it began at the end of the 14th century.

When gunpowder arrived in Europe in the 15th century, Amsterdammers realised that the wooden palisade that surrounded their settlement would offer scant defence against invaders, and so they set about building a new city wall. Watchtowers and gates left over from this wall make up a significant proportion of remaining pre-17th-century architecture, though most have been considerably altered over the years. The **Schreierstoren** (Prins Hendrikkade 94-95; *see pages 42 and 125*) of 1480, however, has kept its original shape, with the addition of

The wedding-cake charm of **Zuiderkerk**.

doors, windows and a pixie-hat roof. The base of
the **Munttoren** (Muntplein; *see page 50*)
originally formed part of the Reguliersspoort, a
city gate built in 1490. Another city gate from
the previous decade, the **St Antoniespoort**
(Nieuwmarkt 4), was converted into a public
weighhouse (or 'Waag') in 1617, then further
refashioned to become a Guild House. It's now
In de Waag, a café-restaurant (*see page 125*).

DUTCH RENAISSANCE

A favourite 16th-century amendment to these
somewhat stolid defence towers was the
addition of a sprightly steeple. Hendrick de
Keyser (1565-1621) delighted in designing such
spires, and it is largely his work that gives
Amsterdam's present skyline a faintly oriental
appearance. He added a lantern-shaped tower
with an openwork orb to the Munttoren, and a
spire that resembled the Oude Kerk steeple to
the **Montelbaanstoren** (Oude Schans 2), a
sea-defence tower that had been built outside
the city wall. His **Zuiderkerk** (Zandstraat 17;
see page 50), built in 1603, sports a richly
decorative spire said to have been much
admired by Christopher Wren. The
appointment of de Keyser as city mason and
sculptor in 1595 had given him free reign, and
his buildings represent the pinnacle of the
Dutch Renaissance style.

Since the beginning of the 17th century,
Dutch architects had been gleaning inspiration
from translations of Italian pattern books,
adding lavish ornament to the classical system
of proportion they found there. Brick façades
were decorated with stone strapwork (scrolls
and curls derived from picture frames and
leather work). Walls were built with alternating
layers of red brick and white sandstone, a style
that came to be called 'bacon coursing'. The old
spout-shaped gables were replaced with
cascading step-gables, often embellished with
vases, escutcheons and masks (before house
numbers were introduced in Amsterdam in the
18th century, ornate gables and wall plaques
were a means of identifying houses).

The façade of the **Vergulde Dolphijn**
(Singel 140-42), designed by de Keyser in 1600
for Captain Banningh Cocq (the commander of
Rembrandt's *Night Watch*), is a lively
combination of red brick and sandstone, while
the **Gecroonde Raep** (Oudezijds Voorburgwal
57) has a neat step-gable, with truly riotous
decoration featuring busts, escutcheons, shells,
scrolls and volutes. However, de Keyser's
magnificent 1617 construction, the **Huis
Bartolotti** (Herengracht 170-72), is the finest
example of the style.

This decorative step-gabled style was to last
well into the 17th century. But, gradually, a
stricter use of classical elements came into play;
the façade of the Bartolotti house features rows
of Ionic pilasters, and it wasn't long before
others followed where de Keyser had led. The
Italian pattern books that had inspired the
Dutch Renaissance were full of the less
ornamented designs of Greek and Roman
antiquity. This appealed to many young
architects who followed de Keyser, and who
were to develop a more restrained, classical
style. Many, such as Jacob van Campen (1595-
1657), went on study tours of Italy, and
returned fired with enthusiasm for the
symmetric designs, simple proportions and
austerity of Roman architecture. The buildings
that they constructed during the Golden Age
are among the finest Amsterdam has to offer.

THE GOLDEN AGE

The 1600s were a boom time for builders as
well as for business. Really, there was no way it
could have been otherwise, as Amsterdam's
population more than quadrupled during the
first half of the century. Grand new canals were
constructed, and wealthy merchants lined them
with mansions and warehouses. Van Campen,
along with fellow architects Philips Vingboons
(1607-78) and his brother Justus (1620-98), were
given the freedom to try out their ideas on a
flood of new commissions.

Stately façades constructed entirely of sandstone began to appear around Amsterdam, but brick still remained the most popular building material. Philips Vingboons's **Witte Huis** (Herengracht 168) has a white sandstone façade with virtually no decoration: the regular rhythm of the windows is the governing principle of the design. The house he built in 1648 at **Oude Turfmarkt 145** has a brick façade adorned with three tiers of classical pilasters – Tuscan, Ionic and Doric – and festoons that were also characteristic of the style. However, the crowning achievement of the period was Amsterdam's boast to the world of its mercantile supremacy and civic might: namely, the Stadhuis (City Hall) on the Dam, designed by Van Campen in 1648 and now known as the **Koninklijk Paleis** (*see page 39*).

There was, however, one fundamental point of conflict between classical architecture and the requirements of northern European building. For obvious practical reasons, wet northern climes required steep roofs, yet low Roman pediments and flat cornices looked rather odd with a steep, pointed roof rising behind them. The architects eventually solved the problem by adapting the Renaissance gable, with its multiple steps, into a tall, central gable with just two steps. These considerably simpler elevated neck-gables had a more suitable classical line. Later, neck-gables were built with just a tall central oblong and no steps. The right angles formed at the base of neck-gables – and again at the step of elevated neck-gables – were often filled in with decorative sandstone carvings called claw-pieces.

Dolphins, sea monsters and other marvels of the world as explored by the Dutch East India Company ships became themes for claw-piece design. At **Oudezijds Voorburgwal 187**, exotic men with feather headdresses recline on bales of tobacco. Later, the space occupied by the claw-piece was filled in with brick, rather than by sandstone carving, to form the aptly named bell-gable. These were often trimmed with sandstone decoration.

On exceptionally wide houses, it was possible to construct a roof parallel to the street rather than end-on, making a much more attractive backdrop for a classical straight cornice. The giant **Trippenhuis** (Kloveniersburgwal 29), built by Justus Vingboons in 1662, has such a design, with a classical pediment, a frieze of cherubs and arabesques, and eight enormous Corinthian pilasters. It wasn't until the 19th century, when zinc cladding became more affordable, that flat and really low-pitched roofs became feasible.

THE 18TH CENTURY

Working towards the end of the 17th century, Adriaan Dortsman (1625-82) had been a strong proponent of the straight cornice. His exceptionally stark designs – such as for the Van Loon house at **Keizersgracht 672-4** – ushered in a style that came to be known as Restrained Dutch Classicism. It was a timely entrance. Ornament was costly, and by the beginning of the 18th century, the economic boom was over.

The great merchant families were still prosperous, but little new building went on. Instead, the families gave their old mansions a facelift or revamped the interiors. A number of 17th-century houses got new sandstone façades (or plastered brick ones, which were cheaper), and French taste – said to have been introduced by Daniel Marot, a French architect living in Amsterdam – became hugely hip. As the century wore on, ornamentation regained popularity. Gables were festooned with scrolls and acanthus leaves (Louis XIV), embellished with asymmetrical rococo fripperies (Louis XV) or strung with disciplined lines of garlands (Louis XVI). The baroque grandeur of the house at **Keizersgracht 444-6**, for example, hardly seems Dutch at all. Straight cornices appeared even on narrow buildings, and became extraordinarily ornate: a distinct advantage, this, as it hid the steep roof that lay behind, with decorative balustrades adding to the deception. The lavish cornice at **Oudezijds Voorburgwal 215-17** is a prime example.

ONE FOOT IN THE PAST

Fortunes slumped even further after 1800, and during the first part of the century, more buildings were demolished than constructed. When things picked up after 1860, architects raided past eras for inspiration. Neo-classical, neo-Gothic and neo-Renaissance features were sometimes lumped together in the same building in a mix-and-match Eclectic style. The **Krijtberg church** (Singel 446) from 1881, for example, has a soaring neo-Gothic façade and a high, vaulted basilica, while the interior of AL van Gendt's **Hollandse Manege** (Vondelstraat 140) from the same year combines the classicism of the Spanish Riding School in Vienna with a state-of-the-art iron and glass roof. On the other hand, the **Concertgebouw** (Van Baerlestraat 98; *see page 222*), another Van Gendt construction from 1888, borrows heavily from the late Renaissance, with the **City Archive** (Amsteldijk 67) from 1892 little more than Hendrick de Keyser revisited. But the most adventurous building of the period is probably the **Adventskerk** (Keizersgracht 676), a mix of different style, it somehow manages to cram

The unique and organic exuberance of the **Tuschinski**.

in a classical rusticated base, Romanesque arches, Lombardian moulding and fake 17th-century lanterns.

The star architect of the period was PJH Cuypers (1827-1921), who landed the commissions for both the **Rijksmuseum** (Stadhouderskade 41; *see page 50*) of 1877-85 and **Centraal Station** (Stationsplein), built between 1882 and 1889. Both are in traditional red brick, adorned with a wealth of Renaissance-style decoration in sandstone and gold leaf. Cuypers made a conscious decision to move away from Eclecticism, and organise each building according to a single coherent principle. This idea became the basis for modern Dutch architecture.

THIS IS THE MODERN WORLD

Brick and wood – good, honest, indigenous materials – appealed to Hendrik Petrus Berlage (1856-1934), as did the possibilities offered by industrial developments in the use of steel and glass. A rationalist, he took Cuypers' ideas a step further in his belief that a building should openly express its basic structure, with just a modest amount of ornament in a strictly supportive role. His **Beurs van Berlage** (Beursplein; *see page 41*), built 1898-1903 – all clean lines and functional shapes, with the mildest patterning in the brickwork – was startling at the time, and earned him the reputation of being the father of modern Dutch architecture.

Apart from the odd shopfront and some well-designed café interiors, the art nouveau and art deco movements had little direct impact on Amsterdam, though there were a few eccentric flourishes at the time: HL de Jong's **Tuschinski** cinema (Reguliersbreestraat 26; *see page 192*) of 1918-21, for example, is a delightful piece of high-camp fantasy. Instead, Amsterdam architects developed a style of their own, an idiosyncratic mixture of art nouveau and Old Dutch using their favourite materials: wood and brick.

> **'The urgent need for housing led to the appearance of soulless, high-rise horrors on the edge of town.'**

This movement, which became known as the Amsterdam School, reacted against Berlage's sobriety by producing whimsical buildings with waving, almost sculptural brickwork. Built over a reinforced concrete frame, the brick outer walls go through a series of pleats, bulges, folds and curls that earned the movement's work the nickname 'Schortjesarchitectuur' ('apron architecture'). Windows may be trapezoid or parabolic; doors are carved in strong, angular shapes; brickwork is decorative and often polychromatic; and brick and stone sculptures are in abundance.

The driving force behind the Amsterdam School came from a pair of young and enthusiastic architects, Michel de Klerk (1884-1923) and Piet Kramer (1881-1961). Commissions for social housing projects from two Housing Associations – one for the **Dageraad** (constructed around PL Takstraat between 1921 and 1923) and another for **Eigen Haard** (in the Spaarndammerbuurt, and built between 1913 and 1920) – allowed them to treat entire blocks as single units. Just as importantly, however, the pair's adventurous clients gave them complete freedom to express their ideas.

Island life

Survival instincts forced the Dutch to conquer the sea centuries ago. Intricate systems of dykes, polders, canals and windmills were continuously and ingeniously engineered to provide a safe haven from the ever-present threat of flooding.

Paradoxically, though, the sea also promised many a source of livelihood, making the Dutch and water rather unlikely neighbours. This relationship has become more peaceable thanks to the engineering advances achieved in the last half-century and might now best be characterised as a love affair. So ingrained is the sea in the collective Dutch psyche that access to – or, preferably, a property with a view of – any waterway has become one of the hallmarks of a desirable address across the western and northern provinces.

Amsterdam, of course, is no exception, and its canal houses represent what might be considered the pinnacle of the good life in the Netherlands. And while the most luxurious of these properties demand rents that only big banks and other multinationals can afford, the less ostentatious residences lining the smaller canals have come to define the character of the city. As these are imited in number and priced dearly, the majority of Amsterdammers can only afford to reside, at best, somewhere around the corner from water.

But at worst, locals have been forced to flee to post-war developments devoid of the city centre's charms, not to mention sound urban planning. Booms in the overall population, the number of families eager to stay in the capital and the number of people interested in buying a home has led the city to address the housing shortage that threatened to drain Amsterdam of one of its most important assets: its middle classes.

The solution is **IJburg**. Also dubbed the 'New East', IJburg is a collection of six man-made islands upon which 18,000 dwellings are to be built. It will offer 45,000 people upscale and affordable shelter, with sea- and canalside views to boot. Of course, the sea is to play the defining role in the development of this neighbourhood, which will be constructed between 2001 and 2015.

Each of the six islands will have its own character. The Haveneiland (Harbour Island) will be the most urban, sporting high-rise apartments and office buildings as well as shopping, restaurants, cafés and recreation options. The Steigereiland (Pier Island) may wind up being the most interesting, as the majority of its dwellings will be houseboats or houses built on piers. The two Rieteneilanden (Reed Islands) and the Buiteneiland (Outer Island) will be primarily residential, with low-rise buildings that won't distract from the surrounding greenery. And the Strandeiland (Beach Island) will offer housing and recreational opportunities, though its actual layout was still being debated in 2000.

While the sea may ultimately play the definitive and seductive role in Amsterdam's newest community, the true stars have to be the plan and the engineering feat themselves. On a par with the laying of the three main canals during the 17th century, this land reclamation project employs the ingenuity of new and traditional techniques, the success of which promises to shift the city's disposition eastward and link the recently gentrified eastern docklands with the south-east of the city. It seems Amsterdam's love affair with water is a long way from being over just yet.

In the early 1920s, a new movement emerged that was the antithesis of the Amsterdam School. Developing on rather than reacting against Berlage's ideas, the Functionalists believed that new building materials such as concrete and steel should not be concealed, but that the basic structure of a building should be there for all to see. Function was supreme, ornament anathema. Their hard-edged concrete and glass boxes have much in common with the work of Frank Lloyd Wright in the USA, Le Corbusier in France and the Bauhaus in Germany.

Unsurprisingly, such radical views were not shared by everyone, and differences of opinion marked this as a turbulent period in Amsterdam's architectural history. Early Functionalist work, such as 1937's **Round Blue Teahouse** (in Vondelpark) and the **Cineac Cinema** (Reguliersbreestraat 31) of 1934, has a clean-cut elegance, and the Functionalist garden suburb of **Betondorp** (literally, 'Concrete Town'), built between 1921 and 1926, is far more attractive than the name might suggest. But after World War II, Functionalist ideology became an excuse for dreary, derivative, prefabricated eyesores. The urgent need for housing, coupled with town-planning theories that favoured residential satellite suburbs, led to the appearance of soulless, high-rise horrors on the edge of town, much the same as in the rest of Europe.

A change of heart during the 1970s refocused attention on making the city centre a pleasant jumble of residences, shops and offices. At the same time, a quirkier, more imaginative trend began to show itself in building design. The **ING Bank** (Bijlmerplein 888), built in 1987 of brick, has hardly a right angle in sight. A use of bright colour, and a return to a human-sized scale, is splendidly evident in Aldo van Eyck's **Moederhuis** (Plantage Middenlaan 33) from 1981. New façades – daringly modern, yet built to scale – began to appear between the old houses along the canals. The 1980s also saw, amid an enormous amount of controversy, the construction of what became known as the **Stopera**, a combined city hall (**Stadhuis**) and opera house on Waterlooplein (*see pages 52 and 223*). The eyecatching brick and marble coliseum of the **Muziektheater** is decidedly more successful than the dull oblongs that make up the City Hall.

Housing projects of the 1980s and 1990s have provided Amsterdam with some of its most imaginative modern architecture. The conversion of a 19th-century army barracks, the **Oranje Nassau Kazerne** (Sarphatistraat and Mauritskade) into studios and flats, with the addition of a row of rather zanily designed apartment blocks, is one of the more successful examples. Building on the KNSM Eiland and other islands in the derelict eastern docklands has combined an intelligent conversion of existing structures with some highly inventive new architecture. It is hoped that the hard lessons of the 1950s and 1960s have been learned, and the architectural mistakes made then will never be repeated.

The **Round Blue Teahouse**, as functional as a teacup.

THE FUTURE

At the municipal information centre for planning and housing in the freshly revamped **Zuiderkerk** (Zuiderkerkhof 72), one can see various models of the many current and future developments set to transform Amsterdam in the next decades; most give some cause for optimism. Those interested are advised to visit the website of **ARCAM** – the Architecture Centrum Amsterdam (*see page 197*) – at www.arcam.nl, where there's a map of all the spatial plans for the region along with around 1,000 projects due to be built between 2000 and 2030. **Bureau Monumentenzorg Amsterdam**, meanwhile, offers an obsessive overview of the city's architecture up to 1940 at www.amsterdam.nl/bmz.

> **'International periodicals now regard the "Dutch Model" as both pragmatic and futuristic.'**

Architectural travesties of the past have politicised the populace, who now keep a sharp eye on development. As such, referendums are now held prior to many new developments. Though 130,000 votes against the construction of IJburg – a residential community currently being built on a series of man-made islands in the IJmeer, just east of Amsterdam – was not enough to stop development around this ecologically sensitive area, it did inspire the promise that ƒ15 million would be invested in 'nature-development'. When completed, the six islands will be home to some 45,000 people in 18,000 dwellings, complete with a total infrastructure of commercial and industrial premises, shops, schools and other facilities. It will also be a showcase for the recently hyped Dutch concept of *wilde wonen* – 'wild living', as it were – where residents themselves get to design and build their own houses.

Similarly, the referendum result against the laying of the North-South Metro line didn't halt the project – still set to begin in the short-term – but it did establish that the city needed to be more diligent in its thinking. The powers that be, after all, apparently skimmed over such details as financing, loss of revenue for proximate shopkeepers and the potential for all this digging to cause the speedier sinking of above-lying historical buildings when planning the line, none of which endeared them to voters.

Now that the facelift of **Museumplein** has at last been completed (*see page 69* **Plein and simple**), all eyes are on the revamping of the

The **Stopera**, a modern block. *See p33.*

Eastern Docklands. A former squat paradise, it's hoped that redevelopments will turn it into a stunning photogenic harbourfront not unlike that in Sydney, Australia. Similarly, construction around the **ArenA** stadium will hopefully pump some much needed economic life into the nearby architectural prison known as the Bijlmermeer. This boulevard, due to be completed in 2006 but already sporting a huge Pathe cinema and rows of lighting poles by Philippe Starck, should become home to many businesses, a huge multifunctional concert hall and – thanks to the recent leaps and bounds made in building vertically on bog – the largest residential tower in the country.

Currently, Dutch architecture – thanks in part to such pundits as Rem Koolhaas – is very much in vogue. International periodicals, no longer casting LA and Hong Kong as the primary visionaries, now regard the 'Dutch Model' – where the boundaries between building, city, and landscape planning have long blurred beyond recognition – as both pragmatic and futuristic. After all, ecological degradation is now a worldwide phenomenon, and the space-constrained Netherlands has long ago begun regarding nature as an artificial construct that needs to be nurtured.

One just has to look at the Dutch pavilion at the Hannover World Expo 2000 to get the general idea. Dubbed the 'Dutch Big Mac', it's a building with water- and windmills for electricity on the roof, a theatre on the fourth floor, an oak forest on the third, flowers on the second, and dunes, cafés and shops on the first. Along the same lines, Amsterdam architect Subash Taneja is getting the opportunity to develop his stacked 'Smart Tower' in Almere, the futuristic satellite city that's already become a pilgrimage site for buffs of modern architecture. The tower is a seven-floor open-sided building with each floor walled into quadrants and each quadrant offering enough room for a single family 'wild-living' dwelling or a small field for animals. Holy cow: now *that's* cutting edge…

Sightseeing

Introduction

Might this be Amsterdam's second Golden Age? With newly expanded
museums and an enlivened city centre, there's never been a better time to visit.

For both casual visitor and long-term resident
alike, Amsterdam has one great advantage
above all others: its size. The compact nature of
the town makes it eminently negotiable,
especially if you're prepared to take your life
into your hands and rent a bike for the duration
of your stay. And even if you're not, then the
city's layout means you'll likely never be much
more than a half-hour's walk from wherever
you're heading, with the tram system providing
back-up if you don't fancy the exertion.

But for whatever reason, few visitors to
Amsterdam go beyond the borders defined by
the Grachtengordel (girdle of canals) – namely,
the area that Albert Camus observed to
resemble 'the circles of hell' – except perhaps to
stroll up to the area around Museumplein and
Vondelpark, where several of the major
museums are situated (see page 67). The further
you travel from the heart of town, the newer the
areas become, and there's plenty out of the
centre worth investigating if you take the time
to escape from the main tourist drag.

Within the centre of town are the medieval
buildings, the old port, the red lights that
denote the world's (flourishing) oldest trade, the
earliest and prettiest canals, the 17th-century
merchants' houses, and the highest density of

greasy snack purveyors. Slightly further out,
though, are quarters built to house the various
waves of incoming workers. Some of these
areas – the Jordaan, the Pijp and the Oost – are
covered below, while others in the south and
west, though not 'sightworthy' enough to cover
in this section, are still worth a visit for their
specific architecture, shopping, eats or
entertainment (see relevant chapters).

After World War II, new self-contained
'garden neighbourhoods' were built even further
out of the centre, including those to the west at
Osdorp and Slotermeer. More recent building
projects have been completed nearer the centre:
in the east, around the old port area, new homes
have been built to replace the old housing, and
many warehouses have been converted from
squats into apartments. And across the River IJ,
behind Centraal Station, lies Amsterdam Noord.
However, apart from the impressive Florapark,
there is little to see in the north, and the most
interesting part of a trip there is probably the
free ferry journey for pedestrians and cyclists,
which leaves from just behind Centraal Station.

See other relevant chapters – including
Architecture, **Shops & Services**, **Bars &
Cafés** and **Restaurants** – for more details on
the highlights of each area.

Neighbourhood watch

THE OLD CENTRE Amsterdam's ground zero
of consumerism, vice, entertainment and
history, the Old Centre has boundaries of
Prins Hendrikkade to the north, Oudeschans
and Waterlooplein to the east, the Amstel
river to the south and Singel to the west.

Within these borders, the Old Centre is split
into the **New Side** (to the west of Damrak and
Rokin) and the **Old Side** (to the east of
Damrak and Rokin). Contained within the Old
Side, roughly within the area bordered by
Zeedijk, Kloveniersburgwal, Oude Hoogstraat,
Damstraat and Warmoesstraat, is the **Red
Light District** (only one of several in the city,
but by far the most famous).

THE PLANTAGE & THE OOST Parts of the
Plantage were once known as Jodenbuurt,

after the Jews who began to settle in this
pocket two centuries ago. For visitors,
though, the Plantage, which lies east and
south-east of Waterlooplein, holds many
delights, among them the Hortus Botanicus
and the Artis Zoo. Further east – or **Oost** –
of the Plantage lies the entirely lovely
Sarphatipark and the splendid
Tropenmuseum, before the city opens up
and stretches further out.

THE GRACHTENGORDEL Translating literally
as 'girdle of canals', the watery ring that
guards the Old Centre is as idyllic and
pleasant an area as you'll find in the city. In
the listings for shops, restaurants and the
like throughout this guide, we've split the
Grachtengordel in half. **Grachtengordel: West**

Amsterdam's canals are every bit as idyllic and lovely as you'd expect.

Museums

If, for most of the world, precious little really changed in the roll-over to 2000, for Amsterdam's museums, 1999 was a year of renewal. Many of the city's collections and their visitors gained new spaces and exhibits in time for the new millennium. It was as if the museums wanted to remake themselves before their definitive 20th-century legacies were committed to history.

A controversial new incarnation of the Museumplein, designed by Dane Sven-Ingvar Andersson, was unveiled in mid-1999. The long expanse of lawn between the **Rijksmuseum** (*see page 67*), the **Van Gogh Museum** and the **Stedelijk Museum** (for both, *see page 68*) features a pool-cum-ice rink, a skaters' half-pipe and a subterranean parking garage. The Van Gogh Museum also reopened after major rebuilding: indeed, the renovation and expansion nearly doubled the museum's size.

denotes the stretch of canals (Singel, Herengracht, Keizersgracht and Prinsengracht) to the west and north of Leidsegracht, while **Grachtengordel: East** covers the area to the east of Leidsegracht, including **Leidseplein** and **Rembrandtplein**. **THE JORDAAN** Located to the east of the Grachtengordel – and bordered roughly by Brouwersgracht, Prinsengracht, Leidsegracht and Lijnbaansgracht – the Jordaan is one of Amsterdam's most charming neighbourhoods. Working-class stalwarts rub shoulders with affluent newcomers to the area in a neighbourhood that, while lacking the grandiose architecture of the Grachtengordel, wants for absolutely nothing in terms of character. **THE MUSEUM QUARTER** Highlighted by its handful of world-class attractions (the Rijksmuseum, the Stedelijk Museum, the Van

Gogh Museum and the Concertgebouw), some stupendously posh fashion emporia (mostly on or very near PC Hooftstraat) and a lovely green space (the Vondelpark), Amsterdam's Museum Quarter is a mix of culture and couture. Located south of Singelgracht, with approximate borders at Overtoom (west) and Hobbemakade (east), it's also home to many pleasant hotels and, at its northernmost tip, is within a stone's throw of Leidseplein. **THE PIJP** Against all odds – notably those of the developers, who have yet to rip the character out of the area – the Pijp has managed to remain a wonderful melting pot of cultures and nationalities. Located to the east of the Museum Quarter and south of the Grachtengordel, it's an area short on traditional sights but defiantly long on character and fun.

The famously cramped **Anne Frankhuis** (*see page 63*) and the **Rembrandthuis** (*see page 50*) breathed sighs of relief in 1999, too, as new wings meant the original houses could undergo more complete restoration work. The Anne Frankhuis's addition, made possible by the demolition of a block of student flats, now houses temporary exhibitions, a new bookstore and café, and even an extra entrance; at last the front house, where Anne Frank's father ran his business, is as it was during the war. And at the Rembrandthuis, a new building has provided a home for the museum's hundreds of etchings and its temporary exhibitions, finally enabling restoration of the artist's house and studios to an atmospheric 17th-century authenticity.

Elsewhere, the **Artis Zoo** (*see page 54*) finally expanded giving animals like the elephants and African wild dogs desperately needed space in which to move around, and the **Amsterdams Historisch Museum** (*see page 42*) renovated a wing, bringing about a new interactive exhibition on the city's diverse 19th- and 20th-century residents, from immigrants to activists to entrepreneurs. The **Bijbels Museum** (*see page 57*), too, spruced up its interior and gained new space that, in 2000, was being filled with items previously not on show.

And it's not over yet. After a flap over a near-miss sponsorship deal whereby part of its space would have been turned into an Audi showroom, the Stedelijk is planning an expansion in the coming few years. The Rijksmuseum is looking into renovations whereby space will be used more in keeping with the original plans of architect PJH Cuypers. And Amsterdam will get a whole new museum in 2006, when the Russian state museum, the Hermitage, plans to open a satellite on the Amstel. There's a lot to get round, then, and museum-lovers would be well advised to get started right away.

TICKETS & INFORMATION

While most Amsterdam museums charge for admission, the prices tend to be reasonable: usually ƒ5 to ƒ10. However, if you're thinking of taking in more than a few, the annual **Museum Card** (or 'Museumjaarkaart') is a steal at ƒ55 or ƒ25 for under-25s. The ticket offers free or reduced admission to around 400 museums throughout the Netherlands, and though special exhibitions are usually not covered by the ticket, cardholders are often entitled to a discount. You can buy the card at many museums, tourist offices and the **AUB** (*see page 283* **Tickets please**).

The money-saving deals don't end there, though: during **National Museum Weekend**, held every April, about 200 small museums around the country offer free or reduced admission (*see page 169*). However, you'll have to vie with all the locals taking advantage of this popular freebie, and the museums can get exceptionally busy. Also to be avoided, if at all possible, are the major museums' temporary exhibitions on the weekends, and almost any museum on Wednesday afternoons: most primary schools have Wednesday afternoons off, and things can get a little hellish.

Other things worth noting include the fact that many museums – though by no means all – are closed on Mondays and public holidays. Always phone to check if you're unsure. And if you're worried about the language barrier, don't be: while museums don't always have captions and explanations in English, many sell English guidebooks, and several also offer guided tours in English for groups, though you'll need to phone ahead to book.

Artis Expres

Office & main boarding point: Stationsplein 8, Old Centre: New Side (530 1090). Tram 1, 2, 4, 5, 9, 13, 16, 17, 20, 24, 25. **Departs** every 30min, 10am-5pm daily. **Stops** at Centraal Station, Artis Zoo. **Day tickets** ƒ15; ƒ10 4-12s. **Map** p306 C/D1/2.
The Artis Expres is a boat that travels between Centraal Station and the Artis Zoo complex, passing the Scheepvaartmuseum and its East India Company ship on the way and taking a scenic canal route on the way back. Tickets include discounts for the Artis, the Scheepvaartmuseum and the Tropenmuseum.

Museumboot

Office & main boarding point: Stationsplein 8, Old Centre: New Side (622 2181). Tram 1, 2, 4, 5, 9, 13, 16, 17, 20, 24, 25. **Departs** *June-mid Sept* every 30min, 10am-5pm daily. *Mid Sept-May* every 45min, 10am-5pm daily. **Stops** at Prinsengracht (Anne Frankhuis, Theatermuseum); Stadhouderskade (Museumplein, Rijksmuseum, Van Gogh Museum, Stedelijk Museum); Herengracht (Bijbels Museum, Amsterdams Historisch Museum, Allard Pierson Museum); Amstel/Zwanenburgwal (Rembrandthuis, Joods Historisch Museum, Hortus Botanicus, Tropenmuseum); Oosterdok/Kattenburgergracht (Scheepvaartmuseum, Werf 't Kromhout); Centraal Station (Madame Tussauds, Museum Amstelkring). **Day tickets** ƒ27,50; ƒ20 4-12s. *After 1pm* ƒ22,50; ƒ15 4-12s. Tickets can also be bought at all stops and on board. **Map** p306 C/D1/2.
The Museumboot is good value, especially for those on a budget. Tickets entitle holders to get on and off at any of six stops serving a host of museums on and near the concentric canals. Bear in mind that the larger museums – such as the Rijksmuseum and the Stedelijk – demand at least half a day each, so the Museumboot is better used to take in more of the smaller ones that are less easily accessible via public transport. Tickets for the Museumboot include discounts of up to 50% on admission prices to assorted museums; phone for details.

The Old Centre

On one side are myriad shopping treats, yet on the other it's sex that's for sale.
Amsterdam's Old Centre is both contradictory and compelling.

With boundaries, at least in theory, of the
harbour behind Centraal Station, the Singel and
the Zwanenburgwal canals, the old city centre
is bisected by Damrak, which turns into Rokin
south of Dam Square. Within the Old Centre
(aka Oud Centrum), the area to the east
containing the Red Light District is the ancient
Old Side (Oude Zijde), while the area to the
west, whose most notable landmark is Spui
Square, is the not-really-that-new-anymore New
Side (Nieuwe Zijde).

Around the Dam

Map p306

Straight up from Centraal Station, just beyond
the once-watery and now-paved and touristy
strip called the Damrak, lies Dam Square, the
heart of the city since the first dam was built
here across the Amstel in 1270. Today, it's a
convenient meeting point for many tourists, the
majority of whom meet under its mildly phallic
centrepiece, the **Nationaal Monument**. This
22-metre (70-foot) white obelisk is dedicated to
the Dutch servicemen who died in World War
II. Designed by JJP Oud, with sculptures by
John Raedecker, it incorporates 12 urns: 11 are
filled with earth collected from the then 11
Dutch provinces, with the 12th containing soil
from war cemeteries in Indonesia, a Dutch
colony until 1949.

Following the refurbishment of the monument
in recent years, the whole square itself is now to
be given a much-needed facelift: the hope is that
it'll become more of a 'people's' square again,
instead of simply a shabby pigeon-filled block
where people dodge careening taxis and errant
cyclists. Indeed, the Dam has certainly lost some
of its social and political spark since 1535, when
the Anabaptists ran naked through the square
to test the boundaries of religious freedom, and
even since the '60s, when it was used as a chill-
out zone by local hippies.

The west side of Dam Square is flanked by
the **Koninklijk Paleis** (literally, 'Royal
Palace'; *listings page 41*). Designed by Jacob
van Campen in the 17th century along classical
lines and famously built on 13,659 wooden piles
that were rammed deep into the sand, it was
originally used as the city hall. The poet
Constantijn Huygens hyped it as 'the world's

Eighth Wonder', a monument to the cockiness
Amsterdam felt at the dawn of its Golden Age.
However, the exterior is only really impressive
when viewed from the rear – where Atlas holds
his load from a great height – and you'll have to
go inside to understand what Huygens meant.
This interior also helps the visitor realise that
the confidence felt at the time was one laced
with fear: God, the devil and their elements
were always on hand to kick you in the teeth
when you least expected it.

Inside the Palace, the epic Citizen's Hall, with
its decoration in grand marble and bronze that
images a miniature universe, is meant to make
you feel about as significant as the nibbling rats
seen carved in stone over the door above the
Bankruptcy Chamber. Though much of the art

The best Museums

For a course in Amsterdam appreciation
From Calvinism to Chinatown, learn how
this amazing city got the way it is today at
the **Amsterdams Historisch Museum**
(see page 49).

For a sumptuous collection
With its limitless collection of art and
artefacts, the **Rijksmuseum** (see page 67)
is the jewel in the Netherlands' glittering
chain of museums.

For virtual travel
Sick of Europe? Spend a few hours in
Africa, Asia and South America at the
Tropenmuseum (see page 54).

For harassed parents
Just don't tell the kids that the
newMetropolis (see page 75) is a museum,
and they'll never be any the wiser.

For emotional impact
Not so long ago, the unthinkable happened
here. The reconstructions and multimedia
displays in the **Anne Frankhuis** (see page
63) and the **Verzetsmuseum** (see page 54)
see to it that the horrors aren't forgotten.

The dope on Cheese

● The yellow and round wheel of Gouda and the orange ball of Edam were already established export products by the 1600s. However, cheese-making has occurred in these parts since the second century BC.

● As the world's largest exporter of cheese, the Dutch are often referred to as *kaaskoppen*, or cheeseheads. Scholars claim that the term originated in the Middle Ages, when farmers would use wooden cheese moulds – also called *kaaskoppen* – as helmets when going into battle.

● Not content with each eating an average of 15 kilograms (33 pounds) per person per year, the Dutch have even found it necessary to open a cheese museum (in Alkmaar; see page 248) to feed their addiction.

● In 1956, a canned Edam left over from a 1912 expedition was found at the South Pole. When eaten, it was found to be merely a tad 'sharp'.

● The typical Dutch cheese-slicing tool – the *kaasschaaf* – is, in fact, a Norwegian invention.

● Dutch language and slang have been hugely enriched by myriad cheese metaphors. Among our favourites: 'He hasn't eaten cheese from there' (he doesn't know anything about that); 'He won't let the cheese be taken from his bread' (he'll make sure he gets what's owed to him); and 'He's selling cheese' (he may well be telling lies). Ask a Dutch friend for the more unprintable ones.

● To try out some Dutch cheese, head to authentic Dutch cheesemakers **Wegewijs** (Rozengracht 32, The Jordaan; 624 4093; see page 157).

reflects the typically jaded humour of a people who have seen it all, the overall impression is one of deadly seriousness: one screw-up and you could end up among the grotesque carvings of the Tribunal and sentenced to die in some uniquely torturous and public way. Kinder, gentler displays of creativity, though, can be seen in the chimney pieces, painted by artists such as Ferdinand Bol and Govert Flinck, both pupils of Rembrandt (who, ironically, had his own sketches rejected). The city hall was transformed into a royal palace in 1808, shortly after Napoleon had made his brother, Louis, King of the Netherlands (*see page 11*), and a fine collection of furniture from this period can be viewed on a guided tour of the building. The Palace became state property in 1936 and is still used occasionally by the royal family.

Beside the Royal Palace stands the **Nieuwe Kerk** (New Church; *listings page 41*). While the 'old' **Oude Kerk** in the Red Light District (*see page 45*) was built in the 1300s, the sprightly 'new' Nieuwe Kerk dates from 1408. It is not known how much damage was caused by the fires of 1421 and 1452, or even how much rebuilding took place, but most of the pillars and walls were erected after that period (*see page 28*). Iconoclasm in 1566 left the church

intact, though statues and altars were removed in the Reformation (*see page 5*). The sundial on its tower was used to set all of the city's clocks until 1890.

In 1645, the Nieuwe Kerk was gutted by the Great Fire; the ornately carved oak pulpit and great organ (the latter designed by Jacob van Campen) are thought to have been constructed shortly after the blaze. Also of interest here is the tomb of naval hero Admiral de Ruyter (1607-76), who initiated the ending of the Second Anglo-Dutch war – seriously wounding British pride in the process – when he sailed up the Thames in 1667, inspiring a witness, Sir William Batten, to observe: 'I think the Devil shits Dutchmen.' Behind the black marble tomb of de Ruyter is a white marble relief depicting the sea battle in which he died. Poets and Amsterdam natives PC Hooft and Joost van den Vondel are also buried here. The Nieuwe Kerk is no longer used as a place of worship, but does host organ recitals, state occasions and consistently excellent exhibitions.

In painfully kitsch contrast is **Madame Tussauds Scenerama** (*listings page 41*), on the south side of Dam Square in the top two floors of the Peek & Cloppenburg department store. Cheese-textured representations from

Holland's own Golden Age of commerce are all depicted alongside a more contemporary golden shower of hits: the Dutch royal family, local celebs and global superstars. One can't help feeling that the materials used should really have been put towards making candles.

Backtrack towards Centraal Station past the shopping frenzy that takes place in the Bijenkorf ('Beehive') department store, and you'll come to the **Beurs van Berlage** (*listings below*). Designed in 1896 by Hendrik Petrus Berlage as the city's palatial stock exchange, the Beurs, while incorporating many different, more traditional, building styles, represents an important break with 19th-century architecture and prepared the way for the modern swoopy brickwork of the Amsterdam School (*see page 31*). The building now operates as a conference and exhibition centre with two concert halls, a café and a restaurant.

If that sounds all a tad too cultural, perhaps your antidote lurks across the Damrak at the **Sex Museum** (*listings below*). Sadly, this den of iniquitous exhibits doesn't boast anything as highbrow as the Lennon drawings at the **Erotic Museum** (*see page 45*), and relies for most of its trade on tourists passing by on their way to and from Centraal Station. Like the worst kind of porn, the Sex Museum is neither erotic nor fun, and succeeds only in boring through a series of tawdry and unilluminating displays.

Beurs van Berlage

Damrak 277, entrance at Beursplein 1 (530 4141). Tram 4, 9, 14, 16, 20, 24, 25. **Open** *Museum* 10am-4pm Tue-Sun; closed Mon. **Admission** *Museum* ƒ7; free Museum Card, under-12s. **No credit cards.** **Map** p306 D2.

Koninklijk Paleis

Dam (624 8698/www.kon-paleisamsterdam.nl). Tram 1, 2, 4, 5, 9, 13, 14, 16, 17, 20, 24, 25. **Open** *June-Aug* 11am-5pm daily; *Sept-May* 12.30-5pm, days vary. **Admission** ƒ8; ƒ6 5-16s free under-4s. **No credit cards. Map** p306 C3.

Madame Tussauds Scenerama

Peek & Cloppenburg, Dam 20 (622 9239/ www.madame-tussauds.com). Tram 4, 9, 14, 16, 20, 24, 25. **Open** 10am-5.30pm daily. **Admission** ƒ19,95; ƒ16 concessions. **Credit** AmEx, DC, MC, V. **Map** p306 D3.

Nieuwe Kerk

Dam (626 8168/www.nieuwekerk.nl). Tram 1, 2, 4, 5, 9, 13, 14, 16, 17, 20, 24, 25. **Open** hours vary. **Admission** free-ƒ15. **No credit cards. Map** p306 C3.

Sex Museum

Damrak 18 (622 8376). Tram 4, 9, 14, 16, 20, 24, 25. **Open** 10am-11.30pm daily. **Admission** ƒ4,50. **Map** p306 D2.

The Old Side & the Red Light District

Maps p306 and p307

The Red Light District, situated in an approximate triangle formed by Centraal Station, the Nieuwmarkt and the Dam, is the root of Amsterdam's international notoriety. The world's desperate and horny imagine breasts eagerly pancaked against red neon-framed windows, canals awash with bodily fluids. As if to give weight to this image, the postcards on sale in local shops depict a sort of small, cutesy Vegas. If truth be told, though, the cheesy joke shop has here become the cheesy sex shop, with electric palm buzzers and comedy nose glasses being replaced by multi-orificed inflatables and huge orbital dildos.

Most of the history of the Red Light District – of which there is plenty, this being the oldest part of Amsterdam – has been greasily veneered with that other of oldest trades: marketing. Sex, while the hook upon which the area hangs its reputation, is actually secondary to window-shopping. People do buy – it's estimated to be a ƒ1-billion per year trade – but mostly they wander in groups, stopping here and there to gawp open-mouthed at the live exhibits. The choice is ample: an astounding 5,000 professionals ply their trade from here, of which 2,000 are available on any given day. Most of these window girls are self-employed, and even though prostitution was only defined as a legal profession since 1988 and bordellos have only been officially legal since October 1999 (a tactic hoped to make taxation still easier), the women have had their own union, De Rode Draad, since 1984. They are, indeed, mostly women: despite attempts to launch male and transsexual prostitution, men have so far found it difficult to get their dicks into this particular door of opportunity.

As at more traditional markets such as the **Albert Cuypmarkt** (*see page 163*), where cheese merchants line up alongside cheese merchants and fishmongers group with fishmongers, women of similar specialisations also tend to clump together. Sultry Latins gather on the Molensteeg and the beginning of Oudezijds Achterburgwal, ambiguously sexed Thais on Stoofstraat, and the vaguely model-ish but definitely anorexic on Trompettersteeg, Amsterdam's smallest street (where you will have trouble passing other punters if you happen to be sporting a woody). But there is much else to absorb in this most iconoclastic of neighbourhoods. Prostitutes, clerics, schoolkids, junkies, carpenters and cops all interact with a strange brand of social cosiness, and the tourists are mere voyeurs. It's all good fun and pretty harmless, just so long as you remember that window girls do not like having their pictures taken and that drug dealers react to eye contact like a dog to a bone.

Zeedijk

Facing away from Centraal Station to the left are two churches, the **St Nicolaaskerk** (whose interior of funky darkness can be viewed from Easter to mid-October, 1.30-4pm Mon, 11am-4pm Tue-Sat) and the dome and skull-adorned exterior of the **St Olafkerk** (known locally as the 'Cheese Church', having housed the cheese exchange for many years). Between the two, you can enter Zeedijk, a street with a rich and tattered history. Before this dyke was built around 1300, Amsterdam was a fishing village with barely enough bog to stand on. But by the 15th and 16th centuries, with the East India Company raking in the imperialist dollars, Zeedijk was where sailors came to catch up on their boozing, brawling and bonking (or 'doing the St Nicolaas' as it was fondly termed in those days, as a tribute to their patron saint, a busy chap who also patrons children, thieves, prostitutes and the city of Amsterdam).

Sailors who had lost all their money could trade in their pet monkey for a bed at Zeedijk 1, which still retains its old name – **In't Aepjen**, meaning 'In the Monkeys' – and is one of the oldest wooden houses in the city (*see also pages 28 and 123*). Just off the street down Oudezijds

Kolk, you can spot the **Schreierstoren**, the 'Weeping Tower' (*see also pages 28, 75 and 125*). It is told that wives would cry there, perhaps with relief, when husbands set off on a voyage, and then cry again if the ship returned with the bad news that the husband was lost at sea. If the latter ever happened, then – conveniently – it was but a short walk to Zeedijk, where the bereaved lady would often continue life as a 'merry widow'. Prostitution was often the female equivalent of joining the navy: the last economic option.

During the 20th century, Zeedijk has been sparked by cultural diversity. In the 1930s, the first openly gay establishments appeared, and at the now-closed – though a replica is now on display in the **Amsterdams Historisch Museum** (*see page 49*) – Café Maandje (Zeedijk 65), there is still a window shrine to legendary owner Bet van Beeren (1902-67), who will surely go down in history as the original Lesbian Biker Chick. In the 1950s, all the jazz greats, from Chet Baker to Gerry Mulligan, came to jam and hang out in the many after-hours clubs around here.

Unfortunately, this subculture marked Zeedijk as a place where heroin could be scored with comparative ease. By the 1970s, the street was crowded with dealers, junkies and indifferent cops, with most of the restaurants and cafés renting their tables to dealers. The junkies' magic number back then was 27: *f*25 for the drugs themselves, and *f*2 for the drink the owners insisted the junkies purchase to maintain the façades of legality.

The neon-lit sleaze and tawdriness of the **Red Light District...**

... sits side by side with the historic and beautiful **Oude Kerk** (*see p45*).

Amsterdam's reputation became littered with needles and bits of foil, never more so than when a wasted Chet Baker made his final moody decrescendo in 1988 on to a cement parking pole from a window of the **Prins Hendrik Hotel** at the entrance of the Zeedijk. A brass plaque commemorating the crooning trumpeter has been installed to the left of the hotel's entrance. But though there was a time when a German tour operator's 'criminal safari' was not even allowed on the Zeedijk, in recent years, police claim to have cleaned the street up; indeed, the scene is today infinitely less intimidating and packed with new and new-ish businesses and restaurants. The famed dance and ambient label **Outland Records** has its store at No.22; **Demask** offers its posh line of leathers and latexes at No.64 (*see page 147*); and excellent cheap Chinese food can be found at **Nam Kee** at Zeedijk 111-13 (*see page 105*). The building of a brand spanking new Chinese Buddhist temple, where monks and nuns will also service a library and Internet café, across the street from Nam Kee, speaks much of this street's continued spiritual growth; it's due to open in late 2000.

Nieuwmarkt

At the bottom of Zeedijk, your eyes will immediately be drawn to the huge and menacing castle-like **De Waag**, or 'the Weigh House'. The Waag, previously called St Antoniespoort, stands in the centre of the Nieuwmarkt and dates from 1488, when it was built as a gatehouse for the city defences. If what motivates your walk through this area is a meditation on humankind's darkest sides, then try to imagine the body parts that used to garnish the Waag's south-east side, and let them act as a baleful warning: this is where the majority of Amsterdam's public executions took place. Here people were tortured, hanged, shot or, when Napoleon's brother held influence, guillotined, and there were always plenty of corpses for the medical guild to dissect, or for Rembrandt to study and paint: *The Anatomy Lesson of Dr Nicolaes Tulp* stands as evidence. One can only hope that none of the leftovers was sold at the open-air market that has always existed here. Still more depressing is to imagine how, in the dark days of the Nazi occupation, this square was surrounded by barbed wire and used as one of the collection points to hold those from the nearby Jewish quarter who were to be shipped off to concentration camps.

More recently, Nieuwmarkt was the site of many riots around 1980, when the city was busy demolishing housing in order to build the Metro. The Waag's **Anatomical Theatre** is now scrubbed clean and is open to the public by appointment, as is a trendy café (**In de Waag**; *see page 125*) and the Society for Old and New Media, complete with free Internet room. The building's 500-year passage from torture to technology is now complete.

"These Americans can take it and they can dish it out"
– Time Magazine

"Rapid-fire improv... a phenomenon"
– Rough Guide

"Funny, fast-paced... a great night out"'
– Time Out

Amsterdam's Comedy Institution 7 Nights a week

We serve great food before the show as well
Reservations essential: (020) 423 0101
Leidseplein Theater ▪ Leidseplein 12 ▪ 1017 PT Amsterdam

The streets leading north-east from Nieuwmarkt contain Amsterdam's small **Chinatown**, while the colourfully named side streets – among them Monnikkenstraat (Monk Street), Bloedstraat (Blood Street) and Koestraat (Cow Street) – on the south-west lead into the reddest part of the Red Light District. Heading south from the Nieuwmarkt along the Kloveniersburgwal canal, though, makes for a more interesting stroll. At Kloveniersburgwal 29 is the **Trippenhuis**, now home to the Dutch Academy of Sciences, and formerly, in the 18th century, home to the Rijksmuseum collection. During the Golden Age, the building was owned by the Trip family, whose fortune was made by arms dealing (witness the cannon-shaped chimneys). Their riches meant they could easily afford the imposing gunpowder grey exterior, and they even indulged themselves in building the House of Mr Trip's Coachman at No.26, erected in response to a one-liner the coachman reputedly made about being happy with a house as wide as the Trip's front door. He got his wish. The house is now home to a trendy clothing store complete with appropriately anorexic display figures in the window.

'De Wallen'

The canals Oudezijds Voorburgwal and Oudezijds Achterburgwal, with their interconnecting streets, are where carnal sin screams loudest. Right in the middle of Sin City, you'll stumble across the **Oude Kerk** (Old Church; *listings page 47*). Originally built in 1306 as a wooden chapel, and constantly renovated and extended between 1330 and 1571, the Oude Kerk is Amsterdam's oldest and most interesting church (*see page 28*). All its original furnishings were removed by iconoclasts during the Reformation, but the church has retained its wooden roof, which was painted all the way back in the 15th century with figurative images. Keep your eyes peeled, too, for the Gothic and Renaissance façade above the northern portal, and the stained-glass windows, parts of which date from the 16th and 17th centuries. Rembrandt's wife Saskia, who died in 1642, is buried under the small organ. The inscription over the bridal chamber, which translates as 'Marry in haste, mourn at leisure', is in keeping with the church's location, though this is more by accident than design. The church is now as much of an exhibition centre as anything, with shows covering everything from Aboriginal art to the annual **World Press Photo** (*see page 169*).

The Oudezijds Achterburgwal offers some of the more 'tasteful' choices for the eroto-clubber. The **Casa Rosso** nightclub (Oudezijds

Achterburgwal 106-8, 627 8954) is certainly worth a look, if only for its peculiar marble cock-and-rotary-ball water fountain at its entrance. A short walk away at No.37 is the **Bananenbar** (622 4670), where Olympic-calibre genitalia can be witnessed night after night working out (and, incidentally, spitting out an average of 15 kilograms (33 pounds) of fruit each evening in the process). A former owner of the Bananenbar once attempted to stave off the taxman – and get round the fact his drinking licence had lapsed – by picking Satan as a deity and registering the Bananenbar as a church. The owner became a black bishop, barmaids were promoted as nuns, drinks became elixirs, and the banana shenanigan became a ritual on a par with the taking of the host during mass. It was a scam that worked for years, until in 1988, when the 'Church of Satan' started to claim a membership of 40,000 overseen by a council of nine anonymous persons. Tax police were called in to find the loopholes and bust the joint: it was to be an exorcism through audit. But the bar was tipped off just in time, and the 'church' disbanded. Now under a new owner, the Bananenbar has kept its name and returned to its roots as a purveyor of specialised sleaze.

If your urges are more academic than participatory, then you can pay tribute to original S&M muse Betty Page at the **Erotic Museum** (*listings page 47*), which has some original photos of the lady on display among its five floors of quasi-erotic gadgetry. However, only the most liberal language student would allow this spot – in a nutshell, five floors of tawdry, asexual tack – into the category 'museum'. The staggering number of sex toys on display are classified as 'collector's items'. If you're not an aficionado, though, the original John Lennon erotic sketches alone are worth the meagre price of admission.

Surprisingly, it's not all sex, sex, sex down here, though you'd be forgiven for thinking otherwise. Body manipulators and defacers, for example, can put their hobby into a cultural and historical perspective by visiting the **Tattoo Museum** (*listings page 47*). In 1996, famous local tattoo artist and convention organiser Henk Schiffmacher moved his Tattoo Museum out of his **Hanky Panky** tattoo parlour in the heart of the Red Light District and into an old tobacco warehouse on the next canal. The surprisingly interesting museum also houses a public library, an archive and an information centre.

The exhibition includes hundreds of ancient and ethnographical tools, thousands of drawings, photographs and prints, and even some preserved pieces of tattooed skin. Financial problems put the Tattoo Museum's fate in the balance in 1999, and Schiffmacher quit running the shop to tend to the museum full-time. A fund-raising drive was still ongoing in mid-2000, and though it looks like the museum will survive, it's best to call ahead before you go. But if skin is really your thing, take the trek to the anatomical **Museum Vrolik** (*see page 78* **The specialists**), which has a few choice clippings of tattooed human rawhide alongside a remarkable collection of skulls and Siamese twin foetuses in brine.

The Oudezijds Voorburgwal was known as the 'Velvet Canal' in the 16th century due to the obscene wealth of its residents. Now, though, the velvet has been replaced by red velour, illuminated by scarlet fluorescent lighting and complemented by a steady stream of bored-looking girls sat twiddling their thumbs in the windows of the lovely canal houses.

It's rather ironic, then, that this canal should be so densely populated with churches, chapels and orders. Reps from the Salvation Army lurk on every corner near the **Agnietenkapel**, at No.231 (*listings page 47*), but if you can successfully negotiate their attentions, you'll be in for a treat once inside. Of Amsterdam's 17 medieval convents, this Gothic chapel is one of a few remnants to have survived intact. Built in the 1470s and part of the university since its foundation in 1632, the chapel has an austere, Calvinistic beauty highlighted by stained-glass windows, wooden beams and benches, and a collection of paintings of humanist thinkers. The

Grote Gehoorzaal ('Large Auditorium'), the country's oldest lecture hall, is where 17th-century scholars Vossius and Barlaeus first taught; its wooden ceiling is painted with soberly ornamental Renaissance motifs including angels and flowers. Exhibitions are held here only occasionally.

The **Museum Amstelkring** (*listings page 47*), meanwhile, can be found at Oudezijds Voorburgwal 40. Undeservedly neglected by most visitors, the building houses the only remaining attic church in Amsterdam, rescued from demolition in the late 1800s by a group of historians called the Amstelkring (hence the museum's name). The church itself – 'Ons' Lieve Heer op Solder', or 'Our Lord in the Attic' – was built in 1663, and was used by Catholics during the 17th century when they were banned from worshipping after the Alteration.

The lower floors of the house include furnished living rooms that could have served as the setting for one of the 17th-century Dutch masters, while the chaplain's room upstairs contains a small cupboard bed. The pilgrimage upwards leads visitors to the highlight of the museum: the beautifully preserved attic church, the altarpiece of which features a painting by 18th-century artist Jacob de Wit. The church is often used for services and a variety of other meetings. Don't miss it.

Amsterdam wouldn't be Amsterdam without a druggie museum, which is where the clumsily named **Hash Marihuana Hemp Museum**

Play ball at the **Casa Rosso**. *See p45.*

The dope on Windmills

- The windmill is not Dutch but, rather, a Spanish invention.
- Many years ago, folks saw the complicated mechanics of a mill as a highly sexually suggestive and diabolical craft. Millers were said to have traded their souls for the secrets of the sprockets and gears, while other tales spoke of demon-sightings and the defilement of virgins occurring under darkness at the neighbourhood windmill.
- Many medieval paintings show windmills grinding up old women and then ejecting them, rejuvenated, as comely young babes. Other illustrations show magical windmills that pulverise shaved and robed monks into grotesque and mutant goblins.
- The original windmills had their number of arms increased from two to four in order to create the suggestion of a crucifix. The idea was to use the windmill as the ultimate protection from possession.
- Back in 19th-century Netherlands, the government levied a wind tax on windmill owners.

- Many Dutch sayings describe insanity and general absurdity in relation to windmills, or 'windmillies', as a child's windwheel was called. A windmill goes round and round in the wind but nothing else: like the brain of the insane or insanely drunk, there's action (twirl twirl) but no connection (fizzle).
- The vast majority of windmills that still remain in the Netherlands serve no actual function, twirling only on government subsidy.
- Among the windmills in Amsterdam, all dating from the 17th or 18th centuries, are **D'Admiraal** (on Noordhollandschkanaaldijk, near Jan Thoméepad); **De Bloem** (on Haarlemmerweg, near Nieuwpoortkade); **De Gooyer**, now home to the splendid brewpub **Bierbrouwerij 't IJ** (at Funenkade 7; see also page 128); **1100 Roe** (on Herman Bonpad, Sportpark, in Ookmeer); **1200 Roe** (the eldest, built around 1632; on Haarlemmerweg, near Willem Molengraaffstraat); and **De Rieker** (on Amsteldijk, near De Borcht).

(*listings below*) comes in. It has its moments, too, with exhibits including smugglers' devices, instructions on how to roll a blunt and a window on the professional grow room next door. Dopers will doubtless find the place fascinating despite the fact that on occasion, it seems to lose sight of the whole point: namely, that you can smoke the stuff, not that you can knit it into a vile pair of sackcloth trousers.

On the Spinhuissteeg is the Spinhuis, another former convent that used to set 'wayward women' to work spinning wool as their penance. The male equivalent was at Heiligeweg 9 – now an entrance to the **Kalvertoren** shopping complex – where audiences once watched prisoners being branded and beaten with a bull's penis. In a further historical foreshadowing of this city's contemporary S&M scene, the entrance gate sports a statue resembling a scolding dominatrix.

Universiteitsmuseum de Agnietenkapel
Oudezijds Voorburgwal 231 (525 3339). Tram 4, 9, 14, 16, 20, 24, 25. **Open** *9am-5pm Mon-Fri; closed Sat, Sun.* **Admission** *ƒ3,50 special exhibitions; free otherwise.* **No credit cards. Map** p306 D3.

Museum Amstelkring
Oudezijds Voorburgwal 40 (624 6604). Tram 4, 9, 14, 16, 20, 24, 25. **Open** *10am-5pm Mon-Sat; 1-5pm Sun.* **Admission** *ƒ10; ƒ6 concessions; free Museum Card, under-5s.* **No credit cards. Map** p306 D2.

Erotic Museum
Oudezijds Achterburgwal 54 (624 7303). Tram 4, 9, 16, 20, 24, 25/Metro Nieuwmarkt. **Open** *11am-1am Mon, Thur, Sun; 11am-2am Fri, Sat; closed Tue, Wed.* **Admission** *ƒ5.* **No credit cards. Map** p306 D2.

Hash Marihuana Hemp Museum
Oudezijds Achterburgwal 148 (623 5961). Tram 4, 9, 14, 16, 20, 24, 25/Metro Nieuwmarkt. **Open** *11am-10pm daily.* **Admission** *ƒ8.* **No credit cards. Map** p306 D3.

Oude Kerk
Oudekerksplein 1 (625 8284/www.oudekerk.nl). Tram 4, 9, 16, 20, 24, 25, 26. **Open** *Dec-Mar 1-5pm Mon-Fri, Sun. Apr-Nov 11am-5pm Mon-Sat; 1-5pm Sun.* **Admission** *ƒ7,50; ƒ5 Museum Card.* **No credit cards. Map** p306 D2.

Tattoo Museum
Oudezijds Achterburgwal 130 (625 1565/ www.tattoomuseum.nl). Tram 4, 9, 16, 20, 24, 25. **Open** *noon-5pm Tue-Sun; closed Mon.* **Admission** *ƒ7,50.* **No credit cards. Map** p306 D3.

Warmoesstraat & Nes

It's hard to believe that Warmoesstraat, Amsterdam's oldest street, was once the most beautiful of lanes, providing a sharp contrast to its then-evil and rowdy twin, Zeedijk. The poet Vondel ran his hosiery business at Warmoesstraat 101; Mozart's dad would try to scalp tickets at the posh bars for his young son's concerts; and Marx would later come here to write in peace (or so he'd claim: cynics point out that he was more likely in town to borrow money from his cousin-by-marriage, Gerard Philips, founder of the corporate capitalist machine, Philips).

But with the influx of sailors, the laws of supply and demand dictated a fall from grace for Warmoesstraat. Adam and Eve in their salad days can still be seen etched in stone at Warmoesstraat 25, but for the most part, this street has fallen to accommodating the low-end traveller. However, hip hangouts such as gay bar **Getto** (*see page 207*) and the **Winston Hotel** (*see page 96*), shops including the **Condomerie Het Guiden Vlies** (*see page 166*) and gallery **W139** (*see page 200*) ensure that the strip retains some brighter and less commercial colours.

Just as Warmoesstraat stretches north from the Nationaal Monument into the Old Side, so Nes leaves the same spot to the south, parallel and to the west of Oudezijds Achterburgwal. Dating from the Middle Ages, this street was once home to the city's tobacco trade and the Jewish quasi-Buddhist Spinoza (1623-77), who saw body and mind as aspects of a single substance. Appropriate, then, that you can now witness the alignment of body and mind on the stages of the many theatres that now grace this street. You can also stop, recharge and realign your own essence at one of the many charming cafés. At the end of the Nes, either turn left to cross a bridge where junkies sell freshly stolen bicycles for next to nothing – though be warned that buying one has you risking jail and deportation – towards the very euroscenic **Oudemanhuis Book Market** (*see page 164*) on the University of Amsterdam campus; or turn right and end up near the archaeologically inclined **Allard Pierson Museum** (*listings below*).

Established in 1934, the Allard Pierson Museum claims to hold one of the world's richest university collections of archaeological exhibits, gathered from ancient Egypt, Greece, Rome and the Near East. The exhibits are undeniably interesting, but the building has a subdued, scholarly atmosphere, and many statues, sculptures, clay tablets and ceramics are unimaginatively presented. More accessible are items such as the scale maquettes (of the pyramids, Olympia and so on), the full-size sarcophagi and the model of a Greek chariot. More often than not, though, the English captions are rather minimal, as if assuming a certain amount of background knowledge. The temporary exhibitions on the first floor (usually costing around ƒ5) draw large-ish crowds.

Allard Pierson Museum

Oude Turfmarkt 127 (525 2556). Tram 4, 9, 14, 16, 20, 24, 25. **Open** 10am-5pm Tue-Fri; 1-5pm Sat, Sun; closed Mon. **Admission** ƒ9,50; ƒ1-ƒ7 concessions; free Museum Card, under-4s. **No credit cards. Map** p306 D3.

The New Side

Map p306

Rhyming, near enough, with 'cow', the Spui is the square that caps the three main arteries that start down near the west end of Centraal Station: the middle-of-the-road walking and shopping street Kalverstraat (called Nieuwendijk before it crosses the Dam), Nieuwezijds Voorburgwal and the Spuistraat.

Coming up Nieuwezijds Voorburgwal – translated literally as 'The New Side's Front of the Town Wall', to distinguish it from the Oudezijds Voorburgwal ('The Old Side's Front of the Town Wall') found in near mirror image in the Red Light District, though both fortress walls have long since been destroyed – the effects of tragically half-arsed urban renewal are immediately noticeable. The **Crowne Plaza** hotel (Nieuwezijds Voorburgwal 5) was formerly the site of the large Wyers squat, which was dramatically emptied by riot police in 1985 after a widely supported campaign by squatters against the mass conversion of residential buildings into commercial spaces that was taking place at the time. The multinational, perhaps predictably, proved victorious, as did the ABN-Amro Bank slightly further up, with its in-your-face glass plaza at the corner with Nieuwezijdskolk.

While an underground car park was being dug on this site, archaeological remains of a 13th-century castle believed to belong to the Lords of the Amstel were found. Once surrounded by marshland, the castle remains have now, unfortunately, been paved over for luxury office, shop and hotel space. However, there are rumours that a new museum may grab a spot on the site in 2001 or thereabouts. Similarly, the interior of the domed **Koepelkerk** (Kattengat 1), once a Lutheran church famously painted by Van Gogh, can now only be viewed if you happen to organise a convention through the **Renaissance Hotel**, which is now its caretaker.

Sightseeing

On yer bike!

South of Dam, still on Nieuwezijds Voorburgwal, is one of the entrances to the **Amsterdams Historisch Museum** (Amsterdam Historical Museum; *listings page 50*). This elegant historical museum is a rambling cluster of buildings and courtyards, located on the site of St Lucy's Convent, which dates from 1414. Indeed, the entrance is a little hard to find: look out for a short alley ending in a lopsided little arch bearing the city's coat of arms. The museum occupies a labyrinthine group of 17th-century buildings and depicts the development of the city from the 13th century to the present through archaeological finds, multimedia displays, models and countless paintings. A new wing completed in late 1999 emphasises the daily life of the town's diverse residents past and present; free attractions nearby include the **Civic Guard Gallery** – a small covered street hung with massive 16th- and 17th-century group portraits of wealthy burghers – and the adjacent **Begijnhof**.

The Amsterdams Historisch Museum is also the starting point for the informal **Mee In Mokum** walking tours (*see page 274*), which leave at 11am (Tue-Sun), last two or three hours and cost *f*5, including coupons that entitle you to a 50 per cent reduction on admission to the museum, among other things. Booking ahead is essential (625 1390, 1-4pm Mon-Fri).

A quiet backwater accessible via the north side of Spui square or, when that entrance is closed, via Gedempte Begijnensloot (the alternating dual entrances have recently been brought in to appease residents), the **Begijnhof** is a group of houses built around a secluded courtyard and garden. Established in the 14th century, it originally provided modest homes for the Beguines, a religious sisterhood of unmarried women from good families who, though not nuns, lived together in a close community and often took vows of chastity. The last sister died in 1971.

Most of the neat little houses in the courtyard were modernised in the 17th and 18th centuries. In the centre stands the **Engelsekerk** (English Reformed Church), built in around 1400 and given over to English-speaking Presbyterians living in the city in 1607. Now one of the principal places of worship for Amsterdam's English community, it's worth a look primarily to see the pulpit panels, which were designed by a young Mondrian. Also in the courtyard is a Catholic church, secretly converted from two houses in 1665 following the banning of the Roman Catholic faith after the Reformation. The wooden house at Begijnhof 34 is dated 1477 and is the oldest house still standing in the city, while Begijnhof 35 is an information centre. This is the best-known of the city's numerous *hofjes* (almshouses); for details of others, *see page 63*.

The Spui square itself plays host to many markets – the most notable being the book market on Fridays – and was historically an area where the intelligentsia gathered for some serious browbeating and alcohol abuse, often after doing an honest day's graft at one of the many newspapers that were once located on the Spuistraat. The Lieverdje ('Little Darling') statue in front of the **Athenaeum Newscentrum** store (*see page 142*) – a small, spindly and pigeon shit-smeared statue of a boy in goofy knee socks – was the site for Provo 'happenings' in the mid-'60s (*see page 19*).

You can leave the Spui by going up either the Kalverstraat or the Singel past Leidsestraat: both routes lead to the **Munttoren** (Mint Tower) at Muntplein. Just across from the floating flower market (the **Bloemenmarkt**; *see page 154*), this medieval tower was the western corner of the Regulierspoort, a gate in the city wall in the 1480s; in 1620, a spire was added by Hendrik de Keyser, the foremost architect of the period. The tower takes its name from the time when it was used to mint coins after Amsterdam was cut off from its money supply during a war with England, Munster and France. There's now a shop on the ground floor selling fine Dutch porcelain (**Holland Gallery de Munt**; *see page 166*), but the rest of the tower is closed to visitors. The Munttoren is prettiest at night when it's floodlit, though daytime visitors may be able to hear its carillon, which often plays for 15 minutes at noon.

Clubbers may want to stop in the area and pay tribute to the former site of the infamous **Roxy** nightclub (Singel 465) that burned down in 1999; rather eerily, in fact, since the fire started during the wake that was taking place there for its deceased designer, the artist and poet Peter Giele. His colourful vision can still be sampled pretty much across the street at the jet-set eaterie **Inez IPSC** (*see page 113*).

From here, walk down Nieuwe Doelenstraat from the **Hôtel de l'Europe** (familiar if you've seen Hitchcock's *Foreign Correspondent*; *see page 81*). This street connects with the scenic – so scenic, in fact, that it's rated the city's most popular film location, having appeared in everything from *The Diary of Anne Frank* to *Amsterdamned* – Staalstraat: walk up here and you'll end up at Waterlooplein market.

Amsterdams Historisch Museum

Kalverstraat 92 (523 1822/www.ahm.nl). Tram 1, 2, 4, 5, 9, 14, 16, 20, 24, 25. **Open** *Museum* 10am-5pm Mon-Fri; 11am-5pm Sat, Sun. *Library* closed until spring 2001. **Admission** ƒ12; ƒ6-ƒ9 concessions; free Museum Card, under-6s. **No credit cards. Map** p306 D3.

Around Waterlooplein

Map p307

Situated to the south-east of the Red Light District, the Waterlooplein and its surrounds are a peculiar mix of old and new architectural styles. If you leave the Nieuwmarkt along St

Antoniebreestraat, you'll pass several bars, coffeeshops and chic clothes shops: it's a good escape route out of the throbbing Red Light District. The modern yet relatively tasteful council housing that lines the street was designed by local architect Theo Bosch.

Pop through the ancient skull-adorned entrance between St Antoniebreestraat 130 and 132, and enter the former graveyard and now restful square around the **Zuiderkerk** (South Church). Designed by the ubiquitous Hendrik de Keyser, it was built between 1603 and 1614, the first Protestant church to appear after the Reformation. Now, it's the municipal information centre for the physical planning and housing of Amsterdam. Development plans are made to look promising with interactive scale models, but as you walk around the neighbourhood – or view it from the vantage of the church's tower (689 2565, open 2pm, 3pm & 4pm Wed-Sat, closed Mon, Tue, Sun) – it becomes obvious that shiny ideals can often create obtuse realities.

Crossing the bridge at the end of St Antoniebreestraat, you'll soon arrive at Amsterdam's new performing arts school, the **Arts Academy** (aka De Hogeschool voor de Kunsten), on the left and the historic and freshly restored Rembrandthuis on the right. Immediately before you reach the Rembrandthuis, though, some steps will take you to the **Waterlooplein Market** (*see page 164*). Though it's a bit touristy, the market can still be a bargain hunter's dream if you're patient and have a couple of hours to spare.

The new wing of the **Rembrandthuis** (*listings page 52*), completed in 1999, has provided space both for the artist's etchings and for temporary exhibitions, as well as freeing up his original three-storey residence (built in 1606) for restoration. The artist's bedroom and kitchen are already outfitted with 17th-century bedsteads and fireplaces, while the studios of Rembrandt and his pupils, along with the art and rarities room where he often found inspiration, are still being equipped with easels, paintbrushes, stuffed animals and art objects. By the end of 2000, the house where Rembrandt lived and worked for almost 20 years should look a lot like it did back in the day.

Aside from all of his most famous paintings – some of which are on permanent display in the **Rijksmuseum** (*see page 67*) – Rembrandt found time to knock up hundreds of etchings, about 250 of which are on display in the new wing here (the museum offers etching demonstrations by arrangement). However, the only paintings on show are by Rembrandt's teacher, Pieter Lastman, and by his pupils and contemporaries.

Piss off

In a 1998 Amsterdam poll, 'wild pissing' – boys urinating willy-nilly across the city – replaced dogshit as the locals' main 'small grievance'. Politicians began talking about the 'watering down' of society's standards, and the council funded research that discovered urine contamination had reached depths of up to two metres in certain canal hotspots.

But more alarming to a city whose sparse selection of iron-trellised and funkily curved 'curly' pissoirs are listed as monuments, some historical buildings are slowly getting slashed away through urine erosion. Wild Pissing Symposiums were held, and 'A Plan of Action: Wild Pissing (1998-2005)' was formulated. Suggested solutions ranged from the distribution of stench-munching microbes to the employment of artists in designing self-cleaning pissbowls.

The initial phase called for the obvious: more public toilets. Some hazarded a return to the Golden Age of the Urinoir that ended in 1960, when the city fathers started to order the mass removal of the city's watering holes at the same time that maps of their locations (complete with ratings) began to appear in gay guides to the city. As if to discourage this diligent charting, the millennial models seem to have been chosen for their openness and potential mobility. The favoured four-bowls-in-one grey plastic moulded 'Rocket' model goes as far as to suggest vertical mobility. However, its phallic mystique draws not only pissers but vandals, who find them easy to push over.

When a wild pisser shot a passer-by who had dissed his method of drainage, some politicians saw another chance to draw a parallel between the urban urinater and the true badass. During a ceremony marking the opening of a new self-cleaning model, a politician commented: 'With these scissors, I relieve the wild pissers of their organ.' In the same vein, the current clampdown has called for the enforcement of a ƒ100 fine with the aid of a campaign featuring posters, stickers and beermats. This approach seems to have been inspired by Singapore, where even a mere non-flusher gets fined and the locals get cajoled each year into participating in a month-long 'Clean Toilet Campaign', which features a scavenger hunt and the very pisstigious People's Choice Award. Granted, boys can always use some aiming training, but we are, after all, dealing here with that very wiggly issue of free expression.

A topic that consistently gets clouded in all the media hype is the age-old question of pee rights for girls. The sanisette, already part of the Paris streetscape – and folklore, as stories circulate of kids getting trapped in its overly enthusiastic self-cleaning system – and the manned outhouse are both considered too expensive for mass implementation. And as things currently stand, there is only one dual sex facility, on Singelgracht behind Leidseplein.

However, there may be hope. Sphinx Sanitair, a Maastricht company, has recently launched the Lady-P, a low-hanging urinoir that takes advantage of the muscles already developed by the inevitable squat that ladies are forced into when faced with unsanitary conditions. The recent development of the cannily funnelled Pee Shooter may even turn females into wild pissers themselves, but most of the authorities' efforts are still aimed at taming the primitive urges of males.

Hopefully in the coming years, Toto, Japan's largest manufacturer of toilets, and its 'human engineering laboratory' can offer some solutions. After all, the company has previously invented a fully featured console toilet that comes complete with a button to press when you want to disguise your own sounds with a recorded flushing noise. But with technological advances come other, more peculiar problems. One news report told of a British woman who was endlessly harassed by silent phone calls. Eventually, it emerged that she was not being stalked: the calls were being made by a self-diagnosing toilet trying to report an overflow to its master.

But are there more spiritual solutions? Certainly, the urine produced from a vegetarian diet lacks the ammonia that eventually forms into building-eating nitrates. And though perhaps disconcerting to fans of Trappist beer, inspiration can be drawn from the self-cleaning fountain that serves as an artistic and functional 'Piss Monument' in a monastery garden in Groenlo. Or is it just a question of recycling, as suggested in an article about a controversial macrobiotic doctor in Amsterdam's newspaper *Het Parool* under the front-page headline 'Milk is Dangerous, Urine is Healthy'? Regardless, given the world's swelling population – and said population's similarly swelling bladders – Amsterdam's struggles to find a solution will be watched by urban planners everywhere.

Next door, the **Holland Experience** (*listings below*) contains a court featuring deliberately constructed examples of various kinds of Dutch café. However, the main attraction is a 30-minute film presentation that covers the gamut of Dutch cultural clichés. Already an assault on several senses, it was set to go 3-D in mid-2000. The movie follows the mishaps of a bunch of tourists while the audience is bombarded with sounds, images and smells from every direction. Images pass by in a half-digested whirl: kids in clogs, windmills and tulips, the best of the Rijksmuseum, a waxen statue of Queen Beatrix. The real street noise outside will seem positively pastoral afterwards. Children might enjoy the show, of course. But as one big cheesy simulation, it raises the question: why? The real Holland experience is, after all, right outside.

Nearby is the 19th-century **Mozes en Aäronkerk**, built on the spot of Spinoza's birth home. This former clandestine Catholic church, where Liszt reportedly played his favourite concert in 1866, has been used as a social and cultural centre since 1970. It's on the corner where Waterlooplein meets Mr Visserplein – the square-cum-traffic roundabout that has as its new showcase the copper-green **Film and Television Academy**. It could be worth checking to see if the plans to temporarily revamp the abandoned traffic tunnel underneath the square as a skateboarding park by day and a nightclub – along the lines of the late and lamented Roxy – by night have been realised.

Close by, too, is the **Joods Historisch Museum** (Jewish Historical Museum; *listings below*). Housed in four former synagogues in the old Jewish quarter near Waterlooplein, the museum is full of religious items, photographs and paintings illustrating the history of Judaism in the Netherlands. Permanent displays concentrate on religious practice and the particularities of Dutch Jewish culture, while temporary exhibitions explore various aspects of Jewish culture and survival. The museum organises walks around the neighbourhood and visits to the nearby **Portuguese Synagogue** (*listings below*). Check out the shop and excellent kosher café off the narrow Shulgass, which runs between the museum buildings, and the Jonas Daniël Meijerplein and its Dock Worker statue commemorating the February Strike of 1941 in protest against Jewish deportations (*see page 17*).

Dominating Waterlooplein is the **Stadhuis-Muziektheater** (the City Hall-Music Theatre; *see page 223*). It wasn't always thus, though: the area where the Stadhuis-Muziektheater now stands was once a Jewish ghetto, and later – in the '70s – home to dozens of squatted gorgeous 16th- and 17th-century buildings. The new

building was dogged by controversy: first mooted in the 1920s, it was not until 1954 that the city council selected Waterlooplein as the site, and it was 1979 before it was decided that the civic headquarters should be combined with an opera house. The decision was a controversial one, as was the design (by Wilhelm Holtzbauer and Cees Dam), and Amsterdammers showed their discontent by organising demonstrations and protesting during construction. In 1982, a riot caused a million guilders' worth of damage to construction equipment. These displays of displeasure are the reasons why the ƒ300-million building, home to the **Nederlands Opera** (*see page 222*) and the **Nationale Ballet** (*see page 245*) is now known as the 'Stopera'.

It's rare that science and art meet on the level, but in the passage between City Hall and the Muziektheater there is a display of geological information, the **Amsterdam Ordnance Project**, which includes a device showing the NAP (normal Amsterdam water level) and a cross-section of the Netherlands showing its geological structure. Architecture buffs should visit the **ARCAM** gallery at Waterlooplein 213 (*see page 197*). Close by is the **Blauwbrug** (Blue Bridge; *see also page 59* **Bridging the gaps**), linking Waterlooplein with Amstel, which used to be the main route into the city from the east. The current bridge was built in 1873, but a plaque depicting the original (taken from a demolished house) has been placed at the entrance of the Muziektheater car park. Current renovation work should return the bridge to the same state as Dutch Impressionist painter Breitner saw it at the turn of the century.

Holland Experience

Waterlooplein 17 (422 2233/www.holland-experience.nl). Tram 9, 14, 20/Metro Waterlooplein. **Open** 10am-6pm daily. **Admission** ƒ17,50; ƒ15 concessions. **Credit** AmEx, DC, MC, V. **Map** p307 E3.

Joods Historisch Museum

Jonas Daniël Meijerplein 2-4 (626 9945/www.jhm.nl). Tram 9, 14, 20/Metro Waterlooplein. **Open** 11am-5pm daily. **Admission** ƒ8; ƒ2-ƒ4 concessions; free Museum Card, under-10s. **No credit cards**. **Map** p307 E3.

Portuguese Synagogue

Mr Visserplein 3 (624 5351/www.esnoga.com). Tram 4, 9, 14, 20. **Open** *Apr-Oct* 10am-4pm Mon-Fri, Sun; closed Sat. *Nov-Mar* 10am-4pm Mon-Thur; 10am-3pm Fri; closed Sat, Sun. **Admission** ƒ7,50; ƒ5 10-15s; free under-10s. **No credit cards**. **Map** p307 E3.

Rembrandthuis

Jodenbreestraat 4 (520 0400/www.rembrandthuis.nl). Tram 9, 14, 20/Metro Nieuwmarkt, Waterlooplein. **Open** 10am-5pm Mon-Sat; 1-5pm Sun. **Admission** ƒ12,50; ƒ2,50-ƒ10 concessions; free Museum Card, under-6s. **No credit cards**. **Map** p307 E3.

The Plantage & the Oost

Museums, a zoo and a mammoth park are among the highlights out east.

Map p307

The mostly residential area known as the Plantage lies south-east of Mr Visserplein and is reached via Muiderstraat, with the Portuguese Synagogue on the right. The wide, attractive Plantage Middenlaan winds past the **Hortus Botanicus**, passes close by the **Verzetsmuseum**, runs along the edge of the **Artis Zoo**, and heads onward towards the **Tropenmuseum** (for all, *see page 54*).

After a period during which the area was largely populated by rich citizens, Jews began to settle here some 200 years ago. Diamond cutting was, back then, one of only a few trades open to Jews, and after an era of poverty, the area was soon redeveloped on 19th-century diamond money. The headquarters of the diamond cutters' union still stands on Henri Polaklaan, and other extant buildings such as the Gassan, the Saskiahuis and the Coster act as reminders that the town's most profitable trade was once based here (*see chapter* **Shops & Services**).

But the ugly spectre of World War II once again raises its head if you visit the **Hollandse Schouwburg** (*listings page 55*), a grand theatre that in 1942 became a main point of assembly for between 60,000 and 80,000 of the city's Jews before they were transported to the transit camp Westerbork. It is now a monument with a small but very impressive exhibition and a memorial hall with 6,700 surnames paying tribute to the 104,000 Dutch Jews who were exterminated. The façade of the Schouwburg has been left intact, with most of the inner structure removed to make way for a memorial monument.

The Plantage is still wealthy, even though its charm has faded somewhat over the years. Its graceful buildings and tree-lined streets provide a residential area much sought after by those who want to live centrally but away from the more touristy areas. The area has already undergone extensive redevelopment, and work is still continuing. As one would expect, results have been mixed: while the housing association flats and houses erected where the army barracks and dockside warehouses once stood (just past Muiderpoort city gate) are decidedly unattractive, Entrepotdok is a scenic and positive example of the renovations. To wander down this stretch is to admire a balance between the new and the old, with docked

Sealed with a kiss: the **Artis Zoo**. *See p54.*

Take a trip to the tropics without leaving town at the **Tropenmuseum**.

post-hippie houseboats and, assuming it manages to survive, the **Kalenderpanden** squat (*see also page 26*) providing a charmed contrast to the condominiums. Still, the area has maintained some of its heritage: the brightly coloured **Van Eyck's Moedershuis** on Plantage Middenlaan was a mother and child refuge during World War II, while on the other side of the road is the attractive Huize St Jacob, an old people's home rebuilt on the site of an earlier one using the original stone portal.

For most visitors, the stretch of Plantage Middenlaan is notable mostly for the lovely collection of museums that dots its sidings. The first and prettiest, though, isn't really a museum at all. However, you don't have to be the green-fingered type to enjoy the beautiful gardens at the **Hortus Botanicus** (*listings page 55*), a true oasis of calm just a stone's throw from Waterlooplein. The Hortus was established in 1632 and moved to this location in 1682. East India Company ships brought back tropical plants and seeds originally intended to supply doctors with medicinal herbs; some of those specimens are still here today in the palm greenhouse, which itself dates from 1912. Three other interesting greenhouses maintain desert, tropical and subtropical climates. The terrace is one of the nicest in Amsterdam: only the distant sounds of the city remind you where you are. The Hortus was part of the University of Amsterdam until 1989, when funding was tightened; now it's run by a foundation and partly supported by the city.

Slightly further to the east – located, to be precise, in an old choral society building in the former Jewish neighbourhood near Waterlooplein – is the **Verzetsmuseum** (Museum of the Dutch Resistance; *listings page 55*), which contains myriad artefacts that tell the story of the Dutch Resistance. False ID papers, clandestine printing presses, spy gadgets, and an authentic secret door behind which Jews hid (*see page 16*) all help to detail the ways people in the Netherlands faced the Nazi occupation. You can

even sit in cinema seats and view a syrupy UFA propaganda movie. Much of today's Dutch press started underground, and early editions of *Het Parool* ('The Password'), *Vrij Nederland* ('Free Netherlands') and *Trouw* ('Loyalty') are on display here. Temporary exhibitions explore wartime themes and modern-day forms of oppression.

The nearby **Artis Zoo** (*listings page 55*) – which also contains a planetarium, aquarium, and zoological and geological museum – is a great day out for children, and anyone else who doesn't mind hanging out with the hordes. Along with the usual range of animals, Artis has an indoor 'rainforest' for nocturnal creatures and a 120-year-old aquarium that includes a simulated Amsterdam canal (the main difference is the clear water, which means the eels are clearly visible). The 160-year-old zoo recently expanded after a long battle for extra land; in 2000, it was completing a mock-up of an African savannah that will wrap around a new restaurant. The narration in the planetarium is in Dutch, but a short English translation is available. Extras for kids include a petting zoo and playgrounds.

Just across Singelgracht, meanwhile, is the **Tropenmuseum** (Tropical Museum; *listings page 55*), which provides a vivid, interactive glimpse of daily life in the tropical and subtropical parts of the world. Ironically, the vast three-storey building was originally designed and erected in the 1920s to glorify the colonial activities of the Dutch. Now, though, other cultures' artefacts, from religious items and jewellery to washing powder and vehicles, have pride of place. The recreated walk-through environments include simulated African and South Asian villages and a Manilan street. A case of spices, taped music and street sounds and the occasional television engage visitors' senses. Temporary arts and photographic exhibitions fill a large central space on the ground floor, while the shop has a good selection of souvenirs and books. Attached to the main museum is the all-Dutch **Kindermuseum**, for children aged six to 12, and a small cinema showing foreign films. It's hugely enjoyable for both adults and kids.

South of Mauritskade is Amsterdam Oost (East), where the happening **Arena** complex (*see page 90*) is located along the edge of another former graveyard that was long ago transformed into the green oasis known as Oosterpark. Just beyond the aforementioned Tropenmusem, also along the park's edge, is the **Dappermarkt** (*see page 164*), which defines one border of the Indische Buurt (Indonesian Neighbourhood), further east. The **Bierbrouwerij 't IJ**, a brewery in a windmill (*see page 47* **The dope on windmills**, *and page 128*), is a good place to sip on a culturally reflective beer.

Artis Zoo

Plantage Kerklaan 38-40 (523 3400). Tram 6, 9, 14, 20. **Open** *Summer* 9am-6pm daily. *Winter* 9am-5pm daily. **Admission** *f*26,50; *f*18,50-*f*24 concessions; free under-4s. **No credit cards**. **Map** p312 G3.

Hollandse Schouwburg

Plantage Middenlaan 24 (626 9945). Tram 7, 9, 14, 20. **Open** 11am-4pm daily. **Admission** free. **No credit cards**. **Map** p307 F3.

Hortus Botanicus

Plantage Middenlaan 2A (625 9021). Tram 9, 14, 20/Metro Waterlooplein. **Open** *Apr-Oct* 9am-5pm Mon-Fri; 11am-5pm Sat, Sun. *Nov-Mar* 9am-4pm Mon-Fri, 11am-4pm Sat, Sun. **Admission** *Apr-Oct* *f*10; *f*5 under-15s. *Nov-Mar* *f*7,50; *f*4,50 under-15s. **No credit cards**. **Map** p312 G3.

Tropenmuseum

Linnaeusstraat 2 (568 8215/www.tropenmuseum.nl). Tram 9, 10, 14/22 bus. **Open** 10am-5pm Mon-Fri; noon-5pm Sat, Sun. **Admission** *f*12,50; *f*7,50-*f*10 concessions; *f*5 Museum Card; free under-6s. *Children's museum f*2,50 extra (6-12s only). **No credit cards**. **Map** p312 H3.

Verzetsmuseum

Plantage Kerklaan 61 (620 2535). Tram 6, 9, 14, 20. **Open** 10am-5pm Tue-Fri; noon-5pm Sat, Sun; closed Mon. **Admission** *f*8; *f*5 6-16s; free Museum Card, under-6s. **No credit cards**. **Map** p307 F3.

The dope on Clogs

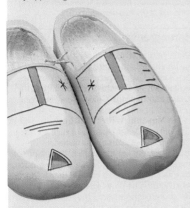

- In the Middle Ages, people known as water-watchers would predict the future by gazing into water-filled *klomp* (or 'clog', a wooden shoe).
- *Klompen* were thought to be a French invention until 1990, when a *klomp* from c.1280 was found in Rotterdam.
- Recyclable as firewood, wooden shoes should be given ultimate millennium-wear status. The EC has already shown its respect by approving it as an official 'safety boot'.

- The nation has over 5,000 stage-performing practitioners of traditional clog-dancing.
- Of the three million pairs of wooden shoes produced each year, two-thirds are sold as souvenirs.
- Very few Dutch people actually work in the *klompen* factories (in Marken and Volendam). Indeed, a quarter of the popular wood used is actually imported.
- In terms of their practical use, *klompen* are sometimes regarded as a fetish item, with every village having its own style and with each individual often applying their own personal markings.
- You can buy *klompen* with attachable skate blades.
- On the corner of Prinsengracht and Vijzelstraat, there is a fully functional, two-person sailing *klomp*.
- Pick up a pair of clogs for yourself at the new branch of the **Wooden Shoe Factory** (Nieuwe Hoogstraat 11, Old Centre: Old Side; 427 3862; see page 166).

The Grachtengordel

There's water, water everywhere, of course, but Amsterdam's canals also hold terrific shops and restaurants amid their gloriously idyllic confines.

The Dutch call them *grachten*. There are 165 of them in Amsterdam. They stretch 75.5 kilometres (47 miles) around the city, and reach an average depth of three metres (ten feet). They function to keep the sea and the surrounding bog at bay. About 10,000 bicycles, 100 million litres of sludge and grunge and 52 corpses (usually tramps, who trip while pissed and pissing) are dredged from their murky depths each year.

The major canals and their radial streets are where the real Amsterdam exists and where its past is most evident. What they lack in specific sights, they make up for as a focus for scenic coffee slurping, quirky shopping, aimless walks and meditative gable gandering. The Grachtengordel – literally, 'girdle of canals' – rings the Old Centre, with its handful of canals providing an eminently trekkable border between the tourist- and shopper-laden centre of town and the more sedate, artsier surrounding locales of the Museum Quarter, the Jordaan and the Pijp.

The Singel was the original medieval moat of the city, while the other three major canals that follow its line outward were part of a Golden Age urban renewal scheme; by the time the building finished, Amsterdam had quadrupled in size. The Herengracht (named after the gentlemen who initially invested in it), the Keizersgracht (named for the Holy Roman Emperor Maximilian I) and the Prinsengracht (named after William, Prince of Orange) are the canals where originally the rich lived, but though they're still residential in parts, many properties have now been given over to offices, hotels and museums.

The radially connecting canals and streets, originally built for workers and artisans, have a higher density of cosy cafés and smaller speciality shops, while the major shopping stretches of Rozengracht, Elandsgracht, Leidsestraat and Vijzelstraat are all former canals, filled in to deal with the advent of motor traffic. Smaller canals worth seeking out include Leliegracht, Bloemgracht, Spiegelgracht, Egelantiersgracht and Brouwersgracht. Throughout this guide, we've split venues on this watery ring into Grachtengordel: West (above Leidsegracht) and Grachtengordel: East (to the east of

Leidsegracht), with the latter area also holding the twin tourist-packed 'delights' of Leidseplein and Rembrandtplein.

The canals

Maps p306, p310 and p311

Singel

One of the few clues to the Singel's past as the protective moat surrounding the city's medieval wall is the bridge that crosses at Oude Leliestraat. It's called the Torensluis and did, indeed, once have a lookout tower; the space under the bridge was supposedly used as a lock-up for medieval drunks. But besides the **Bloemenmarkt** (*see page 154*) by day, there are few specific sights.

Still, while you're here, you may want to join the debate on whether Singel 7 or Singel 166 is the smallest house in Amsterdam. Always good for a snort is the **House with Noses** at Singel 116, though arty types may be more interested in Singel 140-2, once the home of Banning Cocq, the principal figure of Rembrandt's *Night Watch*. Pussy-lovers will adore the **Poezenboot** (or 'cat boat') opposite Singel 20, home to dozens of stray and abandoned felines. You may also want to stake out the town's poshest sex club, **Yab Yum** (Singel 295, 624 9503), to watch the country's elite enter for a good old-fashioned servicing.

Herengracht

As the first canal to be dug in the glory days, the Herengracht attracted the richest of merchants. This is where the houses are the most stately and overblown, especially in the stretch known as the 'Golden Bend' between Leidsestraat and Vijzelstraat.

The **Museum Willet-Holthuysen** (*listings page 58*) is a classic example of such a 17th-century mansion, densely furnished in 18th- and 19th-century styles. Indeed, the interior of this pleasant 1680s merchant's mansion is more reminiscent of a French château than a Dutch canal house. The Willet-Holthuysens, the family that acquired the house in the 1850s, followed the fashion of the time and decorated in the neo-

Louis XVI style. Their passion for over-embellishment is apparent in their legacy of rare objets d'art, glassware, silver, fine china and paintings. English texts accompany the exhibits, and there's also an English-language video explaining the history of the house and the canal system. A view from the first floor into the recently renovated 18th-century garden almost takes you back in time, but the illusion is somewhat disturbed by the adjoining modern buildings. Still, it's well worth a look.

Excess also defines the Louis XVI style of Herengracht 475, while tales of pre-rock 'n' roll excess are often told about Herengracht 527, whose interior was completely trashed by Peter the Great. Mischievous types, meanwhile – and there are plenty in Amsterdam – may like to annoy the town's mayor: to do so, simply park your boat on his personal and pleasantly scenic dock in front of his official residence at Herengracht 502.

If you're caught, quickly douse your spliff and try palming off the authorities with the excuse that you're just visiting **Het Kattenkabinet** (Cat Cabinet; *listings page 58*),

which boasts that it's the only museum in the world to have a permanent exhibition exclusively devoted to cats. The multicultural collection includes paintings, statuettes, posters and more, with some living felines thrown in for good measure. The exhibition is spread over two spacious rooms, and is worth a visit alone for the beautiful location: it's housed in a 17th-century canal mansion.

Alternatively, you could, if caught, be even more angelic and say that you're merely resting before a sojourn to the **Bijbels Museum** (Bible Museum; *listings page 58*). The collection here illustrates life and worship in biblical times with archaeological finds from Egypt and the Middle East, and several models of ancient temples. As you'd expect, there is also a fine collection of Bibles from several centuries. Restoration of the houses and the De Wit paintings was completed in 2000, with some office space converted into exhibition space. More of the collection will be put on show by summer 2002, and a children's area with computers is also planned. Some displays are in English.

Keizersgracht, one of several canals that make up the Grachtengordel. *See p58.*

Having said that, many visit the Bible Museum simply for the two adjoining canal houses that accommodate it. Built in 1660-2 by the renowned Dutch architect Philip Vingboons, they also feature stunning early 18th-century ceiling paintings by Jacob de Wit. A few doors down, stone masons kept themselves busy at Herengracht 380, an exact copy of a Loire mansion, complete with coy reclining figures on the gable and frolicking cherubs and other mythical figures on its bay window. Try, also, to snatch a look into the windows of Van Brienenhuis at Herengracht 284: the excesses of bygone eras will soon become apparent.

Further north on Herengracht is another Vingboons building, this one dating from 1638. Renovated only a few years ago, the **Theatermuseum** (*listings below*) is an architectural gem. The outside is lovely enough, but inside, the 18th-century plasterwork, ceiling paintings by Jacob de Wit and master-craftsman-built spiral staircase are simply magnificent, and would make this museum worth a visit even without the exhibitions of ephemera telling the story of Dutch theatre past and present. In summer, pause in the lovely old garden behind the house for tea and cakes, a practically perfect way to while away a lazy afternoon.

Bijbels Museum

Herengracht 366-8 (624 2436). Tram 1, 2, 5. **Open** 10am-5pm Mon-Sat; 1-5pm Sun, holidays. **Admission** *f*8; *f*5,50 6-17s; free Museum Card, under-6s. **No credit cards. Map** p310 C4.

Het Kattenkabinet

Herengracht 497 (626 5378). Tram 4, 9, 14, 16, 20, 24, 25. **Open** 10am-2pm Mon-Fri; 1-5pm Sat, Sun. **Admission** *f*10; *f*5 concessions. **No credit cards. Map** p310 D4.

Theatermuseum

Herengracht 168 (551 3300). Tram 13, 14, 17, 20. **Open** 11am-5pm Tue-Fri; 1-5pm Sat, Sun; closed Mon. **Admission** *f*7,50; *f*5 students, 6-12s; *f*2,50 Museum Card; free under-6s. **No credit cards. Map** p306 C3.

Museum Willet-Holthuysen

Herengracht 605 (523 1870). Tram 4, 9, 14, 20. **Open** 10am-5pm Mon-Fri; 11am-5pm Sat, Sun. **Admission** *f*8, *f*4 6-16s; free Museum Card, under-6s. **No credit cards. Map** p311 E4.

Keizersgracht

If you walk down Keizersgracht starting at its western end (by Brouwersgracht), you'll soon encounter the 'House with the Heads' at Keizersgracht 123, a classic of pure Dutch Renaissance. The official story has these finely chiselled heads representing classical gods, but the real scoop is supposed to be that these are actually the heads of burglars, chopped off by a vigilante and a lusty maidservant. She decapitated six and married the seventh, or so the story goes.

Another classic can be seen at Keizersgracht 174, an art nouveau masterpiece by Gerrit van Arkels and currently the headquarters of Greenpeace International. Similarly hard to

The legendary **Football Bloke** finds new ways to play keepy-uppy in Leidseplein. *See p60.*

Bridging the gaps

With so many canals, it's logical that Amsterdam should also have a fair number of bridges: there are, in fact, over 1,400 of them. Try to stop off at the point on Reguliersgracht, at the junction with Keizersgracht, where you can see seven parallel bridges. Floodlit by night, it's one of Amsterdam's most beautiful scenes.

One of Amsterdam's more unusual bridges is the Magerebrug ('Skinny Bridge'), built in the 17th century. The story goes that two sisters who lived either side of the Amstel were bored by having to walk all the way round to visit each other, so the bridge was built for them. Uniquely, it's made from wood, and has to be repaired every 20 years. The bridge links Kerkstraat and Nieuwekerkstraat and is opened by hand whenever a boat needs to pass. The main other bridge of note is the **Blauwbrug** (pictured), which links Amstelstraat with Waterlooplein and was inspired by the elaborate Pont Alexandre III in Paris.

ignore is the **Felix Meritis Building** at Keizersgracht 324, given that it's a neo-classical monolith with 'Happiness through achievement' chiselled over its door. And achieve it did: after housing a society of arts and sciences in the 1800s, it went on to house the Communist Party and is now a foundation for experimental art and theatre (*see page 239*). This stretch was also the site in that time of the 'Slipper Parade' every Sunday, where the posh-footed rich strolled about to see and be seen.

A posh and virtually unchanged mid-18th century interior, which illustrates how wonderful it must be to be a wealthy canal house resident, awaits those who choose to visit the **Museum van Loon** (*listings below*) at No.672. Designed by Adriaan Dortsman – the same architect, incidentally, who designed the New Lutheran Church on Singel – the house was the home of Ferdinand Bol, one of Rembrandt's former pupils, and another artist commemorated with a street (Ferdinand Bolstraat, in the Pijp).

Apart from the Louis XV and XVI decor, the museum has an unusually large collection of family portraits from the 17th through 20th centuries, added after the purchase of the house in 1884 by Hendrik van Loon (for whom the museum is named). The 18th-century garden, laid out in the French style, contains a coach house from the same period; it's now, charmingly, a private residence.

Museum van Loon

Keizersgracht 672 (624 5255/www.musvloon.box.nl). Tram 16, 24, 25. **Open** 11am-5pm Mon, Fri-Sun; closed Tue-Thur. **Admission** *f*7,50; free Museum Card, under-12s. **No credit cards. Map** p311 E4.

Prinsengracht

Prinsengracht is the most charming of the canals. Pompous façades have been mellowed with shady trees, cosy cafés and some of the funkier houseboats in town. The streets of Prinsenstraat, Reestraat, Berenstraat and Runstraat, meanwhile, offer a delightfully diverse selection of smaller, artsier speciality shops that perfectly complement a leisurely stroll down by the water.

If it's a Monday morning and you're doing the rounds at the weekly **Noordermarkt** (*see page 164*), stop for coffee at the nearby **Papeneiland** (Prinsengracht 2), a café that has remained unchanged through more than three centuries of service. A tunnel from the Papeneiland used to go under the canal to a Catholic church during the Protestant uprising. The scenic tower of the **Westerkerk** (*see page 62*) is also to be found here.

Near the junction of Prinsengracht and Elandsgracht is one of a handful of only-in-Amsterdam museums, and a charming little spot it is, too. You thought that living on a houseboat was cramped, smelly, cold and uncomfortable? Well, hop inside the **Woonbootmuseum 'Hendrika Maria'** (Houseboat Museum; *listings below*) and be stunned by the space and comfort of this beautiful boat, a former commercial sailing ship built in 1914. Though the museum is rather small, it's an experience not to be missed and gives a good idea of this unique Amsterdam way of life. There are models, photos and a slideshow explaining the perils and maintenance of a houseboat, among other things. The former cargo hold has been transformed into a cosy living space, with all the conveniences one can find in a more conventional home. An illustrated guide in English is available, along with tea, coffee and soft drinks.

Woonbootmuseum

Prinsengracht, near no.296 (427 0750). Tram 13, 14, 17, 20. **Open** *10am-5pm Tue-Sun; closed Mon.* **Admission** *f3,75; f2,50 children under 152cm (5ft).* **No credit cards. Map** p310 C4.

Around Leidseplein

Map p310

Leidseplein is, in a nutshell, the tourist centre of Amsterdam: the bastard child of Times Square in New York City and London's Leicester Square, it's permanently packed with merrymakers drinking at pavement cafés, listening to the buskers and soaking up the atmosphere. It lies on the south-west edge of the Grachtengordel, and though it's called a square, it is, in fact, in an L-shape, running from the end of Leidsestraat to the bridge over Singelgracht. In the current climate of city-centre traffic reduction schemes, Leidseplein is a reminder that such ideas are not new: during the Middle Ages, carts and wagons were banned from the centre of Amsterdam, and people heading for the city had to leave their vehicles in *pleinen*, or squares. At the end of the road from Leiden was a 'cart park', surrounded by warehouses and establishments catering to this captive clientele.

The area around Leidseplein probably has more cinemas, theatres, nightclubs and restaurants than any other part of the city. The square is dominated by the **Stadsschouwburg** (the municipal theatre; *see page 239*), and by the numerous cafés that take over the pavements during the summer. This is also the time of year when fire-eaters, jugglers (including the nigh-on legendary bloke who keeps a football in the air all day and night), acrobats, musicians – everybody from Siberian throat singers to Gypsy jazzsters – and small-time con-artists fill the square, but watch

Aaaaaah. The **Kattenkabinet**. *See p57.*

out for those pesky pickpockets. The development of Leidseplein in recent years has meant that there are now fast food restaurants on every corner, and many locals feel that the essential Dutch flavour of the district has been destroyed for a quick buck.

Leidseplein has always been a focal point of the town for one reason or another. Artists and writers used to congregate here in the 1920s and 1930s, when it was the scene of pre-war clashes between Communists and Fascists. During the war, it was a focus for protests, which were ruthlessly broken up by the occupying Nazis: there's a commemorative plaque on nearby Kerkstraat, where a number of people were killed.

But while the country's most eminent man of letters, Harry Mulisch, still lives around the corner on Leidsekade, Leidseplein's contemporary persona is more jockstrap than literary. This is especially the case when it becomes the venue for celebrations whenever Ajax, the local football team, win anything, which is not as often as it used to be. The police take the mini-riots that usually ensue in their stride (and so they should: they've had enough practice at dealing with them by now).

The café society associated with Leidseplein began in earnest with the opening of the city's first bar incorporating a terrace, the Café du Théâtre. It was demolished in 1877, 20 years before completion of Kromhout's impressive **American Hotel** – now a prominent meeting place for the posh; *see pages 80 and 101* – at the south-west end of the square. Opposite the American is a building, dating from 1882, that reflects Leidseplein's transformation into its current state as architectural billboard. The enormous illuminated Drum and Hitachi adverts add nothing to the building's former grandeur. Just off the square, in the Leidsebos, is the Adamant, a white pyramid-shaped sculpture given to Amsterdam by the city's diamond industry in 1986 to commemorate 400 years of the trade. Designed by Joost van Santen at a cost of ƒ75,000, it uses light to create a rainbow hologram.

Named after the only chess world champion the Netherlands has ever produced – as is the square in which it stands, which is relatively close to Leidseplein – the **Max Euwe Centrum** (*listings below*) harbours a library of works in dozens of languages, various chess artefacts from Euwe's inheritance, vast archives, and chess computers that visitors can use and abuse at their leisure. Housed in the city's old House of Detention, the centre should please chess aficionados from all over the world.

Max Euwe Centrum
Max Euweplein 30A (625 7017/www.maxeuwe.nl). Tram 1, 2, 5, 6, 7, 10. **Open** 10.30am-4pm Tue-Fri, first Sat of mth; closed Mon. **Admission** free. **No credit cards. Map** p310 D5.

Around Rembrandtplein

Maps p310 & p311
Over the Blauwbrug, away from Waterlooplein and on the other side of the Amstel, is Rembrandtplein. Not much to look at now, this area used to be called Reguliersmarkt and once hosted Amsterdam's butter market. In 1876, the square was renamed in honour of Rembrandt; a statue – the oldest in the city – of the Dutch master stands in the centre of the gardens,

Check out the **Max Euwe Centrum**.

gazing in the direction of the Jewish quarter. Though there is no longer a market here, it's still the centre of probably more commercial activity than ever before, with neon signs and loud music blaring out of the cafés, bars and restaurants on all sides.

Even though Planet Hollywood did, rather auspiciously and not a little comically, go under here, the area does remain unashamedly, unconscionably, unbearably tacky. Full of sunbathers by day and fun seekers by night, the square is home to a variety of establishments, from the faded fake elegance of the traditional striptease parlours to the seedy peep-show joints and nondescript cafés and restaurants. Nevertheless, there are a few exceptions to this exuberant display of trash, such as the zoological sample-filled grand café **De Kroon** (*see page 131*) and HL de Jong's extravagantly colourful art deco masterpiece, the **Tuschinski** cinema (*see pages 31 and 192*). Meanwhile, just round the corner on the Amstel is a stretch of lively and largely popular gay cafés and bars (*see pages 203-6*).

The city's oldest graffiti can still be made out on the façade of Amstel 216. The story goes that over 300 years ago, the former mayor Coenraad van Beuningen, drinking buddy of Louis XIV, scrawled – with his own blood, natch – pentagrams, Hebrew letters and magical symbols that, according to his apparent madness, predicted the end of the world. Even modern chemical cleaning products have not been able to erase his ravings, and after 300 years, the word *magog* is still visible as a warning. Coincidentally (or is it?), the nearby alleys between Reguliersbreestraat and Reguliersdwarsstraat were once referred to as the 'Devil's Triangle', in the days when they were still home to the city's rat catchers and petty criminals.

From Rembrandtplein, walk along either the prime mid-range shopping and eating street Utrechtsestraat, or explore the painfully scenic Reguliersgracht and the grotesquely pleasant oasis of Amstelveld. Kerkstraat, which runs along the edge of Amstelveld with the Amstelkerk – the white wooden church that once took a break from its holy duties to act as a stable for Napoleon's horses – is also a fine street for a stroll.

Heading west towards Leidsestraat, you'll encounter a quirky array of funky houses, galleries and shops including 'shroom and smart drugs central **Conscious Dreams** (*see page 137* **Get smart**). Heading east will get you to the **Magerebrug** (which translates as 'Skinny Bridge'; *see page 59* **Bridging the gaps**) over the Amstel, a lovely spot for a stroll on a sunny summer's day.

The Jordaan

To the west of the Grachtengordel lies what is perhaps Amsterdam's most characterful and charming neighbourhood.

Map p305

The Jordaan is roughly sock-shaped, with often-disputed borders at Brouwersgracht, Prinsengracht, Leidsegracht and Lijnbaansgracht. The area emerged when the city was extended in the early part of the 17th century and was originally designated for the working classes, as well as providing a haven for victims of religious persecution, such as Jews and Huguenots. In keeping with the modest economic circumstances of the residents, the houses here tend to be small and densely packed, compared to the magnificent dwellings along the adjacent Grachtengordel.

The area is a higgledy-piggledy mixture of old buildings (many of them listed monuments), bland modern social housing and the occasional eyesore that has somehow sneaked past city planning. There are also many odd, contemporary contributions in the area, such as the large, yellow tap 'sculpture' that protrudes from a house at Tuinstraat 157. Despite its working-class associations, the properties are now highly desirable, and though the residents are mainly proud, community-spirited Jordaanders, the nouveaux riches are slowly moving in and yuppifying the 'hood. Brouwersgracht, arguably still the most charmed and charming canal in the area, is one obvious example, with its trendy warehouse-conversion apartments.

There are several theories as to the origin of the name 'Jordaan': some believe it to be a corruption of *joden*, Dutch for Jews, while others think it's from the French word for garden, *jardin*. The latter seems more plausible: the area was formerly a damp meadow, and many streets have been named after flowers or plants. Other streets are also named after animals whose pelts were used in tanning, one of the main industries in the Jordaan in the 17th century. Looiersgracht ('Tanner's Canal') is surrounded by streets such as Hazenstraat ('Hare Street'), Elandsgracht ('Elk Canal') and Wolvenstraat ('Wolf Street').

One historical occurrence that perhaps helped gel the neighbourhood's fierce sense of community occurred in 1886. Before the Lindengracht was filled in, this small canal was the city's premier venue for the indigenous sport of eel-pulling. The trick to this most

peculiar of games was to yank an eel off a rope from which it was dangling over the canal, while passing in a fast-moving boat. The banning of the sport led to the day when a passing policeman elected to cut the rope from which the eel was hanging. This was perhaps not the wisest idea: the residents of the Jordaan had long felt generally hard done-by, and the cop's interference was the final straw. The Eel Riot of 1886, as the incident came to be known, escalated so quickly that the army had to be called in. After a few days, it was announced that 26 Jordaanders had died, 136 were wounded. And the eel? Astonishingly, it survived the event, and its dry husk was auctioned in 1913 for the princely sum of ƒ1,75.

Before the invention of noise pollution, it was said that if you could hear the bells of the **Westerkerk** (*listings page 66*), you were in the Jordaan. Nowadays, the church tower is merely a good place from which to view the Jordaan's streets and canals, provided you don't suffer from vertigo (the tower sways three centimetres during a good wind). At 85 metres (278 feet) high – one of the tallest structures in Amsterdam – it also makes a useful landmark.

The neo-classical church was built in 1631 by Hendrik de Keyser. Its tower is topped with a somewhat gaudy gold, blue and red crown marked 'XXX'. The story goes that in 1489, Maximilian, the Holy Roman Emperor, in need of medical help during a pilgrimage and grateful for the sanctuary, granted the city the right to include his crown on the city arms. The triple-X came to be used by the city's traders as a seal to denote quality and does not mark something as X-rated, as some people theorise when they witness, for the first time, the 'XXX'-marked and remarkably phallic parking poles – *Amsterdammertjes* – found throughout the city.

It's worth climbing to the top of the tower (186 steps to the sixth floor) for the superb view of the city. While you recover from the exertion, ponder the fate of one of Amsterdam's most famous sons, Rembrandt van Rijn. It's thought that the painter is buried somewhere in the graveyard here, though no one is entirely sure where. Rembrandt died a pauper, and is commemorated inside with a plaque. Though his burial on 8 October 1669 was recorded in the church register, the actual spot was not specified; there's a good chance he shares a grave with his son, Titus, who died the previous year and is buried here. Practical jokers are recommended to take their companions for a coffee at the historical **Chris Café** (Bloemstraat 42), which began as the local for the builders of the Westerkerk. The toilet's flusher has always been located – uniquely – in the bar itself, which makes it all too easy to shock a friend who's having an over-leisurely sit (sic).

A short saunter away from Westerkerk is the expanded **Anne Frankhuis** (*listings page 66*), one of the most visited attractions in town. It's the 17th-century canalside house where the young Jewish girl Anne Frank spent over two years in hiding during World War II, from June 1942 to August 1944. As anyone who's read her diary or seen the film will tell you, Anne Frank's house isn't the largest of properties. But that hasn't stopped it becoming one of the city's most visited sights, attracting about half a million people every year. Having already fled from persecution in Germany in 1933, Anne Frank, her sister Margot, her parents and four other Jews went into hiding on 5 July 1942. Living in an annexe behind Prinsengracht 263, they were sustained by friends who risked everything to help them; a bookcase marks the entrance to the sober, unfurnished rooms that sheltered the eight inhabitants for two long years.

Eventually, on 4 August 1944, the occupants of the annexe were arrested and transported to concentration camps, where Anne died along with Margot and their mother. Her father, Otto, survived, and decided that Anne's moving and perceptive diary should be published. The rest, as they say, is history. Anne Frankhuis is home to an exhibition on the Jews and the persecution they suffered during the war, and other displays charting current developments in racism, neo-Fascism and anti-Semitism, complete with English texts. The museum is managed by the Anne Frank Foundation, which aims to combat prejudice, discrimination and oppression. A statue of Anne Frank by Mari Andriessen (dated 1977) stands nearby, at the corner of Westermarkt and Prinsengracht. Meanwhile, Descartes fans – and if you think, you therefore probably are – can pay tribute by regarding his former house around the corner at Westermarkt 6.

Part of the Jordaan's charm is what is hidden from the uninformed eye: the area has the highest concentration of *hofjes* ('almshouses') in the city. As long as you remain restrained, the residents don't seem to mind folks admiring their inner garden courtyards. The better-known ones in the area are **Claes Claesz Hofje** (1e Egelantiersdwarsstraat 3), **Karthuizerhof** (Karthuizerstraat 21-131), **St Andrieshofje** (Egelantiersgracht 107-14), **Van Brienenhofje** 'De Star' (Prinsengracht 89-133), **Suyckerhofje** (Lindengracht 149-63), **Venetiae** (Elandsstraat 106-36), and the oldest, **Linden Hofje** (Lindengracht 94-112). However, *hofje*-hopping is a bit of a gamble, as their entrances may be sporadically locked in deference to the residents.

The view from the **Westerkerk** (*see p62*). Not suitable for those of a nervous disposition.

Keep on the grass

For such a small city, Amsterdam has a remarkable number of green spaces. Many are found in small residential neighbourhoods: Sarphatipark in the Pijp and Oosterpark in the east are the pride of their respective districts, particularly in spring and summer when the flowers are in full bloom. Still, few of the city's 28 parks – Amstelpark, Amsterdamse Bos, Beatrixpark, Flevopark and **Vondelpark** (pictured; see also page 70-1) – are really worth a visit.

Amstelpark was created for a garden festival in 1972, and now offers recreation and respite to locals in the suburb of Buitenveldert, near the RAI. A formal rose garden and rhododendron walk are among the seasonal floral spectacles, and there's also a labyrinth, pony rides and a children's farm, plus tours on a miniature train. The Rosarium Restaurant serves expensive meals, though its outdoor café is less pricey.

Amsterdamse Bos predates Amstelpark: it was created in the 1930s, partly as a job-creation scheme to ease what was a chronic unemployment problem. The 800-hectare (2,000-acre) Bos ('wood') is a favourite retreat for Amsterdam families, especially at weekends. The man-made Bosbaan is used for boating and swimming, with canoe and pedalo rental available. Other attractions include a horticultural museum, play areas, jogging routes, a buffalo and bison reserve, a bike-hire centre (open March to October), a watersports centre, riding stables and a picnic area. The non-subsidised goat farm sells various cheeses, milks and ice-cream: you can even feed the goats while you're there.

A little off the beaten tourist track, just by the RAI business centre, **Beatrixpark** is one of Amsterdam's loveliest parks. Extended and renovated in 1994, it's a wonderfully peaceful place, and handy if you want to avoid the crowds on a hot summer's day. The Victorian walled garden is worth a visit, as is the pond, complete with geese, black swans and herons. Amenities include a wading pool and well-equipped play area for kids, and there are concerts held here in July and August.

Supremely peaceful and considerably bigger than it first appears on the map, **Flevopark** has both extensive wooded areas and wide open spaces. Its size means that there are always places to sit in peace and quiet; added bonuses are the two open-air swimming pools that, though highly popular in the summer months, somehow always seem to have enough space on the surrounding grass for the late-coming sunbather.

Amstelpark
Bus 8, 48, 49, 60, 158, 173. **Open** dawn-dusk daily.

Amsterdamse Bos
Bus 170, 171, 172. **Open** 24hrs daily.

Beatrixpark
Tram 5. **Open** dawn-dusk daily.

Flevopark
Tram 14. **Open** *Pool* 10am-5pm, 7-9pm (on days warmer than 25°C) daily. **Admission** ƒ4,25.

The Jordaan has no major sights as such, and is more of an area where you just stumble across things. It provides a welcome, relaxing break from the crowded tourist areas: it's constantly surprising to wander through its streets and hardly see a soul. In general, the area north of the shop-dense Rozengracht (formerly a wide canal, now filled in) is more interesting and picturesque, with the area to the south more residential and commercial.

A washed-up Rembrandt, from 1659 until he died ten years later, lived at Rozengracht 184, where all that remains of his former home is a plaque on the first floor bearing the inscription 'Hier Stond Rembrandts Woning 1410-1669' ('Here Stood Rembrandt's Home 1410-1669'). While you're here, look up the gable of Rozengracht 204 to espy an iron stickman wall anchor. In addition to such folksy flourishes, the Jordaan's association with art is still alive today with its many galleries and resident artists. The area also contains some of the city's best hangouts, such as **'t Smalle** (Egelantiersgracht 12; *see page 132*), set on a small, picturesque canal, where Peter Hoppe (of Hoppe & Jenever, the world's first makers of gin) founded his distillery in 1780. For a more unique, local experience, try to sing along with vigour and verve at the marvellously kitschy **Café Nol** (*see page 132*).

Between scenic coffees or debauched daytime beers, check out one of the many specialist shops in this area. Some of the best of the outdoor markets are found nearby: the **Noordermarkt** and the **Boerenmarkt** share the same site around the **Noorderkerk** – the city's first Calvinist church, built in 1623 – on different days. The remains of the former livestock market next to the Boerenmarkt can be a disturbing sight, with cages crammed with tropical birds, ducks and even kittens. Adjacent to the Noordermarkt is the **Westermarkt**, while another general market fills the Lindengracht on Saturday mornings (*for all, see page 164*).

More quirky shopping opportunities are to be found on Haarlemmerdijk, which runs parallel to, and behind, Brouwersgracht. Though not officially part of the Jordaan, the street and its side streets do share a comparable ambience. Where it ends at Haarlemmerplein, you can see the imposing Haarlemmerpoort, built as a city gate for William II's visit in 1840. Behind it, you can enter the eminently wanderable **Westerpark**, which connects up to the **Westergasfabriek** (*see page 240*), a large terrain that's evolved from gas factory to underground squat village to its present state as an official and surprisingly cutting-edge centre for culture, art, exhibitions and music.

The area south of Rozengracht has two excellently browse-worthy indoor antique markets, **Rommelmarkt** and **Looier** (*see page 164*), both of which have cafés. There are also a number of interesting shops, including curio store **Het Winkeltje** (Prinsengracht 228), and the **English Bookshop** (Lauriergracht 71; *see page 143*). Elandsgracht, meanwhile, is lined with a mix of shops that cater to every need.

Bargains galore can be had – if you're lucky – at the **Noordermarkt**.

The dope on Tulips

- Originating in Turkey, the word 'tulip' is said to derive from 'turban'. When written in Arabic, the word auspiciously uses the exact same letters as 'Allah'.
- Conversely, though, the six petals, six stamens and six ovary frills on a tulip form a '666'. In other words, a Beelzebulb. Heh heh.
- The tulip was historically used in Persian arts as the 'Symbol of the Perfect Lover' (much as the devil is reputed to be). There is even a variety of bulb called 'Bacchus'.
- The devilish influence of the tulip inspired the country's 'Tulipmania' of 1636-7, when single bulbs were traded for real estate, piles of cash or thousands of kilograms of cheese. The mania climaxed in a fury of bankruptcies and suicides.
- Turkey's Sultan Ahmed III was deposed in the late 18th century for buying too many bulbs. However, his habit of filling his tulip fields with candle-carrying tortoises and frolicking concubines is thought not to have helped his cause.
- In astrology, the tulip is the 'herb of the moon', and from some photographs taken from the moon, the coloured tulip fields of the Netherlands are clearly visible. Perhaps these fields are not a mere antidote to an otherwise dull landscape but, in fact, a devious code of colours meant to communicate the devil's work to an alien race. Or perhaps not. Whatever.
- Ancient herbalists employed tulip petals as a potent anti-flatulent.
- You can pick up tulips at the colourful **Bloemenmarkt**, which stretches along Singel between Muntplein and Koningsplein (Grachtengordel: East; see page 154).

Elandsgracht 71-7 used to be home to the maze-like Sjako's Fort. Sjako is often referred to as the 'Robin Hood of Amsterdam', glossing over the fact that he usually neglected to give to the poor after stealing from the rich. Still, he had style: robbing houses dressed in white, accompanied by black-clad henchmen. His 24-year-old head ended up spiked on a pole in 1718 where the Shell Building now stands, but a local band (Sjako!) and an anarchist-oriented bookstore (**Fort van Sjako**) keep his name alive. Another tribute can be paid where Elandsgracht hits Prinsengracht: here you'll find statues of Tante Leni, Johnny Jordaan and Johnny Meijer, who all personified the 'Spirit of the Jordaan' by crooning of lost love and spilt

beer in local cafés. Behind these, on the water, is the cosy and charming **Woonbootmuseum** (*see page 60*).

Anne Frankhuis

Prinsengracht 263 (556 7100/www.annefrank.nl). Tram 13, 14, 17, 20. **Open** *Jan-Mar, Sept-Dec* 9am-7pm daily; *Apr-Aug* 9am-9pm daily. **Admission** *f*10; *f*5 10-17s; free under-10s. **No credit cards**. **Map** p306 C2.

Westerkerk

Prinsengracht 279 (624 7766/tower 552 4169). Tram 13, 14, 17, 20. **Open** *Church* Apr-mid Sept 11am-3pm Mon-Fri; also 11am-3pm Sat June-Aug. *Tower* Apr-Sept 10am-5pm Mon-Sat; closed Sun. **Admission** *Tower f*3. **No credit cards**. **Map** p306 C3.

The Museum Quarter

Art for art's sake, money for God's sake: Amsterdam's Museum Quarter is a morass of cash and culture.

Map p310

Part of the Oud-Zuid (Old South) and one of the wealthiest areas in the city, the Museum Quarter's borders run along the Rijksmuseum and Vondelpark in the north, down Emmastraat to Reijnier Vinkeleskade and up along the Hobbemakade in the east. A century ago, the area was still officially outside the city limits and consisted of little more than vegetable patches. Towards the end of the century, though, the city expanded rapidly, and the primarily upper-class city fathers decided to build an swanky neighbourhood between the working-class areas to the west and south. Most of the beautiful mansions, with their characteristic art deco gateways and stained-glass windows, were built around the turn of the century, and the exclusive shopping streets of PC Hooftstraat and Van Baerlestraat are today known throughout the country for their elite selection of designer shops and expensive restaurants.

The heart of the area is the Museumplein, the city's largest square, which is bordered by the **Rijksmuseum**, the **Stedelijk Museum of Modern Art**, the **Van Gogh Museum** (for highlights of all three museums, *see pages 12-13* **Art for art's sake**) and the **Concertgebouw** (*see page 222*). The Museumplein is not really an authentic Amsterdam square, certainly with its recent revamping accenting its more 'park' – or, rather, cow field – aspects. Developed in 1872, it originally served as a location for the World Exhibition of 1883, and was then rented out to the Amsterdam ice-skating club between 1900 and 1936. During the Depression, the field was put to use as a sports ground, and during World War II the Germans built four bunkers and a concrete shelter on it, which remained until 1952. Further annoyance followed with the laying of the country's 'shortest motorway', Museumstraat, in 1953, which cut the plein in two and remained until its recent resurrection with grass, wading pool and the wacky new addition to the Van Gogh Museum.

However, it's the **Rijksmuseum** (*listings page 69*) that remains the city's most popular attraction. Designed by PJH Cuypers – the architect responsible for Centraal Station – and opened in 1885, the Rijksmuseum holds the largest collection of art and artefacts in the Netherlands. The collection was started when William V started acquiring pieces just for the hell of it, and has been growing ever since: it now includes Dutch paintings from the 15th century until around 1900, as well as decorative and Asian art. But if you only have a limited amount of time, head for the Dutch Masters section on the top floor. Here's where you'll find Rembrandt's *Night Watch*, the jewel of the museum's collection, and Johannes Vermeer's *The Kitchen Maid* and *Woman Reading a Letter*, each capturing a moment in the life of a woman from a different background. There are also excellent selections of work by the likes of Frans Hals, Jan Steen, Jacob van Ruysdael and Ferdinand Bol.

Room after room at the Rijks holds a wealth of decorative arts, including 17th-century furniture and intricate silver and porcelain. A room devoted to 17th- and early 18th-century dolls' houses and craftsmen-made furniture gives a glimpse of how canal-house interiors looked. Meanwhile, near the east entrance, the Dutch history collection spans the 15th to mid-20th centuries.

The Rijksmuseum's **South Wing**, meanwhile, has been deemed worthy of its own entrance. One ticket covers the whole museum and an internal corridor connects the two buildings, but it's a complicated procedure: if it's a nice day, go outside and walk around to the south entrance. The South Wing provides a home for 18th- and 19th-century paintings; art objects from all over Asia, including statues, lacquer work, paintings, ceramics, jewellery, weaponry and bronze; and the Textile and Costume collection.

Since the coming of the ARIA computer system, it's much easier to find your way around this enormous place. ARIA offers information on 1,250 items from the collection in sound, film, text and image, and lets you design your own custom museum route around the pieces you want to see. Located in a room behind the *Night Watch*, it's free unless you want to make a printout. The Rijksmuseum is also the only place where you can get tickets for the **Six Collectie**, the Six family's small but perfectly formed collection of paintings by the likes of Rembrandt and Hals. Ask at the information desk, and remember to take your passport as ID.

Art and architecture meet at the Van Gogh Museum.

The **Stedelijk Museum of Modern Art** (*listings page 69*), meanwhile, offers by far and away the best collection of modern art in Amsterdam, with an emphasis on painting. Displays change regularly: some exhibitions are drawn from the collection while others are made up from works loaned to the museum, but each tends to focus on a particular trend or the work of a specific artist. After occupying various locations around the city, the Stedelijk finally settled in its present neo-Renaissance abode, designed by AW Weissman, in 1895. In time, the building became too small for the ambitions of its directors and an ugly new wing was tacked on in 1954.

The rooms at the Stedelijk are agreeably spacious and sympathetically lit; pre-war highlights include paintings by Cézanne, Picasso, Matisse and Chagall. The museum also has a prized collection of paintings and drawings by Russian artist Kazimir Malevich. Post-1945 artists represented here include De Kooning, Newman, Ryman, Judd, Stella, Lichtenstein, Warhol, Nauman, Middleton, Long, Dibbets, Van Elk, Kiefer, Polke, Merz and Kounellis. The Nieuwe Vleugel (New Wing) is used as a temporary space for exhibitions often focusing on design and applied art. CoBrA artist Karel Appel decorated the Appelbar and restaurant; the latter is still in use, and its picture windows make it a nice place to sit on a sunny day.

In 2000, the Stedelijk was granted ƒ55 million for the building of two new wings, to be designed by Portuguese architect Alvaro Siza, and also plans to conduct renovations on its current building to the tune of ƒ60 million. Though nothing had been decided for certain by summer 2000, it is possible that the museum may close for a time in order for the work to be carried out. However, this will not happen before May 2001 at the earliest; after this date, call ahead to check the museum is still open.

Aside from for the bright colours of his palette, Vincent van Gogh is also known for his productivity, and both are clearly reflected in the 200 paintings and 500 drawings that form part of the permanent exhibition at the **Van Gogh Museum** (*listings page 69*), the staple of Amsterdam's museum scene. Aside from this massive collection, there are also examples of his Japanese prints, as well as works by the likes of Toulouse-Lautrec and Gauguin, which add perspective to Van Gogh's own efforts. Changing exhibitions, created from the museum's archives and private collections, also feature here. After a major and impressive refurbishment, the enlarged Rietveld building remains the base for the permanent collection, while Japanese architect Kisho Kurokawa's new wing has been devoted to temporary exhibitions. Add all this together and the whole place becomes a must-visit.

Nearby Roemer Visscherstraat is a quiet street leading into Vondelpark, and is easily passed by. For those interested in architecture, it's worth taking a look at the houses from Nos.20 to 30. Each represents a different country built in the appropriate 'national' style: Russia comes complete with a miniature dome, Italy has been painted pastel pink, and Spain's candy stripes have made it one of the street's favourites. Fans of luxury, though, will probably head for one of the diamond factories in the area; *see chapter* **Shops & Services**.

Rijksmuseum

Stadhouderskade 42 (674 7047/ www.rijksmuseum.nl). Tram 2, 5, 6, 7, 10, 20. **Open** 10am-5pm daily. **Admission** ƒ15; ƒ7,50 6-18s; free Museum Card. **Credit** V. **Map** p310 D5.

Stedelijk Museum of Modern Art

Paulus Potterstraat 13 (573 2911/www.stedelijk.nl). Tram 2, 3, 5, 12, 16, 20. **Open** 11am-5pm daily. **Admission** ƒ10; free Museum Card,

under-7s. **Credit** (shop only) AmEx, EC, MC, V. **Map** p310 D6.

Van Gogh Museum

Paulus Potterstraat 7 (570 5200/ www.vangoghmuseum.nl). Tram 2, 3, 5, 12, 16, 20. **Open** 10am-6pm daily. **Admission** ƒ15,50; ƒ5 13-17s; free Museum Card, under-13s. *Tours* Nov-June by arrangement. **Credit** MC, V. **Map** p310 D6.

Plein and simple

Amsterdam has a revamped park. Where once there stood a nightmarish and unnegotiable stretch of road that hardly encouraged visitors and locals alike to visit the fantastic museums nearby, there now stands the NEW! IMPROVED! **Museumplein**. Indeed, the new park is defined by a refreshing sense of space that compares most favourably with the ugly mess of traffic and greenery it replaced. But will Museumplein ever really compete with Vondelpark as the ultimate people's park?

Unlikely, for Museumplein has already become something of a joke among locals. The grass is in a constant state of near-death. There are constant rumours of dogs and children falling off the 'Donkey Ear' slope covering the Albert Hein grocery store. Taller buses have had their roofs shaved by the low-hanging entrance to the underground parking garage. The glistening skateboard ramp was spraypainted with the slogan 'kut-ramp bedankt a'dam' (a spicy way of saying 'thanks for nothing'). The fountain broke almost immediately, as did the ƒ1.5-million ground-level 'light-line' because people – shockingly – walked on it. The lampposts and benches are both a 1970s Eastern Bloc version of 'colourful' and wimpy enough to entice the local vandals. The list goes on, and on, and on. In time, locals are assured,

many of these problems will be fixed, despite the non-stop bickering between council reps and contractors. Don't hold your breath...

In fact, no one should be surprised by the hassles, for Museumplein has always tended to reflect the social history of the city. While before it played host to the suffragette rally of 1916, the Nazi rallies (and bunkers) of World War II, and the 400,000 who gathered in 1981 to protest against cruise missiles, now it's merely one of many reasons why locals are asking: 'Do the city planners actually know what they're doing?'

Still, besides the new sense of space and the views of the **Concertgebouw** (see page 222), the **Rijksmuseum** (see page 67) and the modern and titanium-roofed expansion of the **Van Gogh Museum** (see page 68), there is one major plus that has come about since the redevelopment of Museumplein: 'the nation's shortest motorway' (the late and not especially lamented Museumstraat) has gone, to be replaced by a wading pool in which dusty travellers can soak their crusty feet. And if you ever have to urinate while in the vicinity, then head to the park's real tour de force. The washrooms of the **Cobra Café** (see page 113) come complete with glass doors that magically 'milk' over when closed. Very high-tech, and, given the area's intrinsic 'openness', very useful.

Sightseeing

Museums further out

Ajax Museum

ArenA Boulevard 3, Zuid Oost (311 1469).
Metro Bijlmer. **Open** 10am-6pm daily (opening
hours on match days vary). **Admission** ƒ15;
ƒ12,50 under-12s. **No credit cards.**
A great outing for footie fans of all ages, the
Ajax Museum takes you on a tour through the
long and rich history of this legendary club.
The exhibitions trace the development of the
team from their humble beginnings to the big
business enterprise of today. Unique
photographs and memorabilia taken from the
club's and players' collections are on display,
as are all the cups, in the trophy cabinet. An
eight-minute film offers footage of the all-time
great goals scored in the last 25 years. Given
the scarcity of tickets – and the fact that
they're an absolute bugger to get hold of if
you don't have a Personal Club Card – it'll
likely be the closest you'll get to seeing the
team in action.

Aviodome

Schiphol Centre, Zuid (406 8000/
www.aviodome.nl). NS rail Schiphol Airport.
Open *Apr-Sept* 10am-5pm daily. *Oct-Mar*
10am-5pm Tue-Fri; noon-5pm Sat, Sun.
Admission ƒ15; ƒ12,50 concessions;
free under-4s.
Aeroplane enthusiasts will loop the loop over
the displays in this exhibition: over 30
historic aircraft are neatly parked or
suspended at the Aviodome museum, a short
trip from Schiphol Airport. The exhibition
starts with the first motorised plane – the
Wright Flyer from 1903 – and the Spider,

designed by Dutch pioneer Anthony Fokker,
and takes in recent aeronautical
developments and space travel. There are
also film screenings and collections of
models, photos and aeroplane parts. The
Aviodome organises markets and fairs as
well as occasional theme weekends.

Bosmuseum

Koenenkade 56, Amsterdamse Bos (676
2152). Bus 170, 171, 172. **Open** 10am-5pm
daily. **Admission** free. **No credit cards.**
The Bosmuseum recounts the history and
use of the Amsterdamse Bos, the extensive
forest built in the 1930s to provide
Amsterdammers with work and a place to
spend their days off. Its mock woodland
grotto, which turns from day to night at
the flick of a switch, is wonderful for kids
(*see page 177*).

CoBrA Museum of Modern Art

Sandbergplein 1, Amstelveen (547 5050).
Tram 5/Metro 51. **Open** 11am-5pm Tue-Sun.
Admission ƒ7,50; ƒ3,50-ƒ5 concessions;
free Museum Card, under-5s. **No credit cards.**
The CoBrA group of artists – who took their
name from the cities in which they worked
(Copenhagen, Brussels and Amsterdam) –
attempted to radically reinvent the language
of paint starting in 1948, preaching an ethos
of participation and believing everyone should
make art, regardless of competence or
education. Artists such as Dane Asger Jorn
and Dutchmen Karel Appel and Corneille –
who's still at it today; he put together a show
of paintings by the mentally disabled for the

Vondelpark

Map p310

The Vondelpark, Amsterdam's largest green
space, is named after the city's most famous
poet, Joost van den Vondel (1587-1679), whose
spicily controversial play *Lucifer* caused a
backlash from the religious powers of the time
against those who engaged in what was
quaintly termed 'notorious living'. The
concerted campaign from the moral majority
helped bring about the downfalls of both
Rembrandt and Vondel, who ended his days as
a pawnshop doorman, a sometimes chilly job
that inspired him to write his own tear-jerking
epitaph: 'Here lies Vondel, still and old/Who
died because he was cold.'

Vondelpark is the most central of
Amsterdam's major parks, though it's slowly
sinking into the bog from which it came. Its
construction was inspired after the development
of Plantage, which had formerly provided the
green background used by the rich for their
leisurely walks. It was designed in the 'English
style' by Zocher, with the emphasis on natural
landscaping; the original four hectares (ten
acres) were opened in 1865.

There are several ponds and lakes in the
park – no boating, though – plus a number of
children's play areas and cafés, the most
pleasant of which are the **Blauwe Theehuis**
(Round Blue Teahouse; *see page 33*) and **Café
Vertigo**, which backs on to the park from the
Nederlands Filmmuseum (*listings page 71*).

newMetropolis (see p75) in 2000 – were long regarded as a troupe of eccentric troublemakers whose work was of little artistic worth. However, time has mellowed their impact and they have now been absorbed into the canon. The CoBrA Museum provides a sympathetic environment from which to trace the development of one of the most influential Dutch art movements of the 20th century.

Electrische Museum Tramlijn Amsterdam

Haarlemmermeerstation, Amstelveenseweg 264, Amstelveen (673 7538/ www.trammuseum.demon.nl). Tram 6, 16. **Open** *Easter-Oct* 1.45-3.15pm Wed; 11am-5pm Sun, public holidays. **Admission** ƒ6,60 round trip; ƒ3,30 children. **No credit cards**.
Both the pride and *raison d'être* of the Electric Tram Museum, housed in a beautiful 1915 railway station, is its rolling stock. The main 'exhibitions' are the Sunday outings during which the colourful antique streetcars, gathered from several European cities, make along their own track through the nearby and surprisingly rural **Amsterdamse Bos** (see p64

Keep on the grass). As of 2000, the museum's 25th anniversary year, the volunteer staff will mount exhibitions in the Haarlemmermeer station building, which also houses an atmospheric bar-restaurant.

Hortus Botanicus (Vrije Universiteit)

Van der Boechorststraat 8, Zuid (444 9390). Tram 5/bus 69, 169, 170, 171, 172. **Open** 8am-4.30pm Mon-Fri. **Admission** free. **No credit cards**.
This small but perfectly formed garden is, rather curiously, wedged between the high buildings of a university and a hospital. Built in 1967, it doesn't have the charm of its counterpart in the city centre (see page 54), but it's enough space place for a stroll if you're in the neighbourhood. The fern collection is one of the largest in the world, while the Dutch garden next door shows the great variety of flora found in this country.

Schipholscoop

Arrivals Hall 1, Schiphol Airport, Zuid (601 2000). NS rail Schiphol Airport. **Open** 10am-5pm Mon-Fri; 12am-5pm Sat, Sun. **Admission** free. **No credit cards**.
The visitors' centre at Schiphol Airport, which opened in July 1994, is no more and no less than a semi-decent way to kill time while waiting for your plane. The Schipholscoop has interactive exhibitions that provide information about the airport's economic and environmental significance, as well as details on noise pollution and job opportunities, should you fancy working in what will be – after the massive programme of renovations has finally been completed – an extremely efficient airport.

A film buff's dream, the NFM is more a cinema than a museum: several films from the museum's collection of 30,000 are shown nightly on its three screens. Occupying a grand former 19th-century tearoom on the edge of the Vondelpark furnished with antique cinema fixtures, the 'museum' very rarely exhibits static objects, but its extensive library around the corner (Vondelstraat 69-71) houses the country's largest collection of film books and magazines, scripts, photos, archives, videos and biographies (though there's no borrowing). Local movie fans rejoiced when a recent decision to move the NFM to Rotterdam was overturned.

Vondelpark gets fantastically busy on sunny days and Sundays, when bongos abound, dope is toked, and impromptu football games take up

any space that happens to be left over. The dicky-tickered can avoid a seizure by keeping one eye out for Rollerbladers, who meet here once a week for the **Friday Night Skate** (*see page 228* **Blade runners**). Film screenings, theatre productions and pop concerts are also held here, including a free festival of open-air theatre in summer (*see page 244* **Park life**).

Nederlands Filmmuseum (NFM)

Vondelpark 3 (589 1400/library 589 1435/ www.nfm.nl). Tram 1, 2, 3, 5, 6, 12, 20. **Open** *box office* 1hr before screenings. *Library* (no loans) 10am-5pm Tue-Fri; 11am-5pm Sat; closed Mon, Sun. *Screenings* 7pm, 7.30pm, 9.30pm and/or 10pm daily; kids' matinée 3pm Sun. **Tickets** *Cinema* ƒ12,50; ƒ10 concessions; ƒ7,50 members. **Membership** ƒ30/yr. **No credit cards**. **Map** p310 C6.

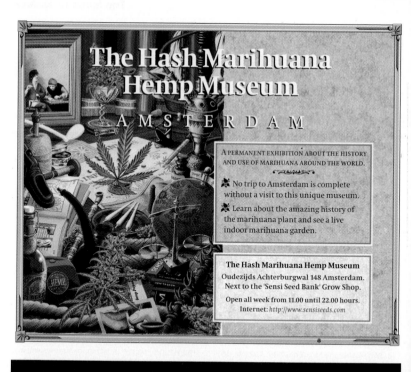

The Pijp

Home to artists, market traders, prostitutes, butchers and giant green gnomes, Amsterdam's most vibrant neighbourhood doesn't want for variety.

Map p311

Not to be confused with the suggestive slang in Dutch for the act of 'piping' – translatable as 'giving a blow job', to be frank – doing the Pijp can still be a fairly colourful experience: the district has definitely got a spunky verve about it. And though it's hardly a treasure trove of history and traditional sights, the Pijp's time is the present, with its reported 168 different resident nationalities keeping its global village vibe very much alive.

The area is the best known of the working-class quarters built in the late 19th century, when a population boom burst the city's seams. Harsh economics saw the building of long, narrow streets, which probably inspired the change in name from the official double yawn-inducing 'Area YY' to its more appropriate nickname, 'The Pipe'. Because rents were still too high for many tenants, they were forced, in turn, to let rooms out to students. And it was the students who gave the area its bohemian character, together with numerous Dutch writers who lived here, including Heijermans, De Haan and Bordewijk, who famously described World War I-era Amsterdam as a 'ramshackle bordello, a wooden shoe made of stone'. Many painters had studios here, too – including Piet Mondrian who lived for a time in the attic of Ruysdaelkade 75 – and the area was packed with brothels and drinking dens. In the basement of Quellijnstraat 64, the Dutch cabaret style, distinguished by its witty songs with cutting social commentary for lyrics, was formulated by Eduard Jacobs and continues to live on through modern proponents like Freek de Jong.

At the turn of the century, the Pijp was a radical socialist area. Though the area has lost much of its radicalism since those halcyon days, the students remain, even though many families with children have fled to suburbia. The number of cheap one- and two-bedroom apartments, combined with the reasonably central location, makes the area very attractive to students, young single people and couples. The area also has the densest gay population in Amsterdam. During the last 40 years, many immigrants have also found their way into the area and set up shop. The Pijp now houses a mix of nationalities, providing locals with plenty of Islamic butchers, Surinamese, Spanish, Indian and Turkish delicatessens, and grocery stores selling exotic food. Restaurants offer authentic Syrian, Moroccan, Surinamese, Thai, Pakistani, Chinese and Indian cuisine. Thanks to all these generally low-priced exotic eats, the Pijp is the best place in town for quality snacking treats, the ingredients for which are mostly bought fresh from the largest daily market in the Netherlands.

Albert Cuypmarkt is the hub around which the Pijp turns, attracting thousands of customers every day. It's the core of the Pijp street life and generally spills merrily into the adjoining roads: the junctions of Sweelinckstraat, Ferdinand Bolstraat and 1e Van der Helststraat, north into the lively Gerard Douplein, and south towards Sarphatipark (*see also page 163*). The chaos will undoubtedly be enhanced over the next few years by the construction of the controversial Noord/Zuidlijn Metro line that will run pretty much underneath the Ferdinand Bolstraat.

The grass-, pond-, and duck-dappled **Sarphatipark** was designed and built as a miniature Bois de Boulogne by the inspired and slightly mad genius Samuel Sarphati (1813-66). Aside from also building the **Amstel InterContinental** hotel and the Paleis voor Volksvlijt, Sarphati also showed philanthropic tendencies as a baker of inexpensive bread for the masses, and as initiator of the city's garbage collection. Fittingly, the park – and its centrepiece fountain, complete with a statue of Sammy himself – received a fresh scrubbing in 1994.

Food for thought:
Albert Cuypmarkt.

Mmmm. Beer. The **Heineken Brewery**.

On the corner of Stadhouderskade and Ferdinand Bolstraat stands the old **Heineken Brewery** (*listings below*). Beer production here stopped at the beginning of 1988 amid some outcry: after all, Heineken is virtually the Dutch national drink, even though connoisseurs refer to it as *paarden pis* due to its resemblance to 'equine urine'. Now the building acts purely as a propaganda centre for the company, which still runs its infamous brewery tours here. The tour climaxes with an all-you-can-drink taste-test, which, for about the same price as real horse piss (or so we reckon) – *f*2 – is a fine deal indeed.

Beyond the stall-filled stretch of Albert Cuypstraat, across Ferdinand Bolstraat, is a cluster of cheap Chinese-Surinamese-Indonesian restaurants excellent for gelling a queasy post-Heineken tour belly. A few doors from here is the famed **Sang Photo Studio** (Albert Cuypstraat 57, 679 6906, closed Sun), where one can have a black and white portrait taken and then painted in by the gentleman proprietor, a sublimely kitsch gift idea for around 40 guilders. And after passing the coach-party attraction of **Van Moppes & Zoon Diamond Factory** (*see chapter* **Shops & Services**), diamond turns to ruby around the corner along the Ruysdaelkade, the location of the Pijp's very own mini red light district. Watch horned-out motorists caught in their own traffic gridlock while you lounge around casually along an otherwise restful canal.

Over 250 artists live in and around the Pijp, and the current crop is slowly gaining more status in a district where most streets are named after their illustrious forebears: Jan Steen, Ferdinand Bol, Gerard Dou and Jacob van Campen are just a few who have been honoured in this way. Steen (1625-79),

barkeeper and painter of rowdy bar scenes, even has a bar named after him (the **Jan Steen Café** at Ruysdaelkade 149), which still represents him well: the beer is cheap and the crowd is loud. And why view his work in the Rijksmuseum when you can see it in action? The new gallery **Art Industry** (*see page 197*), on Ferdinand Bolstraat in the former Heineken Brewery building, may be a good place to start exploring some of the more current of the neighbourhood's great many artistic ventures.

Crossing the Albert Cuypmarkt from Gerard Douplein is 1e Van der Helststraat. This little square, with its cafés, coffeeshops, chip shops and authentic Italian ice-cream parlour, turns into one big terrace during the summer, and is hugely popular with the locals. Bargain second-hand Euro knick-knacks can be bought at the nearby **Stichting Dodo** (No.21, trivia hounds should know that the Dutch – or rather their egg-eating animals – were responsible for this bird's extinction after colonising the island of Mauritius in 1598), while the cheapest raw herring in town can be gotten for the gullet at **Volendammer Vis Handel** at No.60.

On the corner of 1e Van der Helststraat and Govert Flinckstraat is one of the area's best bakeries, **Bakkerij Runneboom** (*see page 155*). Apart from selling a huge variety of Dutch bread – including 'Rembrandt' bread – and pastries, it also stocks various typical Turkish, Moroccan and even Irish (buttermilk) breads. There is always a queue outside the little shop, no matter what time of day. Hidden halfway down 1e Jan Steenstraat is a rather special bric-a-brac shop, **Nic Nic**, a paradise for '50s and '60s freaks (*see page 163*).

Running parallel to Albert Cuypstraat, the Ceintuurbaan offers little of note for the visitor, with the exception of the buildings at Nos.251-5 near the crossing over the Amstel. Why? Well, there aren't many other houses in the city that incorporate giant ball-playing green gnomes with red hats in their wooden façades. The unique exterior of the 'Gnome House' was inspired by the owner's name: Van Ballegooien translates literally (and somewhat clumsily) as 'Of the ball-throwing'. Around the corner from here, on the mighty Amstel river, is the city's archive, **Gemeentearchief Amsterdam** (Amsteldijk 67, 572 0202), at which you can peruse the library or one of its excellent exhibitions.

Heineken Brewery

Stadhouderskade 78 (523 9239/recorded information 523 9666). Tram 6, 7, 10, 16, 20, 24, 25. **Tours** 9.30am, 11am Mon-Fri; closed Sat, Sun. **Admission** *f*2 (goes to charity). **Credit** AmEx, DC, MC, V. **Map** p311 E5.

The Waterfront

Still functioning as an important port for trade, the Waterfront is where Amsterdam's past and present meet in dramatic fashion.

Map p307

Amsterdam's historical wealth owes a lot to the city's waterfront: it was here that all the goods were unloaded, weighed and prepared for storage in the many warehouses still found in the area. During Amsterdam's trading heyday in the 17th century, most maritime activity was centred east of Centraal Station, along Prins Hendrikkade and on the artificial islands east of Kattenburgerstraat. At the time, the harbour and its arterial canals – many of which have been filled in since the rise of land traffic – formed a whole with the city itself. A drop in commerce slowly unbalanced this unity, and the construction of Centraal Station late in the 19th century served as the final psychological cleavage. This neo-Gothic monument to modernity – as it was seen then, at any rate – blocked both the city's view of the harbour and its own past.

This is not to say, though, that the harbour started slacking. While Rotterdam is by far the world's largest port, Amsterdam and the nearby North Sea Canal ports of Zaanstad, Beverwijk and IJmuiden together rank among the world's 15 largest ports, handling 45 million tonnes per year. Amsterdam is now the centre of Nissan's European distribution, and is still the world's largest cocoa port. In 1997, though, a storage warehouse for these most oily of nuts caught fire and stayed burning for a week, spewing dramatic dark smoke over the city.

Since 1876, access to the sea has been via the North Sea Canal, running west from Amsterdam. Because the working docks are also to the west, there is little activity on the IJ behind Centraal Station beyond a handful of passenger ships and the free ferry that runs across to Amsterdam Noord.

The previously mentioned **Schreierstoren**, or 'Weeping Tower' (*see page 42*), is the first thing you'll notice on the right if you walk east from Centraal Station, and is the most interesting relic of what's left of Amsterdam's medieval city wall. Some historians claim that 'schreiers' was actually originally *schreye*, the Dutch word for 'sharp', and, indeed, the tower has a sharp edge where it once formed an acute corner on the city wall. Built in 1487, it was successfully restored in 1966.

In 1927, though, a bronze memorial plaque was added by the Greenwich Village Historical Society of New York: its text states that it was from this point, on 4 April 1609, that Henry Hudson departed in search of shorter trade routes to the Far East. He ended up colonising a small island in the mouth of a river in North America. The river was later named after him and the colony was called New Amsterdam, only to have its name changed by the English to New York. (Today, some of the boroughs still have a nederstamp on them: in particular, Harlem, after Haarlem, and Brooklyn, after Breukelen. Not to mention the fact that the term 'Yankees' comes from the generic Dutch name, 'Jan Kees'.) In 1956, stones from the Schreierstoren were taken to Chicago and placed into the wall of the *Chicago Tribune* building, alongside similar chunks from famous buildings around the world, including the Parthenon in Athens, Paris' Notre Dame cathedral and the Great Wall of China.

The next eye-opener you'll come across is a green building that looks like the *Titanic* in mid-sink. It's the newish **newMetropolis** museum (*listings page 78*), a vast, super-popular spot that aims to get kids interested in learning by offering the usual distractions: movies, TVs, computer games galore, and a host of hands-on exhibits that work like big toys. There's little history here: the lively exhibitions, which cover music, transport, economics, energy and the brain, seem geared towards inspiring the generation of engineers and researchers the Netherlands will need to drive it into an industrious future. However, newMetropolis is great fun, offering kids (and adults) opportunities to make electricity, hook up a mock power grid, run a mixing board, conduct a sort of telepathy experiment with a friend and use microscopes in the Lab (12 and up). All exhibits are well spaced with clear instructions in Dutch and English.

Adults, though, may find just as much joy in the building itself. Renzo Piano's architectural wonder itself is best seen from down the road near the Maritime Museum, where it resembles a green ship rising out of the water of the old harbour. The panoramic views afforded by the building of the water and the houses of the Prins Hendrikkade and surrounds are unequalled.

Sightseeing

Olympic glory

Built in a flash by Jan Wils for the 1928 summer games, Amsterdam's **Olympisch Stadion** (Olympic Stadium) was initially criticised as a cumbersome colossus in stride with current architectural conventions. It was also hailed as the world's first modern sports arena. However, though it was the Netherlands' premier sports facility until the late 1930s, it continually lost profits and respectability to larger-capacity stadiums. Despite the addition of an uninspired encasing construction of concrete bleachers around the ground, both Ajax and the national football team had abandoned the stadium by the 1960s. What events remained failed to generate enough earnings for even rudimentary maintenance, and the stadium fell into a state of disrepair.

Local residents of the respectable Oud Zuid neighbourhood were eager to see the eyesore replaced by much-needed, low-income housing. Ajax would have its ArenA and local officials would enjoy the kudos of a win-win situation. But to the surprise of many, the Netherlands Department for Conservation, in cooperation with the Monuments and Historic Buildings Inventory Project, bestowed monument status on the stadium in 1987. Wils' original design invoked Frank Lloyd Wright's functionalist architectural ideals and captured the spirit of Berlage and the

Amsterdam School of architecture, which dominates the area. Provided it was renovated and became self-sustaining, Olympic Stadium would be saved. Otherwise, the wrecking ball loomed.

Various proposals – including a failed bid to host the 1992 Olympics – were forwarded, rejected based on insufficient funds and re-forwarded. But when it was revealed that plans for the new neighbourhood had been revised to include only a limited number of upscale dwellings, locals sided with the restoration option and more funds became available.

Renovations began in 1998, and were completed two years later. The concrete bleachers have, pleasingly, been removed to expose Wils' original façade, and the outer cycling track has been converted into commercial space. While capacity has been cut to 22,500, the multi-functional sporting facilities have been upgraded to those of an A-status stadium, and a parking garage has been built under the field. A variety of sporting events have been planned, including the Amsterdam Marathon, Amsterdam Admirals matches and other athletic tournaments.

In addition, the stadium's coveted commercial premises have been leased to a variety of firms. There's now a state-of-the-art health club (Medico Vision Sports) on site,

You'll also get to look at a replica of a very 'Shiver me timbers, Matey, ever been masted at sea before?' East India Company sailing ship. Indeed, the wharf of the VOC (the Dutch acronym for the company) was once here and a small naval base remains, though the *Admiralty* has been converted into the **Nederlands Scheepvaartmuseum** (Netherlands Maritime Museum, *listings page 78*). It takes some time to see the collection housed in this monumental Venetian-style building, designed by Daniel Stalpaert and built in the 1650s. Once you've made it all the way round, though, you'll be glad you took the time, for the Scheepvaart houses a collection of naval ephemera second only to that found in London's National Maritime Museum.

Originally used as a warehouse for sails, rope, arms and ammunition for the city's fleet of ships, the Maritime Museum stands in the heart of Amsterdam's nautical district. Wooden models, paintings, drawings and ship parts

illustrate the commercial, military and recreational ways the Dutch have used the water since the 16th century. Most fun is the full-sized replica East India Company ship docked behind the museum. Here you can see a burial at sea while mingling with overacting 'sailors' on the decks and in the holds, who'll happily tell you anything you want to know about life on the 17th-century ship. It's merely the highlight, though, of one of the major museums of its kind in the world.

Nearby is another nautical museum, **Werf 't Kromhout** (*listings page 78*). A nostalgic museum, full of old, silent ship engines and tools. The shipyard is obviously very proud of the fact that it's one of the few remaining original yards still in use, but its 18th-century heritage is no longer very apparent, nor is the yard as active as it once was. The museum has been closed for renovations that were expected to last through mid-2000, so be sure to call ahead and check it's open before setting out.

where injured Ajax players prefer to rehabilitate, as well as a trendy eaterie, **Vakzuid** (see page 115). But whether on a sporting or architectural pilgrimage or simply in for a casual drink, Amsterdam's Olympic Stadium pays homage to its athletic history and proves well worth the trip.

Olympisch Stadion

Stadionplein 20, Zuid (stadium 671 1115/ Medico Vision Sports 379 1961/Vak Zuid 0900 825 9843 premium rate/ www.olympisch-stadion.net). Tram 24/bus 15, 63. **Open** *hours vary. Vakzuid see p115 for details.*

The old harbour is now virtually disused and the whole IJ-Oevers (docklands) are undergoing massive redevelopment, a big issue within the city, concerning both locals and environmental groups. It is said to be the country's only remaining upmarket area for new housing and office development, and plans for development – estimated to cost *f* 6 billion – are continually subject to alteration because of the lack of financial backing, pressure from local residents and new *stadsdeelraden* (local councils), and the ever-changing traffic control plans. Certainly, the city's subculture experienced a great loss with the demise of both the sprawling Silo and Vrieshuis Amerika squats, but the city itself hopes that a transformed harbourfront – complete with the new wave-shaped cruise ship Passenger Terminal – will be as image enhancing as that in Sydney, Australia.

Going east, you'll espy **KNSM Island**, where the KNSM shipping company originally docked its boats and unloaded cargo. In recent years, it's been transformed from a squatters' paradise to a newly developed and largely residential area, featuring some striking modern architecture and some newish bars and venues, such as **Kanis & Meiland** (*see page 132*). As for the squatters in this area, many of them have had to look towards Amsterdam Noord or have made the harsh transition to being legal tenants and homeowners. Further east, you can watch the controversial building of the artificial residential island of **IJburg** (*see page 32* **Island life**).

The Westelijke Eilanden (Western Islands), north-west of Centraal Station, are also artificial islands, created in the 17th century for shipping-related activities. While there are now trendy warehouse flats and a yacht basin on Realeneiland, Prinseneiland and Bickerseiland, where once shipyards, tar distillers, fish-salters and smokers were once located, the area – thanks in part to its large artist community – remains the city's best setting for a scenic stroll.

Nederlands Scheepvaartmuseum

Kattenburgerplein 1 (523 2222). Bus 22, 32. **Open**
late Sept-early June 10am-5pm Tue-Sun; closed Mon.
Mid June-mid Sept 10am-5pm daily. **Admission**
*f*14,50; *f*8-*f*12,50 concessions; free Museum Card,
under-6s. **No credit cards**. **Map** p307 F2.

newMetropolis

*Oosterdok 2 (information 0900 919 1100 premium
rate/www.newmetropolis.nl). Bus 22.* **Open** 10am-

5pm Tue-Fri; 10am-6pm Sat, Sun; closed Mon.
Admission *f*20; *f*15 concessions; free under-3s.
Credit AmEx, DC, MC, V. **Map** p307 F2.

Werf 't Kromhout

Hoogte Kadijk 147 (627 6777). Bus 22.
Open 10.30am-4pm Mon-Fri; closed Sat, Sun.
Admission *f*4; *f*2,50 under-15s. **Closed** for
renovations until mid-2000; call after that for
updated hours and prices.

The specialists

Amsterdam has a variety of small, specialised
collections, dealing with subjects ranging from
the life and times of famous Dutch authors to
embryological specimens. 'Museum' is
perhaps too grand a word for some of the
smaller collections, which will be most
interesting to connoisseurs and which, in any
case, often aren't equipped to deal with many
casual visitors. Many can only be visited by
arrangement; all are free unless otherwise
stated, and none accepts credit cards.

Bedrijfsmuseum ENW Amsterdam

*Spaklerweg 20, Zuid (597 3107). Bus 46,
169/Metro Spaklerweg.* **Open** by
appointment; phone 8am-4pm Mon-Fri.
Industrial artefacts relating to gas and
electricity production and distribution.

Bilderdijk Collection

*De Boelelaan 1105, Zuid (444 5184). Bus 8,
23, 26, 48, 49, 64, 65, 67, 158, 173,
197/51 tram.* **Open** by appointment, in the
Oude Drukken room on the first floor of the
Vrije University.
A collection of manuscripts, etchings and
personal belongings recording the life and
times of Dutch writer and academic Willem
Bilderdijk (1756-1831).

Historisch Documentatiecentrum van de Vrije Universiteit

*De Boelelaan 1105, Zuid (444 7777). Bus 8,
23, 26, 48, 49, 64, 65, 67, 158, 173,
197/51 tram.* **Open** 9am-4.45pm Mon-Fri.
A research centre dealing with the history of
the Dutch Protestant University and its
founder, Abraham Kuyper.

Multatuli Museum

*Korsjespoortsteeg 20, Grachtengordel: West
(638 1938). Tram 1, 2, 5, 13, 17, 20.* **Open**
10am-5pm Tue; noon-5pm Sat, Sun; also by
appointment. **Map** p306 C2.
In the house where he was born, the life of
the 19th-century writer Eduard Douwes-

Dekker (who wrote under the pseudonym
Multatuli) is illustrated by photos and other
objects. There's also a library.

Persmuseum, Instituut voor Sociale Geschiedenis, Nederlands Economisch-Historisch Archief

*Cruquiusweg 31, Oost (668 5866). Tram 6,
10/22 bus.* **Open** 9am-5pm Mon-Fri.
The Persmuseum (Museum of the Dutch
Press) is set to open a permanent exhibition
in late 2000, along with changing temporary
shows, to show off some of its 17,000 items
including newspapers, posters and political
cartoons. Meanwhile, it's one of three
library-archives that are housed in the same
building and share a reading room. The
International Institute for Social History
specialises in the history of world social
movements and has original writings by Marx
and Engels, while the third collection covers
Dutch economic history.

Vakbonds Museum

*Henri Polaklaan 9, Plantage (624 1166).
Tram 7, 9, 14, 20.* **Open** 11am-5pm Tue-Fri;
1-5pm Sun. **Map** p307 F3.
A permanent exhibition showing aspects of
the Labour Union in Dutch history. The
building was designed by Berlage to house
the offices of the country's first trade union.

Museum Vrolik

*Entrance on south side of AMC medical
faculty, Meibergdreef 15, Zuidoost
(566 9111). Bus 59, 60, 61, 120, 126/
Metro Holendrecht.* **Open** 2-5pm Mon-Fri; also
by appointment.
This anatomical embryological laboratory,
contains 18th- and 19th-century specimens of
human embryos, human anatomy and congeni-
tal malformations collected by Professor
Gerardus Vrolik and his son. Not
recommended for those with weak stomachs.

Consumer

Accommodation

A room with a view? No problem. Room at the top? Sure. But when booking a hotel in Amsterdam, massive demand doesn't leave much room for manoeuvre.

Any introduction to accommodation in Amsterdam should advise one thing above all others, and ours is no exception. Book ahead. Book *waaaay* ahead. Accommodation in Amsterdam is at a premium, and unless you want to end up in a cardboard box on Leidseplein, make sure to get your reservation sorted early.

That said, though the town is a little short on rooms for much of the year, what hotels it does have offer a splendid variety of modernity, history, charm and coolness. From **Blakes** to the **Krasnapolsky**, the **Hotel de Filosoof** to the **Flying Pig**, the town has many hotels and hostels that may become as much of an attraction as the sights you're there to see. The vast majority of hoteliers are polite and helpful, and accommodation is generally of a very high standard. If you can find any, that is…

In line with basic economic principles of supply and demand, hotels don't come cheap in Amsterdam. But they're not outrageously expensive, either. Many hotels offer special discounts during the off-peak season, usually November to March (excluding Christmas and New Year). But once again, booking ahead is imperative. All prices listed are exclusive of the five per cent visitors' tax, and are listed in guilders. However, some hotels are already listing their prices in Euros for credit card transactions, and rates are sure to fluctuate when the Single European Currency is introduced in full in 2002.

RESERVATIONS

Aside from going direct to the hotels – and if you do this, be sure to book well in advance – or booking a travel-and-hotel package with your travel agent, there are several ways of making reservations. The **Nederlands Reserverings Centrum** (aka Dutch hoteliers' reservation service) handles bookings for the whole of the Netherlands, as do the **Amsterdam Tourist Board** offices at Centraal Station and Schiphol Airport (*see page 283* **Tickets please**); both organisations charge a booking fee of ƒ20 per person (plus a refundable deposit of 10 per cent), and only take enquiries in person. The Amsterdam Tourist Board also produces a comprehensive guide to hotels in the city, priced at ƒ5.

Nederlands Reserverings Centrum

PO Box 404, 2260 AK Leidschendam (070 419 5500/ www.hotelres.nl). **Open** 9am-5.30pm Mon-Fri.
Bookings can only be made online: the phone number listed is merely for changes or cancellations.

Hotels

Deluxe (ƒ600 and up)

American Hotel
Leidsekade 97, Grachtengordel: East, 1017 PN (556 3000/fax 556 3001/www.interconti.com). Tram 1, 2, 5, 6, 7, 10, 20. **Rates** ƒ395-ƒ450 single; ƒ525-ƒ600 double; ƒ75 extra bed. **Credit** AmEx, DC, MC, V. **Map** p310 C5.
The American's classic art deco exterior, plush, modernised interior and luxurious rooms make it an attractive choice for those seeking deluxe lodgings. Not least among its visitors are numerous rock stars who seem to enjoy the hotel's proximity to the city's two main music venues – the **Melkweg** (*see p217*) and the **Paradiso** (*see p218*) – along with the **Stadsschouwburg** (*see p239*). Situated on the ground floor is **Café Americain** (*see p101*), the hotel's focal point, which overlooks the bustling Leidseplein. In contrast, the tranquil Vondelpark is just two minutes' walk away. Breakfast is an extra ƒ35.
Hotel services *Air-conditioning. Babysitting. Bars. Business services. Concierge. Disabled: adapted rooms. Gym. Limousine service. No-smoking floors. Parking (paid). Restaurants.* **Room services** *Dataport. Minibar. Room service (24hrs).*

Amstel Inter-Continental Amsterdam
Professor Tulpplein 1, Grachtengordel: East, 1018 GX (622 6060/fax 622 5808/www.interconti.com). Tram 6, 7, 10, 20. **Rates** ƒ895-ƒ995 single/double; ƒ1,200-ƒ5,250 suite; ƒ100 extra bed. **Credit** AmEx, DC, MC, V. **Map** p311 F4.
The alluring Grand Hall foyer gives just a hint of what lies beyond in the most luxurious, formal (and, thus, expensive) five-star hotel in the city. With a ratio of two staff to each of the 79 antique- and Delft-adorned rooms and suites, you can expect to be pampered. The high expectations of guests seem to be met, too, given the extraordinary list of returning celebs and royals. The hotel's excellent cuisine can be enjoyed either in sumptuous indoor surroundings or on the riverside terraces, where the spectacular setting – just by the Amstel – can be truly appreciated. Breakfast is an additional ƒ52,50.

Hotel services *Air-conditioning. Bars. Business services. Concierge. Gym. Limousine service. No-smoking rooms. Parking. Restaurants. Swimming pool.* **Room services** *Dataport. Minibar. Room service (24hrs). VCR.*

Amsterdam Hilton
Apollolaan 138, Zuid, 1077 BG (710 6000/fax 710 9000/www.hilton.com). Tram 5, 24. **Rates** ƒ620-ƒ735 single; ƒ650-ƒ765 double; ƒ895-ƒ2,750 suite. **Credit** AmEx, DC, MC, V.

Though it's famed for the John and Yoko 'bed-in' of 1969, the huge five-star Amsterdam Hilton, in terms of style and appearance, is actually pretty unexciting. However, it does offer a wide spectrum of top-brass services: there are no fewer than 271 air-conditioned rooms and the restaurant has great Mediterranean cuisine. The John and Yoko suite can be hired for wedding ceremonies, and is very popular with honeymooners. The hotel's location is ideal, but then again, there's no room for a yacht club and marina in the city centre (though these are not part of the hotel, just a backdrop). Breakfast is an extra ƒ42,50.

Hotel services *Air-conditioning. Babysitting. Bar. Beauty salon. Business services. Concierge. Disabled: adapted rooms. Garden. Gym. Limousine service. No-smoking floors. Parking. Restaurant.* **Room services** *Dataport. Minibar. Refrigerator (suites only). Room service (24hrs).*

Amsterdam Marriott Hotel
Stadhouderskade 12, Grachtengordel: West, 1054 ES (607 5555/fax 607 5511/www.marriotthotels.com/AMSNT). Tram 1, 2, 5, 6, 7, 10, 20. **Rates** ƒ575-ƒ675 room (holds 1-4 people); ƒ895-ƒ1,295 room (holds 1-4 people). **Credit** AmEx, DC, MC, V. **Map** p310 C5.

This five-star hotel is in the centre of the city, overlooking Leidseplein between the Vondelpark and the casino, and near the biggest museums. The very comfortable 392 rooms and suites all offer a feeling of spaciousness: there are no singles, so you'll just have to sit back and let yourself be pampered. Of the two restaurants, Port O' Amsterdam offers a luxurious menu, while Characters includes Pizza Hut pizzas for lunch and dinner, plus a jukebox and pool table. Breakfast is ƒ33,50.

Hotel services *Air-conditioning. Babysitting. Bars. Business services. Concierge. Disabled: adapted rooms. Gym. No-smoking floors. Parking. Restaurants.* **Room services** *Dataport. Minibar. Room service (24hrs).*

Barbizon Palace
Prins Hendrikkade 59-72, Old Centre: Old Side, 1012 AD (556 4564/fax 624 3353/sales@gtbpalace.goldentulip.nl). Tram 1, 2, 4, 5, 7, 9, 13, 17, 20, 24, 25/Metro Centraal Station. **Rates** ƒ452-ƒ584 single; ƒ518-ƒ651 double; ƒ937-ƒ1,873 suite; ƒ132 extra bed. **Credit** AmEx, DC, MC, V. **Map** p306 D2.

Part of the Golden Tulip Group, the Babizon Palace is part of the chain that includes the **Schiller** (*see p89*) and the **Krasnapolsky** (*see p83*). The lavish

Isn't life **Grand**? *See p83.*

surroundings are apparent from first walking into the hall. A canopy creates an exotic impression, one enhanced by the swanky fitness centre, complete with sauna, Turkish bath and solarium. The hotel even has its own landing stage for canal boats. Indulge further at the award-winning restaurant Vermeer. Breakfast is ƒ37,50.

Hotel services *Air-conditioning. Babysitting. Bars. Beauty services. Concierge. Disabled: adapted room. Gym. Limousine service. No smoking floor. Parking. Restaurants.* **Room services** *Dataport. Minibar. Room service (24hrs). VCR (on request).*

Hôtel de l'Europe
Nieuwe Doelenstraat 2-8, Old Centre: Old Side, 1012 CP (531 1777/fax 531 1778/www.leurope.nl). Tram 4, 9, 14, 16, 20, 24, 25. **Rates** ƒ575 single; ƒ655-ƒ755 double; ƒ870-ƒ2,000 suite; ƒ95 extra bed. **Credit** AmEx, DC, MC, V. **Map** p306 D3.

Looking out from one of the 100 individually decorated Victorian rooms, you might think this five-star hotel has a moat. It doesn't; it's just that its location on the Amstel gives a great view of the city centre's main functional waterways. The hotel's charm is further enhanced by the Excelsior restaurant (jacket required), serving haute cuisine and champagne on its river-level terrace facing the historic Munttoren. With its Victorian-period lounge and foyer, this truly is an elegant place, and caters for all, from business types to just-marrieds (the bridal suite comes complete with Jacuzzi). Breakfast costs from ƒ47,50.

Hotel services *Air-conditioning. Babysitting. Bars. Business services. Concierge. Gym. Limousine service. No-smoking rooms. Parking. Restaurants. Swimming pool.* **Room services** *Dataport. Minibar. Room service (24hrs). VCR (on request).*

The Grand

Oudezijds Voorburgwal 197, Old Centre: Old Side, 1012 EX (555 3111/fax 555 3222/www.thegrand.nl). Tram 4, 9, 14, 16, 20, 24, 25. **Rates** *ƒ705 single; ƒ765-ƒ875 double; ƒ1,050-ƒ2,850 suite.* **Credit** AmEx, DC, MC, V. **Map** p306 D3.

Prince William of Orange was among the first of many illustrious guests to stay at this centrally located five-star hotel when it opened as an inn in the late 16th century. Since then, the site has been the home of the great Dutch Admiralty and, contradictorily, the dull city council. You get a glimpse of the history as soon as you enter the spacious courtyard, and the 182 rooms, suites and apartments are decorated accordingly. The restaurant's excellent current chef works under the direction of the mighty Albert Roux (*see p111*).

Hotel services *Air-conditioning. Babysitting. Bar. Business services. Concierge. Disabled: adapted rooms. Garden. Gym. Limousine service. No-smoking rooms. Parking. Restaurant. Swimming pool.* **Room services** *Dataport. Minibar. Room service (24hrs). VCR (on request).*

Grand Hotel Krasnapolsky

Dam 9, Old Centre: Old Side, 1012 JS (554 9111/ fax 622 8607/www.goldentulip.com). Tram 1, 2, 4, 5, 9, 13, 14, 16, 17, 20, 24, 25. **Rates** *ƒ550 single; ƒ625-ƒ1,000 double; ƒ950-ƒ1,500 suite; ƒ100 extra bed.* **Credit** AmEx, DC, MC, V. **Map** p306 D3.

Located in the heart of Amsterdam, this enormous hotel boasts 469 rooms, including 36 fully furnished apartments, and two national monuments. One of these is the Winter Garden, with a high, glass-roofed atrium where guests can breakfast and lunch orangerie-style. There are restaurants for every palate: Mediterranean-influenced dining can be had at Brasserie Reflet, Japanese cuisine at Edo and Kyo, and there are also Italian, Mexican and Middle Eastern options. After a strenuous meeting in one of the 22 convention rooms, business types can have a drink in the Golden Palm Bar, or stroll to the Lounge, which presides over Dam Square, its long windows providing perfect viewing across to the Palace. Breakfast is an extra ƒ38,50.

Hotel services *Air-conditioning. Babysitting. Bar. Beauty salon. Business services. Concierge. Disabled: adapted rooms. Gym. No-smoking rooms. Parking. Restaurants.* **Room services** *Dataport. Minibar. Refrigerator (some rooms). Room service (24hrs).*

Hotel Inntel

Nieuwezijdskolk 19, Old Centre: New Side (530 1818/fax 422 1919/www.hotelinntel.com). Tram 1, 2, 5, 13, 17, 20. **Rates** *ƒ395-ƒ625 single/double; ƒ550-ƒ700 suite; ƒ100 extra bed.* **Credit** AmEx, DC, MC, V. **Map** p306 D2.

Located on a small pedestrian square, the Inntel is quiet enough to ensure a good night's rest, but just one minute away from the shopping on Kalverstraat, and barely five minutes from the Jordaan. All 236 guest rooms are simply but tastefully decorated, cutting a designer-cool edge. The conservatory-style breakfast room overlooks a terrace, making early eating very relaxing. Hotel Inntel guests can use two neighbouring restaurants,

Consumer

and then add dinner to the hotel bill. Staff are incredibly friendly and make every effort to ensure your stay is pleasant. Breakfast is ƒ30.
Hotel services *Air-conditioning (selected rooms). Bar. Disabled: adapted rooms. Limousine service. No-smoking floors. Parking. Restaurant (breakfast only).* **Room services** *Dataport. Minibar. Room service (7-10am Mon-Fri; 7-11am Sat, Sun).*

Okura Hotel Amsterdam
Ferdinand Bolstraat 333, Zuid, 1072 LH (678 7111/ fax 671 2344/www.okura.nl). Tram 12, 25. **Rates** ƒ425-ƒ595 single; ƒ475-ƒ645 double; ƒ715-ƒ2,750 suite; ƒ105 extra bed. **Credit** AmEx, DC, MC, V.
Perfectly situated and equipped for business, the luxury five-star Okura boasts 321 rooms, 49 suites and 16 banqueting and conference rooms. Granted, the location isn't very central, but the fact that it's only a ten-minute walk from the RAI Congress and the World Trade Centre is an obvious advantage to business travellers. Commerce aside, there are two bars and four restaurants, one of which is on the 23rd floor and offers an incredible panoramic view of the entire city. Breakfast is an extra ƒ45.
Hotel services *Air-conditioning. Babysitting. Bar(s). Beauty salon. Business services. Concierge. Disabled: adapted rooms. Garden. Gym. Limousine service. No-smoking rooms. Parking. Restaurant(s). Swimming pool.* **Room services** *Dataport. Minibar. Room service (24hrs). VCR (suites only).*

Hotel Pulitzer
Prinsengracht 315-31, Grachtengordel: West, 1016 GZ (523 5235/fax 627 6753/www.sheraton.com). Tram 13, 14, 17, 20. **Rates** ƒ625-ƒ685 single; ƒ695-ƒ755 double; ƒ1,750 suite; ƒ90 extra bed. **Credit** AmEx, DC, MC, V. **Map** p306 C3.
One of the more centrally located five-star hotels, the Pulitzer is also one of the more traditional. The hotel contains of 226 guest rooms, and occupies an entire block of canal houses (24 in total) from the main entrance on Prinsengracht along Reestraat to Keizersgracht, with a labyrinth of connecting corridors incorporating the covered walkway through the central courtyard gardens. The cultural significance of the Pulitzer goes beyond its architectural essence: the gallery holds regular exhibitions, and the award-winning wine cellar is renowned for harbouring some of the best vino around. Even if you aren't there on business, take a look in the Tuinzaal, decorated in Art Nouveau style, which looks on to the hotel gardens. Breakfast is an extra ƒ45.
Hotel services *Air-conditioning. Babysitting. Bar. Business services. Concierge. Garden. Limousine service. No-smoking rooms. Parking (valet). Restaurant.* **Room services** *Dataport. Minibar. Room service (24hrs).*

Sofitel
Nieuwezijds Voorburgwal 67, Old Centre: New Side, 1012 RE (627 5900/fax 623 8932/www.sofitel.nl/ eng/s/index.html). Tram 1, 2, 5, 13, 17, 20. **Rates** ƒ575-ƒ595 single; ƒ575-ƒ695 double; ƒ975-ƒ995 suite. **Credit** AmEx, DC, MC, V. **Map** p306 C2.

Located on the site of a former monastery, the 148-room Sofitel is remarkably understated, with muted, classical furnishings blending subtly together. The bar, known as the Duke of Windsor, is decorated with lamps and panelling from the Orient Express, reminding drinkers of trans-Europe travel. As the Sofitel is a mere five minutes' walk from Centraal Station and located between the shopping area of Kalverstraat and the canal district, guests won't have to do much travelling to make the most of the superb location.
Hotel services *Air-conditioning. Babysitting. Bar. Concierge. Disabled: adapted room. Gym. No-smoking rooms. Parking. Restaurant.* **Room services** *Dataport. Minibar. Room service (24hrs).*

Expensive (ƒ350-ƒ600)

Ambassade Hotel
Herengracht 341, Grachtengordel: West, 1016 AZ (626 2333/fax 624 5321/www.small-hotel.com/ ambassade). Tram 1, 2, 5. **Rates** ƒ290 single; ƒ350 double; ƒ415 triple; ƒ475-ƒ550 suite; ƒ525 apartment; ƒ60 extra bed. **Credit** AmEx, DC, MC, V. **Map** p310 C4.
Recommended by renowned architect and local professor Thomas van Leewen as one of Amsterdam's most beautiful canal house hotels, the differing structures of the centuries-old houses at the Ambassade mean that no two rooms are alike. To complement this, each bedroom has been individually and exquisitely decorated in keeping with the historic surroundings, as have the drawing and sitting rooms, and the hotel now boasts 59 rooms in its ten canal houses. The hotel offers all the advantages of this modern age, set in the fascinating heritage of a bygone era. Breakfast is ƒ27,50.
Hotel services *Babysitting. Business services (by request, in advance). Concierge. Limousine service.* **Room services** *Room service (24hrs). VCR.*

Best Western AMS Hotel Terdam
Tesselschadestraat 23, Museum Quarter, 1054 ET (612 6876/fax 683 8313/www.bestwestern.nl). Tram 1, 2, 3, 5, 6, 12, 20. **Rates** ƒ280-ƒ390 single; ƒ310-ƒ420 double; ƒ430 triple; ƒ64 extra bed. **Credit** AmEx, DC, MC, V. **Map** p310 C5.
A bit of a longwinded name and a mouthful to say to a taxi driver, but it's worth the effort. This hotel has 95 comfortable rooms in the vicinity of the Vondelpark close to Leidseplein. One wing has been renovated, and now features air-conditioning and revamped bathrooms.
Hotel services *Air-conditioning (selected rooms). Babysitting. Bar. Concierge. Disabled: adapted rooms. Limousine service. Parking nearby.* **Room services** *Dataport. Minibar (selected rooms).*

Hotel Dikker & Thijs Fenice
Prinsengracht 444, Grachtengordel: East, 1017 KE (620 1212/fax 625 8986/www.dikkerenthijsfenice.nl). Tram 1, 2, 5. **Rates** ƒ325-ƒ450 single; ƒ410-ƒ525 double.* **Credit** AmEx, DC, MC, V. **Map** p310 C5.

Blakes: heaven

The latest creation of celebrated designer/ hotelier Anouska Hempel, **Blakes** is the epitome of luxury. It's also something of a model for anyone looking to start a potentially fashionable boutique hotel. Decorated in gorgeous fabrics, each of the 26 rooms and suites has been individually designed to blend colour, texture and atmosphere to perfection. The result is dramatic and elegant, and is complemented by sensational service from a largely youthful staff.

The hotel opened in 1999 in a landmark building: originally a theatre, it dates back to 1617. Two decades later, Joost van den Vondel, the country's greatest poet, penned a play – *Gijsbrecht van Aemstel* – to celebrate the theatre's expansion, and Vivaldi himself conducted the theatre's orchestra at the theatre's centennial celebrations. The following 260-odd years took their toll on the building, but the sumptuous doorway and hall are original, while the restaurant is located in a bakery that dates back to 1787.

The restaurant itself is equally winning (for full details, see page 113), serving an a la carte menu inspired by the 16th-century merchant venturers. The main courses take in a mélange of Japanese and Thai influences, with hints of both Italy and France. The next morning, a continental breakfast will cost an extra ƒ32, while the luxuriant Blakes breakfast, which spans everything from eggs to fruit, comes in at a slightly pricier ƒ48.

Blakes

Keizersgracht 384, Grachtengordel: East (530 2010/fax 530 2030/www.slh.com/ blakesam). Tram 1, 2, 5. **Rates** ƒ475-ƒ575 single; ƒ725-ƒ925 double; ƒ1,300-ƒ2,750 suite. **Credit** AmEx, DC, MC, V. **Map** p310 C4.
Hotel services Air-conditioning. Babysitting. Bar. Concierge. Garden. Limousine service. Parking. Restaurant. **Room services** Dataport. Minibar. Room service (24hrs). VCR.

Views of the city are spectacular from atop the **Okura**. *See p84.*

This four-star hotel is located on the corner of Prinsengracht and Leidsestraat two minutes walk from Leidseplein, making it very handy not only for shopping and social festivities, but also for Museumplein, which is within easy walking distance. Many of the 26 rooms have a canal vista over the Prinsengracht. The hotel's restaurant De Prinsenkelder serves French and Italian food for dinner or a late supper.
Hotel services *Babysitting. Bar. Business services (by advance request). Concierge. Parking. Restaurant.* **Room services** *Dataport. Minibar. Room service (during restaurant hrs).*

Eden Hotel

Amstel 144, Grachtengordel: East, 1017 AE (530 7878/fax 623 3267/www.bestwestern.nl). Tram 4, 9, 14, 20. **Rates** *ƒ225-ƒ335 single; ƒ300-ƒ420 double; ƒ350-ƒ455 triple; ƒ400-ƒ520 quad; ƒ350-ƒ550 apartment (minimum 7 nights).* **Credit** AmEx, DC, MC, V. **Map** p307 C3.

As Amsterdam's largest three-star hotel – 340 rooms, with a further 70 to follow when current renovations are completed – the Eden offers lots of variety. Three special art rooms have been designed by students from the Rietveld Art Academy: ask for the interpretation of Rembrandt's *Night Watch* with luminous sheep on the ceiling to ease your journey to slumberland, but, if you stay in one of these rooms, prepare to pay a supplement of ƒ30. There are also five apartments available for longer stays. Breakfast is an extra ƒ22,50.
Hotel services *Babysitting. Bar. Business services. Concierge. Disabled: adapted rooms. No-smoking rooms. Parking nearby. Restaurant.* **Room services** *Dataport (selected rooms). Minibar (apartments, suites only).*

Esthera

Singel 303-9, Grachtengordel: West, 1012 WJ (624 5146/fax 623 9001/www.estherea.nl). Tram 1, 2, 5. **Rates** *ƒ270-ƒ385 single; ƒ290-ƒ495 double; ƒ400-ƒ550 triple; ƒ450-ƒ605 quad.* **Credit** AmEx, DC, MC, V. **Map** p306 C3.

Tucked round the corner from Spui and still owned and run by the same family that founded the hotel almost 60 years ago, this charming four-star spot is a haven for those who appreciate being looked after. From the luxurious breakfast room overlooking the canal, where tea and coffee are served (free) all day, to the 70 individually and traditionally renovated rooms, meticulous attention to detail is evident. Some 20 rooms spread throughout the plot of eight canal houses are even more deluxe, with the additional bonus of glorious views over the Singel canal. You have to pay a supplement for these, but it's worth the extra. Breakfast is ƒ27,50.
Hotel services *Babysitting. Bar. Concierge. No-smoking rooms.* **Room services** *Dataport. Minibar. Room service (7.30am-10pm).*

Jan Luyken Hotel

Jan Luykenstraat 58, Museum Quarter, 1071 CS (573 0730/fax 676 3841/www.janluyken.nl). Tram 2, 3, 5, 12, 20. **Rates** *ƒ340 single; ƒ370-ƒ540 double; ƒ85 extra bed.* **Credit** AmEx, DC, MC, V. **Map** p310 D6.

In a quiet street between the Vondelpark and the museums, this friendly but formal four-star caters for the more mature, refined customer, and for business travellers. An authentic townhouse atmosphere pervades in the reception area: the hotel has retained its 19th-century style – though there are some quirky decorative elements – and a feeling of hospitality that makes for a pleasant stay. The health

Consumer

spa is a perfect place to unwind, while the 62 well-furnished rooms come with renovated bathrooms, so you can still bathe in luxury if someone else has just booked the jacuzzi.
Hotel services *Air-conditioning. Babysitting. Bar. Business services. Garden. No-smoking floors. Parking nearby.* **Room services** *Dataport. Minibar. Refrigerator. Room service (7am-11pm).*

Omega
Jacob Obrechtstraat 33, Museum Quarter, 1071 KG (664 5182/fax 664 0809/www.omegahotel.nl). Tram 2, 3, 5, 12, 20. **Rates** *ƒ225-ƒ250 single; ƒ275-ƒ325 double; ƒ375 triple.* **Credit** AmEx, DC, MC, V. **Map** p310 C6.
The Omega has recently been refurbished and extended, expanding from a small two-star to an incredibly comfortable four-star hotel. Decor is now a rich, sumptuous array of reds and oranges, and the owner freely admits that you will either love or hate the 'outspoken colour scheme'. Breakfast goes on until 11am, enabling late sleepers to catch up on their zzzs. Staff are so accommodating that they will even arrange for a larger than usual bed if requested. In summer, enjoy drinks in the garden or on the rooftop, which boasts a wonderful panoramic view of the city. Informal, personal and colourful: if only more hotels were like this.
Hotel services *Air-conditioning (selected rooms). Bar. Business services. Concierge. Disabled: adapted rooms. Garden. No-smoking rooms. Parking (street). Restaurant.* **Room services** *Dataport. Minibar. Room service (24hrs).*

Park Hotel
Stadhouderskade 25, Museum Quarter, 1071 ZD (671 7474/fax 664 9455/www.parkhotel.nl). Tram 1, 2, 5. **Rates** *ƒ400-ƒ500 single; ƒ425-ƒ525 double; ƒ515-ƒ565 triple; ƒ725-ƒ750 suite; ƒ90 extra bed.* **Credit** AmEx, DC, MC, V. **Map** p310 D5.
As part of the Principle chain, this four-star hotel proclaims itself to have the 'best city centre location'. A tad biased, perhaps, but it's perfectly positioned for nightlife, with the casino just across the canal and Leidseplein just minutes away. During the daytime, culture vultures can head to nearby Museumplein. The hotel offers wide-ranging facilities, especially for business travellers. Five small boutiques are accessible from inside the hotel, offering hairstyling, Gucci accessories and the like.
Hotel services *Air-conditioning (selected rooms). Babysitting. Bar. Business services. Limousine service. No-smoking floors. Parking. Restaurant.* **Room services** *Dataport. Minibar (selected rooms). Refrigerator. Room service (24hrs).*

Schiller Hotel
Rembrandtplein 26-36, Grachtengordel: East, 1017 CV (554 0700/fax 624 0098/www.goldentulip.com). Tram 4, 9, 14, 20. **Rates** *ƒ350-ƒ400 single; ƒ420-ƒ500 double.* **Credit** AmEx, DC, MC, V. **Map** p311 E4.
Amid the touristy tack of Rembrandtplein lies the refined covered terrace of the four-star Schiller. The hotel was originally renowned for the artists and

poets who lingered over drinks while hotly debating contemporary art. Alas, those days have gone and the artistic guests have given way to business types, though some 40% of the hotel's guests are still tourists. Happily, Schiller has recently been faithfully restored to its former art deco Jugendstil style. The restaurant specialises in French cuisine.
Hotel services *Babysitting. Bar. Business services. Concierge. Gym. No-smoking rooms. Restaurant.* **Room services** *Minibar (selected rooms). Room service (7am-11pm).*

Seven Bridges
Reguliersgracht 31, Grachtengordel: East, 1017 LK (623 1329). Tram 16, 24, 25. **Rates** *ƒ200-ƒ350 single; ƒ240-ƒ380 double.* **Credit** AmEx, MC, V. **Map** p311 E4.
If you think of antiques in terms of heavy tones and dark wood, stay at this stylish hotel near the famed seven bridges, where the furnishings are in light, sunny shades. In fact, some of the pieces in the 11 rooms are real treasures: how about making yourself up in a Napoleonic mirror while your toes sink into a deep, hand-woven carpet? Try to avoid getting into conversation with one of the two proprietors: they'll tell you the financial worth of each item in enormous depth, which kind of spoils the illusion.
Hotel services *No-smoking rooms.*

Toren
Keizersgracht 164, Grachtengordel: West, 1015 CZ (622 6352/fax 626 9705/www.toren.nl). Tram 13, 14, 17, 20. **Rates** *ƒ185-ƒ235 single; ƒ210-ƒ375 double; ƒ270-ƒ375 triple; ƒ400-ƒ425 suite.* **Credit** AmEx, DC, MC, V. **Map** p306 C3.
When deciding upon a renovation scheme, the owner of the family-run four-star Toren decided to make it somewhere he'd like to visit. The thought behind the detailing is fantastic, and with 30 staff looking after the 40 rooms, the exceptionally high standards are maintained effortlessly. Situated on the site where the Free University was founded, the hotel's historic features have been carefully preserved. However, the hotel is equipped with all modern amenities, combining 17th-century atmosphere with 21st-century comfort. The garden suites have a sitting room with French doors opening out into the 'green oasis', while the nine rooms overlooking the canal also have jacuzzis. A terrific hotel, and stupendous value, too. Breakfast is an extra ƒ19,50.
Hotel services *Air-conditioning (selected rooms). Babysitting. Bar. Garden. Parking.* **Room services** *Minibar.*

Victoria Hotel Amsterdam
Damrak 1-5, Old Centre: Old Side, 1012 LG (623 4255/fax 625 2997/www.parkplazaww.com). Tram 4, 9, 14, 16, 20, 24, 25. **Rates** *ƒ435-ƒ540 single; ƒ470-ƒ575 double; ƒ650-ƒ900 suite; ƒ85 extra bed.* **Credit** AmEx, DC, MC, V. **Map** p306 D2.
Conveniently located opposite Centraal Station, this deluxe four-star hotel is a business person's palace. There are so many comforts to enjoy after work,

Consumer

including an indoor pool and a health club. If that's all too much effort, enjoy great views of the Dam as you take afternoon tea on Vic's Terrace. Breakfast is an extra ƒ35.

Hotel services *Air-conditioning. Babysitting. Bar. Beauty salon. Business services. Concierge. Disabled: adapted rooms. Gym. No-smoking rooms. Parking nearby. Restaurants. Swimming pool.* **Room services** *Dataport. Minibar. Room service (7am-11pm).*

Vondel

Vondelstraat 28-30, Museum Quarter, 1054 GE (612 0120/fax 685 4321/www.srsworldhotels.com). Tram 1, 3, 6, 12. **Rates** ƒ425 single/double; ƒ795 suite. **Credit** AmEx, DC, MC, V. **Map** p310 C5.

The impeccable design and stylish interior of this three-star hotel is astounding. The rooms are sumptuously decorated in crimson and cream, with meticulous detailing in a warm walnut wood. Named after Joost van den Vondel (1587-1679), the 'Prince among Poets' who doubled as the Netherlands' most acclaimed playwright, the hotel lies in a quiet sanctuary. Many rooms that look out over Vondelstraat have balconies, enabling guests to hear the occasional busker. But even these accoutrements seem upmarket: not the usual guitar player for this neck of the woods, but a flautist.

Hotel services *Babysitting. Bar. Business services. Concierge. Garden. Limousine service.* **Room services** *Dataport. Minibar. VCR.*

Moderate (ƒ200-ƒ350)

Agora

Singel 462, Grachtengordel: East, 1017 AW (627 2200/fax 627 2202/http://home-1.worldonline.nl/ ~agora). Tram 1, 2, 5. **Rates** ƒ125-ƒ190 single; ƒ160-ƒ225 double; ƒ290 triple; ƒ340 quad. **Credit** AmEx, DC, MC, V. **Map** p310 D4.

After spending a relaxing afternoon in the secluded garden at this canal house hotel, you'll be tempted to go on a spree at the Bloemenmarkt, the floating flower market just up the canal (*see p154*). The friendly staff make this comfortable two-star hotel a home-from-home, though council restrictions prevent major changes being made to the historic building and so there isn't a lift. Five of Agora's 16 rooms look out over Singel, and renovations have left the bathrooms in tiptop condition. Breakfast in bed is gratis.

Hotel services *Bar. Garden.* **Room services** *Room service (8am-10.30pm).*

Amsterdam Wiechmann

Prinsengracht 328-32, Grachtengordel: West, 1016 HX (626 3321/fax 626 8962/www.channels.nl/ amsterdam/wiechman.html). Tram 1, 2, 5 , 7, 17, 20. **Rates** ƒ100-ƒ175 single; ƒ200-ƒ300 double; ƒ350-ƒ450 triple/quad; ƒ450 suite. **Credit** MC, V. **Map** p310 C4.

The friendly owner of Amsterdam Wiechmann prides himself on his antiques, the wooden beams and panelling of the three restored canal houses that make up the hotel, and his good old-fashioned hospitality. The hotel is located in a charming part of town not far from Anne Frankhuis (*see p63*).

Hotel services *Babysitting. Bar. Parking nearby.*

Arena

's Gravesandestraat 51, Oost, 1092 AA (694 7444/ 663 2649/www.hotelarena.nl). Tram 3, 6, 9, 10, 14. **Rates** ƒ110-ƒ240 double; ƒ150-ƒ200 triple; ƒ175-ƒ250 quad. **Credit** AmEx, MC, V. **Map** p312 G3.

Huge renovations have upgraded this hotel to two stars in terms of facilities and comfort; when the restaurant and club are finished in October 2000, it will have a three-star ranking. While the Arena isn't exactly central, the facilities on offer mean you won't want to go elsewhere in the evening. The swanky international restaurant, Al Fresco, serves fine food, and has a terrace in front and a large garden behind. Guests also get a ƒ5 discount to Club Arena (*see p182*). Excursions can be booked at reception, and a pick-up service can be arranged.

Hotel services *Bar. Concierge. Disabled: adapted rooms. Garden. Parking. Restaurant.*

Bridge Hotel

Amstel 107-11, Grachtengordel: East, 1018 EM (623 7068/fax 624 1565/www.thebridgehotel.demon.nl). Tram 4, 6, 7, 9, 10, 20. **Rates** ƒ140-ƒ170 single; ƒ140-ƒ275 double; ƒ215-ƒ275 triple; ƒ275-ƒ375 apartment/ quad. **Credit** AmEx, DC, MC, V. **Map** p307 E3.

Located near the Carré Theatre on the Amstel with a view of the Magerebrug, the Bridge is ideal for explorations to the celebrated Albert Cuypmarkt in and Waterlooplein (*see pp163-4*), as well as for Rembrandtplein (*see p61*). Friendly staff make a stay here very pleasant and, for the cheery country-pine rooms, prices are pretty reasonable.

Hotel services *Parking nearby.*

Canal House Hotel

Keizersgracht 148, Grachtengordel: West, 1015 CX (622 5182/fax 624 1317/www.canalhouse.nl). Tram 13, 14, 17, 20. **Rates** ƒ285 single; ƒ295-ƒ345 double. **Credit** AmEx, DC, MC, V. **Map** p306 C3.

The Canal House is one of the few hotels to refuse children under 12: a relief if you don't have any, but the serenity is carried over with the absence of any TVs. However, that said, this is a gorgeous canal house, with ornate ceilings and antiques liberally sprinkled throughout: even in the bedrooms, which only adds to the homeliness. The view over the garden from the breakfast room is soothing.

Hotel services *Garden.* **Room services** *Dataport.*

Hotel Citadel

Nieuwezijds Voorburgwal 98-100, Old Centre: New Side, 1012 SG (627 3882/fax 627 4684/ hotel.citadel.ams@wxf.nl) Central Station. **Rates** ƒ170-ƒ195 single; ƒ235-ƒ280 double; ƒ315-ƒ360 triple. **Credit** AmEx, DC, MC, V. **Map** p306 C2.

This bright, modern three-star hotel is a two-minute walk from the station, and near the Royal Palace on Dam Square. It's very handy for strolls along the

Minimalist style at the **Arena**. *See p90.*

canals into the quaint Jordaan area, and, in the opposite direction, the Kalverstraat shopping area. All the rooms are comfortable, and most have baths.
Hotel services: *Air-conditioning. Bar. Terrace.*

Concert Inn

De Lairessestraat 11, Museum Quarter, 1071 NR (305 7272/fax 305 7271/www.concert-inn.demon.nl). Tram 16. **Rates** *ƒ230-ƒ315 single; ƒ250-ƒ345 double; ƒ295-ƒ450 studio; ƒ395-ƒ500 apartment.* **Credit** AmEx, DC, MC, V.

Rooms at the Concert Inn are spacious, and current renovations will result in the small singles being knocked into adjacent doubles to create more studios. The revamp has also taken in new TVs, new carpets and drapes that give total blackout, while all rooms have en suite facilities, most with baths. The garden is a mellow chill-out space, perfect in warmer climes, with tons of plants and pretty garden furniture. The chirpy manager offers a discount to *Time Out* readers of 5% in summer and 10% in winter with this guide.
Hotel services *Disabled: adapted rooms. Garden.*
Room services *Dataport.*

Hotel de Filosoof

Anna van den Vondelstraat 6, Museum Quarter, 1054 GZ (683 3013/fax 685 3750/www.xs4all.nl/ ~filosoof). Tram 1, 6. **Rates** *ƒ195-ƒ215 single; ƒ215-ƒ235 double; ƒ265-ƒ285 triple; ƒ315-ƒ325 quad.* **Credit** AmEx, MC, V. **Map** p309 B6.

A fascinating themed hotel that will keep you absorbed for the duration of your stay. Each of the 25 rooms is dedicated to a philosopher or philosophy: the Aristotle room is dreamy, while the Zen room is serene in the extreme. Even the spiral staircase that leads out into the garden encourages guests to pause and look, papered, as it is, in sheet music. Each room contains books on philosophy, with some even containing aphorisms painted on the wall. It comes as little surprise, then, to find that charming owner Ida Jongsma welcomes a local philosophy group to the bar each month for an evening of philosophical chat. A delight.
Hotel services *Babysitting. Bar(s). Garden.*

Owl Hotel

Roemer Visscherstraat 1, Museum Quarter, 1054 EV (618 9486/fax 618 9441/www.owl-hotel.demon.nl). Tram 1, 3, 6, 12. **Rates** *ƒ150-ƒ170 single; ƒ190-ƒ220 double; ƒ235-ƒ265 triple; ƒ265-ƒ295 quad.* **Credit** AmEx, DC, MC, V. **Map** p310 C5.

A small and super-friendly family-run hotel, right next to the gorgeous Filmmuseum (*see p194*) and five minutes from Museumplein and the Rijksmuseum (*see page 67*), the Van Gogh Museum and the Stedelijk Museum (for both, *see page 68*). All 34 of the Owl Hotel's rooms have en suite facilities.
Hotel services *Babysitting. Bar. Garden. Parking (2min away).* **Room services** *Dataport. Room service (breakfast only).*

Consumer

Philosophical chat at the **Filosoof**. See p91.

Hotel Prinsen

Vondelstraat 36-8, Museum Quarter, 1054 GE (616 2323/fax 616 6112). Tram 1, 2, 3, 5, 6, 12, 20. **Rates** ƒ185-ƒ225 single; ƒ250-ƒ275 double; ƒ340-ƒ360 triple; ƒ290-ƒ425 quad; ƒ300-ƒ325 suite; ƒ15 baby bed. **Credit** AmEx, DC, MC, V. **Map** p310 C6.

Brisk and friendly service is on hand at this peaceful hotel, conveniently located minutes away from Leidseplein. Recently renovated and extended by four rooms, this three-star is bright with sunny colours, but also has a secluded garden in which to chill out. Two rooms have balconies, and two have terraces, both offered at no extra charge.

Hotel services *Babysitting. Bar. Garden. Internet connection (not in rooms). Limousine service. Parking (on street).*

Singel Hotel

Singel 15, Grachtengordel: West, 1012 VC (626 3108/fax 620 3777). Tram 1, 2, 5, 13, 17, 20/Metro Central Station. **Rates** ƒ140-ƒ195 single; ƒ240-ƒ295 double; ƒ300-ƒ375 triple. **Credit** AmEx, DC, MC, V. **Map** p306 C2.

Located on Singel, just a short walk from the ancient neighbourhood of the Jordaan, this hotel is the sister of the **Hotel Citadel** (*see p90*), and is just as friendly and welcoming. Many of the 32 rooms have a view of the canal.

Hotel services *Babysitting. Bar. Concierge. Limousine service.* **Room services** *Room service (24hrs).*

Hotel Van De Kasteelen

Frans van Mierisstraat 34, Museum Quarter, 1071 RT (679 8995/fax 670 6604/hotel@kastele.a2000.nl) Amsterdam South then tram 5. **Rates** ƒ95-ƒ150 single; ƒ175-ƒ210 double; ƒ70 extra bed. **Credit** AmEx, MC, V. **Map** p310 D6.

On a quiet, tree-lined street close to Museumplein, this small, scrupulously clean and friendly hotel is popular with visitors to the cultural epicentre of the city. Having drinks in the intimate garden is a welcome haven after a day battling with crowds in the Rijksmuseum. The hotel will be closed for renovations from November 2000, but look out for it from early 2001, when it will be reopened, and is expected to be more popular than ever.

Hotel services *Garden.*

Hotel Wilhelmina

Koninginneweg 169, Museum Quarter, 1075 CN (662 5467/fax 679 2296/ www.euronet.nl/users/wilhlhtl/index.htm). Tram 2, 16. **Rates** ƒ75-ƒ195 single; ƒ125-ƒ255 double; ƒ195-ƒ295 triple; ƒ255-ƒ355 quad; ƒ45 extra bed. **Credit** AmEx, DC, MC, V.

A sister hotel to the **King** (*see p95*), the Wilhelmina offers spacious and recently renovated rooms in bright, happy colours, all with en suite facilities. The excellent location makes it a good base from which to visit the main museums and hang out with Amsterdam's beautiful people in the elegant PC Hooftstraat. A great little find.

Budget (under ƒ200)

Acro

Jan Luykenstraat 40-6, Museum Quarter, 1071 CR (662 0526/fax 675 0811/acro.hotel@wxs.nl). Tram 2, 5, 20. **Rates** ƒ80-ƒ150 single; ƒ110-ƒ195 double; ƒ150-ƒ240 triple; ƒ195-ƒ250 quad. **Credit** AmEx, DC, MC, V. **Map** p310 D6.

This comfortable, modern hotel is handy for the museums and Leidseplein, but if you don't want to go out, the bar is open 24 hours and does basic snacks. The managers often have special off-peak offers, so call ahead to check. If the weather's good, take drinks out to the secluded garden.

Hotel services *Bar. Concierge. Parking (on street). Internet connection at reception.*

De Admiraal

Herengracht 563, Grachtengordel: West, 1017 CD (626 2150/fax 623 4625). Tram 4, 9, 14, 20. **Rates** ƒ105-ƒ145 single; ƒ125-ƒ185 double; ƒ240-ƒ340 triple/quad. **Credit** AmEx, DC, MC, V. **Map** p311 E4.

A friendly and homely hotel by Rembrandtplein. Eight of De Admiraal's nine rooms have canal views and room six has a particularly stunning view of the lovely Reguliersgracht and Herengracht. Make note that the hotel is closed from mid-November to mid-March, except for Christmas and the New Year. The big Dutch breakfasts are ƒ10 extra.

Amstel Botel

Oosterdokskade 2-4, Old Centre: Old Side, 1011 AE (626 4247/fax 639 1952). Tram 1, 2, 5, 9, 13, 17, 20, 24, 25. **Rates** ƒ131-ƒ151 single; ƒ149-ƒ169 double; ƒ180-ƒ190 triple. **Credit** AmEx, DC, MC, V. **Map** p307 E1.

Located to the south-east of Centraal Station, the Botel is moored in an unlikely spot. Were it located a little to the north-east – ie north of the station – it would get fine views of the recently finished manmade islands in the IJ. But from its current morring point, the vistas are noticeably less interesting (though be sure to take the watery side of the boat for the best views). As a three-star hotel, it offers relative comfort at reasonable prices. Breakfast is an extra ƒ13.

Hotel services *Bar. Parking nearby.*

Consumer

Give your regards to Ol' Blue
Eyes and the King at the **Hotel
de Munck**. *See p96.*

Euphemia Hotel

*Fokke Simonszstraat 1-9, Grachtengordel: East,
1017 TD (tel/fax 622 9045). Tram 16, 24, 25.*
Rates *f*100-*f*200 double; *f*120-*f*200 triple;
*f*140-*f*220 quad. **Credit** AmEx, DC, MC, V.
Map p311 E5.
Located in a quiet side street handy for both the bar-
gaintastic Albert Cuypmarkt and Rembrandtplein,
the gay-friendly Euphemia offers cheap and comfortable accommodation for people of all persua-
sions. There's a communal sitting room area, where
you can chill out in front of the TV and video; breakfast will set you back around *f*8,50.
Hotel services *Disabled: adapted rooms.
No-smoking rooms. Internet connection (but not in
rooms).*

Hans Brinker Budget

*Kerkstraat 136-8, Grachtengordel: East, 1017 GR
(622 0687/fax 638 2060/www.hans-brinker.com).
Tram 1, 2, 5, 16, 24, 25.* **Rates** *f*111-*f*113,50
single; *f*121-*f*152 double; *f*196,50 triple; *f*42,50-
*f*52,50 dorm bed per person. **Credit** AmEx, DC, MC,
V. **Map** p311 E4.
This huge, centrally located hotel has a history of
hilarious advertising campaigns, the latest pro-
claiming Hans Brinker is 'close to the best hospital
in Amsterdam': it may not exactly be reassuring, but
gives an indication that you won't have many dull
moments staying here. With 530 beds, it looks massive from Kerkstraat, with another authoritative
sign reminding hostellers that the 'street is not a terrace, so please don't hang around outside – think of
our neighbours'. Inside, staff are friendly, and everything is well maintained and clean.
Hotel services *Bar. Restaurant.*

Hotel Internationaal

*Warmoesstraat 1-3, Old Side: Red Light District,
1012 HT (624 5520/fax 624 4501/michdel@wxs.nl).
Tram 1, 2, 4, 5, 9, 13, 16, 17, 20, 24, 25/Metro
Central Station.* **Rates** *f*80-*f*150 single; *f*120-*f*150
double; *f*180-*f*255 triple. **Credit** AmEx, DC, MC, V.
Map p306 D2.
We might be talking small, but if lively is what you
want, then staying here puts you within two minutes of the thick of the Red Light District, with all
the joy that brings. The bedrooms are pretty light,
but the showers are quite basic, and beware of taking a room on the second floor right under a very
noisy generator.
Hotel services *Bar. Concierge.* **Room services**
Dataport.

Hotel Keizersgracht

*Keizersgracht 15, Grachtengordel: West, 1015 CC
(625 1364/fax 620 7347). Tram 1, 2, 5, 13, 17,
20/Metro Central Station.* **Rates** *f*105 single; *f*150
double; *f*165 triple; *f*210 quad. **Credit** AmEx, DC,
MC, V. **Map** p306 C2.
This charming hotel is at the station end of
Keizersgracht, a short walk through the popular
Nieuwendijk, and along the green garden canal area
of Brouwersgracht. Being in the canal district puts
you two minutes from Anne Frankhuis and the
Jordaan. You'll find the location hard to better, especially at the budget price. Breakfast is *f*15 extra.
Hotel services *Bar. Restaurant.*

King Hotel

*Leidsekade 85-6, Grachtengordel: West, 1017 PN
(624 9603/620 7277). Tram 1, 2, 5, 6, 7, 10, 20.*
Rates *f*85 single; *f*135-*f*150 double; *f*195 triple;
*f*225 quad. **Credit** MC, V. **Map** p310 C5.

Better red than bed: the bar at the **Winston**.

As a budget hotel in a canal house with a smattering of historical intrigue, the King Hotel is a bargain: this was the home of Mata Hari, executed in Paris during WWI for her undercover exploits. The hotel is basic, but its location – really close to Leidseplein – is a massive boon.
Hotel services *Parking (on street).*

Hotel de Munck

Achtergracht 3, Grachtengordel: East, 1017 WL (623 6283/fax 620 6647). Tram 4, 6, 7, 10, 20. **Rates** *ƒ105-ƒ120 single; ƒ165-ƒ195 double; ƒ240-ƒ285 triple; ƒ340-ƒ360 quad.* **Credit** AmEx, DC, MC, V. **Map** p311 F4.
A captain's house from the old East India days, the Munck has been restored to its original style, with traditional furnishings and steep staircases typical of old Amsterdam houses. Original, that is, until you spy the album covers on the walls in the '60s-style restaurant, where you can eat your brekky to the tunes of Nat 'King' Cole or Elvis. This theme spreads to some of the 16 rooms, where neon lamps and clocks kick a bit of kitsch into the surroundings. Very pleasant, and strangely hip to boot.
Hotel services *Bar. Garden.* **Room services** *Minibar. Refrigerator.*

PC Hooft

PC Hooftstraat 63, Museum Quarter, 1017 BN (662 7107/fax 675 8961). Tram 2, 3, 5, 12. **Rates** *ƒ75-ƒ85 single; ƒ110-ƒ120 double; ƒ160 triple; ƒ215-ƒ225 quad.* **Credit** MC, V. **Map** p310 D5.
Pieter Corneliszoon Hooft was a historian who hung out with friend and poet Joost van den Vondel, himself immortalised in the name of the neighbouring park. The street is to Amsterdam what Avenue de la Montaigne is to Paris: this is the beautiful people's shopping area, though it's also close to the major museums. However, the principal reason for the huge number of returning guests is the cheerful atmosphere and delish breakfasts.

Parkzicht

Roemer Visscherstraat 33, Museum Quarter, 1054 EW (618 1954/fax 618 0897). Tram 1, 2, 3, 5, 6, 12, 20. **Rates** *ƒ95 single; ƒ160-ƒ175 double; ƒ240 triple; ƒ260 quad.* **Credit** AmEx, MC, V. **Map** p310 C5.

This Dutch country house is charmingly cluttered with comfortable furnishings. Peaceful and quiet, it's near the park and major museums and offers good value. Unfortunately, it's closed between November and March.
Hotel services *Babysitting.* **Room services** *Dataport.*

Hotel Prinsenhof

Prinsengracht 810, Grachtengordel: East, 1017 JL (623 1772/fax 638 3368/www.xs4all.nl/~prinshof). Tram 4. **Rates** *ƒ85 single; ƒ125-ƒ175 double; ƒ175-ƒ210 triple; ƒ210-ƒ290 quad.* **Credit** AmEx, MC, V. **Map** p311 E4.
Hotel Prinsenhof is a pretty little ten-roomed canal house decorated in traditional old Amsterdam green. The staff, though inundated with requests for rooms, remain pretty friendly. Good value and incredibly clean to boot.
Room services *Dataport.*

Winston Hotel

Warmoesstraat 129, Old Centre: Red Light District, 1012 JA (623 1380/fax 639 2308/www.winston.nl). Tram 4, 9, 14, 16, 20, 24, 25. **Rates** *ƒ120-ƒ142 single; ƒ140-ƒ184 double; ƒ174-ƒ226 triple; ƒ201-ƒ216 quad; ƒ278-ƒ313 5-person room; ƒ325-ƒ372 6-person room.* **Credit** AmEx, DC, MC, V. **Map** p306 D2.
Right in the centre of the constant bustle of the Red Light District, with a 24-hour bar for guests and decent club nights, the Winston is a fun place to stay. Ask if you can be put in one of the 26 funky art rooms: the hotel's philosophy is to get art out of frames and into your head, and these spicily decorated rooms succeed in spades. The atmosphere is laid-back and friendly, and there's always something going on.
Hotel services *Bar. Disabled: adapted room.*

Van Ostade

Van Ostadestraat 123, The Pijp, 1072 SV (679 3452/fax 671 5213/www.bicyclehotel.nl). Tram 3, 12, 24, 25. **Rates** *ƒ90-ƒ110 single; ƒ100-ƒ175 double.* **No credit cards. Map** p311 F6.
This two wheel-friendly hotel in the Pijp offers bicycle hire and has shelter for motorbikes. The rooms are clean and basic and there's also a mellow communal area. Good value all round, and a more than decent option.
Hotel services *Parking.*

Young Budget Hotel Kabul

Warmoesstraat 38-42, Old Centre: Red Light District, 1012 JE (623 7158/fax 620 0869). Tram 4, 9, 14, 16, 20, 24, 25. **Rates** *ƒ45-ƒ65 dorm bed per person; ƒ105-ƒ115 single; ƒ150-ƒ200 double; ƒ190-ƒ250 triple; ƒ275 suite.* **Credit** AmEx, DC, MC, V. **Map** p306 D2.
Don't be put off by the daunting exterior: staff here are friendly. Some big rooms look out over Damrak and let in loads of light, though others are more than a little dark. Better news is the fact that the hotel doesn't operate a curfew.
Hotel services *Bar.*

Hostels

Only two hostels (**NJHC Hostels**, *see page 97*) in town require IYHF membership. This can easily be obtained for an extra ƒ5 per night: you get a stamp on an IYHF card each night, and after six nights you can trade this in for a membership. A few hostels close for a couple of hours in the day and some impose a curfew.

Bob's Youth Hostel
Nieuwezijds Voorburgwal 92, Old Centre: New Side, 1012 SG (623 0063/fax 675 6446). Tram 1, 2, 5, 13, 17, 20. **Rates** *ƒ30 dorm bed per person; ƒ150 2-person apartments.* **No credit cards. Map** p306 D3.
A mellow place in which to meet fellow travellers. Make sure you don't miss the entrance, down a short flight of steps underground to the breakfast bar. Dorms range in size from four to 18 beds, and there are even apartments for two people sharing. Most of the dorms are mixed, though some are women-only. **Hotel services** *Bar.*

Bulldog Budget Hotel
Oudezijds Voorburgwal 220, Old Centre: Old Side, 1012 GJ (620 3822/fax 428 0811/www.bulldog.nl). Tram 4, 9, 14, 16, 20, 24, 25/Metro Nieuwmarkt. **Rates** *ƒ31,50-ƒ42,50 single dorm bed; ƒ60-ƒ70 double dorm bed; ƒ90-ƒ105 single; ƒ115-ƒ135 double; ƒ165-ƒ185 triple; ƒ215-ƒ235 quad.* **Credit** AmEx, MC, V. **Map** p306 D3.
Situated in the city's centre, you can find all manner of pastimes on strolling out from the Bulldog, one of a chain of nine bars and coffeeshops. Currently offering 100 beds, the hotel has plans to expand, incorporating another building and 160 beds. All rooms and dorms have TVs. Breakfast is an extra ƒ7,50. **Hotel services** *Bar. Internet.*

Flying Pig Hostels
Flying Pig Downtown *Nieuwendijk 100, Old Centre: New Side, 1012 MR (420 6822/group reservations 421 0583/fax 421 0811/www.flyingpig.nl). Tram 1, 2, 3, 5, 13, 17, 20.* **Flying Pig Palace** *Vossiusstraat 46-7, Museum Quarter, 1071 AJ (400 4187/group reservations 421 0583/fax 470 5159/www.flyingpig.nl). Tram 2, 5, 20.* **Rates** *Downtown ƒ130 double; ƒ198 quad; ƒ35,50-ƒ46,50 dorm bed per person. Palace ƒ110-ƒ125 double; ƒ150 triple; ƒ47,50 quad per person; ƒ35,50-ƒ45 dorm bed per person.* **Credit** MC, V. **Map** *Downtown p306 D2. Palace p310 C6.*
The Flying Pigs are so popular that reservations can only be made via the Internet, or by ringing reception the morning of the night you want to stay, and asking to be put on the waiting list. Both sites are clean and laid-back, with staff who understand the requirements of the thousands of backpackers who pass through each year. Both also have a fully equipped kitchen and offer a range of tourist information, and almost all rooms have showers and loos. There's no curfew, but if you want to stay in, both sites have lively bars that are open to guests only. **Hotel services** *Bar.*

International Budget Hotel
Leidsegracht 76, Grachtengordel: East, 1016 CR (624 2784/fax 626 1839). Tram 1, 2, 5. **Rates** *ƒ75-ƒ150 double; ƒ25-ƒ40 quad per person.* **Credit** AmEx, MC, V. **Map** p310 C4.
International Budget Hotel is the only inexpensive youth hostel to offer seven rooms with a canal view. All facilities are shared and dorms are mixed unless you ask in advance. There isn't a curfew, so you can party in Leidseplein worry-free. Breakfast is an extra ƒ7.

Meeting Point
Warmoesstraat 14, Grachtengordel: East, 1012 JD (627 7499/fax 330 4774/info@hostel-meetingpoint.etrade.nl). Tram 4, 8, 16, 20, 24, 25. **Rates** *ƒ30-ƒ45 dorm bed per person; ƒ150-ƒ200 quad; ƒ185-ƒ250 5-person room; ƒ210-ƒ300 6-person room.* **No credit cards. Map** p306 D2.
The dark reception area at Meeting Point leads up to rooms with either four, five, six, 12 or 18 beds. The hostel is basic but cheap, with breakfast an extra ƒ5. As with most hostels, reservations have to be made in person. All you need for a fun weekend is right on your doorstep: the spliff-friendly bar is open 24 hours but is for guests only. **Hotel services** *Bar. Concierge. No-smoking rooms.*

NJHC Hostels
Stadsdoelen *Kloveniersburgwal 97, Old Centre: Old Side, 1011 KB (624 6832/fax 639 1035/www.njhc.nl). Tram 4, 9, 14, 16, 20, 24, 25.* **City Hostel Vondelpark** *Zandpad 5, Museum Quarter, 1054 GA (589 8999/fax 589 8955/www.njhc.nl). Tram 1, 2, 5, 6, 7, 10, 20.* **Rates** *Stadsdoelen ƒ31,25-ƒ37 dorm bed per person. City Hostel Vondelpark ƒ75-ƒ90 single; ƒ100-ƒ135 double; ƒ170-ƒ195 triple/quad; ƒ213-ƒ240 5-/6-bed rooms; ƒ35,50-ƒ40 dorm bed per person. Both hostels non-members ƒ5 extra.* **Credit** MC, V. **Map** *Stadsdoelen p306 D3. Vondelpark p310 C6.*
The Stadsdoelen branch of the NJHC is moments from the steamy Red Light District, but is also ideal for Waterlooplein or Rembrandtplein. If you're looking for a bit of green space, then try the Vondelpark branch instead. Both are spotless, friendly and open 24 hours. The bar at Stadsdoelen offers light meals and snacks, but the hostel is closed in January and February. The newly renovated Vondelpark site, meanwhile, is one of Europe's largest and most modern hostels. The two restaurants overlook the park, and there's also an Internet corner and a TV room.
Hotel services *Bar (both). Courtyard (Stadsdoelen only). Disabled: adapted rooms (Vondelpark only). No-smoking rooms (both). Restaurant (both).*

Camping

Vliegenbos and **Zeeburg** are classified as youth campsites, while the other two are more family-oriented campsites with separate areas for youth camping.

Going private

The B&B ideal is growing in the Netherlands, but due to restrictions on the number of rooms and the number of people permitted to stay (officially, four is the maximum), it is still nowhere near as popular – nor as widespread – as in Britain. The best way to track down a B&B is through either **City Mundo** or **Holiday Link**, both of which deal with private accommodation and longer stays. Be sure to book well in advance.

City Mundo

Schinkelkade 47 II, 1075 VK (676 5270/fax 676 5271/www.citymundo.com). **Open** 10am-2pm Mon-Sat.

This excellent network, set up by Christoph and Charlotte Blans, provides visitors with short-term private accommodation, ranging from B&B and studios to flats on boats and even in windmills. Prices vary according to location and amenities and length of stay (the longer, the cheaper). The focus is less on budget and more on providing a specific service for people who relish their surroundings. Stays are for a minimum of two nights and a maximum of 21.

Holiday Link

Postbus 70-155, 9704 AD Groningen (050 313 2424/050 313 3535/050 313 4545/ fax 050 313 3177/www.holidaylink.com). **Open** 10am-3pm Mon-Thur; 10am-noon Fri; closed Sat, Sun.

Holiday Link is an organisation dealing with B&B and budget accommodation. Its annual guide, *B&B and Budget Accommodation in Holland*, is available in bookshops, tourist offices, by post or from its website for ƒ35, and has stacks of information on all types of accommodation, from B&Bs to holiday home swaps. Well worth the money.

Marcel van Woerkom

Leidsestraat 87, Grachtengordel: East, 1017 NX (tel/fax 622 9834/ www.marcelamsterdam.nl). Tram 1, 2, 5. **Rates** ƒ110-ƒ150 per person. **Credit** V. **Map** p310 D4.

Graphic artist Marcel van Woerkom provides a creative exchange in his pristine city-centre home, where four en suite rooms are available. Van Woerkom started letting his rooms out to help him pay the bills and now, 30 years later, the enterprise is an Amsterdam staple. Van Woerkom's favourite art is on the walls; all of it is by his friends. As a people person, he likes to interact with imaginative minds, and guests with an appreciation of creative arts are especially welcome. Be sure to book well in advance, as the rooms are much in demand. Breakfast isn't included, but that's hardly the point.

Hotel services *Garden. No-smoking room. Parking nearby (paid).* **Room services** *Dataport. Refrigerator.*

Het Amsterdamse Bos

Kleine Noorddijk 1, 1432 CC Aalsmeer (641 6868/ fax 640 2378). Bus 171. **Reception open** *Apr-mid Oct* 9am-9pm daily. **Rates** *Per person per night* ƒ8,75; ƒ4,50 4-12s; free under-4s. *Car* ƒ4,75. *Caravan* ƒ6,75. *Camper* ƒ11. *Motorbike* ƒ2,50. *Tent* ƒ5,75; *Electricity for caravan/camper* ƒ4. **No credit cards.**

The site is several miles from Amsterdam. However, half-hourly bus services for the 30-minute trip into town stop 300m from the grounds, which are on the southern edge of the beautiful Amsterdamse Bos, a large park with facilities for horse-riding and watersports. Wooden cabins sleeping up to four people can be hired for ƒ60 per night. These are equipped with stoves and mattresses, but you will have to provide your own cooking utensils and sleeping bags. Site facilities include phones, a shop, a bar and a restaurant, lockers, and bike hire in July and August. In high season, the campsite has its own express bus service one-way to Centraal Station (ƒ5).

Gaasper Camping Amsterdam

Loosdrechtdreef 7 (696 7326). Metro Gaasperplas/59, 60, 158 bus. **Reception open** *July-Aug* 9am-10pm daily. *Sept-Dec, Mar-June* 9am-8pm daily; closed Jan-mid Mar. **Rates** *Per person per night* ƒ7,25; ƒ3,50 under-12s. *Car* ƒ6,50. *Camper* ƒ12. *Caravan* ƒ9,50. *Motorbike* ƒ3,25. *Tent* ƒ7,50-ƒ9,50. *Electrics* ƒ4,50. *Hot showers* ƒ1,50. *Dog* ƒ4. **No credit cards.**

A great campsite on the edge of the Gaasperplas park, which has a lake with a watersports centre and facilities for canoeing, swimming (for children, too), rowing and sailing, plus a surfing school. Ground facilities include a shop, café, bar and restaurant, a terrace, launderette and service station for fuel.

Vliegenbos

Meeuwenlaan 138 (636 8855/fax 632 2723). Bus 32, 36, 110, 111, 114/night bus 73. **Reception open** *Apr-Sept* 9am-9pm daily. **Rates** *Per person per night* ƒ14; ƒ9,25 2-14s; free under-2s. *Car* ƒ15,50. *Camper/caravan* ƒ35,25-ƒ41. *Motorbike* 7,75. *Log cabin for up to 4 people* ƒ85. *Log cabin for up to 12 people* ƒ238. **Credit** AmEx, DC, MC, V.

The grounds are close to the River IJ to the north of Amsterdam, a five-minute bus journey from Centraal Station. Facilities include a bar, a restaurant, a safe at reception, and a small shop with exchange service. Guests staying for less than three nights have to pay a supplement of ƒ1,25 each.

Zeeburg
Zuider Ijdijk 20 (694 4430/fax 694 6238). Tram 14/ bus 22/night bus 97. **Reception open** *Apr-Aug* 8am-11pm daily. **Rates** *Per person per night ƒ7,50; ƒ2,50 5-12s; free under-5s. Tent for 3-4 people ƒ5. Motorbike ƒ5. Car ƒ7,50. Caravan 7,50. Camper ƒ12,50. Electricity ƒ4.* **No credit cards**.
Facilities at these grounds, just north of the River IJ, include a bar, a small restaurant, lockers, a shop and bike hire. Log cabins sleeping two or four people cost ƒ25 per person including bedding, and there is also a dorm with 24 beds for ƒ17,50 per person (including launderette but excluding bedding). Be sure to reserve for the cabins in high season. Tents are available to rent for ƒ12,50 a night.

Flat-hunting

It's all down to supply and demand in this four-storey sardine can of a city: not enough of the former, and way too much of the latter. To get a flat, you need friends, money and bucket loads of luck. In Amsterdam, there are two main price sectors: below ƒ1,000 per month, and above ƒ1,000 per month. Anything above ƒ1,000 is considered free sector housing and can be found through housing agencies or by checking newspapers (in particular, the Wednesday, Thursday and Saturday editions of *De Telegraaf* and *De Volksrant*, and every Thursday in the ads paper *Via Via*). Unfortunately, flatshares are not common, and agency commission is high.

If you're looking for properties under the ƒ1,000 mark, you have two main choices. If you've lived in Amsterdam for over two years or you study in the city and have a resident's permit, register with one of the three main non-commercial housing co-operatives, **Woonwerk** (524 4566), **Archipel** (511 8911) and **Spectrum** (489 0085). For a charge of ƒ35 (registration is an extra ƒ25 with Archipel), these agencies will supply you with a bulletin giving information on available accommodation. However, you'll need even more luck to get anywhere with this method, which can take forever given the shortage of properties and surfeit of clients.

The other alternative is to register with one of the many non-profit housing agencies that hold regular property lotteries. This may seem bizarre, but you do have a chance of eventually obtaining a room in a house with this system: for more details, contact **ASW Kamerbureau** on 523 0130.

Apartment rentals

Amsterdam Apartments
Kromme Waal 32, Old Centre: Old Side (626 5930/ fax 622 9544). Tram 4, 9, 16, 20, 24, 25. **Open** 9am-5pm Mon-Fri; closed Sat, Sun. **Map** p307 E2.
About 20 furnished, self-contained flats in central areas of town. Rates start from ƒ1,120 a week for a one-person studio or one-bed flat. The minimum let is for one week and the maximum one month.

Apartment Services AS
Maasstraat 96, Zuid (672 3013/672 1840/fax 676 4679). Tram 4, 12, 25. **Open** 10.30am-5pm Mon-Fri; closed Sat, Sun.
A wide variety of mainly furnished accommodation, from simple short-let flats to apartments and whole houses. Rentals start at around ƒ1,750 per week and a minimum let of three months is usual. The registration fee of ƒ50 is refundable after one month's rent has been taken as commission.

Intercity Room Service
Van Ostadestraat 348 (675 0064). Tram 3, 4. **Open** 10am-5pm Mon-Fri; closed Sat, Sun. **Map** p311 F6.
The place to try if you require something quickly. Intercity specialises in flatshares, but occasionally offers entire apartments; flatshares in the centre of town cost from ƒ600 per month, with self-contained flats from ƒ2,500. The minimum stay is two months, with one month's rent payable as commission.

Riverside Apartments
Amstel 138 (627 9797/fax 627 9858). Tram 4, 9, 14, 20. **Open** 9am-5pm Mon-Sat; by appointment other times. **Map** p307 E3.
Privately owned, luxurious flats in town that cost ƒ1,800-ƒ2,500 per week with no commision for two people, or, for a minimum of six months, ƒ2,500 per month with a month's rent as commission.

Registration

To register in the city, first you have to go to the **Dienst Vreemdelingenpolitie** (Aliens' Police Service) and register at the immigration desk. If you would like to register for a house from the city council, then you need a housing permit, which means you have to meet certain criteria (for example, you need to show that you are living, working or studying in the city). If you meet these criteria, you can then register with the **Stedelijke Woning Dienst** (City Housing Service). Bank on a very long wait.

Dienst Vreemdelingenpolitie
Johan Huizingalaan 757 (559 6214). Tram 2/19, 63 bus. **Open** 8am-4.30pm Mon-Fri; closed Sat, Sun.

Stedelijke Woning Dienst
Stadhuis, Waterlooplein (552 7511). Tram 3, 10. **Open** 11am-4pm Mon; 9am-4pm Tue, Wed, Fri; 9am-8pm Thur; closed Sat, Sun. **Map** p307 C3.

Consumer

Restaurants

From Dutch basics to the curious tastes of Tibet, you won't have a bored moment in Amsterdam's assorted eateries.

The term 'Dutch cuisine' can often raise a chuckle or two. With a reputation built on the use of the bare essentials – meat/fish, veg and cheese products – and the shunning of 'taboo' herbs and spices, Dutch food has tended to serve but one purpose: to pack bellies. Such a stereotype is born from Calvinism, the scapegoat for all things Dutch. Combine this with the (wrong) assumption that a flat, grey land must surely offer flat, grey food and you soon see why the country is not exactly famed for its cuisine.

Yet you only have to pop into the **Rijksmuseum** (*see page 67*) for the real story. As far back as the Golden Age, gluttony had its grip on the country: take, for example, the works of Jan Steen and Adriaen van Ostade, whose paintings often depict the traditional 'fat kitchen' in their full mouth-watering richness and colour. As always, there's a flipside to the coin, namely an equal number of paintings showing a 'thin kitchen', where the calm and holy occupants and their victuals would give Gandhi a run for his money. Yep, the Dutch,

just like the rest of us, know there's nothing better than a huge blowout to put paid to a bit of abstention.

Time and colonialism have done much to massage the Dutch palate. As the Occupied under Napoleonic rule, they were seduced by the more refined southern cuisine, an influence that is still strongly felt in the city's more highly regarded restaurants. And as the Occupiers, the Dutch took on the spicy cuisine of Indonesia. Add to the mix the influx of workers after World War II, which gave birth to a multitude of Asian, Middle Eastern and Mediterranean eating places, and, more recently, travellers returning from India and Thailand, and the result is that this small corner of the world has finally achieved true culinary diversity.

Today, the gourmand galloping through Amsterdam would hardly know the trouble the country has gone to in order to reach its now high culinary standards. But if you're the galloping type who prefers discovering a restaurant on your own, you might want to

Dine in deco surrounds at the **Café Americain**. *See p101.*

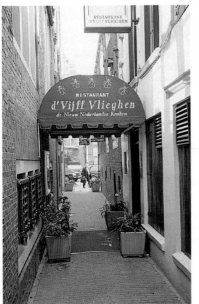

D'Vijff Vlieghen. *See p102.*

know that the Pijp is dense with econo-ethnic eateries, Utrechtsestraat and Nieuwmarkt are both packed with the middle range, the 'Nine Streets' area (the streets linking Prinsengracht, Keizersgracht and Herengracht between Leidsegracht and Raadhuisstraat) and Reguliersdwarsstraat have a greater density of posher restaurants, and the area around Leidseplein – with some notable exceptions – is definitely the hotspot to go for the overpriced, middle-of-the-road scran.

In addition to the restaurants listed below, there are many cafés and bars serving decent – even inspired – food at reasonable prices; for these, *see pages 121-33*. For gay-friendly and gay-owned restaurants and cafés, *see pages 207-8*. And never forget: before leaving, one must indulge in a raw herring or a smoked eel sandwich at one of Amsterdam's many fish stalls. No, really. You *must*.

LEISURELY DINING

Dining in Amsterdam is a laid-back affair, though the uninitiated should note that the Dutch tend to eat early – between 6.30pm and 9pm – with most kitchens closing by 10pm. However, once the meal has been ordered, customers are usually welcome to linger over coffee and dessert for a while, in some cases until after midnight. All bills should by law

include 17.5 per cent tax and a 15 per cent service charge, though it's customary to leave some small change as well, if the service merits it. If you have any special requirements, such as high chairs or disabled access, it's always best to phone the restaurant before setting out. For more places to which to take the kids, *see page 178*.

Given the imminent introduction of the Euro in 2002 and the financial flux that will doubtless bring upon all aspects of life in Amsterdam, the prices listed throughout this section should only be used as a guideline. If you want to find a restaurant in a particular area, *see page 102* **Restaurants by area**. And for a sneaky peak at the menus of many of the eateries listed, head to www.dinnersite.nl/amsterdam or www.dinner-in-amsterdam.nl, both of which offer online menus and, in some cases, reservations services for a wide variety of restaurants in the city.

City landmarks

1e Klas

Centraal Station, Line 2B, Old Centre: New Side (625 0131). Tram 1, 2, 4, 5, 9, 13, 16, 17, 20, 24, 25. **Open** 9.30am-11pm daily. **Main courses** ƒ27-ƒ48. **Credit** AmEx, DC, MC, V. **Map** p306 D1.
The former Grand Café brasserie for first-class commuters is now open to all those who want to kill time in style – with a full meal, or with smaller, snackier, cheaper fare such as sandwiches – while waiting for a train. Its high ceiling and original art nouveau interior can take you back to the turn of the century when Centraal Station was first built. *Very* Euro.

Café Americain

Leidseplein 97, Grachtengordel: East (624 5322/556 3000/www.interconti.com/netherlands/amsterdam/dining_amsame.html). Tram 1, 2, 5, 6, 7, 10, 20. **Open** 7am-1am daily (non-guest breakfast from 10am). **Kitchen** 11am-11.30pm daily. **Main courses** ƒ18,50-ƒ33,50. **Credit** AmEx, DC, MC, V. **Map** p310 C5.
The glorious art deco interior of the Café Americain is a listed monument decorated with murals and marbled lampshades: Mata Hari is said to have held her wedding reception here. Now, theatrical personalities, the theatre crowd and tourists meet under the high, vaulted roof or on the terrace.

Bodega Keyzer

Van Baerlestraat 96, Museum Quarter (671 1441). Tram 3, 5, 12, 16, 20. **Open** 9am-midnight Mon-Sat; closed Sun. **Main courses** ƒ39,50-ƒ72,50. **Credit** AmEx, DC, MC, V. **Map** p310 D6.
Located near the Concertgebouw, Bodega Keyzer caters mainly for posher concertgoers. Don't commit a social blunder by trying to order from a concert violinist, who often have the same style sense as the waiters. The fish is terrific, especially the sole.

Consumer

Restaurants by area

Old Centre: Old Side

De Brakke Grond (Belgian, p105);
Café Bern (Dutch, p105); **Café Roux**
(French, p111); **Excelsior** (French, p109);
Gary's Muffins (Breakfast & lunch stops,
p117); **Morita-Ya** (Japanese, p116);
Poco Loco (Latin American, p117);
Restaurant Pier 10 (Fish, p109);
Thaise Snackbar Bird (Thai/South-east
Asian, p120).

Old Centre: Red Light District

Centra (Portuguese/Spanish, p119);
Nam Kee (Chinese, p105); **New King**
(Chinese, p105); **Oriental City** (Chinese,
p105).

Old Centre: New Side

Al's Plaice (Fish, p107); **Begijntje**
(French, p109); **1e Klas** (City landmarks,
p101); **Keuken van 1870** (Dutch, p107);
Lucius (Fish, p107); **De Roode Leeuw**
(City landmarks, p102); **Sarang Mas**
(Indonesian, p119); **Stereo Sushi**
(Japanese, p116); **Supper Club**
(International, p115); **Vlaamse Friteshuis**
(Belgian, p105); **D'Vijff Vlieghen** (City
landmarks, p102).

The Plantage & The Oost

Kilimanjaro (African, p103).

Grachtengordel: West

't Balkje (Breakfast & lunch stops, p116);
Belhamel (French, p109); **Blakes**
(International, p113); **Café Cox**
(International, p113); **Christophe** (French,
p109); **Gary's Late Night** (Breakfast & lunch
stops, p117); **Gary's Muffins** (Breakfast &
lunch stops, p117); **Goodies** (Breakfast &
lunch stops, p117); **Himalaya** (Indian, p111);
Koh-I-Noor (Indian, p111); **Lof** (International,
p113); **Nostradamus** (French, p111);
Pancake Bakery (Dutch, p107); **Sjaalman**
(Thai/South-east Asian, p120); **De
Struisvogel** (International, p113).

Grachtengordel: East

An (Japanese, p116); **De Blauwe Hollander**
(French, p105); **Bojo** (Indonesian, p118);
Café Americain (City landmarks, p101); **Eat
at Jo's** (International, p113); **Falafel Maoz**
(Middle Eastern, p118); **Indaba** (African,
p103); **Inez IPSC** (International, p113);
Japan Inn (Japanese, p116); **Ka Ya** (Korean,
p117); **Kalinka** (East European, p107); **Kort**
(International, p113); **Le Pêcheur** (Fish,
p107); **Pulitzers** (Breakfast & lunch stops,
p117); **Puri Mas** (Indonesian, p119); **La Rive**
(City landmarks, p102); **Shiva** (Indian,
p113); **Rosa's Cantina** (Latin American,
p117); **Sherpa** (Tibetan, p120); **La Storia**

La Rive

*Amstel Hotel, Prof Tulpplein 1, Grachtengordel: East
(622 6060/www.amstelhotel.nl/netherlands/
amsterdam/dining_amsic.html). Tram 6, 7, 10,
20/Metro Weesperplein.* **Open** 7-10.30am, noon-2pm,
6.30-10.30pm Mon-Fri; 7am-noon, 6.30-10.30pm Sat;
7am-noon Sun. **Main courses** ƒ65-ƒ97,50. **Credit**
AmEx, DC, MC, V. **Map** p311 F4.
Robert Kranenborg, one of the most famous chefs in
the Netherlands, may have departed La Rive with a
view to opening his own restaurant and finally getting that elusive third Michelin star – but this elegant 'two star' waterside restaurant in the Amstel
Hotel should retain its reputation as an unparalleled
purveyor of refined, regional French cuisine under
the able hands of rising star Edwin Kats.

De Roode Leeuw

*Damrak 93-4, Old Centre: New Side (555 0666/
www.hotelamsterdam.nl). Tram 4, 9, 14, 16, 24, 25.*
Open noon-9.30pm daily. **Main courses** ƒ35-ƒ45.
Credit AmEx, DC, MC, V. **Map** p306 D2.
This brasserie, housed in one of the oldest heated
terraces in Amsterdam, takes a step back to posher
times. It specialises in Dutch fare and even has a

selection of Dutch wine on offer, though it's also a
popular meeting place for champagne hounds.

't Swarte Schaep

*Korte Leidsedwarsstraat 24, Grachtengordel: East
(622 3021). Tram 1, 2, 5, 6, 7, 10, 20.* **Open** noon-
11pm daily. **Main courses** ƒ47-ƒ60. **Credit** AmEx,
DC, MC, V. **Map** p310 C5.
Based in this 300-year-old building since 1937, 't
Swarte Schaep is noted for its wines (especially
reds), authentic antiques and blend of classic, nouvelle and postmodern cuisine. An occasional hangout of the Dutch royal family.

D'Vijff Vlieghen

*Spuistraat 294-302 (entrance Vliegendesteeg 1), Old
Centre: New Side (624 8369). Tram 1, 2, 5, 13, 17,
20.* **Open** 5.30-10pm daily. **Main courses** ƒ48-ƒ60.
Credit AmEx, DC, MC, V. **Map** p306 C3.
'The Five Flies' is an institution that sprawls over
five houses and tries hard to pump up a Golden Age
vibe – it has a Rembrandt's Room, featuring some
of his etchings – but that does better as a purveyor
of interactive kitsch. It serves poshed-up Dutch food,
though the boar is no doubt imported.

Della Vita (Italian, p115); **'t Swarte Schaep** (City landmarks, p102); **Tempo Doeloe** (Indonesian, p119); **Tujuh Maret** (Indonesian, p119).

The Jordaan

Albatros (Fish, p107); **Balraj** (Indian, p111); **Bordewijk** (French, p109); **Claes Claesz** (Dutch, p105); **Duende** (Portuguese/Spanish, p119); **Gary's Muffins** (Breakfast & lunch stops, p117); **Groene Lantaarn** (Dutch, p107); **Hostaria** (Italian, p115); **El Huaso** (Latin American, p117); **Ithaca Griekse Traiteur** (Greek, p111); **Kikker** (French, p111); **Moeder's Pot** (Dutch, p107); **Moeders** (Dutch, p107); **Pathum** (Thai/South-east Asian, p120); **Tapasbar a la Plancha** (Portuguese/Spanish, p120); **Toscanini** (Italian, p115); **Yam-Yam** (Italian, p116).

Oud West

Lalibela (African, p103); **Riaz** (Surinamese, p120).

Museum Quarter

Bakkerswinkel van Nineties (Breakfast & lunch stops, p116); **Beddington's** (French, p109); **Bodega Keyzer** (City landmarks, p101); **Cobra Café** (International, p113); **Eetcafé I Kriti** (Greek, p111); **Eetcafé Loetje**

(Dutch, p105); **Enorm** (Breakfast & lunch stops, p116); **Le Garage** (French, p111); **Genet** (African, p103); **De Orient** (Indonesian, p119); **Sama Sebo** (Indonesian, p119).

The Pijp

Albine (Surinamese, p120); **Aleksandar** (East European, p107); **L'Angoletto** (Italian, p115); **Bagels & Beans** (Breakfast & lunch stops, p116); **Balti House** (Indian, p111); **Cambodja City** (Thai/South-east Asian, p120); **District V** (French, p109); **Eufraat** (Middle Eastern, p118); **Falafel Dan** (Middle Eastern, p118); **Koerdistan** (Middle Eastern, p118); **Lokanta Ceren** (Middle Eastern, p119); **Ondeugd** (International, p113); **Warung Spang-Makandra** (Surinamese, p120); **Yamazato** (Japanese, p116).

Zuid

Djago (Indonesian, p119); **Vakzuid** (International, p115); **Vis aan de Schelde** (Fish, p109).

West

Amsterdam (International, p113).

Waterfront

Iberia (Portuguese/Spanish, p120).

African

Genet

Amstelveenseweg 152, Museum Quarter (673 4344). Tram 1, 6. **Open** 5-11pm daily. **Main courses** ƒ16-ƒ55. **No credit cards.**
Located by Vondelpark, this is a great spot to unwind and sample the injera pancake-based food of Ethiopia after a long day of leisure in the greenery. The proprietor is quick to make you feel at home, and the vegetarian-friendly food calls for restraint: you'll want to keep eating regardless of how full you feel.

Indaba

Utrechtsestraat 96, Grachtengordel: East (421 3852). Tram 4, 9, 20. **Open** 6-10pm Mon-Thur; 6-11pm Fri, Sat; 6-9pm Sun. **Main courses** ƒ26,50-ƒ48,50. **Credit** MC, V. **Map** p311 E4.
This South African restaurant/gallery specialises in fragrant wood-grilled dishes, though it also does a mean simmered crockpot of crocodile. History and geography have made this country's food an exotic mix of African, Asian and Dutch sensibilities.

Kilimanjaro

Rapenburgerplein 6, The Plantage (622 3485). Bus 22. **Open** 5-10pm Tue-Sun; closed Mon. **Main courses** ƒ20-ƒ30. **Credit** AmEx, MC, DC, V. **Map** p307 F2.
This relaxed and friendly pan-African eaterie offers an assortment of traditional recipes from Senegal, the Ivory Coast, Tanzania and Ethiopia that can be washed down with the fruitiest of cocktails and the strongest of beers. Go there in summer, when the patio comes into its own.

Lalibela

1e Helmersstraat 249, Oud West (683 8332). Tram 1, 3, 6, 12. **Open** *Kitchen* 5-11pm daily. **Main courses** ƒ14-ƒ25. **No credit cards.** **Map** p310 C5.
This restaurant, located out around the border of the Museum Quarter and the Oud West section of the city (just west of Overtoom and Vondelpark, in other words), claims to be the most authentic Ethiopian eaterie in Amsterdam. It's certainly the most popular: reservations are recommended, especially at the weekend when the place fills up quickly. Prices are temptingly low.

Consumer

THE MUSIC THAT MADE ELVIS FAMOUS

THE FOOD THAT MADE HIM FAT

Hard Rock CAFE®

AMSTERDAM

BETWEEN PARADISO AND THE HOLLAND CASINO
ON THE MAX EUWEPLEIN
TEL: +31 (0)20 523 7625 FAX: +31 (0)20 523 7626
E-MAIL: amsterdam_sales@rank.com

Belgian

De Brakke Grond
Nes 43, Old Centre: Old Side (626 0044). Tram 4, 9, 14, 16, 20, 24, 25. **Open** noon-midnight daily. **Mains** ƒ28,50-ƒ32,50. **Credit** AmEx, DC, MC, V. **Map** p306 D3.
Though **Lieve** (Herengracht 88, Grachtengordel: West, 624 9635) may offer a more sophisticated rendering of Belgian cuisine that cannily straddles northern and southern European aesthetics, De Brakke Grond shows more sensitivity to those already pre-equipped with a love for Belgian beers by recommending the best choice for each dish. Take your pick.

Vlaamse Friteshuis
Voetboogstraat 31, Old Centre: New Side (no phone). Tram 1, 2, 5. **Open** 11am-6pm Mon-Sat; noon-5.30pm Sun. **No credit cards. Map** p310 D4.
Just off the Spui is the best Belgian chip shop in Amsterdam. The chips are crisp and chunky, and are served with a choice of around a zillion toppings. To maximise calories and food groups, choose *oorlog* ('war'): chips with mayonnaise, peanut sauce and onions.

Chinese

Nam Kee
Zeedijk 111-13, Old Centre: Red Light District (624 3470/www.namkee.nl). Bus 51, 53, 54. **Open** 11.30am-midnight daily. **Main courses** ƒ11,50-ƒ30,50. **No credit cards. Map** p306 D2.
A small restaurant with a large circle of regulars who come back again and again because the food is cheap and the fish dishes supreme. Indeed, its ace steamed oysters now even have an equally acclaimed Dutch novel named after them (Kees van Beijnum's *De Oesters van Nam Kee*).

New King
Zeedijk 117, Old Centre: Red Light District (625 2180). Bus 51, 53, 54. **Main courses** ƒ20-ƒ31. **Open** 11am-midnight daily. **Credit** AmEx, DC, MC, V. **Map** p306 D2.
Equatable to **Nam Kee** (*see above*), New King is also handily located next door: if one's too busy, you might get lucky at its neighbour. New King has hundreds of amply portioned choices – including lots of vegetarian options – at bargain basement prices.

Oriental City
Oudezijds Voorburgwal 179, Old Centre: Old Side (626 8352). Tram 4, 9, 14, 16, 20, 24, 25. **Open** 11.30am-10.30pm daily. **Main courses** ƒ17,50-ƒ49,50. **Credit** AmEx, DC, MC, V. **Map** p306 D2.
The views overlook Damstraat, the Royal Palace and the canals. And that's not even the best bit: some of Amsterdam's most authentic dim sum can be had at Oriental City. Understandably, this longtime Amsterdam favourite is popular with Chinese locals as well as tourists.

Dutch

Café Bern
Nieuwmarkt 9, Old Centre: Old Side (622 0034). Tram 4, 9, 14, 16, 20, 24, 25/Metro Nieuwmarkt. **Open** 4pm-1am daily. *Kitchen* 6-11pm daily. **Main courses** ƒ17,50-ƒ26,50. **No credit cards. Map** p306 D2.
Though it's traditionally Swiss, the Dutch long ago appropriated the cheese fondue as their own. This is a suitably cosy brown bar for some 'one pot, many forks' conviviality: the menu is affordable and the bar stocked with a variety of grease-cutting agents.

De Blauwe Hollander
Leidsekruisstraat 28, Grachtengordel: East (623 3014). Tram 6, 7, 10, 20. **Open** 5-10pm daily. **Main courses** ƒ15,50-ƒ30. **No credit cards. Map** p310 D5.
The four big tables – there's no separate seating – are always busy, but small parties seldom have to wait long to be seated in De Blauwe Hollander. One of only a few decent restaurants in a very touristy area, serving rich and tasty food.

Claes Claesz
Egelantiersstraat 24-6, The Jordaan (625 5306). Tram 7, 10, 17, 20. **Open** 6-11pm Tue-Sun; closed Mon. **Main courses** ƒ26,75-ƒ39,75. **Credit** MC, V. **Map** p305 B3.
The guy after whom this restaurant is named was a blanket dealer: he built this as an orphanage, complete with a courtyard (*hofje*), in 1600. Chaos and social cosiness abound as the seasonal menu of modernised Dutch cuisine – including a fine cheese fondue – is served to the sounds of live music.

Eetcafé Loetje
Johannes Vermeerstraat 52, Museum Quarter (662 8173). Tram 16. **Open** 11am-1am Mon-Fri; 5.30pm-1am Sat. *Kitchen* 6-10pm Mon-Sat; closed Sun. **Main courses** ƒ10-ƒ33. **No credit cards. Map** p310 D6.
Sometimes, after an honest day of sightseeing – or for the regulars, ad exec slavery – there's nothing better than a fillet of beef steak, salad, fries and a huge wad of mayo. Loetje is a brown bar that serves just that, and for a nominal price, too. A refreshing antidote to the rarefied air you may have inhaled while gandering at a Rembrandt nearby.

Get the blues at **De Blauwe Hollander**.

FEBO

Branches all over Amsterdam. **Open** hours vary.
No credit cards.

The Dutch answer to fast food, with branches scattered around town like pimples on the face of an adolescent boy. Order *patat* (ie chips), and help yourself to toppings from the counter, or pull a variety of deep fried grease products from the wall via *automaats*. It's junk, sure, but it's culturally educative junk.

Groene Lantaarn

Bloemgracht 47, The Jordaan (620 2088). Tram 10, 13, 17, 20. **Open** 6-9pm Thur-Sun; closed Mon-Wed.
Main courses ƒ29,50-ƒ52,50. **Credit** AmEx, MC, V. **Map** p305 B3.

For the poshest fondues, try the old world vibe of Groene Lantaarn. Bread comes pre-chunked, the desserts are suitably and deliciously decadent, and the menu even stretches out globally to include a dim sum fondue.

Keuken van 1870

Spuistraat 4, Old Centre: New Side (624 8965).
Tram 1, 2, 5, 20. **Open** 1-8pm Mon-Fri; 4-9pm Sat, Sun. **Main courses** (above ƒ25) **Credit** (above ƒ25)
AmEx, MC, V. **Map** p306 C2.

Eating at this former soup kitchen will put you in touch with the Dutch populace: you'll often have to share a table with locals, and the menu contains nothing but authentic Dutch standards such as endive with rashers of bacon or rib of steak.

Moeder's Pot

Vinkenstraat 119, The Jordaan (623 7643).
Tram 3, 10. **Open** 5-10.30pm Mon-Sat; closed Sun.
Main courses ƒ7,50-ƒ23,50. **No credit cards**.
Map p305 B1.

Mother's Pot serves up – you guessed it – simple and honest Dutch farmer's fare in woody and kitsch surrounds. It's not bad, either.

Moeders

Rozengracht 251, The Jordaan (626 7957). Tram 13, 14, 17, 20. **Open** 5-11pm daily. **Main courses** ƒ21,50-ƒ38,50. **Credit** MC, V. **Map** p305 B3.

Traditional Dutch food is best sampled in the mother's home. So here's your chance: in a room full of antiques and photos of 'Mom' (to which you can contribute your own snapshot), allow the charming 'mother's daughters' to serve you simple yet zestily inventive home-grown dishes.

Pancake Bakery

Prinsengracht 191, Grachtengordel: West (625 1333). Tram 13, 17, 20. **Open** noon-9.30pm daily.
Main courses ƒ9,50-ƒ20,95. **Credit** AmEx, DC, MC, V. **Map** p306 C2.

This quaint restaurant in the basement of one of Prinsengracht's lovely old gabled houses claims to serve 'the best pancakes in town'. With Dutch recipes stressing the importance of both thinness and density, it's hard to go wrong, and you can't quibble with the generous portions and over 70 varieties.

East European

Aleksandar

Ceintuurbaan 196, The Pijp (676 6384). Tram 3, 20. **Open** 5-10pm daily. **Main courses** ƒ25,50-ƒ55.
No credit cards. **Map** E6.

Balkan food comes in huge yet refined heaps here, along with heaps of hospitality. Surrender to the grilled selections and the slivovic, a plummy and poetic hard liquor that will soon have you reciting odes to the excellent frog's legs and escargot starters.

Kalinka

Korte Leidsedwarsstraat 49A, Grachtengordel: East (330 5996). Tram 6, 7, 10. **Open** noon-3pm, 5-11pm daily. **Main courses** ƒ23,50-ƒ37,50. **Credit** AmEx, DC, MC, V. **Map** p310 D5.

To dwell on cultural clichés, Russian eaterie Kalinka serves particularly potent (and palate-cleansing) brands of vodka. It also has endearing service and... something else... Right: food, in the form of traditional dishes such as stroganoff and kolebiak.

Fish

Al's Plaice

Nieuwendijk 10, Old Centre: New Side (427 4192).
Tram 1, 2, 4, 5, 9, 14, 16, 17, 20, 24, 25. **Open** 5-10pm Mon; noon-10pm Wed-Sun; closed Tue. **Main courses** ƒ6-ƒ12. **No credit cards**. **Map** p306 D2.

Brits will spot the pun from 50 paces: yep, it's an English fish 'n' chip tent. Besides bargain fish, there's a selection of pies, pasties and peas.

Albatros

Westerstraat 264, The Jordaan (627 9932). Tram 10. **Open** 6-11pm Mon, Tue, Thur-Sun; closed Wed.
Main courses ƒ32,50-ƒ47,50. **Credit** AmEx, DC, MC, V. **Map** p305 B2.

Great fishy cuisine in a fishy setting. All dishes are cooked to perfection, and the fine wine can be bought by the centimetre. The tiramisu is to die for.

Lucius

Spuistraat 247, Old Centre: New Side (624 1831/ www.lucius.nl). Tram 1, 2, 5. **Open** 5pm-midnight daily. **Main courses** ƒ37,50-ƒ87,50. **Credit** AmEx, DC, MC, V. **Map** p306 C3.

A fish-eater's paradise that serves a dinner of fresh ocean fish (as opposed to the normal North Sea variety), poached, grilled or fried, and shellfish in season. Lobster should be ordered in advance.

Le Pêcheur

Reguliersdwarsstraat 32, Grachtengordel: East (624 3121). Tram 1, 2, 5. **Open** noon-3pm, 5.30-10.30pm Mon-Fri; 5.30-10.30pm Sat; closed Sun. **Main courses** ƒ37,50-ƒ77,50. **Set menu** ƒ72,50 (4 courses).
Credit AmEx, DC, MC, V. **Map** p310 D4.

Choose from à la carte or the menu of the day, both of which are provided in Dutch, French and English. The service is friendly but formal, perfect for the mature clientele. The mussels and oysters are particularly excellent.

Consumer

Restaurant Pier 10
De Ruijterkade, Steiger 10 (624 8276). Tram 1, 2, 5, 9, 13, 14, 16, 17, 20, 24, 25. **Open** 6.30pm-1am daily. **Main courses** *f*33,50-*f*37,50. **Credit** AmEx, MC, V. **Map** p306 D1.
This former shipping office combines functional decor, candlelight, watery vistas, innovative fish dishes and a casual atmosphere. Reserve a table in the glass room and you'll be close enough to the herons to talk fish aesthetics with them.

Vis aan de Schelde
Scheldeplein 4, Zuid (675 1583). Tram 5, 25. **Open** noon-2pm, 5.30-11pm Mon-Fri; 5.30-11pm Sat, Sun. **Main courses** *f*37,50-*f*79,50. **Credit** AmEx, MC, V.
In no time, this eaterie, out near the RAI convention centre, has become a fish temple for the connoisseur. The menu sees classy French favourites colliding with more exotic dishes such as Thai fish fondue. A new foodie landmark with restrained deco styling.

French

Beddington's
Roelof Hartstraat 6-8, Museum Quarter (676 5201). Tram 3, 5, 12, 20, 24. **Open** 6-10.30pm Mon, Sat; noon-2pm, 6-10.30pm Tue-Fri; closed Sun. **Main courses** *f*48-*f*55. **Credit** AmEx, DC, MC, V.
The French cuisine here is complemented by original touches gleaned from trips through the Far East. The menu includes some beautifully presented fish dishes and the decor is minimal and restful. Believe it: Jean Beddington is one of the city's best chefs.

Begijntje
Begijnensteeg 6-8, Old Centre: New Side (624 0528). Tram 1, 2, 5. **Open** 1-10pm daily. **Main courses** *f*25-*f*49,50. **Credit** AmEx, DC. **Map** p310 D4.
The 'Little Nun' is the former coach house of the old nunnery in the **Begijnhof** (*see p49*). It has a lovely terrace, where you can eat the set daily meal that relies on French cuisine but also edges towards what can tentatively be termed nouveau Dutch.

Belhamel
Brouwersgracht 60, Grachtengordel: West (622 1095). Tram 1, 2, 5, 13, 17, 20. **Open** 6-10pm daily. **Main courses** *f*31.50-*f*42,50. **Credit** AmEx, MC, V. **Map** p306 C2.
Belhamel offers a fresh approach to French food – dipping into Italy and Holland for inspiration – with a good price/quality ratio and a high art nouveau quotient. As a treat, get a table overlooking the canal.

Bordewijk
Noordermarkt 7, The Jordaan (624 3899). Tram 3. **Open** 6.30-10.30pm Tue-Sun; closed Mon. **Set menus** *f*65-*f*89,50. **Credit** AmEx, MC, V. **Map** p305 B2.
This is a perfectly balanced restaurant, offering the very best original food and palate-tingling wines in a designer interior. Both service and atmosphere are relaxed, and as one of the best and most reliable kitchens in the city, it comes highly recommended.

Nostradamus: the future's bright. *See p111.*

Christophe
Leliegracht 46, Grachtengordel: West (625 0807/ www.christophe.nl). Tram 13, 14, 17, 20. **Open** 6.30-10.30pm Tue-Sat; closed Mon, Sun. **Main courses** *f*55-*f*70. **Credit** AmEx, DC, MC, V. **Map** p306 C3.
Hyper-posh and mega-expensive, Christophe serves inspired French cuisine to movers and shakers with ample expense accounts. Strap a booster to your taste buds and blast off to those Michelin stars.

District V
Van der Helstplein 17, The Pijp (770 0884). Tram 12, 25. **Open** 6pm-1am daily. **Set menu** *f*47,50 (3 courses). **No credit cards.** **Map** p311 F6.
Helping to chart the Pijp as the up-and-coming 'arts' neighbourhood, District V not only offers a divine and econo French-inspired, daily changing menu, but also sells its locally designed plates, cutlery and tables. The patio is truly lovely in summer.

Excelsior
Hôtel de L'Europe, Nieuwe Doelenstraat 2-8, Old Centre: Old Side (531 1777/531 1705/ www.leurope.nl). Tram 4, 9, 14, 16, 20, 24, 25. **Open** 12.30-3pm, 6.30-10.30pm daily. **Main courses** *f*58,50-*f*98. **Credit** AmEx, DC, MC, V. **Map** p306 D3.
Indulgently elegant with a city view to swoon over, this purveyor of formality features the classical – with a tad of modern thrown in – French menu of Jean-Jacques Menanteau. For special occasions.

Restaurants

Café Bern
Fondue with a side of chaos. See page 105.

Nam Kee
Truly legendary oysters. See page 105.

Riaz
The best rice 'n' beans in town, bar none. See page 120.

Supper Club
Dine with the in-crowd in narcoleptic splendour. See page 115.

Vis aan de Schelde
A foodie fish landmark. See page 109.

Le Garage
Ruysdaelstraat 54-6, Museum Quarter (679 7176). Tram 3, 5, 6, 12, 16, 20. **Open** noon-2pm, 6-11pm Mon-Fri; 6-11pm Sat, Sun. **Average** *f*49,50-*f*85. **Credit** AmEx, DC, MC, V. **Map** p311 E6.
Dress up in the latest styles in order to fit in at this trendy brasserie, which is great for Dutch glitterati-watching. The authentic French regional food – and 'worldly' versions thereof – is pretty damn fine.

Kikker
Egelantiersstraat 128-30, The Jordaan (627 9198). Tram 10, 13, 14, 17, 20. **Open** 6-10pm Tue-Thur, Sun; 6-10.30pm Fri, Sat; closed Mon. **Main courses** *f*20-*f*42,50. **Credit** AmEx, DC, MC, V. **Map** p305 B3.
A two-storey restaurant in the Jordaan, where the waiters are friendly, the art deco interior tasteful, the atmosphere intimate and the French/Portuguese/Tunisian dishes fresh. The weekend offers entertainment in the form of music, cabaret or comedy.

Nostradamus
Berenstraat 8, Grachtengordel: West (624 4292). Tram 1, 2, 5. **Open** 6-10pm Mon, Wed, Sun; 6-11pm Fri, Sat. **Closed** Thur. **Main courses** *f*24,50-*f*32,50. **Credit** AmEx, DC, MC, V. **Map** p310 C4.
A cannily themed restaurant that was probably overbooked during the millennial celebrations. The candlelit Middle Ages of Nostradamus are further evoked with astrologically aligned pillars and frescos. The cuisine is reinvented French cuisine with edges of the Orient; veggie options and free Tarot readings round out the schtick.

Café Roux
The Grand, Oudezijds Voorburgwal 197, Old Centre: Old Side (555 3111/www.thegrand.nl). Tram 4, 9, 14, 16, 20, 24, 25. **Open** noon-11pm daily. **Main courses** *f*32,50-*f*40. **Credit** AmEx, DC, MC, V. **Map** p306 D3.

The same food is served in Café Roux as in the Grand Hotel itself, and is supervised by head chef Albert Roux. Despite Roux's superstar status, food here is good value (especially at lunch), as is the afternoon tea. *See also 81.*

Greek

Eetcafé I Kriti
Balthasar Floriszstraat 3, Museum Quarter (664 1445). Tram 3, 5, 12, 16, 20. **Open** 5pm-1am Mon-Thur, Sun; 5pm-3am Fri, Sat. **Main courses** *f*22-*f*32. **No credit cards.**
Eat and party Greek style in this superior invocation of Crete, where a standard choice of dishes is lovingly prepared. Bouzouki-picking legends drop in on occasion and pump up the frenzied atmosphere, which is aided by the *f*2-a-go plate-lobbing option.

Ithaca Griekse Traiteur
1e Bloemdwarsstraat 18, The Jordaan (638 4665). Tram 7, 17, 20. **Open** 1-10pm Tue-Sun; closed Mon. **Main courses** *f*13,50-*f*17,75. **No credit cards.** **Map** p305 B3.
Ithaca enthusiastically serves up stellar Greek treats with a minimum of microwavery. Follow the staff's eager recommendations, and you'll go away replete and joyous. There's only a couple of tiny tables, so you might want to take your grub away and scoff on a canalside bench.

Indian

Balraj
Binnen Oranjestraat 1, The Jordaan (625 1428). Tram 3. **Open** 5-10pm daily. **Main courses** *f*18,75-*f*27,75. **No credit cards.** **Map** p305 B2.
A small, cosy eating house just off Haarlemmerdijk. The food is reasonably priced and particularly well done, with vegetarians generously catered for. Highly recommended.

Balti House
Albert Cuypstraat 41, The Pijp (470 8917). Tram 6, 7, 10, 16, 20, 24, 25. **Open** 4-11pm daily. **Main courses** *f*17,50-*f*35,50. **Credit** AmEx, DC, MC, V. **Map** p311 E6.
The portions at Amsterdam's only balti eaterie are large, though the balti and tandoori dishes are usually mellowed substantially to suit the Dutch palate. If you want the full spicy works, though, let them know and they'll happily oblige.

Himalaya
Haarlemmerstraat 11, Grachtengordel: West (622 3776). Tram 1, 2, 5, 20. **Open** 5-11pm daily. **Main courses** *f*20-*f*49. **Credit** AmEx, DC, MC, V. **Map** p306 C2.
Nothing less than excellent Indian cuisine at nice prices. The staff can make any dish more or less spicy than usual and the service is invariably welcoming and friendly, matching the wonderful art and designs on the walls.

Time Out

'THE GREATEST LONDON AUTHORITY'

Koh-I-Noor

Westermarkt 29, Grachtengordel: West (623 3133).
Tram 13, 14, 17, 20. **Open** 5-11pm daily. **Main**
courses ƒ22,50-ƒ40,50. **Credit** AmEx, DC, MC, V.
Map p306 C3.
Named after the famed diamond (which, coincidentally, an Amsterdam-based Sikh is currently trying
to reclaim for his family from the Brit royals),
Koh-I-Noor is a prime curry house with a cosy interior and friendly service. The food is decent, too.

Shiva

Reguliersdwarsstraat 72, Grachtengordel: East
(624 8713). Tram 4, 9, 14, 16, 20, 24, 25. **Open**
5-10.50pm daily. **Main courses** ƒ22,50-ƒ72.
Credit AmEx, DC, MC, V. **Map** p310 D4.
Air-conditioning keeps the heat down in Shiva's
relaxed and elegant interior. The menu holds a carefully selected choice of dishes, from classic curries
to speciality plates.

International

Amsterdam

Watertorenplein 6, West (682 2666/682 2667/
www.cradam.nl). Tram 10. **Open** 11am-1am daily.
Kitchen 11.30am-10.30pm Mon-Thur, Sun; 11.30am-
11.30pm Fri, Sat. **Main courses** ƒ19,50-ƒ45.
Credit AmEx, DC, MC, V.
This spacious monument to industry pumped water
from the coast's dunes for around a century. Now,
you can eat honest Dutch and French dishes here,
under a mammoth ceiling and beneath floodlighting
culled from the old Ajax and Olympic stadium. A
unique – and child-friendly – experience.

Blakes

Keizersgracht 384, Grachtengordel: West (530
2010). Tram 1, 2, 5. **Open** 6.30-11pm Mon-Sat;
closed Sun. **Main courses** ƒ57-ƒ75. **Credit** AmEx,
DC, MC, V. **Map** p310 C4.
The elegant restaurant of Anoushka Hempel's modish hotel (*see p85*) has received nothing but rave
reviews for its East meets West (but favouring
Japan, including decor) menu, and not without good
reason. Book ahead, sit down and Zen out…

Café Cox

Marnixstraat 429, Grachtengordel: West (620 7222).
Tram 1, 2, 5, 6, 7, 10, 20. **Open** 10am-10.30pm
Mon-Wed, Sun; 10am-1am Thur-Sat. *Kitchen* 10am-
10.30pm Mon-Wed, Sun; 10am-11.30pm Thur-Sat.
Main courses ƒ28-ƒ35. **Credit** AmEx, DC, MC, V.
Map p310 C5.
Imaginative French and modern Dutch cooking in a
lively 'theatrical crowd' environment. The prices are
eminently reasonable.

Cobra Café

Hobbemastraat 18, Museumplein, Museum Quarter
(470 0111). Tram 3, 5, 12, 20. **Open** 10am-8pm
Mon, Tue; 10am-midnight Wed-Sun. *Kitchen* 10am-
8pm Mon, Tue; 10am-10pm Wed-Sun. **Main courses**
ƒ32,50-ƒ39,50. **Credit** AmEx, MC, V. **Map** p310 D6.

Named, with unintentional though hysterical irony,
after an art movement that worshipped spontaneity,
the Cobra Café is a tight ship anchored in the
revamped Museumplein. Pop in for salads, sushi,
yoghurt, and snacks by day, or indulge in the
highly regarded menu by night.

Eat at Jo's

Marnixstraat 409, Grachtengordel: East (420 7469).
Tram 1, 2, 5, 6, 7, 10, 20. **Open** 2-9pm Wed-Sun;
closed Mon, Tue. **Main courses** ƒ9,50-ƒ24,50. **No**
credit cards. Map p310 C5.
Each day sees a different fish, meat and vegetarian
dish on the menu of this cheap and tasty international kitchen. Rock groupies should note that this
is a chance to see your hero chew: whichever artist
is booked to play at the **Melkweg** (*see p217*) will
probably chow down here first.

Inez IPSC

Amstel 2, Grachtengordel: East (639 2899). Tram 4,
9, 20. **Open** noon-3pm, 7-11.30pm daily. **Main**
courses ƒ40-ƒ50. **Credit** MC, V. **Map** p307 E3.
Featuring fantastic urban views and snappily
coloured decor (from designer Peter Giele of the late,
lamented Roxy), Inez is a favoured hotspot of the
well-moneyed artistic set. The food matches the setting: the refined taste and presentation are taken to
new aesthetic heights. Excellent.

Kort

Amstelveld 12, Grachtengordel: East (626 1199).
Tram 16, 24, 25. **Open** 10am-1am daily. *Kitchen*
noon-10pm daily. **Main courses** ƒ33,50-ƒ39,50.
Credit AmEx, DC, MC, V. **Map** p311 E4.
With one of the most painfully scenic terraces in
Amsterdam, this wooden church – once the stable
for Napoleon's horses – is a lovely place in which to
indulge on a sunny day. The set menu is ƒ49,50.

Lof

Haarlemmerstraat 62, Grachtengordel: West (620
2997). Tram 1, 2, 4, 5, 9, 13, 16, 17, 20, 24, 25.
Open 6.45pm-1am Tue-Sun. *Kitchen* 6.45-11pm
Tue-Sun; closed Mon. **Set menu** ƒ60 (3 courses). **No**
credit cards. Map p306 C2.
During daylight hours, you'd be forgiven for mis-
taking Lof for some sort of soup kitchen. At night,
though, it's a different story: the lighting works mir-
acles, as does the chef, who magically improvises
dishes that are drawn equally from Mediterranean
tradition and Far East cuisine. The fish, in particular, is sublime.

Ondeugd

Ferdinand Bolstraat 15, The Pijp (672 0651/
www.ondeugd.nl). Tram 3, 6, 7, 10, 12, 16, 20, 24,
25. **Open** 6pm-1am Mon-Thur, Sun; 6pm-3am Fri,
Sat. *Kitchen* 6-11pm daily. **Main courses** ƒ23,50-
ƒ39,50. **Credit** AmEx DC, MC, V. **Map** p311 E6.
A very popular restaurant in the Pijp, perfect for a
casual and potentially raucous evening out. The
menu is primarily French, but with many outside
influences. Pop in for lobster on Mondays.

Consumer

De Struisvogel

Keizersgracht 312, Grachtengordel: West (423 3817). Tram 13, 14, 17, 20. **Open** 6pm-midnight Mon-Thur, Sun; 6pm-1am Fri, Sat. **Set menu** *f*33 (3 courses). **Credit** AmEx, DC, MC, V. **Map** p310 C4.
The 'Ostrich' is a basement brown café with a simple set-up: for *f*33, choose three courses from a set menu, including, of course, ostrich steak. It's a great deal and many know it, so book ahead.

Supper Club

Jonge Roelensteeg 21, Old Centre: New Side (638 0513/www.supperclub.nl). Tram 1, 2, 5, 13, 17. **Open** 8pm-1am daily. **Set menu** *f*115 (5 courses). **Credit** AmEx, DC, MC, V. **Map** p306 D3.
With its white backdrop, beds replacing traditional seating, irreverent food combinations and themed acts, the Supper Club is a very unique, very arty and very casual – to the point of being a danger to narcoleptics – dining experience. The lounge is similarly chilled and just as hip. *See also p184.*

Vakzuid

Olympisch Stadion 35, Zuid (0900 825 9843/ www.vakzuid.nl). Tram 24/bus 15, 63. **Open** 10am-1am Mon-Thur, Sun; 10am-3am Fri, Sat. **Main courses** *f*25-*f*100. **Credit** AmEx, DC, MC, V.
Already dubbed 'Fuck Zuid' by waggish locals, this new lounge restaurant, located in the recently revamped 1928 Olympic Stadium (*see p76* **Olympic glory**), is hugely popular with the working trendoids. With modish cons and views over the track field, it's a stunning site; hopefully the food – call it Med-Oriental – and service will come to match it in time. DJs pump up the ambience.

Italian

L'Angoletto

Hemonystraat 18, The Pijp (676 4182). Tram 3, 4, 6, 7, 10. **Open** 6-11pm Mon-Fri, Sun; closed Sat. **Average** *f*10-*f*17. **Credit** V. **Map** p311 F5.
The most authentic trattoria in town has a Felliniesque atmosphere. It gets very busy, but the food – often hyped as the best pizza and pasta in Amsterdam – makes the wait for a table worthwhile.

Hostaria

2e Egelantiersdwarsstraat 9, The Jordaan (626 0028). Tram 10, 13, 14, 17, 20. **Open** 6.30-10.30pm Tue-Sun. *Kitchen* 6.30-9.30pm Tue-Sun; closed Mon. **Main courses** *f*31,50. **No credit cards**. **Map** p305 B3.
Owners Marjolein and Massimo Pasquinoli serve a wonderful selection of classic Italian dishes, including salmon carpaccio and a spectacular insalata di polipo (squid salad). Excellent, unpretentious food at good prices.

La Storia Della Vita

Weteringschans 171, Grachtengordel: East (623 4251). Tram 6, 7, 10, 16, 20, 24, 25. **Open** 7-10.15pm daily. **Set menu** *f*65, *f*75 (7 courses). **No credit cards**. **Map** p311 E5.
After a chat, the engaging proprietor will decide which combination of whatever his regional Italian kitchen happens to be fixing that night you'll enjoy. Trust him, sit back in grand brasserie style and enjoy both the food and the animated piano player. Great for a date.

Toscanini

Lindengracht 75, The Jordaan (623 2813). Tram 3, 10. **Open** 6-10pm daily. **Main courses** *f*19-*f*35. *Set menu* *f*59 (3 courses), *f*65 (4 courses). **Credit** AmEx, DC, MC, V. **Map** p305 B2.
The authentic and invariably excellent Italian food at this bustling restaurant is prepared in an open kitchen. Don't go expecting pizza, and book early (from 3pm) if you want to be sure of getting a table at what is undoubtedly one of the most popular eateries in the Jordaan.

Fish is twice the fun at **Stereo Sushi**. *See p116.*

Consumer

Breakfast & lunch stops

Bagels & Beans

Ferdinand Bolstraat 70, The Pijp (672 1610).
Tram 16, 24, 25. **Open** 8.30am-6pm Mon-Fri;
9.30am-6pm Sat; 10am-6pm Sun. **Main
courses** ƒ4-ƒ9,25. **Credit** (over ƒ40 only)
AmEx, DC, MC, V. **Map** p311 E6.
B&B has now consolidated its position in
Amsterdam, thanks in part to this patio-
equipped success story. Perfect for an
econo-breakfast, lunch or snack; sun-dried
tomatoes are employed with particular skill.

Bakkerswinkel van Nineties

*Roelof Hartstraat 68, Museum Quarter (662
3594). Tram 3, 12, 20, 24, 25.* **Open** 7am-
6pm Tue-Fri; 7am-5pm Sat; 10am-4pm Sun;
closed Mon. **Main courses** ƒ5,50-ƒ22.
No credit cards.
A bakery-tearoom where you can indulge in
lovingly prepared hearty sandwiches, soups,
and the divinest slabs of quiche you will
probably ever taste. Dead civilised.

't Balkje

*Kerkstraat 46-8, Grachtengordel: West
(622 0566). Tram 1, 2, 5.* **Open** 9am-5pm
daily. **Average** ƒ3-ƒ13,50. **No credit cards.**
Map p310 D4.
Generous sandwiches, cheeseburgers,
calamares, quiches and Dutch hangover
cures such as uitsmijters, all at low prices,
are offered at this spot just off Leidsestraat.

Enorm

*PC Hooftstraat 87, Museum Quarter (670
9944). Tram 2, 3, 5, 12, 20.* **Open** 8am-8pm
Mon-Fri; 9am-7pm Sat, Sun. **Sandwiches**
ƒ6,75-ƒ13,50. **Credit** AmEx, MC, V.
Map p310 C6.
Designer sandwiches in designer packaging
can be had at this new designer fast-food
outlet. There's a wall of 80 glossies, and
flatscreens on which you can surf the
Internet, check stock quotes or watch MTV.
With a David Carson-designed logo,

Yam-Yam

*Frederik Hendrikstraat 90, The Jordaan (681
5097). Tram 3.* **Open** 6-10pm Mon-Sat; closed Sun.
Main courses ƒ13-ƒ28,50. **No credit cards.**
Map p305 A3.
Yam-Yam, located just west of the Jordaan, offers
unparalleled and shockingly inexpensive pastas and
pizzas. A favourite of clubbers and locals alike, and
more than worth the trip.

Japanese

An

*Weteringschans 199, Grachtengordel: East (627
0607). Tram 6, 7, 10, 20.* **Open** 11.30am-8pm Mon-
Sat; closed Sun. **Main courses** ƒ5-ƒ42. **No credit
cards. Map** p311 E5.
An serves some of the best and most authentic
Japanese cuisine in Amsterdam. Unfortunately, it
now focuses on catering and take-out, which only
acts to the detriment of their restaurant service.

Japan Inn

*Leidsekruisstraat 4, Grachtengordel: East (620
4989). Tram 1, 2, 5, 6, 7, 10, 20.* **Open** 5-11.45pm
daily. **Main courses** ƒ17,50-ƒ50. **Credit** AmEx,
DC, MC, V. **Map** p310 D5.
Something of an oddity in the Leidseplein area, for
Japan Inn offers both quality and quantity. The great
fresh sushi and sashimi are served quickly from the
open kitchen in the back; both are popular both with
students (who appreciate the quantity) and Japanese
tourists (who head there for the quality).

Morita-Ya

*Zeedijk 18, Old Centre: Old Side (638 0756). Tram
1, 2, 5, 13, 17, 20.* **Open** 6-9.30pm Mon, Tue, Thur-
Sun; closed Wed. **Average** ƒ27,50-ƒ45. **Credit**
AmEx, MC, V. **Map** p306 D2.
Morita-Ya is a cheap and cheerful place up near
Centraal Station. The opening hours are, to say the
least, a little erratic, but if you do manage to get there
when it's serving, you'll enjoy some fantastic sushi
and sashimi.

Stereo Sushi

*Jonge Roelensteeg 4, Old Centre: New Side (777
3010). Tram 4, 9, 14, 16, 20, 24, 25.* Open 5pm-
1am Mon-Thur; 5pm-3am Fri; noon-3am Sat, Sun.
Main courses *Sushi & sashimi* ƒ4-ƒ17,50. **Credit**
MC, V. **Map** p306 D3.
A convenient location, a decent vibe and long hours
make Stereo Sushi the perfect snack stop if you're
making a night of it in one of the many hipster bar-
lounges around Nieuwezijds Voorburgwal (for
which, *see pp126-7*).

Yamazato

*Okura Hotel, Ferdinand Bolstraat 333, The Pijp
(678 8351/www.okura.nl/html/yamazato.html). Tram
12, 25.* **Open** 7.30-9.30am, noon-2pm, 6-9.30pm
daily. **Main courses** ƒ38-ƒ65. **Credit** AmEx, DC,
MC, V.
If you want class, head all the way out to Yamazoto
and surrender to the charming kimono-ed service,
the too-neat-to-eat presentation and the restful views
over a fish pond. The lunches are priced more attractively than the dinners.

(sidebar) **Consumer**

Wallpaper* magazine hyping it as a cool hangout and plans for world domination, you'll be hearing a lot more about this place.

Gary's Muffins

Prinsengracht 454, Grachtengordel: West (420 1452). Tram 1, 2, 5. **Open** 8.30am-6pm Mon-Sat; 9am-6pm Sun. **Main courses** *f*1-*f*9,25. **No credit cards. Map** p310 C5.
One of the best snack stops in town, serving bagels, brownies and muffins. In good weather, sit outside by the canal and share your food with the sparrows.
Branches: Jodenbreestraat 15, Old Centre: Old Side (421 5930); Marnixstraat 121, The Jordaan (638 0186); **Late Night** Reguliersdwarsstraat 53, Grachtengordel: West (420 2406).

Goodies

Huidenstraat 9, Grachtengordel: West (625 6122). Tram 1, 2, 5. **Open** 9.30am-10.30pm daily. *Kitchen* 9.30am-4.30pm, 6-10.30pm daily. **Main courses** *f*15-*f*25. *Sandwiches* *f*4-*f*11,50. **Credit** AmEx, DC, MC, V. **Map** p310 C4.
A sandwich and bagel stop by day, with sandwiches named after famous couples (the 'Bill & Hillary' features old cheese) and bagels after cartoon characters (the 'Cartman' is tuna, onions and pickle). In the evening, it serves econo but delish pasta.

Pulitzers

Keizersgracht 234, Grachtengordel: East (523 5283). Tram 13, 14, 17, 20. **Open** 7am-11pm daily. **Main courses** *f*37,50-*f*49,50. **Credit** AmEx, DC, MC, V. **Map** p306 C6.
Spoil yourself with a posh breakfast in one of the many light-infused rooms belonging to this early-opening hotel restaurant (see p84). Sit under a Frans Hals painting, or at least rather a modernised version of one that features mobile phones and empty Heineken cans.

Korean

Ka Ya

Utrechtsestraat 42, Grachtengordel: East (625 9251). Tram 4. **Open** 5.30-11pm Tue-Sun. **Main courses** *f*25-*f*35. *Set menu* *f*55, *f*60 (4 courses). **Credit** AmEx, DC, MC, V. **Map** p311 E4.
Formally known as Mokkalie, this comfortable and friendly eaterie continues to serve the low cal and flash-fried-before-your-eyes food of Korea, a cuisine notable for tripping out your taste buds.

Tex meets Mex at **Rosa's Cantina**.

Latin American

El Huaso

Rozengracht 160, The Jordaan (770 1904). Tram 13, 14, 17, 20. **Open** 4pm-midnight Tue-Sun. **Main courses** *f*13,50-*f*29,50. **No credit cards**. **Map** p305 B3.
Want cheap and tasty Mexican? Good luck, buddy. Instead, try this laid-back Chilean brown café that serves a Mexican-style menu of burritos, tacos et al. Don't miss the garlicky gambas.

Poco Loco

Nieuwmarkt 24, Old Centre: Old Side (624 2937). Tram 4, 9, 14, 20. **Open** 11am-12.30am daily. *Kitchen* 5.30-10.30pm daily. **Main courses** *f*22-*f*32,50. **Credit** AmEx, DC, MC, V. **Map** p307 E2.
This Mexican/Cajun eating café sports a patio with a prime view of the wonderfully scenic Nieuwmarkt square. And, as a bonus, staff cook it right and serve it quick...

Rosa's Cantina

Reguliersdwarsstraat 38-40, Grachtengordel: East (625 9797/www.rosescantina.com). Tram 1, 2, 5, 11, 16, 24, 25. **Open** 5pm-1am daily. *Kitchen* 5-11pm daily. **Main courses** *f*21,50-*f*44,50. **Credit** AmEx, MC, DC, V. **Map** p310 D4.
It's definitely not the place for a quiet night out and it's more Tex-Mex than Mexican, but the ingredients are good enough and the portions are more than generous. Combining a burrito with pitchers of Margarita makes for a merry meal.

Spice world

After Indonesia was granted independence from the Netherlands in 1949, 180,000 residents of the Spice Islands came to the Netherlands to become Dutch citizens. Evenly dispersed, their influence was felt across the country with the result that, even today, the ubiquitous Dutch snack bar serves radically bastardised versions of their cuisine. It's all a very long road from when, as the legend goes, Tumileng first liberated a stalk of rice from the heavens by hiding it between his toes.

As a mirror image of an archipelago of more than 1,000 islands that claims historical influences from the Chinese, Arabs, Portuguese and Dutch, Indonesian cuisine is, in fact, a mélange of many cuisines with an almost infinite range of dishes. Perhaps the only unifiers are the condiments – ketjap (sweet soy sauce) and sambal (crushed chilli pepper paste) – and standard ingredients such as coconut milk, onions, garlic, ginger, cumin, kentjur root, coriander, kunjit saffron, laos root, tamarind, and tembukuntji root.

Adding to the confusion are the many modest Chin-Indo-Suri (or some such combination) eateries serving up cheap and hybridised dishes that have taken on the tones of the many immigrants from China (often via Indonesia) and Surinam, another former colony whose Caribbean style is most often represented by the pancake-like roti. The usual Indo-derived dishes on offer at these places are satay (skewered meat served with a peanut sauce), gado-gado (steamed veg and boiled egg served with rice and satay sauce), nasi goreng (onion fried rice with meat, veg and egg) and bami goreng (the same, with noodles instead of rice).

While these dishes are ultimately satisfying to the monetarily challenged, all visitors should stretch their wallets at least once and go to a purveyor of rijsttafel ('rice-table'). But again, things are not what they seem: a 'rice-table' is actually a Dutch construct that tries to include as many dishes as possible. Every known fish, meat and vegetable is reworked into a micro-extravaganza which, when served en masse with rice, becomes a feast for the gods, albeit gods with asbestos tongues. It's hot shit, whose most efficient antidote is a few gallons of witbier (or 'white beer') and plenty of rice.

Connoisseurs speak highly of The Hague, where Indo cuisine is less watered down to both Dutch and tourist tastes. But for the uninitiated, Amsterdam has ample choices to serve as a frolicsome introduction. You'll inevitably become obsessed. And then, you can go to The Hague…

Bojo

Lange Leidsedwarsstraat 51, Grachtengordel: East (622 7434). Tram 1, 2, 5. **Open** 4pm-2am Mon-Fri; noon-4am Sat, Sun. **Main courses** ƒ8-ƒ25. **Map** p310 C5.
Bojo is a long way from being the best Indo in town. However, it is one of the few eateries – regardless of type – that stays open into the small hours. The price is right, the food's OK, and the portions are large enough to glue your insides together after an evening of excess.

Middle Eastern

Eufraat

1e Van der Helststraat 72, The Pijp (672 0579). Tram 3, 12, 24, 25. **Open** 11am-11pm daily. **Main courses** ƒ18,50-ƒ25,50. **Credit** AmEx, DC, MC, V. **Map** p311 E5.
This family-run Assyrian restaurant is named after one of the rivers that is said to have flowed through the Garden of Eden. The ancient recipes are brought to life with real care and loving attention: Eufraat even makes its own pittas and yoghurts from scratch. Don't miss the supreme Arabic coffee.

Falafel Dan

Ferdinand Bolstraat 126, The Pijp (676 3411). Tram 3, 12, 24, 25. **Open** noon-1am Mon-Thur, Sun; noon-3am Fri, Sat. **Main courses** ƒ6-ƒ17. **No credit cards. Map** p311 E6.

Falafel, naturally enough, plus an all-you-can-stuff salad bar. Absurdity kicks in daily between 3pm and 5pm, when happy hour allows you to cram down all the falafel you can eat. It must be a buyer's market for chick peas.

Falafel Maoz

Reguliersbreestraat 45, Grachtengordel: East (624 9290). Tram 4, 9, 14, 16, 20, 24, 25. **Open** 11am-1am Mon-Thur, Sun; 11am-4am Fri, Sat. **Falafel** ƒ6. **No credit cards. Map** p311 E4.
Pretty similar to **Falafel Dan** (see opposite), only without the happy hour.

Koerdistan

Ferdinand Bolstraat 23, The Pijp (676 1995). Tram 16, 24, 25. **Open** 5pm-midnight Tue-Sun; closed Mon. **Main courses** ƒ15-ƒ27,50. **Credit** DC, MC, V. **Map** p311 E6.

De Orient

Van Baerlestraat 21, Museum Quarter (673 4958). Tram 2, 3, 5, 12, 20. **Open** 5-10pm daily. **Main courses** ƒ24-ƒ65. **Credit** AmEx, DC, MC, V. **Map** p310 C6.
A folklore-decorated restaurant with a large, vegetarian-friendly menu. While the food is not hugely spicy as, its complexity of flavour makes for a good introduction.

Djago

Scheldeplein 18, Zuid (664 2013). Tram 4. **Open** 5-10pm Mon-Fri, Sun; closed Sat. **Main courses** ƒ25-ƒ42. **Credit** AmEx, DC, MC, V.
Djago's West Javanese eats are praised to the hilt by Indo-obsessives. Located near the RAI convention centre, it is a bit out of the way, but it's still closer than The Hague.

Puri Mas

Lange Leidsedwarsstraat 37-41, Grachtengordel: East (627 7627). Tram 1, 2, 5. **Open** 5-11pm daily. **Main courses** ƒ22,50-ƒ42,50. **Credit** AmEx, DC, MC, V. **Map** p310 C5.
Impeccable service and excellent food characterise this classy restaurant. A variety of dishes are served, from light meals to full meals, plus vegetarian meals and rijsttafels.

Sama Sebo

PC Hooftstraat 27, Museum Quarter (662 8146). Tram 2, 3, 5, 12, 20. **Open** noon-2pm, 6-10pm Mon-Sat; closed Sun. **Set meal** ƒ52,50 (16 dishes). **Credit** AmEx, DC, MC, V. **Map** p310 D5.

A comfortable and spacious restaurant with a vibe more akin to that found in a brown café. There's no minimum charge, so even if you just fancy a coffee and a snack between museums, it's a good choice.

Sarang Mas

Damrak 44, Old Centre: New Side (622 2105). Tram 1, 2, 5, 13, 17, 20. **Open** noon-10.45pm daily. **Set meal** ƒ52,75 (18-20 dishes). **Credit** AmEx, DC, MC, V. **Map** p306 D2.
Hidden amid the neon atrocities of Damrak, Sarang Mas is highlighted both by its culinary consistency and by its kitschy interior: check the backlit ceiling of plastic dancing tongues.

Tempo Doeloe

Utrechtsestraat 75, Grachtengordel: East (625 6718). Tram 4, 6, 7, 10. **Open** 6pm-1am daily. **Main courses** ƒ9,50-ƒ85. **Credit** AmEx, DC, MC, V. **Map** p311 E4.
This cosy and rather upmarket restaurant (heck, it even has white linen) is widely regarded as one of the city's best and spiciest Indo eateries, and not without good reason. Book ahead.

Tujuh Maret

Utrechtsestraat 73, Grachtengordel: East (427 9865). Tram 4, 6, 7, 10. **Open** noon-10pm Tue-Sun; closed Mon. **Main courses** ƒ21,50-ƒ49,50. **No credit cards. Map** p311 E4.
A small, relaxed and ratan-chaired gaff that its champions claim is superior to its posher neighbour, **Tempo Doeloe** (see above). Tujuh Maret also does takeaway.

It may be a tad dingy, but this small restaurant is also extremely friendly and most definitely tasty. Koerdistan rarely disappoints with its top-notch Middle Eastern cookery. If you can bear to lay off the snacks all day, then you'll be in perfect shape for its generous daily three-course menu, priced at around ƒ25.

Lokanta Ceren

Albert Cuypstraat 40, The Pijp (673 3524). Tram 4, 16, 20, 24, 25. **Open** 6-10.30pm daily. **Main courses** ƒ26-ƒ35. **No credit cards. Map** p311 E6.
A small, friendly Turkish/Kurdish restaurant with numerous starters (mezes) that are displayed aesthetically on a huge tray. However, they'll all quickly disappear when accompanied by the fresh, warm Turkish bread and a glass of raki. Round off your feast with some fresh fruit for a quick and tasty health kick.

Portuguese/Spanish

Centra

Lange Niezel 29, Old Centre: Red Light District (622 3050). Tram 4, 9, 14, 16, 20, 24, 25. **Open** 1-11pm daily. **Main courses** ƒ33-ƒ40. **No credit cards. Map** p306 D2.
Good, wholesome, homely Spanish cooking. The fluorescent lighting that once sullied the atmosphere, and the tapas, lamb and fish dishes are all great.

Duende

Lindengracht 62, The Jordaan (420 6692). Tram 3. **Open** 4pm-1am Mon-Thur, Sun; 4pm-3am Fri, Sat. **Main courses** ƒ3,50-ƒ17,50. **No credit cards. Map** p305 B2.
This little bit of Andalusia in the Jordaan serves a good and varied selection of tapas. Order at the bar and be prepared to share your table with an amorous

couple or a flamenco dancer who might just offer you some free lessons. Head to the backroom for guitar and dance pyrotechnics.

Iberia

Kadijksplein 16, Waterfront (623 6313). Bus 22. **Open** 5-11pm daily. **Set menu** ƒ55. **Credit** AmEx, DC, MC, V. **Map** p307 F2.

Located close by the **Nederlands Scheepvaart Museum** (*see page 76*) and the simply stunning **newMetropolis** museum (*see page 77*), Iberia offers both Spanish and Portuguese dishes in an appropriately Mediterranean ambience. Indulge in sherry, fresh from the keg, during your meal.

Tapasbar a la Plancha

1e Looiersdwarsstraat 15, The Jordaan (420 3633). Tram 1, 2, 5, 7, 10, 20. **Open** 2pm-1am Tue-Thur, Sun; 2pm-3am Fri, Sat; closed Mon. **Main courses** ƒ5,50 (small tapas dishes)-ƒ45 (tapas platter). **Credit** MC, V. **Map** p310 C4.

The bull's head barely fits into this tiny spot, but its long hours allow you plenty of time to squeeze in and eat some of the best tapas in town. Bring your Spanish phrasebook.

Surinamese

Albine

Albert Cuypstraat 69, The Pijp (675 5135). Tram 16, 24, 25. **Open** 10.30am-10pm Tue-Sun; closed Mon. **Main courses** ƒ7-ƒ21,50. **No credit cards.** **Map** p311 E6.

One in a row of three cheap Suri-Chin-Indo restaurants, Albine – where the Chinese influence predominates – gets top marks for its light-speed service and its solid vegetarian or meat meals of roti, rice or noodles. A perfect place in which to gel your belly back together after the Heineken tour or to ease into the rest of the day following a shopping extravaganza around the Albert Cuypmarkt.

Riaz

Bilderdijkstraat 193, Oud West (683 6453). Tram 3, 7, 12, 17. **Open** noon-9pm Mon-Fri, Sun; closed Sat. **Main courses** ƒ10-ƒ22,50. **No credit cards.** **Map** p309 B5.

Riaz, probably Amsterdam's finest Surinamese restaurant, is where Ruud Gullit scores his rotis when he's in town. The menu has an Indian edge with the inclusion of some curries. If the skies are sunny, take away a takeaway to nearby Vondelpark.

Warung Spang-Makandra

Gerard Doustraat 39, The Pijp (670 5081). Tram 6, 7, 10, 16. **Open** 11am-10pm Mon, Tue, Thur-Sun; closed Wed. **Main courses** ƒ4-ƒ15. **No credit cards.** **Map** p311 E6.

A Java-Suri restaurant out in the Pijp, where the Indo influence comes up trumps with the great Javanese rames. The decor is simple, but the relaxed vibe and beautifully presented dishes will make you want to sit down for your meal as opposed to taking it away.

Thai/South-east Asian

Cambodja City

Albert Cuypstraat 58-60, The Pijp (671 4930). Tram 16, 24, 25. **Open** 5-10pm Tue-Sun; closed Mon. **Main courses** ƒ11,50-ƒ29. **No credit cards.** **Map** p311 E6.

Despite the name, the dishes served here are culled from Thailand, Vietnam and Laos as well as Cambodia. Aside from the 3-D moving waterfall painting, the surrounds are simple, and both the helpful service and the food itself never disappoint.

Pathum

Willemsstraat 16, The Jordaan (624 4936). Tram 3/bus 18, 22. **Open** 5-10pm Mon, Wed-Sun; closed Tue. **Main courses** ƒ16,50-ƒ28,50. **Credit** AmEx, DC, MC, V. **Map** p305 B2.

A cheap and lively Jordaan hangout, offering rather lovely Thai food at rather low prices. Be sure to ask the waiters for advice on how hot the dishes are if you don't want your head blown off. Which you probably don't.

Sjaalman

Prinsengracht 178, Grachtengordel: West (620 2440). Tram 13, 14, 17, 20. **Open** 5.30-10.30pm daily. **Main courses** ƒ18,50-ƒ27,50. **No credit cards.** **Map** p306 C3.

This new Thai restaurant sits on the edge of the Jordaan. The woody and subtle designer atmosphere and personable service are finely tuned to evoke a relaxed and hip ambience, where mellow, grooving modern dance beats accompany conversation and the chewing of excellently prepared dishes.

Thaise Snackbar Bird

Zeedijk 72, Old Centre: Old Side (snack bar 420 6289/restaurant 620 1442). Tram 1, 2, 4, 5, 9, 13, 14, 16, 17, 20, 24, 25. **Open** *Snack bar* 3-8pm daily. *Restaurant* 5-10.30pm daily. **Main courses** ƒ18,50-ƒ36,50. **Credit** (restaurant only) AmEx, DC, MC, V. **Map** p306 D2.

Thaise Snackbar Bird is probably the most authentic and certainly the cheapest Thai place in town. Naturally, then, it's also the most crowded, but it's well worth the wait, whether you settle on a tom yam soup, a snack or a full-blown meal.

Tibetan

Sherpa

Korte Leidsedwarsstraat 58, Grachtengordel: East (623 9495). Tram 1, 2, 5, 6, 7, 10. **Open** 5-11pm daily. **Main courses** ƒ14,50-ƒ26,50. **Credit** AmEx, DC, MC, V. **Map** p310 D5.

Amid the general mediocrity of this tourist-frenzied area is one very special restaurant. Relive your favourite Kathmandu moment by enjoying Sherpa's traditional food and service. The Polish might call them pierogi, the Italians ravioli, but the Tibetan momo – at least as serves at Sherpa – is in a class of its own.

Bars & Cafés

As in most cities, the heart and soul of Amsterdam can be found in its bars: whether modish or trad, the city's watering holes merit attention.

Like it or not, many visitors to Amsterdam show up in the city for one reason and one reason only: the legality and availability of drugs. Dopers, tokers, spliffers and wasters all find a simple solace in the coffeeshops and smart drugs stores of the city, and go home radiant with glee at having been allowed to smoke the wicked weed without fear of arrest.

But don't let such dopetastic frippery get in the way of your enjoyment of another legal drug, for Amsterdam doesn't want for terrific bars and pubs, either. The Dutch are a nation of drinkers far more than they're a nation of tokers, and this fact is reflected in the eclectic and varied excellence of the city's bars.

To sample Dutch culture at its most relaxed and charming, head to one of the plethora of old-style brown cafés around the city. Named for their nicotine-stained walls and ceilings, their woody surrounds are the perfect place in which to lose an afternoon or evening in alcohol and chat. For an equally traditional experience, head out of the centre to a local café for a game of biljarts, cards or cribbage, or make your way to a *proeflokaal*, where beer takes a back seat

and liqueurs – mostly *jenever*, the one truly Dutch spirit – are drunk with a somewhat alarming alacrity and enthusiasm. You'll likely pay more at the town's grand cafés, but it's worth the extra few guilders for a glimpse at the often stunning interiors.

Add in the designer bars, alternative watering holes, Irish (and Oirish) pubs and so-hip-it-hurts nightspots and you'll won't be wanting for imbiberies in which to make merriment during your stay. And even if you don't drink, you'll be well looked after by the plenty of lovely tearooms, cafés and pâtisseries scattered around town. Cheers…

The Old Centre

Around the Dam

Belgique
Gravenstraat 2 (625 1974). Tram 1, 2, 4, 5, 9, 13, 14, 16, 17, 20, 24, 25. **Open** noon-1am Mon-Thur, Sun; noon-3am Fri, Sat. **No credit cards. Map** p306 C3.
A cosy little bar with more than 50 Belgian brews, plus Trappist cheese to make you thirsty for more.

Consumer

Beware of the dog but not the wine at **Henri Prouvin**. *See p122.*

De Drie Fleschjes

Gravenstraat 18 (624 8443). Tram 1, 2, 4, 5, 9, 13, 14, 16, 17, 20, 24, 25. **Open** noon-8.30pm Mon-Sat; 3-7pm Sun. **No credit cards. Map** p306 C3.

A cosy *proeflokaal* just by the Dam. However, though it can be a charming place, be warned that it's often full of tourists getting The Traditional Dutch Drinking Experience™.

Henri Prouvin

Gravenstraat 20 (623 9333). Tram 1, 2, 4, 5, 9, 13, 14, 16, 17, 20, 24, 25. **Open** 3-11pm Tue-Fri; 2-9pm Sat; closed Mon. **No credit cards. Map** p306 C3.

This dark, elegant café offers a spectacular variety of good wines and champagnes either by the bottle or the glass at reasonable prices. It also serves wine-friendly snacks and a few meat dishes.

De Kuil

Oudebrugsteeg 27 (623 4848). Tram 1, 2, 4, 5, 9, 13, 16, 17, 20, 24, 25/Metro Centraal Station. **Open** noon-midnight Mon-Thur, Sun; noon-1am Fri; noon-3am Sat. **No credit cards. Map** p306 D2.

This perfect mix between brown café and coffeeshop is hidden in an alley off Damrak, and is likeable even if you're not a toker. An industrial ventilation system keeps things breezy to a soundtrack of '70s alternative music. One of Amsterdam's best kept secrets.

O'Reilly's

Paleisstraat 103-5 (624 9498). Tram 1, 2, 5, 13, 17, 20. **Open** 10.30am-1am Mon-Thur, Sun; 10.30am-3am Fri, Sat. **No credit cards. Map** p306 C3.

A massive and massively popular Oirish bar. The location makes it a great meeting place, but the place otherwise has little else to recommend it.

Smits Koffiehuis

Stationsplein 10 (623 3777). Tram 1, 2, 4, 5, 9, 13, 16, 17, 20, 24, 25/Metro Centraal Station. **Open** *Café* 9am-9pm Mon-Sat; 10am-9pm Sun. *Kitchen* 11am-8.30pm daily. **Credit** AmEx, DC, MC, V. **Map** p306 D1.

If you have some time to kill around Centraal Station, this vintage tearoom, though a little over-priced, is nicer than most places in the area. The waterside terrace is fine, and the light lunches are serviceable enough.

The Old Side & the Red Light District

De Brakke Grond

Nes 43 (626 0044). Tram 4, 9, 16, 20, 24, 25. **Open** 11am-1am daily. **Credit** AmEx, DC, MC, V. **Map** p306 D3.

Part of the Flemish Cultural Centre, De Brakke Grond has over 20 different kinds of Belgian beer that are slugged back by connoisseurs and laymen alike. There's a fine à la carte restaurant upstairs.

De Buurvrouw

St Pieterpoortsteeg 29 (625 9654). Tram 4, 9, 14, 16, 20, 24, 25. **Open** 8pm-2am Mon-Thur, Sun; 8pm-3am Fri, Sat. **No credit cards. Map** p306 D3.

De Buurvrouw has quietened down considerably in recent years, but remains lively, alternative and popular. A sawdust strewn floor, quirky art – including a figure of de Buurvrouw, 'the woman neighbour' who watches over proceedings below – and a pool table help give the place its atmosphere.

Don't be dictated to by the waiters when you commie to **Café Cuba**. *See p123*.

Café Cuba

Nieuwmarkt 3 (627 4919). Tram 4, 9, 14, 16, 20, 24, 25/Metro Nieuwmarkt. **Open** noon-1am daily. **No credit cards. Map** p306 D2.
Café Cuba is one of the most beautiful cafés on this square. Large and spacious with plenty of snug seating, it's decorated tastefully in a Cuban style: posters of Che Guevara hang next to old black and white photos. Live DJs play occasionally at weekends, it serves wicked Mojito cocktails, and there's a pool table in the 'chill out space' at the back (where you can spliff up). Hemingway would have loved it.

Engelbewaarder

Kloveniersburgwal 59 (625 3772). Tram 4, 9, 14, 16, 20, 24, 25/Metro Nieuwmarkt. **Open** noon-1am Mon-Sat; 2pm-1am Sun. **No credit cards. Map** p306 D3.
Though it has less of a literary bent these days, Engelbewaarder is still popular with quasi-academics and beer-lovers enjoying the fine brews. Others simply admire the views from the huge picture windows. Live jazz brightens up Sunday afternoons.

Café Fonteyn

Nieuwmarkt 13-15 (422 3599). Tram 4, 9, 14, 16, 20, 24, 25/Metro Nieuwmarkt. **Open** 9.30am-1am Mon-Thur, Sun; 9.30am-3am Fri, Sat. **No credit cards. Map** p306 D2.
Something of a home-from-home, the 'Fountain' is perpetually popular for its warm drawing-room feel, and is a good place for breakfasts, light snacks and cosy conversations.

De Hoogte

Nieuwe Hoogstraat 2A (626 0604). Tram 4, 9, 14, 16, 20, 24, 25/Metro Nieuwmarkt. **Open** 10am-1am Mon-Thur; 10am-3am Fri, Sat; noon-1am Sun. **No credit cards. Map** p307 E3.
A small but characterful drinking joint close to the Red Light District, catering to an alternative, hippyish crowd. Drinks are inexpensive compared to most hangouts in the neighbourhood, and the bar is especially popular in the afternoons as a haven from the hustle and bustle of the tourist trap that is Nieuwe Hoogstraat.

In't Aepjen

Zeedijk 1 (626 8401). Tram 4, 9, 14, 16, 20, 24, 25. **Open** 3pm-1am daily. **No credit cards. Map** p306 D2.
Located in one of the oldest remaining wooden houses in Amsterdam, this is a terrific bar. The name – 'In the Monkeys' – comes from the days when the Zeedijk was frequented by sailors: those who couldn't pay their bills would bring back a monkey from the Dutch East Indies. An accordionist plays sea shanties and old Amsterdam songs on Saturdays. *See also p28 and p42.*

Kapitein Zeppo's

Gebed Zonder End 5 (624 2057). Tram 4, 9, 14, 16, 20, 24, 25. **Open** 11am-1am Mon-Thur, Sun; 11am-2am Fri, Sat. **Credit** AmEx, MC, V. **Map** p306 D3.

Use your head

Visitors to Amsterdam are apt to whine about the 'two-fingers' of head that comes with every glass of lager. Well, quit it. No one is trying to rip you off: this is just the way things are done here. And hell, doesn't it look pretty? The Dutch think so: they even regard it as a 'crown'.

However, the reasons behind the crown are more than merely aesthetic. By letting a head form during tapping, some of the beer's carbon dioxide is released. This has the dual effect of freeing up the beer's aroma – connoisseurs know that the head is the best element with which to evaluate the hop-bitterness of a beer – and minimising the client's gas intake (which, in turn, leaves room for more beer). And if the head remains semi-stable for three to four minutes, the consumer can also not only surmise that the beer has been properly brewed and not watered down, but that the glass is clean and free from such froth-busters as fat, soap, milk and other impurities. Such reassurances can only act to amplify your appreciation.

And if one takes the fact that the head is 30 per cent beer anyway, the 'wastage' only comes out to about a thumb's worth. Unless, of course, you have a moustache, which research by Guinness has recently shown to be the true villain when it comes to beer loss. But the biggest advantage of the Dutch head? If a cigarette butt drops in your beer, just spoon it off the froth and take a big quaff...

Used for storing horse-carriages in the 17th and 18th centuries, and as a cigar factory at the turn of the 19th century, the student bar Kapitein Zeppo's – named after a Belgian TV star from the '60s – has retained an olde worlde feel. There's a charming restaurant in the conservatory area.

Lime

Zeedijk 104 (639 3020). Tram 4, 9, 14, 16, 20, 24, 25/Metro Nieuwmarkt. **Open** 5pm-1am Tue-Thur; 5pm-3am Fri; noon-3am Sat; noon-1am Sun; closed Mon. **No credit cards. Map** p306 D2.
A minimalist New York-style café-bar – with the emphasis on 'café' – Lime is perhaps the trendiest bar in the area. However, it's also a surprisingly unpretentious place; in fact, it almost feels like you could be in someone's home. 'Designer' sandwiches, soup and delicious apple pie are served from the open kitchen, and all the usual spirits and beers are present and correct.

WELCOME TO HOTEL ARENA, A GLOBALVILLAGE. DISCOVER, EXPERIENCE & FEEL AT HOME.

restaurant club**arena** hotel**arena** café garden

HOTEL
arena

The marvellous **Maximiliaan**.

Lokaal 't Loosje

Nieuwmarkt 32-4 (627 2635). Tram 4, 9, 14, 16, 20, 24, 25/Metro Nieuwmarkt. **Open** 9.30am-1am Mon-Thur, Sun; 9.30am-2am Fri, Sat. **No credit cards. Map** p306 D2.
Market traders, locals, artists and writers all convene here at this typically Dutch brown café that was formerly a waiting room from the days when trams used to run around the Nieuwmarkt.

Maximiliaan

Kloveniersburgwal 6-8 (624 2778). Tram 4, 9, 14, 16, 20, 24, 25. **Open** 3pm-1am Tue, Wed, Sun; noon-2am Thur; closed Mon. **Credit** AmEx, DC, MC, V. **Map** p306 D3.
In 1544, at this former cloister, nuns began producing beer as the drinking water was so bad. Almost 450 years later, Maximiliaan opened to carry on this worthy tradition. It produces ten different types, and taps on the bar run directly from huge copper vats.

In de Olofspoort

Nieuwebrugsteeg 13 (624 3918). Tram 4, 9, 14, 16, 20, 24, 25. **Open** 5pm-1am Tue-Thur; 5pm-2am Fri, Sat; closed Mon. **No credit cards. Map** p306 D2.
Jenevers and liqueurs from Oud Amsterdam can be found at In de Olofspoort, a renaissance-type building dating from the 17th century. Worth a look if you fancy developing a taste for the hard stuff.

The Tara

Rokin 89 (421 2654). Tram 4, 9, 14, 16, 20, 24, 25. **Open** 11am-1am Mon-Thur, Sun; 11am-3am Fri, Sat. **Credit** AmEx, DC, MC, V. **Map** p306 D3.
This large yet cosy Irish bar has three bars, two pool tables and a couple of log fires. DJs play at weekends, there's regular live music, and TVs – mainly screening football – remain unobtrusive to the non-fan. Spliffers are welcome.

Tisfris

St Antoniesbreestraat 142 (622 0472). Tram 9, 14, 20/Metro Nieuwmarkt. **Open** 9am-6pm Mon, Sun; 9am-7pm (9am-8pm in summer) Tue-Sat. **No credit cards. Map** p307 E3.
A bright, modern, trendy but undaunting split-level café popular with a largely young and arty clientele. It's *the* place for healthy breakfasts and lunches (quiches, salads, soups and so on) in the area, and is handily located by Waterlooplein. The music selection is up-to-date, and DJs play from time to time.

't Tuinfeest

Gelderskade 109 (620 8864). Tram 4, 9, 14, 16, 20, 24, 25/Metro Nieuwmarkt. **Open** 3pm-1am Mon-Thur, Sun; 3pm-3am Fri, Sat. **Credit** AmEx, DC, MC, V. **Map** p306 D2.
This warm, split-level corner café serves delicious, well-presented food at reasonable prices. Music is loud but not intrusive, and the place attracts a young crowd. Unfortunately, its popularity means that at night, it can be hard to get a table. On Fridays, the 'Garden Party' gets going with DJs and cheap drinks.

Van Kerkwijk

Nes 41 (620 3316). Tram 4, 9, 14, 16, 20, 24, 25. **Open** 11am-1am Mon-Thur, Sun; 11am-3am Fri, Sat. **No credit cards. Map** p306 D3.
Formerly Amsterdam's 'wine café', Van Kerkwijk still attracts those with discerning taste. The atmosphere is warm and welcoming, from the surroundings down to the staff and the friendly cat at the bar. Meals, served all day, are delicious and varied.

VOC Café

Schreierstoren, Prins Hendrikkade 94 (428 8291). Tram 4, 9, 14, 16, 20, 24, 25. **Open** 10am-1am Mon-Thur; 10am-3am Fri, Sat; noon-8pm Sun. **No credit cards. Map** p306 D2.
Housed in the city's oldest defence tower (*see p28 and p42*), the VOC Café is a cosy bar with two terraces overlooking Gelderskade. There's regular live music (often from an accordionist), and a good range of *jenevers* and liqueurs: try its own De Zeedijker Schoot An variety, brewed to an old VOC recipe.

In de Waag

Nieuwmarkt (422 7772/www.indewaag.nl). Tram 4, 9, 14, 16, 20, 24, 25/Metro Nieuwmarkt. **Open** 10am-1am daily. **Credit** AmEx, DC, MC, V. **Map** p306 D2.
The building can seem imposing, but walk through the doors of this former weighhouse, originally one of the gates to the old city, and you'll be transported back in time. There's no music here, and candles – a huge circular candelabra hangs from the ceiling – are the only lighting. The sole reminders of 20th-century culture are the (free) Internet facilities. There's also a restaurant here. *See also p29.*

Drink and dine at **Van Kerkwijk**.

Consumer

The New Side

Absinthe Night Bar
Nieuwezijds Voorburgwal 171 (777 4870).
Tram 1, 2, 5. **Open** 8am-3am daily. **No credit
cards. Map** p306 D3.
A thoroughly peculiar little hideaway down on
Nieuwezijds Voorburgwal, offering everyone's
favourite wormwood-infused liquid hallucinogenic.
It's done out like an elf's grotto, which only increas-
es the headfuck quotient.

De Beiaard
Spui 30 (622 5110). Tram 16, 24, 25. **Open** *Mid Apr-
mid Oct* 11am-1am Mon-Thur, Sun; 11am-2am Fri, Sat.
Mid Oct-mid Apr noon-1am Mon-Thur, Sun; noon-2am
Fri, Sat. **Credit** AmEx, MC, V. **Map** p310 D4.

A pleasant enough spot made considerably more
notable by the conservatory at the back: it offers the
perfect sun trap from which to look out over the
canal and watch strollers and cyclists narrowly
missing trams and racing taxis as they navigate the
Singel junction. Marvellous in summer, and not bad
the rest of the time, either.

Bep
*Nieuwezijds Voorburgwal 260 (626 5649). Tram 1,
2, 5.* **Open** noon-1am Mon-Thur, Sun; noon-3am Fri,
Sat. **No credit cards. Map** p306 D3.
A painfully fashionable New Side hangout that sits
very nicely with its similarly cool neighbours **Diep**
and the **Seymour Likely Lounge** (for both, *see
p127*). Go there to be seen, sure, but don't miss the
terrific bar food.

Tasting room only

Once upon a time – around 1650, for the
sake of argument – a doctor in Leiden came
up with the alchemy that allowed juniper
berries to be infused into distilled spirits. The
result was gin; or, rather, *jenever*, as the
Dutch version is called. Less than half a
century later, the Dutch were exporting about
ten million gallons of what was supposed to
be an innocent cure for stomach and kidney
ailments. But like all good inventions, it could
also multitask as a 'blow to the head' (aka
kopstoot) when served with a glass of beer.

Though the basic recipe was swiped by
Gordon's and the like, the Dutch continued to
innovate not only by grading it by age – *jong*,
oud and *zeer oud* ('young', 'old' and
'positively ancient') – but also by adding
various herbs, spices and flavours.
Amsterdam soon was overrun with distilleries
and *proeflokalen* ('tasting houses') where
folks could sample, for free, speciality
distillates – including such evocatively titled
liqueurs as 'Parrot Soup', 'Prunes Prick In'
and 'Assurance for Bitter Suffering' – before
deciding which bottles they wanted to
brownbag and take home.

Thankfully, there are several *proeflokalen* in
the city that have not yet surrendered to
tourism or the dispensing of nouveau cuisine.
However, you will have to pay and, in line with
tradition, remain standing: in days of yore,
proprietors did not want to promote leisure
when dispensing freebies. **Het Proeflokaal
Wynand Fockink** (pronounced as a
Mancunian lad would say 'fucking') is
probably the most charming. **De Ooivaar** is
notable for maintaining a sense of the

'freebie' by passing around plates of cheese
and raw cow. **De Admiraal**, though a tad
dense with yuppie types, does provide
seating in the form of couches carved out of
barrels (two large barrels in the back even
hide the toilets). And while not an official
proeflokaal, **Slijterij Tapperij Oosterling** has
an olde worlde vibe, with barrels as tables
and the fourth generation of the same family
behind the bar. The 'slijterij', incidentally,
denotes it as an off-licence: for a well-
rounded Dutch experience, score some
jenever, head to the hotel and experiment
with the making of a perfect neder-martini.

De Admiraal
*Herengracht 319, Grachtengordel: West
(625 4334). Tram 1, 2, 5.* **Open** 4.30-11pm
Mon-Sat; closed Sun. **Credit** AmEx, MC, V.
Map p310 C4.

De Ooivaar
*Sint Olofspoort 1, Old Centre: Old Side (420
8004). Tram 4, 9, 16, 20, 24, 25.* **Open**
11am-midnight Mon-Thur, Sun; 11am-2am
Fri, Sat. **No credit cards. Map** p310 D2.

Het Proeflokaal Wynand Fockink
*Pijlsteeg 31, Old Centre: Old Side (639
2695/www.wynand-fockink.nl). Tram 4, 9,
16, 20, 24, 25.* **Open** 3-9pm daily. **No credit
cards. Map** p306 D3.

Slijterij Tapperij Oosterling
*Utrechtsestraat 140, Grachtengordel: West
(623 4140). Tram 4, 9, 20.* **Open** noon-1am
Mon-Sat; 1pm-1am Sun (summer 1-8pm
Sun). **Credit** V. **Map** p311 E4.

Surf as you sup at the **Internet Café**.

The mezzanine and the funky green spotlighting make this a mellow place from which to spin emails round the world. Drinks are compulsory, but beware of seemingly oh-so-courteous refills by bar staff pushing a point. It's ƒ2,50 for 20 minutes of Internet use.

Café Luxembourg
Spui 22 (620 6264). Tram 16, 24, 25. **Open** 9am-1am Mon-Thur, Sun; 9am-2am Fri, Sat. **Credit** DC, MC, V. **Map** p310 D4.
Ignore the aloof service and just enjoy the people-watching here, making sure to chuckle at the model-wannabes and the bespoke suits swollen with self-importance. A survivor of a bygone era, with white-aproned waiters and high-ceilinged interiors, Luxembourg has a well-placed terrace for people who need to see and be seen. Afternoons are best.

Ovidius
Spuistraat 139 (620 8977). Tram 4, 9, 14, 16, 20, 24, 25. **Open** 9.30am-9pm Mon-Wed, Fri; 9.30am-11pm Thur; 10am-9pm Sat, Sun. **Credit** AmEx, MC, V. **Map** p306 C2.
This Greek-owned café draws a cosmopolitan crowd. The sandwiches are tasty, and things get busy at lunchtime. Shame about the music.

Café Het Schuim
Spuistraat 189 (638 9357). Tram 13, 14, 17, 20. **Open** 11am-1am Mon-Thur, Sun; 11am-3am Fri, Sat. **No credit cards. Map** p306 C2.
Low, comfy jelly mould-shaped chairs enhance the relaxing atmosphere at this un-signposted café, and the juxtaposition of styles entertains all-comers: a glitzy chandelier hangs by a big glitterball. Chilled music makes it a dreamy hangout on a rainy day.

Seymour Likely Lounge
Nieuwezijds Voorburgwal 250 (627 1427). Tram 1, 2, 5. **Open** 8pm-3am Mon-Thur, Sun; 8pm-4am Fri, Sat. **No credit cards. Map** p306 D3.
Seymour's has held on to its hip reputation for longer than it cares to remember. DJs provide a soundtrack for the regulars, who are noticeably more chilled and approachable than in the past.

De Still
Spuistraat 326 (620 1349). Tram 4, 9, 14, 16, 20, 24, 25. **Open** 3.30pm-1am Mon-Thur; 1pm-3am Fri, Sat; 1pm-1am Sun. **No credit cards. Map** p306 D3.
De Still's selling point is its giant range of whiskies: around 450 in total. Arrange your own tastings at the bar at a price of ƒ45 for a selection of six (minimum two people), or attend a distillery-run slide show.

In De Wildeman
Kolksteeg 3, near Nieuwezijds Kolk (638 2348). Tram 1, 2, 5, 13, 17, 20. **Open** noon-1am Mon-Thur; noon-2am Fri, Sat; 2-9pm Sun. **No credit cards. Map** p306 D2.
A real respite from coffeeshops and chrome-filled interiors. The main bar offers around 200 bottled brews from around the world and around 18 draughts: head here when you've quenched your thirst for Dutch and Belgian brews and fancy an old favourite from home.

Café Dante
Spuistraat 320 (638 8839). Tram 4, 9, 14, 16, 20, 24, 25. **Open** 11am-1am Mon-Thur, Sun; 11am-3am Fri, Sat. **Credit** AmEx, DC, MC, V. **Map** p306 D3.
The bright, sunny, yellow-tinted lighting makes this a spirit-lifting place, even when it's raining. The balcony above hosts a gallery (open office hours and closed Mondays). The Mediterranean light and long list of wines and beers make this charming café an ideal spot in which to idle away the afternoon.

Diep
Nieuwezijds Voorburgwal 256 (420 2020). Tram 1, 2, 5. **Open** 5pm-1am Mon-Thur, Sun; 5pm-3am Fri, Sat. **No credit cards. Map** p306 D3.
Though Diep doesn't quite offer something for everyone, its brown café-meets-opulent disco palace interior should ring a few bells with anyone who likes their bar decor eclectic. DJs play now and then.

La Fruteria
Nieuwezijds Voorburgwal 141 (opposite the Magna Plaza) (no phone). Tram 1, 2, 5, 13, 17, 20. **Open** 10am-6pm Mon-Wed; 10am-7pm Thur; 10am-6pm Fri, Sat; 11am-6pm Sun. **No credit cards. Map** p306 C2.
Choose from milk, yoghurt and non-dairy shakes (from ƒ3) with an added option of honey at this splendid spot. The combos of melon, pineapple, kiwi, banana and mango are drool-inspiring.

Hoppe
Spui 18-20 (420 4420). Tram 1, 2, 5. **Open** 8am-1am Mon-Thur, Sun; 8am-2am Fri, Sat. **Credit** AmEx, DC, MC, V. **Map** p310 D4.
This brown café (serving since 1670) is always popular, though the left-hand entrance leads to the more easygoing and cheerful of the two bars. Old pews as seats and barrels stacked up behind the bar provide a refreshing change from the chrome fittings or generic tawdriness in most New Side haunts.

Internet Café
Martelaarsgracht 11 (627 1052). Tram 4, 9, 16, 20, 24, 25. **Open** 9am-1am daily. **No credit cards. Map** p306 D2.

Consumer

Around Waterlooplein

Dantzig
*Zwanenburgwal 15 (620 9039). Tram 9, 14,
20/Metro Waterlooplein.* **Open** 9am-1am Mon-Fri;
9am-2am Sat; 9am-midnight Sun. *Kitchen* 11am-
10pm daily. **No credit cards**. **Map** p307 E3.
Chandeliers, jazz, a panoramic view of the Amstel
and a terrace in summer make this spacious café-
restaurant an excellent place in which to recuperate
after a day at the adjacent Waterlooplein market.

De Jaren
*Nieuwe Doelenstraat 20-2 (625 5771). Tram 4, 9,
14, 16, 20, 24, 25.* **Open** 10am-1am Mon-Thur, Sun;
10am-2am Fri, Sat. *Kitchen* 5.30-10.30pm daily. **No
credit cards**. **Map** p306 D3.
Located in a beautifully restored building with soaring ceilings, exposed brickwork and warm yellow
lighting, this grand café has an unimpeachable selection of eau-de-vie and other liquors. The waterside
terrace in the back is the place to be in summer.

Café de Sluyswacht
*Jodenbreestraat 1 (625 7611). Tram 9, 14, 20/Metro
Waterlooplein.* **Open** 11.30am-1am Mon-Thur;
11.30am-3am Fri, Sat; 11.30am-7pm Sun. **No credit
cards**. **Map** p307 E3.
Situated just across from the **Rembrandthuis** (*see
p50*), this former lock-keeper's house, built in 1695,
has retained much of its original charm, as well as
its foundations: the building leans heavily. The spacious terrace, overlooking Oude Schans, is one of the
most peaceful settings in Amsterdam.

The Plantage & the Oost

Brouwerij t'IJ
Funenkade 7 (622 8325). Tram 6, 10. **Open** 3-8pm
Wed-Sun; closed Mon, Tue. **No credit cards**.
An excellent local brewery and bar based in a wind-
mill and infested with yuppies from the nearby
condo tower developments. Tours can be arranged.

De Druif
Rapenburgerplein 83 (624 4530). Tram 7, 20. **Open**
11am-1am Mon-Thur, Sun; 11am-3am Fri, Sat. **No
credit cards**. **Map** p307 E2.
A neighbourhood brown bar of immense charm
right on the water's edge, a short walk from the old
harbour. If you make it over here, you'll be the only
non-local, but they're a friendly, if noisy, bunch.

East of Eden
Linnaeusstraat 11 (665 0743). Tram 6, 9, 10, 14.
Open 11am-1am Mon-Fri; 11am-2am Sat, Sun. **No
credit cards**. **Map** p312 H3.
One of the few stylish, youthful bars in a rapidly
gentrifying workaday neighbourhood across from
the **Tropenmuseum** (*see p54*), the spacious East
of Eden is a good place in which to sit and read or
write over a restorative coffee or Pils. Ceiling fans
and archways help extend the sense of escapism.

Now't but the hard stuff at De Still.
See p127.

Eik & Linde
*Plantage Middenlaan 22 (622 5716). Tram 7, 9, 14,
20.* **Open** 11am-1am Mon-Fri; 11am-2am Sat; 2pm-
2am Sun. **Map** p307 F3.
An old-fashioned, tourist-free neighbourhood bar.
Local memorabilia on the walls, including old photographs and posters from radio shows held on the
premises, give it historical appeal; low prices and a
laid-back air make it user-friendly.

The Grachtengordel

Grachtengordel: West

Aas van Bokalen
Keizersgracht 335 (623 0917). Tram 1, 2, 5. **Open**
5pm-1am daily. **No credit cards**. **Map** p310 C4.
A friendly, unpretentious brown café with good
value food and varied, though often young, clientele.

Felix Meritis
Keizersgracht 324 (623 1311). Tram 13, 14, 17, 20.
Open 9am-7pm (during performances 9am-9pm or
later) daily. **No credit cards**. **Map** p310 C4.
The clientele at this open, high-ceilinged room – part
of the theatre, for which *see p239* – varies according to performance. There is also a restaurant, where
you can eat prior to the show.

Café de Gevulde Koe
Marnixstraat 381 (625 4482). Tram 10, 17. **Open**
4pm-1am Mon-Thur, Sun; 4pm-3am Fri, Sat. **Credit**
AmEx, DC, MC, V. **Map** p305 B2.
The pool table has, sadly, been removed, though
there is now a dartboard for gamers. The awning
over the bar is regularly repainted, often themed
with the café's name ('cow'). The downstairs eaterie
serves good food at reasonable prices.

Greenwoods
Singel 103 (623 7071). Tram 1, 2, 5. **Open** 9.30am-
7pm daily. **No credit cards**. **Map** p306 C3.
The slow service means this is hardly a fast food
place, but everything here is freshly prepared, so we
can forgive them: the cakes, scones and muffins are
baked daily on the premises. Try the cheesecake.

Lanskroon

Singel 385 (623 7743). Tram 1, 2, 5. **Open** 8am-5.30pm Tue-Fri; 8am-5pm Sat, Sun; closed Mon. **No credit cards. Map** p310 D4.

The best *banketbakkerij* (pâtisserie) in town? It's a brave man or woman who disagrees. The mouth-watering sacher torte, cakes, savouries, ice-creams and chocolates can be wolfed down in the cramped tearoom or bought as takeaway.

Het Molenpad

Prinsengracht 653 (625 9680). Tram 7, 10, 20. **Open** noon-1am Mon-Thur, Sun; noon-2am Fri, Sat. **No credit cards. Map** p310 C4.

Mellow music wafts through the cigarette smoke at this hangout, as literary types stroll past towards the library a few doors up. Charming staff serve delicious lunches and dinners, and artists' exhibits change monthly.

Pompadour

Huidenstraat 12 (623 9554). Tram 1, 2, 5. **Open** 9.30am-5.45pm Tue-Fri; 9am-5.30pm Sat; closed Mon, Sun. **Credit** MC, V. **Map** p310 C4.

The cakes are ace, but it's the chocolates for which Pompadour is most famous, and justifiably so. You can take your purchases away, but stop to enjoy a bite in the remarkable gilt-and-mirrors interior of the raised tearoom.

De Prins

Prinsengracht 124 (624 9382). Tram 13, 14, 17, 20. **Open** 10am-1am Mon-Thur, Sun; 10am-2am Fri, Sat. **Credit** AmEx, MC, V. **Map** p306 C3.

Friendly and frequented by students, brown café De Prins is a great meeting place. The food is as good as the canalside setting.

Twee Prinsen

Prinsenstraat 27 (624 9722). Tram 3, 10. **Open** 10am-1am Mon-Thur, Sun; 10am-3am Fri, Sat. **No credit cards. Map** p306 C2.

Tweedledum to the Tweedledee of the **Vergulde Gaper** opposite (*see below*). There's a good range of beers here, and the clientele is nicely mixed. The outdoor terrace is heated on chillier evenings.

Van Puffelen

Prinsengracht 377 (624 6270). Tram 1, 2, 5, 7, 10. **Credit** AmEx, DC, MC, V. **Map** p306 C3.

The biggest brown café in Amsterdam and a haunt of the beautiful people, particularly on summer evenings when you can sit on the barge moored outside. There's live jazz on Sundays.

Vergulde Gaper

Prinsenstraat 30 (624 8975). Tram 3, 10. **Open** 10am-1am Mon-Thur, Sun; 10am-3am Fri, Sat. **No credit cards. Map** p306 C2.

A slightly more upmarket and larger version of the **Twee Prinsen** (*see above*), Vergulde Gaper has an excellent selection of drinks, plus some sofas on which to snuggle up on a cold winter's evening.

De Zotte

Raamstraat 29 (626 8694). Tram 1, 2, 5. **Open** 4pm-1am Mon-Thur, Sun; 4pm-3am Fri, Sat. **Credit** AmEx, DC, MC, V. **Map** p310 C4.

De Zotte hums with noisy chatter. Cinema seats line one wall, and the giant selection of beers attracts a lot of samplers. The recently revamped kitchen has shot attendance through the roof: book a table or be deeply disappointed. You'll want to make it your local after just one night. Incomparably *gezelligheid*.

Consumer

The leaning **Café de Sluyswacht** proves disorienting for drunks. *See p128.*

Grachtengordel: East

Café Kalvertoren
Singel 457 (427 3901). Tram 1, 2, 4, 5, 9, 14, 16, 20, 24, 25. **Open** 9am-7pm Mon-Wed, Fri; 9am-9pm Thur; noon-6pm Sat, Sun. **Credit** (above *f*40) AmEx, MC, V. **Map** p310 D4.
A so-so café at the top of the Kalvertoren shopping centre, meriting a mention here purely for its spectacular vistas. Bring plenty of cash, sure, but don't forget your camera, either.

Land van Walem
Keizersgracht 449 (625 3544). Tram 1, 2, 5. **Open** 10am-1am daily. **Credit** AmEx, DC, MC, V. **Map** p310 D4.
One of the first designer bars, this long, narrow and bright filling station is currently being revamped. The food comes in good portions, with excellent vegetarian options.

Metz
Keizersgracht 455 (520 7020). Tram 1, 2, 5. **Open** 9.30am-5.30pm Mon-Sat; noon-5pm Sun. **Credit** AmEx, DC, MC, V. **Map** p310 D4.
The famous department store's café, with a fine lunch-style menu and an even better view over Amsterdam from the sixth floor.

Morlang
Keizersgracht 451 (625 2681). Tram 1, 2, 5. **Open** 10am-1am Mon-Thur, Sun; 10am-2am Fri, Sat. **Credit** AmEx, MC, V. **Map** p310 D4.
Morlang lacks the bright designer looks of **Land van Walem** (*see above*) next door, but it's still a pretty stylish hangout. The food here is good, and the selection of foreign spirits awesome.

Around Leidseplein

De Balie
Kleine Gartmanplantsoen 10 (553 5130/restaurant 553 5131/www.balie.nl). Tram 1, 2, 5, 6, 7, 10. **Open** 11am-1am Mon-Thur, Sun; 11am-2am Fri, Sat. **No credit cards. Map** p310 D5.
The café serving the cultural and political centre of the same name is big and open, crowded with artsy types and the politically involved. Treat yourself to a *koffie verkeerd* (café latte), and check out the elevated view across Leidseplein.

Boom Chicago Lounge
Leidseplein 12 (530 7300/www.boomchicago.nl). Tram 6, 7, 10. **Open** 11am-1am Mon-Thur, Sun; 11am-3am Fri, Sat. **Credit** AmEx, MC, V. **Map** p310 D5.
Stand-up fans pause for a drink at Boom Chicago's bar before adjourning to the theatre out back (*see p238*). The pre-theatre dinner is popular, but you can't go wrong with the pitchers of beer.

Comedy Café
Max Euweplein 43 (620 9164/www.comedycafe.nl). Tram 1, 2, 5, 6, 7, 10, 20. **Open** 9am-1am Mon-Thur, Sun; 9am-3am Fri, Sat; phone for performance times. **Credit** AmEx, DC, MC, V. **Map** p310 D5.
By day, the big windows looking over Singelgracht make the Comedy Café spacious and airy, a complete contrast to the many dark bar interiors in the area. By night, the hilarity kicks in with various comedy shows (*see p238*).

Café Cox
Marnixstraat 429 (620 7222). Tram 10, 17. **Open** 10am-10.30pm Mon-Wed, Sun; 10am-1am Thur-Sat. *Kitchen* 10am-10.30pm daily. **Credit** AmEx, DC, MC, V. **Map** p305 B3.

Get gone with the wind at the **Brouwerij t'IJ**. See p128.

The **Comedy Café** (*see p130*). Har har.

Slightly fragmented by a split level bar, Café Cox is nonetheless pleasant and serves palatable food at reasonable prices. As the café is located in the same building as the city theatre, the **Stadsschouwburg** (*see p240*), it encourages a theatrical crowd, especially in the evenings. Posters advertising forthcoming arts events sprawl across the walls.

Grand Café Raffle's
Kleine Gartmanplantsoen 5 (638 7220). Tram 1, 2, 5, 6, 7, 10. **Open** 9am-1am Mon-Thur, Sun; 9am-3am Fri, Sat. **Credit** AmEx, MC, V. **Map** p310 D5.
The luxurious drapes of the interior, graced with plants and swathes of mosquito netting, give this bar a sumptuously neo-colonial feel. The service is snappy and cheerful, though its grand café attributes mean drinks are a little pricier than usual.

De Tap
Prinsengracht 458 (622 9915). Tram 7, 10, 20. **Open** 4pm-1am Mon-Thur; 4pm-3am Fri; 1pm-3am Sat; 2pm-1am Sun. **No credit cards**.
De Tap is quite a long, dark bar that's sleepy during the day but picks up at night. There's a pleasant ambience, and a good range of snacks on offer.

Around Rembrandtplein

De Duivel
Reguliersdwarsstraat 87 (626 6184/www.deduivel.nl). Tram 4, 9, 14, 20. **Open** 8pm-3am Mon-Thur, Sun; 8pm-4am Fri, Sat. **No credit cards**. **Map** p311 E4.
De Duivel offers something other than the steady diet of Marley that pervades the horrendously tacky coffeeshops nearby. Hip hop is the thing here, with live DJs cuttin' it up on the wheels of steel nightly.

De Kroon
Rembrandtplein 17 (625 2011). Tram 4, 9, 14, 20. **Open** 10am-1am Mon-Thur, Sun; 10am-2am Fri, Sat. *Kitchen* 10am-10pm daily. **No credit cards**. **Map** p311 E4.

Several local TV companies and radio stations are housed in the same building as De Kroon, hence the proliferation of ties and loudmouths here. The high-ceilinged, spacious second-storey room looks down on a square full of daytrippers and tourists.

Mulligans
Amstel 100 (622 1330). Tram 4, 9, 14, 16, 20, 24, 25. **Open** 4pm-1am Mon-Thur; 4pm-3am Fri; 2pm-3am Sat; 2pm-1am Sun. **No credit cards**. **Map** p307 E3.
Yet another theme bar, but this one is more Irish than Oirish. The beer and the craic are both good, and there's a fine programme of Irish music that runs several times a week. The pick of the pack.

L'Opera
Rembrandtplein 27-9 (627 5232). Tram 4, 9, 14, 20. **Open** 10am-1am Mon-Thur, Sun; 10am-2am Fri, Sat. *Kitchen* 11am-10pm daily. **Credit** AmEx, DC, MC, V. **Map** p311 E4.
This grand café features candle lamps, deco fixtures and all the bustle and anonymity of a tourist trap. One of a slew of mammoth, overpriced places on Rembrandtplein, L'Opera serves coffee, booze and indifferent food, and usually has a free table. You could do worse.

Schiller
Rembrandtplein 26 (624 9846). Tram 4, 9, 14, 20. **Open** 4pm-1am Mon-Thur, Sun; 4pm-2am Fri, Sat (opens at 2pm in winter). *Kitchen* 5.30-10pm daily. **Credit** AmEx, DC, MC, V. **Map** p311 E4.
An absolute godsend for anyone feeling like a fish out of water amid Rembrandtplein's discotheques and crass, packed terraces, this renowned art deco café maintains a highbrowed festivity on weekends. Incidentally, Schiller belongs to the hotel of the same name (*see p89*).

't Madeliefje
Reguliersdwarsstraat 74 (622 2510). Tram 4, 9, 14, 16, 20, 24, 25. **Open** 9pm-3am Tue, Thur; 8pm-3am Wed; 9pm-4am Fri, Sat; closed Mon. **No credit cards**. **Map** p310 D4.
A real rarity, this: a smallish, trendy bar that manages to maintain a relaxed atmosphere in the middle of what is a frenzied nightlife district. The music usually ranges from '70s R&B to classic soul, and the Wednesday salsa night is popular. Try one of the shooters.

The Jordaan

Du Lac
Haarlemmerstraat 118 (624 4265). Bus 18, 22. **Open** 4pm-1am Mon-Thur, Sun; 4pm-3am Fri, Sat. **No credit cards**. **Map** p306 C2.
A wildly over-the-top grand café fitted out in an outrageously surrealistic deco style (stuffed alligators, mutant trees and more besides). It packs in trendies by the hundred, each of whom has a favourite spot in either the cosy snugs, the raised gallery or the glass-walled conservatory.

Consumer

Finch

Noordermarkt 5 (626 2461). Tram 1, 2, 5, 13, 17, 20. **Open** 6pm-1am Mon; 11am-1am Tue-Thur; 11am-3am Fri; 9am-3am Sat; 11am-1am Sun. **No credit cards. Map** p305 B2.

Located in one of the city's more scenic squares, Finch attracts the hip and artistic to its vaguely *Wallpaper**-like interior, happily muted by the inclusion of a carefree vibe. Excellent eats, grooving tunes and charming staff make it a top hangout.

Katte in 't Wijngaert

Lindengracht 160 (622 4554). Tram 1, 2, 5, 13, 17, 20. **Open** 10am-1am Mon-Thur, Sun; 10am-3pm Fri, Sat. **No credit cards. Map** p305 B2.

From the 'Cat in the Vinyard', you can spy the spot of the Eel Riot (*see p62*). It's a true neighbourhood café that evokes a truer image of the spirit of the Jordaan than even **Café Nol** (*see below*), with a clientele that represents every walk of life. Purrrfect.

't Monumentje

Westerstraat 120 (624 3541). Tram 13, 14, 17, 20. **Open** 8.30am-1am Mon-Thur; 8.30am-3am Fri, Sat; 11am-1am Sun. **No credit cards. Map** p305 B2.

A nice, cosy brown café in the Jordaan, small but perfectly formed and with a decent range of beers. A useful refreshment stop if you're visiting the **Westermarkt** (*see p164*).

New Deli

Haarlemmerstraat 73 (626 2755). Tram 1, 2, 5, 13, 17, 20. **Open** 10am-10pm daily. **No credit cards. Map** p306 C2.

The minimal yet tightly designed New Deli is the antidote to coffeeshops and brown cafés. The airy and spartan surrounds evoke a vision of Japan, as does the culinary sandwich and salad menu, which features such ingredients as yakitori and shitake.

Café Nol

Westerstraat 109 (624 5380). Tram 10. **Open** 9pm-3am Mon-Thur, Sun; 9pm-4am Fri, Sat. **No credit cards. Map** p305 B2.

Kitsch doesn't come any more hardcore: this over-the-top Jordaan bar/institution, with red leatherette interiors and crowds of lusty-voiced locals, is supposed to sum up the true 'spirit' of the neighbourhood. Be warned: this brand of social cosiness comes with much jolly spittle flying through the air.

De Reiger

Nieuwe Leliestraat 34 (624 7426). Tram 10, 13, 14, 17, 20. **Open** 11am-1am Mon-Thur, Sun; noon-1am Fri, Sat. *Kitchen* 6-10.30pm daily. **No credit cards. Map** p305 B3.

This light and airy brown bar is one of the most popular watering holes in the Jordaan, especially with the vaguely style-conscious. Get here early, particularly if you want to eat from its much-hyped menu.

SAS

Marnixstraat 79 (420 4075). Tram 7, 10, 17, 20. **Open** 2pm-1am Mon-Thur, Sun; 2pm-3am Fri, Sat. **No credit cards. Map** p305 B3.

Grand Café Raffle's. *See p131.*

Comfortable sofas and chairs sit among the wonderfully cluttered and intensely arty interior of this alternabar (decor changes with the owner's moods). Good, homely meals at low prices – and in large portions – are served downstairs and on the canalside terrace on Mondays and Tuesdays. Candlelit, casual and peculiarly romantic, this is a great spot.

't Smalle

Egelantiersgracht 12 (623 9617). Tram 13, 14, 17, 20. **Open** 10am-1am Mon-Thur, Sun; 10am-2am Fri, Sat. **No credit cards. Map** p305 B3.

A delightful café in the Jordaan that's friendly, pleasingly situated by a canal and lovely in summer. Park your boat, and order something cool for your throat.

Café Soundgarden

Marnixstraat 164-6 (620 2853). Tram 10, 13, 14, 17, 20. **Open** 1pm-1am Mon-Thur; 1pm-3am Fri; 3pm-3am Sat; 3pm-1am Sun. **No credit cards. Map** p305 B3.

Popular with a grungy, alternative crowd, Café Soundgarden has one of the best terraces in town, located most introspectively along a quiet stretch of canal. Pool, darts, pinball and table football are on hand to while away those rainy afternoons.

Café Tabac

Brouwersgracht 101 (622 6520). Tram 1, 2, 5, 13, 17, 20. **Open** 10am-6pm Mon; 11am-1am Tue-Thur, Sun; 11am-3am Fri; 10am-3am Sat. **No credit cards. Map** p305 B2.

Despite a change of name – it was formerly called 't Smackzeyl after its 'shipsail' gablestone – and the use of whiter shades, Tabac still evokes the vibe of a restful brown café. Modishness comes from an inventive menu and a youthful but relaxed local crowd.

Thijssen

Brouwersgracht 107 (623 8994). Tram 3. **Open** 9.30am-1am Mon-Thur, Sun; 9.30am-3am Fri, Sat. **No credit cards. Map** p306 C2.

Owned by three local barflys, Thijssen's high windows and brown and nicotine-yellow highlighted interior blend in perfectly with the more ancient neighbouring cafés. Be warned, though: it can get a tad too jockstrap-studenty in the evenings.

De Tuin

2e Tuindwarsstraat 13 (624 4559). Tram 3, 10, 13, 14, 17, 20. **Open** 10am-1am Mon-Thur; 10am-2am Fri, Sat; 11am-1am Sun. **No credit cards. Map** p305 B3.

A classic brown café frequented by slightly alternative locals, De Tuin ('The Garden') is stone-floored, dark and always lively. Excellent apple tarts are served in the afternoon, and there's always someone looking for a game of chess or backgammon.

Café West Pacific

Haarlemmerweg 8-10 (488 7778/ www.westergasfabriek.nl). Tram 10/bus 18, 22. **Open** 11.30am-1am Mon-Thur, Sun; 11.30am-2am Fri, Sat; closed Mon. *Restaurant* 6-10.30pm Tue-Sun. *Members only* after 10pm Thur-Sat. **No credit cards. Map** p305 A2.

This large alternabar has a huge fire, a dancefloor and a decent menu. A mixture of music plays, but after 11pm there's a cover charge and an emphasis on jazz-funky dance music. There's also occasional live music on Sundays. The café is part of the **Westergasfabriek** (*see p240*).

The Museum Quarter

Café Ebeling

Overtoom 52 (689 1218). Tram 1, 3, 6, 12. **Open** 11am-1am Mon-Thur, Sun; 11am-3am Fri, Sat; noon-1am Sun. **No credit cards. Map** p310 C5.

Located in an old bank – the toilets are in the safe – Ebeling is a well laid out, split-level bar that aims itself at the young and trendy without being snobby or needing to have the music so loud you can't think. It's also one of the town's very few non-Irish bars that serves Guinness.

Welling

Jan Willem Brouwerstraat 32 (662 0155). Tram 2, 3, 5, 12, 16, 20. **Open** 4pm-1am Mon-Thur; 3pm-2am Sat; 3pm-1am Sun. **No credit cards. Map** p310 D6.

Just by the Concertgebouw, the brownish Welling offers plenty of choice in the beer department. Its welcoming, relaxed atmosphere contrasts with many of the other overpriced posh spots in the area.

Born to be **Wildschut**.

The Pijp

Carel's Café

Frans Halsstraat 76 (679 4836). Tram 16, 24, 25. **Open** 10am-1am Mon-Thur; 10am-3am Fri, Sat; 11am-1am Sun. **No credit cards. Map** p311 E6.

Though Carel's is basically a large neighbourhood café, people make the special trip from all over town for its excellent lunches and dinners. While you're there, hop about to some of the other ever-evolving selection of bars on this mellow, scenic street.

Gambrinus

Ferdinand Bolstraat 180 (671 7389). Tram 16, 24, 25. **Open** 11am-1am Mon-Thur, Sun; 11.30am-2am Fri, Sat. **No credit cards. Map** p311 E6.

Listen to the crunch of salt underfoot as you enter this pleasant local brown – yet light-infused – café, popular with couples of the young urban professional variety. The snacks and dinners are tasty.

Kingfisher

Ferdinand Bolstraat 23 (671 2395). Tram 6, 7, 10. **Open** 1pm-1am Mon-Thur; 1pm-3am Fri, Sat; closed Sun. **No credit cards. Map** p311 E6.

Of the many local-ish brown cafés that actually let in fresh light and international style, the Kingfisher does the best job, balancing impeccable and neighbourly service with inventive snacks and a daily dinner special that'll take your tastebuds on a global rollercoaster ride. The archetype of the locals' local.

O'Donnells

Ferdinand Bolstraat 5 (676 7786). Tram 16, 24, 25. **Open** 11am-1am Mon-Thur, Sun; 11am-3am Fri, Sat. *Kitchen* 11am-3pm, 5.30-10pm Mon-Fri; 11am-10pm Sat, Sun. **Credit** (above *f*50) AmEx, DC, MC, V. **Map** p311 E6.

A pretty standard Irish formula bar, complete with all the usual Gaelic schtick. There's live music out front, though Brits may be more interested in Sky TV out back. For a cosier, earthier experience, head to the nearby **Dubliner** (Dusartstraat 51, 679 9743).

Wildschut

Roelof Hartplein 1-3 (676 8220). Tram 3, 5, 12, 24, 25. **Open** 10am-1am Mon-Thur, Sun; 10am-2am Fri; 10am-3am Sat. **Credit** (over *f*25) AmEx, DC, MC, V.

This cavernous joint is still one of the places to be seen in town. In summer, take a seat on the large terrace overlooking the Roelof Hartplein, a square surrounded by Amsterdam School architecture.

The Waterfront

Kanis & Meiland

Levantkade 127 (418 2439). Bus 28, 32, 59. **Open** 10am-1am Mon-Thur, Sun; 10am-3am Fri, Sat. **No credit cards.**

Situated on KNSM island (hence the name), Kanis & Meiland is in the middle of Amsterdam's redeveloping docklands. The bright and spacious café is perfect for summer, and the food terrific.

Coffeeshops

Blow by blow, the dope on the dope.

Consumer

If you ain't here for the beer or to shop 'til you drop, you find whores a bore and art a chore, then odds are you've come to partake in a little weed... Amsterdam remains the one city in the world where people can stroll into what is ostensibly a café and purchase, over the counter and in full view of everyone, substances that would lead to arrest and possible criminal charges almost everywhere else in the world.

However, even here, da 'erb is not strictly legal, merely tolerated by the authorities. Coffeeshops can sell soft drugs, but only in amounts of five grams or less; they can stock up to 500 grams (just over a pound) at a time for supply. If individuals are found with up to 30 grams (one ounce) for their own personal use, then it 'will still have no priority as far as investigation is concerned': basically, the police don't mind. The attitude of the locals is, as with most things, a mixture of apathy and amused tolerance: coffeeshops here – and there are over 300 of them in Amsterdam – are used by locals and tourists alike. The gaudier, touristy establishments in the centre of town are to be avoided: steer clear of anything with a nasty neon sign or a poster of Bob Marley in the window. Instead, check out one of the infinitely better places detailed on the following pages.

ATTENTION TO DETAIL

What all coffeeshops have in common is the manner in which hashish and marijuana are sold (anything stronger is definitely frowned upon). Almost all coffeeshops have a menu card either on the bar or just behind it. Most hash and weed is sold in bags of ƒ10 – around a gram's worth, depending on quality – or larger ƒ25 bags. Prices are much of a muchness, but quality can vary hugely.

Good coffeeshops have a bewildering array of comestibles. The hash side of things is fairly clear, as varieties are generally named after the country of origin. Weed is a bit more complicated. It divides roughly into two categories: bush weeds grown naturally, such as Thai; and Nederwiet or Skunk, an indigenous Dutch product grown under UV lights for maximum THC (the active ingredient). As with Guinness in Ireland – well, kinda – the skunk here is worlds away from anything available elsewhere, and caution is advisable if you are at all interested in remembering anything. The

same caution should be exercised when it comes to most of the space cake on offer: return to planet Earth can be a decidedly protracted affair. Don't mix alcohol and smoking if you're not used to it, and if you do overdo it, eat or drink something sweet.

However, the only don't that really needs to be stressed is that you should never, ever buy anything from street dealers. Junkies proliferate in certain areas of town, and if a street deal is not a precursor to a mugging, then you can count yourself lucky. Common sense is all that's needed: there are coffeeshops everywhere. It's also important to bear in mind that there are places where smoking is frowned upon. Not everyone in Amsterdam is going to smile and wave a peace sign if you have a joint in your hand. If in doubt, don't be afraid to ask: the worst you will get is a 'no'. But in the meantime, happy smoking...

Coffeeshops

For the **Otherside**, Amsterdam's only gay coffeeshop, _see page 208_; for details of lesbian bar **Saarein II**'s home-growing contest, _see page 209_. Note that none of the establishments listed in this chapter accept credit cards.

Top five Coffeeshops

Barney's
Hash with mash: they fry while you get high. See page 135.

Greenhouse
One for connoisseurs: good taste in weed, seeds and surroundings. See page 135.

Homegrown Fantasy
Double Dutch: Nederweed and Nederseeds. See page 135.

The Otherside
A perfectly pink joint: the city's only gay coffeeshop. See page 208.

T-Boat
Blow away on the decks of this coffeeshop-boat. See page 139.

'Scuse me while I kiss the skylight: the **Greenhouse Effect**.

Barney's

Haarlemmerstraat 102, Grachtengordel: West (625 9761). Tram 13, 14, 17, 20. **Open** *Nov-Feb* 8am-8pm daily; *Mar-Oct* 7am-8pm daily. **No credit cards. Map** p306 C2.
As with so many hideaways in the city, Barney's is to be filed under 'Only in Amsterdam'. Cannabis and joints are on the menu, sure, but so are massive greasy breakfasts served with HP Sauce and the British tabloids. Vegan and vegetarian breakfasts are also offered.

Greenhouse

Oudezijds Voorburgwal 191, Old Centre: Old Side (627 1739). Tram 4, 9, 14, 16, 20, 24, 25. **Open** 9am-1am Mon-Thur, Sun; 9am-3am Fri, Sat. **No credit cards. Map** p306 D3.
The Greenhouse has a worldwide reputation for its beautiful decor and, particularly, its hash/grass menu that will bring delight to connoisseurs (it's a perpetual winner of the **Cannabis Cup**, for which *see p175*). Knowledgeable staff will talk you through the different highs of each purchase, and alcohol is served at the bar. The Greenhouse Seed Co sells seeds by mail order.
Branches: Tolstraat 91, The Pijp (673 7430); Waterlooplein 345, Old Centre: Old Side (622 5499).

Greenhouse Effect

Warmoesstraat 53, Old Centre: Red Light District (623 7462). Tram 4, 9, 16, 24, 20, 25/Metro Centraal Station. **Open** 9am-1am Mon-Thur, Sun; 9am-3am Fri, Sat. **No credit cards. Map** p306 D2.

Not to be confused with the nearly legendary **Greenhouse** (*see above*), this is a small but very hip joint that also sells alcohol. However, for live DJs, a bit more space, and a 'Cream in your Pants' cocktail, take a trip next door to their bar-hotel of the same name. On the other side is **Getto**, arguably the best gay bar in town (*see p207*).

Grey Area

Oude Leliestraat 2, The Jordaan (420 4301/ www.greyarea.nl). Tram 1, 2, 5, 13, 14, 17, 20. **Open** noon-8pm Tue-Sun; closed Mon. **No credit cards. Map** p306 C3.
A super-friendly atmosphere, wacky owners, top-quality weed and free refills of organic coffee. A particularly popular hangout among travelling musicians and road crews.

Homegrown Fantasy

Nieuwezijds Voorburgwal 87A, Old Centre: Red Light District (627 5683/www.homegrownfantasy.com). Tram 1, 2, 5, 13, 17, 20. **Open** 9am-midnight Mon-Thur, Sun; 9am-1am Fri, Sat. **No credit cards. Map** p306 D2.
When in Rome and all that... For Homegrown Fantasy has one of the widest selections of Dutch-grown weed in Weedsville. The menu and its pleasant environment make it a popular smoker's venue.

Kadinsky

Rosemarijnsteeg 9, Old Centre: Old Side (624 7023). Tram 1, 2, 5. **Open** 10am-1am daily. **No credit cards. Map** p306 D3.

Toking and drinking are best left to experts. Or the very stupid.

Pastels, plants and comfy sofas decorate this split-level coffeeshop, a perpetually popular Amsterdam hangout. The menu lists a wide and impressive selection of hash and grass, including descriptions, tastes and effects (from 'well high' to 'very stoned'). The prices are a little above average, but smaller deals can be done, including some for ƒ5.

't Kruydenhuys
Keizersgracht 665, Grachtengordel: East (427 8282/ www.kruydenhuys.nl). Tram 4, 9, 16, 24, 25. **Open** 10am-1am daily. **No credit cards. Map** p311 E4.
Just a stoner's throw from the Rembrandtplein, the 'Herbs House' occupies two floors of an old canal house and is perfect for the munchies: there's a good

Get smart

It's somewhat ironic that while so-called 'smart drugs' were originally introduced for purposes of 'memory enhancement', they're now mostly just another alternative – and legal – way of getting a little off your face. The smart shops detailed below stock a selection of relatively harmless products such as energy drinks, aphrodisiacs, guarana and echinacea chewing gum, and that centuries-old organic alternative to LSD, magic mushrooms. The latter should be taken with caution: instead of discovering the secrets of the universe, the only trip you could end up taking is one to the toilet. Always ask for advice, and if it isn't forthcoming, go elsewhere.

Also on sale are 'after party' drugs, which aim to counteract the harmful effects of illegal drugs and restore your vitamin, mineral and amino-acid levels. Many of the products, though, such as 'smart oxygen', 'herbal love

joints' and 'life extenders', should be taken with a pinch – nay, a bucketful – of salt. It remains up to the individual to discover whether these drugs are indeed smart or just plain silly.

Chills & Thrills
Nieuwendijk 17, Old Centre: Old Side (638 0015/wholesale mail order 626 6395). Tram 13, 14, 17, 20. **Open** noon-8pm Mon-Wed; 11am-9pm Thur; 11am-10pm Fri, Sat, Sun. **No credit cards. Map** p306 C2.
This store is crammed with an overwhelming selection of products: an innovative range of pipes and bongs sits alongside postcards, T-shirts, mushrooms and hemp products (including a snowboard) and seeds. Staff will happily explain how you can hallucinate from cacti buds, or show you the portable mini-vaporiser that vaporises pure THC, giving you a clean, smokeless hit.

choice of sandwiches, fresh fruit milkshakes and juices. Fall in love with the beautiful views over the canal and nearby bridges, especially at night.

Paradox

1e Bloemdwarsstraat 2, The Jordaan (623 5639). Tram 10, 13, 14, 17, 20. **Open** 10am-8pm daily. **No credit cards. Map** p305 B3.
When judged next to the many dingy, hippie-chic coffeeshops in Amsterdam, it becomes apparent that Paradox lives up to its name. A bright, characterful contradiction in the Jordaan, it serves healthy, organic food, fruit shakes and fresh fruit/vegetable juices on top of all the usual dope.

Pi Kunst en Koffie

2e Laurierdwarsstraat 64, The Jordaan (622 5960). Tram 7, 10, 13, 14, 17, 20. **Open** 10am-8pm Mon-Wed, Sun; 10am-9pm Thur, Fri, Sat. **No credit cards. Map** p309 B4.
A high-ceilinged coffeeshop that looks out on to a canal. The two rooms – one with loud orange and blue walls, the other a mock-Egyptian thing presumably created while under the influence – are linked by a semi-circular bar. There are Internet facilities in the basement, and ace choc chip cookies.

De Rokerij

Lange Leidsedwarsstraat 41, Grachtengordel: East (622 9442). Tram 1, 2, 5, 6, 7, 10, 20. **Open** 10am-1am Mon-Thur, Sun; 10am-3am Fri, Sat. **No credit cards. Map** p310 D5.
A marvellous discovery on an otherwise hideously touristy street by Leidseplein, De Rokerij is a veritable Aladdin's cave: lit by wall-mounted candles and beautiful metal lanterns, it's decorated with colourful Indian art and a variety of seating ranging from mats on the floors to decorative 'thrones'. In line with its central location, it gets very busy on evenings and weekends.
Branches: Amstel 8, Grachtengordel: East (620 0484); Singel 8, Old Centre: New Side (422 6643).

Samenentereng

2e Laurierdwarsstraat 44, The Jordaan (624 1907). Tram 10, 13, 14, 17, 20. **Open** *Summer* noon-midnight daily. *Winter* noon-7pm Mon-Thur, Sun; noon-midnight Fri, Sat. **No credit cards. Map** p309 B4.
If you're after an unusual experience on a par with one of Mr Benn's visits to the fancy dress shop, then pop into what is ostensibly a bric-a-brac shop crammed to the nines. However, tucked away all the way at the back of the store is an African hut-style coffeeshop-cum-conservatory, complete with reggae, rastas and table football.

Siberië

Brouwersgracht 11, Grachtengordel: East (623 5909). Tram 1, 2, 4, 5, 13, 17, 20/Metro Centraal Station. **Open** 11am-11pm Mon-Thur, Sun; 11am-midnight Fri, Sat. **No credit cards. Map** p306 C2.
Siberië is one of the friendliest and most interactive coffeeshops in town. There are regular open mic and poetry nights, frequent exhibitions and occasional jazz gigs, DJs at weekends and free horoscope readings on Sundays. But if you simply want to hang out and chill, there are plenty of board games in this spacious, nicely designed coffeeshop located on a quiet canal.

Conscious Dreams

Kerkstraat 117, Old Centre: New Side (626 6907/www.consciousdreams.nl). Tram 1, 2, 5. **Open** 11am-7pm Mon, Tue, Wed; 11am-8pm Thur, Fri, Sat; 2-6pm Sun. **No credit cards. Map** p310 D4.
Conscious Dreams was the original proponent of the smart drugs wave here, and the owners are keen to point out that they're interested in the idealism behind smart drugs rather than the commercialism. Staff here are knowledgeable – the owner worked as a drugs advisor for five years – and you're more or less guaranteed to find what you're after.

The popularity both of the shop and smart drugs in general is evidenced by the fact that there are three other Conscious Dreams shops in Amsterdam. The newest of the three, **DreamLounge**, is an Internet café, gallery and smart shop. Meanwhile, **Kokopelli** offers a fine selection of smart goodies, Internet terminals and a great canal view at the back; and **Mind Over Matter**, located in the west of the city, also stocks healing stones, tarot cards, incense and the like, as well as selling advance tickets for party nights.
Branches: DreamLounge Kerkstraat 93, Grachtengordel: East (427 2829); **Kokopelli** Warmoesstraat 12, Old Centre: Red Light District (421 7000); **Mind Over Matter** Van Limburg-Stirumplein 24, Westerpark (681 7087).

Siberië, modish and matey. See p137.

T-Boat

*Oudeschans, by No.143, Old Centre: Old Side
(423 3799). Tram 9, 14, 20.* **Open** 11am-6pm
Mon-Thur, Sun; 10am-midnight Fri, Sat. **No credit
cards. Map** p307 E2.
The ultimate 'Amsterdam' experience: a coffeeshop
on a boat. With great views from the deck, it catches
the last of the sun, and it's close to Waterlooplein market. Be warned, though: the cheapest deals are ƒ25.

La Tertulia

*Prinsengracht 312, Grachtengordel: East (no phone).
Tram 7, 10, 13, 14, 17, 20.* **Open** 11am-7pm Tue-Sat;
closed Mon, Sun. **No credit cards. Map** p310 C4.
A stoned-looking Van Gogh is painted on the outer
walls of this charming split-level corner coffeeshop
where Michelle from *EastEnders* took her first toke
many years ago. In summer, the terrace overlooking
the canal is a delightful place in which to spliff up.

Tweede Kamer

*Heisteeg 6, Old Centre: New Side (422 2236/
www.detweedekamer.nl). Tram 1, 2, 5.* **Open** 10am-
1am Mon-Sat; 11am-1am Sun. **No credit cards.
Map** p306 D3.
A bit of an insider's place, frequented by locals as a
result of its deserved reputation for having a wide
range of imported grass. Smoky, poky and 'old Dutch
style', you might do well to purchase your grass here
but head elsewhere to actually smoke the stuff.

Yo-Yo

*2e Jan van den Heijdenstraat 79 (entrance on
Hemonystraat), The Pijp (664 7173). Tram 3, 4.*
Open noon-8pm daily. **No credit cards.
Map** p311 F5.
A popular neighbourhood coffeeshop in the Pijp
area, spacious and simply – but pleasingly –
designed. The atmosphere is intrinsically mellow
and chilling all day, and the weed is organic.

Events

For details of the **High Times Cannabis
Cup**, *see page 175.*

Global Days Against the Drug War

*Stichting Legalize, Postbus 225, 2300 AE Leiden
(070 380 8433/www.legalize.org).*
Events are organised concurrently, usually in late
May or early June, in around 30 cities worldwide in
an attempt to raise awareness of drugs issues. In
Amsterdam, the event includes a remembrance ceremony in Dam Square for victims of drug warfare
and a 'Legalize' street party, attracting both party
and political animals alike. However, it's rumoured
that the party may be shifted to The Hague in future
years, so check the abovementioned website for
more details nearer the time.

Highlife Hemp Exhibition

*Highlife, Discover Publishers BV, Huygensweg 7,
5482 TH Schijndel (073 549 8112/fax 073 547
9732/www.highlife.nl).*
Organised by *Highlife* magazine, this event cele-
brates the cannabis plant, with an emphasis on
the industrial uses of hemp. The exhibition holds
informative displays detailing the many uses for the
plant, and there are around 100 stalls selling smart
drugs, weed tea and coffee and all sorts of soft drugs
paraphernalia. Location – it's usually held outside

Consumer

A growth industry

You strut through the front door of the coffeeshop, smugly engage in a simple cash-for-product transaction, and then smoke the sweet smoke. You exit the front door: wiggly, wasted and most importantly – for you have done no wrong – free of paranoia. The glitch is that the wobbly law that allowed you this simple pleasure neglected to deal with how the wacky weed got there in the first place. The 'back door' where the produce arrived by the kilo is still a gateway to an illegal distribution system, one that in the past had to rely on heavy criminal organisations to smuggle in foreign supplies.

But things have evolved quickly since the 'green wave' that began in the early '90s, when an American-designed reddish weed, Skunk, blew over, and was found to grow very nicely indeed under artificial light. Its sensimillia version – seedless, so that more of the plant's efforts go into producing the magical ingredient, THC – became the basis for all future varieties of seeds (another mega growth industry) and Nederweeds: White Widow, Northern Light, Master Kush, AK47, Bubblegum, Bazooka Joe (a cross between AK47 and Bubblegum) and so on, down a very long list. Technology has even moved on so far that enterprising growers can now viably produce hashes from these locals without the need for foreign markets. Unfortunately, a conservative stream in government back-pedalled against home-growing, allowing only the growing of four plants at a time and banning the use of artificial light. So, the farmer's market has had to go black again.

Among the country's 700,000 regular tokers are enough motivated types not only to run the nation's 900 coffeeshops and 250 growshops, but also to grow somewhere between the government estimate of 50,000 and the insiders' best guess of 250,000 kilos per year. It's also said that half of Europe's cannabis is grown with Dutch-supplied soil, seed and lamps. And while, perhaps naturally, some of the estimated 30,000 home-growers show more initiative than others, the industry in general remains one held together by small businesses. A whole new generation of twentysomething growers is maximising the use of modern technologies to automate the growing process, with the result that yields are skyrocketing and prices are falling. How do you like the sound of the going bulk rate of a guilder a gram?

Of course, the police are also getting more high-tech: sending choppers to scope out greenhouses, or checking after a snowfall to see which roofs are melting faster than others. But though the growers' response to such tactics has been a little less organised, it's been no less effective. Sales of both shovels and red Christmas-tree baubles – which can effortlessly transform ganja plants into tomato plants – are believed to be rising rapidly...

Amsterdam – and dates vary each year: visit the aforementioned *Highlife* website for details. Look out, too, for the **Nederwiet Festival**, *Highlife's* smaller Dutch equivalent of the all-conquering *High Times* Cannabis Cup.

Smoking accessories

Head Shop
Kloveniersburgwal 39, Old Centre: Old Side (624 9061). Tram 4, 9, 14, 16, 20, 24, 25/ Metro Nieuwmarkt. **Open** 11am-6pm Mon-Sat. **No credit cards. Map** p306 D3.
Little has changed at the Head Shop since the 1960s, and the store is well worth a visit for nostalgic reasons, if nothing else. There are wide selections of pipes, bongs, jewellery, incense, clothing, postcards and books, and mushrooms and spores – so greenfingered types can their own – can also be purchased here. Like, *maaan*.

Information

BCD (Cannabis Retailers Association)
627 7050.
The BCD is the coffeeshops' union. Not all coffeeshops belong to it, but members can be identified by a green and white rectangular sticker usually placed near, or on, their door.

Drugs Information Line
0900 1995. **Open** 1-9pm Mon-Fri; Dutch recorded message at other times.
A national advice and information number. When you phone, you'll hear a recorded message in Dutch. Press '4' or stay on the line and you'll be put through to a phone operator, who'll speak English. The DIL deals with a wide variety of enquiries, from specific questions concerning drug laws to the effects and risks of drugs.

Shops & Services

If you thought you'd get away with a cheap holiday, think again: Amsterdam is packed with tempting treats for the discerning and not-so-discerning shopper.

Stereotypes are ugly things. Think 'going Dutch', and you'll be reminded of the reputation the nation has accrued as a bunch of tightwads. Whether this is true or not is a moot point, but the good news is that the prices in Amsterdam shops certainly reflect the fanatical bargain lust that shines bright in Dutch eyes. Don't worry if you've booked the glamour hotel on the breezy canal, have eaten out to your heart's content, or have splashed cash galore getting into any number of museums. The fact is that whether you're a Trump or a tramp, you'll have the power of purchase in Amsterdam. There are great designer duds for those so inclined, but if designer prices leave you weak, there are deals around every corner. Keep your eyes peeled and your wallet stocked, and you'll have a ball.

Art & art supplies

For commercial galleries, *see pages 195-200*. In addition to these and the shops listed below, it's also worth checking out the shops at the main museums (*see chapter* **Sightseeing**) if it's prints and postcards you're after.

Art Unlimited

Keizersgracht 510, Grachtengordel: East (624 8419/www.artunlimited.nl). Tram 1, 2, 5, 20. **Open** 10am-6pm Mon-Wed, Fri, Sat; 10am-9pm Thur; closed Sun. **Credit** AmEx, DC, MC, V. **Map** p310 C4.
Art Unlimited claims to have the largest collection of postcards in western Europe: a gob-smacking 40,000, sorted by artist and subject. The shop also has the most comprehensive collection of international photographs and posters in the country. Calendars and T-shirts complete the picture.

J Vlieger

Amstel 34, Grachtengordel: East (623 5834). Tram 4, 9, 14, 16, 20, 24, 25. **Open** noon-6pm Mon; 9am-6pm Tue-Fri; 11am-5.30pm Sat; closed Sun. **Credit** AmEx, DC, MC, V. **Map** p307 E3.
The ground floor at J Vlieger specialises in papers and cards of every description, weight and colour and a good variety of glues and tapes. Upstairs is a limited selection of paints, pens and inks, as well as small easels and hobby materials.

Peter van Ginkel

Bilderdijkstraat 99, Oud West (618 9827). Tram 3, 7, 12, 17. **Open** 10am-5.30pm Mon-Fri; 10am-4pm Sat; closed Sun. **Credit** MC. **Map** p309 B5.

The biggest art supplier in Amsterdam sells something for every creative persuasion. The rows of shelves are stacked with an inspiring range of paints and pigments, rolls of canvas, stretcher parts and many types of paper, including Fabriano and the shop's own cheaper brand.

Van Beek

Stadhouderskade 63, Museum Quarter (662 1670). Tram 6, 7, 10, 16, 24, 25. **Open** 1-6pm Mon; 9am-6pm Tue-Fri; 10am-5pm Sat; closed Sun. **Credit** AmEx, DC, MC, V. **Map** p310 D5.
A well-stocked shop with everything from oil paints to ready-cut wood and pre-made stretchers. There's always something on special offer if you look around, and the shop runs a discount scheme for regulars. There's a frame-making branch on the same street (Stadhouderskade 62, Museum Quarter; 662 6445), while the branch at Weteringschans 201-5, Grachtengordel: East (623 9647) specialises in graphic art equipment.

Auctions & antiques

Sotheby's (550 2200/www.sothebys.com) and **Christie's** (575 5255/www.christies.com) both have branches in Amsterdam. *See also page 164* **Looier**.

Veilinghuis De Nieuwe Zon

Elandsgracht 68, The Jordaan (623 0343). Tram 7, 10, 17, 20. **Open** to public only for viewings, weekend before auctions. *Auctions* every 2 months; call for details. **Map** p310 D4.
Art, antiques and household goods are auctioned off at Veilinghuis De Nieuwe Zon once a month, except in the summer when sales are less frequent. The organisers claim their household auctions are unique: fine antiques are mixed with house clearance items such as furniture and utensils sold off in boxed lots.

Bookshops

There are two weeks in the Dutch calendar devoted to books: the third week in March, when Dutch literature is celebrated with assorted events and special offers, and the second week in October, when bookshops focus their displays on children's books. Be warned, though: English-language books are expensive in Amsterdam. For book markets, *see page 168*. *See also page 212*.

Where to head

Amsterdam's shopping scene isn't just about chain stores. The streets are lined with speciality shops, many of which hold a quirky and interesting range of goods. However, that's not the whole story. What follows is a 'cheat sheet' detailing the general characteristics of the main shopping districts, to help make your spending spree more of a breeze.

Damstraat

Once a rather sketchy stretch, the Damstraat is evolving into a funky little shopping street. What used to be a sleazy centre for headshops (selling drugs paraphernalia but not drugs) now sells streetwear, slick sneakers and groovy second-hand gear for hip young things.

The Jordaan

The essence, or eau d'Amsterdam. Colourful canals and tiny back streets buzz with local characters and an eclectic array of boutiques, markets, bakeries, galleries and bars, like nowhere else in town. Breath it in.

Kalverstraat & Nieuwendijk

These two streets, divided by Dam Square, have about as much oomph as generic oatmeal, but this is high street heaven and Amsterdammers love it. Luckily, the streets are pedestrian-access only, so you can let down your guard against the dreaded bike and taxi menace and concentrate on shopping. The area is now open seven days a week, but be warned, it gets insanely busy on Sundays.

Magna Plaza

Located just behind Dam Square, this architectural treat was – believe it or not – formerly a post office. Its conversion into a five-floor mall has been embraced by tourists, though the locals are yet to be convinced.

The Pijp

The Pijp is a bustling little neighbourhood, famous for the Albert Cuyp market and scores of ethnic food shops. Even though the upscale crowd is moving in, there are still bargains aplenty.

Leidsestraat

Connecting Koningsplein and the Leidseplein, Leidsestraat is peppered with lots of fine shoe shops and boutiques. Unfortunately, you'll have to dodge the cyclists and trams to reach 'em.

PC Hooftstraat

If money's no object, head here. PC Hooftstraat (the PC stands for Pieter Cornelisz) caters to dedicated followers of fashion who don't bat an eyelid at spending ƒ500 on a shirt. Top designer labels – for men, women or children – are the street's bread and butter.

Spiegelkwartier

Across from the Rijksmuseum and centred on the Spiegelgracht, this area is famous for antique shops offering authentic treasures at accordingly high prices. It's divine, darling, so dress for success and keep your nose in the air.

General

American Book Center

Kalverstraat 185, Old Centre: New Side (625 5537/ www.abc.nl). Tram 1, 2, 4, 5, 9, 14, 16, 20, 24, 25. **Open** 10am-8pm Mon-Wed, Fri, Sat; 10am-10pm Thur; 11am-7pm Sun. **Credit** AmEx, DC, MC, V. **Map** p307 D3.

Since 1972, this shop has specialised in English-language books and magazines from the UK and US, and the four floors are packed with titles on every conceivable subject. Fuel up on bagels at the basement branch of **Gary's Muffins** (*see p117*).

Athenaeum Nieuwscentrum

Spui 14-16, Old Centre: New Side (bookshop 622 6248/news centre 624 2972/www.athenaeum.nl). Tram 1, 2, 5. **Open** *Bookshop* 11am-6pm Mon;

9.30am-6pm Tue, Wed, Fri, Sat; 9.30am-9pm Thur; noon-5.30pm Sun. *News centre* 8am-9pm Mon-Sat; 10am-6pm Sun. **Credit** AmEx, MC, V. **Map** p310 D4.

A favourite hangout among Amsterdam's highbrow browsers, Athenaeum stocks newspapers from all over the world, as well as a wide choice of magazines, periodicals and good-quality books in many languages.

Book Exchange

Kloveniersburgwal 58, Old Centre: Old Side (626 6266). Tram 4, 9, 14, 20/Metro Nieuwmarkt. **Open** 10am-6pm Mon-Fri; 10am-5.30pm Sat; 11.30am-4pm Sun. **No credit cards**. **Map** p306 D3.

An Aladdin's cave of second-hand English and American books (mainly paperbacks). The owner is a shrewd buyer who'll do trade deals, and offers a 10% discount to anyone with a copy of this guide.

English Bookshop

Lauriergracht 71, The Jordaan (626 4230). Tram 7, 10, 17, 20. **Open** 1-6pm Tue-Fri; 11am-5pm Sat; closed Mon, Sun. **Credit** AmEx, DC, V. **Map** p309 B4.
English books, including fiction, non-fiction, children's books and cookbooks, are temptingly displayed here. The proprietor knows his stuff and can offer good reading suggestions.

De Kinderboekwinkel

Rozengracht 34, The Jordaan (622 4761/ www.dekinderboekwinkel.nl). Tram 13, 14, 17, 20. **Open** 1-6pm Mon; 10am-6pm Tue-Fri; 10am-5pm Sat; closed Sun. **No credit cards. Map** p306 D3.
It's (exclusively) children's books here. The large selection of books in English and other languages is attractively displayed and arranged by age.
Branch: Nieuwezijds Voorburgwal 344, Old Centre: New Side (622 7741).

Martyrium

Van Baerlestraat 170, Museum Quarter (673 2092). Tram 3, 5, 12, 20, 24. **Open** 9am-6pm Mon-Fri; 9am-5pm Sat; noon-5pm Sun. **No credit cards. Map** p310 D6.
A high percentage of the stock here is English-language hardbacks and paperbacks, including literature, art , history and philosophy. As 40% of the books are remainders, there are bargains to be had.

Scheltema

Koningsplein 20, Grachtengordel: East (523 1411/ www.scheltema.nl). Tram 1, 2, 5. **Open** 10am-7pm Mon-Wed, Fri; 10am-9pm Thur; 10am-6pm Sat, Sun. **Credit** AmEx, MC, V. **Map** p310 D4.
Six (count 'em) floors of books. Specialist areas are medicine, law, economics and science.

De Slegte

Kalverstraat 48, Old Centre: New Side (622 5933/www.deslegte.nl). Tram 4, 9, 14, 16, 20, 24, 25. **Open** 10am-6pm Mon; 9.30am-6pm Tue, Wed, Fri, Sat; 9.30am-9pm Thur; noon-5pm Sun. **Credit** AmEx, DC, MC, V. **Map** p306 D3.
De Slegte carries a vast number of volumes – including children's books and textbooks – in English, Dutch and other languages. Stock is a mix of antiquarian, remaindered and new, and prices are low.

Waterstone's

Kalverstraat 152, Old Centre: New Side (638 3821/ www.waterstones.co.uk). Tram 1, 2, 4, 5, 9, 14, 16, 20, 24, 25. **Open** 11am-6pm Mon, Sun; 9am-6pm Tue, Wed; 9am-9pm Thur; 9am-7pm Fri; 10am-7pm Sat. **Credit** AmEx, MC, V. **Map** p306 D3.
Waterstone's carries thousands of book titles, as well as magazines and videos, all in English. The children's section is especially delightful.

Specialist

Architectura & Natura

Leliegracht 22, Grachtengordel: West (623 6186/ www.archined.nl/architectura/index.html). Tram 13, 14, 17, 20. **Open** noon-6.30pm Mon; 9am-6.30pm Tue-Fri; 9am-6pm Sat; closed Sun. **Credit** AmEx, MC, V. **Map** p306 C3.
The name says it all: architecture and nature. The stock includes photographic books on architectural history, field guides and animal studies, and many of the books are in English. Leliegracht 22 is also home to **Antiquariaat Opbouw**, which deals in antiquarian books on architecture and related topics.

Au Bout du Monde

Singel 313, Grachtengordel: West (625 1397). Tram 1, 2, 5. **Open** noon-6pm Mon; 10am-6pm Tue, Wed, Fri; 10am-9pm Thur; 10am-5pm Sat; closed Sun. **Credit** MC, V. **Map** p306 C3.
Specialising in Eastern philosophy and religion, Au Bout du Monde stocks a daunting selection of titles, all clearly marked, on subjects ranging from psychology to sexuality. It also sells incense, cards and a handful of specialist magazines, as well as over 100 different packs of tarot cards.

Intertaal

Van Baerlestraat 76, Museum Quarter (575 6756/ www.intertaal.nl). Tram 3, 5, 12, 16, 20. **Open** 9am-6pm Mon-Wed, Fri; 9am-9pm Thur; 10am-5pm Sat; closed Sun. **Credit** AmEx, MC, V. **Map** p310 D6.
This shop deals exclusively in language books, records and teaching aids. Whether grappling with basic Dutch or advancing your English, you'll be well catered for here.

Jacob van Wijngaarden (Geografische Boekhandel)

Overtoom 97, Museum Quarter (612 1901). Tram 1, 6. **Open** 1-6pm Mon; 10am-6pm Tue, Wed, Fri; 10am-9pm Thur; 10am-5pm Sat; closed Sun. **Credit** AmEx, DC, MC, V. **Map** p309 B6.
Every part of our planet comes up for inspection in the geography books, nautical charts, maps and travel guides sold at Wijngaarden, and a great deal of the stock is in English. You can also find cycling maps of the Netherlands and Europe.

De Kookboekhandel

Runstraat 26, Grachtengordel: West (622 4768). Tram 1, 2, 5, 7, 10, 17, 20. **Open** 1-6pm Mon; 11am-6pm Tue, Wed, Fri; 11am-9pm Thur; 11am-5pm Sat; closed Sun. **No credit cards. Map** p310 C4.
This shop sells cookery books on every conceivable subject. There are good 'fresh' and 'green' sections, plus vegan, vegetarian and organic sections. The stock is largely English-language.

Lambiek

Kerkstraat 78, Grachtengordel: East (626 7543/ www.lambiek.nl). Tram 1, 2, 5. **Open** 11am-6pm Mon-Fri; 11am-5pm Sat; 1-5.30pm Sun. **Credit** AmEx, DC, MC, V. **Map** p310 D4.
Established in 1968, Lambiek claims to be the world's oldest comic shop, and has thousands of comic books from around the world. There's a cartoonists' gallery here, too, with new exhibitions of comic art for sale every two months.

Pied-à-Terre

Singel 393, Old Centre: New Side (627 4455). Tram 1, 2, 5, 20. **Open** *Sept-Mar* 11am-6pm Mon-Fri; 10am-5pm Sat. *Apr-Aug* 11am-6pm Mon-Wed, Fri; 11am-9pm Thur; 10am-5pm Sat; closed Sun. **No credit cards. Map** p310 D4.

A wonderful little shop with helpful staff, supplying travel books, international guides and maps (including Ordnance Survey) for active holidays. Adventurous walkers, in particular, should head here before a trip out of town.

Department stores

De Bijenkorf

De Bijenkorf Dam 1, Old Centre: New Side (621 8080/www.bijenkorf.nl). Tram 1, 2, 4, 5, 9, 13, 14, 16, 17, 20, 24, 25. **Open** 11am-6pm Mon; 9.30am-6pm Tue, Wed, Fri, Sat; 9.30am-9pm Thur; noon-6pm Sun. **Credit** AmEx, DC, MC, V. **Map** p306 D3.

De Bijenkorf is to Amsterdam what Harrods is to London and Bloomingdale's is to New York. There's a good range of clothing – both designer and own-label – kidswear, jewellery, cosmetics, shoes, accessories and a wonderful household goods department. The Chill Out department on the fifth floor caters to hip young things in search of streetwear, clubwear, wacky foodstuffs and kitsch accessories, while the store's restaurant, La Ruche, is a good lunch spot. The Sinterklaas and Christmas displays are extravagant and hugely popular.

Hema

Kalvertoren, Singel 457/A1, Old Centre: New Side (422 8988). Tram 1, 2, 4, 5, 9, 13, 14. **Open** 11am-7pm Mon; 9.30am-7pm Tue, Wed, Fri; 9.30am-9pm Thur; 9.30am-6pm Sat; noon-6pm Sun. **No credit cards. Map** p306 D3.

A slightly (but only very slightly) upmarket version of the American five-and-dime store. Prices are low, but the quality is amazingly high: good buys include casual clothes, kids' clothing, swimwear, underwear, household items, stationery and other accessories. Hema also sells pastries, bread, delicatessen foods and reliable wines. The four main branches are listed here, but there are six others in town: call 311 4411 for details.

Branches: Ferdinand Bolstraat 93A, The Pijp (676 3222); Borgerstraaat 142, Oud West (683 4511); Nieuwendijk 174-6, Old Centre: New Side (623 4176).

Maison de Bonneterie

Rokin 140-2, Old Centre: New Side (531 3400). Tram 1, 2, 4, 5, 9, 14, 20, 24, 25. **Open** 1-5.30pm Mon; 10am-5.30pm Tue, Wed, Fri, Sat; 10am-9pm Thur; noon-5.30pm Sun. **Credit** AmEx, DC, MC, V. **Map** p306 D3.

At this venerable institution – 'By Appointment to Her Majesty Queen Beatrix' – you'll find men's and women's clothing of the highest quality. By and large, things are pretty conservative: the Ralph Lauren boutique within the store is about as wild as it gets. There's a fine household goods department.

Disco delicious: **Clubwear House.** *See p146.*

Metz & Co

Leidsestraat 34-6, Grachtengordel: East (520 7020). Tram 1, 2, 5, 20. **Open** 11am-6pm Mon; 9.30am-6pm Tue, Wed, Fri, Sat; 9.30am-9pm Thur; noon-5pm Sun. **Credit** AmEx, DC, MC, V. **Map** p310 D4.

Reminiscent of Heal's in London, Metz & Co is a good place to shop for special gifts: designer furniture, glass and Liberty-style fabrics and scarves are all sold here. The top-floor restaurant is popular for business lunches and has a terrific view of the city. At holiday time, Metz & Co's Christmas shop puts even the most Scroogeian customer back into the spirit of the season.

Branch: Schiphol Airport, Zuid (653 5060).

Vroom & Dreesmann

Kalverstraat 203, Old Centre: New Side (622 0171). Tram 4, 9, 14, 16, 20, 24, 25. **Open** 11am-7pm Mon; 10am-7pm Tue, Wed, Fri; 10am-9pm Thur; 10am-6pm Sat; noon-6pm Sun. **Credit** AmEx, MC, V. **Map** p306 D3.

V&D equals good quality at reasonable prices. You'll find an impressive array of toiletries, cosmetics, small leather goods and watches, clothing and underwear for the whole family, kitchen items, suitcases, CDs and videotapes. The ground-floor bakery, Le Marché, sells excellent bread, ready-made quiches and sandwiches, with La Place restaurant offering just about every other thing you might want to put in your mouth. Prices are a step up from **Hema** (*see above*).

Diamonds

Amsterdam has a long heritage in the diamonds industry (*see page 13*). To be honest, the shops detailed below are as much tourist attractions as retail outlets, but for a brush with luxury, take a tour around any of them and then figure out how you're going to pay for the product.

Amsterdam Diamond Centre

Rokin 1-5, Old Centre: New Side (624 5787). Tram 4, 9, 14, 16, 20, 24, 25. **Open** 10am-6pm Mon-Wed, Fri-Sun; 10.30am-8.30pm Thur. **Credit** AmEx, DC, MC, V. **Map** p306 D2.

Coster Diamonds

Paulus Potterstraat 2-6, Museum Quarter (305 5555). Tram 2, 3, 5. **Open** 9am-5pm daily. **Credit** AmEx, DC, MC, V. **Map** p310 D6.

Gassan Diamond BV

Nieuwe Uilenburgerstraat 173-5, Old Centre: Old Side (622 5333). Tram 9, 14, 20. **Open** 9am -5pm daily. **Credit** AmEx, DC, MC, V. **Map** p307 E2.

Stoeltie Diamonds

Wagenstraat 13-17, Grachtengordel: West (623 7601). Tram 4, 9, 14, 20. **Open** 8.30am-5pm daily. **Credit** AmEx, MC, V. **Map** p307 E3.

Van Moppes & Zoon

Albert Cuypstraat 2-6, The Pijp (676 7601). Tram 16, 24, 25. **Open** 9am-5pm daily. **Credit** AmEx, DC, MC, V. **Map** p311 E6.

Fabrics & trimmings

Capsicum

Oude Hoogstraat 1, Old Centre: Old Side (623 1016). Tram 4, 9, 14, 16, 20, 24, 25. **Open** 1-6pm Mon; 10am-6pm Tue, Wed, Fri, Sat; 10am-9pm Thur; closed Sun. **Credit** AmEx, DC, MC, V. **Map** p306 D3.
The fabrics here are made from splendidly textured natural fibres, such as cotton woven in India. Staff weave the provenance and history of each fabric into the sale, making every purchase an event. A gem.

Ra-ra-ra-ra-**Razzmatazz**. *See p146.*

Coppenhagen 1001 Kralen

Rozengracht 54, The Jordaan (624 3681). Tram 10, 13, 17, 20. **Open** 1-5.30pm Mon; 10am-6pm Tue-Fri; 10am-5pm Sat. **Credit** AmEx, MC, V. **Map** p305 B3.
Create your own designer jewellery or decorate a garment from thousands of different beads: the staff provide all the bits you need for self-assembly.

Het Kantenhuis

Kalverstraat 124, Old Centre: New Side (624 8618). Tram 4, 9, 14, 16, 20, 24, 25. **Open** 11.45am-6pm Mon; 9.15am-6pm Tue, Wed, Fri, Sat; 9.15am-9pm Thur; noon-5pm Sun. **Credit** AmEx, DC, MC, V. **Map** p306 D3.
The 'Lace House' sells tablecloths, place mats, doilies and napkins that are embroidered, appliquéd or printed with Delft blue designs. There are also lace curtain materials, and kits with which to cross-stitch pictures of cutesy Amsterdam canal houses.

Knopen Winkel

Wolvenstraat 14, Grachtengordel: West (624 0479). Tram 1, 2, 5. **Open** 1-6pm Mon (except summer); 11am-6pm Tue-Fri; 11am-5pm Sat; closed Sun. **No credit cards. Map** p310 C4.
This button specialist is reputedly the only shop of its kind in Holland. The vast selection of buttons – one-third old and two-thirds new – comes from all over the world, including Spain, Turkey and Italy.

Stoffen & Fourituren Winkel A Boeken

Nieuwe Hoogstraat 31, Old Centre: Old Side (626 7205). Tram 4, 9, 16, 20, 24, 25. **Open** noon-6pm Mon; 10am-6pm Tue, Wed, Fri; 10am-8pm Thur; closed Sat, Sun. **Credit** MC, V. **Map** p307 E3.
The Boeken family has been hawking theatrical fabrics since 1920, but still manages to keep up to date. Just try to find another shop with as much variety: latex rubber, Lycra, fake fur and sequins galore.

Fashion

Children

Geboortewinkel Amsterdam

Bosboom Toussaintstraat 22-4, Museum Quarter (683 1806). Tram 3, 7, 10, 12. **Open** 1-5.30pm Mon; 10am-5.30pm Tue-Fri; 10am-5pm Sat; closed Sun. **Map** p310 C5.
Beautiful maternity and baby clothes (including pre-mature sizes) in cotton, wool and linen, baby articles, cotton nappy systems and ethnic woven baby slings, and videos about childbirth.

't Klompenhuisje

Nieuwe Hoogstraat 9A, Old Centre: Old Side (622 8100). Tram 4, 9, 14/Metro Nieuwmarkt. **Open** 10am-6pm Mon-Sat; closed Sun. **Credit** AmEx, DC, MC, V. **Map** p307 E3.
A delightful selection of crafted and reasonably priced shoes, traditional clogs and handmade leather and woollen slippers from baby sizes up to size 35.

Prénatal

Kalverstraat 40-2, Old Centre: New Side (626 6392/ www.prenatal.nl). Tram 1, 2, 4, 5, 9, 14, 16, 20, 24, 25. **Open** noon-6pm Mon, Sun; 9.30am-6pm Tue, Wed, Fri, Sat; 9.30am-9pm Thur. **Credit** AmEx, MC, V. **Map** p306 D3.

Goods for expectant mothers and small children (newborns to five-year-olds), such as toys, clothes and furniture. Call for details of branches outside the centre.

Teuntje

Haarlemmerdijk 132, The Jordaan (625 3432). Tram 3/bus 18, 22. **Open** 1-6pm Mon; 10am-6pm Tue-Fri; 10am-5pm Sat; closed Sun. **Credit** AmEx, DC, MC, V. **Map** p305 B1.

Chic mothers-to-be and their bundles of joy get outfitted in high style at this lovely pre/postnatal shop.

't Schooltje

Overtoom 87, Museum Quarter (683 0444). Tram 1, 2, 5, 6. **Open** 1-6pm Mon; 9am-6pm Tue, Wed, Fri; 9am-9pm Thur; 9.30am-5.30pm Sat; closed Sun. **Credit** AmEx, DC, MC, V. **Map** p309 B6.

The well-heeled, well-dressed child is fitted out here. The clothing and shoes for babies and children aged up to 16 are attractive but expensive.

Clubwear

Clubwear House

Herengracht 265, Grachtengordel: West (622 8766/ www.clubwearhouse.nl). Tram 1, 2, 5, 13, 17, 20. **Open** noon-6pm Tue, Wed, Fri, Sat; noon-8pm Thur; closed Mon, Sun. **Credit** AmEx, DC, MC, V. **Map** p306 C3.

Master, servant and some impossibly saucy plastic pants: **Absolute Danny**. *See p147.*

Clothes from around the world, plus from its own label, Wearhouse 2000, and an in-house designer. If it's club information, flyers or pre-sale tickets you want, the staff of enthusiastic clubbers know their proverbial onions and will be able to help. DJ tapes are also available. *See also p189.*

Housewives on Fire

Spuistraat 102, Old Centre: New Side (422 1067/ www.xs4all.nl/~housew). Tram 1, 2, 5. **Open** 10am-7pm Mon-Wed, Fri, Sat; 10am-9pm Thur. *May-Aug* also noon-6pm Sun. **Credit** MC, V. **Map** p306 C3.

New and second-hand clothes and accessories, an in-house hair salon offering colours, extensions and dreads, henna tattoos and gaudy make-up, nail polishes and body paints. Add in-house DJs and flyers galore, and you've got the perfect one-stop club shop.

Designer

Cora Kemperman

Leidsestraat 72, Grachtengordel: East (625 1284/fax 427 8439). Tram 1, 2, 5. **Open** noon-6pm Mon, Sun; 10am-6pm Tue, Wed, Fri, Sat; 10am-9pm Thur. **Credit** MC, V. **Map** p310 D4.

The vast, voluminous avant-garde look is the thing here. Whether you've got something you want to hide or just love to shroud yourself in layer upon layer of fine fabric, let Cora cover you up.

DKNY

PC Hooftstraat 60, Museum Quarter (671 0554). Tram 3, 12. **Open** noon-6pm Mon; 10am-6pm Tue, Wed, Fri; 10am-9pm Thur; 10am-5.30pm Sat; 1-5pm Sun. **Credit** AmEx, DC, MC, V. **Map** p310 C6.

As you'd expect, Donna Karan classics for men, women and children.

Branches: Kalvertoren, Singel 457, Grachtengordel: East (422 7384); Leidsestraat 27, Grachtengordel: East (625 3707).

Khymo

Leidsestraat 9, Grachtengordel: East (622 2137). Tram 1, 2, 5. **Open** noon-6pm Mon; 10am-6pm Tue, Wed, Fri, Sat; 9.30am-9pm Thur; 1-5pm Sun. **Credit** AmEx, DC, MC, V. **Map** p310 D4.

Trendy fashion for twenty- to fortysomethings, both male and female. Labels on offer include Plein Sud, Gaultier and Amaya Arzuaga.

Megazino

Rozengracht 207, The Jordaan (330 1031). Tram 13, 14, 17, 20. **Open** 10am-6pm Tue, Wed, Fri, Sat; 10am-9pm Thur; noon-6pm Sun; closed Mon. **Credit** AmEx, DC, MC, V. **Map** p305 B3.

Versace, DKNY, Cerruti, Guess, Armani and more, at huge discounts. There are no bad quality clothes here, just the classics from last season.

Razzmatazz

Wolvenstraat 19, Grachtengordel: West (420 0483/ www.razzmatazz.nl). Tram 13, 14, 17, 20. **Open** 1-6pm Mon, Sun; noon-6pm Tue, Wed, Fri, Sat; noon-7pm Thur. **Credit** AmEx, DC, MC, V. **Map** p310 C4.

The staff are as nightmarish as ever, but the new collection of designers, from Westwood's Anglomania line to Masaki Matsushima, make Razz a must-see.

2πR

Oude Hoogstraat 10-12, Old Centre: Old Side (421 6329). Tram 4, 9, 14, 16, 24, 25. **Open** noon-7pm Mon; 10.30am-7pm Tue, Wed, Fri, Sat; 10.30am-9pm Thur; noon-6pm Sun. **Credit** AmEx, DC, MC, V. **Map** p306 D3.

Something sizzling just for the lads. These two shops, side by side on Oude Hoogstraat, offer funky threads and urbanwear from the likes of Helmut Lang, Psycho Cowboy, Suspect and Anglomania.

Erotic & fetish

Absolute Danny

Oudezijds Achterburgwal 78, Old Centre: Red Light District (421 0915/www.absolutedanny.com). Tram 4, 9, 16, 20, 24. **Open** noon-8pm Mon-Wed, Sat; noon-9pm Thur; noon-10pm Fri; noon-7pm Sun. **Credit** AmEx, DC, MC, V. **Map** p306 D2.

This saucy shop sells everything from rubber clothes to erotic toothbrushes.

Demask

Zeedijk 64, Old Centre: Red Light District (620 5603/ www.demask.com). Tram 4, 9, 16, 20, 24, 25. **Open** 10am-7pm Mon-Wed, Fri, Sat; 10am-9pm Thur; noon-5pm Sun. **Credit** AmEx, MC, V. **Map** p306 D2.

Demask mainly stocks leather and rubber fetish clothing for both sexes, but it also sells some PVC. High heels, bondage gear and S&M accessories are available. Pre-sale tickets can be bought here for the Demask parties.

Stout

Berenstraat 9, Grachtengordel: West (620 1676). Tram 13, 14, 17, 20. **Open** noon-7pm Tue-Fri; 11am-6pm Sat; 1-5pm Sun; closed Mon. **Credit** AmEx, DC, MC, V. **Map** p310 C4.

A relaxed environment and friendly staff make this shop a haven for women looking for erotic toys, videos, books and the like. Men should also note that the staff love helping fellas help themselves to the perfect gift for their beloveds.

Eyeglasses & contact lenses

Brilmuseum/Brillenwinkel

Gasthuismolensteeg 7, Grachtengordel: West (421 2414). Tram 1, 2, 5. **Open** noon-5.30pm Wed-Fri; noon-5pm Sat; closed Mon, Tue, Sun. **No credit cards. Map** p306 C3.

Though this shop is theoretically an opticians' museum – and a fascinating one, too – don't be put off from browsing. The folks specialise in glasses through the ages, and most exhibits are for sale.

Donald E Jongejans

Noorderkerkstraat 18, The Jordaan (624 6888). Tram 3, 10. **Open** 11am-6pm daily. **No credit cards. Map** p305 B2.

A practically perfect little shop in the Jordaan specialising in frames for glasses and sunglasses dating from the mid-1800s to the present day. The friendly staff stress that they sell not second-hand frames, but rather vintage frames that have never been worn. The vast majority of frames are an absolute steal price-wise, and are built to last. One of the loveliest shops in Amsterdam.

Hans Anders Optitien

Van Woustraat 161, The Pijp (676 8995/ www.hansanders.nl). Tram 4, 20. **Open** 8.30am-6pm Mon-Wed, Fri; 8.30am-6pm, 7-9pm Thur; 9am-5pm Sat; closed Sun. **Credit** V. **Map** p311 F6.

The cheapest contact lenses in town. For ƒ75 you'll get a pair of off-the-peg contacts that'll last about six months.

Branches: Jan Evertsenstraat 84, West (683 4791); Ferdinand Bolstraat 118, The Pijp (664 1879).

De Kinderbrillenwinkel

Nieuwezijds Voorburgwal 129, Old Centre: New Side (626 4091/www.kinderbrillenwinkel.com). Tram 1, 2, 4, 5, 13, 14, 16, 17, 20, 24, 25. **Open** by appointment Tue; 11am-6pm Wed-Fri; 11am-5pm Sat; closed Mon, Sun. **Credit** AmEx, DC, MC, V. **Map** p306 C3.

A vast collection of antique and new children's eyewear at reasonable prices.

Schmidt Optiek

Rokin 72, Old Centre: New Side (623 1981). Tram 4, 9, 16, 20, 24, 25. **Open** 1-5.30pm Mon; 9.30am-5.30pm Tue, Wed, Fri; 9.30am-5.30pm, 7-9pm Thur; 9.30am-5pm Sat; closed Sun. **Credit** AmEx, DC, MC, V. **Map** p306 D3.

An expensive, high-class optician with over 2,000 frames in stock at any one time. Brands and labels include everything from Gaultier to Ray-Ban. If you want it, then Schmidt probably has it.

Handbags

Cellarrich Connexion

Haarlemmerdijk 98, The Jordaan (626 5526). Tram 1, 2, 4, 5, 13, 14, 16, 17, 20, 24, 25. **Open** 1-6pm Mon; 10am-6pm Tue-Fri; 10am-5pm Sat; closed Sun. **Credit** AmEx, DC, MC, V. **Map** p305 B2.

Sophisticated handbags in materials from leather to plastic. Many of the bags on offer are designed and produced locally by four sassy Dutch designers, though the likes of Westwood are also stocked.

Hats

De Hoed van Tijn

Nieuwe Hoogstraat 15, Old Centre: Old Side (623 2759). Tram 4, 9, 14, 16, 24, 25. **Open** 11am-6pm Mon-Sat; closed Sun. **Credit** AmEx, DC, MC, V. **Map** p307 E3.

A vast collection of headgear, including sombreros, Homburgs, bonnets and caps. The range includes period hats dating from 1900, as well as a range of second-hand, new and handcrafted items.

Consumer

Hoeden M/V
Herengracht 422, Grachtengordel: East (626 3038).
Tram 1, 2, 5. **Open** 11am-6pm Tue, Wed, Fri; 11am-
9pm Thur; 11am-5pm Sat; closed Mon, Sun. **Credit**
AmEx, DC, MC, V. **Map** p310 C4.
Dreaming of Ascot in Amsterdam? Look no further.
The top quality hats here come from international
designers such as Philip Treacy, Sandra Phillips,
Patricia Underwood and, for men, Borsalino.

De Petsalon
*Hazenstraat 3, The Jordaan (624 7385). Tram 1, 2,
5, 13, 14, 17, 20.* **Open** noon-6pm Mon-Sat; closed
Sun. **Credit** AmEx, DC, MC, V. **Map** p310 C4.
Show some sass with a kooky handmade hat from
local designer Ans Wesseling, available at this small
shop close to Prinsengracht.

High street

America Today
*Ground floor, Magna Plaza, Spuistraat 137, Old
Centre: New Side (638 8447). Tram 1, 2, 5, 13, 14,
17, 20.* **Open** 11am-7pm Mon; 10am-7pm Tue, Wed,
Fri-Sun; 10am-9pm Thur. **Credit** AmEx, DC, MC, V.
Map p306 C2.
What started out as a tiny venture is now
making millions. America Today is able to sell
new American classics (Converse, Levi's,
Timberland and the like) at lower prices than
anywhere else because it imports stuff straight
from the States under a special tax agreement. It
also has its own clothing label.
Branch: Sarphatistraat 48, Grachtengordel: East
(638 9847).

Exota
*Hartenstraat 10, Grachtengordel: West (620 9102).
Tram 1, 2, 5, 13, 14, 17, 20.* **Open** 11am-6pm Mon;
10am-6pm Tue-Sat; 1-5pm Sun. **Credit** AmEx, DC,
MC, V. **Map** p306 C3.
A funky little shop with an original selection of sim-
ple yet stylish clothes and accessories that crosses
the borders between high street and street fashion.
Branch: Nieuwe Leliestraat 32, The Jordaan
(420 6884).

Hennes & Mauritz
*Kalverstraat 125-9, Old Centre: New Side (624
0624). Tram 1, 2, 4, 5, 9, 14, 16, 20, 24, 25.* **Open**
noon-6pm Mon, Sun; 10am-6pm Tue, Wed, Fri, Sat;
10am-9pm Thur. **Credit** AmEx, DC, MC, V. **Map**
p306 D3.
This chain has clothes for men, women, teens and
kids. Prices: reasonable to jaw-droppingly low.
Quality: reasonable to jaw-droppingly low. There
are loads of items that will appeal to trend-conscious
guys and gals, plus updates of timeless standards.
Only the branches at Kalverstraat 114-118 and
Nieuwendijk 141 have Big is Beautiful departments.
Branches: Kalverstraat 114-18, Old Centre: New
Side (520 6090); Kalvertoren, Singel 415, Old Centre:
New Side (530 1030); Nieuwendijk 141, Old Centre:
New Side (520 6000).

Jewel personality: **BLGK**.

Sissy Boy
*Kalverstraat 199, Old Centre: New Side (638 9305/
www.sissy-boy.nl). Tram 1, 2, 4, 5, 9, 14, 16, 20, 24,
25.* **Open** noon-6pm Mon, Sun; 10am-6pm Tue, Wed,
Fri, Sat; 10am-9pm Thur. **Credit** AmEx, DC, MC, V.
Map p306 D3.
Simple urban basics for men and women. Own-label
clothes are cleverly crafted by a team of international and Dutch designers and hang next to staples
from French Connection and Migel Stapper.

Jewellery

See also page 145 **Diamonds**.

BLGK
*Hartenstraat 28, Grachtengordel: West (624 8154).
Tram 13, 14, 17, 20.* **Open** 11am-6pm Tue, Wed,
Fri; 11am-8.30pm Thur; 11am-5pm Sat; closed Mon,
Sun. **Credit** AmEx, DC, MC, V. **Map** p306 C3.
Byzantinesque gold and silver jewellery: magnifi-
cent one-offs and commissioned works, as well as
serious pieces at reasonable prices.

De Blue Gold Fish
*Rozengracht 17, The Jordaan (623 3134). Tram 13,
14, 17, 20.* **Open** 11am-6.30pm Mon-Sat; closed Sun.
Credit AmEx, DC, MC, V. **Map** p305 B3.
The staff can be a little arsey, but De Blue Gold Fish
has a great selection of funky jewellery and house-
wares for those lucky enough to have it all.

Grimm Sieraden
*Grimburgwal 9, Old Centre: Old Side (622 0501).
Tram 16, 20, 24, 25.* **Open** 11am-6pm Tue-Fri;
11am-5pm Sat; closed Mon, Sun. **Credit** AmEx, DC,
MC, V. **Map** p306 D3.
Owner Elize Lutz has a talent for bringing the fresh-
est jewellery designers into her gallery shop, keep-
ing the wearable pieces at the cutting edge of design.

Jorge Cohen Edelsmid
*Singel 414, Grachtengordel: East (623 8646). Tram
1, 2, 5, 10.* **Open** 10am-6pm Mon-Fri; 11am-6pm Sat;
closed Sun. **Credit** AmEx, DC, MC, V. **Map** p310 D4.
This shop, founded by the late Jorge Cohen and now
run by Ilja de Bruin, uses a combination of salvaged
jewellery, antique and new stones and silver to
produce art deco-inspired jewellery you'd be proud
to pass off as the real thing.

You know what they say about men with big feet: **Big Shoe**.

Large sizes

G&G Special Sizes

Prinsengracht 514, Grachtengordel: East (622 6339). Tram 1, 2, 5. **Open** *9am-5.30pm Tue, Wed, Fri; 9am-5.30pm, 7-9pm Thur; 9am-5pm Sat; closed Mon, Sun.* **Credit** *AmEx, DC, MC, V.* **Map** *p310 D5.*
A full range of men's clothing from sizes 58 to 75 is stocked by G&G. Staff also tailor garments to fit, though this service costs a bit extra.

Mateloos

Bilderdijkstraat 62, Oud West (683 2384). Tram 3, 12, 13, 14, 17, 20. **Open** *1-6pm Mon; 10am-6pm Tue, Wed, Fri; 10am-9pm Thur; 10am-5pm Sat; closed Sun.* **Credit** *AmEx, DC, MC, V.* **Map** *p309 B5.*
Two fabulous shops brimming with an enormous variety of large-sized clothing for women from sizes 44 to 60. Mateloos I offers a sumptuous collection of eveningwear and business clothes, while **Mateloos II** (Kinkerstraat 77, 689 4720) has a dizzying array of leisure- and sportswear, fake fur coats, hip hop pants, polyester shirts and denims.

Lingerie

Hunkemöller

Kalverstraat 162, Old Centre: New Side (623 6032). Tram 1, 2, 4, 5, 9, 14, 16, 20, 24, 25. **Open** *11am-6pm Mon; 9.30am-6pm Tue, Wed, Fri, Sat; 9.30am-9pm Thur; noon-6pm Sun.* **Credit** *AmEx, DC, MC, V.* **Map** *p306 D3.*
A women's lingerie chain with six branches in and around Amsterdam (call 035 646 5413 for details of others). It deals in attractive but simply designed and good quality underwear at reasonable prices.
Branches: Bilderdijkstraat 67, Oud West (618 2503); Ferdinand Bolstraat 61, The Pijp (670 4114).

Robin's Bodywear

Nieuwe Hoogstraat 20, Old Centre: Old Side (620 1552). Tram 4, 9, 14, 16, 24, 25. **Open** *1-6pm Mon-Wed; 11am-6pm Thur, Fri; 11am-5.30pm Sat; closed Sun.* **Credit** *AmEx, MC, V.* **Map** *p307 E3.*
Sizeable for a women's lingerie shop, Robin's has an extensive selection of underwear, swimwear and hosiery by Naf-Naf, Calvin Klein, Lou and others.

Tothem Underwear

Nieuwezijds Voorburgwal 149, Old Centre: New Side (623 0641). Tram 1, 2, 4, 5, 9, 13, 14, 16, 17, 20, 24, 25. **Open** *1-5.30pm Mon; 9.30am-5.30pm Tue, Wed, Fri; 9.30am-9pm Thur; 9.30am-5pm Sat; closed Sun.* **Credit** *AmEx, DC, MC, V.* **Map** *p306 D3.*
This men's underwear shop mainly sells designer items by Hom, Calvin Klein and Body Art.

Shoes

The best selections of shoes can be had at shops on **Leidsestraat** or **Kalverstraat**, while the best bargains in second-hand shoes are to be had at **Waterlooplein**, and **Noordermarkt** on Mondays; for both, *see page 164.*

Big Shoe

Leliegracht 12, Grachtengordel: West (622 6645). Tram 13, 14, 17, 20. **Open** *10am-6pm Wed, Fri, Sat; 10am-9pm Thur; closed Mon, Tue, Sun.* **Credit** *AmEx, DC, MC, V.* **Map** *p306 C3.*
Fashionable footwear for men and women in large sizes only. Every women's shoe on display is available in sizes 42-46.

Free Lance Shoes

Rokin 86, Old Centre: New Side (420 3205). Tram 4, 9, 14, 16, 20, 24, 25. **Open** *1-6pm Mon; 10am-6pm Tue, Wed, Fri; 10am-9pm Thur; noon-5pm Sat, Sun.* **Credit** *AmEx, DC, MC, V.* **Map** *p306 D3.*
The imaginative façade and decor set Free Lance apart from other similar retailers. Shoes are created by two French designers in classic and modern styles.

Kenneth Cole

Leidsestraat 20-2, Grachtengordel: East (627 6012/www.kencole.com). Tram 1, 2, 5. **Open** *noon-6pm Mon-Wed, Fri, Sat; 10am-9pm Thur; 1-5pm Sun.* **Credit** *AmEx, MC, V.* **Map** *p310 D4.*

Kenneth Cole stocks its own conservatively styled shoes, plus a good range of boots from the likes of Timberland and Doc Martens. Stock changes often, and bargains can be had during the frequent sales.
Branch: Leidsestraat 29-33, Grachtengordel: East (422 6060).

Seventy Five
Nieuwe Hoogstraat 24, Old Centre: Old Side (626 4611). Tram 4, 9, 14/Metro Nieuwmarkt. **Open** noon-6pm Mon; 10am-6pm Tue-Sat; closed Sun. **Credit** MC, V. **Map** p307 E3.
Trainers for folk who don't have sporting in mind: high fashion styles from Nike, Puma, Converse, Acupuncture, Diesel and many more.

Shoe Baloo
Koningsplein 7, Grachtengordel: East (626 7993). Tram 1, 2, 5. **Open** noon-6pm Mon; 10am-6pm Tue, Wed, Fri, Sat; 10am-9pm Thur; noon-5pm Sun. **Credit** AmEx, DC, MC, V. **Map** p310 D4.
Shoes for men and women that make your mouth water: Gucci, Prada and more. The friendly staff make parting with your cash that much easier.
Branch: PC Hooftstraat 80, Museum Quarter (671 2210).

Street

Henxs
Sint Antoniebreestraat 136, Old Centre: Old Side (416 7786). Tram 4, 9, 14/Metro Nieuwmarkt. **Open** 11am-6pm Tue-Sat; 1-6pm Mon, Sun. **No credit cards**.
Live DJs, graffiti mags and hip hop-influenced styles make this a skaters' paradise. Check out urban gear from local label g.sus, and casual duds from Carhartt.

RMF Streetwear
Oudezijds Voorburgwal 189, Old Centre: Old Side (626 2954). Tram 4, 9, 14, 16, 20, 24, 25. **Open** 10am-6pm Mon-Wed, Fri; 10am-9pm Thur; 10am-5pm Sat, Sun. **Credit** AmEx, MC, V. **Map** p306 D3.
RMF stocks a selection of American brands – South Pole, Sir Benni Miles, Menace – that were once hard to find over here. It's not a place for bargains, but you can be confident that when you go out, you won't meet four other people in the same shirt.

RDL's
Top floor, Magna Plaza, Spuistraat 137, Old Centre: New Side (623 1214/www.rdlfs.nl). Tram 1, 2, 5, 13, 17, 20. **Open** 11am-7pm Mon; 10am-7pm Tue, Wed, Fri, Sat; 10am-9pm Thur; noon-7pm Sun. **Credit** AmEx, MC, V. **Map** p306 C3.
An inline skate and skateboard outlet selling all the accessories needed to look the part: this is the best place to buy what's hip on any given day of the week. There's a large choice of T-shirts as well as the latest in trainers.
Branches: De Bijenkorf, Dam 1, Old Centre: New Side (621 8080 ext 894); Utrechtsestraat 107, Grachtengordel: East (626 0980); Sarphatistraat 59, Grachtengordel: East (622 5488).

Stillet
Damstraat 14, Old Centre: Old Side (625 2854). Tram 1, 2, 4, 5, 9, 13, 14, 16, 17, 20, 24, 25. **Open** noon-6pm daily. **Credit** MC, V. **Map** p306 D3.
T-shirts with imaginative logos and designs, including eco and political themes as well as cartoon images and club styles. Be warned, though: opening times can vary wildly.

Vintage & second-hand

Lady Day
Hartenstraat 9, Grachtengordel: West (623 5820). Tram 1, 2, 5, 20. **Open** 11am-6pm Mon-Wed, Fri, Sat; 11am-9pm Thur; noon-5pm Sun. **Credit** AmEx, MC, V. **Map** p306 C3.
Highly fashionable designs, including beautifully tailored second-hand and period suits, and sportswear classics (including swimming costumes from the '40s and '50s). Period wedge shoes, pumps and accessories complete the collection.

Laura Dols
Wolvenstraat 7, Grachtengordel: West (624 9066). Tram 1, 2, 5. **Open** 11am-6pm Mon-Wed, Fri, Sat; 11am-9pm Thur; closed Sun. **No credit cards**. **Map** p310 C4.
This shop is packed with period clothing, much of it from the '40s and '50s. The emphasis is on women's clothing (including some sumptuous dresses), though there is a limited selection of menswear.

Hipper than thou: **Henxs**.

Designs for life

After strolling the streets of Amsterdam, many first-time tourists observe how reluctant the Dutch are to draw their curtains, blinds or shades. This openness may seem logical given their reputation for tolerance, but the Dutch actually prefer to maintain a comfortable degree of distance from neighbours, strangers and especially tourists.

In fact, the locals's open-curtain practices are all down to Calvinism. The Calvinist doctrine of predestination kept people constantly aware of their standing in society. Success indicated God's favour, and failure the opposite. The distinction was more nuanced than this, though, and it was presumed that drawn curtains hid less than pious deeds.

At the dawn of the new century, the practice is outdated, especially considering the city's reputation for the less than pious deeds of its locals. Nonetheless, the Dutch still leave their curtains open until deep in the night. Hell, some homes don't even *have* curtains. A lack of (functional) window treatments affords the apartment-dweller the maximum amount of daylight, an excellent view and the illusion of a more spacious home. It also affords the passer-by a representative exhibition of trends in Dutch interior design.

Having taken its cues from Scandinavian and Italian design, Dutch design is all the rage. The aesthetics of modern Dutch architecture and furniture had long been established in their own right since the early half of the last century. Mondrian and Berlage figured prominently in art, architecture and design movements that enjoyed high visibility, yet remained exclusive.

A rather abrupt change occurred in the 1970s, when Swedish furniture giant Ikea entered the Dutch market. Furniture that mimicked Scandinavian design principles of form and functionality became affordable and so could be replaced in a few years in good conscience. As a result, the Dutch public became aware of trends in interior design and could afford to upgrade and update.

At about the same time, Rietveld Academy graduate Jan des Bouvrie took national design fairs and households by storm. Insisting on bringing the outdoors in, he managed to convince people to abandon their darkened interiors – still found in many of Amsterdam's brown cafés – in favour of natural light, the colour white and a minimalist aesthetic. His approach has been revolutionary in its simplified integration of loose elements from a variety of traditions into a coherent and understated style that permeates the whole of the interior. His influence can be observed by glancing through many Amsterdam windows.

Des Bouvrie and a score of others have inspired a hard-working generation of Dutch designers who enjoy international acclaim at design shows throughout Europe. The good news is that it's all for sale. Amsterdam boasts a number of reputable furniture shops featuring the latest in Dutch and international design, the highest concentration of which can be found along the Rozengracht. The serious shopper may want to head further afield to one of the many *woonboulevards* (furniture malls) that dot the suburbs, while true trendsetters should keep an eye open for *woonbeurzen* (design shows) that take place from time to time at a variety of large venues throughout the country.

● For Dutch designs, head to Rozengracht in the Jordaan, and specifically to **Abai** (No.231, 421 3893), **De Kasstoor** (No.202-10, 521 8112), **Koot Light** (No.8-12, 626 5000), **Koot Living** (No.101-103, 625 0770), **Wonen 2000** (No.219-23, 521 8710) and **Wulf Meubelen** (No.74-78 (626 5011); **Frozen Fountain** (see page 162) in Grachtengordel: East; and **Pro-Wonen** (Hobbemakade 89, 664 5369) in the Museum Quarter.

Consumer

Wini

Haarlemmerstraat 29, Grachtengordel: West (427 9393). Tram 1, 2, 4, 5, 9, 13, 14, 16, 17, 20, 24, 25. **Open** noon-6pm Mon; 10am-6pm Tue, Wed, Fri, Sat; 10am-9pm Thur; closed Sun. **Map** p306 C2.
Newish to Amsterdam's hugely competitive second-hand market, Wini sizzles with retro clothes that reflect today's tastes. Original pimp jackets, hipsters, Adidas and lots of polyester have made it the flavour of the moment.

Zipper

Huidenstraat 7, Grachtengordel: West (623 7302). Tram 1, 2, 5. **Open** 11am-6pm Mon-Wed, Fri, Sat; 11am-9pm Thur; 1-5pm Sun. **Credit** AmEx, MC, V. **Map** p310 C4.
An excellent selection of jeans, cowboy shirts, '80s revival, as well as 1970s hipsters and flares. It's not cheap, but the odd treasure here is worth the price. **Branch**: Nieuwe Hoogstraat 8, Old Centre: Old Side (627 0353).

Get kitted out at **Zipper**. *See p153.*

Flowers

It's tempting to bring home bulbs from Amsterdam, where bouquets and blooms are a part of everyday life. Unfortunately, import regulations often either prohibit the entry of bulbs entirely or require them to have a phytosanitary (health) certificate. An unlimited amount of bulbs can be taken into the UK and the Irish Republic without a certificate, and you can also carry an unlimited amount into the USA and Canada with the appropriate certificate(s). However, Australia and New Zealand allow no import of bulbs whatsoever, while Japan allows the import of no more than 100 certified bulbs. Some bulb packaging is marked with national flags, indicating the countries into which they can safely be taken. By and large, Dutch wholesale dealers know the regulations and can ship bulbs to your home. This can be arranged at the **Keukenhof Flower Show** (held from the end of March to the end of May; call 025 246 5555 for details) or by mail order from **Frans Roozen Nurseries** (023 584 7245), where the minimum order varies depending on where you live.

You are allowed to take an unlimited quantity of cut flowers back to the UK and Eire, as long as none are gladioli or chrysanthemums. In the US, regulations on cut flowers vary from state to state. You can buy flowers and bulbs at **Bloemenzaak Fleurtiek** (653 1702/ www.fleurtiek.nl) at Schiphol Airport. However, you must buy a minimum of ten bulbs, and prices are higher than in the city.

Bloemenmarkt (Flower market)

Singel, between Muntplein and Koningsplein, Grachtengordel: East. Tram 1, 2, 4, 5, 9, 14, 16, 20, 24, 25. **Open** 9.30am-5pm Mon-Sat; closed Sun. **No credit cards. Map** p310 D4.

The world's only floating flower market is a fascinating collage of colour stretching along the southern side of Singel, with 15 florists and garden shops permanently ensconced on barges. The plants and flowers generally last well and are good value.

Plantenmarkt (Plant market)

Amstelveld, on Prinsengracht between Utrechtsestraat and Vijzelstraat, Grachtengordel: East. Tram 4, 6, 7, 10. **Open** 9.30am-6pm Mon; closed Tue-Sun. **No credit cards. Map** p311 E4. Though the emphasis at the Plantenmarkt on plants, vases and pots, there are some flowers for sale. In spring, most plants are meant for the balcony or living room, while later in the year, there are more garden plants and bedding plants for flower boxes.

Florist

Jemi

Warmoesstraat 83A, Old Centre: Red Light District (625 6034). Tram 4, 9, 16, 20, 24, 25. **Open** 9am-6pm Mon-Sat; closed Sun. **No credit cards. Map** p306 D2. The first stone-built house in Amsterdam is now home to this colourful florist, which makes stunning bouquets, offers courses in arranging, hosts floral brunches and stocks loads of pots and plants.

Food & drink

Bakeries

For bread, rolls and packaged biscuits, go to a *warme bakker*; for pastries and wickedly delicious cream cakes, you need a *banketbakker*.

JG Beune

Haarlemmerdijk 156, The Jordaan (624 8356). Tram 3/bus 18, 22. **Open** 8.30am-6pm Mon-Fri; 8am-4.30pm Sat; closed Sun. **No credit cards. Map** p305 B2. A full range of cakes and chocolates, as well as speciality items such as chocolate tulips and wooden shoes. It also has the technology to take a photo and transfer the image on to a cake. The results will have you both smiling and licking your lips.

Mediterranee

Haarlemmerdijk 184, The Jordaan (620 3550). Tram 3/bus 18, 22. **Open** 8am-8pm daily. **No credit cards. Map** p305 B2. French, Moroccan and Dutch baking traditions are all practised under one roof here, and the results are delicious. Famous for the best croissants in town.

Oldenburg

Beethovenstraat 17, Oud West (662 5520). Tram 5. **Open** 9am-6pm Mon-Fri; 9am-5pm Sat; closed Sun. **No credit cards.** Dessert cakes, *bavarois* and chocolate mousse tarts, plus home-made chocolates and marvellous marzipan confections in winter and chocolate eggs at Easter. **Branch**: Maasstraat 84, Zuid (662 2840).

Puccini Bomboni

Staalstraat 17, Old Centre: Old Side (626 5474).
Tram 9, 14, 20/Metro Waterlooplein. **Open** noon-
6pm Mon; 9am-6pm Tue-Sat; noon-5pm Sun. **No**
credit cards. Map p307 E3.
This highly regarded bakery specialises in sweets
and gorgeous desserts made on the premises without artificial ingredients.
Branch: Singel 184, Grachtengordel: West (427 8341).

Runneboom

1e Van der Helststraat 49, The Pijp (673 5941).
Tram 16, 24, 25. **Open** 7am-5.30pm Mon-Fri;
7am-5pm Sat; closed Sun. **No credit cards.**
Map p311 E5.
This tiny bakery in the Pijp is a favourite with locals,
and after just one bite, you'll know why. An enormous selection of French, Russian, Greek and
Turkish loaves is offered, with rye bread the house
speciality. Delicious cakes and pastries are also sold.

Cheese

It's considered derogatory to call the Dutch
'cheese heads', but you are what you eat, and the
Dutch average 14 kilograms (31 pounds) per
person per year. Luckily, there is plenty to
choose from. In general, the younger (*jong*) the

cheese, the creamier and milder it will be, while
riper cheeses (*belegen*) will be drier and sharper,
especially the old (*oud*) cheese. The most popular
cheeses are Goudse (from Gouda), Leidse,
flavoured with cumin seeds, and Edammer (aka
Edam), with its red crust. However, don't miss
Friese Nagelkaas, a ripe cheese whose sharp
flavour is enhanced by cumin seeds and cloves;
Kernhem, a dessert cheese; and Leerdammer
and Maaslander, which are both very mild with holes.

De Kaaskamer

Runstraat 7, Grachtengordel: East (623 3483). Tram
1, 2, 5. **Open** *Oct-Mar* noon-6pm Mon; 9am-6pm
Tue-Fri; 9am-5pm Sat; closed Sun. *Apr-Sept* noon-
6pm Mon; 9am-6pm Tue-Fri; 9am-5pm Sat; noon-5pm
Sun. **No credit cards. Map** p310 C4.
Over 200 domestic and imported cheeses, plus pâtés,
olives, pastas and wines. Make a game of quizzing
staff on cheese types and trivia: they know their stuff.

Kef, French Cheesemakers

Marnixstraat 192, The Jordaan (626 2210). Tram 3,
10. **Open** 10am-6pm Tue-Thur; 9am-6pm Fri; 9am-
5pm Sat; closed Sun. **No credit cards. Map** p305 B3.
French cheesemaker Abraham Kef started this business over 40 years ago and his shop still imports the
finest selection of French cheeses in Amsterdam.
The range of goat's cheeses is particularly good.

The nigh-on miraculous cakes at **Oldenburg**. Don't eat 'em all at once. *See p154.*

Wegewijs
Rozengracht 32, The Jordaan (624 4093). Tram 13, 14, 17, 20. **Open** 8.30am-6pm Mon-Fri; 8.30am-5pm Sat; closed Sun. **No credit cards. Map** p305 B3.
This authentic cheese emporium has been run here by the Wegewijs family for over a century. On offer are 50 foreign cheeses and over 100 domestic types, including *gras kaas*, a grassy-tasting cheese available in summer. Try the Dutch ones before you buy.

Chocolate
You might not find true love in Amsterdam, but you can get at least halfway there with a piece or seven of fabulous Dutch chocolate. Once you've tasted these beauties, you'll forget the Swiss and the Belgian varieties in a heartbeat.

Hendrikse Le Confiseur
Overtoom 448-50, Oud West (618 0260). Tram 1, 6. **Open** 8.30am-5.30pm Mon-Fri; 8.30am-4.30pm Sat; closed Sun. **No credit cards. Map** p309 B6.
Hendrikse specialises in excellent handmade chocolates: try gianduja, a fudge-like chocolate log made with ground hazelnuts and almonds. Marzipan and chocolate figures are a forte (and can be designed to order), as are the delicious fruit preserves.

Huize van Wely
Beethovenstraat 72, Oud West (662 2009). Tram 5. **Open** 9am-6pm Mon-Fri; 8.30am-5pm Sat; closed Sun. **Credit** V.
Huize van Wely has been making sweet treats by hand at its factory in Noordwijk, on the west coast of Holland, since 1922. Its confections are so sublime that it's the only Dutch company invited to become a member of the prestigious Relais Desserts and Académie Culinaire de France.

Pâtisserie Pompadour
Huidenstraat 12, Grachtengordel: West (623 9554). Tram 1, 2, 5, 7. **Open** 9.30am-5.45pm Tue-Fri; 9am-5.30pm Sat; closed Mon, Sun. **Credit** MC, V. **Map** p310 C4.
This small bonbonnerie and tearoom – with an 18th-century interior imported from Antwerp – is likely to bring out the little old lady in anyone, even men. The handmade chocolates and pastries are inspired by traditional Belgian, French and German recipes, and offer the best price/quality ratio in town.

Delicatessens

Eichholtz
Leidsestraat 48, Grachtengordel: East (622 0305). Tram 1, 2, 5. **Open** 10am-6.30pm Mon; 9am-6.30pm Tue, Wed, Fri; 9am-9pm Thur; 9am-6pm Sat; 1-5pm Sun. **Credit** (over ƒ50 only) AmEx, MC, V. **Map** p310 D4.
This is the place where Yanks will find their chocolate chips and Brits their Christmas puddings. There are lots of imported foods here – including some from the UK and US – plus Dutch souvenirs.

Loekie
Prinsengracht 705A, Grachtengordel: East (624 4230). Tram 1, 2, 5. **Open** 9am-5pm Mon-Sat; closed Sun. **No credit cards. Map** p310 D4.
Premium sandwiches at premium prices. Whether it's Parma ham, Parmesan or pesto, Loekie will serve it in distinctive combinations on French bread, fresh ciabatta or rye. There's also a selection of wines, sauces and flavoured cooking oils.

De Pepperwortel
Overtoom 140, Museum Quarter (685 1053). Tram 1, 6. **Open** 4-9pm daily. **No credit cards. Map** p309 B6.
Pop out of the luvverly Vondelpark and into De Pepperwortel for luscious sandwiches and salads, a tasty selection of wines and complete picnic hampers from late spring until early autumn.

Ethnic

Casa Molero
Gerard Doustraat 66, The Pijp (676 1707). Tram 16, 24, 25. **Open** 10am-6pm Tue-Fri; 8.30am-5.30pm Sat; closed Sun. **No credit cards. Map** p311 E6.
Aside from stocking cheeses, spices, sausages and hams from Spain, Casa Molero is also the exclusive Dutch distributor for several Spanish and Portuguese wines, hence its vast Iberian wine collection.

Oriental Commodities
Nieuwmarkt 27, Old Centre: Old Side (638 6181). Tram 4, 9, 14, 16, 20, 24, 25/Metro Nieuwmarkt. **Open** 9am-6pm Mon-Sat; closed Sun. **No credit cards. Map** p306 D2.
The largest Chinese food emporium in Amsterdam covers the full spectrum of Asian foods and ingredients, from shrimp- and scallop-flavoured egg noodles to fried tofu balls, spicy crisp snacks and fresh vegetables. It also has a fine range of Chinese cooking appliances and utensils.

Pinoj Pindaihan: Filipino Foodstore & Toko
1e Sweelinckstraat 20, The Pijp (673 4309). Tram 3, 4, 16, 20, 24, 25. **Open** 1-6pm Mon; 10am-6pm Tue-Sat; closed Sun. **No credit cards. Map** p311 F5.
A fantastic selection of Filipino food, from shrimp fry to coconut vinegar to dried salted fish. Sweets include cassava cookies and halo-halo (mixed fresh fruits in crushed ice, milk and ice-cream), all perfect for hot summer days.

A Taste of Ireland
Herengracht 228, Grachtengordel: West (638 1642). Tram 13, 14, 17, 20. **Open** 11am-6pm Mon-Fri; 11am-5pm Sat; closed Sun. **No credit cards. Map** p306 C3.
This shop stocks many of the goodies you may be missing from home: fresh sausages, bacon and puddings are flown in fresh from Ireland every week, and there is also an extensive selection of British and Irish beers and ciders on sale.

De Thai Shop

*Koningsstraat 42, Old Centre: Old Side (620 9900).
Tram 4, 9, 14, 16, 20, 24, 25/Metro Nieuwmarkt.*
Open 10am-6.30pm Mon-Fri; 10am-6pm Sat; closed
Sun. **No credit cards**. **Map** p307 E2.
A small shop stocking a selection of Thai ingredi-
ents, including freshly made curry, imported salted
fish and fresh ingredients such as lemongrass and
other herbs.

Toko Ramee

*Ferdinand Bolstraat 74, The Pijp (662 2025).
Tram 16, 20, 24, 25.* **Open** 9am-6pm Tue-Fri;
9am-5pm Sat; closed Mon, Sun. **No credit cards**.
Map p311 E6.
All the spices and ingredients used in Indonesian
cooking are sold here, along with Chinese and Thai
ingredients and some takeaway dishes. Dead handy
for a night in.

Fish

Viscenter Volendam

*Kinkerstraat 181, Oud West (618 7062). Tram 7,
17.* **Open** 9am-6pm Mon-Fri; 9am-5pm Sat; closed
Sun. **No credit cards**. **Map** p309 B5.
The family that runs this popular shop commutes
from Volendam, a major fishing village on the east
coast of Holland. Choose from a large selection of
freshwater and sea fish, shellfish, cured fish (try the
smoked eels, or *gerookte paling*), takeaway snacks
and seafood salads.

Health food

See also page 164 **Noordermarkt**.

Biologische Boerenmarkt

*Noordermarkt, corner of Noorderstraat and
Brouwersgracht, The Jordaan. Tram 3, 10/bus 18,
22.* **Open** 9am-3pm Sat; closed Mon-Fri, Sun. **No
credit cards**. **Map** p306 B2.
A weekly market up in the Jordaan, and a terrific
place to find organic fruit, veg, cheese, breads and
dairy products.

Deshima Freshop

*Weteringschans 65, Grachtengordel: East (423
0391). Tram 6, 7, 10, 16, 24, 25.* **Open** 10am-6pm
Mon-Fri; 10am-5pm Sat; closed Sun. **No credit
cards**. **Map** p310 D5.
This basement macrobiotic shop sells foods that
contain no dairy products, meat or sugar, and also
offers macrobiotic cookery courses in Friesland as
part of the Kushi Institute (phone 625 7513 for
details). Above the shop is a curiously – even, perhaps, eerily – subdued restaurant serving macrobiotic lunches from noon until 2pm on weekdays.

De Bast

*Huidenstraat 19, Grachtengordel: West (624 8087).
Tram 1, 2, 5.* **Open** 11.30am-6.30pm Mon; 9.30am-
6.30pm Tue-Fri; 9am-5pm Sat; closed Sun. **No credit
cards**. **Map** p310 C4.

A popular and centrally located health food shop
with organic fruit and veg and excellent freshly
baked bread, cakes and savouries. The place to head
if you've overdone it at **Febo** (*see p105*) and want
to get your body back on an even keel.

De Natuurwinkel

*Weteringschans 133, Grachtengordel: East (638
4083/www.denatuurwinkel.nl). Tram 6, 7, 10.* **Open**
7am-8pm Mon-Wed, Fri, Sat; 7am-9pm Thur; 11am-
6pm Sun. **Credit** AmEx, MC, V. **Map** p311 E5.
De Natuurwinkel is easily the largest health food
supermarket in Amsterdam, with branches scattered across town. You'll find everything wholesome
here, from organic meat, fruit and veg (delivered
fresh to the stores daily) to surprisingly tasty sugar-
free chocolates and organic wine and beer.
Branches: 1e Constantijn Huygensstraat 49-55,
Museum Quarter (685 1536); 1e Van Swindenstraat
30-2, Oost (693 5909); Haarlemmerdijk 174, The
Jordaan (626 6310).

Night shops

It's 11pm, and you're in dire need of ice-cream/
cigarettes/toilet roll/condoms/beer/chocolate
(delete as applicable). This is where the city's
night shops come in handy. Although prices are
often pretty steep, you're paying for the
convenience, and let's face it: shops that stay
open until 2am are worth their weight in gold.

Avondmarkt

De Wittenkade 94-6, West (686 4919). Tram 10.
Open 4pm-midnight Mon-Fri; 3pm-midnight Sat;
2pm-midnight Sun. **No credit cards**. **Map** p305 A2.
The Avondmarkt is the biggest and best night shop
in town: it's basically a supermarket, albeit a late-
opening one. Recommended, and worth the trek.

Big Bananas

*Leidsestraat 73, Grachtengordel: East (627 7040).
Tram 1, 2, 5.* **Open** 10am-1am Mon-Fri, Sun; 10am-
2am Sat. **No credit cards**. **Map** p310 D4.
An OK selection of wine, some dubious-looking
canned cocktails and a variety of sandwiches are
stocked here. Expensive, even for a night shop.

Begorrah! It's **Taste of Ireland**. *See p157*.

Dolf's Avondverkoop

*Willemsstraat 79, The Jordaan (625 9503). Tram
3.* **Open** *4pm-1am daily.* **No credit cards.**
Map *p306 B2.*
One of the best night shops in the Jordaan, Dolf's
stocks all the urgent products you might suddenly
need late at night, including toilet paper, toothpaste
and bread. As pricey as most night shops.

Heuft's First Class Night Shop

Rijnstraat 62, Oost (642 4048). Tram 4, 25.
Open *5pm-1am Mon-Fri; 3pm-1am Sat, Sun.*
Credit AmEx, DC, MC, V.
If you can't make it all the way out to Heuft's – it's
just beyond the Pijp – you can phone for a delivery
of anything from champagne and oysters to full
meals: Heuft's has it all, if you're willing to pay over
the odds. Definitely the classiest night shop in
Amsterdam.

Sterk

*Waterlooplein 241, Old Centre: Old Side (626 5097).
Tram 9, 14, 20/Metro Waterlooplein.* **Open** *8am-
2am daily.* **Credit** MC, V. **Map** *p307 E3.*
Sterk is more of a deli than a night shop: quiches,
pastries, salads and more are made on the premises,
and there's even a range of fresh fruit and veg. It's
also a good bet for a decent bottle of plonk and some
nice confectionery. Be prepared to ask for whatever
you want here, as there's no self-service. Its branch
is known as 'Champagne Corner', which may give
you some idea as to what's on offer.
Branch: De Clercqstraat 1-7, Oud West (618 1727).

Off-licences (Slijterijen)

De Bierkoning

*Paleisstraat 125, Old Centre: New Side (625 2336/
www.bierkoning.nl). Tram 1, 2, 5, 13, 14, 16, 17,
20, 24, 25.* **Open** *1-7pm Mon; 11am-7pm Tue, Wed,
Fri; 11am-9pm Thur; 11am-6pm Sat; 1-5pm Sun.*
Credit AmEx, DC, MC, V. **Map** p306 C3.
'The Beer King', named for its location behind the
Royal Palace, stocks approximately 850 different
brands of beer from around the world, and a range
of nice beer glasses.

Chabrol, Adviseurs in Wijnen en Gedistilleerd

*Haarlemmerstraat 7, Grachtengordel: West
(622 2781/www.chabrol.nl). Tram 1, 2, 5.* **Open**
*9.30am-8pm Mon-Fri; 9.30am-7pm Sat; noon-5.30pm
Sun.* **Credit** *(over ƒ50 only)* AmEx, MC, V.
Map *p306 C2.*
Offering wine, beer and spirits from all over the
world as well as expert advice, this clumsily named
shop is great value for money. Added bonuses include
free delivery within Amsterdam and glasses available for rent.

De Cuyp

*Albert Cuypstraat 146, The Pijp (662 6676). Tram
4, 16, 24, 25.* **Open** *9am-6pm Tue-Sat; closed Mon,
Sun.* **Credit** MC, V. **Map** p311 F5.

De Cuyp stocks a large assortment of international
wines and spirits, including drinks from Brazil,
Surinam, and the owner's favourite, Pisco, from
Chile. It also specialises in extremes: there are over
3,000 miniatures in stock, plus some huge bottles,
such as a 21 litre bottle of champagne. There's free
delivery in Amsterdam, and rental glasses are on
offer if you're the partying type.

Supermarkets

That the Netherlands is one of the world's most
densely populated countries is perhaps most
apparent on Saturday afternoons at the
supermarket. Thankfully, because Amsterdam
is a city that stays up late, Saturday mornings
are a different story and are a good time to get
out and get the goods. Otherwise, prepare to
brave the horrendously crowded aisles and long
queues at the cash registers.
A few tips: unless a per piece (*per stuk*) price
is given, fruit and vegetables must be weighed
by the customer. Put your produce on the scale,
press the picture of the item, and press the
'BON' button to get the receipt. You must pack
your groceries yourself, and if you want a
plastic bag (usually 35¢), you have to ask for it.

Albert Heijn

*Nieuwezijds Voorburgwal 226, Old Centre: New Side
(421 8344/www.ah.nl). Tram 1, 2, 4, 5, 9, 13, 14,
16, 17, 20, 24, 25.* **Open** *8am-10pm Mon-Sat; 11am-
7pm Sun.* **No credit cards.** **Map** p306 D3.
This massive branch of Albert Heijn, aptly named
the 'Food Plaza', is located behind Dam Square.
There are over 40 branches of Heijn within
Amsterdam (some of which are listed below), but
the extended hours at this branch are an exception
to those of most others. It should contain most
everything you need in terms of household goods,
though prices on some ranges are more expensive
than at some of its competitors.
Branches: Van Baerlestraat 33A, Museum Quarter
(662 0416); Haarlemmerdijk 1, The Jordaan (625
6931); Kinkerstraat 89, Oud West (618 0088);
Koningsplein 4-6, Grachtengordel: East (624 5721);
Nieuwmarkt 18, Old Centre: Old Side (623 2461);
Overtoom 454, Oud West (618 3065); Vijzelstraat 113,
Grachtengordel: East (625 9405); Jodenbreestraat 21,
Old Centre: Old Side (624 1249); Westerstraat 79-87,
The Jordaan (623 6852).

Dirk van den Broek

*Marie Heinekenplein 25, The Pijp (673 9393).
Tram 16, 24, 25.* **Open** *8am-9pm Mon-Fri;
8am-8pm Sat; 1-7pm Sun.* **No credit cards.**
Map *p311 E5.*
A perfectly decent, unflashy grocery store. There's
less choice and less luxury than at **Albert Heijn**
(*see above*), but it's far cheaper.
Branches: Bilderdijkstraat 126, Oud West (612
2658); 2e Nassaustraat 23, Westerpark (686 0132);
Wittenburgerstraat 18, Oost (620 0070).

Groceries and all manner of household goods can be had at **Albert Heijn**. See p159.

Hema

Kalvertoren, Singel 457/A1, Old Centre: New Side (422 8988). Tram 1, 2, 4, 5, 9, 20. **Open** 11am-7pm Mon; 9.30am-7pm Tue, Wed, Fri; 9.30am-9pm Thur; 9.30am-6pm Sat; noon-6pm Sun. **No credit cards. Map** p306 D3.

Hardly the place for weekly basics – it doesn't sell milk, for one thing – but everything you need for a picnic, along with a terrific range of cheap snacks. **Branches**: *See page 144.*

Marks & Spencer

Kalverstraat 66-72, Old Centre: New Side (531 2468). Tram 4, 9, 14, 16, 20, 24, 25. **Open** 11am-6pm Mon; 10am-6pm Tue, Wed, Fri, Sat; 10am-9pm Thur; noon-6pm Sun. **Credit** MC, V. **Map** p306 D3.

Full of the food and underwear Brits know and love, albeit at higher prices than in the UK. There's also a currency exchange.

Tea & coffee

Brandmeester's Koffie

Van Baerlestraat 13, Museum Quarter (675 7888). Tram 3, 12, 20, 24. **Open** 9am-6pm Mon-Wed, Fri; 9am-9pm Thur; 9am-5.30pm Sat; noon-5pm first Sun of mth. **Credit** AmEx, DC, MC, V. **Map** p310 D6.

Coffee beans from around the globe, roasted on the premises. The smell, as you'd imagine, is fantastic.

Geels & Co

Warmoesstraat 67, Old Centre: Red Light District (624 0683). Tram 4, 9, 14, 16, 20, 24, 25. **Open** *Shop* 9.30am-6pm Mon-Sat; closed Sun. **No credit cards. Map** p306 D2.

Coffee beans and loose teas, plus a large stock of brewing contraptions and serving utensils. Upstairs is a small museum of brewing equipment, open on Saturday afternoons.

Branch: 't Zonnetje, Haarlemmerdijk 45, The Jordaan (623 0058).

Simon Levelt

Prinsengracht 180, Grachtengordel: West (624 0823). Tram 13, 14, 17, 20. **Open** noon-6pm Mon; 9am-6pm Tue-Fri; 9am-5pm Sat; closed Sun. **No credit cards. Map** p305 B3.

The tea and coffee specialist. The wonderful shop, which dates from 1839 and which still has much of the original tiled decor in place, carries anything and everything to do with brewing and serving.

Branches: Centraal Station, Old Centre (428 5887); Ferdinand Bolstraat 154, The Pijp (400 4060).

Games, models & toys

Joe's Vliegerwinkel

Nieuwe Hoogstraat 19, Old Centre: Old Side (625 0139). Tram 4, 9, 16, 20, 24, 25/Metro Nieuwmarkt. **Open** 1-6pm Mon; 11am-6pm Tue-Fri; closed Sun. **Credit** AmEx, DC, MC, V. **Map** p307 E3.

Kites, kites and more kites, plus a quirky array of boomerangs, yo-yos and kaleidoscopes can be found at the wonderfully colourful Joe's Vliegerwinkel.

Kramer/Pontifex

Reestraat 18-20, Grachtengordel: West (626 5274). Tram 13, 14, 17, 20. **Open** 10am-6pm Mon-Fri; 10am-5pm Sat; closed Sun. **No credit cards. Map** p306 C3.

Mr Kramer is a doctor for old-fashioned dolls and teddies who has held his surgery on these premises for 25 years; he can fix anything from a broken Barbie to a battered bear. It is all impossibly sweet. Pontifex, on the same premises, sells a multitude of candles.

Schaal Treinen Huis
Bilderdijkstraat 94, Oud West (612 2670). Tram 3, 7, 12, 13, 14, 17, 20. **Open** 9.30am-5.30pm Tue-Sat; closed Sun. **Credit** AmEx, DC, MC, V. **Map** p309 B5.
With a DIY kit from here, you can build a replica of St Peter's Basilica or the Arc de Triomphe. The ready-made parade includes electric trains plus tracks, stations, houses and scenery. There is also a huge variety of modern and vintage vehicles, dolls' houses and dolls' house accessories.

Schaak en Go het Paard
Haarlemmerdijk 147, The Jordaan (624 1171). Tram 3/bus 18, 22. **Open** 10.30am-5.30pm Tue-Fri; 10.30am-5.30pm Sat; closed Mon, Sun. **Credit** MC, V. **Map** p305 B1.
A fine selection of beautiful and exotic chess sets, ranging from African to ultra-modern, as well as the Japanese game Go. One for the more cerebral game-player, but none the worse for it.

De Zeiling
Ruysdaelstraat 21-3, The Pijp (679 3817). Tram 2, 3, 5, 12, 16, 20. **Open** noon-6pm Mon; 9am-6pm Tue, Wed; 9am-8pm Thur; 9am-5pm Fri, Sat; closed Sun. **Credit** AmEx, DC, MC, V. **Map** p311 E6.
This gem of a shop is stocked with Rudolf Steiner-inspired artefacts, including handmade wooden toys, rattles, puzzles, music boxes and night lights, baby clothes in natural materials, dyes, doll-making materials, cards and candles.

Health & beauty

Body Shop
Kalverstraat 157-9, Old Centre: New Side (623 9789/www.thebodyshop.co.uk). Tram 4, 9, 14, 16, 20, 24, 25. **Open** 11am-6pm Mon; 9.30am-6pm Tue, Wed, Fri; 9.30am-9pm Thur; 10am-5.30pm Sat; 1-5pm Sun. **Credit** AmEx, DC, MC, V. **Map** p306 D3.
The usual array of shampoos, lotions and soaps for pampering your body, along with gift-wrapping and refill services. Prices are higher than in Britain.
Branches: Kinkerstraat 251, Oud West (683 7157); Nieuwendijk 196E, Old Centre: New Side (626 6135).

Boots
Kalverstraat 31-3, Old Centre: New Side (530 8860/www.boots.co.uk). Tram 4, 9, 14, 16, 20, 24, 25. **Open** 11am-6pm Mon; 9.30am-6pm Tue, Wed, Fri; 9.30am-9pm Thur; 9am-6pm Sun. **Credit** AmEx, DC, MC, V. **Map** p306 D3.
Hip hip hooray! The mighty British chain Boots has finally made it to Holland, offering the Dutch the usual selection of great hair, body and make-up lines from the UK, as well as pharmaceuticals. It's all too exciting for words.

Homeopathie De Munt
Vijzelstraat 1, Grachtengordel: East (624 4533). Tram 4, 9, 14, 16, 20, 24, 25. **Open** 9.30am-6pm Mon-Wed, Fri, Sat; 9.30am-9pm Thur; 1-6pm Sun. **Credit** AmEx, DC, MC, V. **Map** p310 D4.
This tiny, picturesque store is choc-a-bloc with all it takes to turn your bathroom into a spa, including a wide range of essential oils and treatment products from Neal's Yard, Kiehl's and Weleda. If you have a taste for herbs you can't find in coffeeshops, come here for Celestial Seasonings teas, Solgar Vitamins and bee pollen in capsule form.

Consumer

Never say Neder again

If kitsch is the cultivation of the artificial and unnatural, then the Netherlands – which should be a bog – is, in fact, the ultimate kitsch country. And, naturally, part of the joys of travelling is to laugh at a nation's kitsch. And much Nederkitsch ranks among the world's finest and most exuberant souvenirs.

However, one can also glean plentiful historical and sociological insights into the town in question through nothing more than a gander at its gift shops. And so it is with Amsterdam, whose kitsch yields many home truths. How large chocolate penises speak of the city's openness and willingness to share, say. Or how the model tallships made of Heineken cans speak less of shabby taste in interiors and more of the nation's seafaring

past and its ever-ready-for-a-beer present. And even how the tallest European nation's obsession for miniatures has not only led to the building of **Madurodam**, 'the world's largest miniature village' (see page 260), but also to scientific innovations such as the invention of the modern microscope, and the laying of the foundations for the discipline of scientific study known as entomology.

So instead of simply scoffing at souvenirs, shake off that cynicism, narrow your ironic distance, step up and take a closer look. And then take the memory of your gaze home with you. Hell, they might be educational, but you certainly wouldn't want to *buy* such ugly tat. What sort of sociological insight into their foreign guests would that give the Dutch?

Candle sales and doll repairs at the adorable **Kramer** and **Pontifex**. *See p160.*

Interiors & housewares

Frozen Fountain
Prinsengracht 629, Grachtengordel: East (622 9375). Tram 1, 2, 5. **Open** 1-6pm Mon; 10am-6pm Tue-Fri; 10am-5pm Sat; closed Sun. **No credit cards. Map** p310 D4.
Frozen Fountain defies description, though its thing is largely cutting-edge designer furnishings that are deeply seated in tradition. Don't miss.

Galerie KIS
Paleisstraat 107, Old Centre: New Side (620 9760). Tram 1, 2, 4, 5, 9, 11, 13, 16, 17, 20, 24, 25. **Open** noon-6pm Wed-Sun; closed Mon, Tue. **No credit cards. Map** p306 C3.
Masses of sensational furniture, lighting and house-wares from independent designers, artists and architects. KIS keeps the numbers in each series small, so you can be sure you'll be the only one on the block with one of these original pieces.

Kitsch Kitchen
Rozengracht 183, The Jordaan (622 8261). Tram 13, 14, 17, 20. **Open** 10am-6pm Mon-Sat; closed Sun. **Credit** AmEx, DC, MC, V. **Map** p306 B3.
Kitsch Kitchen sends even the most hardy tat queens weak at the knees. A staggering variety of culinary and household objects (including wacky '60s wallpapers) have been imported from Mexico, Guatemala, India, China and parts of Africa, and there's also tons of plastic stuff.
Branch: 1e Bloemdwarsstraat 21, The Jordaan (428 4969).

Marañón Hangmatten
Singel 488-90, at the flower market, Grachtengordel: East (420 7121). Tram 1, 2, 5, 20. **Open** 9.30am-6pm Mon; 10am-6pm Tue-Fri; 9am-6pm Sat; 10.30am-6pm Sun. **Credit** AmEx, DC, MC, V. **Map** p310 D4.
Europe's biggest collection of hammocks, available in a variety of colours and designs. The most expensive and colourful are the hand-woven ones from South America and Mexico (from ƒ60).

Santa Jet
Prinsenstraat 7, Grachtengordel: West (427 2070). Tram 1, 2, 5, 20. **Open** 11am-6pm Mon-Fri; 10am-5pm Sat; noon-5pm Sun. **Credit** AmEx, DC, MC, V.
Live la vida loca with wild Mexican housewares, mini altars, day of the dead puppets and much more Mexican kitsch madness. Olé!

What's Cooking
Reestraat 16, Grachtengordel: West (427 0630). Tram 13, 14, 17, 20. **Open** noon-6.30pm Tue-Fri; 11am-6pm Sat; closed Mon, Sun. **Credit** AmEx, MC, V. **Map** p306 C3.
Every object in this zingy culinary gift shop seems chosen for its retina-searing colours: vivid pink salad bowls, kiwi green sauces, and acid orange peppermills are just the tip of the proverbial iceberg; all are capable of putting pep into the most humdrum of kitchens. Cooking will never be the same again.

Xenos
Kalverstraat 228, Old Centre: New Side (422 9163). Tram 1, 2, 4, 5, 9, 14, 16, 20, 24, 25. **Open** 11am-6pm Mon; 9.30am-6pm Tue, Wed, Fri, Sat; 9.30am-9pm Thur; noon-6pm Sun. **No credit cards. Map** p306 D3.
If you're setting up house on a tight budget or for a short period of time, this is the place to find much of what you'll need at very low prices.
Branch: Nieuwendijk 200-6, Old Centre: New Side (427 4153).

Glass & crystal

Glasgalerie Kuhler
Prinsengracht 134, Grachtengordel: West (638 0230). Tram 13, 14, 16, 20. **Open** noon-6pm Wed-Sat; 1-4pm first Sun of mth; closed Mon, Tue. **Credit** AmEx, DC, MC, V. **Map** p305 B3.
A large collection of contemporary European glass and crystal is available at Glasgalerie Kuhler. Most pieces are unique, dated and signed by well-known artists. Glass-blowing is well represented, along with pate verre and cold laminated sculptures. Prices range from ƒ85 to a cool ƒ10,000.

Van Tetterode

Singel 163, Grachtengordel: West (620 6382).
Tram 1, 2, 5, 13, 17, 20. **Open** 10.30am-6pm
Tue-Sun; closed Mon. **Credit** AmEx, DC, MC, V.
Map p306 C3.
Since 1919, Van Tetterode's atelier has been turning
out unique glass objets d'art, as well as monumen-
tal commissions and public pieces. One-day glass
workshops are available by appointment.

Vintage

Bebob Design Interior

Prinsengracht 764, Grachtengordel: East (624
5763/www.bebob.nl). Tram 4. **Open** 1-6pm Mon;
10am-6pm Tue-Fri; 10am-5pm Sat; closed Sun.
Credit AmEx, DC, MC, V.
Highly sought-after vintage furnishing from Eames
on up. The quality is fantastic, the selection superb,
and the prices high.

Nic Nic

Gasthuismolensteeg 5, Grachtengordel: West (622
8523). Tram 1, 2, 5, 13, 17, 20. **Open** noon-6pm
Mon-Fri; 10am-5pm Sat; closed Sun. **Credit** AmEx,
MC, V. **Map** p306 C3.
There's certainly no shortage of shops of this ilk in
Amsterdam, but this one definitely has the best
selection of '50s and '60s furniture, lamps, ashtrays
and kitchenware, mostly in mint condition. Opening
times can vary, so phone first to check.
Branch: 1e Jan Steenstraat 131, The Pijp (675 6805).

Quadra Original Posters

Herengracht 383-9, Grachtengordel: West (626
9472). Tram 1, 2, 4, 5, 14, 16, 20, 24, 25.
Open 10.30am-4.30pm Tue-Sat; closed Mon, Sun.
Credit MC, V. **Map** p310 D4.
Celebrate the millennium with an original *fin de*
siècle advertising poster, or decorate your room with
a '30s circus poster. Whatever your tastes – from
beer ads to B-movies – you're sure to find it here.

Markets

The biggest and best market of all is held on
Queen's Day (*see page 172*). Amsterdam's
neighbourhood markets, particularly **Albert**
Cuypmarkt and the **Dappermarkt**, are the
best places to find cheap food and clothes, while
aficionados of second-hand goods should head
to Monday's **Noordermarkt**. For flower
markets, *see page 154*.

Albert Cuypmarkt

Albert Cuypstraat, The Pijp. Tram 4, 16, 24, 25.
Open 9.30am-5pm Mon-Sat; closed Sun. **No credit**
cards. Map p311 E5.
Amsterdam's biggest general market sells everything from pillows to prawns at excellent prices. It's
also worth visiting for the material stalls, a firm
favourite with painters, who can pick up untreated
canvas from around ƒ3,95 a metre. Clothes tend to
be run-of-the-mill cheapies, with the odd bargain.

Experience a whole new taste sensation at **Kitsch Kitchen**. *See p162.*

Viva Mexico! **Santa Jet**. *See p162*.

Boerenmarkt
Westerstraat/Noorderkerkstraat, The Jordaan.
Tram 3, 10. **Open** 9am-3pm Sat; closed Mon-Fri,
Sun. **No credit cards**. **Map** p306 B2.
Every Saturday, the Noordermarkt is transformed
into the organic farmers' market. Products include
organic fruit and vegetables (with opportunities for
food- and wine-tasting) as well as essential oils,
herbs, candles and the like. Groups of singers or
medieval musicians sometimes make a visit here feel
more like a day trip than a mere shopping excursion.

Dappermarkt
Dapperstraat, Oost. Tram 3, 6, 10, 14. **Open**
9am-5pm Mon-Sat; closed Sun. **No credit cards**.
Map p312 H3.
A true locals' market, far less touristy than its
famous counterparts: for a start, prices don't seem
to rise in accordance with the number of visitors. It
sells the usual market fodder, with plenty of cheap
clothes and underwear.

Looier
Elandsgracht 109, The Jordaan (624 9038).
Tram 7, 10, 17, 20. **Open** 11am-5pm Mon-Thur,
Sat, Sun; closed Fri. **Credit** AmEx, DC, MC, V.
Map p310 C4.
The Looier is more upmarket than the nearby
Rommelmarkt (*see below*): it's mainly antiques
here, with plenty of collectors' items on offer. It's easy
to get lost in the quiet, warehouse-like premises and
find yourself standing alone by a stall crammed with
antiquated clocks eerily ticking away.

Hey good-looking: **What's Cooking** (*p162*).

Noordermarkt
Noordermarkt, The Jordaan. Tram 3, 10. **Open**
7.30am-1pm Mon; closed Tue-Sun. **No credit cards**.
Map p306 B2.
A bargain hunter's paradise. Tagged on to the end
of the utilitarian **Westermarkt** (*see below*), the
Noordermarkt is compact and frequented by the
serious market shopper. The piles upon piles of new
and (mainly) second-hand clothes, shoes, jewellery
and hats need to be sorted through with a grim
determination in order to sift the dross from the
delights. Prices can be laughably low, but like all the
best second-hand markets, if you don't arrive early,
the best stuff will already have been snapped up.

Oudemanhuis Book Market
Oudemanhuispoort, Old Centre: Old Side. Tram 4, 9,
14, 16, 20, 24, 25. **Open** 11am-4pm Mon-Fri; closed
Sat, Sun. **No credit cards**. **Map** p306 D3.
People have been buying and selling books, prints
and sheet music at this arcade since the 19th century. When the alley was built in 1601, it was the
entrance to a home for the elderly, hence the name.

Postzegelmarkt
Nieuwezijds Voorburgwal, by No.276, Old Centre:
New Side. Tram 1, 2, 5, 13, 17, 20. **Open** 11am-
4pm Wed, Sun; closed Mon, Tue, Thur-Sat.
No credit cards. **Map** p306 D3.
A specialist market for collectors of stamps, coins,
old postcards and commemorative medals.

Rommelmarkt
Looiersgracht 38, The Jordaan. Tram 7, 10, 17, 20.
Open 11am-5pm daily. **No credit cards**. **Map**
p310 C4.
A flea market where, nestled among the household
junk, you are likely to come across dubious bargains
such as a boxed set of Demis Roussos discs.

Waterlooplein
Waterlooplein, Old Centre: Old Side. Tram 9, 14,
20/Metro Waterlooplein. **Open** 9am-5pm Mon-Sat;
closed Sun. **No credit cards**. **Map** p307 E3.
Amsterdam's top tourist market, but no less entertaining for that. Basically a huge flea market, it's
great for clothes (though they can be a bit pricey and,
at many stalls, decidedly naff), with the usual selections of jeans, leathers and batik T-shirts and some
excellent second-hand stuff. Bargains can be had,
but they're often hidden among defunct toasters and
down-at-heel (literally) shoes. Musos will enjoy
rifling through the boxes of battered vinyl, though
everyone should beware of pickpockets.

Westermarkt
Westerstraat, The Jordaan. Tram 3, 10. **Open**
9am-1pm Mon; closed Tue-Sun. **No credit cards**.
Map p306 B2.
A general market, selling all sorts of things. The
amount of people packing the pavement is proof as
to the entirely reasonable prices and the range of
goods, which includes new watches, pretty (and not
so pretty) fabrics and cheap factory reject clothes.

Music

Blue Note From Ear & Eye
Gravenstraat 12, Old Centre: New Side (428 1029).
Tram 1, 2, 4, 5, 9, 13, 16, 20, 24, 25. **Open** 11am-
7pm Mon-Sat; noon-5pm Sun. **Credit** AmEx, DC,
MC, V. **Map** p306 C3.
The full spectrum of jazz, from '30s stompers to
mainstream, avant-garde and Afro jazz, can be seen
on the packed shelves here. Mmmm. Niiiice.

Boudisque
Haringpakkerssteeg 10-18, Old Centre: New Side
(623 2603/www.boudisque.nl). Tram 1, 2, 4, 5, 9,
13, 14, 16, 17, 20, 24, 25. **Open** noon-6pm Mon,
Sun; 10am-6pm Tue, Wed, Fri, Sat; 10am-9pm Thur.
Credit AmEx, DC, MC, V. **Map** p306 D2.
Pop, rock, heavy metal, ambient house, jungle and
world music CDs, plus T-shirts and CD-Roms.

Charles Klassiek en Folklore
Weteringschans 193, Grachtengordel: East (626
5538). Tram 6, 7, 10, 16, 24, 25. **Open** 1-6.30pm
Mon; 10am-6.30pm Tue, Wed, Fri; 10am-9pm Thur;
10am-5.30pm Sat; closed Sun. **Credit** AmEx, DC,
MC, V. **Map** p311 E5.
Literally, 'classical and folk'. A good place for some
of the smaller German and French labels, and, buck-
ing trends, for good, old-fashioned vinyl.

Concerto
Utrechtsestraat 54-60, Grachtengordel: East (626
6577/624 5467/623 5228). Tram 4. **Open**
10am-6pm Mon-Wed, Fri, Sat; 10am-9pm Thur;
noon-6pm Sun. **Credit** (over ƒ25 only) AmEx, DC,
MC, V. **Map** p311 E4.
New and second-hand records and CDs of all types:
this is where to look for historic Bach recordings,
obscure Beatles items, or that favourite Diana Ross
album that got lost in the move. There's also a large
section of second-hand 45s and new releases at
decent prices. Nick Hornby types will love it.

Get Records
Utrechtsestraat 105, Grachtengordel: East (622
3441). Tram 4. **Open** 10am-6pm Mon-Wed, Fri, Sat;
10am-9pm Thur; noon-6pm Sun. **Credit** AmEx, DC,
MC, V. **Map** p311 E4.
The space liberated by the clearout of much of the
vinyl at Get Records has been filled with a consid-
erable selection of alternative and independent-label
CDs. The back of the shop is deceptive: a little corner to the left is partially dedicated to cheapies and
is well worth investigating.

Midtown
Nieuwendijk 104, Old Centre: New Side (638 4252).
Tram 1, 2, 5, 13, 17, 20, 24, 25. **Open** 1-6pm Mon,
Sun; 10am-6pm Tue, Wed, Fri, Sat; 10am-9pm Thur.
Credit AmEx, DC, MC, V. **Map** p306 D2.
Dance music galore: hardcore, gabber, trance, club,
mellow house and garage are among the styles on
the shelves. Midtown is also a good source of infor-
mation and tickets for hardcore parties.

Sound of the Fifties
Prinsengracht 669, Grachtengordel: East (623 9745).
Tram 6, 7, 10, 20. **Open** 1-6pm Mon; noon-6pm
Tue-Sat; closed Sun. **Credit** AmEx, MC, V.
Map p310 C4.
Collectable vinyl from the '50s, from Liberace to
Yma Sumac. Records and sleeves are in good con-
dition, but prices are accordingly high.

Virgin Megastore
Magna Plaza, Nieuwezijds Voorburgwal 182, Old
Centre: New Side (622 8929). Tram 1, 2, 5, 13, 17,
20. **Open** 11am-7pm Mon; 10am-7pm Tue, Wed, Fri,
Sat; 10am-9pm Thur; noon-7pm Sun. **Credit** AmEx,
DC, MC, V. **Map** p306 C3.
There's no vinyl, but Virgin does have splendid selec-
tions of CDs, videos, computer games and T-shirts.

New Age & Eco

See also page 158 **Health food.**

Greenlands, Hemp Eco Store
Utrechtsestraat 26, Grachtengordel: East (625 1100/
www.greenlands.nl). Tram 4. **Open** 1-6pm Mon;
11am-6pm Tue-Sat; closed Sun. **Credit** AmEx, DC,
MC, V. **Map** p311 E4.
Greenlands' stock includes clothes, food, a small
selection of stationery and lots of other bits and bobs
made from hemp.

Hemp Works
Niewendijk 13, Old Centre: New Side (421 1762).
Tram 1, 2, 5, 13, 17, 20. **Open** 11.30am-7pm daily.
Credit AmEx, DC, MC, V. **Map** p306 C2.
A whole lot of hemp: from streetwear styles to basic
jeans, and baseball caps to bubble bath.

Himalaya
Warmoesstraat 56, Old Centre: Red Light District
(626 0899/www.himalaya.nl). Tram 1, 2, 4, 5, 9, 16,
17, 20, 24, 25/Metro Centraal Station. **Open** 1-6pm
Mon; 10am-6pm Tue, Wed, Fri, Sat; 10am-8.30pm
Thur; 12.30-5pm Sun. **Credit** AmEx, MC, V.
Map p306 D2.
Shop-gallery-teahouse Himalaya is a haven of
calm amid seedy, bustling surroundings. The shop
stocks an extensive range of books and magazines,
crystals, tarot cards and jewellery.

Get jazzy at **Blue Note From Ear & Eye.**

Consumer

Jacob Hooy & Co

Kloveniersburgwal 12, Old Centre: Old Side (624 3041). Tram 4, 9, 14, 16, 20, 24, 25/Metro Nieuwmarkt. **Open** 10am-6pm Mon; 8.15am-6pm Tue-Fri; 8.15am-5pm Sat. **Credit** V. **Map** p306 C3.

Established in 1743, this chemist sells around 600 kitchen and medicinal herbs, spices, natural cosmetics, health foods and homeopathic remedies.

De Roos-Centrum voor Creatieve en Spirituele Groei

Vondelstraat 35, Museum Quarter (689 0081/shop 689 0436/teahouse 689 5477). Tram 1, 2, 3, 5, 6, 12. **Open** *Centre* 8.15am-10.45pm Mon-Fri; 9am-6pm Sat, Sun. *Shop* 10am-9.30pm Mon-Fri; 11.30am-5.30pm Sat; noon-4pm Sun. *Teahouse* 9am-10.30pm Mon-Fri; 9am-5pm Sat, Sun. **No credit cards. Map** p310 C5.

A New Age centre with regular workshops and daily open sessions in yoga, Zen meditation and healing. There's a great range of books and leaflets on esoteric subjects, as well as magazines, candles, crystals, herbs, tarot cards and incense.

Vitals Vitamine-Advieswinkel

Nieuwe Nieuwstraat 47, Old Centre: New Side (625 7298). Tram 1, 2, 5, 13, 17, 20. **Open** 9.30am-6pm Mon-Fri; 11am-5pm Sat; closed Sun. **Credit** AmEx, DC, MC, V. **Map** p306 C2.

The emphasis at this friendly shop is on educating yourself about food supplements and vitamins.

Souvenirs

C-Cedille

Lijnbaansgracht 275, Grachtengordel: East (624 7178). Tram 6, 7, 10. **Open** noon-6pm Thur, Fri; 11am-6pm Sat; closed Mon-Wed, Sun. **Credit** AmEx, DC, MC, V. **Map** p310 D5.

In one half of this lovely shop, you'll find designer jewellery, mostly made by hand in the Netherlands. The other half has wooden toys, mobiles, puppets, music boxes and dolls in Dutch costumes, plus etchings and aquarelles of typical (for which, read tourist-friendly) Amsterdam scenes.

Holland Gallery De Munt

In the Munttoren, Muntplein 12, Old Centre: New Side (623 2271). Tram 4, 9, 14, 16, 20, 24, 25. **Open** 10am-6pm Mon-Sat; closed Sun. **Credit** AmEx, DC, MC, V. **Map** p310 D4.

Antique Delftware and royal and Makkumer pottery, plus other hand-painted objects such as traditional tiles and decorated wooden trays and boxes. Other highlights include miniature ceramic canal houses and dolls in traditional Dutch costume.

Tesselschade: Arbeid Adelt

Leidseplein 33, Grachtengordel: East (623 6665). Tram 1, 2, 5, 6, 7, 10, 20. **Open** 10am-6pm Tue-Fri; 10am-5pm Sat. **Credit** AmEx, MC, V. **Map** p310 D5.

Toys, decorations and more utilitarian items – such as tea cosies and decorated clothes hangers – are crafted and sold on a non-profit basis by an association of Dutch women, Arbeid Adelt ('work ennobles').

Wooden Shoe Factory

Nieuwe Hoogstraat 11, Old Centre: Old Side (427 3862/www.woodenshoefactory.nl). Tram 1, 2, 5. **Open** 9am-6pm daily. **Credit** AmEx, DC, MC, V. **Map** p307 E3.

A brand new location for this splendid little shop that does exactly what you'd expect from its name. It was due to open in autumn 2000 and hours may change, so call ahead before you make the trek.

Speciality

Christmas World

Damrak 33, Old Centre: New Side (420 2838). Tram 1, 2, 5, 13, 17, 20. **Open** 10am-6pm Mon-Wed; 10am-7.30pm Thur, Sun; 10am-8pm Fri, Sat. **Credit** AmEx, MC, V. **Map** p306 D2.

Nothing but Christmas decorations, all year round. Very, very merry, and positively packed with tidings of comfort and joy.

Condomerie Het Gulden Vlies

Warmoesstraat 141, Old Side: Red Light District (627 4174). Tram 4, 9, 14, 16, 20, 24, 25. **Open** 11am-6pm Mon-Sat; **Closed** Sun. **Credit** AmEx, DC, MC, V. **Map** p306 D2.

Located – but of course – in the Red Light District, this jolly emporium offers a trouser-boggling variety of rubbers for all shapes and sizes.

Olivaria

Hazenstraat 2A, The Jordaan (638 3552). Tram 7, 10. **Open** 1.30pm-6pm Mon; 11am-6pm Tue-Sat; closed Sun. **No credit cards. Map** p310 C4.

A shop devoted exclusively to olive oils, with an astounding array of them from around the world on show and for sale.

PGC Hajenius

Rokin 92-6, Old Centre: New Side (625 9985). Tram 4, 9, 14, 16, 20, 24, 25. **Open** noon-6pm Mon; 9.30-6pm Tue, Wed, Fri, Sat; 9.30am-9pm Thur; noon-5pm Sun. **Credit** AmEx, DC, MC, V. **Map** p306 D3.

A smoker's paradise (tobacco, not dope) for well over 250 years, Hajenius offers all manner of cigarabilia, from traditional Dutch pipes (14in or 20in stem) to own-brand cigars.

Waterwinkel

Roelof Hartstraat 10, Museum Quarter (675 5932). Tram 3, 24. **Open** 1-6pm Mon; 10am-6pm Tue-Fri; 10am-5pm Sat; closed Sun. **Credit** AmEx, DC, V.

Mineral water galore, both native and imported. Both product variety and shop decor are enough to make the weak of bladder want to head straight for the nearest toilet.

De Witte Tandenwinkel

Runstraat 5, Grachtengordel: West (623 3443). Tram 1, 2, 5. **Open** 1-6pm Mon; 10am-6pm Tue-Fri; 10am-5pm Sat; **Closed** Sun. **Credit** AmEx, DC, MC, V. **Map** p310 C4.

Everything you need to keep your teeth in perfect nick, from brushes to pastes and other gimmickry.

Arts &
Entertainment

Amsterdam by Season

From high culture to lowlife insanity, Amsterdam's calendar has something for everyone.

When the original settlers of Amsterdam, the Batavians, arrived in the city, they brought with them a rich heritage of partying that involved song, dance and the slurping of brew from the skull of the slain enemy. As Amsterdam entered its Golden Age in the 17th century, parties tended to last for weeks. The Zottenfeesten ('Fool Fests'), in particular, were mass, drawn-out, drunken mind games that promoted insanity by role reversal: the kids hammered authority, while the adults went berserk and acted, as the saying had it, as if 'hit on the head by the windmill'.

The centuries-long ingraining of Calvinist morals may be the root of the Netherlands' healthy economy, but it did little for the survival of ancient off-the-wall traditions. Today, Amsterdammers' inner partying pagan beast only comes raging out on to the cobbled streets for **Koninginnedag** (Queen's Day; see page 172 **A right royal party**) and **Oudejaarsavond** (New Year's Eve; see page 175), the year's two consistently best bets for experiencing frolicsome mass psychosis. These only get topped when Ajax win an important championship match and thousands of supporters gather in and around Leidseplein and Rembrandtplein to tread that delicately fine line between celebratory partying and raucous rioting. But whether you want to get off your head on cannabis or on art, there is enough to interest all but the pickiest punters.

Where possible, exact dates are given; check the dates of others by phone. The **AUB Ticketshop** and **Uitlijn** (0900 0191) and the **Amsterdam Tourist Board** (0900 400 4040) have information on all events in the city; the latter publishes a calendar in its *What's On In Amsterdam* magazine (f5). Also, check out *Time Out* magazine in London and New York, which has a pick of the town's events, and its more choice-rich website, at *www.timeout.com/ amsterdam*. For a list of public holidays, see page 289. Unless stated, all events are free.

Frequent events

Arts & crafts markets
Spui, Old Centre: New Side (tram 1, 2, 4, 5, 9, 14, 16, 20, 24, 25) & Thorbeckeplein, Grachtengordel: East (tram 4, 9, 14, 20). **Date** *Mar-Oct* 10am-5pm Sun. **Map** p310 D4 (Spui); p311 E4 (Thorbeckeplein).

Two open-air arts and crafts markets are held every Sunday from March until October or November (depending on the weather). These are decent places to browse if you're into pleasant browsing, but don't come here to buy elephant dung, a bovine in brine or a crucifix in urine: most of the jewellery, paintings, vases and bargain ornaments are rather more mediocre. Buskers touting CDs and tapes enhance the laid-back vibe.

Rowing contests
Amsterdamse Bos (information 646 2740). Bus 170, 171, 172. **Date** Apr-July.

Come to this lovely green expanse to watch participants get wet. There are various rowing contests held here from April through to December; check local press or phone the Amsterdam Tourist Board for details.

Book markets
Information 627 5794. **Date** May-Aug.

Four book markets spring up in summer: two along the Amstel (art book market, mid-June; religion, mid-Aug) and two on Dam (children's, mid-May; mysteries, mid-July).

Antiques market
Nieuwmarkt, Old Centre: Old Side. Tram 9, 14, 20/ Metro Nieuwmarkt. **Date** *Mid May-Sept* 9am-5pm Sun. **Map** p306 D2.

Lovers of antiques and bric-a-brac should head for this small antiques market. There's a fair amount of naffness, but also a few gems, especially books, furniture and objets d'art.

Spring

Spring is when the tulips and crocuses start cracking through the earth, and a winter's worth of doggy-do defrosts: those who know about this sort of thing estimate the amount at 20 million kilograms. However, it's also when the population of Amsterdam shrugs off the weight of existential drag that often defines the northern European mindset during winter. Motivated by a visible sun, the city-dwellers take on the more shiny *joie de vivre* vibe that's usually associated with the southern European terrace-café cultures. On the downside, bicycle paths start to clog up, not only with increased traffic, but also with lost, doe-eyed tourists stopping to check their maps. Cycling lanes are often a dull red asphalt, so pedestrians be warned: avoid them or be prepared to take on road pizza position. Otherwise, relax and enjoy a city in a season when lounging in a park or on a terrace is seen as a well-deserved and respected thing to do after a long winter's cold rain and mental drain.

Next Five Minutes: Conference on Tactical Media

Information 557 9898/www.n5m.org. **Date** Mar 2002.
The N5M conference on tactical media brings together media theorists, artists, activists and media-makers from around the world with the hope of providing an inspiring environment for the exchange of ideas and strategies for social change in the digital age. Though the scheduled workshops, exhibitions and performances take place in a variety of locations in Amsterdam and Rotterdam, most of the action should be found at Amsterdam's **Paradiso** (*see p218*) and **De Balie** (*see p237*).

Stille Omgang (Silent Procession)

Information 023 524 6229. **Date** end Mar.
Every year on a Sunday in March, local Catholics commemorate the 1345 Miracle of Amsterdam with a silent night-time procession through the city. The apparently true story of the Miracle begins graphically: a dying man vomited up the bread given to him in communion as part of the last rites. The purged host was tossed on the fire, but was then found the next morning undamaged among the ashes, and the sick man is reputed to have recovered. The procession, with the very same piece of toast in tow (yum!), follows the road that pilgrims have used for centuries, called, for that reason, Heiligeweg (Holy Way). The sight of the procession moving through the

bustling Red Light District at night is decidedly surreal. The route begins and ends at Spui, via Kalverstraat, Nieuwendijk, Warmoesstraat and Nes. For information, write to Gezelschap van de Stille Omgang, Zandvoortseweg 59, 2111 GS Aerdenhout, or phone the above number after 7pm.

World Press Photo

Oude Kerk, Oudekerksplein 23, Old Centre: Red Light District (information 625 8284/ www.worldpressphoto.nl). Tram 4, 9, 16, 20, 24, 25. **Map** p306 D2. **Admission** f10; f7 concessions.
Date Apr-May.
With exhibits chosen from tens of thousands of photos taken by thousands of different photojournalists, the world's largest photo competition takes place in the already sight-worthy confines of the **Oude Kerk** (*see p45*). Each year it kicks off in Amsterdam, before moving on to another 70 locations around the world.

National Museum Weekend

Information 670 1111. **Date** mid-Apr. **Admission** varies.
During National Museum Weekend, many state-run museums offer reduced or free admission and mount exhibitions and activities. Though opening hours are often extended, most museums are busy. Phone the Vereniging Museum Jaarkaart on the above number for further information, or pick up the free Museum Weekend paper at the Amsterdam Tourist Board, the ANWB (auto association) and at the museums themselves. *See also p38.*

Herdenkingsdag & Bevrijdingsdag (Remembrance Day & Liberation Day)

Remembrance Day *National Monument, Dam, Old Centre: Old Side.* Tram 1, 2, 4, 5, 9, 13, 14, 16, 17, 20, 24, 25. **Date** 4 May. **Map** 2 D3.
Liberation Day *Vondelpark (tram 1, 2, 3, 5, 6, 12, 20) & Leidseplein (tram 1, 2, 5, 6, 7, 10, 20).* **Date** 5 May. **Map** p310 C6 (Vondelpark); p310 C5 (Leidseplein).
On 4 May, those who died during World War II are remembered at the National Monument on Dam Square. The service starts at 7.30pm, with the Queen laying a wreath half an hour later. A two-minute silence then follows, after which the Chief of the Armed Forces and other dignitaries lay wreaths.

Though homosexuals who died during World War II are also now remembered in this ceremony, the Dutch gay organisation COC organises its own remembrance service at the **Homomonument** (*see p201*). Liberation Day is celebrated on 5 May, with various activities throughout the city. Vondelpark, Museumplein, Leidseplein and Rokin are the best places to head: expect to find performances by local and national bands, speeches and information stands organised by political and ideological pressure groups, and a free market where you can sell everything you bought in a drunken stupor on Queen's Day a week earlier.

Top five Events

Holland Festival
Where highbrow meets cutting-edge.
See page 170.

Koninginnedag (Queen's Day)
Yoo-hoo! Civilisation! Where are you?
See page 172 **A Right Royal Party**.

Open Studios
Peak into the funky surrounds of Amsterdam's arty types. See page 170.

Oudejaarsavond (New Year's Eve)
The fall of Saigon recreated annually.
See page 175.

Parade
An arty vision of an Old World carnival.
See page 171.

Arts & Entertainment

Oosterparkfestival

Oosterpark, Oost. Tram 3, 6, 9, 14. **Date** first wk in
May. **Map** p312 H3.

Located in the centre of the culturally eclectic east
of Amsterdam, Oosterpark plays host to a one- or
two-day free festival that emphasises community
between nationalities. It has its own links with
Remembrance Day (4 May), since many local Jews
were deported during World War II, and is a great
opportunity to experience different music, customs,
food, games and sports.

National Windmill Day

Information 623 8703. **Date** second Sat in May.
Admission free; donations welcome.

About 600 of the country's 1,035 windmills and
75 watermills turn their Ministry of Tourism-
subsidised sails and open to the public, among them
Amsterdam's half-dozen working mills. Windmills
open to the public carry a blue banner, but for
full details, contact the Vereniging de Hollandse
Molen on the above number. *See also p47* **The
dope on windmills**.

National Cycling Day

Information 071 560 5959. **Date** second Sat in May.
On National Cycling Day, the roads are even more
full of cyclists than usual (if that's possible). More
than 200 routes are set up especially for the occasion, and if you want to be part of the two-wheeled
action – or, of course, avoid it completely – contact
the Amsterdam Tourist Board for details close to
the date of the event.

KunstRAI (RAI Arts Fair)

*RAI Congresgebouw, Europaplein, Zuid (549 1212).
Tram 4, 25/NS rail to RAI station.* **Open** *Office/
enquiries* 8am-6pm Mon-Fri. **Dates** mid May-early
June. **Admission** varies.

This huge (and hugely mainstream) annual exhibition of contemporary art includes everything from
ceramics and jewellery to paintings and sculpture.
All in all, about 100 Dutch and international galleries
take part.

Open Studios: Kunstroute de Westelijke Eilanden

*Prinseneiland, Bickerseiland & Realeneiland
(information 625 6482).* **Date** late May/early June.

Many neighbourhoods with large artist populations
and artists' studio complexes hold open days in the
spring or autumn, when, over a weekend or more,
dozens of artists – both starving and successful –
open their doors to the public. The annual Westelijke
Eilanden is the largest and most popular, situated
on the wonderfully picturesque and peaceful islands
around Prinseneiland, all connected by traditional
'skinny bridges'. Be sure, also, to check out the
Jordaan Open Ateliers that usually occur on the
same weekend. You can find out about the times and
venues of all the Open Ateliers by picking up the
Kunstladder (the official list) at Amsterdam Tourist
Board or the AUB Ticketshop on Leidseplein.

Vondelpark Openluchttheatre (Open-air theatre)

*Vondelpark, Museum Quarter (information 523
7790/673 1499).* *Tram 1, 2, 3, 5, 7, 10, 12, 20.*
Date *End May-end Aug* Wed-Sun. **Admission** free.
Map p310 C6.

Throughout the summer months, Vondelpark hosts
a wide variety of theatre and music at its open-air
theatre, in the middle of the park by the fountain.
Cabaret, drama, concerts, kids' programmes and
dance all feature. The atmosphere alone is worth
experiencing, even if the performances themselves
turn out to be crap.

Summer

With the consistent sunshine that summer
brings, Amsterdammers move outdoors for
their leisure time. Liberally undressed bodies
pack like sardines on the nearby beaches at
Bloemendaal and Zandfoort, and Vondelpark
gets gridlocked with skaters, joggers, sun-
worshippers and bongo players. Many locals
vacate to vacationsville, while the city's tourist
load reaches critical density.

Echo Grachtenloop (Canal Run)

Information 585 9222. **Date** late May/early June.
Admission ƒ10 participants; free spectators.

Close on 5,000 people take part in either a 5½-, 9½-
or 18km (three-, six- or 11-mile) run along the city's
canals (Prinsengracht and Vijzelgracht). Though
you can sign up from mid-May at VSB banks
(there's one at Rozengracht 207; 638 8009), you can
also register on the spot half an hour before the 11am
start at the **Stadsschouwburg** (*see p239*), where
the run starts and finishes. However, if you've left
your sports gear at home or would rather – perhaps
understandably – sit outside with a beer and observe
the runners getting knackered, then there are
plenty of decent vantage points. Avoid the usually
crowded Leidseplein and head, instead, for the
banks of Prinsengracht. *See also p230.*

Holland Festival

*Stadsschouwburg, Leidseplein, Grachtengordel: East
(information 530 7110/www.hollandfestival.nl).*
Tram 1, 2, 5, 6, 7, 10, 20. **Date** early-mid June.
Admission ƒ18-ƒ85. **Map** p310 C5.

A perennial fixture in the diaries of the Netherlands'
posh, civilised and thoroughly cultured folk, the
world-renowned Holland Festival features art,
dance, opera, theatre and a whole lot more. The programme includes both mainstream and experimental works, and is held in the Stadsschouwburg and
assorted venues around Amsterdam, with other
events in The Hague. Advance programme information is available from Holland Festival, Kleine
Gartmanplantsoen 21, 1017 RP Amsterdam (530
7110). There are also direct sales (from May) from
the AUB Ticketshop, Amsterdam Tourist Board
offices and individual theatres.

Catholics commemorate the Miracle of Amsterdam with the **Stille Omgang**. *See p169.*

Open Garden Days

Information 422 1870. **Date** *mid-June.*
Similar to the **Open Monument Days** (*see p172*), this weekend event sees owners of beautiful, hidden backyard gardens open their doors to the general public, who file in and emit admiring 'Oohs' and 'Aahs' in honour of their hosts's landscaping skills.

Parade

Martin Luther Kingpark, Zuid (information 033 465 4577/www.mobilearts.nl). Tram 25/Metro Amstel station. **Date** *first 2wks of Aug (3pm-1am Mon-Thur, Sun; 3pm-2am Fri, Sat).* **Admission** *varies.*
One of the highlights of the cultural year, this outdoor theatre festival (*see also p240*) comes pretty darn close to re-enacting the vibes of ancient carnivals. Enter into another – alcohol-fuelled – world, where a tree-shadowed beer garden is surrounded by kitschily decorated tents that each feature a different cabaret, music, spectacle or theatre act. Afternoons are child-friendly. There's also a **Winter Parade** in December on the grounds of the **Westergasfabriek** (*see p240*).

Hartjesdag Zeedijk

Zeedijk, Old Centre: Old Side (information 625 8467). **Date** *mid-Aug.* **Map** *p306 D2.*
'Heart Day' is an ancient Amsterdam celebration, traditionally held on the last Monday of August, that for a long time involved a great deal of drinking, cross-dressing and firecrackers. Though it wasn't celebrated for decades, some resourceful folk resurrected the event on Zeedijk in 1999, primarily to focus on the drinking and cross-dressing aspects. Marvel at the parade of boys dressed as girls and girls dressed as boys at this event that proven understandably popular with the city's seemingly burgeoning transvestite population.

Uitmarkt

Various locations, including Museumplein, Dam & sites along the Amstel (www.uitmarkt.nl). **Date** *last weekend of Aug.*
The chaotic Uitmarkt previews the Netherlands' coming cultural season with a huge fair on and around Museumplein, Leidseplein, Dam and Nes, giving information on amateur and professional theatre, opera, dance and music of all sorts. There are also performances on outdoor stages and in the city's various theatres. Everything is free, so, not surprisingly, it gets very crowded. Theatres, performing artists and companies preview and sell their programmes for the coming season. From Friday to Sunday, several outdoor stages are set up in squares around the centre of Amsterdam, with free music, dance, theatre and cabaret performances.

Autumn

Amsterdam has been known to have the occasional Indian summer, but otherwise this season's sometime stormy disposition is a warning of the winter's despair that is sure to follow. It's a time when Amsterdammers renew their Prozac prescriptions and start storing any razor blades out of sight. As a visitor, though, this might be just the right time to visit the city. With the tourist tide finally beginning to depart in preparation for winter, and touring bands arriving in their droves to play the **Melkweg** or **Paradiso**, the true essence and spirit of Amsterdam comes right to the surface.

Aside from the events detailed below, parents with their offspring in tow may care to investigate **Cinekid** (*see page 177*).

Arts & Entertainment

Jordaan Festival

Information 626 5587. **Date** Sept.

This annual neighbourhood festival features performances from local talents following in the footsteps of Johnny Jordaan (no, really) and Tante Leen, artists who personified the spirit of the Jordaan by singing about lost love and spilt beer. Fun.

Bloemen Corso (Flower Parade)

Information 029 732 5100. Route leaves from Aalsmeer at 9.30am; Olympic Stadium, Stadionplein, at 1pm (tram 16); Overtoom (tram 1, 6); Leidseplein (tram 1, 2, 5, 6, 7, 10, 20); Leidsestraat (tram 1, 2, 5); Spui (tram 1, 2, 5); Spuistraat (tram 1, 2, 5); Dam (tram 1, 2, 4, 5, 9, 13, 14, 16, 17, 20, 24, 25) around 4pm; Rembrandtplein (tram 4, 9, 14, 20); Vijzelstraat (tram 16, 24, 25); Weteringschans (tram 6, 7, 10). **Date** first Sat of Sept.

Since the 1950s, a spectacular parade of floats bearing all kinds of flowers – except tulips, amazingly, as they're out of season – has made its way from Aalsmeer (the home of Holland's flower industry; *see p249*) to Amsterdam. Crowds line the pavements for a glimpse of the beautiful and fragrant displays; then, at 4pm, the parade reaches a packed Dam for a civic reception. At 9pm, it begins an hour-long illuminated cavalcade back through Aalsmeer.

Open Monument Days

Information 552 4888/www.openmonumentendag.nl. **Date** second weekend of Sept. **Admission** free.

Every year, the private owners of some of Amsterdam's most historic buildings – including the windmills, natch – open their doors to the public, who can then open their eyes to the past in what is a unique opportunity to gander behind the gabled façades and into the lives lived and living in Golden Age grandeur. It's a national event: wherever you find yourself in the Netherlands, look out for the flying Monumenten flag that means free entrance to another world.

Chinatown Festival

Nieuwmarkt, Old Centre: Old Side (information Mr Man 06 2553 7077 mobile). **Date** mid-Sept.

The ancient square of Nieuwmarkt gets covered with stalls of Chinese food and enlivened with many acts and artists. It's an especially valuable event in the calendar since the Chinese New Year festivities, which were held here in January, were cancelled due to the repeatedly (if predictably) inclement weather.

Kunstroute/Exchange WG Terrein

WG Terrein, Marius van Bouwdijk Bastiaansestraat, Oud West (information 618 7848). Tram 1, 3, 6, 12. **Date** mid-Sept. **Map** p309 A6.

This event is held in a former women's hospital turned artists' studios/living complex. One year it's a Kunstroute (meaning that an exhibition of local work is shown here), and the next year it's an exchange exhibition with another European city (they all exhibit here and then go off for a jolly old time over there: any excuse for a trip abroad). A combined route map and catalogue can be obtained from the Amsterdam Tourist Board or the AUB Ticketshop.

A right royal party

Party-lovers, bric-a-brac collectors and students of the stupendously surreal, listen up. If you only go to Amsterdam once in your life, make sure your visit coincides with 30 April. **Queen's Day** (aka Koninginnedag, in the local lingo) is, in theory, a one-day celebration of Beatrix's birthday. In reality, though, the Queen is soon forgotten amid the wild revelry. More than a million folk pour into the city, making every single street and canal dense with different sounds, suspicious smells and second-hand sellers in the process.

It's a day of excess when the communal vision of a city becomes blurred. You might stagger along and discover a leather-boy disco party on one side street, boogie through and get to some local crooner singing of broken hearts and spilt beer on another, when suddenly a boat bellows by with a heavy metal band, whose amps get short-circuited at the next bridge as a gang of gabber-loving boys in orange (the royal colour) with shaven heads urinate directly on to it. If nothing else, you'll at least come away with a fair few stories to tell your grandkids.

Even though Mayor Patijn played party pooper a few years ago by banning street-selling on the Queen's Eve (29 April), he does have a point: you should really try to get some rest before the big day. If you've got kids in tow, head to Vondelpark, which is dedicated to children; gay and lesbian celebrations are focused around Reguliersdwaarsstraat and the Homomonument (see page 201); and Dam becomes a fairground. The mind gets clogged with an overdose of senses and pockets slowly empty as punters get tricked into buying just what they always (read: never) wanted: a fetching pair of orange clogs or silver platforms, a brain implant or some processed uranium, all for next to nothing. With performances, markets, crowds and, of course, alcohol, the scenic streets of Amsterdam have it all for one day only. Come and see what the fuss is all about. But don't make too many plans for the next day.

Koninginnedag (Queen's Day)

Date 30 Apr.

Perverting the course

The naughty '90s? You betcha. The last decade of the 20th century saw fetishistic sauciness edge its way into popular culture as never before. The happily perverted strutted their leathery stuff within whipping distance of the mainstream. S&M imagery slithered out from its secretive, hidden grottos to the boardwalks of Milan and the front covers of the world's more fashionable magazines. Becoming a full-time dominatrix became something approximating to a savvy career move. Even people lacking entirely in depravity who had not yet grown bored of the missionary position started to clue in to the fact that the S&M scene was less Marquis de Sade and more theatrical role-playing, where all the world's a stage with remarkably few extra slippy bits.

At the vanguard of this sea-change was the Amsterdam fetish outlet **Demask** (see page 147), which organises the annual **EuroPerve** event. Europerve herds together thousands of Europe's most sexually adventurous folks – with the Germans and the English seemingly the most needy for a buttock-blushing – for a long evening of fashion, performance, dancing, naughty games and friction fun. Formal dress has always been required – in the form of leather, latex, PVC and/or adult-sized nappies – and the unwritten etiquette was not BYOB, but BYOS (Bring Your Own Slave, natch). Old skool S&M-ers speak of the scene reaching its peak in the mid '90s, when it surreally took over the Artis Zoo for an evening of frolics. But the next year, they had to move from there. Not because they were acting like animals, but because the scene, remarkably, outgrew it. The year 2000 saw the tenth EuroPerve leaving the confines of the city centre in order that it might find a venue big enough. But more than that, the event is even expanding to fetish-friendly New York, where it hopes to get an annual franchise going in the infamous Club 54. Next stop: the White House. Maybe.

EuroPerve

Information from Demask, Zeedijk 64, Old Centre: Red Light District (620 5603). **Date** last Sat in May. **Admission** varies.

Crossing Border Festival

www.crossingborder.nl. **Date** beginning of Oct.
A rocking literary festival that, after many years in The Hague, is set to move to Amsterdam. Although, among the 120 or so acts, there are 'authors' in the strictest sense of the word, the majority of participants come from the world of music and perform a mix of music and spoken word. Featured acts have included Arab Strap, Henry Rollins Can, Kinky Friedman and Michael Franti. Not to be missed.

High Times Cannabis Cup

Information 624 1777/www.hightimes.com. **Date** Oct/Nov. **Admission** varies.
It's harvest time, and therefore time for *High Times* magazine's annual – and heavily commercialised – Cannabis Cup where all things related to wastedness are celebrated. There are banquets, bands, product expos, cultivation seminars and a competition where hundreds of judges (including you, if you so wish) try to ascertain which of the hundreds of weeds are the wickedest, dude. The event is scattered – as are the minds – all over town, but is focused around the **Melkweg** (*see p217*).

Sinterklaas Intocht

Date mid-Nov. **Route** *Barbizon Palace Hotel, Prins Hendrikkade (tram 1, 2, 4, 5, 9, 13, 16, 17, 20, 24, 25); Damrak (tram 4, 9, 14, 16, 20, 24, 25); Dam (tram 1, 2, 4, 5, 9, 13, 14, 16, 17, 20, 24, 25); Raadhuisstraat (tram 13, 14, 17); Rozengracht (tram 13, 14, 17, 20); Marnixstraat (tram 7, 10); Leidseplein (tram 1, 2, 5, 6, 7, 10, 20).*
In mid-November, Sinterklaas (St Nicholas, the Dutch equivalent of Santa Claus) marks the beginning of the Christmas season when he steps ashore from a steamboat at Amsterdam's Centraal Station. St Nick – with his white beard, bishop's robes and rigid staff – is every Dutch kid's favourite uncle, playing good cop by controlling the distribution of sweets at this annual parade of the city. Meanwhile, his assisting bad cops, Zwarte Pieten ('Black Peters', Al Jolson-style elves) represent a threat to the naughty kids. Each year, people note how staggeringly politically incorrect all this is. Klaas warriors, on the other hand, maintain that the elves are part of the tradition that darkness represents evil: Black Peter is actually the devil, and his colour and predilection for mischief-making are the only leftovers of an evil beaten out of him by St Nick. Others still reckon that the colour of Black Peter's skin is a result of his assigned job of delivering sweets via a chimney, on the eve of 6 December. *See also below.*

Triple X Festival

Information 420 5316/www.triplex.nl. **Date** ten days in autumn. **Admission** varies.
Triple X, which takes place at the Westergasfabriek, prides itself as being on the global cutting edge of developments in the worlds of theatre, dance, music, art and electronic media. Funding problems delayed the event in 1999, however: call ahead to check the event's status before you make plans.

The conversion of Leidseplein from patio into ice rink signals the advent of winter. With a little luck, the canals also turn solid enough for scenic skating. Otherwise, it's only two family-oriented festivals – St Nicholas's Day, as important to the Dutch as Christmas, and New Year's Eve – that break up the potential monotony of this most sleety of seasons.

Sinterklaas

Date 5, 6 Dec.
While the St Nicholas prototype, Sinterklaas, is directing his 'Black Peter' helpers down chimneys on the eve of his day, 6 December, families celebrate by exchanging small gifts and poems. This tradition started when the Church decided to tame the wild pagan partying that had always accompanied the end of the slaughter season. It began by ruling that the traditional celebration should be based around the birthday of St Nicholas – or 'Sinterklaas' – the patron saint of children (and, ironically, also prostitutes and thieves). Cakes were baked, poems were exchanged, and a once-violent tradition was slowly reborn as a Christian family feast. Sinterklaas, as we all know, eventually emigrated to the States, mutated into Santa Claus, and shifted his birthday to 25 December in order to fill in for Jesus' failings of character when it came to the spirit of gross revenue.

Oudejaarsavond (New Year's Eve)

All over Amsterdam. **Date** 31 Dec.
Along with **Koninginnedag** (*see p172* **A right royal party**), New Year's is Amsterdam's wildest celebration. There's happy chaos throughout the city, but the best spots are Nieuwmarkt and Dam, both of which get seriously crowded. It's an evening to be avoided by those who suffer from combat flashbacks: the ample use of firecrackers is suggestive of the fall of Saigon (and almost as dangerous). The Dutch often begin their celebration with an evening of coffee, spirits and *oliebollen* ('oil-balls', which taste better than they sound: they're deep-fried blobs of dough, apple and raisins, made yummier with a sprinkle of icing sugar) with the family until midnight, which is why many bars don't open until the witching hour.

Commemoration of the February Strike

Jonas Daniël Meijerplein, Old Centre: Old Side. Tram 9, 14, 20/Metro Waterlooplein. **Date** 25 Feb. **Map** p307 E3.
A ceremony commemorating the dockworkers' protest strike of 1941, held at the Dokwerker statue.

> ▶ For more on **film festivals**, see page 193.
> ▶ For more on **music festivals**, see pages 219 and 225.

(Arts & Entertainment)

Children

Where to take the young and the young at heart.

Unlike its northern European neighbours, the Netherlands has maintained a consistently positive population growth. More recently, thanks to a thriving economy, there has even been talk of a baby boom. Of course, there are downsides to this, including long crèche waiting lists and professional education and healthcare shortages. But there are also a great deal of advantages. For one thing, travelling to Amsterdam with child in tow won't draw strange looks from locals. Amsterdam actually has a long tradition of children's activities and entertainment: you simply need to know where to look. Listed in this chapter is a selection of sites and services that could prove useful for families travelling to Amsterdam for short or long visits.

Amsterdam is bursting with cultural events for children all year round, from concerts to theatrical events. The **AUB Ticketshop** on Leidseplein (0900 0191; *see also page 283* **Tickets please**) is a good source of information, as is *Uitkrant* (look under 'Jeugd'). Its listings are mostly in Dutch, but a call to the relevant organisation will normally clear up anything you're not sure about. For children's bookshops, clothing and shoe stores, and toy shops, *see chapter* **Shops & Services**.

Transport

Amsterdam is small and compact, making a visit with kids far easier than, say, a trip to London. Its size and layout make most of the interesting places for youngsters reachable by foot, though manoeuvring a pushchair over the older cobbled sections can be frustrating. A faster way to get around is by tram, bus or Metro. The newer buses and trams are very easy to board with tots, but some of the older vehicles can be difficult: remember that the bottom step on a tram must be pressed down to hold the doors open. Most locals are willing to lend a helping hand.

Children, understandably, love Amsterdam's myriad waterways. Water taxis might be expensive, but what they lack in value for money they make up for in fun. Not quite as pleasant but better value for money – it's free – is a trip on the River IJ ferry to Amsterdam Noord; boats leave from behind Centraal Station about every ten minutes. If you have older children, then you might enjoy renting a canal bike, but remember to navigate on the right-hand side of the waterway. For more information on all aspects of public and private transport in Amsterdam, *see page 270*.

Electrische Museum Tramlijn Amsterdam

Haarlemmermeerstation, Amstelveenseweg 264 (673 7538). Tram 6, 16. See p71 **Museums further out** for full listings information.
Less of a museum than a pleasure ride, particularly for youngsters. Its antique electric tram carriages come from cities across Europe; the 60-minute round trip in one of the old trolleys along the edge of the Amsterdamse Bos (*see p177*) is great fun.

Outdoor entertainment

When winter arrives, many parents take their kids skating at the **Jaap Edenhal** rink (*see page 232*), though the more daring head to the canals: when the weather is cold enough, many of the city's canals freeze over. However, if in doubt, check with the locals if it's safe to skate.

Walk with the animals at urban farms (*p177*).

The **Kindermuseum**. *See p55.*

To the disappointment of many inline skaters and skateboarders, the famed half-pipe at Museumplein has been replaced by a new version that, unfortunately, has failed to match the quality of the old one. There are other facilities scattered throughout the city, but without the hubbub of Museumplein.

Parks

One of the greenest cities in Europe, Amsterdam has 28 parks. Another huge one will eventually open near IJburg, while many existing parks have received funding for renovations and expansions. In a city of cramped quarters, parks consistently cater to children. Almost every park has a playground with a sandpit and, sometimes, a paddling pool. But beware of unleashed pooches and their droppings: dog owners seem to think their canines have as much right to these areas as humans.

Quite aside from boasting the best children's park in Amsterdam, **Vondelpark** (information 673 1499; *see page 70*) is famous for its summer programme of free afternoon entertainment, which includes children's theatre, concerts, mime artists and acrobatic displays (most children's programming takes place on Wednesday; *see also page 244* **Park life**).

Amstelpark's attractions include a miniature train, a maze, a small children's farm and pony rides. **Flevopark** is the wildest and least used of the city's parks, and, as such, is a nice peaceful spot for a picnic or a kickabout. The adjacent **Flevoparkbad** has two fantastic outdoor swimming pools and a toddlers' paddling pool in a spacious grassy recreation area (*see page 233*).

Amsterdam's largest green areas are on the edge of town. The **Amsterdamse Bos** is easily the pick of the bunch, with boating lakes, an open-air theatre and large playgrounds. It's also home to the magical **Bosmuseum** (*see page 70*

Museums further out), which has maps of the park, including walking routes, and **Bio Dyn Geitenkaasboerderij** (645 5034, open 10am-5pm Mon, Wed-Sun, closed Tue), a goat farm with 120 milk goats and loads of cute goatlets. Finally, **Gaasperplas Park** has some superb sport and playground facilities, including a paddling pool and lake for swimming (*see page 235*). For more on Amsterdam's green spaces, *see page 64* **Keep on the grass**.

Urban farms

The children's farm at the **Artis Zoo** (*see page 54*) has a variety of animals, including pigs, calves, chickens, sheep and goats, plus a great (dog-free) play area. All the usual beasts can be found at **De Pijp Kinderboerderij** (Lizzy Ansinghstraat 82, The Pijp, 664 8303, open 11am-5pm daily). Look out for the children's activity days, held on some Wednesdays and, occasionally, on Saturdays and Sundays. There's a children's farm in Rembrandtpark, **De Uylenburg** (Staalmeesterslaan 420, Oud West, 618 5235, open 9am-5pm daily), which has a simple play-and-do area for children, plus pony rides and grooming.

Smaller farms are listed in the *Amsterdam Yellow Pages* under 'Kinderboerderijen'. Admission to all farms is often free.

Indoor entertainment

Children's films

There are a few special children's film shows at the **Kriterion**, the **Rialto** (for both, *see page 193*) and the **Filmmuseum** (*see page 194*), though most films for under-tens are dubbed into Dutch (indicated by the words 'Nederlands Gesproken' in the film listings). However, many other family-oriented films are in English with Dutch subtitles. In the autumn holidays, many theatres and cinemas take part in **Cinekid** (624 7110), a children's film festival with quality films from across the globe, many in English.

Museums

Not all of Amsterdam's museums are suitable for children. However, many make for a terrific day out, with the best two the **newMetropolis** (*see page 75*) and the **Tropenmuseum** (which incorporates the **Kindermuseum**; *see page 54*). At the **Nederlands Scheepvaartmuseum** (*see page 76*), children can handle exhibits on the docked ships, including a reproduction of an 18th-century trading vessel, while the **Woonbootmuseum** (*see page 60*) offers a glimpse at what it's like to live on a houseboat.

Big top fun at **Circustheater Elleboog**.

Of the rest, the **Aviodome** (*see page 70* **Museums further out**) at Schiphol Airport boasts an exciting flight simulator; the **Allard Pierson** (*see page 48*) archaeological museum has a small but worthwhile mummy collection and regular educational exhibitions; and **Madame Tussauds Scenerama** (*see page 40*) is always a good shot for keeping the kids happy. For full details on Amsterdam's museums, *see chapter* **Sightseeing**.

Restaurants

Aside from the specific kids' restaurants listed below, most cheaper restaurants and pizzerias welcome kids. Youngsters are normally allowed in licensed bars and cafés, as long as they don't run amok. When in doubt, ask the staff if children are welcome. Be forewarned, though, that most Dutch restaurants and cafés do not have changing facilities, and toilets are often in the cellar at the bottom of a steep flight of stairs. *See also pages 100-20 and pages 121-33.*

KinderKookKafé

Oudezijds Achterburgwal 193, Old Centre: Old Side (625 3257). Tram 1, 2, 4, 5, 9, 14, 17, 20, 24, 25/ Metro Nieuwmarkt. **Open** Sat, Sun; phone for details and book ahead. **No credit cards. Map** p306 D3.
This small restaurant – whose name translates as 'Children's Cooking Café' – offers cooking courses in Dutch to children during the week. At weekends it is entirely run by children: they cook, serve, present the bill and wash up, all with a little help from the grown-up staff, of course. The simple set menu includes a main course and dessert: ingredients are fresh, the food is healthy, and prices for diners are very low (ƒ5 1-4s; ƒ10 5-12s; ƒ15 over-13s; ƒ2,50 drinks). Kids, who can cook for their own guests, pay ƒ20. Book at least two weeks in advance.

Kinderspeelcafé Toet-Toet

Tussenmeer 94, Osdorp (610 4921/06 5025 2150 mobile). Tram 1. **Open** *telephone enquiries* 10am-6pm daily. **Rates** ƒ15 per child. **No credit cards.**
This café, which offers a variety of planned games and activities, can only be booked in advance, but promises to keep your kids entertained. Private, off-premises parties can also be arranged in advance.

Pizzeria Capri

Lindengracht 63, The Jordaan (624 4940). Tram 3, 10/bus 18, 22. **Open** 5-10pm daily. *Kitchen* open from 6pm. **No credit cards. Map** p305 B2.
Children are welcome at this pizzeria-cum-gelateria with a small pavement terrace. Staff and customers remain unfazed by kids dropping pasta on the floor, and there's plenty of real Italian ice-cream on hand for blackmail purposes. High chairs are available.

Swimming pools & saunas

Good pools for kids are **De Mirandabad** (a subtropical pool with a wave machine, whirlpool, toddler pool and slide), the **Zuiderbad** and **Marnixbad** indoor pools, and the **Brediusbad** and **Flevoparkbad** outdoor pools. For local pools, consult the phone directory under 'Zwembad' and check by phone for special children's hours. Most saunas tolerate quiet children, especially at off-peak hours. For saunas and pools, *see page 233.*

Theatre & circus

The Dutch pride themselves on their cultural development, something that holds true for the way they stimulate their children's appreciation of art and entertainment. The **Children's Theatre Phoneline** (622 2999) offers recorded information in Dutch on kids' theatre, though you can also check under 'Jeugd' in *Uitkrant* for information on ongoing productions.

If you're in town with young 'uns in tow, try and pick up a copy of *Maanvahanda*. A free paper produced by six children's theatres including the **Krakeling** (*see page 179*), it features full listings and up-to-date programme information for kids' theatre in Amsterdam. In addition to children's theatre companies, many theatres and music venues hold special children's concerts and the like throughout the year: check with the **Uitlijn** (0900 0191) for full details.

Circustheater Elleboog

Passeerdersgracht 32 (626 9370). Tram 1, 2, 5, 7, 10. **Open** 10am-5pm phone bookings; times vary activities/sessions. **Shows** call for times.
Admission *Non-members* ƒ15/day. *Membership* ƒ140/6mths; ƒ45/3-morning pass, or ƒ90 adult plus child (selected mornings). *Shows* ƒ15; ƒ10 under-17s. **No credit cards. Map** p310 C4.

Kids aged from four to 17 can try out circus and clowning skills, learning tricks, make-up skills, juggling and tightrope walking. Activity days end in a performance for parents and friends. Non-member sessions are always busy, mostly with Dutch kids, but staff speak English. Children's birthday parties can also be arranged (phone for details).

De Krakeling

Nieuwe Passeerdersstraat 1 (625 3284/reservations 624 5123). Tram 7, 10. **Shows** *2pm Wed, Sun; 8pm Thur-Sat.* **Admission** ƒ16 unaccompanied adult; ƒ12 adult with child; ƒ8 children; ƒ3 extra some performances. **No credit cards. Map** p310 C5.
De Krakeling has separate productions for over-12s and under-12s: phone to check what's going on at any given time. For non-Dutch speakers, there are puppet and mime shows and sometimes musicals. Shows are listed in a programme available from the theatre, as well as in *Uitkrant*.

Out of town

Local Amsterdam Tourist Board offices, ANWB shops and the Netherlands Railways have excellent ideas for day trips out of town. Though the information offered is primarily in Dutch, staff should be able to steer you in the right direction with train maps and ideas. If weather permits, inquire about short walking and cycling routes in the area that promise to keep children entertained (and wear them out so you can have the evening off). The Netherlands

Top five Kids' stuff

Cook at the KinderKookKafé

Kiddies can practice their culinary skills in this charming restaurant. See page 178.

Play in Vondelpark

Amsterdam's loveliest green spot is a welcome and exciting respite from the city streets. See page 177.

Take a canal ride

What trip to Amsterdam would be complete without spending some time on the water? See page 176.

Tour an urban farm

Any of the city's petting zoos will entice your youngster. See page 177.

Visit the newMetropolis

All ages are catered for in Amsterdam's state-of-the-art science and technology museum. See page 75.

Railways also sells **NS Rail Idee** tickets that cover the cost of the maps and transport to and from the walking or cycling location.
All the attractions below can be reached by rail with an NS Rail Idee ticket that may include the admission price. For details of other out-of-town attractions, *see pages 248-68.*

Archeon

Archeonlaan 1, Alphen aan den Rijn (0172 447744). 50km (31 miles) from Amsterdam; A4 to Leiden, then N11 to Alphen aan den Rijn. **Open** *Apr-July, Sept, Oct 10am-5pm Tue-Sun; closed Mon. Aug 10am-5pm daily; closed Nov-Mar.* **Admission** ƒ24,50 adults; ƒ17,50 concessions; free under-4s. **Credit** MC, V.
The Archeon offers a trip through history, from when dinosaurs walked the earth, via the Bronze Age, to Roman times. There are loads of interactive and hands-on displays, plus an open-air plunge pool. It's all great fun.

Efteling

Europalaan 1, Kaatsheuvel, Noord Brabant (0416 288111/UK agent 01242 528877). 110km (68 miles) from Amsterdam; take A27 to Kaatsheuvel exit, then N261. **Open** *Apr-June, Sept, Oct 10am-6pm daily. July-late Aug 10am-9pm daily; closed Nov-Mar.* **Admission** ƒ39; free under-4s. **Credit** AmEx, DC, MC, V.
An enormous fairy-tale forest peopled with dwarves and witches, characters from Grimms' stories and the *Arabian Nights*, enchanted and haunted castles, and even talking rubbish bins. The massive (and massively popular) amusement park is packed with state-of-the-art thrills, as well as more traditional fairground rides for tinies. It gets busy in summer.

Linnaeushof

Rijksstraatweg 4, Bennebroek (023 584 7624). 20km (13 miles) from Amsterdam); take A5 to Haarlem, then head south on N208. **Open** *Apr-Oct 10am-6pm daily; closed Nov-Mar.* **No credit cards.** **Admission** ƒ12; free under-1s.
A huge leisure park near Haarlem, host to an astonishing 300 attractions: there's a Wild West train, cable cars, mini-golf, trampolines, a water play area and go-karts. Children under five are happy in the new play area, and the price is most certainly right.

Madurodam

George Maduroplein 1, The Hague (070 355 3900). 57km (35 miles) from Amsterdam; take A4 to The Hague. **Open** *Apr-June 9am-8pm daily; July, Aug 9am-11pm daily; Sept-Mar 9am-6pm daily.* **Admission** ƒ21; ƒ14 4-11s; ƒ18,50 over-65s; free under-4s. **Credit** AmEx, DC, MC, V.
It says it's the 'largest miniature village in the world', and who are we to argue? Kids adore the scale models of Holland's most famous sights – anything from Rotterdam's Erasmus Bridge to Schiphol Airport – all of which are built to scale on a 1:25 ratio. The best time to go is on a summer's evening, when the models are lit from inside by over 50,000 tiny lamps.

Museum van Speelklok tot Pierement

Buurkerkhof 10, Utrecht (030 231 2789). 38km (24 miles) from Amsterdam; take A2 to Utrecht. **Open** 10am-5pm Tue-Sat; noon-5pm Sun. **Admission** ƒ12,50; ƒ7,50 4-12s; under-4s free. **No credit cards.**
A unique antique collection of mechanical music boxes, circus, fairground and street organs and wondrous tin toys. A great double day out for junior machine freaks.

Nederlands Spoorwegmuseum

Maliebaanstation 16, Utrecht (030 230 6206). 38km (24 miles) from Amsterdam; take A2 to Utrecht. **Open** 10am-5pm Thur, Fri; 11.30am-5pm Sat, Sun; closed Mon-Wed. **Admission** ƒ15 adult; ƒ12,50 over-65s; ƒ9,50 4-12s; free under-4s. **No credit cards.**
The Netherlands Railway Museum is housed in an historic station, where over 60 old and new locomotives can be admired from inside and outside. There are also rides on a miniature Intercity and TGV line for under-12s.

Six Flags Holland

Spijkweg 30, Biddinghuizen (0321 329991/0321 329999). 72km (45 miles) from Amsterdam); take A1 towards Amersfoort, then A6 towards Lelystad, then follow signs for Six Flags. **Open** Apr-Aug from 10am daily, closing times vary. *Sept, Oct* from 10am Fri-Sun, closing times vary; closed Mon-Thur. **Admission** ƒ39 over 1.4m; ƒ19,50 1m-1.40m; free under 1m. **Credit** AmEx, MC, V.
Opened in 2000, Six Flags Holland caters to bigger kids with the Netherlands' largest collection of rollercoasters, including one made of wood. Tots are sure to be entertained by the Looney Tunes characters and some tamer attractions. Opening hours are complicated and change often, though it's always open until at least 5pm and, during peak season, until 10pm.

Parenting

Babyminders

Check the *Amsterdam Yellow Pages* under 'Oppascentrales' for babysitting in the suburbs.

Oppascentrale Kriterion

(624 5848). **Bookings** 5-8pm daily. **Rates** ƒ10/hr 8pm-midnight; ƒ12,50/hour midnight-8pm; ƒ6 admin charge; ƒ7,50 supplement for Fri & Sat evenings. *Minimum charge* ƒ30. **No credit cards.**
This reliable service has been running for 45 years and uses male and female students aged over 18, all of whom are individually vetted. Book in advance.

Children's rights

Kinderrechtswinkel

Staalstraat 19, Old Centre: Old Side (626 0067/ info@krwa.demon.nl). Tram 4, 9, 14, 16, 20, 24, 25. **Open** *Walk-in consultations* 3-6pm Mon; 2-5pm Wed, Sat; closed Tue, Thur, Fri, Sun. **Map** p307 E3.

This children's rights office supplies under-18s with information about legal matters and the responsibilities of teachers, parents and employers. Kids may phone or visit, and while staff will answer questions from adults, they prefer dealing directly with the children involved.

Kindertelefoon (Childline)

0800 0432/office 672 2411. **Open** 2-8pm daily.
Young people from eight to 18 are welcome to phone this free line to get information on bullying, sexual abuse, running away from home and so on. Staff are keen to stress that they do not give information on children's entertainment.

Crèches & playgroups

Crèches take children aged from three months to four years. There are long waiting lists for both council crèches (*kinderdagverblijven*) and playgroups (*speelzalen*). Though private, unsubsidised crèches have shorter waiting lists, they're more expensive and often non-deductable. For a list of childcare facilities in your area and a registration form (register early in pregnancy), contact your local Welfare Department office.

Kinderbijslag (Family Allowance)

Parents from EU countries who live and/or work in the Netherlands are entitled to claim family allowance from the Dutch state for their children. For information and an application form, call the Sociaal Verzekerings Bank on 665 5856.

Schools

Primary schooling is optional for children from four years of age, and compulsory from those over five years old. The vast majority of schools are open from 8.45am to 3.15pm, and primary schools have Wednesday afternoons free. Due to severe teacher shortages in the late '90s and early '00s, some schools started experimenting with four-day school weeks, though this may change back to the standard five-day week in time depending on recruitment.
For more information about schools in your area, contact your local council office (*stadsdeelkantoor*). For information on specifically English-speaking or international schools, contact the British Council directly on 550 6060.

Toy libraries

There are several toy libraries in Amsterdam. There is a registration fee and a small borrowing charge. For details of your nearest toy library, consult the *Amsterdam Yellow Pages* under 'Speel-o-theek'.

Clubs

When you think of Dutch clubbing, don't just think of gabber: Amsterdam's eclectic after-hours scene is moving into the 21st century in rude health.

If you don't arrive in **Time**, you'll find the dancefloor packed. *See p185.*

See p185.

With the arrival of the new millennium has come a groundswell of change on Amsterdam's clubbing circuit. In 1999, the Roxy, one of the city's most enduring nightspots, burned down just days after the death of Peter Giele, its designer and one of its founders. Spookily, the cause of the fire was said to be debris from a little sparkler that worked its way into the air-conditioning vent system – he was apparently a big fan of fireworks – at Giele's own wake. And still more spookily, Giele's own (self-chosen) life motto was 'Ab igne ignem campere'. Translation? 'One fire starts another'…

Just days after the Roxy's demise, with many clubbers still in mourning, the **iT** (*see page 183*) as raided by the police and closed down for several months after accusations that its door staff were corrupt and dealer-friendly (just imagine the bounty awaiting the cleaners on the floor the next day). The claims, though, were never proven, and the iT is now proudly back in business. And then in early 2000, Club 114, which claimed to be Amsterdam's longest running *discotheek*, announced its closure. For a

while, it seemed as though Mayor Patijn's desire to clean up the city was becoming a self-fulfilling prophecy.

It's not all bad news. As the website of the now-defunct Roxy proudly requests, clubbers should 'keep the fire burning', which is exactly what the city's remaining clubs are attempting to do. The holes that the mishaps left in the circuit have at least enabled new places to spring into life and forced existing clubs to smarten up their act. Fans of the Roxy style find many crazy offshoots all over the city, from NL, a lounge opened by one of the Roxy's ex-doormen, to Roxy nights in other venues: Planet Pussy, for example, which now takes a monthly bow at the **Melkweg** (*see page 184*). Though techno and house still pervades, other musical styles have now carved themselves out a niche: the ragga night at **Time** (*see page 185*), hosted by the Controverse Allstars, is a perfect example of this horizon-broadening.

On a practical note, when you're out and about, make sure you have some small change so that you can pay to pee: each trip to the toilet

Clubs

For a mega-Euro clubbing experience

Chemistry, every Saturday night at Escape (see page 182).

For fun in the sun

Woodstock, Solaris and other beach cafés at **Bloemendaal** (see page 187).

For super-hip grown-ups

Club de Ville at the **Westergasfabriek** (see page 185).

For a modern, friendly night out

Any night of the week at **Mazzo** in the Jordaan (see page 185).

For a cheap, cheerful knees-up

Head directly to Singel, and the **Odeon** (see page 184).

will set you back about ƒ1. And don't forget to press some money into the palm of the friendly door person as you leave, unless you don't ever plan on returning. The latter is not compulsory, just good Amsterdam club etiquette. And though the country is renowned for its liberal drug policies, make no mistake about it: hard drugs are illegal. You're welcome to light up a joint in any of the clubs listed in this section, but this is not late-'70s New York: as the iT and **Mazzo** will shamefacedly attest, the police enforce the no-hard-drugs rule with an iron fist.

Clubbing in Amsterdam is largely a weekend hobby. The population of the city is only about a million and it can't really compete in the mega-clubbing stakes with the likes of London and Berlin, but there are still plenty of chances to go wild and happen upon a night to remember… or, at least, one that's hard to forget. For as the T-shirts plagiarise: 'If you can remember clubbing in Amsterdam, you weren't really there.'

Club venues

Club Arena

's Gravesandestraat 51, Oost (694 7444). Tram 3, 6, 7, 10. **Open** 11pm-4am Thur; 10pm-4am Fri, Sat; closed Mon-Wed, Sun. **Admission** ƒ12,50 Fri; ƒ15 Sat. **No credit cards. Map** p312 G3.
Club Arena used to be just a dinky club adjoining a mammoth hostel (it's now a smarter hotel; *see p90*), but in the last couple of years it's become a club in its own right. Despite its location away from the centre of town, many twentysomethings gladly make the trek eastwards each weekend to get down to the

mostly nostalgic fare played by decent resident DJs. Friday is '80s and '90s night – a '90s revival night? Already? – with Saturdays promising goodies from the '60s, '70s and '90s.

Dansen bij Jansen

Handboogstraat 11, Old Centre: New Side (620 1779/www.dansenbijjansen.nl). Tram 1, 2, 5. **Open** 11pm-4am Mon-Thur, Sun; 11pm-5am Fri, Sat. **Admission** ƒ2,50-ƒ7,50. **No credit cards. Map** p310 D4.
Dansen bij Jansen is packed most nights with up to 500 students – indeed, the club was founded by students – enjoying the unthreatening music, cheap entry, cheap drinks and cheap company (jus' kiddin'). Think of it as a Clubbing 101, a handy accessory to any degree. If you're a student and you like hanging with other students, then it's a blast. However, you'll need proof that you're a bona fide student to get in.

Escape

Rembrandtplein 11, Grachtengordel: East (622 1111/www.escape.nl). Tram 4, 9, 14, 20. **Open** 11pm-4am Thur, Sun; 11pm-5am Fri, Sat; closed Mon-Wed. **Admission** ƒ15-ƒ35. **No credit cards. Map** p311 E4.
With a capacity of 2,000, Escape is as big as it gets. Yet despite its size, the queues can be long and the door policy selective. Techno and its assorted offshoots are played by resident DJs Dimitri and Marcello along with frequent international guests at the award-winning Chemistry Saturday-nighter. Sunday's Impact is also popular, though look out for Salsa Lounge, held on the second Sunday of every month (from 4pm): it includes a free salsa workshop and performances by experts. Other nights are run by different party organisers and vary from student events to fashion openings.

Exit

Reguliersdwarsstraat 42, Grachtengordel: East (625 8788). Tram 1, 2, 4, 5, 9, 14, 16, 20, 24, 25. **Open** 11pm-4am Mon-Thur, Sun; 11pm-5am Fri, Sat. **Admission** free-ƒ10. **No credit cards. Map** p311 E4.
Though predominantly a gay club, Exit is hetero-friendly. It's open all week and gets packed at the weekend with buffed, sweaty, mainly masculine bodies. Music is top 40 Europop and techno, and the crowd is always looking for an excuse to git on down 'n' party. *See also p206.*

Havana

Reguliersdwarsstraat 17-19, Grachtengordel: East (620 6788). Tram 1, 2, 5, 16, 20, 24, 25. **Open** 4pm-1am Mon-Thur; 4pm-2.30am Fri; 2pm-2.30am Sat; 2pm-1am Sun. **Admission** free-ƒ5. **No credit cards. Map** p310 D4.
This gay bar, on the main trendy gay drag, tends to get very busy at the weekend before other clubs open. It hosts a glamorous Hollywood party once a year and has occasional 'Musical Theatre Showcases' when stars of the Dutch stage sing numbers from Lloyd Webber et al in Dutch. Cute. *See also p206.*

House of Soul
Amstelstraat 32, Grachtengordel: East (620 2333).
Tram 4, 9, 14, 20. **Open** 11pm-4am Thur; 11pm-
5am Fri, Sat; closed Mon-Wed, Sun. **Admission**
ƒ10-ƒ15. **No credit cards. Map** p307 E3.
The Club Formerly Known As Soul Kitchen is a
friendly spot with plenty of room for self-expression
on the dancefloor, a relaxed door policy and a nice
atmosphere. Its recently revamped music programme
caters for more than just lovers of soul and funk:
Thursdays are Paradise Garage, Fridays offer Club
Utopia, and if it's Saturday, it must be Soul Kitchen.

Industry
Pardenstraat 17, Grachtengordel: East (no phone).
Tram 9, 14, 20. **Open** 11pm-4am Thur, Sun; 11pm-
5am Fri, Sat; closed Mon-Wed. **Admission** ƒ10-ƒ20.
No credit cards. Map p307 E3.
Industry's music policy is focused on R&B and the
occasional theme night. Located just off the
Rembrandtplein, its two levels include a bar upstairs
and dancefloor downstairs. Baseball caps are not
allowed – though thick and ugly gold chains are
encouraged – but there are no further dress restrictions and staff are generally attitude-free zones.

iT
Amstelstraat 24, Grachtengordel: East (625 0111/
www.it.nl). Tram 4, 9, 14. **Open** 11pm-4am Thur;
11pm-5am Fri, Sat (with 'cool-down' 5am-6am);
closed Mon-Wed, Sun. **Admission** free-ƒ20. **No
credit cards. Map** p307 E3.
Holland's favourite gay club for over ten years, the
iT is filled with people who live by the mantra 'all
the world's a stage' and who believe in dressing to
impress. They rub shoulders with tourists and other
locals, all of whom are hoping to experience the
myth of iT. Saturday is for gay men only; gays go
free on Thursday, though straights are allowed, as
on Friday. Club nights alter from time to time, but
the music is always the same: happy Ibiza house,
played mainly by DJ Jean. Sportswear – and that
includes trainers – is not allowed. *See also p204.*

Kalenderpanden
Enrepotdok 98, The Plantage (420 6645/
www.squat.net/entrepotdok). Tram 9, 14. **Open**
free-ƒ10. **No credit cards.**
Map p307 F2.
Currently going through a court battle to ensure its
survival, this squatted building (*see also p26*) is host
to some great parties. A gothic event is held every
second Saturday of the month (10pm-5.30am);
Wednesdays offer experimental music; and on
Thursdays, food is served, followed by a film and
DJ. Visit Kalenderpanden to get a glimpse of what
former squats the **Paradiso** and the **Melkweg** (for
both, *see p204*) were like way back when.

Korsakoff
*Lijnbaansgracht 161, Grachtengordel: West (625
7854/www.korsakoff.nl). Tram 10, 13, 14, 17.*
Open 10pm-3am Mon-Thur, Sun; 11pm-4am
Fri, Sat. **Admission** usually free. **No credit cards.**
Map p310 C4.
An alternative grunge club, within walking distance
of the Leidseplein. You may feel a little out of place
here if you're not gothic, dreadlocked, pierced or, at
least, clothed in black. Sounds include hip hop, metal
and heavy alternative rock. The venue is small but
boozy and friendly, ideal for an all-night drinking
session. If you've got a Cure T-shirt, wear it.

Like the idea of dancing to techno with 2,000 others? Here's where to **Escape**. *See p182.*

Mazzo

Rozengracht 114, The Jordaan (626 7500/ www.mazzo.nl). Tram 13, 14, 17, 20. **Open** 11pm-4am Wed, Thur, Sun; 11pm-5am Fri, Sat; closed Mon, Tue. **Admission** ƒ10-ƒ15. **No credit cards**. **Map** p309 B4.

This smallish, friendly club has long been highly regarded for its progressive, cutting-edge musical policy, and for its championing of VJs as opposed to DJs. Trance and techno is played by residents and an impressive line-up of international guests. On Saturdays, you'll hear techno and progressive trance; Fridays it's drum 'n' bass; and Thursday's sound is progressive techno. The club sometimes fills up quickly, so it's a good idea to show up in good time. However, one point in its favour is that the door policy is refreshingly relaxed.

Melkweg

Lijnbaansgracht 234A, Grachtengordel: East (531 8181/www.melkweg.nl). Tram 1, 2, 5, 6, 7, 10. **Open** varies. **Admission** ƒ10-ƒ30. *Membership* ƒ5/mth (compulsory). **No credit cards**. **Map** p310 C5.

A bunch of hippies in the '70s thought it would be a good idea to turn this one-time milk factory into a cultural venue. How right they were, and how grateful we are: though the hippies have gone – except for when Melkweg hosts the *High Times* Cannabis Cup each November (*see p175*) – the 'Milky Way' has been an Amsterdam staple for years. Variety is the key here: Saturdays offer Dance Arena, while every Thursday it's the Controverse Allstars's Soundclash – 100% Jamaican Crossover, showcasing everything from reggae and ska to ragga, jungle, dub and house. Monthly Friday-nighter Sabotage brings you drum 'n' bass from local heroes DJs Chaos and L-Dopa, with Planet Pussy, a women-only event that used to be held at the Roxy, staged monthly on Sundays. *See also p193, 217 and 244.*

Ministry

Reguliersdwarsstraat 12, Grachtengordel: East (623 3981/www.ministry.nl). Tram 16, 24, 25. **Open** 10pm-4am Thur, Sun; 11pm-5am Fri, Sat; closed Mon-Wed. **Admission** free-ƒ15. **No credit cards**. **Map** p310 D4.

A small club in a classy environment with different music every night. As with many clubs, Saturdays are the busiest night: Ministry regularly has a speed garage gig, often with guest DJs from the UK.

Odeon

Singel 460, Grachtengordel: East (624 9711). Tram 1, 2, 5. **Open** 10pm-4am Mon-Thur, Sun; 10pm-5am Fri, Sat; 4-10pm Sun. **Admission** ƒ2,50-ƒ10. **No credit cards**. **Map** p310 D4.

Odeon, one of the few clubs open all week, has three floors offering different musical styles for three times the fun: R&B and hip hop in the basement, top 40 housey hits on the ground floor, and disco classics in the beautiful room up top. It's cheap and casual, though there's often something of an office-workers-largeing-it sort of feel.

Paradiso

Weteringschans 6-8, Grachtengordel: East (626 4521/www.paradiso.nl). Tram 1, 2, 5, 6, 7, 10, 20. **Open** varies. **Admission** ƒ10-ƒ35. *Membership* ƒ5/mth (compulsory). **No credit cards**. **Map** p310 D5.

Though this beautiful venue was once a church, the worshipping that goes on here is now of an entirely different nature. Paradiso usually hosts bands or films during the week, with a DJ following on. Among the popular regular nights are Friday's VIP Club and Saturday's Paradisco, which attracts a youngish, up-for-it crowd. Various party organisers use the venue, though look out in particular for events by the Balloon Company, whose off-the-wall happenings are usually well worth experiencing.

Sinners in Heaven

Wagenstraat 3-7, Grachtengordel: East (620 1375/ www.sinners.nl). Tram 4, 9, 14, 20. **Open** 11pm-4am Thur, Sun; 11pm-5am Fri, Sat; closed Mon-Wed. **Admission** free-ƒ20. **No credit cards**. **Map** p307 E3.

Sinners in Heaven is a trendy club on a side street across from **iT** (*see p183*) that attracts a chic and wealthy crowd. The club isn't enormous by any means, but the beautiful interior – all mirrors and designer benches – and the three floors of different music more than compensate. Thursday's Pure Grooves features hip hop with a touch of two-step; Friday night is 'TGIF', with classics, disco, garage and happy grooves (the preferred night of many Dutch soap stars); and Positive Love Energy on Saturday showcases the best in garage. Entry is free before midnight.

Supper Club Lounge

Jonge Roelensteeg 21, Old Centre: New Side (638 0513/www.supperclub.nl). Tram 4, 9, 16, 20, 24, 25. **Open** 7pm-1am Mon-Thur, Sun; 7pm-3am Fri, Sat. **Admission** free. **No credit cards**. **Map** p306 D3.

Lounge about in style at the super-chilled

This small and *très* cool bar beneath the Supper Club restaurant (*see p115*) is decked out in the eatery's famous minimalist style, with mirrors, pillars and lush couches making up what management describe as a 'sultry atmosphere'. Live DJs spin chilled, modern tunes. The SC crew are going to try and apply their golden touch to the Salad Bowl club – located on Nieuwezijds Voorburgwal, just next door to **Time** (*see below*) – which should be reopening in autumn or winter 2000.

Time

Nieuwezijds Voorburgwal 163-165, Old Centre:
New Side (06 2606 0693 mobile). **Open** 11pm-4am
Thur, Sun; 11pm-5am Fri, Sat; closed Mon-Wed.
Admission *f*10-*f*25. **No credit cards. Map**
p306 C3.
The main attraction of this refurbished club is its great open-level layout: the view down onto the dancefloor through the lighting rig from the third floor is often hypnotising. On Tuesdays, there's a popular Jamaican night that mainly plays ragga and pulls a mostly black crowd. Wednesday is drum 'n' bass night, while the weekend concentrates on more mainstream techno. The water running down the back of the mirrored bars gives the place a somewhat spacey feel.

Trance Buddha

Oudezijds Voorburgwal 216, Old Centre: Old Side
(422 8233). Tram 4, 9, 14, 16, 20, 24, 25/Metro
Nieuwmarkt. **Open** 11pm-4am Mon-Thur, Sun;
11pm-5am Fri, Sat. **Admission** free-*f*35. **No credit
cards. Map** p306 D3.
This low-key club is decorated like an Indian-influenced student pad: batik sheets hang from the ceiling, with pictures of Shiva sticky-taped to the walls. Drinks are served in plastic cups and purchased with a token, while the door staff are a little off-putting, but the club still fills up with wide-eyed late-teens at the weekend. Trance music dominates.

Supper Club. *See p184.*

Vakzuid

Olympisch Stadion 35, Zuid (570 8400/
www.vakzuid.nl). *Tram 1, 6.* **Open** 10pm-1am
Mon-Thur, Sun; 10pm-3am Fri, Sat; 4pm-1am Sun.
No credit cards. Admission free-*f*10.
Vakzuid is a sleek, clever space of the type you'd expect to find in Berlin. A small but nattily designed bar-cum-lounge-cum-restaurant-cum-club, it's built under old grandstands at the stadium that was erected for when Amsterdam hosted the Olympics in 1928 and that has recently been renovated and spruced up a treat. Indeed, there's even a fantastic terrace that looks out over the track, though – and this is a nice touch – blankets are available if you get too chilly. DJs spin at the weekend, with Quincy Lounge, a cool Sunday gig (4-10pm) that features DJs such as Enrico Riva, a highlight. A modern clubbing/dining experience for grown-ups. *See also p76 and p115.*

Westergasfabriek

Haarlemmerweg 8-10, Westerpark (597 4458/
www.westergasfabriek.nl). *Bus 18, 22.* **Open** varies.
Admission varies. *Membership f*5 (compulsory).
No credit cards. Map p305 A1.
An old gas factory that is home to many interesting cultural events and festivals (*see also p240*). The Café West Pacific, one of the buildings on the site (*see p133*), holds a variety of dance parties, usually nightly Thursday to Sunday. Look out for the funky Club de Ville and the excellent garage night Speedfreax. It fills up quickly, though, so go early.

Out of town

Many hardcore clubbers regularly take a trip out of Amsterdam, especially for large-scale events billed as parties. Though the clubs listed below are not too far out of town, and some run free, regular bus services in and out of Amsterdam, the best way to travel is invariably by car, so try and blag a lift. Flyers and the ever-elusive word-of-mouth are the best sources of up-to-date information.

De Hemkade

Hemkade 48, Zaandam (075 614 8154/
www.hemkade.nl). *NS rail Zaandam.* **Open** usually
10pm-8am, days vary. **Admission** *f*40-*f*50. **No
credit cards.**
Once known as the Fun Factory, De Hemkade, just north of Amsterdam, is basically a huge hall with adjoining rooms hosting different styles of music. While there's no regular club night here, expect at least one gig a week: check flyers or the club's website to see what's happening.

De Waakzaamheid

Hoogstraat 4, Koog aan de Zaan (075 628 5829/
party info 06 5069 3485 mobile/www.waakzaamheid.
A2000.nl). *NS rail Koogzanddijk.* **Open** 11pm-10am
Sat; closed Mon-Fri, Sun. **Admission** *f*20-*f*27,50.
No credit cards.

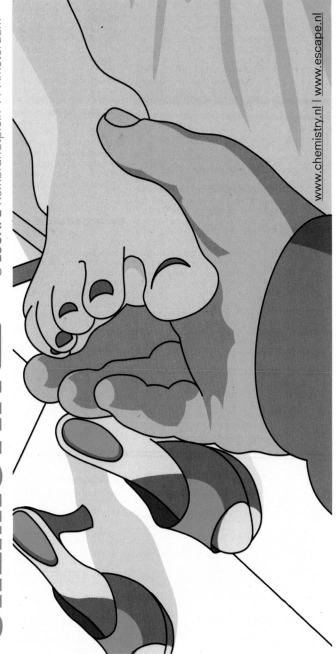

CHEMISTRY

Lazy, crazy Sundays

In recent years, Sunday has been admitted as an honorary member of the weekend on Amsterdam's clubbing circuit after years of underuse, though its style tends to be more chilled and loungey than that found out and about on Fridays and Saturdays. That said, some nights will leave you wondering how anyone is able to work on a Monday.

Beatlounge

De Kring, 1st Floor, Kleine Gartmanplantsoen 7-9, Grachtengordel: East (330 2369). Tram 1, 2, 5, 6, 7, 10, 20. **Open** 4pm-9.30pm last Sun of the month. **Admission** ƒ10. **No credit cards. Map** p310 D5.

Most of the time de Kring is a members-only club, but non-members are allowed in for Beatlounge. Expect a mixture of live music, DJs, non-Western food, movies, slide shows and spoken word (oh, and lots of 'I've got an art degree' poseur types). Worth checking out if just to see the beautifully designed and usually off-limits space in which it's held.

Club Vegas

Winston Kingdom, Warmoesstraat 129, Old Centre: Red Light District (623 1380/
www.winston.nl). Tram 4, 9, 16, 20, 24, 25. **Open** 9pm-3am Sun. **Admission** ƒ10. **No credit cards. Map** p306 D2.

More like a strange private party than a club, Vegas has been going strong for over two years and claims to have started the trend in Amsterdam for easy, loungey Sunday nights. Sundays offer cheesy listening music, performances, competitions, snacks and an 'anything-can-happen' kinda feel. The dress code is 'glamorous, sexy, suave, Las Vegas!' and you may be refused entry if you come looking too plain. The crowd is unpretentious and mischievous.

De Club

Odeon, Singel 460, Grachtengordel: East (624 9711). Tram 1, 2, 5. **Open** 4pm-10pm Sun. **Admission** ƒ10. **No credit cards. Map** p310 D4.

De Club attracts a glitzy, solvent crowd of thirtysomething media types, TV personalities and assorted wannabes with live bands – Herman Brood, Amsterdam's answer to Iggy Pop, has performed here – and rock 'n' roll top-40-ish music. You don't even need to organise a babysitter: there's a creche on site.

A cosy and perpetually packed club right in the middle of a housing estate in Koog aan de Zaan. Pulling power comes in the form of great DJ line-ups, with top international names often putting in an appearance. The club is generally only open on Saturdays, but there are also monthly club nights. There's a separate bar area, and in warm weather you can sit outside on the terrace.

Woodstock, Republiek & Solaris

Beach pavilions, Bloemendaal aan Zee (023 5732 152). NS rail to Haarlem, then taxi (ƒ25) or train taxi to Bloemendaal aan Zee. **Open** May-Oct times vary. **Admission** free. **No credit cards.**

These three beach cafés, open in summer, are worth a visit if the weather's nice. Soul and easy-listening icon Piet Popcorn spins discs at Woodstock on Monday nights to an up-for-anything crowd of regulars, an amiable mix of students, locals, ex-hippies and escaping city slickers. When the dancefloor gets full, the action spills on to the beach.

If Woodstock is a little San Francisco, the less kitschily funksome Solaris is a baby Ibiza, with techno played to a younger crowd. Outdoor stages go up in September and October, as both cafés join forces and throw big beach parties for six straight weeks on Sundays (from 1pm). Republiek falls in between the two, and tends to be inhabited by trendsetting types.

After hours

Though the clubs in town have to close by 5am at the latest, there are a handful of late night and early morning events to keep insomniacs satisfied. Most clubs and bars have permission to hold about five after-hours parties every year, and there's normally at least one super-late wing-ding going on: look out for flyers and keep your ear to the ground. **Delta/Dino's** (Coenhaveweg 26; no phone) and **After Hour Power Supreme** (Overtoom 65, Westzaan; 400 3391), the latter held every first Sunday of the month, are two worth looking out for: kicking off around 5am, the final stragglers are booted out during the afternoon. Expect to pay upwards of ƒ25 to get in. **Something 2 Go 2**, launched in 2000 at the **Winston Hotel** (*see page 96*) kicks off on Saturday nights and can run through until 8am: though it's not strictly a club, decent DJs can usually found here, spinning the night away for punters who've paid under ƒ10 at the door.

If you're feeling peckish after a night on the town, and you're the sort of person who likes a vodka and orange alongside your bacon and eggs, then head for **Het Dobbertje Café**

Relaxed punters **Havana** ball down on Reguliersdwarsstraat. *See p182.*

(Marnixstraat 325), open from 6am. Expect to see a mishmash of early morning folk and messed-up party people who just can't stop.

All of this, though, comes with one major caveat. Given Mayor Patijn's apparent desire to clamp down on some of the city's prevalent naughtiness, it's hard to say how Amsterdam's after-hours scene is going to look in the future. One late-night/early-morning hangout, **Club Zoo**, closed after a period of inspired lunacy in the Red Light District, and Patijn's hardline approach may result in other underground enterprises being forced to shut up shop (or, of course, having to move even further underground). But in general, keep your ears to the ground and you should find something to satisfy the round-the-clock cravings of even the hardiest clubber.

Club night organisers

Look out for one-off events organised by the following companies. Flyers can be picked up and tickets bought in the stores listed under **Tickets & information** (*see page 189*). The excellent free English 'zine *Shark*, available in many bars and clubs around the city as well as on the Internet at www.underwateramsterdam.com, lists many of the bigger underground events, as does the **Clubwear House** site (*see page 189*).

Club Risk
www.clubrisk.nl.
Risk's resident DJs are Eric de Man and the seemingly ubiquitous Dimitri, with international guests completing the bill. Its website carries news of upcoming events.

Dance Valley
Spaarnwoude Recreation Area (tickets 0900 300 1250/travel information 038 423 5222/ www.dancevalley.nl). NS rail to Sloterdijk, then free buses to Spaarnewoude. **Tickets** ƒ80-ƒ100.
Begun in 1995, Dance Valley has expanded to become the biggest dance festival in Holland. Once a year, on a Saturday in August, up to 30,000 people gather at Spaarnwoude Recreation Area outside Amsterdam to chill out and listen to everything from techno and hard house to speed and garage. During the day, over 100 DJs and bands perform on the main stage and in eight huge tents. The Dance Valley gang also organise the monthly **HQ** at the **Melkweg** (*see 184*) and occasional parties at other venues. Check out its website for information on travel, camping and tickets.

Healers
Tickets Uitlijn 0900 0191 premium rate.
Several times a year, Healers' two **Love Boats** board near Centraal Station for a unique clubbing experience on Amsterdam's waterways. On certain holidays – such as Queen's Day, Christmas and New Year – the boats are joined together, with DJs on the decks on deck spinning all sorts of stuff for an enthusiastic and up-for-it crowd.

MTC
www.tedmtc.nl.
The most hyped and extravagant parties in the Netherlands. Most MTC gigs take place in Rotterdam, but are well worth the hour's drive. The only drawback is that the events sell out about a month in advance; even if you can get a ticket, there's no guarantee you'll be let in due to MTC's erratic door policy. Still, if you manage to get in, you'll have a blinding night. Information on events can be gleaned from the MTC website.

Monumental

Tickets 0900 300 1250/www.awakenings.nl.
Monumental hosts the hugely popular Awakenings parties at the **Westergasfabriek** (*see p185*) five times a year. Gabbers and clubbers come together as a line-up of international DJs play techno until the early hours. The nigh-on legendary Andrew Weatherall and Paul van Dijk are but two of the excellent guests to have graced the turntables.

Silly Symphonies

Tickets Clubwear House 622 8766.
The long-running Silly Symphonies hold parties right across Holland. In particular, though, look out for the beach parties held annually at Scheveningen near The Hague (for details on how to get to the town, *see p261*), where DJ Remy and guests spin techno and trance.

Tickets & information

Detailed below are the best places in which to pick up flyers and tickets for clubs and parties in Amsterdam. Smart shop **Conscious Dreams** (*see p137* **Get smart**) also has flyers for some events.

Korsakoff. High-class it ain't. *See p183*.

Clubwear House

Herengracht 265, Grachtengordel: West (622 8766/ www.clubwearhouse.nl). Tram 1, 2, 5, 13, 17, 20. **Open** noon-6pm Tue, Wed, Fri, Sat; noon-8pm Thur; closed Mon, Sun. **Credit** AmEx, DC, MC, V. **Map** p306 C3.
A large fashion shop with flyers and tickets for a massive variety of events, plus DJ mix taps and other goodies. *See p146.*

Dance Tracks

Nieuwe Nieuwstraat 69, Old Centre: New Side (639 0853). Tram 1, 2, 5. **Open** 1-7pm Mon; 11am-7pm Tue, Wed, Fri, Sat; 11am-9pm Thur; 1-6pm Sun. **No credit cards. Map** p306 D2.
A record shop with flyers and some tickets for events on the hardcore house scene.

Groove Connection

Sint Nicolaasstraat 41, Old Centre: New Side (624 7234). Tram 1, 2, 5. **Open** 2-6pm Mon, Sun; 11am-6pm Tue, Wed, Fri, Sat; 11am-9pm Thur. **Credit** MC, V. **Map** p306 C2.
Another record store that holds some tickets and flyers for underground events.

Housewives on Fire

Spuistraat 102, Old Centre: New Side (422 1067/ www.xs4all.nl/~housew). Tram 1, 2, 5. **Open** Sept-Apr 10am-7pm Mon-Wed, Fri, Sat; 10am-9pm Thur. *May-Aug* also noon-6pm Sun. **Credit** MC, V. **Map** p306 C2.
Cool clothes and accessories, plus a hairdressing salon in the back and live DJs on some days. Cute, friendly staff proffer flyers and pre-sale tickets.

Midtown Records

Nieuwendijk 104, Old Centre: New Side (638 4252). Tram 1, 2, 5, 13, 17, 20, 24, 25. **Open** 1-6pm Mon, Sun; 10am-6pm Tue, Wed, Fri, Sat; 10am-9pm Thur. **Credit** AmEx, DC, MC, V. **Map** p306 D2.
This record shop for serious music-lovers – there are always one or two DJs at the listening booths – has tickets and flyers for the hardcore and gabber scenes. *See also p165.*

Outland Records

Zeedijk 22, Old Centre: Red Light District (638 7576). Tram 1, 2, 5, 13, 17, 20, 24, 25. **Open** 11am-6pm Mon-Wed, Fri, Sat; 11am-9pm Thur. **Credit** AmEx, DC, MC, V. **Map** p306 D2.
A very popular record shop that offers tickets for house events. Flyers are available only with record purchases.

Hairpolice

Kerkstraat 113, Grachtengordel: East (420 5841/ www.channels.nl/amsterdam/hairpo.html). Tram 1, 2, 5, 16, 24, 25. **Open** noon-7pm Tue, Wed, Fri; noon-8pm Thur; noon-6pm Sat; closed Mon, Sun. **Credit** V. **Map** p310 D4.
A Californian store that offers clubwear, flyers, presale tickets and the like. **Hairpolice**, located upstairs, specialises in extensions, and there's an adjoining tattoo parlour.

Arts & Entertainment

Film

The Dutch are finally waking up to their nation's filmic talent: it's hello to the Netherlands and farewell to the US of A.

Things are stirring in the Dutch film world. True, the average cinema continues to play mostly standard Hollywood fodder, but Dutch movies are becoming more popular and, as a consequence, more are being made. In 1999, a specialist cinema, soley devoted to Dutch films and documentaries, opened in Amsterdam. However, perhaps more pertinently, a new tax law designed to encourage investment in Dutch films and documentaries was introduced in the same year. The benefits of the law will hopefully become apparent in the next few years, but it's certainly a step in the right direction.

The international success of films such as *Antonia* and *Character* – both winners of the Best Foreign Language Film prize at the Oscars, in 1996 and 1998 respectively – has also helped fuel interest in national cinematic products, and what's on offer is often worth a look. Watch out for anything that bears the names of commercially-oriented directors Jos Stelling (*The Flying Dutchman*), Dick Maas (*Flodder, Amsterdamned*) and Jean van de Velde (*All Stars*), or artsier types Alex van Warmerdam (*Abel, The Dress*), Eddy Terstall (*Hufters en Hofdames, Rent-a-Friend*), Ian Kerkhof (*Wasted!*) and Robert Jan Westdijk (*Zusje*).

Still, some Dutch film folk have found a wider public – and a larger bank account – over in the US. Paul Verhoeven, director of *Robocop* and *Basic Instinct*, is probably the most famous, but don't forget Robby Muller (Wim Wenders' preferred cameraman), screenwriter Menno Meyes, and, of course, Jan de Bont, a former cameraman on films like *The Jewel of the Nile* and *Ruthless People,* who's seen his flashy directorial efforts – *Speed* and *Twister* in particular – clean up all over the globe. As for Dutch actors, Famke Janssen rubbed shoulders (and limbs) with Pierce Brosnan in *GoldenEye*, while Jeroen Krabbé, who starred next to Harrison Ford in *The Fugitive*, turned director with the beautifully crafted and prize-winning international production *Lost Luggage*.

THE CINEMAS

Amsterdam's cinemas offer as balanced and substantial a cinematic diet as any other European city, from Hollywood blockbuster junk food to the indigenous flavours of home-grown produce. As in many major cities, the cinemas can be divided into two main categories: First run cinemas, which show exactly what you'd imagine, and Revival and art houses (or 'filmhuizen'). Amsterdammers have a healthy appetite for foreign and art house fare: the venues offer both a cosmopolitan mix of art films, documentaries and retrospectives (as well as an informed selection of the more intelligent Hollywood flicks) in characterful settings. With the exception of the **Uitkijk**, all have marvellous cafés, while **The Movies**, especially notable for its lavish art deco interior, also has an enchanting restaurant.

Of the mainstream cinemas, the **Tuschinski**, with its sumptuous original deco architecture and fittings, is a marvel in itself. The recently opened **Pathé ArenA** is Amsterdam's first multiplex, with 14 screens. It will be followed by another multiplex, **Pathé de Munt**, due to open on Vijzelstraat (around the corner from Tuschinski) in late

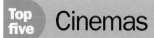

Top five Cinemas

Kriterion
Catch a surpise film at this cinema's weekly preview slot on Thursdays. See page 193.

The Movies
Dinner and a movie? You can have both at this café-restaurant. See page 193.

Nederlands Filmmuseum
The NFM's outdoor screenings in summer are as close as you'll get to a drive-in, but without the horrible Hollywood flicks. See page 194.

Pathé ArenA
If you're in the mood for a mega-blockbuster and a mega-Coke, this mega-multiplex offers it all. See page 192.

Tuschinski
Something to celebrate? Splash out on the eight-seater box and sip champagne while watching a movie. See page 192.

Mega-films, mega-venue: head to **Pathé ArenA** for the mega-blockbuster. *See p192.*

2000. There are also plans to build an art house cinema on water, aptly named **CineShip** and slated to contain four screens, a terrace and a restaurant. Located on Oostelijke Handelskade – right by Centraal Station – it should be up and running by 2002.

TICKETS & INFORMATION

Cinema programmes in the multiplexes change every Thursday. Weekly listings of the main venues are prominently displayed in virtually every café, bar and cinema, while other reliable sources of information include *Uitkrant*, the Wednesday and Saturday editions of *Het Parool*, the *Amsterdams Stadsblad* and, for independent and quirky art house films, the free English listings mag *Shark*. Look out, too, for excellent monthly Dutch film mag *De Filmkrant*, which also has comprehensive movie information – mostly in Dutch, but easily understood by the non-native – and the websites of the individual cinemas.

Commercial-haters should be warned that while art houses go straight into the movie without the often unwelcome appetiser of half-a-dozen soft drinks ads, the publicised starting time in multiplexes allows 15 minutes' grace while pre-film commercials are shown. It's advisable to reserve your tickets in advance if you think the movie of your choice is likely to be popular (on opening weekends, for example). Cinemas usually charge a nominal fee of 50¢, though credit cards are not accepted by any cinemas in Amsterdam.

Worse still for those who count English as a first language, all Pathé-owned cinemas – all of those listed under **First run & Mainstream** below – now use a computer-operated telephone reservation line in Dutch only, which will set you back 50¢ per minute. If you don't speak Dutch and want to reserve tickets, then you may well have to journey to the cinema itself in order to do it.

All films are shown in the original language (normally English) with Dutch subtitles. Films in Dutch are indicated by the words 'Nederlands Gesproken' after the title. Some movie houses offer student discounts with the appropriate ID. Purists should also note that for some inexplicable reason, many Dutch cinemas stick an interval in the middle of every film; call ahead if you really can't face it.

Cinemas

First run & mainstream

Bellevue Cinerama/Calypso

Marnixstraat 400-2, Grachtengordel: East (0900 1458 premium rate). Tram 1, 2, 5, 6, 7, 10, 20. **Tickets** *ƒ8-ƒ17.* **Screens** 2 each. **No credit cards. Map** p310 C5.

Two separate and glitzy Pathé complexes next door to each other, with a shared box office. As with all cinemas in this section, the ƒ8 ticket price is only for screenings before noon; ordinarily, tickets for evening shows will cost the top rate ƒ17, with day-time screenings ƒ4 or ƒ5 cheaper.

The classic and charming **De Uitkijk**, Amsterdam's oldest cinema. *See p193*.

City

Kleine Gartmanplantsoen 15-19, Grachtengordel: East (0900 1458 premium rate). Tram 1, 2, 5, 6, 7, 10, 20. **Tickets** *f8-f17.* **Late shows** around midnight Fri, Sat. **Screens** 7. **No credit cards.** **Map** p310 D5.

The large frontage and huge electronic advertisement hoarding of the City dominate the Kleine Gartmanplantsoen. Inside, a bank of TV sets in the foyer runs a constant diet of trailers. Because of its central location and its policy for action flicks, City is hugely popular with loud youngsters.

Pathé ArenA

ArenA Boulevard 600, South-East (0900 1458 premium rate). Metro Bijlmer. **Tickets** *f8-f17.* **Screens** 14. **No credit cards.**

This glitzy multiplex, next to the Ajax stadium, offers a staggering 14 screens, 3,250 seats, a digital sound system and spacious foyers. Expect blockbusters, action films and other Hollywood success stories, playing to a crowd drawn largely from the surrounding suburbs. Screenings start every 15 minutes.

Pathé de Munt

Vijzelstraat 15, Grachtengordel: East (0900 1458 premium rate). Tram 4, 9, 14, 16, 20, 24, 25. **Tickets** *f8-f17.* **Screens** 7. **No credit cards.** **Map** p310 D4.

A brand new complex near the **Tuschinski** (also Pathé-owned; *see below*), the Pathé de Munt multiplex is expected to boast seven screens and eminently comfortable decor. It was scheduled to open in 2000; phone the above number for more details.

Tuschinski

Reguliersbreestraat 26-8, Grachtengordel: East (0900 1458 premium rate). Tram 4, 9, 14, 16, 20, 24, 25. **Tickets** *f8-f17.* **Guided tours** Mon, Sun mornings by appointment; *f10.* **Screens** 6. **No credit cards.** **Map** p311 E4.

Built in 1921 as a variety theatre, the Tuschinski is now Amsterdam's most prestigious movie house, which inevitably means box-office queues at evenings and weekends. Home to regular premières and occasional royal screenings, it offers a lively and often inspired choice of films. The building's stunning art deco design (*see p31*) attracts many visitors, which explains the need for guided tours. If you've come with a group, splash out on the eight-person box, complete with champagne all round. The Tuschinki was scheduled to add three more screens in late 2000, bringing its tally up to nine.

Revival & art houses

Cinecenter

Lijnbaansgracht 236, The Jordaan (623 6615). Tram 1, 2, 5, 6, 7, 10, 20. **Tickets** *f7-f15.* **Screens** 4. **No credit cards.** **Map** p310 C4.

The Cinecenter is a welcoming venue, with recently revamped decor. Each screen has its own name – check out the tiny 52-seater Jean Vigo room – and the programme is pleasingly international.

Het Ketelhuis

Haarlemmerweg 8-10, The Jordaan (684 0090/ www.ketelhuis.nl). Bus 18, 22. **Tickets** *f15.* **Screens** 1. **No credit cards.** **Map** p305 A1.

Devoted to Dutch films and documentaries – sometimes with subtitles – this project of Marc van Warmerdam (producer and brother of filmmaker Alex) is an asset for film fans. It's located by **Café West Pacific** (*see p133*), a restaurant-club where you can enjoy a meal beforehand or a drink after.

Kriterion

Roetersstraat 170, Oost (623 1708/ www.kriterion.nl). Tram 6, 7, 10/Metro Weesperplein. **Tickets** ƒ12,50-ƒ13,50; ƒ10 children's matinées; ƒ8,50 previews. **Late shows** 12.15am Fri, Sat. **Screens** 2. **No credit cards. Map** p312 G3.

Run by volunteer students, this local knows how to pick 'em: the ever-intriguing programme includes children's matinées (Wednesdays, Saturdays and Sundays) and preview screenings (Thursdays). Student flicks are shown here, while late shows cover cult US or erotic French films.

The Movies

Haarlemmerdijk 161, The Jordaan (624 5790/ www.themovies.nl). Tram 3. **Tickets** ƒ13,50-ƒ15. **Late shows** 12.15am Fri, Sat. **Screens** 4. **Credit** *Restaurant* MC, V. **Map** p305 B1.

Don't be fooled by the insipid name: the Movies is a great place to visit if you like, um, the movies. Built in 1928, it's a fine building: the 1930s-style café is worth a visit even if you're not catching a flick. If you do see a film, it will probably be international in origin and interesting in content. Make an evening of it: if you have a meal in the restaurant, your seats for the show will be reserved, allowing you to slip in at the last minute.

Rialto

Ceintuurbaan 338, The Pijp (662 3488/ www.rialtofilm.nl). Tram 3, 12, 24, 25. **Tickets** ƒ12,50-ƒ15; ƒ50 5-visit card; ƒ90 10-visit card. **Screens** 2. **No credit cards. Map** p311 F6.

This stylish, alternative cinema out in the Pijp offers a mixed diet of new and old international flicks and the occasional European première. Thematic blocks change monthly, and there's always at least one classic oldie on show.

De Uitkijk

Prinsengracht 452, Grachtengordel: East (623 7460/ www.uitkijk.nl). Tram 1, 2, 5, 6, 7, 10, 20. **Tickets** ƒ13-ƒ16. **Screens** 1. **No credit cards. Map** p310 D5.

Amsterdam's oldest cinema – the set-up dates from 1913 – is a charming 158-seat converted canal house; films that prove popular tend to stay put for a while. Movie snobs, pay attention: de Uitkijk doesn't serve snacks, so you're unlikely to be disturbed by annoying gits in the back row flicking popcorn at your head.

Film festivals

Amnesty International Film Festival

Information 626 4436. **Dates** Sept, even-numbered years only. **Tickets** call for prices.

This five-day biennial event centres around **De Balie** (*see p237*) and features films, documentaries, clips, discussions, lectures and a workshop. Even though the theme for 2000 is 'torture', organisers try to include some lighter material as well.

Multimedia centres

Biotoom at Akademie

Overtoom 301, Oud West (06 2478 4791/ www.go.to/overtoom301). Tram 1, 6. **Tickets** ƒ5-ƒ7,50. **Screens** 1. **No credit cards. Map** p309 B6.

The former Nederlandse Filmacademie was squatted in 2000 and turned into, among other things, an organic vegan restaurant, a club and – you guessed it – a cinema. Biotoom offers indie and experimental films and children's movies (every other Wednesday afternoon), plus gay and lesbian flicks. Though the future looks promising, it's not known how long the squatters will be allowed to stay, so phone before setting out.

Melkweg

Lijnbaansgracht 234A, Grachtengordel: East (531 8181/www.melkweg.nl). Tram 1, 2, 5, 6, 7, 10, 20. **Tickets** ƒ10; **membership** ƒ5. **Late shows** 12.15am Fri, Sat. **Screens** 1. **No credit cards. Map** p310 C5.

The multipurpose, multifunction, multimedia Melkweg (see also p184, p217 and p244) runs a consistently imaginative film programme in its cosy first-floor cinema, taking in anything from mainstream trash to cult fare and avant-garde art house flicks. There's a café-bar here, too.

Tropeninstituut Kleine Zaal/ Grote Zaal

Kleine Zaal *Linnaeusstraat 2, Oost;* **Grote Zaal** *Mauritskade 63, Oost (568 8500/www.kit.nl/theater/html/film.htm). Tram 9, 10, 14, 20.* **Open** *reservations* 10am-4pm. **Screens** 2. **No credit cards. Map** p312 H3.

Located right next to the **Tropenmuseum** (see p54), this venue stages regular ethnic music and theatre performances, and, occasionally, interesting documentaries and feature films from developing countries. A worthy enterprise, but an interesting one, too.

Festival van de Fantastische Film

www.fff2000.nl. **Date** Apr. **Tickets** ƒ12,50 per film; ƒ250 all films. *Night of Terror* ƒ47,50.

The annual Festival of the Fantastic Film is a week-long extravaganza held in various cinemas around the city. Offering premières, sneak previews, retrospectives and a youth programme, it should appeal to all lovers of horror, fantasy and SF. The Night of Terror, which spotlights some of the goriest movies imaginable in front of an up-for-it crowd, is not to be missed.

International Documentary Filmfestival Amsterdam

626 1939/www.idfa.nl. **Dates** 22-30 Nov 2000; 21-29 Nov 2001. **Tickets** ƒ12,50; ƒ180 week-long pass.

As the name suggests, documentaries are the staple of this fascinating annual festival. A ƒ25,000 prize in the name of the late Dutch documentary maker Joris Ivens is awarded to the best film. Each afternoon, the public gets the opportunity to put questions to a few of the directors in the central festival location at De Balie (for which, *see p237*).

International Film Festival Rotterdam

PO Box 21696, 3001 AR Rotterdam (information 010 890 9090/reservations 010 890 9000/ www.filmfestivalrotterdam.nl). NS rail to Rotterdam Centraal Station. **Date** 31 Jan-11 Feb 2001; every year late Jan/early Feb. **Tickets** ƒ10-ƒ15.

The Rotterdam Film Festival is easily the biggest film festival in the Netherlands. It is international in scope, boasting around 90 films in the main programme and up to 100 others, thoughtfully compiled in retrospectives. The series of lectures and seminars by guest directors, actors, producers and other industry figures is normally a highlight, while aspiring movie-makers should check out the afternoon workshops on film technique. The festival is non-competitive with an emphasis on what can loosely be termed 'art' movies, and is held in a number of different locations, all within walking distance of each other (for more details on the city of Rotterdam, *see p262*). Enjoy the festival, which exposes Cannes as the mere schmoozefest that it undoubtedly is.

Among the highlights of the festival is the **Exploding Cinema** series, which focuses on the future of film with a mix of live performances, installations, exhibitions, VJs and DJs, plus a forum where directors such as Peter Greenaway field questions from viewers. Exploding Cinema also occasionally organises alternative events around Amsterdam, where self-produced VHS, 8mm and 16mm films are screened. Keep your eyes peeled for flyers about the events.

Nederlandse Film Festival

PO Box 1581, 3500 BN Utrecht (030 232 2684/ www.filmfestival.nl). NS rail to Utrecht. **Dates** 20-29 Sept 2000; every year in late Sept. **Tickets** call for prices.

The grand **Nederlands Filmmuseum (NFM)**.

An all-Dutch affair, aimed at the Dutch public and film industry and held in late September, the Nederlandse Film Festival spotlights around 100 features in a variety of venues, along with selections of shorts, documentaries and TV programmes. Each new Dutch production is shown here, along with a selection of flicks by students from Dutch Film and Art Academies. The festival presents its own awards to the year's best films and holds an annual retrospective of a Dutch film personality. Lectures and seminars also feature. For more on Utrecht, *see p266*.

World Wide Video Festival

Information 420 7729/www.wwvf.nl. **Dates** Sept. **Tickets** call for prices.

This annual festival takes place at various locations in the city, such as the Paradiso and the Stedelijk Museum. Aside from showing videos and DVDs, the festival also features CD-Roms, web-based projects, installations and seminars on a plethora of film- and video-related subjects.

Film museum

Nederlands Filmmuseum (NFM)

Vondelpark 3, Museum Quarter (589 1400/ library 589 1435/www.nfm.nl). Tram 1, 2, 3, 5, 6, 12, 20. **Open** *Library* 10am-5pm Tue-Fri; 11am-5pm Sat. *Screenings* 7pm, 7.30pm, 9.30pm, 10pm daily. *Children's matinées* 3pm Sun. **Tickets** ƒ12,50; ƒ10 students, groups (min 10 persons); ƒ7,50 members. **Membership** ƒ30/yr. **Screens** 3. **No credit cards. Map** p310 C6.

This government-subsidised movie museum was established in the 1940s and has over 35,000 films in its vaults, culled from every period, cinematic style and corner of the world. Dutch films and children's matinées take care of the Sunday programmes, and the occasional screenings of silent movies are accompanied by live piano music. On balmy evenings during the summer, there are outdoor screenings on the first-floor terrace. Students of cinema can often be found poring over the unique archives, parts of which have been transferred on to video. The museum's Café Vertigo, in the basement, has one of Amsterdam's most charming terraces. *See also pp70-71.*

Galleries

Rembrandt may be gone, but the Dutch art scene is still exceeding expectations.

Amsterdam's abnormally large concentration of galleries and art dealers has led many to suspect that the scene is more given to laundering drug money than actually promoting the arts. However, the city has, in fact, teemed with art since those heady days of Rembrandt and the Golden Age, when paintings of bowls of fruit were often cheaper than what they depicted. The riches wrought from colonial conquests allowed the early formation of a large middle class that quickly warmed to art; not only for its snazzy decorative powers, but also for the aura of status it imbued, with the attached bonus of tweaking that status if the painting's guilder value happened to rise. Even today, the average Amsterdammer often betrays a shocking amount of knowledge of the arts, both past and painfully contemporary, and one would be hard pressed to find a home or a workplace that does not feature an original work of art.

THE 20TH CENTURY

While drawing ideas from the major 20th-century art movements – and, in particular, Cubism – Dutch artists have come up with a few of their own unique contributions, some of which have had a major global influence. The bold yet pristine abstraction of De Stijl ('the Style'), founded in 1917 and involving the illustrious likes of Theo van Doesburg, Piet Mondrian and Gerrit Rietveld, sought rules of equilibrium that would be just as useful in the design of daily life as it would be in art. But while De Stijl had a global impact on modern art in all its forms, it was actually a much messier crew of artists that probably proved to be the most relevant art movement that has occurred in the Netherlands this century, from inspiring the Provo 'happenings' of the '60s to explaining the escalating market prices of Outsider Art in the '90s.

It all began in 1948, when a group of like-minded artists combined the initial letters of the cities in which they worked – Copenhagen, Brussels and Amsterdam – to come up with **CoBrA** (*see page 70* **Museums further out**). For three years, this striking label described the efforts and collaborations of such (now singularly famed) artists as Karel Appel, Eugene Brands, Doutrement, Constant, Corneille and Lucebert. While their Surrealist forebears had embraced Freud, CoBrA artists were more inspired by those who seemed directly wired into Jung's collective unconscious: primitives, children and the mentally deranged. Vaguely humanoid monsters, both happy and scary, became the CoBrA trademark. They sought to further define the 'freedom' that had recently been regained by Liberation. The goal was to express immediate sensual urges, and the key was spontaneity. Ragged excess drips of paint – with poetry often scrawled in – was the movement's standard; the action always transcended the product. CoBrA's brand of revolutionary thought did not call for art for the masses, but rather art by the masses.

Techniques from this form of abstract expressionism can be found echoed in the more figurative work of Amsterdam artists such as Peter Klashorst, Jurriaan van Hall, Gijs Donker and Ernst Voss, who gained ascension in the '80s as an antidote to the modernist conceptual art that had essentially taken over the market at this time (and that had made their art school buddy, Rob Scholte, rich and famous). By painting, 'After Nature' – as the group was called – sought a return to 'reality'. While fundamental in seeing in a return of the figurative to Dutch art, the movement's founder Klashorst came to see a little too much reality in the spring of 2000 when he fled Senegal after spending three weeks in jail for the painting of some nude portraits.

THE CONTEMPORARY SCENE

While not enjoying the huge cash infusions of a decade or two ago – when artists were getting paid for basically just calling themselves artists – the arts are relatively well subsidised in this country, with the folks holding the purse strings also cannily funnelling funds to the younger artists who are exploring new media and technologies. With the decline of inner city squat locations, the local government is – albeit belatedly – showing some more sensitivity to younger artists, with talk of establishing 'breeding grounds of the arts' equipped with affordable studio space. While it would be brash in these complicated times to actually speak of movements, perhaps the most interesting current phenomenon is the blurring of borders between different and once-rigid scenes: where graphic designers (*see page 199* **Digital dynamism**) can

make Mercedes logos without losing the respect
they receive in more purely arty circles, where
celeb snapper Anton Corbijn can get a
retrospective at the Groninger Museum, and
where nightclub names such as Micha Klein and
Dadara are now raking in cash on the
international gallery scene.

WHAT'S IN A NAME?
In addition to its galleries, the Netherlands
boasts five globally statured museums: the
Stedelijk Museum in Amsterdam (*see page
68*), the **Haags Gemeentemuseum** in The
Hague (*see page 259*), the **Rijksmuseum
Kröller-Müller** in Otterlo, the **Groninger
Museum** in Groningen and the **Van
Abbemuseum** in Eindhoven (for all three, *see
pages 264-5* **Beyond Holland**). All attempt to
curate not only established international names,
but also artists of a more local and youthful
nature, the result being competition for the
smaller galleries that already share the art trade
with *kunsthandels* (art dealers). While the
kunsthandels, who rarely put on exhibitions, buy
directly from the artist, galleries generally sell
work on a commission basis. As an artist, which
would you choose?

The result of this is that galleries open and
close in Amsterdam all the time. For the most
up-to-date list, buy the monthly *Alert* magazine
(available at **Athenaeum Nieuwscentrum**;
see page 142): though it's in Dutch, galleries are
sorted into areas and clearly marked on maps.

You can also check the art listings in the listings
magazine *Uitkrant* (www.uitkrant.nl), or the art
listings pamphlet published every four months
by AKKA, whose website (www.akka.nl) also
provides some direct links to the websites of the
city's more relevant galleries. Many of the
galleries listed below close during July or
August and have a relaxed attitude to opening
hours the rest of the time, so it's advisable to call
ahead. For **KunstRAI**, the city's annual art fair,
and the **Open Ateliers**, *see page 170*.

Galleries

Galerie Akinci
*Lijnbaansgracht 317, Grachtengordel: East (638
0480/www.akinci.nl). Tram 16, 20, 24, 25.* **Open**
1-6pm Tue-Sat; closed Mon. **No credit cards.**
Map p311 E5.
Part of a complex that includes Lumen Traven, Art
Affair, Oele and the Foundation for Indian Art,
Akinci thrives on surprising with diverse shows that
might include the video art of Emmanuelle Antille
or the body hair art of Yael Davids.

Amsterdamse Centrum voor Fotographie
*Bethaniënstraat 9, Old Centre: Old Side (622 4899).
Tram 16, 24, 25.* **Open** noon-5pm Wed-Sat;
closed Mon, Tue, Sun & July, Aug. **No credit
cards.** **Map** p306 D3.
Photo hounds should go directly to this sprawling
exhibition space, within flashing distance of the
Red Light District. Besides showing the work of

photographers – of both Magnum and up-and-coming varieties – it also has workshops and a black and white developing room available for hire.

Annet Gelink Gallery

Laurierstraat 187-9, The Jordaan (330 2066). Tram 13, 14, 17, 20. **Open** 11am-6pm Tue-Sat; 2-5pm 1st Sun of mth; closed Mon. **No credit cards.**
As one of the former owners of Bloom Gallery, Annet Gelink knew what she wanted when she decided to open her own gallery: space and light, to best reflect some of the latest highways and byways of Dutch and international art. Some notable names: Mat Collishaw, Ed van der Elsken, Alicia Framis and Kiki Lamers.

De Appel

Nieuwe Spiegelstraat 10, Grachtengordel: East (625 5651/www.deappel.nl). Tram 16, 24, 25. **Open** noon-5pm Tue-Sun; closed Mon. **No credit cards. Map** p310 D4.
An Amsterdam institution that showed its mettle early as one of the first galleries in the country to embrace video art. It's maintained a good sense of the bleeding edge by featuring the likes of Christine Borland and Araki, and by allowing both international and rookie guest curators freedom to follow their muse.

ArCam

Waterlooplein 213, Old Centre: Old Side (620 4878/www.arcam.nl). Tram 9, 14, 20/Metro Waterlooplein. **Open** 1-5pm Tue-Fri; closed Mon, Sat, Sun. **No credit cards. Map** p307 E3.
'Architecture Centrum Amsterdam' is obsessed with the promotion of Dutch architecture, and happily organises tours, forums, lectures and exhibits on the subject. Besides its more central exhibition space, it now also has a second space on the harbourfront (Oosterdok 14, 620 4878, open 1-5pm Fri-Sun).

Art Industry

Ferdinand Bolstraat 1, The Pijp (777 9910). Tram 6, 7, 10. **Open** 11am-6pm Wed-Sat; closed Mon, Tue, Sun. **No credit cards. Map** p311 E5.
A good starting point from which to explore the smaller art initiatives of the Pijp. Expect anything, from established figures such as Marlene Dumas, Rob Scholte and Rob Birza to younger artists – such as Ottograph – who are helping bring club culture to the mainstream. Thanks to the sponsorship of its neighbours Heineken, its openings are legendary.

Galerie Binnen

Keizersgracht 82, Grachtengordel: West (625 9603). Tram 1, 2, 5, 13, 17, 20. **Open** noon-6pm Tue-Sat; closed Mon, Sun. **No credit cards. Map** p306 C2.
These industrial and interior design specialists have plenty of room in which to show some of the more unusual Dutch and international names. With ties to Germany's Vitra Design Museum and relationships with the likes of Starck, Sottsass, Kukkapuro and Studio Atika, exhibits can include anything from toilet brushes to full-blown installations.

Clement

Prinsengracht 845, Grachtengordel: East (625 1656). Tram 16, 24, 25. **Open** 11am-5.30pm Tue-Sat; closed Mon, Sun. **No credit cards. Map** p310 D5.
While also exhibiting drawings and paintings, Clement is best known as a heaven for print collectors, having first begun as a printing studio in 1958 before the opening of the gallery in 1968. Walk your eyes through a selection that includes work by the likes of Penck, Sierhuis, Lucebert, Mira and Cremer.

Collection d'Art

Keizersgracht 516, Grachtengordel: East (622 1511). Tram 1, 2, 5, 20. **Open** 1-5pm Wed-Sat; closed Mon, Tue, Sun. **No credit cards. Map** p310 C4.
Another old school gallery founded in 1969, which supplements its established Dutch – and often CoBrA-related – names of Westerik, Armando and Constant with a German expressionist or two.

Consortium

Oostelijke Handelskade 29, Waterfront (421 2408). Bus 32. **Open** 2-6pm Fri-Sun; closed Mon-Sat. **No credit cards.**
In the once squat-rich and now quickly transforming stretch of the eastern Docklands, the converted warehouse space of Consortium puts on exhibitions dedicated to international up-and-comers, with a seeming penchant for those from Italy.

Gallery Delaive

Spiegelgracht 23, Grachtengordel: East (625 9087/www.delaive.nl). Tram 6, 7, 10. **Open** 11am-5.30pm Tue-Sat; noon-5pm Sun; also by appointment. **Credit** AmEx. **Map** p310 D5.
An acclaimed, upmarket joint renowned for its over-reliance on 'names'. But hell, it's a top one-stop-shop if you're out for a collection of all your favourite CoBrA and Surrealist painters and sculptors, and you can even grab a Picasso or a Warhol to boot.

Donkersloot Galerie

PC Hooftstraat 127, Museum Quarter (572 2722/www.virga.net/donkersloot). Tram 2, 3, 5, 12, 20. **Open** 10am-9pm Mon-Sat; 9am-9pm Sun. **Credit** AmEx, DC, MC, V. **Map** p310 C6.
Hyping itself as a 'night gallery', Donkersloot is often home to After Nature artists such as Jurriaan Van Hall and Peter Klashorst, VJ-ing artists such as REL and Ottograph, and – perhaps misguidedly – *Rolling Stone* art. Its openings are a 'who's who' of the city's more potentially decadent artists.

Espace

Keizersgracht 548, Grachtengordel: East (624 0802). Tram 1, 2, 5, 20. **Open** 1-5pm Wed-Sat; 2-5pm 1st Sun of mth; closed Mon, Tue. **No credit cards. Map** p310 C4.
Founded in 1960 by the city's premier arts maven Eva Bendien, Espace has a near-legendary reputation. Most stories derive from a past when Lucebert, Alechinsky, Dubuffet and de Kooning represented the cutting edge. Still, some of the more recent exhibitions have been known to surprise.

Galerie Fons Welters

Bloemstraat 140, The Jordaan (423 3046/ www.fonswelters.nl). Tram 13, 14, 17, 20. **Open** 1-6pm Tue-Sat; 2-5pm 1st Sun of mth; closed Mon. **No credit cards. Map** p305 B3.

Fons Welters knows what he likes, and what he likes is to 'discover' the latest new (and often local) talent. He shows remarkable taste in both sculpture and installation, too, having provided a home to Atelier van Lieshout, Rob Birza, Roy Villevoy and Matthew Monahan. Even the entrance is a tour de force.

Frozen Fountain

Prinsengracht 629, Grachtengordel: West (622 9375). Tram 1, 2, 5, 20. **Open** 1-6pm Mon; 10am-6pm Tue-Fri; 10am-5pm Sat; closed Sun. **No credit cards. Map** p309 C4.

A mecca for lovers of contemporary furniture and design items. While staying abreast with innovative young Dutch designers who show a taste for bizarre materials and odd forms, the 'Froz' also exhibits and sells stuff by the likes of Droog Design and Marc Newsom, 'modern classics' and even photography.

Gate Foundation

Keizersgracht 613, Grachtengordel: East (620 8057/ www.gatefoundation.nl). Tram 1, 2, 5. **Open** 10am-5pm Mon-Fri. **No credit cards. Map** p311 E4.

This 'intercultural contemporary art multicultural society' was founded in 1988 to focus on – you guessed it – the role of (multi)cultural identities in (mostly non-Western) contemporary arts. It has initiated many projects and websites that promote the exchange of ideas between artists from around the world: check out its monumental site for the scoop.

GO Gallery

Prinsengracht 64, Grachtengordel: West (422 9580/ www.gogallery.nl). Tram 13, 14, 17, 20. **Open** noon-6pm Wed-Sat; 1-5pm 1st Sun of mth. **Credit** AmEx, DC, MC, V. **No credit cards. Map** p305 B2.

Curator Oscar van den Voorn has shown bottomless energy in popularising the local arts scene without becoming unfunny-trendy. Expect the likes of a show themed around Mother's Day, the stained glass of Jan Brokkelkamp, or the work of such local bad boys as Ottograph and Paul Smit.

Huis Marseilles

Keizersgracht 401, Grachtengordel: West (531 8989/www.huismarseille.nl). Tram 1, 2, 5. **Open** 11am-5pm Tue-Sun; closed Mon. **No credit cards. Map** p310 C4.

Located in a monumental 17th-century house, this foundation for photography, which opened in 1999, has the space in which to curate insightful exhibitions, such as a Wim and Donata Wenders show themed around the Buena Vista Social Club. Admission is ƒ5, or ƒ2,50 concessions.

Melkweg

Lijnbaansgracht 234A, Grachtengordel: East (624 1777/www.melkweg.nl). Tram 1, 2, 5, 6, 7, 10, 20. **Open** 2-8pm Wed-Sun; closed Mon, Tue. **No credit cards. Map** p310 D5.

The Melkweg gallery reflects the broad interests of director Suzanne Dechart, with her quality exhibitions culled from the world of contemporary photography. Expect anything from meditative studies of twins to portraits of your favourite punk rockers. *See also p184, p217 and p244.*

It's local artists who get hung at the **GO Gallery**.

Digital dynamism

When peeking out the window of a plane as it descends towards the Netherlands, one is struck by the sheer neatness of the landscape below. And it certainly does make sense that a dense and tiny land would evolve innate organisational skills. Centuries ago, these skills were able to be readily transfered on to the artist's canvas, with its more purely aesthetic possibilities. This savvy and typically Dutch sense of space led to much global acclaim: first with the realist painters of the Golden Age, then with the paper-bound graphic designers of the 20th century, and currently with the new breed of multimedia designers who are manipulating the now near-infinite spatial possibilities offered by the Internet.

The history of Dutch design has always betrayed a double edge, where the intrinsic orderliness – which was additionally reinforced by Calvinism – would get refreshingly undermined by a strong desire for personal expression. Nearly a century ago, De Stijl (see page 195) sought an equilibrium by balancing austere precision with almost pure abstraction. Today, the approach is not so very different, especially since the Internet plays nicely into this past by requiring a certain orderliness in order to deal with the sheer mass of information that is often involved while at the same time flaunting its own democratic sense of the

individual. The contemporary Dutch digital designer seems well equipped to find a new sense of equilibrium where potential bulkiness is reined in by an intrinsic graphical elegance. Of course, in this age of irony and free association, you might have to use your brain a bit to find this often highly personalised sense of elegance, but that's just part of the visual fun.

The scene is very quickly evolving its own unique – yet ultimately international – visual language. Amsterdam, as the global village, certainly has itself played a part, but the nation's art colleges have also helped the process by not only often forcing artists and designers to study together, but also allowing up to one third of its student body to hail from outside the country. A remarkable number of designers actually thank graffiti and flyer art for instilling their now profitable sense of the visual. After all, just like the graffiti tag and party flyer are often encrypted so that it can only be recognised by a few 'insiders', the optimum corporate logo now includes an 'in-joke' to be recognised by the target audience.

● For a flavour of modern Dutch design, head to any of the following sites: www.artmiks.nl; www.caulfield.nl; www.dept.nl; www.dietwee.nl; www.jetset.nl; www.lava.nl; www.ottograph.com; www.xs4all.nl/~petr/; www.75b.nl; and www.una-design.nl.

Montevideo/TBA

Keizersgracht 264, Grachtengordel: West (623 7101/ www.montevideo.nl). Tram 13, 14, 17, 20. **Open** 1-6pm Tue-Sat; closed Mon, Sun. **No credit cards.** **Map** p306 C3.

Montevideo subtitles itself as the 'Netherlands Institute for the Media Arts', and dedicates itself to works that apply the latest technologies to visual arts alongside photography and installations. Admire cutting-edge tech in an old world-vibed canalside location, or do some old-fashioned book learning in the reference room.

Galerie Paul Andriesse

Prinsengracht 116, Grachtengordel: West (623 6237). Tram 13, 14, 17, 20. **Open** 11am-6pm Tue-Fri; 2-6pm Sat; 2-5pm 1st Sun of mth; closed Mon. **No credit cards.** **Map** p306 C2.

While perhaps no longer as innovative as in it was the past, one can interpret a reborn sense of savvy through the early relationship Galerie Paul Andriesse forged with the now much-lauded artist Fiona Tan.

Ra

Vijzelstraat 80, Grachtengordel: East (626 5100). Tram 4, 9, 14, 16, 20, 24, 25. **Open** noon-6pm Tue-Sat; closed Mon, Sun. **Credit** AmEx, DC, MC, V. **Map** p310 D4.

Paul Derrez's acclaimed gallery for contemporary jewellery is a healthy antidote to the conservative approach of the city's diamond industry. Geared to a broad variety of tastes and with an equal emphasis on both Dutch and international designers, this is the place to put your finger on the pulse while, at the same time, decorating it.

Reflex Modern Art Gallery

Weteringschans 79A, Grachtengordel: East (627 2832/www.reflex-art.nl). Tram 6, 7, 10. **Open** 11am-6pm Tue-Sat; closed Mon, Sun. **Credit** AmEx, DC, MC, V. **Map** p310 D5.

A New York flavour exudes from Reflex, which not only deals with such international names as Christo and Chris Verene, but also local lads like Dadara and photographer Paul Blanca. Check out the gallery shop across the street (at No.83) where you can score graphics and lithos by Appel and his ilk while picking up an inflatable Edvard Munch *Scream* doll (open 11am-6pm Tue-Sun; closed Mon).

Serieuze Zaken
Elandsstraat 90, The Jordaan (427 5770/ www.serieuzezaken.demon.nl). Tram 7, 10, 17, 20. **Open** noon-6pm Tue-Sat; 1-5pm 1st Sun; closed Mon. **No credit cards**. **Map** p310 C4.
Rob Malasch had already established his name as a quirky theatre type and journalist before opening this gallery. You might walk in on a show featuring Brit Art, contemporary Chinese painters or an odd theme, such as was the case with his 'Whiteass European Cowboy' show that had European artists playing with the imagery of country music.

Stedelijk Museum Bureau Amsterdam
Rozenstraat 59, The Jordaan (422 0471/ www.smba.nl). Tram 13, 14, 17, 20. **Open** 11am-5pm Tue-Sun; closed Mon. **No credit cards**. **Map** p309 B4.
The Stedelijk's space for the work of younger and mostly Amsterdam-based artists. The results are occasionally mixed, but with its group shows, there is invariably at least one jaw-dropper. Ask if it still has its fascinating map covering 'abandoned locations' in Amsterdam.

Steendrukkerij Amsterdam
Lauriergracht 80, The Jordaan (624 1491/ http://steendrukkerij.cjb.net). Tram 13, 14, 17, 20. **Open** 1-5.30pm Wed-Sat; 2-5pm 1st Sun of mth; closed Mon, Tue & July, Aug. **No credit cards**. **Map** p309 B4.
This gallery-cum-printshop specialises in the hands-on work of woodcuts and lithography, and usually only gives thrills to the pre-initiated. However, more interesting is when guest artists – such as Koen Vermeule and Claes Oldenburg – are asked to collaborate with the more technique-bound printers.

Stichting Oude Kerk
Oudekerksplein, Old Centre: Red Light District (625 8284/www.oudekerk.nl). Tram 4, 9, 14, 16, 20, 24, 25. **Open** 11am-5pm Mon-Sat; 1-5pm Sun. **No credit cards**. **Map** p306 D2.
The 'Old Church' is now the home of World Press Photo. Its other shows have ranged from Aboriginal art to artists installing work inspired by the thousands of graves that lie under its stone floor (in one of which lies Saskia Rembrandt). Admission is usually ƒ7,50, or ƒ5 for concessions. *See also p45.*

Torch
Lauriergracht 94, The Jordaan (626 0284/ www.torchgallery.com). Tram 7, 10, 20. **Open** 2-6pm Thur-Sat; also by appointment; closed Mon-Wed, Sun. **Credit** AmEx, DC, MC, V. **Map** p309 D4.
If you like your art edgy, you'll love Torch, which has shown the likes of Richard Kern, Annie Sprinkle, Cindy Sherman, Jake and Dinos Chapman and Anton Corbijn.

Galerie Van Gelder
Planciusstraat 9A, off Haarlemmerplein, The Jordaan (627 7419). Tram 3. **Open** 1-5.30pm Tue-Sat, 1st Sun of mth; closed Mon. **No credit cards**. **Map** p305 A1.
Taking on conceptual art in the broadest sense of the term, Van Gelder is usually one step ahead in picking the latest up-and-comer in the world of video, film and installation. Names include Sylvie Fleury, David Powell and Wolfgang Timmins.

De Veemvloer
Van Diemenstraat 410, Waterfront (638 6894/ www.xs4all.nl/~veemvlr). Bus 35. **Open** 1-6pm Wed-Sat; closed Mon, Tue, Sun. **No credit cards**.
This waterfront warehouse retains some squat persona, not only with its evocative location but through its dedication to younger artists, many culled from Amsterdam's Gerrit Rietveld arts academy.

W139
Warmoesstraat 139, Old Centre: Red Light District (622 9434/www.w139.nl). Tram 4, 9, 14, 16, 20, 24, 25. **Open** 1-7pm Wed-Sun; closed Mon, Tue. **No credit cards**. **Map** p306 D2.
In its nearly two decades of existence, W139 has never lost its squat edge. This remarkable space has room to deal with installations, and though the work is occasionally too conceptual for some tastes, a visit is always worthwhile, especially during one of its chaotic openings.

De Zaaier
Keizersgracht 22, Grachtengordel: West (420 3154). Tram 1, 2, 5, 13, 17, 20. **Open** 10.30am-6pm daily. **No credit cards**. **Map** p306 C2.
This imposing canalside building, which once hid a clandestine church, is now a large open space dedicated to contemporary group exhibitions of both local (Foundation Amsterdam Artists have a home here) and international natures.

Artoteeks

In town for a while? Then rent some art just as you would a library book, but with a bonus 'to buy' option. The **SBK** (Stichting Beeldende Kunst, or 'Visual Arts Foundation') has 20,000-plus works by over 2,000 artists.

SBK Kunstuitleen
Nieuwe Herengracht 23, Grachtengordel: East (623 9215/www.sbk.nl). Tram 4, 9, 20/Metro Waterlooplein. **Open** noon-8pm Tue, Thur; noon-5pm Fri, Sat; 1-5pm Sun. **Cost** ƒ8-ƒ40/mth. **Map** p307 F3.
You'll need to show your passport and proof of address to borrow art from the SBK Kunstuitleen. Of your fee, 60-75% is banked by the SBK and can be used if you buy a work later on.
Branches: Zeilmakerstraat 15, Bickerseiland (427 5862); KNSM-laan 307-9, KNSM Eiland (419 0064); Wingardweg 28A/B, Noord (632 1336); Keurenplein 28-30, Osdorp (619 5782); Van Limburg Stirumstraat 15, Westerpark (688 0520); Van Eeghenstraat 59, Zuid (673 2640).

Gay & Lesbian

If it's queer, it's here…

Whether Amsterdam is, as many claim, the 'Gay Capital of Europe' is a moot point. However, less arguable is the fact that for gay men, the opportunities are just about endless in this veritable gay mecca, from the Reguliersdwarsstraat and its bars for the body beautiful, via the leather-lovers' paradise of the Warmoesstraat, to the area around the Amstel frequented by camp queens. However, for 'dam-bound dykes, the city may prove to be quite an anti-climax, as the scene – though not the women – is surprisingly limited. There are a couple of lesbian-owned, but mixed, bars but amazingly no lesbian-only clubs, merely one-nighters at various venues in town. Former women-only bar Saarein was reopened as a mixed bar in 1999 (and renamed **Saarein II**), though its still predominately women who frequent it. Even so, Amsterdam's legendary reputation as a city where just about anything is tolerated makes it one of the most popular cities in Europe for both the lesbian and gay traveller.

For information on gay and lesbian resources, including health resources, helplines, meeting groups, libraries and other useful organisations, *see pages 280-1.*

Landmarks

Homomonument
Westermarkt. Tram 13, 14, 17. **Map** p306 C3.
The Homomonument is the world's first memorial to persecuted gays and lesbians. Designed by Karin Daan, its three triangles of pink granite together form one large triangle that juts out into the Keizersgracht. Those victimised in World War II are commemorated here every year on 4 May, but flowers are laid daily in memory of more private grief, and also on World AIDS Day (1 Dec).

Pink Point of Presence
Westermarkt. Tram 13, 14, 17. **Open** *June-Aug* noon-6pm daily. **Map** p306 C3.
Located by the **Homomonument** (*see above*), this funky little kiosk serves as both an information point and a souvenir shop for gay and lesbian visitors to the city. All the free gay publications are stocked here alongside maps, flyers, magazines and books, and the friendly staff will help you with any questions you may have. Though only currently open three months a year, the organisers are busy trying to keep it open all year round.

Media & cinema

Broadcast media
The radio and TV stations below, all broadcasted on Amsterdam cable, are mainly run by volunteers, which means quality can be a little dodgy at times. However, they can be a good source of information and entertainment. Try, also, to check out **Urania**'s nationwide gay and lesbian Teletext page, on page 447 of NOS Teletext (on Nederland 1, 2 and 3 channels), or **De Gay Krant**'s Teletext service: it has pages 137, 138 and 139 on SBS6. In addition, **MVS** (*see below*) also has an informative website at www.mvs.nl, though it's all in Dutch.

MVS Radio
Cable 103.8 or 106.8 FM ether (620 0247).
Times 6-9pm daily.
The major local gay and lesbian radio station, with news, events, interviews, and a gay music chart on Saturdays. There are English-language programmes every Sunday evening.

MVS TV
Cable 62.25 (620 0247). **Times** 8-9pm Mon.
This mainly Dutch station offers coverage of the latest developments on the scene plus lifestyle, gay culture, events, health, etc. MVS Teletext can be found on pages 437 and 601 via Salto.

Cinema
Independent cinemas the **Rialto** (*see page 193*) and the Cavia regularly screen gay and lesbian movies, as does highbrow cultural centre, **De Balie** (*see page 237*). The **Akademie** squat (*see page 193* **Multimedia centres**) also has gay and lesbian themed nights in its fully operational cinema.

Smaller gay porn cinemas can be found in the centre of Amsterdam; for more information, check the ads in local gay publications. In addition, the **Gay & Lesbian Switchboard** (*see page 280*) has a list of cinemas and theatres with special gay and lesbian programmes.

De Roze Filmtoer
One of two annual gay and lesbian film festivals, the 'Pink Film Tour' sweeps across the whole of the Netherlands, stopping off in Amsterdam for a few days at the beginning of December. Generally speak-

Cruise along to **De Spyker** for some splendidly seedy goings-on. *See p203.*

ing, the films are already available on video, but it usually includes a couple of new gems. Screenings are held at **De Balie** and **Cavia**.

De Roze Filmdagen

Fast establishing itself as underground, alternative and cutting edge, the 'Pink Film Days' festival is held over a few days during the second or third week of December. The main idea is to present (short) films and documentaries with gay and lesbian content that aren't yet on general release in the country. Check www.rozefilm.w3.to for more details.

Publications

Gay News Amsterdam, in both Dutch and English, comes out monthly, and can be picked up for free in many gay establishments (it costs *f*4,95 in some newsagents); you can also find it on the web at www.gaynews.nl. Catering for both tourists and locals, it's almost always an interesting read. Its main rival is **Gay & Night**, which hit the shelves during 1997. Published by a splinter group from *Gay News Amsterdam*, both look remarkably similar, though the latter makes for a more colourful read. It's published monthly, is free in bars (it costs *f*3,95 in some newsagents), and is on the web at www.gay-night.nl.

In addition, there's also bi-weekly English-language magazine **Shark** – distributed free across Amsterdam, with a website at www.underwateramsterdam.com – that

includes a *Queer Fish* centrefold with regularly updated listings of bars and clubs as well as a diary of events. The **SAD-Schorerstichting** (*see page 281*) also produces a free gay tourist map and a safer-sex booklet (with a gay male bias) in English every year. Good Dutch-language publications include **De Gay Krant**, **sQueeze** and **Culture & Camp**.

Clubs & bars

The gay scene in Amsterdam is mainly concentrated around four areas in the city, each with its own unique identity. Clubs and bars are listed here by area, with specialist establishments – bar-restaurants, cafés and lesbian bars – and the pick of the city's one-off club nights and sex parties listed below that.

Kerkstraat

This quiet, innocuous street that crosses Leidsestraat near the busy Leidseplein has no specific identity, unlike the other gay areas across amsterdam. However, it is home to a wide variety of gay establishments, and frequented by a larger number of locals than other areas tend to be.

As well as the bars listed below, other hangouts can be found on 'Church Street', such as the **Greenwich Village Hotel** (Kerkstraat 25, 626 9746), the **Bronx** (*see page 212*) and **Thermos Night** (*see page 210*). In addition, a couple of mixed, low-key bars frequented mainly by more mature, gay men are **Camp Café** (Kerkstraat 45, 622 1506) and **Meia Meia** (Kerkstraat 63, 623 4129).

Cosmo Bar
Kerkstraat 42 (624 8074). Tram 1, 2, 5.
Open 1pm-3am Mon-Thur; 1.30pm-4am Fri, Sat; closed Sun. **Credit** (over *f*25) AmEx, DC, MC, V.
Map p310 D4.
A tarty, late-night hangout for those who don't want to go on to a club but don't want to go home, either.

De Spyker
Kerkstraat 4 (620 5919). Tram 1, 2, 5.
Open 1pm-1am Mon-Thur, Sun; 1pm-3am Fri, Sat.
No credit cards. Map p310 C4.
A friendly, American-style bar where, though there is no dress code, you won't look out of place in your jeans, leathers or army outfit. Expect a delightfully seedy and dimly lit place, that can be cruisey and rowdy. Porn videos and cartoons are shown side by

side, and there is an upstairs darkroom; more balls are knocked around on the pool table. De Spyker is one predominantly male place that is also welcoming to women.

Rembrandtplein

This area, centred around the ghastly, neon-lit, touristy Rembrandtplein, has traditionally long been associated with the camp scene: most of the gay bars, all within earshot of each other, belt out either oompah music or Dutch pop songs and feature occasional drag acts. Paardenstraat (full of rent boys) is close by, as are women's bar **Vive la Vie** (*see page 209*), popular café **Le Monde** (*see page 208*) and the infamous **iT** (*see page 204*).

Aside from the recommended bars listed below, there are a cluster of other bars located along the Amstel that provide a bit of a

The queer year

For more information on gay events, phone the **Gay & Lesbian Switchboard** (see page 280).

Spring
Gay celebrations on **Queen's Day**, held annually on 30 April (see page 172 **A right royal party**), are based around the Homomonument, with drag acts, bands and stalls. The day closes with a huge open-air disco. Most gay and lesbian bars and clubs also organise their own celebrations, so head for your favourite bar or gay area.

Remembrance Day takes place on 4 May. Though gay and lesbian victims from WWII are remembered at the event on Dam, the **NVIH/COC** stage their own quiet tribute at the Homomonument. The next day, there's a celebratory open-air party for **Liberation Day**.

AIDS Memorial Day is held at the Beurs van Berlage (see page 41) on the last Saturday of May. Names of deceased loved ones are read and candles lit. Everyone then walks to Dam, where symbolic white balloons are released.

Summer
The **Midsummer Canal Party** in Utrecht is held on or around 21 June. This three-day extravaganza includes performances on the canals with stages set up on the water.

Gay Pride Day Nederland is generally held on the last Saturday in June, but takes place in a different town each year. On 30 June 2001, it will be held in Rotterdam.

Amsterdam Diners is a huge, celebrity-oriented one-day HIV/AIDS fund-raiser that usually takes place on the last Saturday of June. The venue, and the date, seem to change each year, so log on to the website, www.aidsfonds.nl for more information nearer the time.

Held on the first weekend in August, **Amsterdam Pride** is probably the most fun event of the year. This three-day extravaganza includes street parties, performances and a gay parade on boats around the canals.

The **Hollywood Party**, held in August at **iT** (see page 204), usually brings traffic to a complete standstill. Glitzy transvestite 'stars' gather together before making their way to the club itself in limousines.

Autumn
Amsterdam Leather Pride takes place annually at the end of October and usually encompasses ten days' worth of parties and events. There's also a range of events for women, organised by **Wild Side** (see page 281). For more details, log on to www.leatherpride.nl nearer the event.

Winter
Various activities are organised by the Nationale Commissie AIDS-Bestrijding on and around **World AIDS Day** on 1 December. Events to look out for include Theater Action, a series of fund-raising performances by stars of the stage.

breather from the frantic square behind.

Gaiety (Amstel 14, 624 4271) was originally an underground bar in the '50s; **Mix** (Amstel 50, 420 3388) is a fairly nondescript place, as is **Macho Macho** (Amstel 102, 622 8335), which hosts a happy hour every Sunday evening from 6pm to 9pm.

Amstel Taveerne

Amstel 54 (623 4254). Tram 4, 9, 14, 16, 20, 24, 25. **Open** 4pm-1am Mon-Thur, Sun; 4pm-2.45am Fri, Sat. **No credit cards**. **Map** p307 E3.

If you want a real Dutch experience, head directly to Amstel Taveerne, a spacious brown café on the corner of the Amstel and Halvemaansteeg. A TV monitor displays the song currently being played and hollered along to: a mixture of both old and new Dutch singalong songs get heavy rotation, with the odd Eurovision tune thrown in for bad measure. Get ready to exercise those vocal chords.

iT

Amstelstraat 24, Grachtengordel: East (625 0111/ www.it.nl). Tram 4, 9, 14. **Open** 11pm-4am Thur; 11pm-5am Fri, Sat (with 'cool-down' 5am-6am); closed Mon-Wed, Sun. **Admission** ƒ15-ƒ20 (free for gays Thur; Sat gay men only). **No credit cards**. **Map** p307 E3.

Once one of Europe's most famous gay clubs, this converted cinema has definitely lost most of its glamorous appeal, especially since a drugs raid in 1999 that resulted in its temporary closure. Having said that, it is still packed at weekends (on Saturdays, it's gay men only, though the odd fag hag may slip in). Every July, the iT makes a splash with its famous Swimming Pool Party. *See also p182.*

Lellebel

Utrechtsestraat 4 (427 5139). Tram 4, 9, 14. **Open** *May-Sept* 9pm-3am Mon-Thur, Sun; 9pm-4am Fri, Sat. *Oct-Apr* 9pm-3am Mon-Thur, Sun; 8pm-4am Fri, Sat. **No credit cards**. **Map** p311 E4.

Go Dutch at the **Queen's Head**. *See p207.*

Get your glad rags out and stilettos on for Lellebel, Amsterdam's first tranny bar, just off the rowdy Rembrandtplein. Exchange make-up, fashion tips and girlie gossip with Desiree dello Stiletto, Mayday, Babette LaFayette or any of the other divine divas who perform from Friday to Sunday at 9pm. And you can neck a few discounted drinks during happy hour every Sunday, 8pm to 10pm.

Le Montmartre

Halvemaansteeg 17 (620 7622). Tram 4, 9, 14, 16, 20, 24, 25. **Open** 5pm-1am Mon-Thur; 5pm-3am Fri; 4pm-3am Sat; 4pm-1am Sun. **No credit cards**. **Map** p307 E3.

This deliciously cheesy bar advertises itself with the slogan 'voted most popular bar in 1997, 1998, 1999', though the ad doesn't say by whom. All the same, this claim is backed up by the lively crowd who clearly loves the pop and Dutch music played here, singing along and showing off on the tiny raised dancefloor at the back.

Le Shako

's Gravelandseveer 2 (624 0209). Tram 4, 9, 14, 16, 20, 24, 25. **Open** 10pm-3am Mon-Thur, Sun; 8pm-4am Fri, Sat. **No credit cards**. **Map** p307 E3.

Across the water from the rest of the camp-oriented bars on the Amstel, Le Shako is a friendly, late-opening night bar, and a favourite among locals.

Reguliersdwarsstraat

On the other side of Rembrandtplein is Reguliersdwarsstraat, a quite tremendously gay street: there are more pansies here than in the flower market on Singel. A posey, young crowd of gays hangs out here, and the bars and clubs reflect the trend: **Café April**, **Exit**, **Soho**, **Havana** (*for all see page 206*), and **Downtown** (*see page 208*) are owned by the same people. It's also where the town's only gay coffeeshop,

Bingo at **Getto** will send your balls spinning with excitement. *See p207.*

the **Otherside** (*see page 208*), and **Reality** (Reguliersdwarsstraat 129, 624 7532), a tropical, multicultural gay bar, can be found.

Café April

Reguliersdwarsstraat 37 (625 9572). Tram 1, 2, 4, 5, 9, 14, 16, 20, 24, 25. **Open** 2pm-1am Mon-Thur, Sun; 2pm-2am Fri, Sat. **No credit cards**. **Map** p309 D4.

Thanks to the recent opening of **Soho** (*see below*) across the street (*see below*), this bar has lost much of its clientele. Or is the reason, in fact, the staff who seem to work here just to entertain their visiting friends? Either way, it doesn't get crowded until after 11pm. One quirky feature of the café is its back bar, which revolves when the premises gets busy.

Exit

Reguliersdwarsstraat 42, Grachtengordel: East (625 8788). Tram 1, 2, 4, 5, 9, 14, 16, 20, 24, 25. **Open** 11pm-4am Mon-Thur, Sun; 11pm-5am Fri, Sat. **Admission** free-*f*10. **No credit cards**. **Map** p311 E4.

This smart disco for trendy young gays (women are allowed in, but only in small numbers) is reached via a comfortable bar area. The disco room was once a hayloft, and plenty of haymaking activity still goes on. An enthusiastic crowd. *See also p182.*

Havana

Reguliersdwarsstraat 17-19, Grachtengordel: East (620 6788). Tram 1, 2, 5, 16, 20, 24, 25. **Open** 4pm-1am Mon-Thur; 4pm-2.30am Fri; 2pm-2.30am Sat; 2pm-1am Sun. **Admission** free, upstairs *f*5. **No credit cards**. **Map** p310 D4.

One of the most popular gay bars along this stretch, Havana is a people-watcher's paradise where Gaultier clashes with Gucci. However, it gets very busy from around 10pm. On Fridays and weekends from 11pm, DJs play soul, house and R&B in the Havana Upstairs dance area. *See also p182.*

Soho

Reguliersdwarsstraat 36 (330 4400). Tram 1, 2, 4, 5, 9, 14, 16, 20, 24, 25. **Open** 8pm-3am Mon-Thur; 8pm-4am Fri, Sat; 4pm-3am Sun. **No credit cards**. **Map** p311 E4.

Packed since its opening in 1999, this two-floor English-style pub (complete with comfy Chesterfield sofas) has become the pub pulling the most punters on this street. DJs play on weekends. During the week at midnight is 'Midnight Hour', offering two drinks for the price of one. Be warned, though: Soho can be a little intimidating if you're on your own.

Red Light District: Warmoesstraat

The Warmoesstraat is a seedy street running along the edge of the Red Light District and attracts all sorts of lowlife. At best, they'll try to sell you dubious drugs; at worst, they'll try to rob you. Though there is a high police profile and a police station on the street itself, it's advisable to take care when walking here at night. Sleazy geezers and junkies dominate the area: avoid engaging in conversation with them.

Apart from the fabulously kitsch **Getto** (*see page 207*) and the trad Dutch bar **Casa Maria** (Warmoesstraat 60, 627 6848) this strip is dominated by most of the city's leather bars. **The Web** and **Cuckoo's Nest** (Nieuwezijds Kolk 6, 627 1752), a daytime opening bar (1pm-1am daily) that boasts Europe's largest playroom in its cellar, are located just a couple of streets away, as is the popular **Queen's Head** (*see below*).

Argos

Warmoesstraat 95 (622 6595). Tram 4, 9, 16, 20, 24, 25. **Open** 10pm-3am Mon-Thur, Sun; 10pm-4am Fri, Sat. **No credit cards. Map** p306 D2.
The oldest and most famous leather bar in the city, Argos is also the cruisiest. The basement darkroom with cabins, one of which has a sling, is often busier than the upstairs bar. Wednesday night is poppers night, and every last Sunday of the month is SOS (Sex on Sunday): doors are open between 3pm and 4pm, it costs ƒ10 to get in, and the dress code is 'nude/shirtless'. Men only.

Cockring

Warmoesstraat 96 (623 9604/ www.clubcockring.com). Tram 4, 9, 16, 20, 24, 25. **Open** 11pm-4am Mon-Thur; 11pm-5am Fri, Sat. **No credit cards. Map** p306 D2.
Despite charging the best part of ƒ6 for a near-frozen beer, this club is one of the few gay venues for which you need to queue at weekends, particularly after 1am. Though situated in the leather district, the Cockring attracts all types of gays aged 40 or under. It's a cruisey place, with a darkroom and a hard house music policy. There are regular live sex shows, raffles and free massages, and every first Wednesday of the month there's an 'underwear party'. Men only.

Queen's Head

Zeedijk 20 (420 2475/www.queenshead.nl). Tram 4, 9, 16, 20, 24, 25/Metro Centraal Station. **Open** 5pm-1am Mon-Thur; 5pm-3am Fri; 4pm-3am Sat; 4pm-1am Sun. **No credit cards. Map** p306 D2.
A row of action men and a Dusty doll line the window of this traditional '50s Dutch bar, opened by gay couple Johan and Willem (aka Dusty). There's a beautiful view out the back on to old Dutch canal houses: you could almost forget which century you're in. Every Monday is 'beer night' with unlimited beer for ƒ25, and every Tuesday, Dusty drags up and dons her magical wig to host her popular bingo night from 10pm. Sportslounge, on the first Wednesday of the month, is for soccer or sports-outfit lovers, and features large-screen sport videos and a free beer for those wearing a full sports outfit.

The Web

Sint Jacobsstraat 6 (623 6758). Tram 1, 2, 3, 5. **Open** 2pm-1am Mon-Thur, Sun; 2pm-2.30am Fri, Sat. **No credit cards. Map** p306 D2.
Close to Centraal Station, this is another popular leather bar. Attractions include a pool table and a DJ on most nights, but more popular is the darkroom upstairs and the porn videos in the downstairs bar.

The Web has a reputation for throwing wild parties and for having the cleanest toilets of any leather bar in town. Sundays from 5pm is snack afternoon, and Wednesday night is lottery night. Men only.

Bar-restaurants

Getto

Warmoesstraat 51, Old Centre: Red Light District (421 5151). Tram 4, 9, 16, 20, 24, 25. **Open** 5pm-1am Tue-Sun. *Kitchen* 6-11pm Tue-Sun; closed Mon. **Main courses** ƒ18,50-ƒ27,50. **Credit** DC, MC, V. **Map** p306 D2.
Undoubtedly the most exciting initiative to open on the gay scene in recent years, and a place where gays and lesbians really do mix. Getto is a trendy, kitsch establishment with a candlelit restaurant at the back (delicious meals, including vegetarian options, cost around ƒ18,50 and are available until 11pm) and a cool bar at the front. Cocktail Happy Hour is 5-7pm and there's a popular bingo night every Thursday. Every first Monday of the month is Club Fu, a karaoke night, and every second Monday of the month is Getto Girls Lounge, a women-only night.

Hemelse Modder

Oude Waal 9, Old Centre: Old Side (624 3203). Tram 1, 2, 4, 5, 9, 13, 16, 17, 20, 24, 25/Metro Nieuwmarkt. **Open** 6pm-midnight Tue-Sun. *Kitchen* 6-10pm Tue-Sun; closed Mon. **Set menu** ƒ50 (3 courses); ƒ62,50 (5 courses). **Credit** AmEx, DC, MC, V. **Map** p307 E2.
This gay-owned, mixed restaurant comes highly recommended for its romantic, candlelit vibe, good food, nice interior and friendly staff. In fact, the only complaint we've heard is that the tablecloths aren't long enough to conceal a discreet shag under the table. Food is Mediterranean, with veggie options available.

Huyschkaemer

Utrechtsestraat 137, Grachtengordel: East (627 0575). Tram 4, 6, 7, 10. **Open** 4pm-1am Mon-Thur, Sun; 4pm-3am Fri, Sat. *Kitchen* 5-11pm daily. **Main courses** ƒ20-ƒ27. **Credit** AmEx, MC, V. **Map** p311 E4.
Huyschkaemer's split-level designer interior – with huge windows and wrought-iron features – attracts a mixed, mainly young and artistic gay and lesbian crowd. The delicious food costs around ƒ20-ƒ25 for a main dish. The staff are friendly and usually willing to turn a starter of your choice into a main dish. DJs play on Fridays and Saturdays.

La Strada

Nieuwezijds Voorburgwal 93-5, Old Centre: New Side (625 0276). Tram 1, 2, 5, 13, 17, 20. **Open** 4pm-1am Tue-Thur; 2pm-1am Fri, Sat; closed Mon, Sun. **Main courses** ƒ25,50-ƒ34,50. **Credit** AmEx, DC, MC, V. **Map** p306 D2.
La Strada, a spacious and centrally located culinary café, attracts an artistic crowd and is particularly popular with lesbians. Food here is delicious: a three-course meal costs around ƒ25,50, with vegetarian dishes available. Every Monday night is the

Gay hangouts

Argos
Denim and leather, darkroom and lust, dicks
and lips... See page 207.

Backstage
Coffee, cake, crochet and chat with
'Christmas Twin' Gary. See page 208.

Downtown
Heavenly cakes, hot coffee and hot gossip.
See page 208.

Getto
Bingo, cocktails, karaoke and kitsch.
See page 207.

Havana
Home to hip homos and their happy high-
heeled friends. See page 206.

Lellebel
Heels and squeals at the city's campest café.
See page 204.

MR B
For kinky essentials, party info and service
with a smile. See page 212.

Saarein II
Split-level and sweetly Sapphic.
See page 209.

Thermos
Steamy saunas for sexy boys.
See page 210.

De Trut
Cheap entry and booze, quirky art and
designer loos. See page 210.

popular, themed Mstry Mnday Move (from around
6pm to 11pm). With an emphasis on mingling,
guests often have to share tables, serve the food
themselves, or even go down into the kitchen to fetch
it. Retro DJ Eddy PolyeSter plays oldies, camp and
kitsch tunes, and invites guests to inspect his collection and place requests.

Cafés

Backstage
Utrechtsedwarsstraat 67, Grachtengordel: East
(622 3638). Tram 4, 6, 7, 10. **Open** 10am-5.30pm
Mon-Sat. **No credit cards. Map** p311 E4.
Donning a pair of sunglasses would be a definite
bonus in this multicoloured café/knitwear boutique
that serves almost as a museum to the half-Mohawk
'Christmas Twins'. Although Greg died in 1997, his
identical twin Gary continues to run the place in his
own unique way, selling knitwear, chatting to the
customers and giving spontaneous horoscope readings. A fabulous place.

Downtown
Reguliersdwarsstraat 31, Grachtengordel: East
(622 9958). Tram 1, 2, 4, 5, 9, 14, 16, 20, 24, 25.
Open 10am-7pm daily. **No credit cards.**
Map p310 D4.
Good-value snacks, healthy salads and cakes are
served by friendly staff in this small split-level café.
Ever since its opening 30 years ago, it gets packed
during weekends when friends meet for late lunch
or afternoon coffee after their shopping sprees. Great
for eavesdropping on other people's conversations
or just reading from its selection of magazines and
newspapers. During summer, the outdoor terrace is
one of the most popular gay haunts on the street.

Le Monde
Rembrandtplein 6, Grachtengordel: East
(626 9922). Tram 4, 9, 14, 20. **Open** 8.30am-1am
Mon-Thur, Sun; 8.30am-2am Fri, Sat. *Kitchen*
8.30am-10.30pm daily. **No credit cards.**
Map p311 E4.
A popular, early-opening and late closing café on
Rembrandtplein, and a great place to have break-
fast, lunch, dinner (including vegetarian options), a
snack, or a drink.

Coffeeshop

The Otherside
Reguliersdwarsstraat 6, Grachtengordel: East
(421 1014). Tram 1, 2, 5. **Open** 11am-1am daily.
No credit cards.
The Otherside is a bright and modern coffeeshop
with a good, varied hash/weed menu – single
joints are available from ƒ6 to ƒ11, depending on
strength – with space cake priced at ƒ7,50 a
slice and cannabis tea at ƒ10 a cup. Staff here are
friendly and informative: don't hesitate to ask if you
have any doubts about whether you should have
your cake and eat it, too. For more on coffeeshops in
Amsterdam, *see page 134.*

Lesbian nightlife

Unfortunately, there is currently no lesbian
club in Amsterdam, and the rather tacky
You II ('bi-het-les lady's dancing club') is a
sorry excuse for one. However, its conveniently
central location at Amstel 178 (421 0900) does
mean that it draws a largely post-**Vive la Vie**
crowd (*see below*).

However, there is a thriving (though small) lesbian scene in the bars and clubs. On Saturdays, lesbians head for the women-only night at the **COC** (*see page 280*), though more by habit than by choice. On the second Saturday of the month, there's also an over-30s party (they're very strict about age, so take ID); younger babes can be found upstairs in another part of the building.

Among the regular monthly parties are **Bimbo Night**, hosted by DJ Bo and held at Toon (Korte Leidsedwarsstraat 26, Grachtengordel: East, no phone) every first Sunday of the month. **Getto Girls Lounge** is held on the second Monday of the month in **Getto** (*see page 207*), while the perpetually popular **Planet Pussy** is now held at the **Melkweg** (*see page 184*) on the third Sunday of the month. For information on the scene in general, head to www.lesbianamsterdam.nl.

Saarein II

Elandsstraat 119, The Jordaan (623 4901). Tram 7, 10. **Open** *5pm-1am Tue-Thur, Sun; 5pm-2am Fri, Sat; closed Mon.* **No credit cards. Map** p310 C4.
Once a legendary women-only bar, Saarein was taken over and reopened as a mixed café in April 1999. Still predominantly frequented by women, this split-level brown bar now serves delicious food (average ƒ14-ƒ17,50) from 6pm to 9.30pm (tapas available until midnight). The infamous pool table remains, as does the weed-growers contest on the last Friday in November. Though the resident cat has left, there is still plenty of pussy to be had.

Vandenberg

Lindengracht 95, The Jordaan (622 2716). Tram 3, 10. **Open** *5pm-1am Mon-Thur, Sun; 5pm-2am Fri; 11am-2am Sat. Kitchen 5.30-10pm daily.* **Main courses** ƒ19,50-ƒ25. **No credit cards. Map** p305 B2.

Eel-baiting may have been a popular 'sport' along this canal before it was filled in at the turn of the century, but, fortunately, it's one thing you won't find on the menu at Vandenberg, a vegetarian bar-restaurant. Small but glowingly cosy, this lesbian-owned place attracts a crowd of older locals, though the younger bar staff pull in a few admirers and contemporaries. The vicious cat is to be avoided at all costs.

Vive la Vie

Amstelstraat 7, Grachtengordel: East (624 0114). Tram 4, 9, 14, 20. **Open** *3pm-1am Mon-Thur, Sun; 3pm-3am Fri, Sat.* **No credit cards. Map** p310 E4.
On the edge of the bustling neon jungle that is Rembrandtplein, this lively bar – which turned 20 in August 2000 – attracts a largely lipstick/femme clientele, though men are also welcome. Don't be put off by the women dancing and singing along to the traditional Dutch music: it's guaranteed that after a few beers, you'll be joining in (or at least trying to pick up the language). Though the bar is a little on the small side, the pavement terrace outside is great in the summer.

One-off club nights

A few of Amsterdam's clubs hold one-off gay club nights, the pick of which have been detailed below. For more on Amsterdam's clubbing scene, *see pages 181-9.*

BPM

Rembrandtplein 17, Grachtengordel: East (625 1329). Tram 4, 9, 14/Metro Waterlooplein. **Open** *11pm-4am Wed.* **Admission** ƒ15. **No credit cards. Map** p311 E4.
The weekly BPM (Beats Per Minute) opened in spring 2000, and attracts a hedonistic crowd whose aim is to show off and party hard.

Arts & Entertainment

Looking for a **Downtown** man. *See p208.*

De Trut

Bilderdijkstraat 165, Oud West (no phone). Tram 3, 7, 12, 17. **Open** 11pm-4am Sun. **Admission** *f*2,50. **No credit cards. Map** p309 B5.

De Trut is probably the best gay night in Amsterdam, attracting a good, mixed and attitude-free crowd. This – and the cheap drinks – makes it eternally popular, which means you have to start queueing outside no later than 10.40pm to ensure you get in: doors open at 11pm and shut when it's full, which could be just 20 minutes later. The club night is held in a bricked, industrial basement of a former squat, and features quirky art works, UV lighting, videos and, occasionally, performances. The club is run on a non-profit basis – staff are all volunteers – and proceeds are donated to suitably PC causes. Strictly no heterosexuals.

Zociëteit

VOC Café, Schreierstoren, Prins Hendrikkade 94, Old Side (428 8291). Tram 4, 9, 16, 20, 24, 25/Metro Centraal Station. **Open** 9pm every third Sat. **Admission** *f*10. **No credit cards. Map** p307 D2.

Every third Saturday of the month in the lower floors of the Schreierstoren, men-only club Zociëteit stages parties with music and live acts for those looking for something a little different than what the scene has to offer. Women aren't allowed to join the club, though they're welcome at the parties.

Sex parties

Apart from **Wild Side** events (*see page 281*), there are currently no women-only sex parties in Amsterdam, just occasional, mixed fetish parties. There are regular sex parties for men, though, with smaller parties generally taking place in bars on Warmoesstraat.

The **Stablemaster Hotel** (Warmoesstraat 23, Old Centre: Red Light District, 625 0148) hosts jack-off parties almost every night, while SOS is held every last Sunday of the month at the **Argos** (*see page 207*). **Club Jaecques** (Warmoesstraat 93, Old Centre: Red Light District, 622 0323) holds Naked Parties on every first Sunday of the month, and on every third Sunday of the month it's the Horsemen and Knights party. At the latter, admission is relative to, um, 'size': for most it's *f*10, but it's free if you have more than 18 centimetres (roughly seven inches) for you – or others – to play with.

Just as popular as these Red Light District fandangos are the more regular and larger parties at venues that offer a wide range of facilities from private cabins and sling and bondage rooms to golden shower areas. Held on the third Saturday of the month in the **Roothaanhuis** (Rozengracht 133, The Jordaan, 623 5969), Club Trash draws a big crowd; the

dress code is leather/rubber, and tickets cost *f*30 in advance from **MR B** or **Black Body** (*see page 212*). A less hardcore alternative is the Hot Leather/Rubber Night, held every two months at the **COC** (*see page 280*, or www.stop.demon.nl).

Saunas

Fenomeen

1e Schinkelstraat 14, Zuid West (671 6780). Tram 6. **Open** 1-11pm daily. *Women's day* Mon. **Admission** *f*11-*f*13,50. **No credit cards.**

This relaxed squat sauna is very popular with lesbians on Monday's women-only day. It's open-plan and split level with a sauna, a steam bath, a cold bath, a chill-out room with mattresses, showers in the courtyard outside, and a café serving wholefood snacks, organic juices and herbal teas. Extras include massage and a sunbed.

Thermos Day

Raamstraat 33, The Jordaan (623 9158). Tram 1, 2, 5, 7, 10. **Open** noon-11pm Mon-Fri; noon-10pm Sat, Sun. **Admission** *f*30; *f*25 under-24s with ID. **Credit** AmEx, DC, MC, V. **Map** p310 C4.

Busy during the week and crowded during weekends, this relaxed sauna offers a load of facilities, including a tiny steam room, a large dry-heat room, a small cinema showing porn, private cubicles, a bar and restaurant, a hairdresser, a masseur and a gym (well, three battered weightmachines). Look out for the occasional performances by drag artist Vera Springveer.

Thermos Night

Kerkstraat 58-60, Grachtengordel: East (623 4936). Tram 1, 2, 5. **Open** 11pm-8am Mon-Sat; 11pm-10am Sun. **Admission** *f*30; *f*25 under-24s with ID. **Credit** AmEx, DC, MC, V. **Map** p310 D4.

Just a stone's throw away from the **Spijker** bar (*see p203*), Thermos Night's facilities include a spacious bar, a small jacuzzi, a dry sauna and a steam room, a darkroom and a maze of cubicles. It gets absolutely packed on weekends.

Shops & services

Accommodation

It's illegal for Amsterdam hotels to refuse accommodation to gays and lesbians, but those detailed below are all specifically gay-owned. The **Gay & Lesbian Switchboard** (*see page 280*) can provide more information on hotels that are gay and lesbian friendly. For more hotels, *see pages 80-99*.

Black Tulip Hotel

Geldersekade 16, Old Centre: Old Side (427 0933/ www.blacktulip.nl). Tram 1, 2, 4, 5, 9, 13, 16, 17, 20, 24, 25/Metro Centraal Station. **Rates** *f*195 single; *f*265-*f*350 double. **Credit** AmEx, DC, MC, V. **Map** p306 D2.

The men-only Black Tulip Hotel has mastered the art of serving and accommodating the leather man: SM facilities are included in all the rooms, as is a TV and VCR. The fully equipped Black Body Fantasy Room costs a whopping (or is that a whipping?) ƒ290 a night. Located in a convenient spot near Centraal Station.

Hotel New York
Herengracht 13, Grachtengordel: West (624 3066). Tram 1, 2, 3, 5, 13, 14. **Rates** *ƒ150 single; ƒ200-ƒ250 double; ƒ275 triple.* **Credit** AmEx, DC, MC, V. **Map** p306 C2.

A beautiful, modernised 17th-century building in a charming, picturesque canalside location. Room rates are reasonable.

ITC Hotel
Prinsengracht 1051, Grachtengordel: East (623 0230). Tram 4, 6, 7, 10. **Rates** *ƒ95-ƒ115 single; ƒ155-ƒ185 double; ƒ245 triple.* **Credit** AmEx, DC, MC, V. **Map** p311 E4.

Located on the plushest canal in the city and close to the Kerkstraat, Reguliersdwarsstraat and Amstel areas, this canalside house is a popular stopover for gays and lesbians.

The bare essentials

Amsterdam's reputation as an exceedingly liberal city didn't come about by accident: the town's tolerant policies on drugs and prostitution are well documented. Just as importantly, though, Amsterdam is also more tolerant of gays and lesbians than most major world cities. The good news: the Netherlands originally decriminalised homosexuality in 1811, with the age of consent for gay men lowered to 16 in 1971.

Cruising
Cruising is generally tolerated in Amsterdam: public expressions of affection and even discreet sex in open spaces are all allowed, within reasonable limits and in places where offence is unlikely to be taken. Particularly popular spots for cruising are Vondelpark (by the rose garden: watch out for them thorns) and the wooded Nieuwe Meer, in the south-west of the city. However, things are changing: the last few years have seen the emergence of an increasingly less tolerant attitude towards cruising areas: the Nieuwe Meer area has been redesigned to make it more open, largely due to public concern about the possibility of stumbling across amorous couples and used condoms.

Darkrooms
Darkrooms, found in assorted bars and clubs around Amsterdam, must comply with strict regulations that force proprietors to make both safer sex information and condoms readily available.

Marriage
Gay and lesbian marriage was introduced from 1 January 1998. However, it's little more than a legal contract in the form of a registered partnership dealing with practical matters such as finance and property rights.

Custody rights of same-sex couples and their children differ greatly from heterosexuals, and adoption, too, is still not possible for married gay or lesbian couples, though it is possible for unmarried heterosexual couples, and – since April 1998 – for individuals. If you are unable to get married officially but would like some sort of ceremony, the Remonstrantse Broederschap (Nieuwegracht 27A, 3512 LC Utrecht, 030 231 6970) is allowed to bless gay relationships even if the couple are not Dutch or don't belong to its church. Make sure to get in contact on the above number six to 12 months in advance.

Prostitution
The well-advertised, super-liberal prostitution laws in Amsterdam also apply to gays: there are several male brothels scattered throughout the city, and 'rent boy bars', mainly to be found on Paardenstraat, are legal. However, Paardenstraat is full of exploited, mainly Eastern European boys and can be rather dangerous, in terms of both personal safety and unsafe sex. Caution is strongly advised.

Safer sex
Since the advent of HIV and AIDS, the Dutch have developed a highly responsible attitude towards the practice and promotion of safer sex, and condoms are available from most gay bars. See page 280 for details of HIV- and AIDS-related organisations.

SM
The practice of SM is legal here. Men should head for the Warmoesstraat area, where there are many leather bars with darkrooms and cellars, while women interested in SM should contact **Wild Side** (see page 281), based at the COC .

Orfeo Hotel
Leidsekruisstraat 14, Grachtengordel: East (623 1347). Tram 1, 2, 5, 6, 7, 10. **Rates** *ƒ90-ƒ195 single; ƒ120-ƒ195 double; ƒ195 triple.* **Credit** AmEx, MC, V. **Map** p310 D5.

The Orfeo is handily located by the Leidseplein. Though the breakfast area looks uninspiring, the rooms are good value.

Bookshops

Aside from the specialist bookshops listed below, the **American Book Center** (*see page 142*) has a well-stocked English language gay and lesbian section in its basement, with a wide range of fiction and non-fiction titles, magazines (including porn) and postcards. And though **Waterstone's** (*see page 143*) has no actual gay section, the occasional homoerotic window display has been spotted from time to time. There are also two charming second-hand women's bookstores in the city in **Antiquariaat Lorelei** (Prinsengracht 495, Grachtengordel: East, 623 4308) and **Vrouwen in Druk** (Westermarkt 5, The Jordaan, 624 5003), both with a large number of titles in English.

Intermale
Spuistraat 251, Old Centre: New Side (625 0009). Tram 1, 2, 5, 13, 14, 17, 20. **Open** 11am-6pm Mon; 10am-6pm Tue, 9pm Tue; closed Sun. **Credit** AmEx, MC, V. **Map** p306 C3.

This split-level gay men's bookstore is crammed with literature, porn and books on history and sexuality, as well as a sexy selection of cards, magazines and newspapers.

Vrolijk
Paleisstraat 135, Old Centre: New Side (623 5142). Tram 1, 2, 5, 13, 14, 17, 20. **Open** 11am-6pm Mon; 10am-6pm Tue, Wed, Fri, Sat; 10am-9pm Thur; 10am-5pm Sat; closed Sun. **Credit** AmEx, DC, MC, V. **Map** p306 C3.

Vrolijk offers a wide range of gay and lesbian books, from politics to fiction and anything in between. Many titles are in English – some in the second-hand section – while there are also good selections of international magazines, T-shirts, CDs by gay and lesbian artists, and videos.

Xantippe Unlimited
Prinsengracht 290, Grachtengordel: West (623 5854). Tram 1, 2, 5, 10, 13, 14, 17, 20. **Open** 1-7pm Mon; 10am-7pm Tue-Fri; noon-5pm Sat. **Credit** AmEx, DC, MC, V. **Map** p310 C4.

Despite having disposed of its '70s feminist bookstore image and gone for a designer look (it now considers itself to be a general bookstore), Xantippe Unlimited continues to have a comprehensive Women's Studies section (many books are in English), as well as many international women's/lesbian magazines.

Hairdressers

Cuts & Curls
Korte Leidsedwarsstraat 74, Grachtengordel: East (624 6881). Tram 1, 2, 5, 6, 7, 10. **Open** 10am-8pm Mon-Wed; 10am-9pm Thur; 10am-7pm Fri; 10am-4.30pm Sat; closed Sun. **Credit** AmEx, DC, MC, V. **Map** p310 D5.

OK, so what male hairdresser isn't gay? But a butch hairdresser? There you go. Cuts & Curls leather men offer 'men's cuts' and 'blockheads' for ƒ33. No appointments.

Leather-rubber/sex shops

Within the Red Light District lies the leather district, home to a handful of gay leather and rubber shops such as **MR B** (Warmoesstraat 89, Old Centre: Red Light District, 422 0003) and **RoB Accessories** (Warmoesstraat 32, Old Centre: Red Light District, 420 8548). Rubber-lovers should also visit **Black Body**, a specialist rubber shop at Lijnbaansgracht 292 in the Jordaan (626 2553) and the main **RoB** shop (Weteringschans 253, Grachtengordel: East, 625 4686). Other gay sex shops worth a look include the **Bronx** (Kerkstraat 53-5, Grachtengordel: East, 623 1548) and **Drakes** (Damrak 61, Old Centre: New Side, 627 9544), both of which have a porn cinema.

Women's erotica can be found at **Female & Partners** (Spuistraat 100, Old Centre: New Side, 620 9152) and **Mail & Female** (Prinsengracht 489, Grachtengordel: East, 623 3916), while **Demask** (Zeedijk 64, Old Centre: Old Side, 620 5603) is also popular with both men and women. For erotic and fetish shops, *see pages 147.*

Life is good at **Vive La Vie**. See p209.

Music

Don't believe the hippie hype: Amsterdam is one of the best cities to experience live music, whether maddeningly jazzy or artfully classical.

Rock, Roots & Jazz

It certainly has the sex. It undoubtedly has the drugs. So it follows, then, that Amsterdam ought to have rock 'n' roll. And – wouldn't you know – it has a ton of the stuff. Amsterdam has always been a mecca to rock, reggae and jazz types, who regard the city – with its casual vibe when it comes to, well, just about everything – as the nearest thing to rock heaven you're likely to find on God's merry earth. Predictable, maybe, but hey: these are musicians we're talking about. Slip 'em some dope, a sizeable bar tab and sex on tap, and they'll get their manager to see to it that they return to the city again and again.

In the 1950s, Zeedijk was the groovy hepcat strip of the day. After making their bread at the Concertgebouw earlier in the evening, jazz legends such as Gerry Mulligan, Count Basie and Chet Baker would gather and jam at one of the many after-hours places around here. The most famous is the **Casablanca** (*see page 219*),

whose spiritual void has long been filled by the **Bimhuis** (*see page 218*), now the best place to catch current jazz legends in intimate confines.

Multimedia centres the **Melkweg** and the **Paradiso** (for both, *see page 217*) came into being in the heady '60s. Condoned by the city as an alternative hangout for the hippies who were overrunning Vondelpark at the time, both clubs have always received huge council subsidies, allowing them to rise above the clouds of weed smoke and chart every trend ever since, from hippie and punk to techno and drum 'n' bass.

With the world's biggest bands clamouring to play here, the local outfits are often forgotten. Few bands ever get beyond the Dutch club circuit, perhaps understandable given that some acts sing in Dutch (the cheek of it!), as is the case with the infamously intense Raggende Manne and the hip hop – or, rather, nederhop – Osdorp Posse. Most Amsterdam-based bands, though, either remain instrumental or opt for the more universal tongue of English.

The international respect garnered in the past by the likes of Urban Dance Squad, Bettie Serveert and the Ex, and the more recent appearance of such bands such as Junkie XL, Anouk, Caesar and Solex – who runs a record shop in the city – suggest that the ongoing renaissance in the home-grown music scene isn't letting up. It's all a very long way from traditional Dutch musical culture, which can be witnessed in many brown cafés in the Jordaan night after night. Incidentally, it's even further away from the live music sessions in the city's myriad Irish bars: for details on **Mulligan's**, which has arguably the best Irish music in the city, *see page 131*.

For full listings of all musical genres, check out the **AUB Ticketshop** (*see page 283* **Tickets please**) and its own free Dutch-listings magazine, *Uitkrant*; Dutch-language website *Uitgaanagenda* (http://agenda.welcome.nl), alternative 'zine *Shark* (free in bars, and online at www.underwateramsterdam.com), or the Dutch national music magazine *Oor*. Details of the town's more notable gigs are posted on *Time Out*'s website (www.timeout.com/amsterdam). Take note that few concert bookings are made in advance in Amsterdam, and, as a result, most rock, roots and jazz music venues do not accept credit cards.

Alternative sounds at **De Buurvrouw** '*p215*'.

Arts & Entertainment

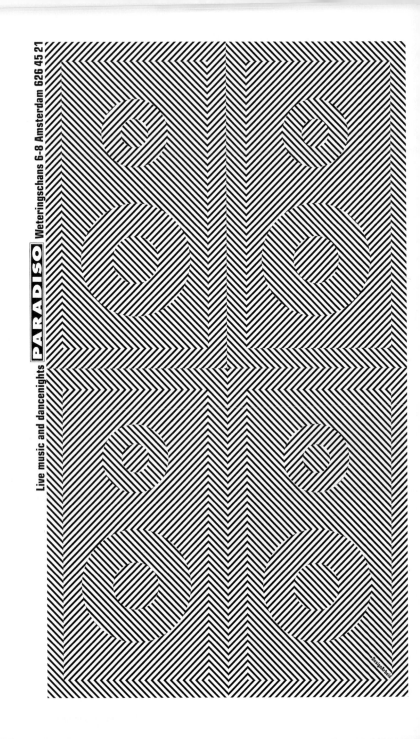

Live music and dancenights **PARADISO** Weteringschans 6-8 Amsterdam 626 45 21

General venues

Aside from those venues listed below, keep an eye out for squat gigs – usually of a more experimental nature – which may be listed in *Shark* (*see page 213*) or on www.squat.net.

Akhnaton

Nieuwezijdskolk 25, Old Centre: New Side (624 3396/www.akhnaton.nl). Tram 1, 2, 5, 13, 17, 20. **Open** 11pm-5am Fri, Sat; closed Mon-Thur, Sun. **Admission** *f*10-*f*15. **No credit cards. Map** p306 D2.
Renowned for its world music, and host to regular African dance nights and salsa parties. Not exactly on the palatial side, the club is often bursting at the seams, so prepare to make like a sardine.

AMP Studios

KNSM-laan 13, Waterfront (418 1111/ www.xs4all.nl/~ampmail). Bus 28. **Open** noon-1am daily. **Admission** free-*f*15. **No credit cards.**
AMP Studios started out as a rehearsal space for bands and now offers regular concerts and parties as well as full recording facilities (both analogue and MIDI) plus a fully licensed café/bar.

ArenA

ArenA Boulevard 1, Bijlmermeer (311 1333/ www.amsterdamarena.nl). Metro Bijlmer. **Open** times vary. **Admission** *f*40-*f*60. **No credit cards.**
Amsterdam's 50,000-seat mega-stadium for those mega-acts (U2, the Rolling Stones et al) who occasionally deign to pass through town. Ambience, to put it mildly, isn't all that it might be.

Bamboo Bar

Lange Leidsedwarsstraat 66, Grachtengordel: East (624 3993). Tram 1, 2, 5, 6, 7, 10, 20. **Open** 8pm-3am Mon-Thur, Sun; 9pm-4am Fri, Sat. **Admission** free. **No credit cards. Map** p310 D5.
A small bar with a friendly crowd of regulars enjoying Brazilian and world music. Squeeze in for local blues and jazz every night except Sunday.

De Buurvrouw

St Pieterpoortsteeg 9, Old Centre: Old Side (625 9654). Tram 4, 9, 14, 16, 20, 24, 25. **Open** 8pm-3am Mon-Thur, Sun; 9pm-4am Fri, Sat. **Admission** free. **No credit cards. Map** p306 D3.
Imaginative decor, occasional live performances from local rock bands and a particularly eclectic record collection make up this pocket-sized watering hole. The place draws an alt-rock clientele. *See p122.*

Club Arena

's Gravesandestraat 51, Oost (694 7444/ www.hotelarena.nl). Tram 3, 6, 7, 10, 14/Metro Weesperplein. **Open** 11pm-4am Thur; 11pm-5am Fri, Sat; closed Mon-Wed, Sun. **Admission** *f*10-*f*15. **No credit cards. Map** p312 G3.
This former hostel is now a sparkling new multimedia cultural centre (complete with a hotel, for which *see p90*). Not to be confused with the **ArenA**

Bimhuis
The Mount Zion of jazz: balancing legends with skwonking up-and-comers. See page 218.

Café Meander
Jazz 'n' funk that'll make you jump. See page 217.

Concertgebouw
Posh and with stunning acoustics: the musician's choice... See page 222.

IJsbreker
Cutting-edge with a patio to boot. See pages 219 and 222.

Melkweg
Milks all the latest sounds. See page 217.

(*see above*), the cosier Arena has an excellent alternative party venue in the old nuns' quarters high in the rafters along with a small concert hall, which tends to rely on decade-themed club nights.

Cruise Inn

Zeeburgerdijk 271-3, Oost (692 7188/www.cruise-inn.com). Tram 6, 10. **Open** 9pm-3am Fri, Sat; closed Mon-Thur, Sun. **Admission** usually free. **No credit cards.**
James Dean clones twist the night away in this gloriously pink wooden club house, where DJs and visiting bands often appear on Saturday nights. Brothel creepers abound.

Last Waterhole

Oudezijds Armsteeg 12, Old Side: Red Light District (624 4814/www.lastwaterhole.nl). Tram 4, 9, 16, 20, 24, 25/Metro Centraal Station. **Open** 11am-2am Mon-Thur, Sun; 11am-4am Fri, Sat. **Admission** free. **No credit cards. Map** p306 D2.
This largish bar caters mainly for the Amsterdam chapter of the Hell's Angels. Temporary residents of the adjoining youth hostel venture in to play pool and listen to native rockers and bluesters jamming live, almost every night.

Maloe Melo

Lijnbaansgracht 163, Grachtengordel: West (420 4592/www.maloemelo.com). Tram 7, 10, 13, 14, 17, 20. **Open** 9pm-3am Mon-Thur, Sun; 9pm-4am Fri, Sat. **Admission** free. **No credit cards. Map** p311 E5.
A cosy hangout for musicians and hangers-on. Wednesday, Friday and Saturday nights feature rock, country and blues bands; other nights play host to jam sessions featuring shit-hot musicians, many of whom are of international stature and claim Melo's as their local when they're in town.

Flying solo

American jazz musicians of the '50s and '60s must have been blown away when they gigged in Amsterdam for the first time. Many were booked to play at the city's most prestigious venue, the **Concertgebouw** (see page 222), and were greeted by a seemingly straight and suited crowd. Fair enough, they must have thought. Until said crowd went absolutely apeshit. In March of 1956, for example, the locals' enthusiasm was so great that Lionel Hampton needed a police escort to get off the stage, as a frothing mob screamed 'Hey-Ba-Be-Re-Bop'. But the reactions were only slightly muted for other A-list performers such as Louis Armstrong, Velma Middleton, Miles Davis, Lester Young, Count Basie, Modern Jazz Quartet, Art Blakey, Lee Morgan, Stan Getz, Gerry Mulligan, Sarah Vaughn, Duke Ellington, Sonny Rollins, Thelonius Monk, John Coltrane and Eric Dolphy.

It was, perhaps, unsurprising that many of these performers sought to come down after the show by hanging and jamming at the more intimate clubs around the infamous Zeedijk. And naturally, there are a million jazz tales that have entered the city's mythology. Bud Powell standing on a streetcorner, screaming 'I wanna fuck!'. Louis Armstrong arriving at Schiphol Airport and giving the waiting crowd a testimonial – complete with free samples – for his sponsor Swiss Kriss, a maker of laxative powders. Archie Shepp causing a panic at one jazz hotspot by *actually showing up on time.*

But two musicians, in particular, came to be regarded by locals as native sons. As many know, Amsterdam was the town in which crooning trumpet-player **Chet Baker** (pictured) toppled to his death from a hotel window (see page 43). But before that tragic event, Amsterdam was the only place in the world where he could be counted on to turn up to play one of his legendary shows. Anywhere else, and he'd frequently vanish, often hopping a train or plane back to Amsterdam for a fix.

A victim not of junk but of alcohol, which led to him being blacklisted in American clubs, **Ben Webster** lived a fairly mellow life with the widow Hartlooper at Waalstraat 77 between 1966 and '69. While his prime years as Duke Ellington's sidekick and as discoverer of Charlie Parker were long behind him, he was still able to show who was boss when sharing the stage in 1967 with his rival and fellow Amsterdammer Don Byas. Byas took the first solo with flourishes galore, before giving Webster a jeering 'Top that' look. Webster calmly waited a few bars before releasing two 'magnificent sighs' – as they're invariably described – which set witnessing spines a-tingling. It is said these two notes were actually responsible for Webster having a street named after him in Amsterdam West, out near Chet Bakerstraat, Count Basiestraat, Duke Ellingtonstraat, Billie Holidaystraat, Charlie Parkerstraat, John Coltranestraat, Louis Armstrongstraat and Boy Edgarstraat.

While Amsterdam always had its own truly native jazz legends, the most characterful was, without doubt, accordionist **Johnny Meijer** (1912-1992) who, in the '50s, backed up the illustrious likes of Maurice Chevalier, Josephine Baker, Joe Venuti and Archie Shepp. But locally, he is remembered mostly as a quaffer of beer who, endearingly, preferred to entertain in the small brown cafés of the Jordaan backed by his bassist brother-in-law Nelis – known by the knowers as 'the worst bassist in the world' – than to accept high-dollar recording contracts in the US. Like the expats, he knew a good steady gig when he saw one.

Café Meander

Voetboogstraat 3, Old Centre: New Side (625 8430/ www.cafemeander.com). Tram 1, 2, 5. **Open** 8.30pm-3am Mon-Thur; 8.30pm-4am Fri-Sun. **Admission** ƒ5-ƒ10. **No credit cards. Map** p310 D4.

This cosy bar in the heart of Amsterdam provides jazz, dance, soul, funk, disco and trip hop for an enthusiastic crowd. The club is handily divided into three floors for three different vibes. Regular gigs by Saskia Laroo, New Cool Collective and DJ Graham B give the place a busy but relaxed 'local' feeling. Monday and Tuesday are jazzy, Wednesday has a funky edge, Thursday is fairly studenty, Friday and Saturday explore the funk in soul, and Sunday is salsa night.

Melkweg

Lijnbaansgracht 234A, Grachtengordel: East (531 8181/www.melkweg.nl). Tram 1, 2, 5, 6, 7, 10, 20. **Open** *Box office* 1-5pm Mon-Fri; 4-6pm Sat, Sun. *Club* times vary; usually 9pm-4am daily. **Admission** ƒ5-ƒ40. *Membership* ƒ5/mth; ƒ30/yr (compulsory). **No credit cards. Map** p310 D5.

Once a dairy (the name means 'Milky Way'), the Melkweg opened in the late '60s as a hippie hangout but is now a slickly run venue. Completely remodelled in the last few years with the addition of the Pepsi-sponsored 'Max' hall – the opening of which coincided with the removal of its weed stall – the multimedia centre can now play host to a double helping of international acts of all imaginable genres, plus theatre, art, video, dance and film events. *See p184, p193* and *p244* for details on the Melkweg's other functions.

OCCII

Amstelveenseweg 134, Vondelpark (671 7778). Tram 2, 6. **Open** 9.30pm-3am Mon-Thur, Sun; 9pm-2am Fri, Sat. **Admission** ƒ7,50. **No credit cards.**

A former squat venue, this cosy and friendly bar-cum-music hall makes you feel at home immediately and invites you to pull up a chair and take in some great local talent. Comfortably tucked away at the end of a delightful cycle ride through Vondelpark, it's a fine excuse to escape the hubbub of the city centre and catch an eclectic mix of quirky cabaret acts, flailing punk rock and world music.

Paradiso

Weteringschans 6-8, Grachtengordel: East (626 4521/www.paradiso.nl). Tram 1, 2, 5, 6, 7, 10, 20. **Open** times vary. **Admission** ƒ10-ƒ60. *Membership* ƒ5/mth; ƒ35/yr (compulsory). **No credit cards. Map** p310 D5.

Like the **Melkweg** (*see above*), the Paradiso tries its absolute hardest to hide its hippie past. The weekly programme caters for a wide range of musical tastes, from local band nights to bigger names on tour: even the Stones and Prince have graced the 'Pop Temple' – as the Paradiso is also called – with their presence. The small upstairs podium and bar hosts small, cultish bands. *See also p184.*

Tropeninstituut

Kleine Zaal: *Linnaeusstraat 2, Oost;* **Grote Zaal:** *Mauritskade 63, Oost (568 8500/ www.kit.nl/theater). Tram 9, 10, 14, 20.* **Open** *Box office* noon-4pm Mon-Sat, from 1hr before performance; closed Sun. *Theatre* times vary. **Admission** ƒ20-ƒ35. **Credit** MC, V. **Map** p312 H3.

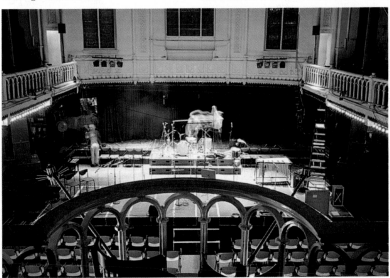

Once a hippie haven, now a 'Pop Temple': the **Paradiso**.

Mmmm. Niiiiiiice. Get horny at the **Bimhuis**.

Two theatres attached to the **Tropenmuseum**, which exhibits artefacts from all over the world (*see p55*). The Tropeninstituut follows the same policy as the museum in its programming, featuring international folk musicians in its formal, all-seater halls.

Vondelpark

Vondelpark, Museum Quarter (open-air theatre 673 1499/park office 523 7790). Tram 1, 2, 3, 5, 6, 7, 10, 12, 20. **Open** dawn-dusk daily. **Admission** free. **No credit cards. Map** p310 C6.

Wander down to Vondelpark and spy on some of the more unusual examples of artistry and musicianship. Aside from the array of buskers, there is an organised agenda of entertainment for the outdoor podium; flyers and posters are usually plastered over trees and gates in the park. *See also p170, and p244* **Park life.**

Winston Kingdom

Warmoesstraat 129, Old Centre: Red Light District (623 1380/www.winston.nl). Tram 4, 9, 16, 20, 24, 25. **Open** 9pm-3am Mon-Thur, Sun; 9pm-4am Fri, Sat. **Admission** free-*f10.* **No credit cards. Map** p306 D3.

Part of the **Winston Hotel** (*see p96*), this bar attracts a mix of residents, locals and tourists. A quirky booking policy means that on any given week one might luck upon a '70s disco, a local band, a poetry reading and an underrated international legend (the late Townes van Zandt strummed one of his last shows here). Loungey types should head for Club Vegas (*see p187* **Lazy, crazy Sundays**).

Jazz venues

Throughout the year, venues play host to big international stars, while local groups and jam sessions sneak into the early hours in snug bars on most nights of the week.

Alto Jazz Café

Korte Leidsedwarsstraat 115, Grachtengordel: East (626 3249). Tram 1, 2, 5, 6, 7, 10, 20. **Open** 9pm-3am Mon-Thur, Sun; 9pm-4am Fri, Sat. **Admission** free. **No credit cards. Map** p310 D5.

A cosy and relaxed traditional brown bar in an otherwise commercialised tourist area just off Leidseplein. Live jazz and blues is played every night of the week by in-house musicians and guests.

Bimhuis

Oudeschans 73-77, Old Centre: Old Side (623 3373/ box office 623 1361/www.bimhuis.nl). Tram 9, 14, 20/Metro Waterlooplein. **Open** Box office 8-11pm on performance nights. **Admission** *f20-f35.* **No credit cards. Map** p307 E2.

The city's major jazz venue stages a mix of well-known international artists and local talent. It's often hard to get a seat, so arrive early. Tickets are available on the day from the **AUB** or **Amsterdam Tourist Board**, or on the door one hour before performances. However, take note that the Bimhuis is moving to the soon-to-be-built **Centrum voor Moderne Muziek** on the eastern docklands in 2002: phone or check the website nearer the time for more information.

Bourbon Street

Leidsekruisstraat 6-8, Grachtengordel: East (623 3440). Tram 1, 2, 5, 6, 7, 10. **Open** 10pm-4am Mon-Thur, Sun; 10pm-5am Fri, Sat. **Admission** *f*2,50-*f*5. **No credit cards. Map** p310 D5.

A spacious bar with a podium for jazz most nights of the week and a very late licence. The friendly staff and customers will make you feel right at home. Performances can border on the poetic.

Casablanca

Zeedijk 26, Old Side: Red Light District (625 5685). Tram 4, 9, 16, 20, 24, 25. **Open** 8pm-2am Mon-Thur, Sun; 10pm-4am Fri, Sat. **Admission** free. **No credit cards. Map** p306 D2.

This formerly legendary home to jamming junkie jazz musicians has sadly lost its edge: it now has karaoke from 10pm until closing from Thursday to Saturday. However, it still has something going for it: Sunday to Wednesday nights are dedicated to live jazz, from big band to trio.

IJsbreker

Weesperzijde 23, The Pijp (box office 693 9093/ administration 668 1805/www.ysbreker.nl). Tram 3, 6, 7, 10/Metro Weesperplein. **Box office** phone enquiries 9.30am-5.30pm Mon-Fri & from 1hr before performance. *Café* 10am-1am Mon-Thur, Sun; 10am-2am Fri, Sat. **Admission** *f*17,50-*f*35. **No credit cards. Map** p312 G4.

Situated on the picturesque banks of the Amstel just east of the Pijp, this venue is especially pleasant on summer evenings. The programming concentrates on contemporary classical music and experimental jazz. It's worth a visit for the bar alone, even when there's no live shows. Like the **Bimhuis** (*see p218*), it will be moving to the new Centrum voor Moderne Musiek in 2002. *See also p222.*

Festivals

Maybe it's the flat terrain. Maybe it's the Netherlands' festival-friendly narcotics legislation (okay, it's almost undoubtedly the Netherlands' festival-friendly narcotics legislation). It certainly ain't the weather. Whatever the reason, Holland is host to a myriad of music festivals, held throughout the year and catering for all tastes. Tickets for most festivals are available from **Amsterdam Tourist Board** (0900 400 4040) and the **AUB** (0900 0191; *see also page 283* **Tickets please**).

Amsterdam Blues Festival

Meervaart, Meer en Vaart 300 (410 7700/box office 410 7777/www.meervaart.nl). Tram 1, 17/bus 19, 23, 64, 68. **Date** mid-Mar. **Tickets** phone for details. **No credit cards.**

This two-day blues festival in Meervaart has been gradually growing in status with its mix of young local names and international cult legends. They got it bad. And that's good.

Amsterdam Pop Prijs/Wanted R&B & Hip Hop Prijs Finals

Information 420 8160/www.grap.nl. **Date** *Pop Prijs* Mar-Jun. *Wanted* Apr-Jun. **Tickets** *Pop Prijs f*15. *Wanted f*20. **Credit** varies by venue.

Local music talent (pop, R&B and hip hop) can be watched – and heard – around town during these events. Phone the above number for full details.

Amsterdam Roots Festival

Tickets Uitlijn 0900 0191 premium rate. **Date** June. **Tickets** free-*f*60. **Credit** AmEx, DC, MC, V.

Initiated by the **Melkweg**, the **Tropeninstituut** (for both, *see p217*), the **Concertgebouw** (*see p222*) and the **Holland Festival** (*see p170*), the Roots Festival feature some of the greatest 'world music' acts on the planet. A 'world village' in Oosterpark, with a collection of different podiums, hosts a selection of lesser-known names.

A Camping Flight to Lowlands

Walibi Park, Flevoland (information 015 284 0740/tickets 0900 300 1250/www.lowlands.nl). NS rail Lelystad. **Tickets** *f*175. **Date** last weekend of Aug. **No credit cards.**

The alternative festival of the year, where tens of thousands descend to many metres below sea level on the polder (reclaimed land) of Walibi Park in Flevoland for three days to camp and groove to the hippest bands and DJs. The price includes camping and a bus to the site from Lelystad train station: for details on the Dutch rail system, *see p274.*

Drum Rhythm Festival

Westergasfabriek, Haarlemmerweg (information 015 215 7756/www.drumrhythm.com). Tram 3, 10/bus 18, 22. **Date** May. **Tickets** *f*100 2-day pass; *f*60 1-day pass. **No credit cards. Map** p305 A1.

This annual festival of roots and modern rhythms takes place at the **Westergasfabriek** (*see p240*). It often features well known bands and artists in its proudly eclectic line-ups: one year, for example, it managed to slot George Clinton, Lee 'Scratch' Perry and Youssou N'Dour together on the same bill.

Dynamo Open Air Festival

Goffertpark, Nijmegen (information 040 211 7878/ www.dynamo-open-air.com). NS rail Nijmegen, then shuttle bus to festival. **Date** end May or mid-June. **Tickets** *f*87,50. **No credit cards.**

With a turnout of roughly nine billion stage-diving, skateboarding adolescent devotees of MTV culture, the Dynamo Open Air Festival may give visitors the distinct impression that the Dutch language contains at least 50 per cent US slang. The loudest three days in a field you're ever likely to experience.

North Sea Jazz Festival

Netherlands Congress Centre, Churchillplein 10, The Hague (information 015 215 7756/tickets 010 591 9000/www.northseajazz.nl). NS rail to Den Haag Centraal Station, then tram 7, 8 or bus 4, 14; NS rail to Den Haag HS, then tram 8. **Date** 2nd weekend in July. **Tickets** *f*270 3-day pass. **No credit cards.**

Arts & Entertainment

This three-day mega-event in The Hague, supposedly the biggest jazz festival in the world, is a fantastic opportunity to see a large hatful of bona fide jazz legends: up to a thousand artists perform each year, all hoping to land one of the special festival awards. The three-day pass covers the main hall, where the big names – from the instrumental twiddlings of Oscar Peterson to the triumphant croonings of Tony Bennett – take curtain call after curtain call for educated audiences. The pass for the entire festival covers the whole shebang: shows by the big names, plus entry to all the smaller halls and fringe events.

Parkpop

Zuiderpark, Den Haag (0900 340 3505/ www.parkpop.nl). NS rail Den Haag Centraal Station. **Date** late June. **Tickets** free. **No credit cards**.
The biggest of the numerous free, one-day festivals held each year in Holland, Parkpop is one of the few festivals that caters for both Dutch and international music in equal amounts. The crowd is very mixed, due largely to the fact that the festival is basically a family day out: the music is just thrown in for good measure. The eclectic programming reflects this, and often comes up with bills you're unlikely to find anywhere else: Bloodhound Gang, the Levellers, the Bomfunk MCs and Rich Wyman all played in 2000.

Pink Pop

Landgraaf (046 475 2500/ www.wanadoo.nl/ pinkpop). NS rail Landgraaf, then shuttle bus to festival. **Date** May/June. **Tickets** ƒ145 3-day pass. **No credit cards**.
Held near Landgraaf, a small village in the south of Holland, this increasingly popular three-day outdoor festival usually has an impressive line-up of famous Dutch and international pop stars. Expect to find a diverse mixture of artists: Gomez, Moby and 16 Horsepower were among those that played here in 2000.

Sonic Acts

Paradiso, Weteringschans 6-8, Grachtengordel: East (626 4521). Tram 1, 2, 5, 6, 7, 10. **Date** varies. **Tickets** ƒ17,50. **No credit cards. Map** p310 D5.
The **Paradiso** (*see p217*) hosts this three- or four-day festival for new electronic music, which in the past has featured Stockhausen, Scanner, David Toop and Zoviet France as guests. Workshops and an Image and Sound Lab for remixing complete the cutting-edge ambience.

Tracks & Traces

Paradiso, Weteringschans 6-8, Grachtengordel: East (626 4521). Tram 1, 2, 5, 6, 7, 10. **Date** varies. **Tickets** ƒ17,50. **No credit cards. Map** p310 D5.
Another so-hip-it-hurts festival organised by the **Paradiso** (*see p217*), Tracks & Traces is dedicated to 'unusual music', an open term that may include unique DJs (à la David Shea), postrockers (such as Rex or Kriedler) or any other inspired mutants from the world of sound.

Classical & Opera

In an age when governments around the world are slashing arts funding in a frighteningly casual way, it's always a thrill to find a city in which the arts are not only fighting back, but holding their own. Amsterdam is such a city: the local arts scene is on the up-and-up; serious theatre is back on track again despite competition from trashy musicals and the like; and classical music is most definitely alive and well, following the financial flux of a decade or two ago.

Anyone with a half-decent classical music CD collection probably has at least one disc by the **Royal Concertgebouw Orchestra**. The famed ensemble – based at the **Concertgebouw**, funnily enough – has gone from strength to strength in recent years under Riccardo Chailly's direction. It's not all Chailly, though: despite the fact that the international conducting circuit is starting to get out of hand – how many guest appearances from 'star' conductors do audiences really need? – a roster of visiting baton-wielders that includes Mstislav Rostropovich, Nikolaus Harnoncourt and the orchestra's honourary conductor, Bernard Haitink, cannot fail to catch the eye.

Across town at the Beurs van Berlage, the **Netherlands Philharmonic**, directed by Hartmut Haenchen, plays a symphonic series alongside its regular productions at the **Nederlands Opera**, and is normally good value for a night out. The other major ensembles shouldn't be forgotten, either: the **Rotterdam Philharmonic Orchestra** has as its chief conductor the exceptional Valery Gergiev, while the **Radio Philharmonic Orchestra**, based in Hilversum but a regular visitor to Amsterdam, continues to work at the highest levels under the skilled baton of the internationally acclaimed Edo de Waart.

Almost everyone in Amsterdam has finally started to forget about the ruckus over the construction of the 'Stopera' – Muziektheater/ City Hall – building, which opened in 1985 and is now home to the **Nederlands Opera**. Good thing, too, for the company is on something of a roll under the acclaimed artistic direction of Pierre Audi, a man who demands much of his audience (as evidenced by his take on Wagner's highly dense 'Ring' cycle).

ENSEMBLES

Although it would be exaggerating to say that all small classical music ensembles in Amsterdam fall into one of two camps, it's undeniable that two types of music stand out above all others in this city of extremes.

On the one hand, there's the old school. Dutch musicians were the founders of authentic performance practice – performances using authentic period instruments – and the innovation has now almost become a tradition. Ton Koopman still holds the torch as harpsichordist and 'director who doesn't conduct' of the Amsterdam Baroque Orchestra, founded in 1979, while the Amsterdam Bach Soloists, formed by members of the Concertgebouw Orchestra, is led by principle violinist Henk Rubingh when it's not employing a collaborating guest conductor. Recorder-player and director Frans Brüggen extends authentic practice into the classical era with his Orchestra of the 18th Century, whose daring tempi, brilliant strings and valveless natural horns make for exciting performances. Look out for concerts organised by **Organisatie Oude Muziek** – literally, the 'Organisation for Old Music' – whose early music events at the Waalse are normally excellent and often unmissable.

On the flipside, there is a burgeoning modern music scene in Amsterdam. Holland's most important post-war composer Louis Andriessen still lives in the city (*see page 222* **Louis Louis: oh yeah**), and his work is occasionally performed before reverential audiences at the excellent **IJsbreker** (*see page 222*), Amsterdam's nominal centre for new music. There are, in fact, around 20 new music ensembles based in the city. Two that are

particularly worth investigating are the Asko Ensemble led by Reinbert de Leeuw, and the Schönberg Ensemble, which is often directed by noted muso Oliver Knussen. Both the Nieuw Music Ensemble and the Nieuw Sinfonietta also make noises worth listening out for, as do minimalist eccentrics Orkest de Volharding. Contemporary music fans should also keep an ear open for the Proms. Kind of a low-down and dirty version of the British proms, it's a series of contemporary concerts held, oddly, in the grimy confines of the **Paradiso** (*see page 217*).

TICKETS & INFORMATION

Ticket prices in Amsterdam are reasonable compared with other European cities. However, this bonus is tapered by the fact that tickets for many of the larger venues are sold on a subscription system, and even though some concerts are announced up to a year ahead, it can be difficult to get tickets on an ad hoc basis. For the big concerts and operas, try to book as far in advance as you can, but if you're just passing through, it's always worth phoning up for returns.

For full listings information, pick up a copy of the free Dutch listings magazine *Uitkrant*, published by the **AUB Ticketshop** (0900 0191; *see page 283* **Tickets please**), which accepts all major credit cards, or call in at the **Amsterdam Tourist Board** (0900 400 4040), which has information on upcoming concerts. Discounts on tickets are often available for students, over-65s and CJP card-holders.

Arts & Entertainment

Ladies both thin and fat sing at the **Beurs van Berlage**. *See p222*.

Louis Louis: oh yeah

Widely regarded as the nation's greatest living composer, **Louis Andriessen** was born in Utrecht in 1939 to a family that would have given the Bach posse a run for their money: both father Hendrik and brother Juriaan enjoyed acclaim as composers. Extending his familial resources, he came to study under Kees van Baaren at the Hague Conservatory (where he would start teaching in 1974), and then under Berio in Milan and Berlin.

Besides the general headiness of the leftist '60s, the influences that perhaps had the optimum effect in establishing Andriessen as a pivotal figure in new music would be his appreciation of jazz, Charles Ives and Igor Stravinsky (about whom he later co-wrote a definitive study, *The Apollonian Clockwork*). It's interesting that all three influences are equatable by their savvy – and very 20th century – sense of montage, where 'high' and 'low' culture are given equal credence.

Indeed, if there is one typical Andriessen trademark, it's his willingness to uninhibitedly cruise the full stretch of musical history.

Besides the Dutch A-list of ensembles and orchestras and his own uniquely instrumented groups, such international performers as the San Francisco and BBC Symphony Orchestras, the Kronos Quartet, the London Sinfonietta, Ensemble Modern, Bang on a Can and the California EAR Unit have all performed and/or commissioned works by Andriessen.

Andriessen first made an impression in 1968 with a 'Politically Demonstrative Experimental Concert' in the Carre Theatre, where he performed an opera based on the life of Che Guevara that he had co-composed with Reinbert de Leeuw, Misha Mengelberg, Peter Schat and Jan van Vlijmen. Certainly, his willingness to take on 'big subjects' would come to define his own later, more realised, works. *De Staat* (1973) used the ideas of Plato to 'democratise' composition by arranging all instruments to play at the same time. This approach would still be apparent in *De Tijd* (1981) and *De Snelheid* (1983), works that also meditated on the nature of 'time' and 'velocity';

Concert halls

Where a telephone number is given in the listings below, tickets are sold at the venue's box office. Tickets are also available from the AUB Ticketshop, from its Uitjin phone service (0900 0191) and website (www.uitlijn.nl). Look out for their annual publication *Uitgids*, which details subscription series concerts.

Beurs van Berlage: AGA Zaal & Yakult Zaal

Damrak 213, Old Centre: New Side (627 0466). Tram 4, 9, 14, 16, 20, 24, 25. **Open** *Box office* 2.30-5pm Tue-Fri; 12.30-5pm Sat; also from 75min before performance for sales and collection; closed Mon, Sun & June-mid Aug. **Tickets** *f*15-*f*35; concessions with CJP card. **No credit cards. Map** p306 D2.

This former stock exchange is now a cultural centre, housing a large exhibition hall, two concert halls, one of Holland's dedicated classical radio stations, the Concertzender, and the offices of the resident orchestras: the Netherlands Philharmonic and the Netherlands Chamber Orchestra. Entered from the Damrak, the medium-sized **Yakult Zaal** offers comfortable seating, a massive stage and controllable but not ideal acoustics. The 200-seat **AGA Zaal** is an odd-looking free-standing glass box within the walls of a side room, which is sometimes referred to as the 'diamond in space'. *See p31 and p41.*

Concertgebouw

Concertgebouwplein 2-6, Museum Quarter (reservations 671 8345 10am-5pm daily/24-hour information in Dutch 675 4411). Tram 2, 3, 5, 12, 16, 20. **Open** *Box office* 10am-7pm daily. **Tickets** *f*10-*f*250. **Credit** AmEx, DC, MC, V. **Map** p310 D6.

The Concertgebouw is the favourite venue of many of the world's top soloists and orchestras, including its own **Concertgebouw Orchestra** (which, aside from its regular year-round programme, plays a lovely Christmas matinée concert here every 25 December). The acoustics of the **Grote Zaal** (Great Hall) are second to none and a seat anywhere in the house offers great sound. The **Kleine Zaal** (Recital Hall) is less comfortable, but features top-class chamber groups and soloists. Visiting stars push prices up, but for 75% of the remaining concerts, tickets cost less than *f*35. The matinées on Saturdays at 3pm are renowned for concert performances of opera. Throughout July and August, tickets for the Robeco Summer Concerts – featuring high-profile artists and orchestras – are an excellent bargain.

IJsbreker

Weesperzijde 23, The Pijp (box office 693 9093/administration 668 1805/www.ysbreker.nl). Tram 3, 6, 7, 10/Metro Weesperplein. **Open** *Box office* phone enquiries 9.30am-5.30pm Mon-Fri & from 1hr before performance. *Café* 10am-1am Mon-Thur, Sun; 10am-2am Fri, Sat. **Tickets** *f*17,50-*f*35. **No credit cards. Map** p312 G4.

subjects dear to such allied colleagues of the avant garde as Terry Riley, Steve Reich and Philip Glass. But never one to remain rigid, *De Materie* (1989), a full-length theatre piece he created with Robert Wilson for the Nederlands Opera, musically fused writings on both shipbuilding and atomic theory.

More recent acclaim has come from his collaborations with film-maker Peter Greenaway, which began in 1991 with the soundtrack to the film, *M is for Man, Music, Mozart*. Greenaway would later provide the production and libretto for *Rosa, A Horse Opera* which premiered in the Nederlands Opera in 1994, and the libretto for *Writing to Vermeer*, first staged in 1999. Best of all, though: Nonesuch Records has begun releasing an ambitious series that should make all Andriessen's major works available on CD during the first couple of years of the 21st century. And not before time.

One of Europe's most innovative venues. Aside from its regular programme of ensembles and concerts, many of which feature obscure and avant-garde Dutch works and musicians, the venue co-produces several concerts with the **Holland Festival** (*see p170*). It also organises other concerts in both the **Tropeninstituut** (*see p245*) and the **Melkweg** (*see 217*). The IJsbreker's café boasts one of the best outdoor terraces in town, with a fantastic view of the Amstel. But stay alert: it's planning to move to a new location on the harbourfront in 2002.

Opera

Koninklijk Theater Carré

Amstel 115-25, Grachtengordel: East (622 5225). Tram 4, 6, 7, 10, 20. **Open** *Box office* 10am-7pm Mon-Sat; 1-7pm Sun. **Tickets** *f*25-*f*250. **Credit** AmEx, DC, MC, V. **Map** p311 F4.

This former circus theatre hosts large-scale musicals such as *Cats* and *La Cage aux Folles*, alongside reputable opera and ballet companies on tour from, in particular, Eastern Europe that usually perform popular classics.

Muziektheater

Waterlooplein 22, Old Centre: Old Side (625 5455). Tram 9, 14, 20/Metro Waterlooplein. **Open** *Box office* 10am-6pm Mon-Sat; 11.30am-6pm Sun; or until start of performance. **Tickets** *f*25-*f*140. **Credit** AmEx, DC, MC, V. **Map** p307 E3.

The modern Muziektheater is home to the **Nationale Ballet** (*see p245*) and the **Nederlands Opera**, as well as visiting guest productions. The emphasis is on high-quality opera and dance productions at reasonable prices. The big staircases make an impressive sweep around the auditorium, that has floor-to-ceiling glass and marble-faced pillars, giving a wonderful view of the Amstel. The stage's spaciousness invites particularly ambitious ideas from world-famous stage directors such as Willy Decker (*Wozzeck and Werther*), Harry Kupfer (*Die Frau ohne Schatten*) and Peter Sellars (*Pelléas et Mélisande*).

Stadsschouwburg

Leidseplein 26, Grachtengordel: East (624 2311). Tram 1, 2, 5, 6, 7, 10, 20. **Open** *Box office* 10am-6pm or until start of performance Mon-Sat; from 1½hrs before start of performance Sun. **Tickets** *f*20-*f*80. **Credit** AmEx, MC, V. **Map** p310 C5.

Because its productions are designed for portability and hence rarely get much of a chance to become established for any length of time, the **Nationale Reisopera** (National Travelling Opera) receives less attention than it perhaps deserves. The Reisopera usually stages two or three performances of each production in the red velvet surroundings of this municipal theatre, which also occasionally hosts other opera performances by visiting companies, often from abroad.

Arts & Entertainment

Churches

Many musicians in Amsterdam take advantage of the monumental churches around the city. The bonus for concertgoers is obvious: aside from hearing largely excellent music, you get a chance to see the interiors of these wonderful buildings at the same time. During the summer, the city's many bell-towers resonate to the intricate tinkling of their carillons: thumping the 'keyboard' mechanism triggers a whole array of smaller bells into surprisingly rapid renderings of tunes. But churches are not just for organ and carillon recitals. The refurbished Amstelkerk and Lutherse Kerk, and the intimate Bethanienklooster are also used for concerts. Most churches have no box office, but tickets and information are available from the **AUB Ticketshop** (*see page 283* **Tickets please**).

Engelse Kerk

Begijnhof 48, Old Centre: New Side (624 9665). Tram 1, 2, 4, 5, 9, 14, 16, 20, 24, 25. **Open** times vary. **Tickets** free. **Map** p310 D4.

Nestled in an idyllic courtyard, the Academy of the **Begijnhof** (*see p49*) arranges weekly concerts of baroque and classical music at its English Reformed Church, with particular emphasis on the use of authentic period instruments in performances. The series of free lunchtime concerts in July and August features young players and new ensembles. The acoustics are vibrant and clear.

Nieuwe Kerk

Dam, Old Centre: New Side (Nieuwe Kerk Foundation 626 8168). Tram 1, 2, 5, 9, 13, 14, 16, 17, 20, 24, 25. **Open** 10am-5pm daily. **Tickets** *f*12,50; *f*10 concessions. **No credit cards**. **Map** p306 C3.

The Nieuwe Kerk has a magnificent 16th-century organ and hosts organ concerts by top Dutch and international players. Gustav Leonhardt, grandfather of baroque performance practice, is the resident organist. On Saturdays (at 8.15pm) between May and September, it has a programme of guest organists. *See p28 and p40.*

Oude Kerk

Oudekerksplein 23, Old Centre: Red Light District (625 8284). Tram 4, 9, 14, 16, 20, 24, 25. **Open** 11am-5pm Mon-Sat; 1-5pm Sun. **Tickets** *f*7,50-*f*15; *f*5-*f*12,50 concessions. **No credit cards**. **Map** p306 D2.

Jan Sweelinck, the Netherlands' most famous 17th-century composer, was once organist at this stunning church in the heart of the Red Light District. Concerts today, staged between June and August, include organ and carillon recitals, choral and chamber music. The Oude Kerk (*see also p45*) organises a summer 'wandering' concert series (three pieces in three venues, with promenades and coffee breaks) together with the **Museum Amstelkring** (*see p46*).

Waalse Kerk

Oudezijds Achterburgwal 157 (information from Organisatie Oude Muziek 030 236 2236). Tram 4, 9, 16, 20, 24, 25. **Open** times vary. **Tickets** *f*22,50; *f*18,50 concessions. **No credit cards**. **Map** p306 D3.

Small, elegant and intimate, concerts at the Waalse Kerk are organised by the Organisatie Oude Muziek, a group devoted to early music played on period instruments. Musicians from both the Netherlands and abroad play here on a relatively regular basis.

Out of town

Anton Philipszaal, The Hague

Spuiplein 150, The Hague (box office 070 360 9810/information 070 360 7927). NS rail Den Haag Centraal Station. **Open** Box office 10am-6pm Mon-Sat; also from 45 min before performance. **Tickets** *f*27,50-*f*65; concessions with CJP card, over-65s. **Credit** AmEx, DC, MC, V.

Home of The Hague's Residentie Orchestra since 1987, and situated amid the modern architecture of the city centre. Inside, it's a soundly designed hall with excellent acoustics.

De Doelen, Rotterdam

Kruisstraat 2, Rotterdam (010 217 1717). NS rail Rotterdam Centraal Station. **Open** Box office 10am-6pm Mon-Thur, Sat, Sun; 10am-9pm Fri. **Tickets** *f*15-*f*400 (average *f*50). **Credit** AmEx, MC, V.

The Doelen, which is home to the **Rotterdam Philharmonic Orchestra** (RPO), contains both a large and small concert hall. It hosts about two dozen series a year, ranging from contemporary orchestral work to jazz and just about everything in between, including the RPO's own season. There are also plenty of concerts featuring visiting and guest orchestras from home and abroad.

Vredenburg Music Centre, Utrecht

Vredenburgpassage 77, Utrecht (box office 030 231 4544/24-hour information 0900 9203). NS rail Utrecht. **Open** Box office noon-7pm Mon; 10am-7pm Tue-Sat; also from 45min before performance. **Tickets** *f*35-*f*55. **Credit** AmEx, MC, V.

Many performers make their only Dutch appearances here. Despite the horribly ugly setting – by a shopping mall, bizarrely – the Vredenburg attracts plenty of orchestras, with the Radio-Philharmonisch playing more than its fair share of concerts every year. Vredenburg remains fully subsidised by the government, which means ticket prices are cheaper than in Amsterdam. The occasional pop concerts held here tend to sell out quickly.

Lunchtime menus

Many of Amsterdam's lunchtime concerts are free and run throughout the standard September to June season. Most venues have a weekly concert: among the best are the **Boekmanzaal** at the **Muziektheater** (*see* *page 223*), which has a recital each Tuesday at 12.30pm. Most famous of all is the lunchtime concert at the **Concertgebouw** (*see page 222*) on Wednesdays at 12.30pm, with up-and-coming ensembles or soloists and even previews of evening concerts by visiting world-famous orchestras. Get there early to fight your way in. In addition, the **Stedelijk Museum** (*see page 68*) stages occasional concerts, often of innovative contemporary music, on Thursday and Saturday afternoons at 3pm. But it's best first to check with the Amsterdam Tourist Board for information on these events.

Festivals & events

Further details on the events listed below can be obtained from the **AUB** (0900 0191) and the **Amsterdam Tourist Board** (0900 400 4040). Two other festivals that feature a whole range of arts including classical music are the **Holland Festival** and the **Uitmarkt** (*for both, see page 170-71*).

Grachtenfestival
(421 4542). **Date** mid-Aug. **Tickets** free.
What began as a single free concert by an orchestra floating on a pontoon in front of the **Pulitzer Hotel** (*see p84*) has become the 'Canal Festival', involving over 70 chamber concerts in 20 different canalside locations. The line-up balances some of the larger international names with local up-and-comers. Not to be missed.

International Gaudeamus Music Week
Postal & telephone enquiries Stichting Gaudeamus, Swammerdamstraat 38, 1091 RV Amsterdam (694 7349). **Date** early Sept. **Tickets** *f*15 per concert. **No credit cards**.
An annual competition for young composers organised by the Centre for Contemporary Music, which includes a whole week of intense discussion of the state of the art, plus performances of selected entries and works by established composers. Also of interest is the International Gaudeamus Interpreters Competition (usually in Rotterdam during October), a similar competition for performers of contemporary repertoire. Contemporary music devotees should not miss either; classicists, on the other hand, would do well to plug their ears and run away as fast as their legs can carry them.

Utrecht Early Music Festival
Various venues in Utrecht; information from Stichting Oude Muziek, Postbus 734, 3500 AS Utrecht (030 236 2236). **Date** late Aug-early Sept. **Tickets** *f*15-*f*65. **No credit cards**.
Top baroque and classical artists and ensembles from around the world, performing in churches and concert halls throughout the city. Many ensembles use period instruments, which satisfies the trainspotters no end. There's normally something interesting going on, and the festival is rightfully a popular one.

Other organisations

Network for Non-Western Music
Pauwstraat 13A, 3512 TG Utrecht (030 233 2876).
Indonesian, Turkish, African and Middle Eastern culture is brought to the Netherlands courtesy of this organisation. It arranges tours by visiting musicians. Expect six or seven concerts a year.

STEIM (Stichting for Electro-Instrumental Music)
Achtergracht 19, 1017 WL Amsterdam (622 8690).
Amsterdam's electronic music institution is a unique research team examining the interface between man and music. Prototype MIDI controllers (Michel Waisvisz's gloved 'Hands' have the biggest claim to fame), novel sensors and hard- and software packages that can convert any manner of signals into MIDI data. They also organise many bleeding-edge concerts and performances to give technophobes an intriguing glimpse into the future.

The **IJsbreker**: innovative, eclectic and with a fab bar, too. *See p222.*

Sport & Fitness

Fitness freaks take note: Amsterdam is a splendidly sporty city, even if you daren't get on your bike and brave the roads.

While the relaxed disposition of the typical Amsterdam native may stand in stark contrast to the zeal of most sports enthusiasts, the average Dutch person is at least aware of, and at most active in, some kind of sport. This is evidenced by Holland's international prominence in professional and semi-professional sports, as well as its many municipal and private facilities for recreational sport and fitness. Traditionally, the weather and landscape shaped which sports became popular; today, an ageing population, a shift from nine-to-five work routines and a trend towards using free time constructively are also determining factors.

Professional football, tennis, skating and cycling have earned the Dutch international respect, but tickets for top professional events are pricey and hard to come by. However, a number of semi-professional leagues and sports have been gaining in popularity, a rundown on which is given below. For further information, contact the **Municipal Sport and Recreation Department** on 552 2490, or head to www.sport.amsterdam.nl (mostly in Dutch) for maps, schedules and links concerning almost every sport imaginable. The *Amsterdam Yellow Pages* (also mostly in Dutch) is another valuable resource when trying to determine what's on where. And try not to miss the **Nederlands Sportmuseum** in Lelystad. Aside from all the usual exhibits, it holds comprehensive archives of books, cuttings and photos, all of which are open by appointment.

Nederlands Sportmuseum
Museumweg 10, Lelystad (0320 261010). NS rail Lelystad. **Open** 10am-5pm Tue-Fri; noon-5pm Sat, Sun; closed Mon. **Admission** ƒ9,50; ƒ7 Museum Card, under-13s. **No credit cards**.

Spectator sports

American football

Though American football may still seem a little out of place in the Netherlands, it's beginning to take root in the Dutch sporting psyche. The Admirals are the city's pro team, while the **Amsterdam Crusaders** represent the city in the amateur league, and can be reached on 617 7450. The season runs from

March to June. Full details of American football in the Netherlands are available from the governing body, the **NAFF**, on 0229 214801.

Amsterdam Admirals
Amsterdam ArenA, Arena Boulevard 1, South-East (465 4545). Metro Strandvliet or Metro/NS rail Bijlmer. **Admission** ƒ27,50-ƒ75. **Season** Mar-June. **Matches** 7pm Sat, Sun. **Credit** AmEx, DC, MC, V.
Members of NFL Europe, the Admirals regularly draw crowds of 15,000. Attending an Admirals match may be one of the only ways to actually get into the ArenA.

Baseball

The dozen or so baseball and softball clubs that compete in and around Amsterdam deliver a splendid mix of excitement and relaxation during the long days of summer. Baseball is played to a variety of standards, and the season runs from April to October. For details, contact the regional **KNBSB** on 023 539 0244.

Cricket

Cricket's popularity has been increasing steadily over the years. With an underdog national team capable of upsetting established teams, the Dutch are making a name for themselves in international circles. Throughout the Netherlands, there are over 100 men's and women's teams affiliated to the Royal Dutch Cricket Board (**KNCB**).

There are several clubs in Amsterdam, the best of which is the **VRA** (645 9816). Most Dutch clubs have junior, veteran and women's teams as well as their main sides, and welcome new players. Interested parties should contact the KNCB, based at the VRA (645 1705).

Cycling

The Netherlands is a cycling nation, and produces many pro cyclists, both sprinters and, in particular, climbers: the Dutch still talk with awe and affection about Joop Zoetemelk who, after finishing second six times, finally won the Tour de France in 1985.

There's plenty to watch, too: Dutch cycling fans turn out for stage, *criterium* (road circuit) and one-day road races, plus track, field, cyclo-cross and ATB/mountain biking. The biggest Dutch races are the **Amstel Gold Race** around Limburg in late April; the **RAI Derny Race**, held at the RAI in Amsterdam in mid-May; the popular **Acht van Chaam**, a 100-kilometre (62-mile) *criterium* held in Noord Brabant on the first Wednesday after the Tour de France (late July or early August); and the **Tour de Nederland**, a five-day race – it passes through Amsterdam – held in late August. For more details on all types of cycle racing, contact the **KNWU** (Dutch Cycle Racing Association) at Postbus 136, 3440 AC Woerden (0348 484084), or the Amsterdam rep, Bert de Bruin, on 496 3621.

Of course, there's always the option of cycling yourself. If you have a racing bike and are looking for competition, head for Sportpark Sloten. Two cycle clubs are based here – **ASC Olympia** (617 7510/secretary 617 3057), the oldest cycling club in Europe, and **WV Amsterdam** (secretary 619 3314) – and there is a 2½-kilometre (1½-mile) circuit round the park. The 200-metre track has also recently been rebuilt as a hyper-modern velodrome. If it's information on recreational cycling you're after, contact the **ENFB**, a national cyclists' group: the Amsterdam branch can be reached on 685 4794.

Don't miss Sports

Amsterdam ArenA
Trading your right arm could be your only chance to step inside this venue... and it may well be worth it. See page 228.

Dutch football mania
No tickets? No problem... Experience a new form of nationalism by donning team colours and going with the flow at any bar broadcasting the match.

Field hockey
Head south to Amstelveen and find out what all the fuss is about. The Dutch are tops in this sport. See page 229.

Friday Night Skate
Locals colour the streets of Amsterdam, but anyone's welcome to take part. See page 228.

Olympisch Stadion
Sydney who? Amsterdam's landmark stadium just had a facelift, and is much the better for it. See page 76.

Darts

Darts has undergone a renaissance of sorts in Holland since Amsterdam's own Raymond 'Barny' van Barneveld won the world title in 1998 and 1999, with local tram driver Co Stompe also helping to raise the sport's profile. Now, most competitions are televised. The Dutch Darts Federation (**NDF**) looks after the sport nationally, but much of the organisation is done by regional affiliates.

Some 150 cafés in Amsterdam boast 180 teams and 1,300 members affiliated to **DORA** (662 0247), which organises leagues from September to May plus smaller summer competitions. The **ADB** (682 1970) is smaller, but still has 400 members who play in cafés in and around the city. It's usually easy to find a café in which to play, but if you're serious, try **De Vluchtheuvel** (Van Woustraat 174; 662 5665) or **Matchroom Sloten** (Slimmeweg 8; 617 7062).

Football

Nothing brings out Dutch sports enthusiasm more than football. This is, of course, not all that surprising. For years, Dutch teams have excelled, making even friendly matches exciting national events. Considering its relatively small population, the Netherlands has cultivated and produced a extraordinary number of star players, coveted throughout the world.

Just as in other countries, there's a huge gap between the big football clubs in the Netherlands and the smaller teams. After Ajax, PSV and Feyenoord, it's a long way down to the rest. The Dutch season runs from late August until late May, with a break from Christmas until early February. Pleasingly, you can still watch the big games on network TV, though following games at local cafés surrounded by partisan supporters may prove a viable and exciting alternative if you can manage to peer over the heads.

Unfortunately, the reputation of Dutch football has been tarnished somewhat thanks to hooliganism. The main source of tension lies between small groups of supporters who have repeatedly and violently clashed in the past. Hooliganism has become a political issue and heated matches always spark debates between organisers, police and supporters. Thanks to the efforts to keep a tighter rein on hooliganism, purchasing tickets for pro matches is nearly impossible, with possession of a Personal Club Card now a prerequisite for securing tickets to any Dutch football league event. The waiting lists for the cards are discouragingly long, and you'll be lucky if you get in.

Ajax

Amsterdam ArenA, Arena Boulevard 29, South-East (311 1444). Metro Strandvliet or Metro/NS rail Bijlmer. **Matches** 2.30pm Sun, plus some other games midweek. **Tickets** ƒ27,50-ƒ57,50. **Credit** AmEx, DC, MC, V (advance bookings only).

Thinking about going to an Ajax game? Think again: tickets for Ajax are worth more than their weight in gold. However, while many star players have departed for more lucrative contracts abroad and the team isn't the super-dominant force it once was, the matches are still exciting and the team's future looks bright.

Feyenoord

De Kuip, Van Zandvlietplein 3, Rotterdam (information 010 292 6888/tickets 010 292 3888). NS rail Rotterdam Centraal Station, then bus 46. **Matches** 2.30pm Sun, plus some other games midweek. **Tickets** ƒ27,50-ƒ42,50. **Credit** AmEx, DC, MC, V.

Much as it has been for years, Feyenoord is still struggling to keep up with its illustrious rivals **PSV** (*see p229*) and **Ajax**. The local fans are loyal almost beyond the call of duty, but the 52,000-capacity stadium doesn't always fill up. Even so, tickets are hard to come by without a Personal Club Card.

Blade runners

Upon first hearing the shrill whistling and chanted countdown while strolling through Vondelpark, you may find yourself drawn into the belief that you're about to be stampeded by a herd of excitable marathon runners. Don't panic, though: it'll only be the skate-mad Dutch and their contagious enthusiasm as they prepare for the start of the **Friday Night Skate**.

With the possible exception of the few who still prefer the ice version, Amsterdammers have taken inline skating to their hearts like ducks to a gracht. During peak season, some 3,500 skaters take part in the weekly Friday Night Skate (or FNS). In summer, the sheer size of the crowd slows the pace to manageable levels, and the experience is rather pleasant.

However, a dry Amsterdam night in February draws a very different crowd, and makes for a very different experience. Close to 100 hardcore skaters take part during the winter months, and a scarily competent bunch they are, too. You'll find yourself practically running in your skates in order to keep up, but once you're in the middle of the pack, be prepared for some serious trick-dodging, as skaters jump and spin past you, tear through the park backwards and offer a hand with which they'll tow you up to some stomach-churning speeds. Be prepared for some seriously sore thighs, but also for a great social scene at the end of the blade; assuming you can keep up with the pace, that is. New routes are selected each week, always looping around the city.

PSV

Philips Stadium, Frederiklaan 10A, Eindhoven (040 250 5501). NS rail Eindhoven, then bus 4, 13. Matches 2.30pm Sun, plus some other games midweek. **Tickets** ƒ27,50-ƒ70. **Credit** AmEx, DC, MC, V.

Eindhoven's team now dominates Dutch football. Unsurprisingly, tickets are tough to get hold of.

Other teams

Though stadiums may not be full, the Personal Club Card is sure to prove a big obstacle for any visitors wanting to see a Premier League game. Instead, try the First Division, which has a rather more flexible policy on the card. Failing that, some of the top amateur clubs in the city – **Blauw Wit**, **DGC** and **Elinkwijk** among them – play surprisingly decent football. For information, or if you fancy a game, contact the Amsterdam **KNVB** on 487 9130.

Hockey

While both ice and field hockey are played in the Netherlands, the word 'hockey' is synonymous with field hockey to the Dutch, and is immensely popular. The Dutch Hockey Association (**KNHB**) boasts the largest

Pleasingly, the stewards who lead the Friday Night Skate put a premium on safety. Some skate on ahead to clear junctions so skaters have short waits at traffic lights; others act as look-outs to keep the group together, making sure no one falls behind; and there are even skating medics on hand.

Assuming you're a reasonably competent skater, it's well worth turning out, if not for the beauty of the floodlit Filmmuseum, then to see the spectacular attire worn by one infamous skater. Come rain or come shine, this particular gentleman skates in a G-string, 'for maximum freedom of movement'. Almost as entertaining are the expressions on the faces of passers-by as they catch sight of him in cropped leather jacket, sky-blue rollerboots and silver thong showing off his taut butt, toned thighs and well-packed pouch. Yikes.

And if you can't make the FNS – which kicks off at 8pm every Friday from Vondelpark, near the Filmmuseum entrance, and lasts around three hours – then don't despair: there is a Tuesday night version from the first week in July to the start of September in Spaarnwoude, a short train ride north-west of the city. The **Tuesday Night Skate** kicks off at 8pm from outside Het Buitenhuis in Spaarnwoude.

Other events during the year include marathons, midnight skates, roller discos, and the **Liptonice Inline Challenge**, held annually in Zandvoort, on the coast west of Amsterdam, on the last Sunday in August. Organised by Consultations In Sport (CIS), the event incorporates demonstrations and clinics, hosts inline basketball and street hockey games, and publicises new products and fitness skating. There are several routes offering something to suit everyone, plus a half-pipe for tricksters.

The **Dam-to-Dam Inline** is another annual event, held in mid-September, and is extremely popular among the skating fraternity. In 1999, though, there was an accident in the IJ Tunnel after some of the 3,000 participating skaters lost control on the incline. The ensuing pile-up involved 70 people, though the majority were, thankfully, only slightly injured. While the FNS does not take bladers under the IJ Tunnel – and has a reassuringly accident-free record – CIS, the organisers of the Dam-to-Dam, plan to use the IJ Tunnel again in the future, though as of mid-2000, it wasn't known what preventative measures they plan to take.

Still, in this bike-friendly – for which, read 'largely traffic-free' – town, skaters should rest assured that their whims will on the whole be catered for extremely well. G-strings, though, are optional.

Dam-to-Dam Inline

070 418 2114/www.cis.nl.

Friday Night Skate

www.fridaynightskate.nl/ info@fridaynightskate.nl.

Liptonice Inline Challenge

070 418 2125/www.cis.nl

Marathons

663 0781/www.amsterdammarathon.nl.

Midnight skates (Utrecht)

030 286 2871.

Roller discos

682 3456/620 6767.

Tuesday Night Skate

www.xs4all.nl/~justb/skating/wheels/html/ events.html.

Arts & Entertainment

number of affiliated teams of any equivalent association in the world. They're good, too: both the Dutch men's and women's teams are consistently ranked at the top. The 7,000-capacity Wagener Stadium in Amstelveen is used for club games and internationals. The many clubs in the area welcome players and spectators; details of the local teams are available from Mr A Flokstra of the North Holland district of the KNHB (644 3830) or from the KNHB Bunnik (030 656 6444). The season runs from September until May.

While ice hockey's popularity is nowhere near that of field hockey, matches can be exciting. Contact the **Jaap Edenhal** (694 9894) to find out when Amsterdam's Boretti Tigers are playing. The **Dutch Ice Hockey Union** can be reached on 079 341 7574.

Recent variations on hockey combine Dutch field prowess with new twists. Interest in inline and floor hockey has taken off in the city, though it may be too early to speak of pro leagues. For further information, contact Rob de Kooning of the **Netherlands Floorball and Unihockey Federation** on 618 7345, or log on to www.unihockey.nl/nefub.

Kaatsen

A forerunner to tennis, but using the hands to hit the ball, kaatsen was banned between 1500 and 1750 because of the nuisance it caused. However, this authentic Dutch sport – played on a 60-metre by 32-metre (197-foot by 105-foot) field, with two teams of three players – is still popular in Friesland, where many competitions are held. Contact governing body the **KNKB** (0517 397300) or the **KC Amsterdam Kaatsclub** (613 5679) for details of events in the city.

Korfball

Korfball was developed by an Amsterdam teacher in 1902, and is best described as a quirky form of basketball. Its appeal has always been strong in the Netherlands and has grown considerably abroad. The season has three stages: from September to mid-November and from April to June, games are played outdoors, while from mid-November to March, it heads indoors. Contact the **North Holland KNKV** (075 635 4065) for more details.

Motor sport

TT Races

De Haar Circuit, Assen (0592 321321/race day information 0592 380367). Exit Assen south off A28, then follow signs. **Date** *Grand Prix late June.* **Tickets** *ƒ60; ƒ25 children.* **No credit cards.**

More than 100,000 people come to the TT, with the Grand Prix races for sidecars and assorted bikes particularly popular. Tickets can be booked in advance from TT Assen, Postbus 150, 9400 AD Assen (fax 0592 356911).

Zandvoort

Circuit Park Zandvoort, Burgemeester Van Alphenstraat, Zandfoort (023 574 0740/information 023 574 0750). NS rail Zandvoort. **Tickets** *ƒ15-ƒ55.* **No credit cards.**
This racing track, about 40 minutes' drive from Amsterdam, was once a venue for Formula One racing. A programme of international races runs roughly every other weekend from March to October, with tickets available from 8am on the day.

Rugby

More than 100 clubs take part in various competitions throughout the country, with four clubs active in and around Amsterdam. The season runs from September until May. For information on the Heineken Rugby Sevens tournament, matches or clubs that welcome new members, contact the **National Rugby Board** on 480 8100.

Volleyball

Thanks to the success of both men's and women's national teams, volleyball is on the up and up in Holland. For details of events and local clubs, contact the **NeVoBo** on 0348 411994 (national office) or 693 6458 (Amsterdam office).

Fitness & leisure

Athletics

There are four athletics tracks in Amsterdam: Elzenhagen, Olympiaplein, Ookmeer and Chris Bergerbaan. The *Trimloopboekje*, published every August, lists all running events in the Netherlands. The four major events in Amsterdam are the **Vondelparkloop** in January; June's **Grachtenloop** around the city's canals (*see also page 170*); the **Dam tot Damloop** from Amsterdam to Zaandam in late September; and the **Amsterdam Marathon**, which will celebrate its 25th anniversary in October 2000. Further details on athletics in Holland are available from the **KNAU** on 030 608 7300.

Badminton

There are several badminton clubs in Amsterdam. Contact the **Amsterdam Badminton Union** on 697 3758 for more details on the sport in the city.

Basketball

While public basketball courts are a rarity in the city centre, there are several clubs in Amsterdam that welcome players: call the **NBB** Amsterdam district office on 675 0462 for more information.

Golf

The exclusive reputation golf used to have in Holland is fading. These days, courses are crowded with players from all walks of life, especially at weekends. A safety certification is required for professional courses, but public courses are open to everyone, with many courses also offering driving ranges. You can play at a private club if introduced by a member, or if you belong to a British club; otherwise, there are several public courses open to everyone. For details, see the *Amsterdam Yellow Pages*, or contact the **Amsterdam Golf Club** (497 7866).

De Hoge Dijk

Abcouderstraatweg 46, Amsterdam ZO (0294 281241/285313). Metro Nieuw Gein; from Holendrecht stop, take bus 120, 126 to Abcoude. **Open** dawn-dusk daily. **Rates** ƒ65. *Club hire* ƒ25. **Credit** AmEx, DC, MC, V.
A public 18-hole polder course on the edge of Amsterdam. Reservations are required.

Golfbaan Sloten

Sloterweg 1045, Sloten (614 2402). Bus 145. **Open** *Mid June-mid Aug* 8.30am-dusk daily. *Mid Aug-mid June* 8.30am-6pm Mon-Fri; closed Sat, Sun. **Rates** *Golf* ƒ21,50; ƒ17,50 after 6.30pm. *Driving range* ƒ7 (incl 60 balls). *Club hire* ƒ12,50 half-set. **No credit cards**.
A nine-hole public course, with a driving range and practice green. Booking is advisable on weekends.

Golfpark Spaarnwoude

Het Hogeland 2, Velsen-Zuid, Spaarnwoude (023 538 5599). Bus 82. **Open** *Summer* 6.30am-8.30pm daily. *Winter* 8.30am-3.30pm daily. **Rates** *18-hole course* ƒ50. *9-hole courses* ƒ25. *Pitch & putt* ƒ10. **No credit cards**.
An 18-hole course, with two short courses and a pitch and putt. Reservations can be made up to three days ahead.

Health & fitness

Look under 'Fitnesscentra' in the *Amsterdam Yellow Pages* for a full listing of health centres.

A Bigger Splash

Looiersgracht 26-30, Jordaan (624 8404). Tram 7, 10, 17, 20. **Open** 7am-midnight daily. **Admission** ƒ35/day; ƒ87,50/wk; ƒ150/2 wks; ƒ140 (plus ƒ100 membership)/mth. **Credit** AmEx, DC, V. **Map** p310 C5.

Facilities at A Bigger Splash include a weights room, Turkish baths, a massage service and a sauna, all included in the price. There are ten aerobics classes daily, and personal trainers are available.

The Garden

Jodenbreestraat 158, Old Centre: Old Side (626 8772). Tram 9, 14, 20/Metro Waterlooplein. **Open** 9am-11pm Mon, Wed, Fri; noon-11pm Tue, Thur; 11am-6.30pm Sat; 10am-7pm Sun. **Admission** *Training & shower* ƒ16,50/day; ƒ120/10 visits. *Training & sauna* ƒ23,50/day; ƒ160/10 visits. *Sauna* ƒ19,50/day. **No credit cards**. **Map** p307 E3.
The cheapest all-in-one price in town gives you the choice of high- and low-impact and step aerobics, bodyshape, callisthenics and stretching. There's also a sun studio and hairdressers, and masseurs are available.

Sporting Club Leidseplein

Korte Leidsedwarsstraat 18, Grachtengordel: East (620 6631). Tram 1, 2, 5, 6, 7, 10, 20. **Open** 9am-midnight Mon-Fri; 10am-6pm Sat, Sun. **Admission** ƒ25/day; ƒ110/mth. **No credit cards**. **Map** p310 C5.
A central health club with weights, aerobics classes and a sauna. Individual training programmes can be put together.

Horse riding

The two main centres – **De Amsterdamse Manege** (643 1342) and **Nieuw Amstelland Manege** (643 2468) – both offer rides daily in the Amsterdam Bos at ƒ30 an hour for adults; lessons are available for kids. For more details, see 'Maneges' in the *Amsterdam Yellow Pages*.

Saunas

Most Dutch saunas are mixed, and covering up is frowned upon. But most offer women-only times as well. See also the *Amsterdam Yellow Pages* under 'Saunas', **Health & fitness** *opposite, and page 210*.

Deco Sauna

Herengracht 115, Grachtengordel: West (623 8215). Tram 1, 2, 5, 13, 17, 20. **Open** 11am-11pm Mon-Sat; 1-6pm Sun. **Admission** ƒ27,50; ƒ18,50 Mon-Fri before 2pm, plus ƒ2 each hr after 2pm; half-price under-12s before 8pm. **No credit cards**. **Map** p306 C2.
The most beautiful sauna in town, with art deco glass panels and murals. Facilities include a Turkish bath, a Finnish sauna, a cold plunge bath and a solarium. Massages, Shiatsu, and skin and beauty care are by appointment.

De Keizer

Keizersgracht 124, Grachtengordel: West (622 7504). Tram 1, 2, 5, 13, 17, 20. **Open** noon-11pm Mon, Wed, Fri, Sat; 10am-11pm Tue, Thur; noon-8pm Sun. **Admission** ƒ26. **No credit cards**. **Map** p306 C2.

Tucked away in the servants' quarters of this 18th-century canal house is a full sauna that conjures up Hollywood interpretations of ancient Rome.

Skateboarding, inlining & rollerskating

While the new half-pipe at Museumplein is considered by locals to be too dangerous, there are others scattered throughout neighbourhoods just outside the city centre. Inliners and rollerskaters flock to Amsterdam for the miles of bike paths and the Vondelpark.

If conditions are dry enough, check out the **Friday Night Skate**, an informal and popular tour through Amsterdam. Wearing protective gear and blinkers is strongly encouraged, and you must be able to stop at intersections. *See page 228* **Blade runners**.

Consult the *Amsterdam Yellow Pages* (under 'Sport en Spelartikelen') for a complete list of specialist shops and rental locations.

Balance
Overtoom 464-6, Museum Quarter (489 4723). Tram 1, 6. **Open** 1-6pm Mon; 10am-6pm Tue, Wed, Fri; 10am-9pm Thur; 9.30am-5pm Sat; closed Sun. **Rates** ƒ17,50/day; ƒ65/week; plus ƒ100 deposit with ID. **Credit** MC, V.
The rates for skate hire here include protection for the wrists, knees and elbows, but not helmets, which cost ƒ2,50 a day or ƒ10 a week to hire.

Rent A Skate
Vondelpark 7; entrance at Amstelveenseweg, Museum Quarter (06 5466 2262 mobile). Tram 1, 2, 3, 5, 6, 12, 20. **Open** Apr-Oct 11am-9.30pm Mon-Fri; 10.30am-8pm Sat, Sun. **Rates** ƒ7,50/hr; ƒ15/3 hrs; ƒ25/day; plus ƒ50 deposit with ID. **No credit cards**. **Map** p310 C6.
There are two branches of in Vondelpark: one at the café by the Amstelveenseweg, the other over at the Melkgroothuis.

Skating

Skating in the Netherlands is all about blades, not wheels, and we're not talking figure skating either. Dutch skating is about long-distance treks and tours, and it's not for the faint-hearted. However, conditions are rarely right nowadays: the scenes depicted by the old masters of people skating on the canals are, in general, a thing of the past.

If conditions are right – the ice must be very thick, which is why the race hasn't been held since 1997 – look out for the **Elfstedentocht**, a 200-kilometre (124-mile) race round Friesland. With up to 10,000 people taking part – starting early and finishing by dusk – it's a massive national event. You must be a member of the Elfstedenvereniging association to compete, and even then, lots are drawn as numbers are limited. However, exceptions are sometimes made for foreigners.

If the canals freeze over in Amsterdam and you fancy a skate, then be careful: the ice is often weak, particularly under the bridges. If in doubt, ask one of the locals or head to the **Jaap Edenhal** 400-metre ice track at Radioweg 64 (694 9652). Some of the ponds and lakes in and around Amsterdam may offer safer opportunities: contact the **KNSB** in Amersfoort (0334 621784) for information on conditions and organised events.

Snooker & carambole

There are several halls in Amsterdam where you can play snooker or pool fairly cheaply. Carambole, played on a table without pockets, is a popular variation. Traditionally, billiards (*biljart*) has been associated with cafés: outside the centre of town, there are many cafés with billiards and pool tables, while in town, many bars have pool tables, though they're often pretty scruffy and ill-maintained. A full listing of clubs can be found in the *Amsterdam Yellow Pages* under 'Biljartzalen'.

Snookercentre Bavaria
Van Ostadestraat 97, De Pijp (676 4059). Tram 3, 12, 20, 24, 25. **Open** 11am-1am Mon-Thur, Sun; 11am-2am Fri, Sat. *Pool tables* from 2pm. **Rates** ƒ15/hr snooker; ƒ13,70/hr pool; ƒ10/hr carambole. **No credit cards**.
Spread over four floors here, the Bavaria boasts one carambole table, 26 billiards tables and seven snooker tables, with the first floor a pool hall. Some nights are reserved for members only.

De Keizer
Keizersgracht 256, Grachtengordel: West (623 1586). Tram 13, 14, 17, 20. **Open** noon-1am Mon-Thur; noon-2am Fri, Sat; 1pm-1am Sun. **Rates** ƒ10/hr before 7pm; ƒ13-ƒ16/hr after 7pm. *Membership* ƒ100/yr. **No credit cards**. **Map** p306 C3.
There are two professional-size pool tables and seven snooker tables here, all of which are in separate rooms. There are phones in all rooms, so players can phone orders down to the bar and have drinks or sandwiches sent up. Members pay less for tables, but all are welcome. The most civilised snooker club in Amsterdam.

Snooker Club OudWest
Overtoom 209, Museum Quarter (618 8019). Tram 1, 6/bus 171, 172. **Open** noon-1am Mon-Thur, Sun; noon-2am Fri, Sat. **Rates** ƒ10/hr before 2pm; ƒ15/hr after 2pm. *Membership* ƒ50/yr. **No credit cards**. **Map** p309 B6.
The atmosphere in this former church is quiet, making it a club for the serious snooker player. Members pay ƒ2,50 less an hour.

Orange/squash at the **Sporting Club Leidseplein**. *See p231*.

Sports centre

Borchland Sportcentrum

Borchlandweg 6-12, South-East (696 1441). Metro Strandvliet. **Open** 7.30am-midnight daily. **Rates** varies with activity; phone for details. **Credit** AmEx, DC, MC, V.

The only big *omni-sportcentrum* (sports centre) in Amsterdam – a Metro ride out of the centre – offers squash, outdoor and indoor tennis, ten-pin bowling, badminton and, on a non-sporting level, a restaurant. It's impossible to list all the prices here, but rates are higher in the evening and at weekends.

Squash

For details of local clubs, phone the **Amsterdam Squash Rackets Club** on 662 8767. Details of squash courts can be found in the *Amsterdam Yellow Pages* under 'Squashbanen'.

Dicky Squash

Gustav Mahlerlaan 16, Zuid (646 2266). Tram 5/ Metro 51. **Open** 9.30am-12.30am Mon-Fri; 9.30am-6pm Sat, Sun. **Rates** ƒ25-ƒ35/hr; ƒ15-ƒ20/half-hr. **Membership** ƒ425-ƒ645. **No credit cards**.

This wonderfully named place caters for experienced players, with 12 courts and a sauna.

Squash City

Ketelmakerstraat 6, West (626 7883). Bus 18, 22. **Open** 8.45am-midnight Mon-Fri; 8.45am-9pm Sat, Sun. **Rates** ƒ14-ƒ18,50/45min (incl sauna). **Credit** AmEx, MC, V.

The place to head if you see squash as more of a hobby than a battle. There are 12 courts, a sauna, a

weights room and two aerobics rooms. Keep an eye out for the Amsterdam Admirals' Cheerleading Squad that trains here.

Swimming

The opening times of both indoor and outdoor pools in Amsterdam vary hugely, with hours set aside for various groups, including women, babies, toddlers and those who like to swim nude. While it's best to phone ahead, most pools set aside lanes for swimming lengths in the early morning, mid-afternoon and evening. Look in the *Amsterdam Yellow Pages* under 'Zwembaden' for a full list of pools.

Flevoparkbad (outdoor)

Zeeburgerdijk 630, Oost (692 5030). Tram 14. **Open** May-early Sept 10am-5.30pm (10am-7pm in hotter weather) daily. **Admission** ƒ4,75; ƒ4,50 concessions; from 1hr before closing ƒ2,50. **No credit cards**.

Two huge pools with kids' areas, a playground and a sunbathing area.

Marnixbad (indoor)

Marnixplein 9, The Jordaan (625 4843). Tram 3, 7, 10. **Open** daily, times vary. **Admission** ƒ4,75; ƒ3-ƒ4 concessions. **Map** p305 B3. **No credit cards**.

As well as a 25m indoor pool with water slides and a whirlpool, Marnixbad also boasts a sauna.

Mirandabad (indoor & outdoor)

De Mirandalaan 9, Zuid (622 8080/644 6637/ www.mirandabad.nl). Tram 15/bus 169. **Open** 7am-10pm Mon-Fri; 9.30am-5pm Sat, Sun. **Admission** ƒ6,25; ƒ4,50 over-65s. **No credit cards**.

Pool your resources at the splendid **Marnixbad**. *See p233.*

The only sub-tropical pool in Amsterdam, De Mirandabad is very clean, with a stone beach and a wave machine. It's not good for swimming lengths, but there's fun to be had on the waterslide and in the whirlpool and outdoor pool. There's also squash courts here, and a restaurant if you get peckish.

Zuiderbad (indoor)

Hobbemastraat 26, Museum Quarter (671 0287). Tram 2, 16, 24, 25. **Open** times vary; call for details. **Admission** ƒ4,75; ƒ4,25 4-11s; ƒ3 over-65s; ƒ2,75 1-3s. **No credit cards. Map** p310 D5.
One of the country's oldest pools, the Zuiderbad was built in 1912. Exhibitionists should note that there's nude swimming on Sundays, 4-5pm.

Table tennis

For full details of clubs and facilities in Amsterdam, contact the **Nederlandse Tafeltennis Bond** on 079 341 4811.

Tafeltennis Centrum Amsterdam

Keizersgracht 209, Grachtengordel: West (624 5780). Tram 13, 14, 17, 20. **Open** 2pm-1am Mon-Sat; 1-8pm Sun. **Rates** ƒ14/hr (incl bats and balls). **No credit cards. Map** p306 C3.
One of the few places where you can both ping *and* pong in town. As such, it can get busy and booking is advisable. In addition to the tables, there are also showers and a bar.

Amstelpark
*Koenenkade 8, Amstelveen (301 0700). Bus 170,
171, 172 from Amsterdam Centraal Station; 169
from Amstel Station.* **Open** 8am-11pm daily. **Rates**
*ƒ35/hr Apr-Sept; ƒ45 Oct-Mar. Membership ƒ280
Apr-Sept.* **Credit** AmEx, DC, MC, V.
All in all, 42 courts: during the summer, there are
ten indoor courts, and in the winter six of the outdoor courts are covered over. There are also 12
squash courts, a Turkish bath, a sauna, a swimming
pool and a shop. Rackets can be hired for ƒ5.

Tennishal Kadoelen
*Sportpark Kadoelen 5, Kadoelenweg, Noord (631
3194). Bus 92.* **Open** 9am-11pm daily. **Rates** *Mid
Sept-mid Apr ƒ30-ƒ40/hr. Mid Apr-mid Sept
ƒ27,50/hr.* **No credit cards.**
Kadoelen is subsidised by the local council, so the
nine indoor courts cost less to hire than elsewhere.
Tennis lessons can be arranged in advance.

Ten-pin bowling

Several places mentioned above, such as the
Borchland Sportscentrum (*see page 233*),
have lanes; see the *Amsterdam Yellow Pages*
under 'Bowlingbanen'. Phone the **Nederlandse
Bowling Federatie** on 010 473 5581 for more
details on all aspects of the sport, including
competitions and leagues.

Knijn Bowling
Scheldeplein 3, Zuid (664 2211). Tram 4. **Open**
10am-1am Mon-Fri; noon-1am Sat; noon-midnight
Sun. **Rates** *ƒ30-ƒ40/hr Mon-Thur; ƒ30-ƒ45/hr Fri,
Sat; ƒ42,50/hr Sun.* **Lanes** 18; max 6 persons per
lane. **Credit** AmEx, MC, V.

Watersports

Holland has loads of water, and watersports are
accordingly very popular: sailboards are normal
holiday luggage for the Dutch. If you want to go
sailing, visit Loosdrecht (25km/15 miles south-
east of Amsterdam) or go to the IJsselmeer.
Catamarans can be rented in Muiden (20km/12
miles east of Amsterdam). For details on
canoeing, phone the **NKB** on 033 462 2341.
Most watersports schools ask for a deposit and
ID when you rent a boat.

ROWING
There are rowing clubs on the Amstel and at the
Bosbaan (the former Olympic rowing course) in
the Amsterdam Bos. For full details, call the
Dutch Rowing Union (**KNRB**) on 646 2740.

Gaasperplas Park
*Gaasperplas Park, South-East. Metro
Gaasperplas/bus 59, 60, 174.* **Open** 24hrs daily.
Tucked away behind the Bijlmermeer, this park's
large lake is a centre for watersports and windsurf-
ing. There's also a campsite.

Tennis

For full information on competitions – including
the popular Dutch Open, held in Hilversum
every August – and clubs, call the **KNTLB
Amsterdam Office** on 301 0743 (open 11am-
3pm Mon-Fri); the national office can be reached
on 033 454 2600. A full listing of courts, both
indoor and outdoor, can be found in the
Amsterdam Yellow Pages under 'Tennisparken
en -hallen'. If your serve is a little rusty or
your forehand has gone backwards, then
you'll be pleased to know that many of the
courts offer lessons.

Theatre & Dance

The whole world's a stage, and heaps of its performers are in Amsterdam.

Theatre

The origins of Dutch theatre are twofold. The first is found in the liturgy of Catholic worship way back at the beginning of the 12th century, the other in the rituals that marked the beginning of a new season, including the festivities held at annual fairs. Hence the tent show tradition that's survived in the likes of **Parade** and **Boulevard** (*see pages 240-2*).

Dutch theatre, though, became far more developed in the 17th century, a period now referred to as 'the Golden Age of Dramatic Art'. The significance of this period is underlined by the opening of the Amsterdamse Schouwburg in 1638 (now the **Stadsschouwburg**; *see page 239*), the Municipal Theatre. The 18th century found a transition from a declamatory style of acting to a relatively realistic style, and, though the 19th century saw comic shows dominate, it also saw the founding, in 1874, of the Royal Dutch Drama Society. Consisting of a drama school, a magazine and a theatrical company, its aim was to re-establish theatre as an art.

In line with European trends, Dutch theatre saw a change, to a more socially conscious and politically motivated art form, in the early part of the 20th century. It was at this time that the uniquely Dutch cabaret style developed: a mix of earthy, witty songs and monologues infused with social commentary, it's still very much evident in the work of Freek de Jong and Hans Teeuwen. After World War II, though, theatre increasingly became viewed as a necessary instrument in the education of the population, and it was deemed important to produce some works that were free from commercial constraints. The government soon became directly involved in theatre by supplying subsidies to companies; indeed, in the bigger cities, repertory companies were guaranteed subsidies on the condition that they took time to perform outside their own theatres, in an attempt to ensure that they reached a wider audience throughout the country.

However, the 1960s were highlighted by Aktie Tomaat ('tomato campaign'), a fierce attack against what protesters saw as the lack of social involvement by establishment theatre

A panorama of talent plays at the **Bellevue**. See p237.

Information & bookings

Uitlijn, run by the AUB, offers nationwide information on theatre performances and concerts, as well as selling tickets. From within Amsterdam – and, for that matter, anywhere else in the Netherlands – call 0900 0191 (open 9am-9pm daily, premium rate number). If you're calling from abroad, dial +31 20 621 1288 (calls charged at standard rates; this number can only be used from outside the Netherlands). All major credit cards are accepted, and tickets will either be sent out by post or left at the theatre on the night of the performance. A booking fee of ƒ6 is charged per ticket.

Otherwise, log on to **www.uitlijn.nl**, where commission is ƒ5,50 per ticket, or visit the **AUB Ticketshop** (Leidseplein 26, open 10am-6pm Mon-Wed, Fri-Sun, 10am-9pm Thur), which has plentiful information on events and sells tickets (with a booking fee of ƒ3,50 per ticket) and theatre gift vouchers.

Look out, too, for *Uitkrant*, a free monthly magazine that offers details of all manner of performances and events, available from theatres, bookshops and the AUB Ticketshop; it's online at www.uitkrant.nl.

The **Amsterdam Tourist Board** also sells theatre tickets over the counter, but not via the phone. For information on events, head to its offices (at Stationplein, at the corner of Leidseplein and Leidsestraat, and at Stadionplein opposite the Olympic Stadium), email info@amsterdamtourist.nl or phone 0900 400 4040 (+31 20 551 2525 if calling from abroad).

The **GWK Ticket Network** operates from most post offices and GWK money exchange offices across the Netherlands. Theatre tickets can be purchased at most branches, though many smaller post offices are unable to offer such a service. For more information, call 569 0690, or log on to www.gwk.nl.

groups. Radicals threw tomatoes at the offending casts, causing the closure of the Nederlandse Comedie and the Rotterdamse Toneel. The movement, though, was in part responsible for more cash being pumped into theatre. Groups such as Werktheater were set up as mini-laboratories for practical theatre research, and adventurous groups such as the Festival of Fools, which took its inspiration from carnival-style sideshows, became popular. But the '80s and '90s saw a turnaround in this situation: cuts in subsidy meant that more established groups retained their power while smaller companies struggled to stay afloat. The situation that many companies were left in led to them experimenting with such essentials as locations – many groups squatted buildings, while others worked on the streets.

The 21st century has got off on a better footing with the redevelopment of the NSDM Shipyard into a huge cultural centre (*see page 240*). Many groups and companies that had been turfed out of squatted arts centres will now have a place to settle without the threat of eviction. In addition, there are now better support systems to assist with production and promotion of theatre as a whole, while the International Theaterschool has kept a new stock of performers ready to hit the stage.

A note of caution: unless non-Dutch speakers fancy spending the evening wondering what the hell is going on, it's advisable to always phone and check if your chosen show is in English.

Venues

Badhuis Theater de Bochel
Andreas Bonnstraat 28, Oost (668 5102). Tram 3, 6, 7, 10, 20. **Box office** open half-hour prior to performance; reservations taken until 30min before start of performance. **Performances** times vary. **Tickets** ƒ7,50-ƒ15. **No credit cards. Map** p312 G4. Located in a square, this old bathhouse is now a cultural centre of sorts. On Fridays and Saturdays, the venue hosts cult dance parties, but during the rest of the week, there are multicultural events including children's theatre activities and workshops. The space is set to be classified as a state monument in 2000, when renovations will begin.

De Balie
Kleine Gartmanplantsoen 10, Grachtengordel: East (553 5100/www.balie.nl). Tram 1, 2, 5, 6, 7, 10, 20. **Box office** 1-6pm or until start of performance Mon-Fri; 5pm-start of performance Sat; 90min before performance Sun. **Performances** times vary. **Tickets** ƒ10-ƒ18,50. **No credit cards. Map** p310 D5. This cultural centre stages theatre, new media, cinema and literary events, plus lectures, debates, discussions and special projects on political issues. All informally influence Amsterdam's public opinions and lifestyle. There's a café here, too. *See also p129.*

Bellevue
Leidsekade 90, Grachtengordel: East (530 5301/ www.theaterbellevue.nl). Tram 1, 2, 5, 6, 7, 10, 20. **Box office** 11am-6pm or until start of performance daily. **Performances** 8.30pm. **Tickets** ƒ17,50-ƒ25. **Credit** AmEx, DC, MC, V. **Map** p310 C5.

Arts & Entertainment

A glimpse at the stunning 18th-century architecture of **Felix Meritis.**

A medium-sized venue just a short walk from Leidseplein, the Bellevue offers dance, serious spoken theatre and cabaret, performed by a mix of hot Dutch talent and imported international artists.

Boom Chicago

Leidseplein Theater, Leidseplein 12, Grachtengordel: East (423 0101/www.boomchicago.nl). Tram 1, 2, 5, 6, 7, 10, 20. **Box office** noon-8.30pm Mon-Thur, Sun; noon-11.30pm Fri, Sat; noon-5pm Sun in winter. **Performances** 8.15pm Mon-Fri, Sun; 7.45pm, 11.15pm Sat. *Late show* 11.30pm Fri. **Open** *Bar & lounge* noon-1am Mon-Thur, Sun; noon-3am Fri, Sat. *Restaurant* noon-9pm daily. **Tickets** ƒ29,50-ƒ32,50. *Late show* ƒ18. **Credit** AmEx, MC, V. **Map** p310 D5.
An American improv troupe – whose theatre, right on Leidseplein also serves as an unofficial meeting point for wayward Americans – Boom Chicago is one of Amsterdam's biggest success stories. With several different shows seven nights a week (except Sundays in winter), the troupe offers a mix of rehearsed sketches and audience-prompted improvisation. The **Boom Chicago Lounge** (*see p130*) in the lobby offers cocktails, snacks and DJs (the latter Thursday through Sunday only), and there's a bar and restaurant here, too.

Theater de Cameleon

3e Kostverlorenkade 35, West (489 4656). Tram 1, 6. **Box office** from 8pm performance days only. **Performances** times vary. **Tickets** ƒ5-ƒ17,50. **No credit cards. Map** p305 A3.
A relatively new theatre in the old western part of town. Besides a wide variety of theatre performances, often in English, the Cameleon hosts music productions every Sunday at 3.30pm, and also offers theatre and voice workshops.

Comedy Café Amsterdam

Max Euweplein 43-5, Grachtengordel: East (638 3971/www.comedycafe.nl). Tram 1, 2, 5, 6, 7, 10, 20. **Box office** 9am-5pm Mon-Fri. **Performances** 9.30pm Wed; 9pm Thur, Fri, Sun; 9pm, 11.30pm Sat. **Tickets** free Wed; ƒ20 Thur-Sat; ƒ15 Sun. **Credit** AmEx, MC, V. **Map** p310 C5.
Stand-up has never been as wildly popular in Amsterdam as it is in, say, London or New York, but the Comedy Café has been doing a decent job at

getting the art a wider audience. From Thursday to Saturday, there's a stand-up show in a mix of Dutch and English. On Wednesdays, when admission is free, comics try out new material at the venue's Open Mic Night, while Sundays offer an improv show, *Off Your Head.*

Cosmic Theater

Nes 75, Old Centre: Old Side (622 8858). Tram 4, 9, 14, 16, 20, 24, 25. **Box office** *By phone* 10am-6pm Mon-Fri; from 1hr before performance. **Performances** 8.30pm. **Tickets** ƒ17,50; ƒ10 concessions. **No credit cards. Map** p306 D3.
Cosmic formed 15 years ago in the Caribbean and, after a spell in New York, ended up in Amsterdam. The company has toured widely and has developed an international reputation for its productions that address the multicultural reality of the modern world.

De Engelenbak

Nes 71 (626 3644/box office 626 6866/ www.engelenbak.nl). Tram 4, 9, 14, 16, 20, 24, 25. **Box office** *By phone* 1-7.30pm Mon-Sat. *In person* from 1hr before performance. **Performances** 8.30pm. **Tickets** ƒ12,50-ƒ18. **No credit cards. Map** p306 D3.
De Engelenbak is best known for 'Open Bak', an open-stage event each Tuesday where virtually anything goes. It's the longest-running theatre programme in the Netherlands, where everybody gets their 15 minutes of potential fame; arrive at least half an hour before the show starts in order to get a ticket. Otherwise, the best amateur groups in the country perform between Thursday and Saturday.

Felix Meritis

Keizersgracht 324, Grachtengordel: West (623 1311). Tram 1, 2, 5, 13, 17, 20. **Box office** 9am-7pm Mon-Fri, or until start of performance; 3pm-start of performance Sat, Sun. **Performances** usually 8.30pm. **Tickets** ƒ10-ƒ30. **No credit cards. Map** p310 C4.
The Felix Meritis stages a variety of international dance and theatre performances alongside its noted programme of discussions, lectures and courses about Europe and other subjects. Worth visiting, if just to see the building: built in 1787, it's situated overlooking Keizersgracht in central Amsterdam.

Gasthuis Werkplaats & Theater

*Marius van Bouwdijk Bastiaanstraat 54;
entrance opposite 1e Helmerstraat 115, Museum
Quarter (616 8942).* Tram 1, 3, 6, 12. **Box office**
noon-5pm Mon-Fri. *In person* from 1hr before start of
performance. **Performances** usually 9pm. **Tickets**
ƒ15; ƒ7,50-ƒ12,50 concessions. **No credit cards.**
Map p305 B6.

An adaptable, stageless space situated on the
grounds of an old squatted hospital – it's now fully
legit – the Gasthuis Werkplaats is often used by
young theatre students to try out their talent, as well
as being home to smaller productions. The programme is mainly of an experimental nature, it's a
good idea to check beforehand if the production is
in English. There's an open day held here once a
year: call the theatre for more information.

Koninklijk Theater Carré

*Amstel 115-25, Grachtengordel: East (622 5225).
Tram 4, 6, 7, 10, 20/Metro Weesperplein.*
Box office 10am-7pm Mon-Sat; 1-7pm Sun.
Performances 8pm. **Tickets** ƒ25-ƒ100.
Credit AmEx, DC, MC, V. **Map** p311 F4.

Formerly home to a circus, Koninklijk Theater Carré
now hosts some of the best Dutch comedians and
cabaret artists around. However, if mainstream theatre is more your thing, then look out for the Dutch
versions of popular British and American musicals
such as *42nd Street*, *Les Misérables*, *Cats*, *Fame* and
Oliver, which almost invariably end up here. Other
offerings include folk dance events, revues and even
backstage tours on Wednesdays and Saturdays
(3pm, ƒ7.50, ƒ5 children), phone for more information and reservations.

De Nieuw Amsterdam

*Grote Bickersstraat 2/4, Westerdok (627 8672). Bus
18, 22.* **Box office** 10am-5pm Mon-Fri; 7.30pm-start
of performance on performance days only.
Performances 8.30pm. **Tickets** ƒ15; ƒ12,50
students. **No credit cards. Map** p305 B1.

The brainchild of director Rufus Collins, De Nieuw
Amsterdam is the leading socially concerned theatre
company in the Netherlands. Aside from its shows,
it also runs a programme for young people set on
becoming the next big thing, known as ITS DNA.
The ensemble of actors and teachers from ITS are
overseen by Aram Adriaanse.

De Stadsschouwburg

*Leidseplein 26, Grachtengordel: East (624 2311).
Tram 1, 2, 5, 6, 7, 10, 20.* **Box office** 10am-6pm or
until start of performance Mon-Sat; from 1½hrs
before start of performance Sun. **Performances**
8.15pm. **Tickets** prices vary. **Credit** AmEx, MC, V.
Map p310 C5.

The Stadsschouwburg – 'Municipal Theatre' – is into
its third incarnation, the first two buildings having
been destroyed by fire in the 17th and 18th centuries.
The present theatre, which opened in 1894, is a beautiful and impressive baroque building, built in the
traditional horseshoe shape and seating about 950.
Aside from nurturing traditional Dutch theatre, it
also stages a wide variety of contemporary national
and international productions. The programme consists of mostly theatre but there is also dance, modern music and some light opera productions. The
theatre's Bovenzaal space plays host to small-scale
productions that are often in English.

Arts & Entertainment

Bright lights, big... horseshoe? **De Stadsschouwburg**.

Zaal 100

De Wittenstraat 100, Westerpark (688 0127). Tram 3, 10/bus 18, 22. **Box office** 1hr before start of performance. **Performances** usually 9pm. **Tickets** prices vary. **No credit cards. Map** p305 A2.

This neighbourhood cultural centre, in an ex-squat building, offers a sporadic programme in its small but cosy theatre space. The in-house group, Sub Theatre, usually performs one show every month. There's live jazz nights on Tuesdays, a big band gig, the Tri-tone Festival, every third Wednesday of the month, and performance poetry every third Thursday of the month.

Cultural complexes

Kinetic Nord at the NSDM Shipyard

The redevelopment of this old abandoned ship-building site is one of Amsterdam's most ambitious recent projects. The construction of Kinetic Nord began at the NSDM Shipyard in mid-2000; when finished, it'll be an enormous cultural centre, possibly the biggest of its kind in Europe. There'll be two main halls on the site – one for large events and concerts, and the other housing a labyrinth of spaces that will eventually include studios, a cinema, a theatre, a gallery, an art market, a skate park, performance areas and cafés. The large outdoor area, meanwhile, will afford spectacular views over the IJ river of Amsterdam.

The list of prospective residents is impressive. The **Over Het IJ** festival (*see p242*) will set up here in 2001; **Dogtroep** (*see p240*) are setting up a studio space; *Bimbotown*, Jim Whiting's unique installation of moving furniture and robots, will relocate here from Leipzig; and several local theatre companies, including Silo Theatre and the Theatre of Hell, will stage regular shows. When the site opens, hopefully in 2001, it should become one of the city's most unusual attractions. More information can be obtained by calling **Uitlijn** (0900 0191) or logging on to the website (www.uitlijn.nl).

Westergasfabriek

Haarlemmerweg 8-10, West (681 3068/ www.westergasfabriek.nl). Bus 18, 22.

This former gas factory originally supplied all of Amsterdam with gas for its street lighting. But when huge gas reserves were discovered north of Holland, it became redundant, and has since been converted into a multimedia arts complex. The site consists of 13 monumental buildings of various sizes and shapes, which variously play host to film and theatre companies, fashion shows, corporate functions, movie shoots, operas, techno parties and assorted festivals, plus bars, nightclubs and restaurants.

The site, which is still undergoing renovations, is a classic visual example of the changes that occurred throughout the 20th century, and specifically the change from industrial age to information age. In 2000, a new park is being landscaped around the buildings that will be able to hold outdoor events,

an exhibition area and café terraces. For details on the varied programme of activities and events, log on to the Westergasfabriek website (of which, pleasingly, there's an English version available).

Theatre groups

Dogtroep

632 1139/www.dogtroep.nl.

Dogtroep formed informally in 1975, when it improvised its shows on the streets. Over a quarter-century on, and it's a world-famous performance/ spectacle group that usually comes up with one site-specific production a year. Expert at visually stunning but simple theatrical effects, the group sees its work as a form of experimentation and starts each new show with just some general ideas. It then gathers a group of artists, designers, musicians and technicians to explore all the creative possibilities, with the end result invariably being a sell-out show.

Vis à Vis

073 690 0999/www.visavis.nl.

Near enough unique among Dutch theatre groups, Vis à Vis's shows are grand spectacles, with incredible moving sets and constructions. The company began in 1990, and has made a name for itself worldwide with shows such as *Central Park* and *Topolino* (in which the stage was a mobile reservoir containing 300,000 gallons of water). In 2000, it toured with *Picnic* as part of the **Over Het IJ** festival (*see p242*), and shows no signs of slacking.

Warner & Consorten

663 2656/www.warnerenconsorten.nl.

A theatre group consisting of ten Amsterdam artists from different creative backgrounds, Warner & Consorten performs mostly in unusual sites rather than in conventional theatre spaces, often tailoring its work around the site itself. Its productions have an (intentionally) rough edge to them – improvisation is a common element in the creation of its works – but are unusual chiefly for the total lack of a spoken word element: the only language W&C use is visual. In addition to creating up to 20 shows a year, the group also works with local artists, gives workshops and offers training in interdisciplinary theatre art.

Festivals

Parade

Martin Luther Kingpark, Zuid (033 465 4577/ www.mobilearts.nl). **Date** first 2wks of Aug. **Admission** free 3-5pm; *f*5 5-7pm; *f*7,50 7pm-midnight. *Shows f*2,50-*f*25. **No credit cards.**

This unique event has captured the essence of the old circus/sideshow atmosphere that's so conspicuous by its absence in today's commercial fairgrounds. Held every year in the Martin Luther Kingpark just a short tram ride out of the centre – it also takes place in Rotterdam, The Hague and

Warner & Consorten: bold, strong and visual.

Arts & Entertainment

International Theatre and Film Books (*p243*): look up and you won't believe your eyes.

Utrecht – Parade offers a plentiful selection of bizarre shows, many in beautiful circus tents. Spread between the tents is a range of cafés, bars and restaurants, as well as the odd roving performer. The event has become very popular, and many shows sell out quickly: go early, have dinner and book your tickets at the Parade Kiosk for the night (some of the smaller shows, however, sell their own tickets separately).

In 1999, Parade introduced a winter version of the festival, WinterParade, held in the gasholder of the Westergasfabriek in late December. It's a more theatrical event than its summer counterpart, and consists of a grand performance every night, plus a selection of shows from the summer season. The admission price for WinterParade includes the grand performance, with the smaller shows charging separately.

Boulevard

's Hertogenbosch (information 073 613 7671/ www.bossenova.nl). **Date** early Aug. **Admission** varies by event. **No credit cards**.

Held every summer over a period of ten days, Boulevard finds actors, musicians, dancers and performers of visual arts taking over the centre of the medieval town of Den Bosch ('s Hertogenbosch). The main festival venues are tents erected in the square next to St Jan Cathedral, though performances are also staged in the town's theatres and in other, more unlikely locations. An exciting and innovative event, Boulevard is devoted mainly to new circus acts, contemporary theatre, visual acts and dance: among the companies who've taken part in recent years are La Fura dels Baus (Spain), Circus Oz (Australia), **Vis à Vis** (Netherlands, *see p240*) and Stomp (UK). Tickets for the festival are available at Theater aan de Parade/Bosch (073 612 5125) and at all Amsterdam Tourist Board and GWK offices (*see p237* **Information & booking**).

Oerol

Terschelling (Amsterdam Tourist Board 056 244 3000/www.oerol.nl). **Date** June. **Admission** varies by event. **No credit cards**.

Terschelling, one of the five Frisian islands that sit off the north coast of Holland, has a unique landscape shaped by wind dunes, dykes and woodlands. It's usually a peaceful place, but for ten days each year, it's transformed into a cultural free state for the Oerol festival. Approximately 200 different acts perform amid the mayhem and merriment, from international theatre groups creating their own environments influenced by the landscape to world music events on the beaches, theatre expeditions through the woods to bicycle tours (cars are outlawed on the island). Oerol has a different theme each year: in 2000, it was 'When the Tide Turns'. There are regular ferries to the island (*see also p264*).

Triple X

Information 420 5316/www.triplex.nl. **Date** ten days in autumn. **Admission** varies. **No credit cards**.

Dealing in original international theatre and multi-disciplinary artistic events, Triple X is a mix of contemporary performing and visual arts. Usually held at the Westergasfabriek, funding problems delayed the event in 1999 and may have left it in a state of flux: check the website or with the AUB for full details.

Over Het IJ

NDSM Shipyard, Neveritaweg, Noord (0900 0191/ www.ijfestival.nl). Ferry from Centraal Station/bus 35, 94. **Date** June-Aug. **Tickets** *f*20-*f*35. **No credit cards**.

A summer festival of large-scale theatrical projects and avant-garde mayhem, Over Het IJ is usually interesting and frequently compelling. The highlight in 2000 was **Vis à Vis**'s predictably large-scale *Picnic* (*see p240*), while previous years have offered **Dansgroep Krisztina de Châtel** (*see p245*) in a theatrical deconstruction of Tomb Raider's Lara Croft. In other words, expect the unexpected. In 2000, the festival was held at Florapark in the north of the city, but is scheduled to return to its regular location, the NSDM Shipyard (*see p240*), in 2001.

ITs Festival

various venues in Amsterdam (527 7613/ www.its.ahk.nl). **Dates** late June. **Admission** *f*5-*f*15. **No credit cards**.

Something of a talent-spotter's dream, the International Theaterschool Festival is where students from all over the world show what they've learned during their studies. A mix of cabaret, dance, mime and drama takes place in the Theaterschool and at several other venues in town. During the festival, many congregate at the ITs lounge in the Theaterschool building (Jodenbreestraat 3).

Bookshop

International Theatre & Film Books

Leidseplein 26 (in the Stadsschouwburg building, to the right of the main entrance; 622 6489). Tram 1, 2, 5, 6, 7, 10, 20. **Open** noon-6pm Mon; 10am-6pm Tue, Wed, Fri, Sat; 10am-7pm Thur. **Credit** (min *f*100) AmEx, DC, MC, V. **Map** p310 C5.

A wide variety of international magazines and books on stage, screen, dance and opera. There's everything from books on circuses and musicals to production and technical manuals, often in English, plus texts of current theatre productions. The store also has the biggest collection of dance books and videos in Europe. A great place for a browse, but be warned: it's hard to leave without buying something.

Dance

Amsterdam's role as cultural meeting point and leading European short-stay city inevitably affects its dance culture. Thanks in part to its accessible geographical location, world-famous international companies perform frequently in and around the city. The likes of Ohad Naharin, Pina Bausch, Min Tanaka, Anna Teresa de Keersmaker, Trisha Brown, William Forsythe, Lloyd Newson and Saburo Teshigawara have all made relatively recent appearances performing in Amsterdam.

Many foreign choreographers and lead dancers are even invited to join Dutch companies for temporary engagements, and the local Theaterschool has an international student and teacher body. Indeed, many of the companies are led by international choreographers, and the bigger companies import repertoires abroad. But little of this international influence becomes a part of the Dutch society at large, as most of it flies by in passing fads and fashions.

Dance festivals

In July each year, the **Stadsschouwburg** (see page 239) hosts **Julidans**, a month-long showcase of international dance. The **International Concours for Choreographers** in Groningen, meanwhile, is a competition event at which prizes are awarded for ensemble choreographies. Details about festivals, competitions, performances, courses and workshops are available from the **Theater Instituut Nederland** (Herengracht 168, Grachtengordel: West, 623 5104, open 11am-5pm Tue-Fri, 1-5pm Sat, closed Mon, Sun).

For details of the **Holland Festival** and **Uitmarkt**, two multicultural festivals that both include a number of noteworthy dance performances in modern dance, film and music from around the world, see pages 170-1.

Spring Dance

Post Box 111, 3500 AC Utrecht (030 233 2032/www.wxs.nl/~spdance). **Dates** Apr-May. **Tickets** *f*17,50; *f*12,50 concessions.

Spring Dance, held annually in Utrecht in late April and early May, attempts to give an overview of recent developments in contemporary dance, film and music from around the world.

Holland Dance Festival

Nobelstraat 21, 2513 BC Den Haag (070 361 6142/www.wxs.nl/~hdf). **Dates** biennial; 15 Nov-1 Dec 2001, then again in 2003. **Tickets** prices vary.

Held every two years, the Holland Dance Festival takes place at three different venues, including The Hague's **Lucent Danstheater** (see p245). Many of the world's larger companies are attracted to the event, and the quality of the work is consistently high. **Nederlands Dans Theater** (see page 245) is usually the country's main representative.

Cadans

Korzo Theater, Post Box 13407, 2501 EK Den Haag (070 363 7540/www.korzo.nl). **Dates** biennial; 9-25 Nov 2000, then again in 2002. **Tickets** prices vary.

The Hague's exciting international festival of contemporary dance takes place every other November. Each work is choreographed specifically for the festival.

Arts & Entertainment

The dance scene in Amsterdam is not only international: it's also highly eclectic. Granted, passing trends leave their mark and, occasionally, contribute to a new style of dance. But trends do not just come from dance companies and choreographers: influences also flow from other media. In recent years, for example, collaborations with visual and video artists have become more and more popular. This kind of influence is at its strongest among new, up-and-coming dancers and choreographers, but is also occasionally seen on larger, more established stages. Even taking out the collaborative pieces, the Dutch dance scene is a versatile one. A wide range of styles is to be seen, from more traditional choreography to the most experimental and underground dance.

The highly developed Dutch arts subsidy system keeps many of the more acknowledged artists busy, while beginners – choreographers and dancers – are paying their bills themselves. But, luckily, this is only half the truth, since the small- and medium-scale theatres offer the newcomers a stage and, sometimes, a space in which to rehearse. And some of the more established companies invite new innovators to choreograph on their experienced dancers.

But though many associate Dutch dance with a mere two names – the **Nationale Ballet** and **Nederlands Dans Theater** (for both, *see page 245*) – there's far more to the scene than just this eminent pair. It's impossible to give a full list here, but among the Amsterdam-based choreographers worth checking out are **Krisztina de Châtel**, **Beppie Blankert**, **Truus Bronkhorst**, **Shusaku Takeuchi**, **Andrea Leine** and **Harijono Roebana**, **Itzik Galili**, **Gonnie Heggen**, **Anouk van Dijk**, **Suzy Blok and Chris Steele**, **Marcello Evelin** and **Katie Duck**.

INFORMATION & BOOKINGS

Tickets for the vast majority of performances can be reserved and purchased at the venues themselves, or from any of the various phone, online or drop-in AUB operations – such as the AUB Ticketshop and www.uitlijn.nl – or the Amsterdam Tourist Board (*see page 237* **Information & booking**), both of which will charge a booking fee for each ticket bought. *Uitkrant* (*see page 222*) offers information on dance events in the city.

(*see page 245*)

(*see page 237*

(*see page 222*)

Venues

Dance is performed at a variety of venues in Amsterdam, the biggest of which are detailed below. For information on other venues, such as the **Bellevue**, **Stadsschouwburg** and **Cosmic** theatres, *see pages 237, 238 and 239*.

see pages 237, 238 and 239.

Park life

Skaters, joggers, cyclists and sun-worshippers gather in Vondelpark each summer to do nothing. However, for three months, they're joined by culture vultures, who head to the park for its programme of music, theatre and children's events; theatrical events have, in fact, been held in the park since 1865). During the festival, Wednesdays offer a lunchtime concert and a mid-afternoon children's show; Thursday nights find a concert on the bandstand; there's a theatre show every Friday night; various events (including another theatre show) take place on Saturdays; and theatre events and pop concerts are held on Sunday afternoons.

Vondelpark Openluchttheater

Vondelpark (673 1499/ www.openluchttheater.nl). Tram 1, 2, 3, 6. **Dates** late May-Aug. **Admission** free.

Danswerkplaats Amsterdam

Arie Biemondstraat 107B, Museum Quarter (689 1789/www.euronet.nl/~dwa). Tram 1, 17. **Box office** *By phone* 10am-5pm Mon-Fri. *In person* 7.30pm-15min before start of performance. **Performances** usually 8.30pm. **Tickets** *f*12,50. **No credit cards.**
The dance studio at Danswerkplaats stages performances once a month, both here and elsewhere in the city or country.

Melkweg

Lijnbaansgracht 234A, Grachtengordel: East (531 8181/www.melkweg.nl). Tram 1, 2, 5, 6, 7, 10, 20. **Box office** 1-5pm Mon-Fri; 4-6pm Sat, Sun; also 7.30pm-start of performance. **Performances** 8.30pm. **Tickets** *f*15, plus *f*5 membership. **No credit cards. Map** p310 C5.
This interdisciplinary venue – a one-time milk factory, hence the name, which translates as 'Milky Way' – opened its doors to national and international dance and theatre groups in 1973. For many years, the small stage hosted mainly dancers and choreographers at the start of their careers. However, the recently renovated theatre now has capacity for more ambitious projects; and there's a café here, too. A special focus is placed on multimedia performances, *see also p184, 217 and 193*.

see also p184, 217 and 193.

Muiderpoorttheater

2e Van Swindenstraat 26 (668 1313). Tram 4, 6, 9, 14. **Tickets** *f*15. **No credit cards. Map** p312 H2.
Muiderpoorttheater is known primarily for its performances by international acts. Every January, this small theatre hosts the Go Solo festival, a showcase

of solo works. The monthly MAD interdisciplinary improvisation event, in which pioneers of dance and music invite and get invited to perform by new faces on the scene, is worth checking out.

Muziektheater

Amstel 3, Old Centre: Old Side (625 5455/ www.muziektheater.nl). Tram 4, 9,14, 16, 20, 24, 25/Metro Waterlooplein. **Box office** 10am-6pm or until start of performance Mon-Sat; 11.30am-6pm or until start of performance Sun. **Tickets** *f*25-*f*140. **Credit** AmEx, DC, MC, V. **Map** p307 E3.
Amsterdam at its most ambitious. This plush, crescent-shaped building, which opened in 1986, has room for 1,596 people and is home to both the **Nationale Ballet** (*see below*) and the **Nederlands Opera** (*see p221*), though the big stage is also used by visiting companies such as the Royal Ballet, the Martha Graham Company and Sankai Juku. The lobby's panoramic glass walls offer impressive views of the Amstel.

International Theaterschool

Jodenbreestraat 3, Old Centre: Old Side (527 7700/ www.ahk.nl/the). Tram 4, 9, 14, 16, 20, 24, 25/ Metro Waterlooplein. **Box office** times vary. **Tickets** prices vary. **No credit cards.** **Map** p307 E3.
Handily located near the Waterlooplein, the Theaterschool of Amsterdam brings together students and teachers from all over the world to share their experiences, and both to learn and create in the fields of dance and theatre. Dance performances – some of which are announced in *Uitkrant* – vary from studio shots to evening-long events in the Philip Morris dans zaal. Worth checking out.

Tropeninstituut Theater

Kleine Zaal: *Linnaeusstraat 2, Oost;* **Grote Zaal**: *Mauritskade 63, Oost (568 8500/ www.kit.nl/theater). Tram 9, 10, 14, 20.* **Box office** noon-4pm, from 1hr before start of performance Mon-Sat. **Performances** usually 8.30pm. **Tickets** *f*20-*f*35. **Credit** MC, V. **Map** p312 H3.
Affiliated to the Royal Tropical Institute, the Tropeninstituut Theater organises performances related to non-Western cultures. The dance programmes vary from classical Indian dance to South African modern dance, from Indonesian dance to Argentinian tango.

Out of town

Lucent Danstheater

Spuiplein 152, The Hague (070 360 9931/box office 070 360 4930/www.ndt.nl/Lucent/LucentInfo.html). NS rail Den Haag Centraal Station. **Box office** 10am-6pm Mon-Sat. **Performances** around 8pm. **Tickets** *f*30-*f*65. **Credit** AmEx, DC, MC, V.
The Lucent Danstheater, located in the centre of The Hague, is the home of the world-famous **Nederlands Dans Theater** (*see below*). Thanks to its high-quality productions in dance, ballet and opera, it's also one of the country's most important

international venues. With its excellent acoustics, fine visibility and stage that compares favourably in size to the Metropolitan in New York, the theatre offers wonderful facilities to go with its exceptional performances. A real treat.

Rotterdamse Schouwburg

Schouwburgplein 25, Rotterdam (010 411 8110/ www.schouwburg.rotterdam.nl). NS rail Rotterdam Centraal Station. **Box office** 11am-7pm Mon-Sat; noon-5pm Sun. **Performances** usually 8.15pm, 8.30pm. **Tickets** *f*18-*f*90. **Credit** AmEx, DC, MC, V.
This large, square-shaped theatre opened in 1988 and quickly became known as 'Kist van Quist' ('Quist's box') after its architect. Rotterdamse Schouwburg offers a large variety of classical ballet and modern dance, from both Dutch and international troupes, in its two auditoria (one of 900 seats, the smaller other of 150 seats). There's also a bar, café and a shop.

Toneelschuur

Smedestraat 23, Haarlem (023 531 2439/ www.toneelschuur.nl). NS rail Haarlem Centraal Station. **Box office** 3-7pm or start of performance Mon-Sat; 1.30-2.30pm Sun. **Performances** around 8pm. **Tickets** *f*10-*f*30. **Credit** AmEx, DC, MC, V.
Many dance- and theatre-lovers from Amsterdam head straight to Haarlem for performances at the Toneelschuur. There are two halls here (plus a bar and café, if you arrive early) and the venue is nationally renowned for its programmes of theatre and modern dance.

Dance companies

Nationale Ballet

Muziektheater 625 5455/www.het-nationale-ballet.
The largest company in the Netherlands boasts over 20 Balanchine ballets in its repertoire (the largest collection outside New York). However, since moving to the **Muziektheater** (*see above*) in 1986, its repertoire has included the more popular classical ballet as the company attempts to fill the theatre on a regular basis. Toer van Schayk and Rudi van Dantzig have been instrumental in developing this company's distinctive style within contemporary ballet.

Nederlands Dans Theater

Lucent Danstheater 070 360 9931/www.ndt.nl.
Nederlands Dans Theater was founded in 1959 and is now one of the most successful modern dance companies in the world. With two world-famous choreographers – Jiri Kylian and Hans van Manen – the company has a very firm artistic foundation, and the many works created each year have undoubtedly contributed to its enormous international success. Apart from the main company, look out for NDT2, made up of novices and up-and-coming dancers, and NDT3, which comprises veterans.

Dansgroep Krisztina de Châtel
669 5755/www.dechatel.nl.
Over the last quarter-century or so, Dance Company Krisztina de Châtel has grown into a modern international company boasting an exquisite list of dancers, all led by Hungarian choreographer de Châtel. Most productions last an entire evening, during which dance, music and visual art enter into a combined play.

Dance Company Leine & Roebana
627 0455.
Harijono Roebana and Andrea Leine's company performs its exciting, inventive modern dance works at various venues across Amsterdam.

Het Internationale Danstheater
Klovenierburgwal 87-9, Old Centre: Old Side (box office 623 5359/company 623 9112). Tram 9, 14, 20/Metro Nieuwmarkt. **Box office** from 1hr before start of performance. **Tickets** *f*16. **No credit cards. Map** p307 E3.
This Amsterdam-based company performs original dance from all over the world. The corps of 24 dancers works with guest international choreographers on a regular basis.

Magpie Music Dance Company
616 4794/companymagpie@hotmail.com.
Magpie uses improvisation to mix up a remarkable blend of dance, music and text into surprising whole-night events. Founded by dancer Katie Duck and musician Michael Vatcher in 1994, the company has toured extensively in Europe and the US, though it maintains both a season of performances at the **Melkweg** (*see p244*) and a programme of workshops at the **Theaterschool** building (*see p245*).

Jazzscool
681 5766/www.jazzscool.nl.
Jazzscool is the only company in the country whose speciality is jazz dance. The energetic and fairly young company is based at the Theaterschool of Amsterdam (*see p245*); indeed, many of the company members have only recently graduated. Performances take place at various venues around the city.

Out of town

Amsterdam performances by the companies detailed below are usually held in the **Stadsschouwburg** (*see page 239*).

RAZ/Hans Tuerlings
013 583 5929/www.raz.nl.
Hans Tuerlings regards his performances as narratives without a set story through a language of nonchalant, yet pure and especially well-measured, precisely timed movement. The RAZ dance company, meanwhile, consists of international dancers and performs regularly at the **Bellevue** (*see p237*).

Rotterdamse Dansgroep
010 436 4511/www.drd.org.
The Rotterdamse Dansgroep is one of the most vigorous exponents of New York modern dance in the Netherlands. Imported dance routines are mixed with work by young Dutch choreographers.

Scapino Ballet
010 414 2414/www.scapinoballet.nl.
Scapino is the oldest dance company in the country. Until recently, the company's work was more oriented towards youth dance and 'family' programmes, but Scapino's image is now more in tune with current, modern trends.

Movement theatre

Griftheater
419 3088/www.grif.nl.
Griftheater is a giant on the international mime scene. The company produces both location movement theatre and productions for existing theatre spaces. An excellent combination of plastic arts and modern mime.

Shusaku & Dormu Dance Theater & Bodytorium
662 4692.
Veteran Japanese choreographer Shusaku Takeuchi has been producing fascinating work for over 20 years. He specialises in massive location spectacles, often on or near bodies of water, that frequently feature huge constructions, fire, impressive lighting, plus live music. His indoor work is on a less grandiose scale, and is influenced by his background in plastic arts.

Courses & workshops

Dansstudio Cascade
Koestraat 5, Old Centre: Red Light District (623 0597/689 0565). Tram 4, 9, 14, 16, 20, 24/Metro Nieuwmarkt. **Classes** 6-10.30pm Mon-Fri. **Cost** varies. **Map** p306 D3.
Modern dance technique, capoeira, contact improvisation and Pentjak Silat are all taught at Dansstudio Cascade. Most teachers work within the new dance technique.

Henny Jurriens Foundation
Gerard Brandtstraat 26-8, Museum Quarter (412 1510/www.euronet.nl/~hjs). Tram 1, 6. **Classes** 10.30am, 12.15pm Mon-Fri; 11am Sat. **Cost** *f*12,50 per class; *f*100 ten-class card. **Map** p309 B3.
The Henny Jurriens Foundation provides open training for professional dancers in both classical and modern dance techniques throughout the year, with modern classes taking place at **Danswerkplaats Amsterdam** (*see p244*). Teachers are a mix of locals and guest teachers from abroad, and the foundation also offers workshops (pre-registration is necessary); phone for more information.

Trips Out of Town

Excursions in Holland

You want cheese? You want tulips? You want windmills? Well, guess what: you've come to the right place.

The majority of the Netherlands' most popular (and stereotypical) sights are concentrated in the two provinces around Amsterdam: Noord and Zuid Holland. Both provinces are small, and many of the sights are close to each other and easily reached by public transport. For more information on getting around the country, *see* chapter **Directory**. None of the establishments listed in this chapter accept credit cards.

Charming Clichés

Cheese

Ah, yes. Cheese. Food of the gods. Well, food of the Dutch, anyway. Aside from eating mountains of the stuff each year, they export well over 400,000 tonnes of cheese every year. It's also quite a tourist industry, too: the summer cheese markets, museums and traditional farms capture the flavour of how this commodity used to be made and sold.

Alkmaar Cheese Market, which runs 10am-noon every Friday (mid-Apr to mid-Sept only), is as much a ritual for tourists as it is for members of the cheese porters' guild. Garbed in pristine white uniforms and straw hats with coloured ribbons denoting the competing guilds, the porters weigh the cheeses and carry them on wooden trays hung from their shoulders. Buyers then test a core of cheese from each lot before the ceremony, which takes place at the Waag (weighhouse); here you can also find craft stalls and a **Cheese Museum** (*listings below*).

But Alkmaar has more to offer than just cheese. The VVV offers a written walking tour of the medieval centre: dating from 935, it often resounds to the sound of a carillon concert. There's a beer-tasting cellar at the **Biermuseum** (*listings below*); and an impressive art and toy collection at the **Stedelijk Museum** (*listings below*).

Edam was a prosperous port during the Golden Age, and still has exquisite façades and bridges. The famous red-skinned cheese is sold at the cheese market, held every Wednesday in July and August from 10am until noon.

Over in **Gouda**, meanwhile, golden wheels of cheese are traded at the cheese market every Thursday from 10am in July and August in front of the 1668 Waag – whose gablestone depicts cheese-weighing – and the Gothic city hall of 1450. There are many thatched-roof *kaasboerderijen* (cheese farms) near Gouda, several of which are on the picturesque River Vlist. If you're passing, keep your eyes peeled for signs reading *kaas te koop* ('cheese for sale'): this indicates a farm shop where you may be able to look behind the scenes as well as buy freshly made Gouda.

But though the cheese is justly famed the world over, Gouda does have points of interest beyond the yellow stuff. Its other famous products include clay pipes and pottery, which can be seen in the **De Moriaan Museum** (*listings below*); interested visitors shouldn't miss the popular pottery festival, held each year in the second week of May. Gouda's candles are another city classic: 20,000 of them illuminate the square during the Christmas tree ceremony.

Alkmaar Biermuseum
Houttil 1, Alkmaar (072 511 3801). **Open** 10am-4pm Tue-Fri; 1-4pm Sat, Sun; closed Mon. **Admission** ƒ4; ƒ2,50 concessions.

Alkmaar Cheese Museum
De Waag, Alkmaar (072 511 4284). **Open** Apr-Oct 10am-4pm Mon-Thur, Sat; 9am-4pm Fri; closed Sun & Nov-Mar. **Admission** ƒ5, ƒ3 under-11s.

De Moriaan Museum, Gouda
Westhaven 29, Gouda (0182 588444). **Open** 10am-5pm Mon-Sat; noon-5pm Sun. **Admission** ƒ5; ƒ3,50 over-65s; free children.

Stedelijk Museum, Alkmaar
Doelenstraat 5, Alkmaar (072 511 0737). **Open** 10am-5pm Tue-Fri; 1-5pm Sat, Sun; closed Mon. **Admission** ƒ3; free Museum Card, 10-17s.

Getting there

Alkmaar
By car 37km (22 miles) north-west. *By train* direct from Amsterdam Centraal Station.

Edam
By car 10km (5 miles) north. *By bus* 110, 112, 114 from Amsterdam Centraal Station.

Gouda
By car 29km (18 miles) south-west. *By train* direct from Amsterdam Centraal Station.

Bloemen Corso (*see p250*): say it with flowers. And leaves. And some old bits of hedge.

Tourist information

Alkmaar VVV

Waagplein 2, Alkmaar (072 511 4284). **Open** 10am-5.30pm Mon; 9am-5.30pm Tue, Wed; 9am-9pm Thur; 9am-6pm Fri; 9.30am-5pm Sat; closed Sun.

Edam VVV

Stadhuis, Damplein 1, Edam (0299 315125). **Open** *Apr-Oct* 10am-5pm Mon-Sat. *July, Aug* also 10am-5pm Sun. *Nov-Mar* 10am-3pm Mon-Sat.

Gouda VVV

Markt 27, Gouda (0182 513666). **Open** 9am-5pm Mon-Sat. *End June-mid Aug* also noon-3pm Sun.

Flowers

Ask any visitor what springs to mind when they hear the word 'Holland', and you can be pretty sure that tulips will be top of the list or thereabouts. But that's not the end of the story: the Netherlands produces 70 per cent of all the world's flowers, and many types of blooms can be seen all year round in markets, botanical gardens, auctions and parades. For export rules on bulbs and flowers, *see page 154*.

Each year, more than 3.5 billion cut flowers and 370 million pot plants are handled, mostly for export, at the **Verenigde Bloemenveilingen** in Aalsmeer (*listings page 250*), the world's biggest flower auction. The perishable nature of the flowers demands high speed action, the result being a chaotic scene. To bid, dealers push a button to stop a 'clock' that counts from 100 down to one: unusually, the price is lowered, rather than raised, until a buyer is found. Bidders risk either overpaying or not getting the goods if time runs out. This procedure gave rise to the English phrase 'Dutch auction'. The best action here is usually before 9am, except on Thursdays when very little happens.

Broeker Veiling (*listings page 250*), the oldest flower auction in the world, is a bit of a tourist trap. Bidding is at done as at a 'proper' auction, and the admission price includes a museum of old farming artefacts, and – for a small extra fee – a boat trip round the area.

The greenhouse and extensive fields of the 200-year-old **Frans Rozen Nursery** (*listings page 250*) are open to the public, and allows visitors an insight into commercial cultivation and the meticulous development of new hybrids. You can also purchase bulbs for export, and there's a tulip show in April and May.

Since 1949, it's been flowers everywhere at the **Keukenhof Bulb Gardens** (*listings page 250*). This former 15th-century royal 'kitchen garden' contains over 500 varieties of tulip and over six million bulbs in 32 hectares (80 acres), but the glass flower pavilion – all 6,500sq m (70,480sq ft) of it – is just as interesting, as are the various statues and works of art. With the help of a VVV map, you can tour the bulb district (in bloom from March to late May), from which over half of the world's cut flowers and pot plants originate. The gardens and café get overrun, so arrive early with a picnic lunch. The bulb district's history is covered at the **Museum de Zwarte Tulp** in Lisse (*listings below*).

Broeker Veiling
Museumweg 2, Broek-op-Langerdijk (0226 313807). **Open** *Apr-Nov* 10am-5pm Mon-Fri; 11am-5pm Sat, Sun; closed Dec-Mar. **Admission** *Auction & museum* ƒ10,50; ƒ6 under-15s. *Auction, museum & boat trip* ƒ17,50; ƒ9,50 under-15s.

Frans Rozen Nursery
Vogelenzangseweg 49, Vogelenzang (023 584 7245). **Open** *Mid Mar-mid May* 8am-6pm daily. *Mid May-Sept* 9am-5pm Mon-Fri; 10am-5pm Sat, Sun; closed Oct-mid Mar. **Admission** ƒ6,60; ƒ3,25-ƒ5 concessions.

Keukenhof Bulb Gardens
Keukenhof, near Lisse (0252 465555). **Open** *Mid Mar-mid May* 8am-7.30pm daily (ticket office 8am-6pm daily); closed late May-early Mar. **Admission** ƒ19; ƒ9,50 4-12s.

Museum de Zwarte Tulp
Grachtweg 2A, Lisse (0252 417900). **Open** 1-5pm Tue-Sun; closed Mon. **Admission** ƒ4; ƒ3 under-12s.

Verenigde Bloemenveilingen
Legmeerdijk 313, Aalsmeer (0297 393939). **Open** 7.30-11am Mon-Fri; closed Sat, Sun. **Admission** ƒ7,50; ƒ4 under-12s.

Getting there

Aalsmeer
By car 15km (9 miles) south-west. *By bus* 172 from Amsterdam Centraal Station.

Broek-op-Langerdijk
By car 36km (22 miles) north. *By train* from Amsterdam Centraal Station to Alkmaar, then bus 155; from Amsterdam Centraal Station to Heerhugowaard, then taxi.

Keukenhof/Lisse
By car 27km (17 miles) south-west. *By train* from Amsterdam Centraal Station to Leiden, then bus 54.

Vogelenzang
By car 25km (16 miles) west. *By train* from Amsterdam Centraal Station to Heemstede, then bus 90 to Café Rusthoek.

Floral calendar

Spring
The flower trade's year kicks off in mid- to late February with the indoor **Westfriese Flora** (0228 511644) at Bovenkarspel, near Enkhuizen. From late March to late May, the bulb district from Den Helder to The Hague is carpeted with blooms of the principal crops: daffodils, crocuses, gladioli, hyacinths, narcissi and – of course – tulips. The **Noordwijk-Haarlem Flower Parade** (0252 434710) is held on the first Saturday after 19 April, departing Noordwijk at 10am and arriving in Haarlem (via Sassenheim) at 7pm. The suitably florid loats are on show in Lisse and Hobahohallen for two days prior to the parade.

Summer
In mid- to late May, golden fields of rapeseed brighten Flevoland, Friesland and Groningen. In The Hague, the Japanese Garden at **Clingendael Gardens** is in full flower from early May to mid-June, while the rose garden in Westbroek Park (which contains 350 varieties) bursts into colour during July and August. In late June, there's the Floralia exhibition at the Zuider Zee Museum in

Enkhuizen (see page 252). And on the first weekend in August, it's the **Rijnsburg Parade** (071 409 4444). The floats leave Rijnsburg at 11am on Saturday, reach Leiden at 1pm and then journey to Nordwijk by 4pm, where they show at the Boulevard that evening and the next day.

Autumn
Heather purples the landscape – especially in **Veluwe**, in the province of Gelderland – during August and September, when greenhouse flowers also emerge. The **Bloemen Corso** (0297 325100), Europe's biggest flower parade, winds from Aalsmeer to Amsterdam and back on the first Saturday in September, with float viewing taking place the day before and after the parade in Aalsmeer. See also page 172.

Winter
In November, the public and florists from all over the world view new varieties at the Professional Flower Exhibition at **Aalsmeer Flower Auction** (see page 249). At Christmas, there's the Kerstflora show at Hillegom near Lisse.

Dutch Traditions

The Dutch may be modern-thinking, unsentimental people, but they also understand commerce and how to give customers what they want. Small historic towns, where the main industry is tourism, accordingly make the most of their traditions, right down to the lace caps, wooden shoes and working windmills that churn out souvenirs like flour and mustard.

Zuid-Holland & Utrecht

High fashion it ain't, but about one-fifth of **Bunschoten-Spakenburg** residents still wear traditional dress on midsummer market Wednesdays (from mid-July to mid-August); Some older people even wear it every day. Costumes are also worn at the special summer markets in Hoorn, Medemblik and Schagen (*see pages 252-3*), and on folkloric festival days in Middelburg, Zeeland.

Over in Alblasserdam, the sight of the 19 **Kinderdijk Windmills** (*listings below*) under sail is amazing, particularly when they're illuminated during the second week in September. To drain water from reclaimed land, windmills were usually clustered in a group called a gang. They now operate for the benefit of tourists (2-5pm Sat in July and Aug, and first Sat in May and June). From April to September, you can take a boat trip out to see them (*f*4).

Schoonhoven has been famous since the 17th century for its silversmiths, who crafted items to be worn with traditional costume. You can see antique pieces in the **Nederlands Goud-, Zilver- en Klokkenmuseum** (*listings below*) and the **Edelambachtshuis** (Museum of Antique Silverware; *listings below*). Olivier van Noort, the first Dutchman to sail around the world, and Claes Louwerenz Blom, who locals believe introduced the windmill to Spain in 1549, are buried in the 14th-century **Bartholomeuskerk**, the tower of which leans 1.6m (5ft) off-centre and offers great views.

Dating from the 11th century, **Oudewater** (north of Schoonhoven) was once known for its rope-making and its particularly honest merchants. However, an epidemic of witch-hunting broke out in the 1480s, lasting until the beginning of the 17th century, and Oudewater achieved fame for its honest weighing of suspected witches and warlocks in the **Witches' Weigh House** ('Heksenwaag'; *listings below*); today, swarms of tourists step on to the scales.

Edelambachtshuis

Haven 13, Schoonhoven (0182 382614). **Open** 10am-5pm Tue-Sat; closed Mon, Sun. **Admission** *f*1.

Kinderdijk Windmills

Molenkade, Alblasserdam (078 691 5179). **Open** Apr-Sept 9.30am-5.30pm daily; closed Oct-Mar. **Admission** *Windmills f*3,50; *f*2 under-16s.

Nederlands Goud-, Zilver- en Klokkenmuseum

Kazerneplein 4, Schoonhoven (0182 385612). **Open** noon-5pm Tue-Sun; closed Mon. **Admission** *f*7,50; *f*5 under-12s.

Witches' Weigh House

Leeuweringerstraat 2, Oudewater (0348 563400). **Open** *Apr-Oct* 10am-5pm Tue-Sat; noon-5pm Sun; closed Mon & Nov-Mar. **Admission** *f*3; *f*2,50 Museum Card, over-65s; *f*1,50 4-12s; free under-4s.

Getting there

Alblasserdam

By car 55km (34 miles) south-west. *By train* from Amsterdam Centraal Station to Utrecht, then bus 154.

Bunschoten-Spakenburg

By car 35km (22 miles) south-east. *By train* from Amsterdam Centraal Station to Amersfoort, then bus 116.

Oudewater

By car 40km (25 miles) south. *By train* from Amsterdam Centraal Station to Utrecht, then bus 180.

Schoonhoven

By car 50km (31 miles) south. *By train* from Amsterdam Centraal Station to Utrecht, then bus 195.

Tourist information

Alblasserdam VVV

Cortgene 2, inside City Hall, Alblasserdam (078 692 1355). **Open** 9am-4pm Mon-Fri; closed Sat, Sun.

Bunschoten-Spakenburg VVV

Oude Schans 90, Spakenburg (033 298 2156). **Open** *Apr-Sept* 10am-5pm Mon-Fri; 10am-4pm Sat; closed Sun. *Oct-Mar* 1-5pm Mon-Fri; 10am-3pm Sat; closed Sun.

Oudewater VVV

Kapellestraat 2, Oudewater (0348 564636). **Open** *Apr-Oct* 10am-4.30pm Tue-Sat; noon-3.30pm Sun; closed Mon. *Nov-Mar* 10am-1pm Tue-Sat; closed Mon, Sun.

Schoonhoven VVV

Stadhuisstraat 1, Schoonhoven (0182 385009). **Open** *May-Sept* 1.30-5pm Mon; 9am-5pm Tue-Fri; 10am-3pm Sat; closed Sun. *Oct-Apr* 9am-4pm Tue-Fri; 10am-3pm Sat; closed Mon, Sun.

Waterland

Until the IJ Tunnel opened in 1956, the canal-laced peat meadows of Waterland north of Amsterdam were accessible mainly by ferry

Trips Out of Town

and steam railway. This isolation preserved much of the area's heritage, which is best seen from a bicycle: for a prime example, take a look around the old wooden buildings over in **Broek in Waterland**. For more on the similarly charming **Edam**, *see page 248*.

Reached via a causeway, **Marken**, once full of fishermen, is now bursting with costumes, souvenir shops and tourists. However, out of season, it's quieter and more authentic than Volendam (*see below*). Many houses are built on mounds or poles to protect against flooding. Visit the **Marker Museum** (*listings below*) for a glance at the history of the island.

The most remarkable thing about **Monnickendam** is its number of preserved ancient buildings, from Golden Age merchants' houses to its famous herring smokehouses. History-lovers should enjoy the collection of music boxes at the **Stuttenburgh** fish restaurant (Haringburgwal 3-4, 0299 651869), and there's a delightful antique carillon on the bell-tower of the old town hall.

Volendam was such a successful fishing village that it's said the town flag was lowered to half-mast when the Zuider Zee was enclosed in 1932, cutting off access to the sea. The village's enterprise was soon applied to creating a theme park from its historic features, but, unfortunately, the gaily garbed locals can barely be seen for the coachloads of tourists that are dumped there on a daily basis.

De Zaanse Schans (*listings below*) is a museum village with a difference: people live in it. One of the world's first industrial zones, the small Zaan district was once crowded with 800 windmills that powered the manufacture of paint, flour and lumber. Today, amid the gabled green and white houses, attractions include an old-fashioned Albert Heijn store.

Marker Museum
Kerkbuurt 44-7, Marken (0299 601904). **Open** *Apr-Oct* 10am-5pm Mon-Sat; noon-4pm Sun; closed Nov-Mar. **Admission** ƒ4; ƒ2 under-12s.

De Zaanse Schans
Information from **Zaandam VVV** *below.* **Open** *times vary, generally: Museums* 10am-5pm Tue-Sun; closed Mon. *Shops & windmills* 9am-5pm Tue-Sun; closed Mon. **Admission** free-ƒ20; free-ƒ9 under-13s.

Getting there

Broek in Waterland
By car 10km (6 miles) north-east. *By bus* 110, 111, 114 or 116 from Amsterdam Centraal Station.

Marken
By car 20km (12 miles) north-east. *By bus* 111 from Amsterdam Centraal Station to Marken, or 110, 114 or 116 to Monnickendam, then boat to Marken.

Monnickendam
By car 15km (9 miles) north-east. *By bus* 110, 114 or 116 from Amsterdam Centraal Station.

Volendam
By car 20km (12 miles) north-east. *By bus* 110 from Amsterdam Centraal Station.

De Zaanse Schans
By car 15km (9 miles) north-west. *By train* to Koog-Zaandijk. *By bus* 89 from Marnixstraat.

Tourist information

Monnickendam VVV
Nieuwpoortslaan 15, Monnickendam (0299 651998). **Open** 10am-5pm Mon-Sat; closed Sun.

Volendam VVV
Zeestraat 37, Volendam (0299 363747). **Open** *Mid Mar-Oct* 10am-5pm daily. *Nov-mid Mar* 10am-3pm Mon-Sat; closed Sun.

Zaandam VVV
Gedempte Gracht 76, Zaandam (075 616 2221). **Open** 9am-5.30pm Mon-Fri; 9am-4pm Sat; closed Sun.

West Friesland

Facing Friesland across the northern IJsselmeer is West Friesland. Though it's been part of Noord Holland for centuries, it has its own customs, and fewer visitors than its near-neighbour. One scenic way to get there is to take a train to Enkhuizen, then a boat to Medemblik. From here, take the **Museumstoomtram** ('Steam Railway Museum'; *listings page 253*) to Hoorn.

Enkhuizen, a once-powerful fishing and whaling port, has many relics of its past, but most people come here for the remarkable **Zuider Zee Museum** (*listings page 253*). It has two separate sections: the indoor Binnenmuseum features exhibits on seven centuries of seafaring life around the IJsselmeer, while the Buitenmuseum is an open-air reconstructed village of authentic late 19th- and early 20th-century buildings transplanted from towns around the Zuider Zee.

An ancient port dating from the early Middle Ages, **Medemblik** is dominated by the Gothic Bonifaciuskerk and Kasteel Radboud. The 13th-century castle is smaller than when it defended Floris V's realm, but still retains its knights' hall and towers. Glassblowers, smiths and leatherworkers demonstrate their skills at the Saturday market (held during July and August). Nearby is the 'long village' of Twisk, with its pyramid-roofed farm buildings, and the circular village of Opperdoes, built on a mound.

The pretty port of **Hoorn**, which dates from the 1310s, grew rich on the Dutch East Indies trade; its success is reflected in its grand and

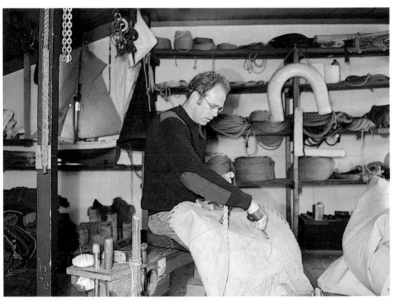

History comes alive at Enkhuizen's **Zuider Zee Museum**. *See p252.*

ancient architecture. Local costumes and crafts can be seen at the weekly historic market, Hartje Hoorn (10am-5pm Wed, July and Aug), while the grandly named **Museum van de Twintigste Eeuw** ('Museum of the 20th Century'; *listings below*) has a permanent exhibit of daily life from the last hundred years. The Statencollege (council building), built in 1632, houses the **Westfries Museum** (*listings below*), which focuses on art, decor and the region's past.

Museumstoomtram Hoorn-Medemblik
Tickets behind the railway station at Van Dedemstraat 8, Hoorn (0229 214862), or **Hoorn VVV** *below.* **Admission** ƒ14,50-ƒ23,50.

Museum van de Twintigste Eeuw
Bierkade 4, Hoorn (0229 214001). **Open** 10am-5pm Tue-Sun; closed Mon. **Admission** ƒ5; ƒ4 concessions.

Westfries Museum
Rode Steen 1, Hoorn (0229 280028). **Open** 11am-5pm Mon-Fri; 2-5pm Sat, Sun. **Admission** ƒ5; ƒ2,50 concessions; free Museum Card.

Zuider Zee Museum
Wierdijk 12-22, Enkhuizen (0228 351111). **Open** *Binnenmuseum* Apr-Jun, Sept, Oct 10am-5pm Mon-Sat, 10am-6pm Sun; July, Aug 10am-6pm daily; Nov-Mar 10am-5pm daily. *Buitenmuseum* Apr-Oct as Binnenmuseum; Nov-Mar closed. **Admission** ƒ18,50; ƒ13 concessions.

Getting there

Enkhuizen
By car 55km (34 miles) north-east. *By train* direct from Amsterdam Centraal Station.

Hoorn
By car 35km (22 miles) north-east. *By train* direct from Amsterdam Centraal Station.

Medemblik
By car 50km (31 miles) north. *By train* direct from Amsterdam Centraal Station.

Tourist information

Enkhuizen VVV
Tussen Twee Havens 1, Enkhuizen (0228 313164). **Open** Apr-Oct 9am-5pm daily. Nov-Mar 9am-5pm Mon-Fri; 9am-2pm Sat; closed Sun.

Hoorn VVV
Veemarkt 4, Hoorn (0229 218343). **Open** *Apr, May* 1-5pm Mon; 9.30am-5pm Tue-Sat; 1-5pm Sun. *June-Aug* 1-6pm Mon; 9.30am-6pm Tue-Fri; 9.30am-5pm Sat; 1-5pm Sun. *Sept-Mar* 1-5pm Mon; 9.30am-5pm Tue-Sat; closed Sun.

Medemblik VVV
Dam 2, Medemblik (0227 542852). **Open** *Apr-Jun, Sept, Oct* 10am-5pm Mon-Sat; closed Sun. *July, Aug* 10am-5pm Mon-Sat; noon-5pm Sun. *Nov-Mar* 10am-noon, 2-4pm Mon-Sat; closed Sun.

Trips Out of Town

Ancient Castles

The Netherlands is studded with 400 castles, and many fortress towns retain large parts of their defences. Many of the best are in the province of Utrecht, within half an hour of Amsterdam. Almost 100 of the castles are open for tourists or business conferences: the 15th-century **NJHC Slot Assumburg** at Heemskerk, between Haarlem and Alkmaar, is a youth hostel (025 123 2288), while the ultimate power lunch can be had at either **Château Neercanne** in Maastricht (043 325 1359) or **Kasteel Erenstein** in Kerkrade (045 546 1333).

De Haar (*listings below*) looks like the quintessential medieval castle. However, its fairy-tale embellishments are relatively recent recreations: in 1892, the baron who inherited the ruins of De Haar (dating from 1391), and his Rothschild wife, recreated the original building on a majestic scale, moving the entire village of Haarzuilens 850 metres (259 feet) to make room for the formal grounds. The lavish interior boasts medieval weaponry, stone carvings, ancient tapestries, Louis XIV-XVI furniture and Far Eastern art, and spectacular stained-glass in the hall. The castle is open by guided tour only.

The **Muiderslot** (*listings below*) is legendary: many Dutch historical events took place in this moated rectangular castle, strategically situated at the mouth of the River Vecht. It was originally built in 1280 for Count Floris V, who was murdered nearby in Muiderberg in 1296 (*see page 4*). Rebuilt in the 14th century, the fortress has been through many sieges and frequent renovations. The 17th-century furnishings may seem out of context, but they originate from the period of its most illustrious occupant, PC Hooft, who entertained in the castle's splendid halls.

Naarden is a moated, star-shaped stronghold with arrowhead-shaped bastions, and a very well-preserved fortified town; it was in active service as recently as 1926. All is explained in the **Vestingmuseum** (*listings below*), located partly underground in the Turfpoortbastion (Peat Gate). The fortifications date from 1675, after the inhabitants were massacred by the Duke of Alva's son in 1572; the slaughter is depicted above the door of the Spaanse Huis (Spanish House), now a part-time conference venue.

Meandering up the River Vecht into **Utrecht** (*see page 266*), boat passengers can glimpse some of the plush country homes built in the 17th and 18th centuries by rich Amsterdam merchants. Two of the trips afford close-up views of castles. The first stops on the way back downriver for a one-hour tour of Slot Zuylen, a 16th-century castle that was renovated in 1752. The boat company, **Rondvaartbedrijf Rederij**

Schuttevaer (*listings below*), can arrange an English guide in advance. The collection of furniture, tapestries and objets d'art gives an idea of the lives of the castle's residents. Another boat trip deposits passengers in the charming town of Loenen, which the restored castle of Loenersloot, complete with a 13th-century keep. Sadly, this castle is not open to the public.

De Haar
Kasteellaan 1, Haarzuilens, Utrecht (030 677 3804). **Open** *June-Sept* 11am-4pm Mon-Fri; 1-4pm Sat, Sun. *Mid Mar-May & Oct-mid Nov* 1-4pm Tue-Sun; closed Mon. *Jan-mid Mar & late Nov* 1-4pm Sun; closed Mon-Sat. *Dec* groups only (by arrangement). *Grounds open* 10am-5pm daily. **Admission** *Castle & grounds* ƒ15; ƒ10 5-12s (no under-5s); free Museum Card. *Grounds only* ƒ5; ƒ2,50 5-12s; free Museum Card, under-5s.

Muiderslot
Herengracht 1, Muiden (0294 261325). **Open** *Apr-Oct* 10am-4pm Mon-Fri; 1-4pm Sat, Sun. *Nov-Mar* 1-3pm Sat, Sun; closed Mon-Fri. **Admission** ƒ10; ƒ7,50 concessions; free Museum Card.

Rondvaartbedrijf Rederij Schuttevaer
Oudegracht, opposite No.85, Utrecht (030 272 0111/030 231 9377). **Times** *June-Sept* leaves Utrecht for Slot Zuylen 10.30am Tue & 11.30am Thur, returning 4pm. *June-Sept* leaves Utrecht for Loenen 10.30am Wed, (July, Aug also Fri) returning 6pm. **Tickets** ƒ32,50-ƒ49; ƒ30,50-ƒ47 under-13s; reservations mandatory.

Vestingmuseum Turfpoortbastion
Westvalstraat 6, Naarden (035 694 5459). **Open** *Mar-Oct* 10.30am-5pm Tue-Fri; noon-5pm Sat, Sun; closed Mon. *Nov-Feb* noon-5pm Sun; closed Mon-Sat. **Admission** ƒ10; ƒ7,50-ƒ9 concessions; free Museum Card, under-4s.

Getting there

De Haar
By car 30km (19 miles) south. *By train* Amsterdam Centraal Station to Utrecht, then bus 127.

Muiderslot
By car 12km (7.5 miles) south-east. *By bus* 136 from Amstel Station.

Naarden
By car 20km (12 miles) south-east. *By train* direct from Amsterdam Centraal Station. *By bus* 136 from Amstel Station.

Tourist information

Naarden VVV
Adriaan Dortsmanplein 1B, Naarden (035 694 2836). **Open** *May-Oct* 10am-5pm Mon-Fri; 10am-3pm Sat; noon-3pm Sun, public holidays. *Nov-Apr* 10am-2pm Mon-Sat; closed Sun.

City Breaks

Amsterdam is by no means the only town worth visiting in the Netherlands: the nearby cities of the Randstad hold an assortment of delights.

The Randstad – or 'Edge City', named for its coastal location on the Netherlands' western edge – is essentially a ring-shaped conurbation bounded by Amsterdam, Delft, Haarlem, The Hague, Leiden, Rotterdam and Utrecht, though in recent years, **Gouda** (*see page 248*) and Dordrecht have also come to be considered part of the area. Though separately administered and fiercely independent, the individual towns work together by choice for their common good. Somewhat surprisingly, it's also one of the most densely populated areas in the world: no less than 40 per cent of the Dutch population inhabit this urban sprawl.

The road, rail and waterway networks are impressive, and the area's strong economy accounts for at least half of the national turnover. The Randstad's importance is based on several factors: Rotterdam's port, which handles more tonnage than any other in the world; Amsterdam's Schiphol Airport and the city's role as financial and banking centre; the seats of government and royalty at The Hague; and a huge agricultural belt.

Regarded with awe and sometimes resentment by the outlying provinces, the Randstad is often accused of monopolising government attention and funds. However, it has no formally defined status and is still prone to bitter rivalries between cities and municipalities. The cities within it provide ample and welcome contrast to Amsterdam, and are ideal for a short break from the Dutch capital.

Delft

Imagine a miniaturised Amsterdam – canals reduced to dinky proportions, bridges narrowed down, merchants' houses shrunken and altogether less forbidding – and you have the essence of Delft. However, though it's a small town, scoffed at for its seeming sleepiness, it is, in fact, teeming with social carryings-on if you know where to look.

Everything you might want to see in this compact city is in the old centre, where the best views are also to be found. As soon as you cross the road from the station towards the city centre, you encounter the first introduction to Delft's fascinating past: a modern representation of Vermeer's *Melkmeisje* (*Milk Maid*) in white stone on the junction of Phoenixstraat and Binnen Watersloot.

Delft, though, is of course most famous for its blue and white tiles and pottery, known as Delft Blue. There are still a few factories open to visitors – among them **De Delftse Pauw** and **De Porceleyne Fles** (*listings page 257*) – but for a historical overview of the industry, head for the **Museum Lambert van Meerten** (*listings page 257*). A 19th-century mansion, it houses fine pieces of tin-glazed earthenware as well as a vast collection of magnificent ebony-veneered furniture. The huge range of tiles, depicting everything from battling warships to copulating hares, contrasts dramatically with today's mass-produced trinkets.

Delft was traditionally a centre for trade, producing and exporting butter, cloth, Delft beer – at one point in the past, almost 200 breweries could be found beside the canals – and, later, pottery. The town's illustrious history incorporates stories of prosperity and murder; of how lightning bolts caused disastrous fires; of plague outbreaks; of art treasures lost when bombs destroyed part of a convent; of how the declining quality of the canal water drastically reduced the number of breweries… And all this before 1630, when Chinese ceramic imports spawned Delftware, which in turn rescued the economic situation. Delft's loss in trade has been Rotterdam's gain, but the aesthetic benefits can be seen in the city's centuries-old gables, humpback bridges and shady canals.

To appreciate how little has changed, walk to the end of **Oude Delft**, the oldest and most prominent canal in Delft, which has some impressive mansions incorporated into its terrace. Cross the busy road to the harbour, for it was on the far side of this big canal that **Johannes Vermeer** (1632-75) stood while painting his famous *View of Delft*, which is now on display in the **Mauritshuis** in The Hague (*see page 258*).

Delft also has two spectacular churches that can be seen for miles around. The first, the **Nieuwe Kerk** (the New Church), stands in the Markt (the Market Place) and contains the mausolea of William of Orange and the lawyer-philosopher Hugo de Groot. It took almost 15

Het Princenhof, where William of Orange breathed his last breath. Nice place to die, though.

years to construct and was finished in 1396. Across the Markt is architect Hendrick de Keyser's 1620 **Stadhuis** (or City Hall), which was built after the previous one was razed to the ground. De Keyser also designed Prince William's black and white marble mausoleum. Not to be outdone, the town's other splendid house of worship, the Gothic **Oude Kerk** (c1200), stands proudly with its tower some two metres off-kilter. Art-lovers should note that it's the last resting place of Vermeer.

Museums in Delft have the air of private residences and are, thankfully, pretty much crowd-free. **Het Princenhof** (*listings page 257*), located in the former convent of St Agatha, holds permanent exhibitions about Prince William of Orange, who was allegedly assassinated in 1584 by Philip II of Spain in the midst of Holland's turbulent 80-year fight for independence. The fatal bullet holes are still visible on the stairs.

Following the decline of the pottery workshops, Delft's depression lifted when the **Technical University of Delft** was founded in 1842. The university is recognised as being part of a concentration of advanced technology-involving research institutes such as the Dutch TNO. Of the city's current population of 95,000, some 13,000 are students, which goes to create a very laid-back feeling in the bars in the centre of town.

But if museums and bars don't appeal, then content yourself with a stroll around town. The historic town centre has more than 600 national monuments in and around the preserved merchants' and traders' houses. Pick up a historical walk guide from the VVV and wander around this delightful little town to see all it has to offer, stopping off for coffee and/or beer along the way. Just one of the many places that may draw your attention is the **Oostpoort** (East Gate), dating from 1394. And while at the VVV, ask if you can visit the **Windmill de Roos** and the torture chamber in **Het Steen**, the 13th-century tower of the historic city hall in the market square. Both will fascinate and enchant.

De Delftse Pauw

Delftweg 133 (015 212 4920/www.delftsepauw.com). **Open** *Apr-Oct* 9am-4.30pm daily. *Nov-Mar* 9am-4.30pm Mon-Fri; 11am-1pm Sat, Sun. **Admission** free. **No credit cards.**

De Porceleyne Fles

Rotterdamseweg 196 (015 256 9214). **Open** *Apr-Oct* 9am-5pm Mon-Sat; 9.30am-5pm Sun. *Nov-Mar* 9am-5pm Mon-Sat; closed Sun. **Admission** ƒ5. **Credit** AmEx, DC, MC, V.

Museum Lambert van Meerten

Oude Delft 199 (015 260 2358). **Open** 10am-5pm Tue-Sat; 1-5pm Sun; closed Mon. **Admission** ƒ3,50; ƒ1,75 12-18s; free under-12s. **No credit cards.**

Het Princenhof

Sint Agathaplein 1 (015 260 2358). **Open** 10am-5pm Tue-Sat; 1-5pm Sun; closed Mon. **Admission** ƒ5; ƒ2,50 12-16s; free under-12s. **No credit cards.**

Where to eat and drink

Though many of the bars and cafés may appear to outsiders as survivors of a bygone era – white-aproned waiters and high-ceilinged interiors abound – it's the norm in Delft. While other cities offer hot chocolate finished with whipped cream, cafés here use real cream and pop a biscuit on the saucer. These small details emphasise the difference between city culture and this town's attention to detail.

In summer, delicious sandwiches are served on a canal barge moored alongside **Klijwegs Koffiehuis** (Oude Delft 133, 015 212 4625). **De Wijnhaven** (Wijnhaven 22, 015 214 1460) and **The V** (Voorstraat 9, 015 214 0916) both offer reasonably priced and rather delicious lunches and dinners.

Where to stay

De Ark (Koornmarkt 65, 015 215 7999) is upmarket, with single rooms priced from ƒ140 for a small single to ƒ375 for the priciest double. **Dish** (Kanaalweg 3, 015 256 9358) is a little more reasonable, priced at ƒ165 for a single, ƒ193 for a double.

Budget travellers could try the camp site at **Delftse Hout** (Korftlaan 5, 015 213 0040), where a site for two costs ƒ43,50 (plus ƒ1 per person tourist tax). During the colder weather, try **De Kok** (Houttuinen 14, 015 212 2125), where singles range from ƒ135 to ƒ175, and doubles from ƒ145 to ƒ185.

Getting there

By car
60km (37 miles) south-west on A4, then A13.

By train
1hr from Amsterdam Centraal Station, changing at The Hague if necessary.

Tourist information

VVV
Markt 83-5 (015 212 6100/www.vvvdelft.nl). **Open** *Mid Apr-Sept* 9am-5.30pm Mon-Sat; 11am-3pm Sun. *Oct-mid Apr* 9am-5.30pm Mon-Fri; 9am-5pm Sat; closed Sun.

Haarlem

Lying between Amsterdam and the coastal resort of Zandvoort, Haarlem is a stone's throw from the dunes and the sea, and attracts flocks of beachgoing Amsterdammers and Germans every summer. All trace of Haarlem's origins as a 10th-century settlement on a choppy inland sea disappeared with the draining of the Haarlemmermeer in the mid-19th century. But the town hasn't lost its appeal: the historic centre is beautiful with its lively main square, canals and charming almshouse courtyards. Plenty of high-quality restaurants and shops cater for well-to-do locals, and people tend to be more friendly than in nearby Amsterdam.

To catch up with Haarlem's history, head to **St Bavo's Church**, which dominates the main square. It was built around 1313 but suffered severe fire damage in 1328; rebuilding and expansion lasted another 150 years. It's surprisingly bright inside: cavernous white transepts stand as high as the nave and make for a stunning sight. Music buffs will swoon at the sight of the famed Müller organ (1738): boasting an amazing 5,068 pipes, it's been played by both Handel and the young Mozart.

Haarlem's cosy but spacious **Grote Markt** is one of the loveliest squares in the Netherlands. A few blocks away is the former old men's almshouse and orphanage that currently houses the **Frans Halsmuseum** (*listings page 258*). Though it holds a magnificent collection of 16th- and 17th-century portraits, still lifes, genre paintings and landscapes, including works by Pieter Claesz, Jacob van Ruisdael and Adriaen van Ostade, the highlight is Frans Hals's eight group portraits of militia companies and regents. (Hals, incidentally, is buried in the aforementioned St Bavo's Church.) The museum also houses a large collection of period furniture, Haarlem silver and ceramics, an 18th-century

Trips Out of Town

apothecary with Delftware pottery, and an extensive modern art collection. Nearby is **De Hallen** (*listings page 258*), whose two buildings, the Verweyhal and the Vleeshal, house a collection of modern and contemporary art, including outstanding examples of work by artists from Haarlem and surrounding areas.

Though it's rather in the shadow of the Frans Halsmuseum, the **Teylers Museum** (*listings page 258*) is equally excellent. Founded in 1784, it's the country's oldest museum and has a mix of exhibits: fossils and minerals sit alongside antique scientific instruments, while there's also a superb collection of 10,000 drawings by 16th- to 19th-century masters including Rembrandt, Michelangelo and Raphael.

Haarlem is more than a city of nostalgia, of course. The **Patronaat** (Zijlsingel 2, 023 532 6010) is a fine rock music venue: it's Haarlem's answer to the Melkweg in Amsterdam, though without the really big bands.

De Hallen

Grote Markt 16 (023 511 5840). **Open** 11am-5pm Mon-Sat; noon-5pm Sun. **Admission** ƒ7,50; ƒ5 over-65s; free Museum Card, under-19s. *Combination ticket with Frans Halsmuseum* ƒ12,50; free Museum Card, under-19s. **No credit cards**.

Frans Halsmuseum

Groot Heiligland 62 (023 551 5775). **Open** 11am-5pm Mon-Sat; noon-5pm Sun. **Admission** ƒ7,50 over-65s; free under-19s. *Combination ticket with De Hallen* ƒ12,50; free Museum Card, under-19s. **No credit cards**.

Teylers Museum

Spaarne 16 (023 531 9010). **Open** 10am-5pm Tue-Sat; noon-5pm Sun; closed Mon. **Admission** ƒ10; ƒ2,50 5-18s; free Museum Card, under-5s. **No credit cards**.

Where to eat & drink

The best Greek food in town can be had at **Zorba de Griek** (Smedestraat 47, 023 531 5188). One of the tiniest restaurants in town, **De Keuken** (Lange Veerstraat 4, 023 534 5343) offers European cuisine in a quiet atmosphere, though, if you have money to burn, don't miss **De Componist** (Korte Veerstraat 1, 023 532 8853), where main courses start at ƒ44. **Grand-Café Brinkmann** (Brinkmannpassage 41, 023 532 3111) serves a range of bistro food and drink; most tables look out on to the Grote Markt and there's plenty of sun on nice afternoons. The nearby **Café Studio** (Grote Markt 25, 023 531 0033) serves an assortment of strong Belgian ales and has live music a couple of times a week, while at **Stalker** (Kromme Elleboogsteeg 12, 023 531 4652), house and techno DJs spin from Thursday to Sunday.

Where to stay

The beautiful **Carlton Square Hotel** (Baan 7, 023 531 9091) is as pricey as Haarlem gets, with single and double rooms from ƒ340. The **Carillon** (Grote Markt 27, 023 531 0591) is more reasonable, with single rooms for ƒ60, and doubles with in-room shower and toilet for ƒ142, while outside the centre, the **NJHC Hostel Jan Gijzen** (Jan Gijzenpad 3, 023 537 3793) offers bed and breakfast starting at ƒ31,50 (members) and ƒ36,50 (non-members).

Getting there

By car

10km (6 miles) west on A5.

By train

15min, direct from Amsterdam Centraal Station.

Tourist information

VVV

Stationsplein 1 (0900 616 1600). **Open** 9.30am-5pm Mon-Fri; 10am-2pm Sat.

The Hague

Once the hunting ground of the Counts of Holland, The Hague (aka Den Haag) was founded in 1248 when William II built a castle on the site of the present parliament buildings, the **Binnenhof** (*listings page 260*). It was here that the De Witt brothers were lynched after being accused of conspiring to kill William of Orange. The buildings have retained a bastion-like appearance to this day.

Queen Beatrix arrives at the Binnenhof in a golden coach every **Prinsjesdag** (third Tuesday in September) for the annual state opening of parliament. Guided tours are organised daily to the **Knights' Hall**, where the ceremony takes place and where the Queen sits on her throne. **Huis ten Bosch Palace**, the Queen's residence, **Noordeinde Palace** and **Kneuterdijk Palace** are, unfortunately, not open to the public, but **Voorhout Palace**, on the elegant Lange Voorhout avenue has recently been opened as a museum. The **Mauritshuis** (*listings page 260*), a former regal home, is also open to the public and has an excellent art collection including works by Rubens, Rembrandt, Van Dijck, Vermeer (most notably his *View of Delft*) and Jan Steen.

The Hague's city centre is lively, offering – among other things – a good selection of shops on the small streets and squares around the palaces. And while architects are currently and

Vermeer's *View of Delft* (1658-60), now on display in the **Mauritshuis**. *See p258.*

continually working to bring the city into a bigger and brighter cultural sphere, The Hague is also one of the greenest cities in Europe, and has a number of lovely parks. **Clingendael** has a Japanese garden; **Meijendael**, a little further out of town, is part of an ancient forest; and the **Scheveningse Bosje** is big enough to occupy an entire day. Between the Bosje and the city is **Vredes Paleis** (the Peace Palace), a gift from Andrew Carnegie that is now the UN's Court of International Justice.

Just beyond Scheveningse Bosje is **Scheveningen**, a former fishing village. It's now a huge resort with high-rise hotels and, in summer, a massive choice of beach cafés. The architectural highlight of the beach is the **Steigenberger Kurhaus Hotel**. Built in 1887, it's a legacy of Scheveningen's days as a bathing place for European high society. The main salon, with its enormous chandeliers and glass cupola, is a wonderful and intimidating place to take tea. The town's history as a spa has been resurrected with the opening of **Kuur Thermen Vitalizee** (Strandweg 13F, 070 416 6500, www.vitalizee.nl), a spa bath that offers a range of treatments in which to indulge.

Also in Scheveningen is the highly acclaimed 'Sculptures by the Sea' exhibition, a multi-dimensional collection of statues portraying emotions and hailed as 'a silent sensation', at the **Museum Beelden aan Zee** (*listings page 260*). The recently renovated **Panorama Mesdag** (*listings page 260*) houses works from The Hague (marine style) and Barbizon (peasant life and landscape) schools.

None, though, is worth quite as much as the *Victory Boogie Woogie*, Piet Mondrian's last work which went for a cool ƒ80 million in 1998. *Victory Boogie Woogie* is part of the modern art collection at the **Gemeentemuseum** (*listings page 260*), housed in newly restored buildings masterminded by Dutch architect Berlage. The museum now has its own Fashion Gallery, with temporary exhibitions focusing on designers whose work transcends fashion to become art objects. The Gemeentemuseum is also linked to the **Museon**, a popular science museum, and the **Omniversum IMAX Theatre**, a state-of-the-art planetarium, while Gemeente's sister museum, **Het Paleis** (*listings page 260*) on the Lange Voorhout, has special temporary exhibitions and, during the summer only, a

Groszer Maskierter Kopf by Rainer Kreister, at **Museum Beelden aan Zee** (*see p259*).

fine selection of 20th-century sculptures on display along the tree-lined avenue in front of the museum.

For all those who want to explore the cities in Holland but haven't got enough time or energy, visit **Madurodam** (*listings below*). An insanely detailed miniature city, it depicts, among other attractions, Amsterdam's merchants' houses and the Alkmaar cheese market, both of which are replicated in minute detail. Windmills turn, ships sail and modern trains speed around on the world's largest miniature railway.

The Hague also offers a decent calendar of seasonal events, the most entertaining of which is the **Queen's Day** on 30 April (though it's not as wild as Amsterdam's equivalent celebrations). The **North Sea Regatta** is held at the end of May, falling in the middle of the **International Sand Sculpture Festival**, which takes place from early May to the beginning of June. Add to this the **Hague Horse Days**, equestrian displays held in the Lange Voorhout over the last weekend in May, **Parkpop**, an enormous free pop festival held in Zuiderpark during June, and the **North Sea Jazz Festival** in early July, and the old cliché about there being something for everyone rears its ugly but relevant head.

Museum Beelden aan Zee
Harteveltstraat 1 (070 358 5857). **Open** 11am-5pm Tue-Sun; closed Mon. **Admission** ƒ7,50; ƒ4 under-13s. **No credit cards**.

Binnenhof
Binnenhof 8 (070 364 6144). **Open** 10am-3.45pm Mon-Sat; closed Sun. **Admission** ƒ10; ƒ8,50 under-13s. **No credit cards**.

Gemeentemuseum
Stadhouderslaan 41 (070 338 1111/ www.gemeentemuseum.nl). **Open** 11am-5pm Tue-Sun; closed Mon. **Admission** ƒ12,50; ƒ7,50 13-18s; free Museum Card, under-13s. **No credit cards**.

Madurodam
George Maduroplein 1 (070 355 3900/ www.madurodam.nl). **Open** *Mid Mar-June* 9am-8pm daily. *July, Aug* 9am-11pm daily. *Sept-mid Mar* 9am-5pm daily. **Admission** ƒ21; ƒ14 4-11s; ƒ18,50 over-65s; free under-4s. **No credit cards**.

Mauritshuis
Korte Vijverberg 8 (070 302 3456/ www.mauritshuis.nl). **Open** 10am-5pm Tue-Sat; 11am-5pm Sun; closed Mon. **Admission** ƒ12,50; ƒ6,50 concessions; free Museum Card, under-7s. **No credit cards**.

Het Paleis Museum
Lange Voorhout 74 (070 362 4061). **Open** 11am-5pm Tue-Sun; closed Sat. **Admission** ƒ10; ƒ5-ƒ7,50 concessions; free Museum Card, under-13s. **No credit cards**.

Panorama Mesdag
Zeestraat 65 (070 310 6665/www.mesdag.nl). **Open** 10am-5pm Mon-Sat; noon-5pm Sun. **Admission** ƒ7,50; ƒ4 3-13s; free under-3s. 11am-5pm. **No credit cards**.

Where to eat & drink

Juliana's (Plaats 11, 070 365 0235) is where the beautiful people enjoy lunch and dinner. **Surakarta Indonesische Brasserie** (Prinsestraat 13, 070 346 6999) offers traditional Indonesian cuisine in a supremely swish setting. **De Zwart Ruiter** (Grote Markt 27, 070 364 9549), previously a brown café, is now the proud possessor of a revamped bar, and its decor is now more stylish than ever. Right next door is the grubby and down-at-heel but very lively **September** (Grote Markt 26, 070 362 3862).

Havana (Buitenhof 19, 070 356 2900), meanwhile, has a brilliant combination of bright colours, tons of candles, and boppy tunes. As well as being a decent spot for a drink, it's also a club. With its funky music, the mellow crowd in **Greve** drinks, eats and parties all hours (Torenstraat 138, 070 360 3919). While you're there, try and remember to check out the mad tiled ceiling (and toilets).

Where to stay

Des Indes InterContinental (Lange Voorhout 54-56, 070 361 2345) is the most luxurious hotel in town, with prices to match its facilities: singles cost ƒ450, doubles ƒ575. The **NJHC City Hostel Den Haag** charges ƒ35,50-ƒ40 per person, plus ƒ5 extra if you are not a member (Scheepmakersstraat 27, 070 315 7878).

Getting there

By car

50km (31 miles) south-west on A4, then A44.

By train

50min from Amsterdam Centraal Station to Den Haag Centraal Station, changing at Leiden if necessary.

Tourist information

VVV

Koningin Julianaplein 30, outside Centraal Station (0900 340 3505 premium rate/ www.denhaag.com/indexdh.html). **Open** 9am-5.30pm Mon-Sat. *July, Aug* 11am-3pm Sun.

Leiden

Canal-laced Leiden derives a good deal of its charm from the Netherlands' oldest university, which was founded here in 1575 and which boasts alumni such as Descartes, US president John Quincy Adams and many a Dutch royal. The old town teems with bicycles and cosy bars, boasts the most historic monuments per square metre in the country, and is, accordingly, a rewarding place for a stroll and a short weekend away from the relative madness of Amsterdam.

William the Silent gave the university to the townspeople as a reward for their resistance during the Spanish siege in 1574. The population had nearly been starved into submission when William opened the dykes, flooding the ground around Leiden and scaring off the southerners. **Het Ontzet van Leiden** (the Relief of Leiden) is still celebrated every 3 October with a carnival-like festival of which *hutspot*, a stew said to have been found in the Spaniards' garrison, is a big feature.

The heart of the student quarter sprawls around the Pieterskerk, in the neighbourhood in which the American Pilgrim Fathers settled before sailing to Plymouth on the *Mayflower*. Their leader, John Robinson, stayed and was buried in the church. For more history, visit the **Leiden American Pilgrim Museum** at Beschuitsteeg 9.

In the Dutch Golden Age of the late 16th and 17th centuries, Leiden grew fat on the textile trade. It also spawned three great painters of the time: Rembrandt, Jan van Goyen and Jan Steen. Although few works by these three artists remain in Leiden today, the **Stedelijk Museum de Lakenhal** (Lakenhal Municipal Museum; *listings below*), where the Golden Age clothmakers met, does have a Rembrandt, as well as other Old Masters and collections of pewter, tiles, silver and glass.

Perhaps Leiden's most notable museum, though, is the **Rijksmuseum van Oudheden** (National Museum of Antiquities; *listings below*), which houses the largest archaeological collection in the Netherlands: the Egyptian mummy collection should not be missed. The **Rijksmuseum voor Volkenkunde** (National Museum of Ethnology; *listings below*), meanwhile, showcases the cultures of Africa, Oceania, Asia, the Americas and the Arctic. Fans of Dutch clichés should visit the **Molenmuseum de Valk** (Windmill Museum The Falcon; *listings below*), a windmill-turned-museum where you can see restored living quarters, machinery and a picturesque view of Leiden. An even better view of the city can be had from the top of the **Burcht**, a 12th-century fort on an ancient artificial mound. And the latest addition to Leiden's many sights is the natural history museum **Naturalis** (*listings below*), which houses displays including full-scale dinosaurs, minerals and stuffed animals.

Molenmuseum de Valk

2e Binnenvestgracht 1 (071 516 5353). **Open** 10am-5pm Tue-Sat; 1-5pm Sun; closed Mon. **Admission** ƒ5; ƒ3 concessions; free Museum Card, under-6s. **No credit cards**.

Naturalis, Nationaal Natuurhistorisch Museum

Darwinweg (071 568 7600). **Open** noon-6pm Tue-Sun; closed Mon. **Admission** ƒ12,50; ƒ5 6-12s. **No credit cards**.

Rijksmuseum van Oudheden

Rapenburg 28 (071 516 3163). **Open** 10am-5pm Tue-Fri; noon-5pm Sat, Sun; closed Mon. **Admission** ƒ7; ƒ6 6-18s, ƒ5 over-65s; free Museum Card. **No credit cards**.

Rijksmuseum voor Volkenkunde

Steenstraat 1 (071 516 8800). **Open** 10am-5pm Tue-Fri, Sun; noon-5pm Sat; closed Mon. **Admission** ƒ10; ƒ7,50 concessions; free Museum Card. **No credit cards**.

Stedelijk Museum de Lakenhal

Oude Singel 28-32 (071 516 5360). **Open** 10am-5pm Tue-Fri; noon-5pm Sat, Sun; closed Mon. **Admission** ƒ8; ƒ5 over-65s; free Museum Card, under-18s. **No credit cards**.

Trips Out of Town

Where to eat & drink

Full of trad atmosphere, the cosy **In Den Bierbengel** (Langebrug 71, 071 514 8056) specialises in meat, fish and wines. Bar-restaurant **Annie's Verjaardag** (Hoogstraat 1A, 071 512 5737) occupies eight close, candlelit cellars underneath a bridge in the centre of town. Its main selling point is the canal barge terrace, where you can savour a relaxing view down a canalised bit of the Rhine. Expect to pay around ƒ23. For ultra-cheap and cheerful, try **La Bota** (Herensteeg 9, 071 514 6340) near the Pieterskerk. The sign says 'sherry bodega', but it's really a dark, fun, studenty bar that does homestyle meat and vegetarian dishes, salads and snacks for around ƒ15.

If you're after a drink and a dark place to sit, plenty of traditional bars dot Leiden. But for a walk on the grungy side, try student standby the **WW** (Wolsteeg 4-6, 071 512 5900), with dartboards and graffiti. **The Duke** (Oude Singel 2, 071 512 1972) has live jazz, and **LVC** (Breestraat 66, 071 566 1059) hosts touring acts specialising in reggae, hip hop and metal.

Where to stay

Top of the range is the **Golden Tulip** (Schipholweg 3, 071 522 1121), which has rooms from ƒ225 to ƒ355. Cheaper is the **Mayflower** (Beestenmarkt 2, 071 514 2641), which offers singles for ƒ135 and doubles for ƒ185 (both including breakfast), while the **Pension De Witte Singel** (Witte Singel 80, 071 512 4592) is cheaper, at ƒ57,50-ƒ85 for a single and ƒ90-ƒ115 for a double.

Getting there

By car
40km (24 miles) south-west on A4.

By train
35min from Amsterdam Centraal Station, direct.

Tourist information

VVV
Stationsweg 2D (0900 222 2333). **Open** 10am-6.30pm Mon-Fri; 10am-2pm Sat.

Rotterdam

A skate city; a harbour city; an artists' haven; an architectural inspiration; the Cultural Capital of Europe for 2001; a historical museum centre; a jazz-lover's dream… Rotterdam is, it's fair to say, all things to all people.

Rotterdam: either lots of cars at night, or the biggest neon striplight in the world.

When Rotterdam's city centre and harbour were destroyed in May 1940, the authorities decided to start anew rather than try to reconstruct its maze of canals. The imposing, futuristic skyline along the banks of the River Maas has been developing since, and one of the success stories is the **Oude Haven** (Old Harbour), a work of imaginative modernism, the pinnacle of which is Piet Blom's witty **Kijk-Kubus** (*listings page 266*). These bright yellow cubic houses are tilted cater-corner and stand, a little goofily, on stilts. Of the houses, No.70 is open to visitors. Another architectural wizard, Rem Koolhaas, designed the **Museum Park**, referred to as the cultural heart of Rotterdam, with five museums and many outdoor sculptures.

An often overlooked feature of Rotterdam is the quirky, humorous art that is found all over the city. A huge storage tank in the oil refinery complex, on the road towards Europoort, has

been painted as a giant hat box, complete with
ribbons; while on the **Willemsbrug**, the old red
bridge linking the north of the river with Nord
Island, is a more controversial piece of art. Called
the *Washing Line*, it's a large sea-chain painted
black, with bits of sea junk hanging off it. The
only people who can see it are pedestrians on the
bridge and those passing below in boats, leaving
many to wonder as to its purpose.

The Old Harbour districts such as **Kop van
Zuid** and **Entrepot** are currently undergoing
reconstruction and renovation, as part of
Rotterdam's ongoing architectural
development. Take one of the various Spido
boat tours (Leuvehoofd 5, 010 275 9988) to
check out what's new; in summer, trips are
extended to **Europoort**, the world's biggest
harbour, and the new flood barrier. The **Prins
Hendrik Maritime Museum** (Leuvehaven 1,
010 413 2680) offers plenty of perspective on

seafaring: with its background of modern and
historical maritime objects, the seafaring ways
of old Rotterdammers will make more sense. If
you're around at the start of September, don't
miss the **Wereldhavendagen** (World Harbour
Days), a three-day festival during which a
myriad of activities related to the harbour are
staged around the city.

The **Netherlands Architecture Institute**
(*listings page 266*), in seven temporary
exhibition spaces, gives an overview of the
history and development of architecture,
especially the urban design and spatial
planning of Rotterdam. Be stimulated by the
urban development yourself and go up the
Euromast (*listings page 265*) for a spectacular
view, if you can handle the height (185 metres,
or 607 feet). The park at the base of the
Euromast is where many Rotterdammers hang
out when the weather holds up.

One of the shopping areas, **Beurstraverse**, is a modern development itself. It has the usual bright chains such as Sting, the Bijenkorf (the biggest Dutch department store, whose ground-floor Chill Out zone has a great mix of lesser-known labels), international chains including Esprit and Benetton, and a particular favourite, the divine lingerie shop Heaven Lingerie (Beurstraverse 160). Meanwhile, **Van Oldenbarneveltstraat** offers more upmarket shopping and the lovely **Jan Evertsenplaats**, a green square where you can take a rest from all that spending before heading off to have a look at some of the city's sights.

Delfshaven, a solitary tree-lined canal, is one of the few remnants of Rotterdam's old city centre; a plaque on the quay marks where the Pilgrim Fathers set sail for America in 1620. Close by is the **Oude Kerk** (the Old Church), the last stop of the Pilgrim Fathers, where they are also commemorated, having held a final service here. The **Historical Museum de Dubbelde Palmboom** (Double Palm Tree;

(*listings page 265*) is housed in an old granary in Delfshaven, and features life and work in the Meuse delta from 8000 BC to the present. As part of the **Rotterdam City Museum**, it's also linked to **Het Schielandshuis** (*listings page 266*), a 17th-century palatial mansion and another of the few buildings spared in the bombing. Now placed in bizarre juxtaposition to Quist's Robeco Tower built in 1992 and the giant Hollandse Bank Unie, it displays historic rooms and clothing from the 18th century to the present. Across town, the **Museum Boijmans-Van Beuningen** (*listings page 265*) offers a beautiful collection of traditional and contemporary art (including works by Van Eyck and Rembrandt), with a sizeable design collection. Though work on the pavilion has at last been finished, the museum will be closed for restoration work until 7 April 2001.

Poles apart from this is Rotterdam's role as the only city in the Netherlands home to a growth in youth population. Rent inline skates or rollerskates for ƒ15 a day – though you'll

Beyond Holland

The country's attractions don't begin and end with the province of Holland and the cities of the Randstad. The other provinces offer a variety of attractions that provide a cultural education for those looking to explore the Netherlands beyond all the usual stops.

Drenthe

Fens, moors and forests highlight this historical province: humans have lived here for some 50,000 years. The **Drents Museum** in Assen (Brink 1, Assen, 0592 312741) offers a glimpse of the area's past with a terrific exhibition of prehistoric artefacts.

For information on attractions in Drenthe, call the **Provincial VVV** (0592 373755) or visit the **Assen VVV** (Brink 42, Assen, 0592 314324).

Friesland

Once an independent tribal nation that reached along the coast from North Holland to East Germany, Friesland's main attraction is its network of waterways; boating is now focused around the town of **Sneek**. To the north and west of Friesland are the desolate **Frisian Islands**, which nature-lovers will love for its collection of nature and bird reserves.

The **Provincial VVV** is at Stationsplein 1 in Leeuwarden (0900 202 4060 premium rate). The **Sneek VVV** can be found at Markstraat 18

(0515 414096). For information on the Frisian Islands, visit the **Texel VVV** at Emmelaan 66 on the island of Texel (0222 312847).

Gelderland

The largest of the Dutch provinces, Gelderland is dominated by the **Veluwe**, a 4,600-hectare (11,400-acre) stretch of forest and moorland. It's here you'll find the country's biggest national park, the **Hoge Veluwe** (entrances at Otterlo, Schaarsbergen and Hoenderloo, visitors' centre 0318 591627), and the terrific **Rijksmuseum Kröller-Müller** (near Otterlo entrance of Hoge Veluwe, 0318 591041).

The **Provincial VVV** can be reached on 026 333 2033, and offers full information on the area's attractions.

Groningen

Arguably the most staid and conservative of the Dutch provinces, Groningen has little to recommend it save for its wonderful collection of ancient rural churches in towns such as **Garmerwold**, **Ten Boer**, **Stedum**, **Appingedam** and **Uithuizen**. The pick of them, though, is the **Martinikerk** in the capital, Groningen.

The **Provincial VVV** and the **Groningen VVV** share a building at Gedempte Kattendiep 6 in Groningen (0900 202 3050 premium rate).

need to show a passport and leave a ƒ300 deposit – and try out the largest outdoor skate park in the country, completed in May 2000. Get your skates on at **Rotterdam Sport Import** (Witte de Withstraat 57, 010 461 0066).

Events-wise, it's one festival after another from the beginning of June until late September. The summer carnival, **Streetlife**, a sporty lifestyle event for young people, takes place at Blaak in late June (029 734 444). Don't miss the **Dunya Festival** (World Festival), with music, poetry, stories and street theatre, held at the Park (near the Euromast) in June. For **De Parade** (033 465 4577), the Museumpark is taken over by a travelling theatre, and on the occasion of the **Fast Forward Dance Parade** in mid-August, Rotterdam becomes one massive street party.

The first few years of the 21st century look exciting. The **New World Museum** on the Willemskade opens in autumn 2000, and plans to feature exhibitions of world cultures. The following year sees the opening of **Asklepion**, where visitors will be able to make a spectacular journey through the human body. And as the officially designated Cultural Capital of Europe for 2001, Rotterdam will be hosting many events, covering exhibitions, theatre, music, poetry, design and literature. For full information, log on to www.rotterdam01.nl.

Museum Boijmans-Van Beuningen
Museumpark 18-20 (010 441 9400). **Open** 10am-5pm Tue-Sat; 11am-5pm Sun; closed Mon. **Admission** ƒ10; ƒ4 4-16s; free Museum Card, under-4s. **No credit cards**.

Dubbelde Palmboom
Voorhaven 12 (010 476 1533/ www.hmr.rotterdam.nl/nl/ddp/ddp.htm). **Open** 10am-5pm Mon-Fri; 11am-5pm Sat, Sun. **Admission** ƒ6; ƒ3 concessions. **No credit cards**.

Euromast
Parkhaven 20 (010 436 4811/www.euromast.nl). **Admission** ƒ15,50; ƒ10 4-11s. **Open** *Apr-June, Sept* 10am-7pm daily. *July, Aug* 10am-10.30pm daily. *Oct-Mar* 10am-5pm daily. **Credit** AmEx, DC, MC, V.

Limburg
Limburg is arguably most notable for the town of **Maastricht**, a lovely spot to explore quite aside from its European political ties. The **Maastricht VVV** is at Kleine Straat 1 (043 325 2121), while the **Provincial VVV** can be found at Kerkstraat 31 in Valkenburg (043 601 7321).

Noord Brabant
Bordering Belgium to the south, Noord Brabant's main attractions are the **Safaripark Beekse Bergen** in Hilvarenbeek (0900 233 5732 premium rate) and **De Efteling Theme Park** in Kaatsheuvel (0416 288111). However, it's also home to the city of **Eindhoven**, which offers a fine football team (PSV) and a better modern art museum (the **Stedelijk van Abbemuseum**, Vonderweg 1, 040 275 5275).

The **Provincial VVV** can be found in the town of Tilburg (Stadhuisplein 128, 013 535 1135); the **Eindhoven VVV** is at Stationsplein 17 (0900 112 2363 premium rate).

Overijssel
Known as the 'Garden of the Netherlands', Overijssel is crisscrossed by long, winding rivers and 400 kilometres (249 miles) of canoe routes. Among its attractions are the **Hellendoorn Adventure Park** (0548 655555), the splendid modern art museum the **Rijksmuseum Twenthe** in Enschede (Lasondersingel 129-31, 053 435 8675) and the summer carnivals that are held in almost every town in the province.

For more information, contact the **Enschede VVV** (Oude Markt 31, 053 432 3200) or the **Provincial VVV** (0546 535535).

Utrecht
Utrecht's main attractions – the province's capital (see page 266) and the assorted castles (see page 254) – have been covered elsewhere in this chapter. The beautiful medieval town of **Amersfoot** is also worth a look; its **VVV** can be found at Stationsplein 9-11 (0900 112 2364 premium rate).

Zeeland
Many old buildings and farms in Zeeland were swept away in the floods in 1953. As a result, the province is now home to the **Delta Works**, the world's biggest flood barrier that was completed in 1986 at a cost of ƒ14 billion. Among the province's less useful but more entertaining attractions are the **Stedelijk Museum** in Vlissingen (Bellamypark 19, 0118 412498) and the historical **Zeeus Museum** in Middelburg (Abdij, 0118 626655). The **Provincial VVV** is at Nieuwe Burg 42 in Middelburg (0118 659965).

Trips Out of Town

Kijk-Kubus
Overblaak 70 (010 414 2285). **Open** 11am-5pm daily. **Admission** *f*3,50; *f*2,50 concessions; free under-4s. **No credit cards.**

Netherlands Architecture Institute
Museumpark 25 (010 440 1200/www.nai.nl). **Open** 10am-9pm Tue; 10am-5pm Wed-Sat; 11am-5pm Sun; closed Mon. **Admission** *f*7,50; *f*4 4-16s; free Museum Card, under-4s. Free to all Tue 5-9pm. **No credit cards.**

Het Schielandshuis
Korte Hoogstraat 31 (010 217 6767). **Open** 10am-5pm Tue-Fri; 11am-5pm Sat, Sun; closed Mon. **Admission** *f*6; *f*3 4-16s; free under-4s. **No credit cards.**

Where to eat & drink

Oude Haven, the Entrepot district and Delfshaven all offer a wide choice of (grand) cafés and restaurants. For veggies, **Bla Bla** (Piet Heynsplein 35, 010 477 4448) is expensive but busy (make sure you book ahead). At one end of Beurstraverse, the department store **V&D** has a market stall-type takeaway, **Le Marché**, offering a tempting variety of sandwiches. On the top floor, a café transforms the roof into a sunny terrace. If you want the ultimate rooftop view of the city, head for the other end of Beurstraverse to the **World Trade Centre** and up to the 23rd floor, where the swish restaurant offers spectacular panoramic views of the city (Beursplein 37, 010 405 4465).

De Schouw (Witte de Withstraat 80, 010 412 4253) is a stylish brown café, a former journalists' haunt and now a mix of artists and students. Lofty ceilings give **Café Duodok** (Meent 88, 010 433 3102) an artsy, warehouse feel, making it a mellow spot for its delicious lunches; it's just round the corner from the Beurs shopping centre but well worth the trek. Jazz fiends should head for **Dizzy** ('s Gravendijkwal 127, 010 477 3014), one of the best jazz venues in the country, while the trendy set should venture to **Nighttown** (West-Kruiskade 26-8, 010 436 1210). Other options include **Sister Moon** (Nieuwe Binnenweg 89B, 010 436 1508) and **Club Vibes** (Westersingel 50A, 010 436 6389).

Finally, young travellers would do well to visit **Use-it** (Conradstraat 2, 010 240 9158, www.jip.org/use-it), located outside the central rail station, on an island surrounded by Eurolines bus bays. Kind of a young person's VVV, it offers a feast of ideas for stuff to do in the city, as well as free lockers if you want to ditch your backpack and take the weight off your shoulders as you roam around the city.

Where to stay

The **Hotel New York** is one of the most luxurious places in town (Koninginnenhoofd 1, 010 439 0500): doubles cost from *f*165 up to *f*400 a night for the boardroom (they're charging for the view). Perhaps the most unusual way to spend the night in Rotterdam is on **De Clipper** (Leuvehaven, accessible via Terwenakker, 065 185 7380), a boat moored in the centre of the city. It'll set you back *f*51,50 a night with breakfast. For budget travellers, there is the **NJHC City Hostel Rotterdam** (Rochussenstraat 107-9, 010 436 5763); for *f*32,25 a night, you also get the use of a kitchen.

Getting there

By car
73 km (45 miles) south on A4, then A13.

By train
1hr from Amsterdam Centraal Station, direct.

Tourist information

VVV
Coolsingel 67 (0900 403 4065 premium rate/www.vvv.rotterdam.nl). **Open** 9.30am-6pm Mon-Thur; 9.30am-9pm Fri; 9.30am-5pm Sat. *Apr-Sept* also noon-5pm Sun.

Utrecht

One of the oldest cities in the Netherlands, Utrecht was also, in the Middle Ages, the country's biggest. It was a religious centre for centuries, where bishops lived and built their churches. At the end of this period, there were around 40 houses of worship in the city. All had towers and spires: from a distance, Utrecht must have resembled a giant pincushion.

However, there's more to Utrecht than history and scenery. **Utrecht University** is one of the largest in the Netherlands, and as a result the city centre is bustling with trendy shops and relaxed cafés. The city boasts the largest covered shopping centre in the country, the **Hoog Catharijne**, though unfortunately it's also one of the biggest eyesores. However, try not to be too put off by its labyrinthine layout. It might be big enough to lose yourself in for a day, but if you follow signs for 'centrum' (town centre), you will eventually come out on Achter Clarenburg. For tourist information, turn left outside and follow the shopping centre to the corner of Vredenburg and Lange Viestraat, where you'll find the VVV on your left.

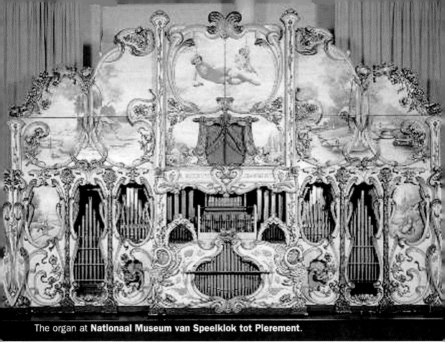

The organe at **Natlonaal Museum van Speelklok tot Pierement**.

Lovers of luxury should instead head for the boutiques and galleries tucked down the small streets along the canals; linger especially on **Oudkerkhof**, where there is a concentration of designer shops, or go to **La Vie**, the shopping centre on Lange Viestraat. Bargain hunters will enjoy the markets at **Vredenburg** on Wednesdays and Saturdays, and at St Jacobsstraat on Saturdays, or the flower and plant markets along **Janskerkhof** and **Oudegracht** on Saturdays.

Though bikes can be hired from **Rijwiel Shop** (030 296 7287), the city is so compact that practically everything is within walking distance. A good place to start a stroll around town is the **Domtoren** (the cathedral tower). At over 112 metres (367 feet) high, not only is it the highest tower in the country, but with over 50 bells it's also the largest musical instrument in the Netherlands. Visitors are allowed to climb the tower, but make sure you feel capable of scaling 465 steps. The panoramic view is worth the effort, stretching 40 kilometres (25 miles) to Amsterdam on a clear day.

The entire space between the tower and the **Domkerk** was originally occupied by the nave of the huge church, destroyed in a freak tornado in 1674. Many other buildings were damaged, and the exhibition inside the Domkerk shows interesting 'before' and 'after' sketches. Outside is the **Pandhof**, a cloister garden planted with many medicinal herbs. The garden, with its

beautiful statuette of a canon hunched over his writing, is a tranquil spot to sit and rest a while.

Another fascinating place to explore is the **Oudegracht**, the canal that runs through the centre of the city. Unlike Amsterdam, where the water is at street level, the people of Utrecht have been blessed with waterside footpaths and cellars, which allow them to use the basements of their canalside houses. Many of those cellars now house cafés and shops, and are excellent places to have a snack and watch boats navigate their way under the narrow bridges. There are regular boat trips, and *waterfietsen* (pedal boats) can also be hired.

Of Utrecht's several museums, the **Museum Catharijnecovent** (St Catharine Convent Museum; *listings page 268*) is located in a beautiful late medieval building and gives an account of the country's religious history. The *bogenkelder* (vaulted cellar), which contains many old Bibles with silver cast covers, and the beautiful stained-glass windows in the adjoining church should not be missed. The **Nationaal Museum van Speelklok tot Pierement** (*listings page 268*), meanwhile, has an extensive collection of automated musical instruments dating back to as far as the 17th century, and the **Universiteitsmuseum** (University Museum; *listings page 268*) focuses on the interaction between science and education, past and present. At the **Nederlands Spoorwegmuseum** (Dutch Railway Museum;

listings below) visitors can drive on an intercity train simulator and look at old locomotives. The biggest rock garden in the Netherlands is a striking part of **Fort Hoofddijk** (*listings below*); on a cold day, the tropical greenhouse is a perfect place to thaw out.

There are various blues and jazz weekends throughout the year, starting in April with a **Jazz Festival** at the beginning of the month and **Blues Roots** in mid-April. Music is central to the hectic **Queen's Day** celebrations on 30 April, the **Midsummer Night's** pop and classical concert, and the **Festival of Music** at the end of August. There are specific days when monuments and museums throw their doors open to the public for free (check with the VVV) and, during July and August, there are informative walking tours through the city.

Utrecht is located in a neighbourhood abundant with castles, forests and arboretums. In the outskirts of the city, **Slot Zuylen** (Zuylen Castle, Tournooiveld 1, Oud Zuilen, 030 244 0255) presides over exquisite ornamental waterfalls and gardens. Check out the concerts and exhibitions in **Kasteel Groeneveld**'s gorgeous gardens (Groeneveld Castle, Groeneveld 2, 035 542 0446), just north-east of Utrecht. Stroll in the lovely **Arboretum von Gimborn** (Vossensteinsesteeg 8, 030 253 1826) in Doorne, then pop across the town to **Kasteel Huis Doorn** (Doorn Castle, Langbroekerweg 10, 034 341 2244) to see how royalty lived at the end of the 19th century. In Haarzuilens, west of Utrecht, **Kasteel de Haar** is a sumptuous fairy-tale castle with purple-tiled turrets.

Fort Hoofddijk

Budapestlaan 17, De Uithof (030 253 5455). **Open** *Mar, Apr, Oct, Nov* 10am-4pm daily. *May-Sept* 10am-5pm daily; closed Dec. **Admission** ƒ7,50; ƒ2,50 4-12s; free Museum Card. **No credit cards**.

Museum Catharijnecovent

Lange Nieuwstraat 38 (031 231 3835/7296/ www.catharijneconvent.nl). **Open** 10am-5pm Tue-Fri; 11am-5pm Sat, Sun; closed Mon. **Admission** ƒ10; ƒ5-ƒ7,50 concessions; free Museum Card, under-6s. **No credit cards**.

Nationaal Museum van Speelklok tot Pierement

Buurkerkhof 10 (030 231 2789/ www.museumspeelklok.nl). **Open** 10am-5pm Tue-Sat; noon-5pm Sun; closed Mon. **Admission** ƒ12; ƒ7,50-ƒ9 concessions. **No credit cards**.

Nederlands Spoorwegmuseum

Maliebaanstation 16 (030 230 6206/ www.spoorwegmuseum.nl). **Open** 10am-5pm Tue-Fri; 11.30am-5pm Sat, Sun; closed Mon. **Admission** ƒ15; ƒ9,50-ƒ12,50 concessions; free Museum Card, under-4s. **No credit cards**.

Universiteitsmuseum

Lange Nieuwstraat 106 (030 253 8008/ www.museum.ruu.nl). **Open** 11am-5pm Tue-Sun; closed Mon. **Admission** ƒ7,50; ƒ3,75 concessions; free Museum Card. **No credit cards**.

Where to eat & drink

Het Grachetenhuys (Nieuwgracht 33, 030 231 7494) is a busy restaurant with a good menu; dinner costs from ƒ70. Budget travellers should try **De Zakkendrager** (De Zakkendragerssteeg 26, 030 231 7578), close to the station; with dinner at ƒ40 for two, you can't go wrong in this cosy restaurant. If you want something lighter, try the **Pancake Bakery de Oude Munt Kelder** (Oudegracht aan de Wer, 030 231 6773), which serves pancakes from ƒ13 and a has lovely view of the canal.

Most of the bars in the city centre are well populated by students and are pretty relaxed. The **Havana Bar** (Oudkerkhof 29, 030 231 5040) is a bit more international, and **Jacqmotte Coffee** (Steenweg 37, 030 233 3410) approximates to Starbucks with a smile, if you want a change from brown cafés.

Where to stay

The four-star **Malie Hotel** (Maliestraat 2, 030 231 6424) is a beautiful old merchant's house and one of the most characterful address in which to stay on a short-term basis in the city; if you really want to pamper yourself, a double costs ƒ225-ƒ255 a night. **Park Hotel** (Tolsteegsingel 34, 030 251 6712) is a one-star budget hotel, where a double room will set you back from ƒ125 a night.

Those on an even tighter budget should take a ten-minute bus ride out from the city centre to Bunnik, where the **NJHC Youth Hostel** (Rhijnauwenselaan 14, Bunnik, 030 656 1277) offers a night in a shared room for ƒ28-ƒ31,50.

Getting there

By car

40km (25 miles) south-east.

By rail

30min from Amsterdam Centraal Station, direct.

Tourist information

VVV

Vredenburg 90 (0900 414 1414 premium rate/ www.tref.nl/utrecht/vvv). **Open** 9am-6pm Mon-Fri; 9am-5pm Sat.

Directory

Directory

Getting Around

Getting around Amsterdam is fairly easy. The city has an efficient and reasonably priced tram and bus system, though if you're staying in the centre of town, most places are easily reachable on foot. Locals tend to get around by bike: the streets are busy with cycles all day and most of the evening. There are also pleasure boats, commercial barges and water taxis on the canals.

If you're thinking of bringing a car to Amsterdam for a short stay, don't. The roads aren't designed for them, and parking places are elusive. Unfortunately, public transport provision for those with disabilities is dire: though there are lifts at all Metro stations, staff can't always help people in wheelchairs.

To & from the airport

KLM Hotel Bus Service

Main exit, Schiphol Airport, Zuid (653 4975). **Times** buses every 30min 6.30am-3pm, then on the hr until 10pm daily. **Tickets** *Single* ƒ17,50. *Return* ƒ30.
This service is available to anyone; you don't need to have travelled on the airline or be staying at one of the hotel stops. The route starts at Schiphol, then goes to the Golden Tulip Barbizon (Leidseplein), Pulitzer (Westermarkt-Keizersgracht), Krasnapolsky (Dam Square), Holiday Inn and Renaissance (Nieuwezijds Voorburgwal), Barbizon Palace (Zeedijk) and back to Schiphol again. There is also a route that leaves from the south of the city: details are available from the above number or from the Amsterdam Tourist Board.

Schiphol Airport Rail Service

Schiphol Airport/Centraal Station (information 0900 9292). **Times** Trains daily every 15min 4am-

midnight; then every hr from 12.44am. **Tickets** *Single* ƒ6.50; ƒ2,50 under-12s with adult; free under-4s. *Return* ƒ11; ƒ2,50 under-12s with adult; free under-4s.
The journey to Centraal Station takes about 20 minutes. You'll probably want a single ticket; a return is valid only for that day.

Taxis

There are always plenty of taxis outside the main exit. It's pricey, however: about ƒ70 from the airport into Amsterdam is average.

Airline information

For general airport enquiries, ring Schiphol Airport on 0900 0141 or go to www.schiphol.nl. Staff at the airlines listed below usually speak English.

British Airways 346 9559/ www.britishairways.nl.
British Midland 346 9211/ www.britishmidland.com.
EasyJet 023 568 4880/ www.easyjet.co.uk.
KLM 474 7747/ http://nederland.klm.com.

Left luggage

There is a staffed left-luggage counter at Schiphol Airport, open from 7am to 10.45pm daily. There are also lockers in the arrival and departure halls, while in Amsterdam itself, there are lockers at Centraal Station with 24-hour access. Expect to pay ƒ5-ƒ10 per item per day.

Cycling

Cycling is the most convenient means of getting from A to B in Amsterdam: there are bike lanes on most roads, marked out by white lines and bike

symbols. Some drivers insist on using bike lanes (which are often paved red) as parking spaces, but most motorists are used to the abundance of cyclists and collisions are rare. Remember, though, that cycling two abreast is illegal, as is going without reflector bands on both front and back wheels.

Never leave your bike unlocked: there's a thriving trade in stolen bikes. Use a sturdy lock: some thieves are equipped with powerful cutters that will make short work of thin chains. Always lock your bike to something unmovable, preferably using two locks: one around the frame and one through the front wheel. If someone in the street offers you a bike for sale ('fiets te koop'), don't be tempted: it's almost certainly stolen, and there's no shortage of firms where a good bike can be hired for ƒ10-ƒ15 a day. Aside from the bike hire firms listed below, check the *Amsterdam Yellow Pages* (*Gouden Gids*) under 'Fietsen en Bromfietsen Verhuur'.

Bike City

Bloemgracht 68, The Jordaan (626 3721). Tram 10, 13, 14, 17, 20. **Open** 9am-6pm daily. **Rates** ƒ12,50/ first day; ƒ10/extra days; ƒ50/wk; plus ƒ50 deposit (basic bikes; others are more expensive) and passport/ID card or credit card imprint. **Credit** AmEx, DC, MC, V. **Map** p305 B3.
Opening times may vary in winter.

Rent-A-Bike

Damstraat 22, Old Centre: Red Light District (625 5029). Tram 4, 9, 14, 16, 20, 24, 25. **Open** 9am-6pm daily. **Rates** ƒ15/day; plus ƒ50 deposit and passport/ID card or credit card imprint. **Credit** AmEx, DC, MC, V. **Map** p306 D3.
A 10% discount (excluding deposit) to anyone mentioning *Time Out* when they hire a bike here.

Take-A-Bike

Centraal Station, Stationsplein 12,
Old Centre: New Side (624 8391).
Tram 1, 2, 4, 5, 9, 13, 16, 17, 20,
24, 25. **Open** 8am-midnight daily.
Rates *f*10/day; *f*40/wk; plus *f*200
deposit. **Map** p306 D1.
Here you can either hire a bike (until
10pm) or store one (until midnight).

Driving

If you absolutely must bring a
car to the Netherlands, join a
national motoring organisation
beforehand. These provide
international assistance
booklets, which explain what
to do in the event of a
breakdown in Europe. To drive
in the Netherlands you'll need
a valid national driving
licence, although the Dutch
motoring club, **ANWB** (*see
below*), and many car hire firms
favour a photocard ID or an
international driving licence,
available from selected Post
Office branches around
Britain: phone the AA
information line (0990 500600)
for a full list.

Major roads are usually
well-maintained and clearly
signposted. Motorways are
labelled 'A'; major roads 'N';
and European routes 'E'. Brits
in particular should note that
the Dutch drive on the right,
while everyone should
remember that drivers and
front-seat passengers must
always wear seatbelts. Speed
limits are 50kmh (31mph)
within cities, 70kmh (43mph)
outside, and 100kmh (62mph)
on motorways. If you're
driving in Amsterdam, look
out for cyclists, who'll come at
you from every which way. To
complicate things further,
many Amsterdam streets are
now one-way.

To bring your car into the
Netherlands, you'll need an
international identification
disk, a registration certificate,
proof of the vehicle having
passed a road safety test in its
country of origin, and
insurance documents.

Royal Dutch Touring Club (ANWB)

Museumplein 5, Museum Quarter
(070 314 1420/24hr emergency line
0800 0888). Tram 2, 3, 5, 12, 16,
20. **Open** 9.30am-6pm Mon-Wed,
Fri; 9.30am-9pm Thur; 9am-4pm
Sat; closed Sun. **Credit** MC, V.
Map p310 D6.
If you haven't joined a motoring
organisation, enrol here for *f*140,
which covers the cost of assistance
should your vehicle break down. If
you're a member of a foreign
motoring organisation, you're
entitled to free help. Emergency
crews may not accept credit cards or
cheques at the scene.

Car hire

Dutch car hire (*auto-verhuur*)
companies generally expect at
least one year's driving
experience and will want to see
a valid national driving licence
and passport. All companies
will require a deposit through
a credit card, and you'll
generally need to be over 21.
Prices given below are for one
day's hire of the cheapest car
available excluding insurance,
unless otherwise stated.

Adam's Rent-a-Car

Nassaukade 344-346, Oud West
(685 0111). Tram 7, 10, 17, 20.
Open 8am-6pm Mon-Fri; 8am-8pm
Sat; closed Sun. **Credit** AmEx, DC,
MC, V. **Map** p310 C5.
One-day hire costs from *f*65; the first
100km (62 miles) are free, and after
that the charge is 35¢/km.

Dik's Autoverhuur

Van Ostadestraat 278-280, The
Pijp (662 3366). Tram 3, 4. **Open**
8am-7.30pm Mon-Sat; 9am-12.30pm,
8-10.30pm Sun. **Credit** AmEx, DC,
MC, V. **Map** p311 F6.
Prices start at *f*57 per day. The first
100km are free, then it's 22¢/km.

Hertz

Overtoom 333, Oud West (612
2441). Tram 1, 6. **Open** 8am-6pm
Mon-Thur; 8am-7pm Fri; 8am-4pm
Sat; 9am-2pm Sun. **Credit** AmEx,
DC, MC, V. **Map** p309 B6.
Prices start at *f*119 per day
including insurance and mileage.

Ouke Baas

Van Ostadestraat 362-372, Oost
(679 4842). Tram 3, 4. **Open** 7am-
8pm Mon-Fri; 7.30am-9pm Sat; 8am-
1pm, 7-10.30pm Sun. **Credit** AmEx,
DC, MC, V. **Map** p312 G5.

Inclusive of VAT and the first
100km, Ouke Baas' cheapest car
costs *f*56 per day. After the first
100km, it costs 22¢/km.

Clamping & fines

Amsterdam's wheel-clamp
(*wielklem*) teams are swift to
act and show little mercy if
they see a car parked illegally.
A yellow sticker on the
windscreen informs you where
to go to pay the fine (*f*140).
Once you've paid, return to the
car and wait for the traffic
police to remove the clamp.
Luckily, the declampers
normally arrive promptly.

If you park illegally and fail
to pay your parking fine
within 24 hours, your car will
be towed away. It'll cost over
*f*400 – plus parking fine – to
reclaim it from the pound if
you do so within 24 hours, and
*f*98 for every 12 hours
thereafter. The pound is at
Daniel Goedkoopstraat 7-9.
Take your passport, licence
number and enough cash or
travellers' cheques to pay the
fine. All major credit cards are
accepted. If your car has been
clamped or towed away, head
to any of the following offices
to pay the *f*140 fine.

Head office

Weesperstraat 105A, Old Centre: Old
Side (553 0300). Tram 6, 7, 9, 10,
14, 20. **Open** 8.30am-4.30pm Mon-
Fri; closed Sat, Sun. **Map** p307 F3.

Branches

Weesperstraat 105A, Old Centre:
Old Side (553 0333). Tram 6, 7, 9,
10, 14, 20. **Open** 8am-8pm Mon-Sat;
closed Sun. **Map** p307 F3.
Beukenplein 50, Oost (553 0333).
Tram 9, 14. **Open** 8am-8pm Mon-
Sat; closed Sun. **Map** p312 H4.
Jan Pieter Heijestraat 94, Oud West
(553 0333). Tram 3, 12. **Open** 8am-
8pm Mon-Sat; closed Sun.
Daniel Goedkoopstraat 7-9, Oost
(553 0333). Metro Spaklerweg.
Open 24hrs daily.

Parking

Parking in central Amsterdam
is a nightmare: the whole of the
town centre is metered from

9am to 7pm and meters are difficult to find. Meters will set you back up to ƒ5,50 an hour depending on how central you are. Illegally parked cars get clamped or towed away without any warning (*see above*). Car parks (*parkeren*) are indicated by a white 'P' on a blue square. After 7pm, parking at meters is free. Below is a list of central car parks where you're more likely to find a space during peak times. Be sure to empty your car completely of all valuables and the radio: cars with foreign number plates are particularly vulnerable to break-ins.

ANWB Parking Amsterdam Centraal

Prins Hendrikkade 20A, Old Centre: New Side (638 5330). **Open** 24hrs daily. **Rates** ƒ5/hr; max ƒ50/day; ƒ195/wk (from noon Sat to noon following Sat). **Credit** AmEx, DC, MC, V. **Map** p306 D2.
Many nearby hotels give 15% discount on parking here.

Europarking

Marnixstraat 250, Oud West (623 6694). **Open** 6.30am-1am Mon-Thur; 6.30am-2am Fri, Sat; 7am-1am Sun. **Rates** ƒ4/hr; ƒ50/24hrs. **Map** p309 B4.

De Kolk Parking

Nieuwezijds Voorburgwal 12, Old Centre: New Side (427 1449). **Open** 24hrs daily. **Rates** ƒ5/hr; ƒ55/24hrs. **Map** p306 C2.

Petrol

The main 24-hour petrol stations (*benzinestations*) within the city limits are at Gooiseweg 10-11, Sarphatistraat 225, Marnixstraat 250 and Spaarndammerdijk 218.

A basic map of the tram network is on page 314. For information, tickets, maps and an English-language guide to the city's ticket system, visit the GVB, Amsterdam's municipal transport authority.

GVB

Stationsplein 15, Old Centre: New Side (0900 9292). Tram 1, 2, 4, 5, 9, 13, 16, 17, 20, 24, 25. **Open** *Phone enquiries* 6am-midnight Mon-Fri; 7am-midnight Sat, Sun. *Personal callers* 7am-9pm Mon-Fri; 8am-9pm Sat; closed Sun. **Map** p306 D1.
The GVB runs Amsterdam's Metro, bus and tram services, and can provide information on all.
Branches: GVB Head Office, Prins Hendrikkade 108, Old Centre: New Side; Amstel Railway Station, Julianaplein, Zuid.

Metro

The Metro system uses the same ticketing system as trams and buses (*see below*), and serves suburbs to the south and east. There are three lines, all terminating at Centraal Station (which is sometimes abbreviated to CS). Trains run from 6am Monday to Friday (6.30am Sat, 7.30am Sun) to around 12.15am daily.

Trams & buses

As a visitor to Amsterdam, you will find buses and trams a particularly good way to get around the city centre. Tram services run from 6am Monday to Friday, 6.30am on Saturday and 7.30am on Sunday, with a special night bus service taking over after midnight. Night buses are numbered from 71 to 79; all go to Centraal Station, except 79. Night bus stops are indicated by a black square at the stop with the bus number printed on it. Night buses run from 1am to 5.30am from Monday to Friday, and until 6.30am on weekends.

Yellow signs at tram and bus stops indicate the name of the stop and further stops. There are usually maps of the entire network in the shelters and diagrams of routes on board the trams and buses. The city's bus and tram drivers are generally courteous and will give directions if asked; most are sufficiently fluent to do this in English.

The yellow and decorated varieties of tram are as synonymous with Amsterdam as the red double-decker bus is with London. The vehicles make for fast and efficient travel, but other road users should be warned that they will stop only when absolutely necessary. Cyclists should listen out for tram warning bells – as well as being careful to avoid crossing tramlines at an angle that avoids the front wheel getting stuck – and motorists should avoid blocking tramlines: cars are allowed to venture on to them only if they're turning right.

To get on or off a tram, wait until it has halted at a stop and press the yellow button by the doors, which will then open. On some trams you can buy a ticket from the driver at the front; on others from either a machine in the middle, or a conductor at the back.

Tram 20, also known as the Circle Line tram, departs from two stops outside Centraal Station. Its route stays within a fairly central area and is convenient for all the major museums and sights. In mid-2000, though, rumours were rife that the 20 route would soon be cancelled due to financial losses, so don't make plans to rely on it.

Note that Metro 51, 53 and 54 are, confusingly, fast trams that run on Metro lines. This is not the same as the number 5 tram, actually called a *sneltram* (which translates literally as 'fast tram').

Tickets

Beware of travelling on a bus or tram without a ticket. Uniformed inspectors make regular checks and passengers without a valid ticket – or an exceptional excuse – will be asked for ID and fined ƒ60 (plus a fare of ƒ4,50) on the spot. Playing the ignorant foreigner rarely works.

Strippenkaarten

A 'strip ticket' system operates on trams, buses and the Metro. It's initially confusing, but ultimately good value for money. Prices range from ƒ3 for a strip of two units to ƒ12 for 15 units and ƒ35,25 for 45 units; children under four travel free, and older children (aged 4-18) pay reduced fares (ƒ7 for a 15-strip card). Prices increase annually.

Tickets can be bought at GVB (public transport) offices, post offices, train stations and many tobacconists. The tickets must be stamped upon boarding a tram or bus and on entering a Metro station. The city is divided into five zones: Noord (north), West, Centrum, Oost (east) and Zuid (south); most of central Amsterdam falls, not surprisingly, within zone Centrum. Strip tickets are also valid on trains that stop at Amsterdam stations, with the exception of Schiphol.

For travel in a single zone, two units must be stamped, while three are stamped for two zones, four for three zones and so on. On trams, you can stamp your own tickets in the yellow box-like contraption near the doors: fold the ticket so the unit you need to stamp is at the end. Some trams, though, now only allow passengers to enter at the rear, where a conductor will stamp the ticket for you. On buses, drivers stamp the tickets, and on the Metro there are stamping machines at the entrance to stations.

An unlimited number of people can travel on one card, but the appropriate number of units must be stamped for each person. The stamps are valid for one hour, during which time you can transfer to other buses and trams without having to stamp your card again. If your journey takes more than an hour, you have to stamp more units, but no single tram journey in central Amsterdam is likely to take that long. Strippenkaarten are valid for one year from the first stamp.

Dagkaarten

A cheaper option for unlimited travel in Amsterdam, a 'day ticket' costs ƒ12. Dutch pensioners, the unwaged and children aged four to 18 pay less. Child day tickets are valid on night buses. A day ticket is valid on trams, buses and Metro on the day it is stamped until the last bus or tram runs. You need to buy a new ticket for night buses. Only the one-day ticket can be bought from drivers on trams and buses. After stamping the day ticket on your first journey, you do not need to stamp it again.

The extended form of the day ticket costs ƒ31,50: aside from entitling the bearer to use trams, buses and the Metro, it also includes all-day use of the Canal Bus network (*see p274*) and offers ƒ300 worth of vouchers valid in museums, attractions and restaurants.

Another, cheaper ticket costs ƒ4 and is valid on the system for two hours. Returns – which are valid for four hours – cost ƒ7.

Sterabonnement

'Season tickets' can be bought from GVB offices, tobacconists and post offices, and are valid for a week, a month or a year. A weekly pass for the central zone (Centrum) costs ƒ18, a monthly one ƒ59,50 and a yearly one ƒ590,50. Children aged from four to 18 get cheaper season tickets: ƒ10,75 for a day, ƒ37,50 for a month and ƒ370,50 for a year. You'll need a passport photo to get a season ticket.

Taxis

There are a few ground rules that visitors would do well to follow. Be sure to check that the meter initially shows no more than the minimum charge (ƒ4,80). Ask the driver for an estimate of how much the journey will cost before setting out. Even short journeys are expensive: on top of ƒ4,80, you will be expected to pay ƒ3,40 per kilometre for the first 25 kilometres, then ƒ2,80 per kilometre thereafter.

If you feel you have been ripped off, ask for a receipt, which you are entitled to see before handing over cash. If the charge is extortionate, phone the central taxi office (677 7777) or contact the police. Rip-offs are relatively rare.

You're not supposed to hail a taxi in the street – though occasionally one may stop – as there are ranks dotted around the city. The best places to find taxis are outside Centraal Station, the bus station at the junction of Kinkerstraat and Marnixstraat, Rembrandtplein and Leidseplein. You can't book cabs in advance, but if you call Amsterdam's 24-hour central taxi control on 677 7777, a taxi will arrive almost immediately. The line is often busy on Friday and Saturday nights, but there's a telephone queueing system.

Wheelchairs will only fit in taxis if folded. If you're in a wheelchair, phone the car transport service for wheelchair users on 633 3943 (generally open 9am to 5pm, Monday to Friday). You'll need to book your journey one or two days in advance and it costs around ƒ4 per kilometre.

Tours

Bike tours

Cycling may be the best way to get around Amsterdam, but be careful of resident cyclists and car drivers who delight in cutting up tourists (*see page 270*). However, if you stick with one of the tours and are careful to follow the guide's instructions, you should be OK. Rental of a bicycle for the duration of the tour is included in the prices listed.

Yellow Bike

Nieuwezijds Voorburgwal 66, Old Centre: New Side (620 6940). Tram 1, 2, 5, 13, 17, 20. **Open** *Apr-Nov* 8.30am-5.30pm daily. **No credit cards. Map** p306 C2.
Glide past Amsterdam's main sights with Yellow Bike's City Tour: it takes three hours, departs at 9.30am and 1pm every day from Nieuwezijds Kolk 29, and costs ƒ32,50. The Waterland Tour takes you further afield and lasts about six hours: the trip includes a visit to a windmill and lunch at a pancake house. Waterland Tours depart at 11am daily also from Nieuwezijds Kolk 29, and cost ƒ42,50 (not including lunch).

Boat tours

Best of Holland

Damrak 34; cruises depart from Rederij Lovers landing stage, opposite Centraal Station, Old Centre: New Side (623 1539). Tram 4, 9, 16, 20, 24, 25. **Open** 8.30am-11pm daily. **Cruises** *Day cruise* approx every 30min 10am-5pm daily. *Candlelight cruise* (reservation required) summer 9pm daily; winter 9pm Wed, Fri, Sat. **Duration** *Day cruise* 1hr. *Candlelight cruise* 2hrs. **Tickets** *Day cruise* ƒ13; ƒ6,50 under-13s. *Candlelight cruise* ƒ47,50; ƒ23,75 under-13s. **Credit** AmEx, MC, V. **Departs Map** p305 D2.

Holland International

Prins Hendrikkade 33A; cruises depart from opposite Centraal Station, Old Centre: New Side (622 7788). Tram 1, 2, 4, 5, 9, 13, 16, 17, 20, 24, 25. **Summer cruises** every 20min 9am-6pm, every 30min 6-10pm daily. *Brunch cruise* (reservation required) 11am Sat, Sun. *Candlelight cruise* (wine & cheese; reservation required) 9.30pm daily. *Dinner cruise* (4-course dinner; reservation required) 8.30pm daily. **Winter cruises** approx every 30min, 10am-6pm daily. *Brunch cruise* 11am Sat, Sun. *Candlelight cruise* 8pm daily. *Dinner cruise* 7pm Tue, Thur, Fri, Sat. **Duration** *Day cruise* 1hr. *Brunch cruise* 3hrs. *Candlelight cruise* 2hrs. *Dinner cruise* 2½hrs. **Tickets** *Day cruise* ƒ15 (ƒ17,50 from 27 Mar 2001); ƒ10 under-13s. *Brunch cruise* ƒ65; ƒ60 under-13s. *Candlelight cruise* ƒ50; ƒ25 under-13s. *Dinner cruise* ƒ150; ƒ100 under-13s. **Credit** AmEx, MC, V. **Departs Map** p305 D2.

Lindbergh

Damrak 26, Old Centre: New Side (622 2766). Tram 4, 9, 16, 20, 24, 25. **Cruises** *Day cruise* Mar-Oct every 15min 10am-6pm daily; Nov-Apr every 30min, 9am-4pm daily. *Dinner cruise* 7.30pm daily. *Candlelight cruise* (wine & cheese) 9pm daily (May-Oct); 9.30pm Wed, Fri, Sat (Nov-Apr). **Duration** *Day cruise* 1hr. *Dinner cruise* 2hrs. *Candlelight cruise* 2hrs. **Tickets** *Day cruise* ƒ13; ƒ8 4-13s. *Dinner cruise* ƒ132,50. *Candlelight cruise* ƒ47,50. **Credit** AmEx, DC, MC, V. **Departs Map** p305 D2.

Lovers

Prins Hendrikkade, Old Centre: New Side (opposite 25-27), by Centraal Station (622 2181). Tram 1, 2, 4, 5, 9, 13, 16, 17, 20, 24, 25. **Cruises** *Day cruise* every 30min, 9am-6pm daily. *Dinner cruise* (reservation required) 7.30pm daily. *Candlelight cruise* (reservation required) 9pm daily. **Duration** *Day cruise* 1hr. *Dinner cruise* 2½hrs. *Candlelight cruise* 2hrs. **Tickets** *Day cruise* ƒ15; ƒ10 under-13s. *Dinner cruise* ƒ132,50; ƒ86 under-13s. *Candlelight cruise* ƒ47,50; ƒ30 under-13s. **Credit** AmEx, MC, V. **Departs Map** p305 D2.

Rondvaarten

Kooy BV Rokin, Old Centre: New Side (opposite No.125), at corner of Spui (623 3810). Tram 4, 9, 16, 20, 24, 25. **Cruises** *Mar-mid Oct* every 30min 9am-10pm daily. *Mid Oct-Feb* every 30min 10am-5pm daily. *Candlelight cruise* Apr-mid Oct 9pm daily. **Duration** 1hr. *Candlelight cruise* 2hrs. **Tickets** ƒ13; ƒ8 under-14s. *Candlelight cruise* (wine & cheese) ƒ40. **No credit cards. Departs Map** p306 D3.

Walking tours

Amsterdam is a great city to explore on foot, though its uneven streets and tramlines mean it isn't the world's best city if you're wearing stilettos, pushing pushchairs or in a wheelchair. The **Amsterdam Tourist Board** (*see page 289*) has a series of brochures (in English) outlining easy-to-follow walks.

Archivisie

Postbus 14603, 1001 LC (625 8908). Archivisie organises tailor-made architectural tours, and runs regular theme tours. Phone for appointments and details of charges.

Mee in Mokum

Hartenstraat 18, Grachtengordel: West (625 1390). Tram 13, 14, 17, 20. **Tours** (last 2-3hrs) 11am Tue-Sun. **Cost** ƒ4; free under-12s. **Map** p306 C3.

Long-time residents of Amsterdam, all over 55, give highly personal and individual tours of the old part of the city and the Jordaan: each guide has his or her own route and his or her own story to tell about the city (in English as well as Dutch). Tours leave from the **Amsterdams Historisch Museum** (*see p49*); advance booking is necessary.

Water travel

Boats to rent

Canal Bike

Weteringschans 24, Grachtengordel: East (626 5574). **Open** *Summer* 10am-9.30pm daily. *Winter* 10am-6pm daily. **Moorings** Leidsekade at Leidseplein, between Marriott and American Hotels; Stadhouderskade, opposite Rijksmuseum; Prinsengracht, by Westerkerk; Keizersgracht, on the corner of Leidsestraat. **Hire rates** *4-person pedalo* if 1 or 2 people, ƒ12,50/person/hr; if 3 or 4 people, ƒ10/person/hr. **Deposit** ƒ50/canal bike. **No credit cards. Office Map** p310 D5.

Roell

Mauritskade 1, by the Amstel, Plantage (692 9124). Tram 6, 7, 10. **Open** *Apr-Sept* 11am-7pm Tue-Fri; 11am-4pm Sat; closed Mon, Sun; *Oct-Feb* 11am-6pm Wed-Fri; also by appointment. **Hire rates** *2-person pedalo* ƒ27,50/hr. *4-person pedalo* ƒ35/hr. *4-person motor boat* ƒ55/1hr (ƒ95 for 2 hrs). *Group boat* (Mar-Dec only; max 30 persons incl captain):

ƒ225/1hr; ƒ200/hr for subsequent hours. **Deposit** *Pedalos* ƒ50. *Motor boat* ƒ250 (ID required). **No credit cards. Map** p312 H2.

Canal buses

Canal Bus

Weteringschans 24, Grachtengordel: East (623 9886). Tram 6, 10. **Open** *Summer* 9am-7pm Mon-Sat. *Winter* 10am-6pm Mon-Fri. **Cost** *Day ticket* ƒ25; ƒ17,50 under-12s. *2-day ticket* ƒ29,75. *Combination day ticket incl entrance to Rijksmuseum* ƒ32 (not available during special exhibitions). **No credit cards. Map** p310 D5.

Water taxis

Water Taxi Centrale

Stationsplein 8, Old Centre: New Side (622 2181). Tram 1, 2, 4, 5, 9, 13, 16, 17, 20, 24, 25. **Open** 8am-midnight daily. **Cost** *8-person boat* ƒ125 for first 30min, then ƒ75/30min. *16-person boat* ƒ225 for first 30min, then ƒ125/30min. *25-person boat* ƒ250 for first 30min, then ƒ150/30min. **Credit** AmEx, MC, V (accepted only prior to boarding). **Map** p305 D1.

Try and book in advance.

Travel from Amsterdam

Hitch-hiking

An accepted practice, but caution is advised.

Starting points

Towards The Hague/Rotterdam: between RAI station and the RAI on Europa Boulevard, by the motorway. **Towards Utrecht**: the corner of Rijnstraat and President Kennedylaan. **Towards Arnhem & Germany**: at Gooiseweg, by Amstel station.

Trains

From Centraal Station, one of the biggest railway terminals in Europe, you can get direct trains to most major cities across the continent. As most of the city's bus and tram services begin and end here, it's also an ideal starting point for trips around the city. On the down side, beware of pickpockets and hustlers.

The options for travelling within the Netherlands are many. Nederlandse Spoorwegen (aka NS, and translatable as Netherlands Railway) offers a largely excellent service in terms of cost, punctuality and cleanliness. Aside from the usual singles and returns, you can also buy tickets that entitle you to unlimited travel in the Netherlands on any given day (Dagkaarten), one that also entitles you to use buses, trams and the Metro (OV

Dagkaarten) and, for selected places, NS Rail Idee tickets, which are usually all-in-one tickets that'll get you to a destination and also include the admission fee to one or more of the local sights. Many attractions covered in the **Trips Out of Town** chapter are covered by NS Rail Idee tickets, the purchase of which will invariably involve a discount on separate rail and admission tickets. Ask at Centraal Station or call 0900 9292 for more details.

You must reserve tickets for international trains, but be warned: the office gets very crowded during the summer season. Tickets can be reserved over the phone (620 2266), but this should be done at least a week ahead of travel.

Centraal Station Information Desk

Stationsplein 15, Old Centre: New Side (information 0900 9292). Tram 1, 2, 4, 5, 9, 13, 16, 17, 20, 24, 25. **Open** *Information desk* 6.30am-10pm daily. *Reservations office* 24hrs daily. **Credit** MC, V. **Map** p306 D1.

Resources A-Z

In the following entries we have listed credit cards where relevant; if no credit cards are listed, none are taken.

Information

Many of the agencies listed below are in The Hague (Den Haag), though they are able and willing to deal with basic enquiries on the telephone or by post. For full information on country embassies, and consulates, *see above* **Embassies**.

American Chamber of Commerce

Van Karnebeeklaan 14, 2585 BB The Hague (070 365 9808). **Open** 9am-5pm Mon-Fri; closed Sat, Sun.

British Embassy

Commercial Department, Lange Voorhout 10, 2514 ED The Hague (070 364 5800/www.britain.nl). **Open** 9am-1pm, 2.15-5.30pm Mon-Fri; closed Sat, Sun.
This office cooperates with the British Department of Trade and Industry to assist British companies operating in the Netherlands.

Commissariaat voor Buitenlandse Investeringen Nederland

Bezuidenhoutseweg 2, 2594 AV The Hague (070 379 7233/fax 070 379 6322/www.nfia.nl). **Open** 7am-5pm Mon-Fri; closed Sat, Sun.

The 'Netherlands Foreign Investment Agency' is probably the most useful first port of call for business people wishing to relocate to Holland.

EVD: Economische Voorlichtingsdienst

Bezuidenhoutseweg 181, 2594 AH The Hague (070 379 8933/www.hollandtrade.com). **Open** 8am-5pm Mon-Fri.; closed Sat, Sun.
The 'Netherlands Foreign Trade Agency' offers a useful library and information centre for business people. It incorporates the Netherlands Council for Trade Promotion (NCH), another handy source of information.

Kamer van Koophandel

De Ruijterkade 5 (531 4000/www.kvk.nl). Tram 1, 2, 4, 5, 9, 13, 16, 17, 24, 25. **Open** 8.30am-5pm Mon-Fri; closed Sat, Sun. **Map** p306 C1.
Amsterdam's Chamber of Commerce has lists of import/export agencies, government trade representatives and companies by sector. They will also advise on legal procedure, finding an office and hiring locals.

Ministerie van Economische Zaken

Bezuidenhoutseweg 30, 2594 AV The Hague (070 379 8911/www.minez.nl). **Open** 8am-5pm Mon-Fri; closed Sat, Sun.
The Ministry of Economic Affairs can provide answers to general queries concerning the Dutch economy. Detailed enquiries tend to be referred to the EVD; *see above*).

Ministerie van Buitenlandse Zaken

Bezuidenhoutseweg 67, Postbus 20061, 2500 EB The Hague (070

348 6486/www.bz.minbuza.nl). **Open** 9am-5pm Mon-Fri; closed Sat, Sun.
The Ministry of Foreign Affairs. As with the Ministry of Economic Affairs, detailed enquiries may be referred to the **EVD** (*see above*).

Netherlands-British Chamber of Commerce

Oxford House, Nieuwezijds Voorburgwal 328L, Old Centre: New Side (421 7040/www.nbcc.co.uk). Tram 1, 2, 5, 13, 14, 17. **Open** 9am-5pm Mon-Fri; closed Sat, Sun. **Map** p306 D3.

Banking

The branches listed below are head offices. Most do not have general banking facilities, but staff will be able to provide a list of branches that do. For information about currency exchanges, *see page 286*.

ABN-Amro

Vijzelstraat 68, Grachtengordel: East (628 9393/www.abnamro.nl). Tram 6, 7, 10, 16, 24, 25. **Open** 9am-5pm Mon-Fri; closed Sat, Sun. **Map** p310 D4.
The main offices of this super-bank, which has branches all over Amsterdam.

Citibank NA

Hoogoorddreef 54B, Zuid (651 4211). Metro Bijlmer/Sneltram 51, 52, 53/62, 137, 158, 163, 164, 174, 175, 176, 187, 188, 189 bus. **Open** 9am-5pm Mon-Fri; closed Sat, Sun.
Citibank NA is affiliated to the US Citibank, and deals with business transactions only.

'Spreekt u Nederlands?'

A brief guide to the Dutch language…

PRONUNCIATION GUIDE

ch – like 'ch' in 'loch'
ee – like 'ay' in 'hay'
g – similar to 'ch' (above)
ie – like 'ea' in 'lean'
ei – like 'i' in 'line'
j – like 'y' in 'yes' except when preceded by 'i', in which case it should be pronounced as a 'y' (see below)
oe – like 'o' in 'who'
oo – like 'o' in no
ou, au, ui – like 'ow' in 'cow' (have to be heard to be imitated)
tie – like 'tsy' in 'itsy bitsy'
tje – like 'ch' in 'church'
v – like 'f' in 'for'
w – like 'w' in 'which', with a hint of the 'v' in 'vet' thrown in
y/ij – (written as either) a cross between 'i' in 'hide' and 'ay' in 'way'

WORDS & PHRASES

hello – hallo (hullo) or dag (daarg)
goodbye – tot ziens (tot zeens)
bye – dag (daarg)
yes – ja (yah)
yes please – ja, graag (ya, graag)

no – nee (nay)
No thank you – nee, dank je (nay, dank ye)
please – alstublieft (als-too-bleeft); also commonly used to replace the phrase 'there you are' when exchanging items such as money with others
thank you – dank u (dank-oo)
thanks – bedankt
excuse me – pardon (par-don)
Excuse me, do you speak English? – Sorry, spreekt u Engels? (sorry, spraykt oo Engels?)
I'm sorry, I don't speak Dutch – Het spijt me, ik spreek geen Nederlands (et spite meh, ik spraykhane nayderlants)
I don't understand – Ik begrijp het niet (ik begripe et neet)
What is that? – Wat is dat? (vot is dat?)
My name is… – Mijn naam is…(mine naam is…)
I want… – ik wil graag…
How much is…? – Wat kost…?
Could I have a receipt? – Mag ik een bonnetje alstublieft?
How far is it to…? – Hoe ver is het naar…?
waiter – ober
nice, tasty (only food) – lekker (lecker)

nice (non-food) – mooi (moy)
open – open
closed – gesloten/dicht
inside – binnen
outside – buiten (bowten)
left – links
right – rechts (reks)
straight ahead – rechtdoor
far – ver (fair)
near – dichtbij (dikt-bye)
street – straat (straart)
canal – gracht
square – plein (pline)
good – goed
bad – slecht
big – groot
small – klein (kline)

NUMBERS

0 – nul; **1** – een; **2** – twee;
3 – drie; **4** – vier; **5** – vijf;
6 – zes; **7** – zeven; **8** – acht;
9 – negen; **10** – tien;
11 – elf; **12** – twaalf;
13 – dertien; **14** – veertien;
15 – vijftien; **16** – zestien;
17 – zeventien; **18** – achttien;
19 – negentien; **20** – twintig;
21 – eenentwintig;
22 – tweeëntwintig;
30 – dertig; **31** – eenendertig;
32 – tweeëndertig;
40 – veertig; **50** – vijftig;
60 – zestig; **70** – zeventig;
80 – tachtig; **90** – negentig;
100 – honderd;
101 – honderd een;
110 – honderd tien;
200 – tweehonderd;
1,000 – duizend.

Fortis Bank

Singel 548, Old Centre: New Side (624 9340/www.fortisbank.com). Tram 4, 9, 14, 16, 20, 24, 25. **Open** 1-5pm Mon; 9.30am-5pm Tue-Fri; closed Sat, Sun. **Map** p310 D4.
Full banking facilities in 50 branches.

ING Group

Bijlmerplein 888, Bijlmermeer (563 9111). Metro Bijlmer/59, 60, 62, 137 bus. **Open** 9am-4pm Mon-Fri; closed Sat, Sun.
The ING Group incorporates the 50 Amsterdam branches of the **Postbank** (*see below*).

Lloyds TSB Bank

PO Box 3518, 1001AH (581 5912/www.lloydsbank.nl). Tram 12/NS rail Sloterdijk. **Open** 9am-6pm Mon-Fri (by appointment only); closed Sat, Sun. **Map** p310 C5.
This branch of Lloyds TSB is open for business transactions only.

Postbank

Postbus 94780, 1090GT Amsterdam (565 5012/www.postbank.nl). **Open** 9am-6pm Mon-Wed, Fri; 9am-8pm Thur; 10am-1.30pm Sat; closed Sun.
There is a Postbank housed in every post office in Amsterdam.

Rabobank

Dam 16, Old Centre: New Side (530 4630/www.rabobank.nl). Tram 1, 2, 5, 9, 13, 14, 16, 17, 20, 24, 25. **Open** 9.30am-5pm Mon-Wed, Fri; 9.30am-6pm Thur; 11am-3pm Sat; closed Sun. **Map** p306 D2.
Some 30 branches in Amsterdam.

Conferences

Most major hotels offer full conference facilities. The **World Trade Center** (*see page 277*) should also offer excellent facilities when renovations are completed in late 2001.

Congrex Convention Services

AJ Ernststraat 595 K, Grachtengordel: East (504 0200/fax 504 0225/ www.congrex.nl). Tram 5/Metro 51. **Open** 9am-5.30pm Mon-Fri; closed Sat, Sun. **Credit** AmEx, DC, MC, V. **Map** p311 E4.
Specialists in teleconferencing.

Grand Hotel Krasnapolsky

Dam 9, Old Centre: New Side, 1012 JS (554 9111/fax 622 8607/ www.goldentulip.com). Tram 1, 2, 4, 5, 9, 13, 14, 16, 17, 20, 24, 25. **Map** p306 D3.
The most comprehensive in-hotel meeting facilities. *See also p83.*

RAI Congresgebouw

Europaplein 8-22, Zuid (549 1212/ www.rai.nl). Tram 4, 25/NS rail to RAI Station. **Open** 24hrs daily.
A self-contained congress and trade fair centre in the south of the city. The building contains 11 halls totalling 87,000sq m of covered exhibition space and 22 conference rooms that can seat up to 1,750 people.

Stichting de Beurs van Berlage (Berlage Exchange Foundation)

Damrak 277, Old Centre: New Side (530 4141/fax 620 4701/ www.beursvanberlage.nl). Tram 4, 9, 14, 16, 20, 24, 25. **Open** *Office & enquiries* noon-5pm Mon; 9am-5pm Tue-Fri; closed Sat, Sun. **Map** p306 D2.
Used for cultural events and smaller trade fairs (up to 2,500 visitors can be provided with buffet dinners). Berlage Hall is a conference venue for between 50 and 2,000 people.

Couriers & shippers

FedEx

Berquetlaan 20-2, Oudemeer (0800 022 2333). **Open** 8am-6.30pm Mon-Fri; closed Sat, Sun. **Credit** AmEx, DC, MC, V.
Even from Amsterdam, packages can be delivered to the US by 10.30am the next morning. Your package will be picked up by a multilingual driver.

TNT

(0800 1234). **Open** 24hrs daily. **Credit** AmEx, DC, MC, V.
You can send packages within the Netherlands by TNT by either taking it yourself to the post office or having it picked up from you.

Exchanges

Effectenbeurs (Stock Exchange)

Beursplein 5, Old Centre: New Side (550 4444). Tram 4, 9, 14, 16, 20, 24, 25. **Open** for free tours (mainly groups only; phone for details). **Map** p306 D2.
Stock for officially listed Dutch companies is traded here, plus Nederlandse Termijnhandel, the commodity exchange for trading futures in potatoes and pigs, and Optiebeurs, the largest options exchange in Europe. Phone to arrange a guided tour.

Office relocation

Formula Two Relocations

Stadionweg 131, Museum Quarter (672 2590/fax 672 3023). Tram 24. **Open** 8.30am-5.30pm Mon-Fri; closed Sat, Sun. **Map** p310 C6.
This is an independent company, established in 1983, offering a comprehensive relocation service to companies and individuals moving into and out of the Netherlands.

Home Abroad

Weteringschans 28, Grachtengordel: East (625 5195/fax 624 7902). Tram 6, 7, 10. **Open** 10am-5.30pm Mon-Fri. **Map** p311 E5.
A company that assists in all aspects of living and doing business in the Netherlands. There's a fixed hourly rate for advice and assistance; rates for other services, such as seminars on the Dutch way of doing business, are negotiable; phone for details.

Office services

Lots of tobacconists and copy shops also have fax facilities. Many hotels have fax services for guests, but prices are high.

Avisco

Stadhouderskade 156, The Pijp (671 9909). Tram 3, 4, 16, 20, 24, 25. **Open** 9am-5pm Mon-Fri; closed Sat, Sun. **Map** p311 F5.
Slide projectors, video equipment, screens, cameras, overhead projectors, microphones and tape decks hired out or sold.

Euro Business Center

Keizersgracht 62, Grachtengordel: West (520 7500/fax 520 7510). Tram 1, 2, 5, 13, 14, 17, 20. **Open** 8.30am-5.30pm Mon-Fri; closed Sat, Sun. **Credit** AmEx, DC, MC, V. **Map** p306 C2.

Fully equipped offices for hire (long- or short-term) including the use of fax, photocopier, phone and mailbox services plus multilingual secretaries. For a minimum of three months, fully equipped offices cost between ƒ1,500 and ƒ6,000 per month. Private offices cost around ƒ125-ƒ200 per day.

World Trade Center

Strawinskylaan 1, Zuid (575 9111/ fax 662 7255). Tram 5/NS rail RAI Station. **Open** *Office & enquiries* 9am-5pm Mon-Fri; closed Sat, Sun.
Office space in the World Trade Center is let by the Dutch Business Center Association Strawinskylaan 305 (571 1800/fax 571 1801). Offices can be hired long or short term. While their conference services have been suspended until the end of 2001, secretarial services, fax and photocopying facilities are still offered. Audio and projection equipment is also for hire.

Printing & duplicating

Grand Prix Copyrette

Weteringschans 84A, Grachtengordel: East (627 3705). Tram 16, 24, 25. **Open** 9am-6pm Mon-Fri; closed Sat, Sun. **No credit cards.** **Map** p310 D5.
Colour and monochrome copying, binding, fax services and printing. **Branch:** Amsteldijk 47, The Pijp (671 4455).

Multicopy

Weesperstraat 65, Oost (520 0720/fax 520 0722). Tram 4, 9, 14, 20/Metro Waterlooplein. **Open** 8.30am-6pm Mon-Fri; closed Sat, Sun. **No credit cards.** **Map** p307 F3.
Colour and monochrome copies in A4, A3 and A2 sizes, on white or coloured paper.

Translators

Berlitz Language Center

Rokin 87, Old Centre: New Side (639 1406/fax 620 3959). Tram 4, 9, 10, 16, 24, 25. **Open** 9am-6pm Mon-Fri; closed Sat, Sun. **Map** p306 D3.
Specialists in commercial, technical, legal and scientific documents. All European languages are translated, plus Japanese and Arabic. English/Dutch translation costs a minimum of ƒ150.

Mac Bay Consultants

PC Hooftstraat 15, Museum Quarter (24-hr phoneline 662 0501/fax 662 6299). Tram 2, 3, 5, 12, 20. **Open** 9am-7pm Mon-Fri; closed Sat, Sun. **Map** p310 C6.

Directory

WATERSTONE'S
The home of English Books in the Netherlands
Haven't you got anything better to read than this?
We have.
Our store, in the very heart of Amsterdam, has four floors of books, all in English. With over 60,000 titles to browse through, you certainly won't be stuck for choice. We also carry videos, tapes and all the major English language magazines and newspapers. See you soon!
Waterstone's
Kalverstraat 152, 1012 XE Amsterdam
Tel: 020 6383821 Fax: 020 6384379
E-mail: books@amsterdam.waterstones.nl
Free ordering service/mail order Open seven days a week

Specialists in translating financial documents. Dutch/English translations cost ƒ225 an hour. Other languages are also translated and there is a copywriting service.

Customs

EU nationals over the age of 17 may import limitless goods into the Netherlands for their personal use. Other EU countries may still have limits on the quantity of goods they permit on entry. For citizens of non-EU countries, the old limits still apply. These are:
● 200 cigarettes or 50 cigars or 250g (8.82oz) tobacco;
● 2 litres of non-sparkling wine plus 1 litre of spirits (over 22 per cent alcohol) or 2 litres of fortified wine (under 22 per cent alcohol)
● 60cc/ml of perfume;
● Other goods to the value of ƒ368.

The import of meat or meat products, fruit, plants, flowers and protected animals to the Netherlands is illegal.

Disabled

The most obvious difficulty people with mobility problems face in the Netherlands is negotiating the winding cobbled streets of the older towns. Poorly maintained and broken pavements are widespread, and canal houses, with their narrow doorways and steep stairs, can also present access problems. But the pragmatic Dutch don't have preconceptions about people with disabilities, and any problems are generally solved quickly and without fuss.

Most of the large museums have reasonable facilities for disabled users but little for the partially sighted and hard of hearing. Most cinemas and theatres also have an enlightened attitude and are accessible. However, if you're going to any venue where you fear access may be limited, it's advisable to check in advance.

The metro is accessible to wheelchair users who 'have normal arm function'. There is a taxi service for wheelchair users (*see page 273*). Most trams are inaccessible to wheelchair users, especially because of their high steps.

The AUB and the Amsterdam Tourist Board produce brochures listing accommodation, restaurants, museums, tourist attractions and boat excursions with facilities for the disabled.

Drugs

The Amsterdam authorities have a relaxed attitude towards soft drugs, but you should note that smoking isn't acceptable everywhere in the city, so use some discretion. Many bars and cafés will not tolerate the practice and will eject offenders. Outside Amsterdam, public consumption of cannabis is largely unacceptable.

Foreigners found with any amount of hard drugs – cocaine, speed, ecstasy, LSD and especially heroin – should expect prosecution. Organisations offering advice to users can do little to assist foreigners with drug-related problems, though the Drugs Prevention Centre is happy to provide help in several languages, including English. Its helpline, on 626 7176 (1-5pm Mon, Tue, Thur), offers advice and information on drugs and alcohol abuse. Visitors caught dealing in drugs are likely to be swiftly prosecuted and repatriated.

Electricity

The voltage in the Netherlands is 220, 50-cycle AC, so it's compatible with British equipment, but because the Netherlands uses two-pin continental plugs you'll need an adaptor. American visitors may need to convert their equipment or buy a transformer, plus a

new plug: Dutch sockets require a larger plug than those used in the USA.

Embassies & consulates

The **Amsterdam Tourist Board** offices (*see page 289*) have lists of all embassies and consulates in the country; most are based in The Hague (Den Haag).

American Consulate General
Museumplein 19, 1071 DJ Amsterdam (664 5661/679 0321). Tram 3, 5, 12, 16, 20. **Open** 8.30am-noon Mon-Fri for US citizens & visa applications; closed Sat, Sun. **Map** p310 D6.

Australian Embassy
Carnegielaan 4, 2517 KH The Hague (070 310 8200). **Open** 8.30am-4.50pm Mon-Fri; closed Sat, Sun. *Visa enquiries* 8.45-11.45am Mon-Fri; closed Sat, Sun.

British Consulate General
Koningslaan 44, 1075 AE Amsterdam (676 4343). Tram 2. **Open** 9am-noon, 2-3.30pm Mon-Fri for British citizens; 9am-noon Mon-Fri for visa enquiries; closed Sat, Sun.

British Embassy
Lange Voorhout 10, 2514 ED The Hague (070 364 5800). **Open** 9am-5.30pm Mon-Fri; closed Sat, Sun.
The Embassy deals with political and economic crises only. For visa and tourist information, contact the Consulate General.

Canadian Embassy
Sophialaan 7, 2514 JP The Hague (070 311 1600). **Open** 10am-noon Mon-Fri; 2.30pm-4pm Mon, Tue, Thur, Fri for Canadian nationals; closed Sat, Sun.
For all visa enquiries, contact the consulate in Berlin.

Eire Embassy
Dr Kuyperstraat 9, 2514 BA The Hague (070 363 0993). **Open** 10am-12.30pm, 2.30-5pm Mon-Fri; closed Sat, Sun.

New Zealand Embassy
Carnegielaan 10, 2517 KH The Hague (070 346 9324). **Open** 9am-12.30pm, 1.30-5pm Mon-Fri; closed Sat, Sun.

Directory

Emergencies

Emergencies

112.
A 24-hr switchboard for ambulance, fire and police. In phone boxes, you don't have to insert coins or a card to dial this number.

Afdeling Inlichtingen Apotheken

694 8709.
A 24-hr service that can direct you to your nearest chemist.

Centraal Doktorsdienst/Atacom

592 3434.
A 24-hr English-speaking line offering advice about medical symptoms. Sympathetic to people who've overdone it on the weed.

TBB

570 9595.
A 24hr service which refers callers to a dentist. Operators can also give details of chemists open outside normal hours.

Lost or stolen credit cards

Use the following relevant 24-hr numbers:
American Express 504 8666.
Diners Club 557 3407.
Mastercard/Eurocard 030 283 5555 if card was issued in the Netherlands; freephone 0800 022 5821 if card was issued outside of the Netherlands.
Visa 660 0611 if card was issued in the Netherlands; freephone 0800 022 4176 if card was issued outside of the Netherlands.

Gay & lesbian

Help & information

COC Amsterdam

Rozenstraat 14, 1016 NX (information 626 3087). Tram 13, 14, 17, 20. **Open** *Phone enquiries* 10am-5pm Mon-Fri. *Info-Coffeeshop* 1-5pm Sat. *Café* 9pm-midnight Tue-Thur, Sun; 10pm-4am Fri, Sat. *Discos* 11pm-4am Fri, Sat. **Admission** *Disco* f5. **Map** p305 B3.
The Amsterdam branch of the COC deals largely with the social side. Many groups meet here, including the English-speaking Wild Side group and Love2Love (see p281), and a regular HIV café is also held here every Thursday (8pm-midnight). In addition, the Info-Coffeeshop is a useful place to get help with any enquiries you may have about the COC or the gay scene in general.

COC National

Rozenstraat 8, The Jordaan (postal address: Postbus 3836, 1001 AP) (623 4596/textphone 620 7541/www.coc.nl). Tram 13, 14, 17, 20. **Open** 9am-5pm Mon-Fri; closed Sat, Sun. **Map** p306 C3.
COC's head office deals with all matters relating to gays and lesbians; the organisation has strong social and activist tendencies. However, many locals find it hard to have confidence in a gay and lesbian group that, in 1998, appointed an unashamedly heterosexual woman as chair. Cox Habbema justified her position to gay men by saying, 'You do it with men. Me too.' Er, quite.

Gay & Lesbian Switchboard

Postbus 11573, 1001 GN (623 6565/text phone 422 6565/fax 38 0407/www.switchboard.nl). **Open** 10am-10pm daily.
Whether it's information on the scene or safe sex you're after, the friendly, English-speaking Dutch men and women on this line are well informed when it comes to giving information and advice.

Het Vrouwenhuis (The Women's House)

Nieuwe Herengracht 95, Oost (625 2066/fax 638 9185/www.vrouwenhuis.nl). Tram 7, 9, 14, 20/Metro Waterlooplein. **Open** *Office* 10am-5pm Mon-Fri. *Info-Café* 5-8pm Tue (except school holidays); noon-5pm Wed, Thur; closed Sat, Sun.* **Map** p307 F3.
There's a well-stocked library here (around 4,000 books; membership is just f15 a year) plus free Internet facilities (12-5pm Wed, Thur). But if you want to take one of the classes held here, such as web design, you'll have to learn the local lingo.

Archives

Homodok–Lesbisch Archief Amsterdam

Nieuwepoortkade 2A, Westerpark (606 0712/fax 606 0713/www.homodok-laa.nl). Tram 10, 12, 14. **Open** 9.30am-4pm Mon-Fri; closed Sat, Sun.
After the Homodok relocated from the University of Amsterdam at the beginning of 1999, it merged with the Lesbisch Archief (Lesbian Archives) at this new location in the west of the city. A wealth of audio-visual material, books, journals, magazines, newspaper articles and theses are housed here, as well as a large video collection. However, though the archives will definitely stay here for

2000, the location is by no means permanent; check the website for any future developments.

IIAV

Obiplein 4, Oost (665 1318/www.iiav.nl). Tram 3, 6, 10, 14/bus 15, 22. **Open** noon-5pm Mon; 10am-5pm Tue-Fri; closed Sat, Sun.
This women's archive has a fascinating history. Confiscated during the World War II Nazi occupation, it was removed to Berlin where it then disappeared. In 1992, it was found in Moscow, but, in contravention of international law, the Russians are still refusing to return it. Though the current collection, started after the war, is officially an archive, there's a huge amount of other resources, including several online databases.

HIV/AIDS

The Netherlands was one of the first countries to pour money into research once the HIV virus was recognised. The liberal Dutch government took a progressive approach towards HIV/AIDS, with active research complemented by high-profile fundraising events and regular national campaigns. However, 'bareback sex' (unprotected sex) is gaining popularity in this country, so there's still a need for safer sex campaigns. And, strangely, though the country was swift to take action and promote safe sex, condoms are still not distributed free in clubs and bars as they are in the UK.

For people living in the country with HIV or AIDS, there are a number of organisations in Amsterdam. On the social side, there is an HIV café held at the COC (see above) every Thursday evening, often with informal, themed talks, and another at the **HIV Vereniging** every Tuesday and Sunday (see page 281).

Aside from the organisations listed below, the free **AIDS Helpline** (0800 022 2220, open 2-10pm Mon-Fri) offers advice by phone (including information on STDs), part of the Stichting

AIDS Fonds. More information can be found on its website, www.aidsfonds.nl.

HIV Vereniging

1E Helmersstraat 17, Oud West (616 0160/fax 616 1200). Tram 1, 2, 3, 5, 6, 12. **Open** 9am-5pm Mon-Fri; closed Sat, Sun. **Map** p310 C5.
The Netherlands HIV Association supports the individual and collective interests of all those who are HIV positive, including offering legal help. It produces a bi-monthly Dutch magazine, *HIV Nieuws* (ƒ50/ƒ80 per year, subscription only, online at www.hivnet.org/hvn), and also runs the Internet service, HIVNET, and a help line, HIVpluslijn (685 0055, open 1-4pm Mon, Wed, Fri, 8-10.30pm Tue, Thur; for Spanish and Portuguese: 3-5pm Tue). There's an HIV Café for men and women every Tuesday and Sunday (4-8pm), plus regular lunches and dinners for people with HIV; call for information and reservations one day in advance on 412 3635 (after 1pm).

SAD-Schorerstichting

PC Hooftstraat 5, Museum Quarter (662 4206). Tram 2, 3, 5, 6, 7, 10, 12, 20. **Open** 9am-5pm Mon-Fri; closed Sat, Sun. **Map** p310 D5.
This state-funded agency offers psycho-social support, education and HIV prevention advice for gays and lesbians. Examinations and treatment of sexually transmitted diseases, including an HIV test, are free. The clinic is held at the city's health department, the GG&GD (Groenburgwal 44), but call the SAD-Schorerstichting help desk (10am-5pm Mon-Thur) to make an appointment. Lesbians and gay men can also call the help desk for general information regarding mental and physical health, and referral. Staff speak English.

Stichting AIDS Fonds

Keizersgracht 390, 1016 GB (626 2669/fax 627 5221/ www.aidsfond.nl). Tram 1, 2, 5. **Open** 9am-5pm Mon-Fri; closed Sat, Sun. **Map** p310 C4.
This active organisation, responsible for such high-profile fund-raisers as the AmsterdamDiners (*see p203* **The queer year**), was set up to channel money into research and safer sex promotion, as well providing grants for the more personal needs of people with AIDS. They also run a telephone helpdesk for gay and lesbian-specific health questions (662 4206, open 10am-5pm Mon-Thur) and organise regular workshops such as the 'F*CKSH*P', an info/safer sexer workshop on the ins and outs of anal sex. English information is available on its website.

Other groups & organisations

Amsterdam Stetsons

683 7333/http://people.a2000.nl/ tfokker/saloon/eng/saloon.html.
A country and western dance club for gays and lesbians, which meets regularly at the Cruise Inn at Zeeburgerdijk 271. Open evenings are held every last Tuesday of the month at 8pm, while it also has a monthly Gay Western Salon held every last Saturday of the month at 7pm at the Crea Café (Turfdraagsterpad 17, 627 2412). Its location may change in 2000 or 2001, so be sure to check the website before you set out.

Dikke Maatjes

c/o COC (Amsterdam): see above for address (0343 531791 /http://home.eu.org/~bignbear.nl).
'Dikke Maatjes' means 'close friends,' though its literal translation is 'fat friends'. That's exactly what this gay club is for: chubbies, bears and their admirers.

Groep 7152

023 527 4299/www.geocities.com/ WestHollywood/Stonewall/2951/ engels.html#algemeen.
This national organisation for lesbians and bisexual women started with a classified ad (number 7152) placed in a publication back in 1971. In Amsterdam, they meet every third Sunday of the month (except June-Aug) for bridge (1-4pm), information and introductions (4-5.30pm), and dancing (4-8pm) at the Crea Café (Turfdraagsterpad 17, 627 2412). Entrance is ƒ7,50 (members ƒ5). More of an older women's scene.

Long Yang Club Holland

Postbus 58253, 1040 HG (023 571 5788).
The Dutch branch of this worldwide organisation for Asian and oriental gays and their friends meets regularly in town.

Love2Love

c/o COC (Amsterdam): see above for address (626 3087).
A non-profit-making mixed gay and lesbian youth group for under 27s based at the COC (*see page 279*). The group meets every Thursday (8pm-midnight) and puts a lot of energy into creating themed evenings.

Mama Cash

Postbus 15686, 1001 ND Amsterdam (689 3634/fax 683 4647/www.antenna.nl/mamacash). **Open** 9am-5pm Mon-Fri.

Founder Marjan Sax put her ƒ2.5 million inheritance into setting up this organisation supplying funding for women-run businesses (it has sponsored many lesbian organisations and events in the city).

Netherbears

c/o Le Shako, Postbus 15495, 1001 ML (625 1400/www.xs4all.nl/~elza/ netherbears/club.htm).
This hairy men's club meets at Le Shako (*see p205*) every second Sunday of the month, 5-9pm.

Sjalhomo

Postbus 2536, 1000 CM Amsterdam (023 531 2318 evenings only).
This national organisation for Jewish gays, lesbians and bisexuals regularly organises cultural, social and political activities on and around Jewish feast days.

Spellbound Productions

(682 7228/http://huizen.dds.nl/ ~deplanet).
A non-profit-making group of gays and lesbians that organises the Planet, a series of alternative, underground parties every few months. Location and frequency vary, so check the website.

Stichting IPOTH

Postbus 59564, 1040 LB (684 2121).
Based at the **HIV Vereniging** (*see above*), IPOTH organises activities specifically for multicultural gay and lesbians, as well as acting as a resource centre for ethnicity and homosexuality. It is also active in HIV/AIDS counselling/prevention (specifically targeted at Arab and Turkish men), and runs a support group specifically for immigrants affected by HIV/AIDS.

Sportclub Tijgertje

Postbus 10521, 1001 EM (673 2458/ www.xs4all.nl/~tijgertj).
Tigertje organises a wide variety of sports activities, from yoga to wrestling, for gays and lesbians, including an HIV swimming group.

Wild Side

c/o COC (Amsterdam) (626 3087/ www.dds.nl/~wildside).
A social and educational support group for woman-to-woman SM. Every first Saturday of the month it holds SM workshops, and every third Saturday of the month, there's a members' meeting. Wild Side organises regular 'play parties', and publishes *Wild Side News*, a free bi-monthly, bilingual newsletter that's a useful source for SM/fetish events. It's available from the COC (*see p279*) and the **Vrolijk** bookshop (*see p212*).

Health

As with any visit to any city, it's advisable to take out medical insurance before you journey to Amsterdam. For emergency services and medical or dental referral agencies, *see above* **Emergencies**. For AIDS/HIV information, *see page 280*.

In the case of minor accidents, try the outpatients' departments at the following hospitals (*ziekenhuis*), all of which are open 24 hours a day, 365 days a year.

Academisch Medisch Centrum
Meibergdreef 9, Zuid (566 9111/566 3333). Bus 59, 60, 120, 126, 158/ Metro Holendrescht.

Boven IJ Ziekenhuis
Statenjachtstraat 1, Noord (634 6346). Bus 34, 36, 37, 39, 171, 172.

Onze Lieve Vrouwe Gasthuis
's Gravesandeplein 16, Oost (599 9111). Tram 3, 6, 10/Metro Weesperplein or Wibautstraat. **Map** p312 G4.

St Lucas Andreas Ziekenhuis
Jan Tooropstraat 164, West (reception 510 8911/first aid 510 8160). Tram 13/bus 19, 47, 80, 82, 97.

VU Ziekenhuis
De Boelelaan 1117, Zuid (444 4444). Bus 142, 147, 148, 149, 170, 171,172/Metro Amstelveenseweg.

Dentists

For a dentist (*tandarts*), phone the dentist administration bureau on 0900 821 2230. An operator can put you in touch with your nearest dentist; lines are open 24 hours daily. The Central Medical Service may also be of help (*see above* **Emergencies**).

AOC
Wilhelmina Gasthuisplein 167, Oud West (616 1234). Tram 1, 2, 3, 5, 6, 12. **Open** 9am-4pm Mon-Fri; closed Sat, Sun. **Map** p309 B5.
Emergency dental treatment.

Contraception & abortion

MR '70
Sarphatistraat 620-626, Plantage (624 5426). Tram 6, 9, 10, 14/22 bus. **Open** 9am-4pm Mon-Thur; 9am-1pm Fri; closed Sat, Sun. **Map** p312 G3.
An abortion clinic which offers help and advice.

Polikliniek Oosterpark
Oosterpark 59, Oost (693 2151). Tram 3, 6, 9. **Open** *Advice services* 9am-5pm daily. *Phonelines* 24hrs daily. **Map** p312 H4.
Information and advice on contraception and abortion. Abortions are carried out (on Tue and Fri only), though non-residents without appropriate insurance will be charged from ƒ600 for the operation. The process is prompt and backed up by sympathetic counselling.

Rutgersstichting
Aletta Jacobshuis, Overtoom 323, Museum Quarter (616 6222). Tram 1. **Open** by appointment 9am-4.30pm Mon-Fri; 6-9pm Tue, 7-9pm Thur; closed Sat, Sun. **Map** p310 C6.
Besides giving information on health issues, the staff at this family planning centre can help visitors with prescriptions for contraceptive pills, morning-after pills and condoms, IUD fitting and cervical smear tests. Prescription costs vary.

Prescriptions

Chemists (*drogists*) sell toiletries and non-prescription drugs and are usually open 9.30am to 5.30pm, Monday to Saturday. For prescription drugs go to a pharmacy (*apotheek*), usually open 9.30am to 5.30pm Monday to Friday.

Outside these hours, phone the **Afdeling Inlichtingen Apotheken** (*see above*) or consult the daily newspaper *Het Parool*, which publishes details of which *apotheken* are open late that week. Details are also posted at local *apotheken*.

Helplines

Alcoholics Anonymous
(625 6057). **Open** 24-hr answerphone.
A lengthy but informative message details times and dates of meetings, and contact numbers for counsellors.

SOS Telephone Helpline
(675 7575). **Open** 24hrs daily.
A counselling service – comparable to the Samaritans in the UK and Lifeline in the US – for anyone with emotional problems, run by volunteers. English isn't always understood at first, but keep trying and someone will be able to help you.

Narcotics Anonymous
(662 6307). **Open** 24hr answerphone message with direct numbers of counsellors.

ID

Regulations concerning identification require that everyone carries some form of ID when opening accounts at banks or other financial institutions, when looking for work, when applying for benefits, when found on public transport without a ticket, and when going to a professional football match. You then have to register with the local council, which is in the same building as the Aliens' Police.

Insurance

EU countries have reciprocal medical treatment arrangements with the Netherlands. British citizens will need form E111, which can be obtained by filling in the application form in leaflet SA30, available in all Department of Social Security (DSS) offices and the Post Office. Make sure you read the small print on the back of form E111 so you know how to obtain medical or dental treatment at a reduced charge: you'll probably have to explain this to the Dutch doctor or dentist who treats you. If you need treatment, photocopy your insurance form and leave it with the doctor or dentist who treats you. Not all treatments are covered by these forms, so it's best to take out private travel insurance to cover both health and personal belongings.

Tickets please

Though both the Amsterdam Tourist board and the GWK sell tickets for concerts, plays and myriad other events, the main ticket retailer in Amsterdam is the AUB. It offers a variety of services, from ticket sales via the Internet to a free listings publication. Here's a summary of its services.

Uitlijn

0900 0191 premium rate/+ 31 20 621 1288 from abroad. **Open** *Phone enquiries* 9am-9pm daily. **Credit** AmEx, DC, MC, V. A national telephone information and booking line for theatre productions and music concerts. Commission is *f*6 on each ticket, and staff will speak English.

AUB Ticketshop

Leidseplein 26, Grachtengordel: East. **Open** 10am-6pm Mon-Wed, Fri-Sun; 10am-9pm Thur. **Credit** AmEx, DC, MC, V. **Map** p310 C5. Tickets can be purchased from here in person with a charge of *f*3,50 per ticket.

AUB Ticketshop will also give information (in English) on most events.

Uitkrant

A free monthly magazine detailing events in Amsterdam available at theatres, bookstores and the AUB Ticketshop.

Uitgids

An free annual publication offering details of subscription series concerts and other information on venues and events. Available at theatres, bookstores and the AUB Ticketshop.

www.uitlijn.nl

An online version – in Dutch, sadly – of the phone service detailed above, only with a reduced commission of *f*5,50 per ticket.

www.uitkrant.nl

A new online version of the magazine of the same name. Again, it's all in Dutch.

Citizens of other EU countries should make sure they have obtained one of the forms E110, E111 or E112. Citizens of the following non-EU countries can also receive medical treatment at reduced rates by producing the appropriate form: Morocco, form MN111; states of the former Yugoslavia, YN111; Tunisia, TUN/N111; Turkey, TUR/N111. Citizens from all other countries should take out private medical insurance before their visit. Dutch medical treatment costs about half of what it would in the USA, which is still more than enough to make travelling without insurance unwise.

Internet

The city has several ISPs if you're planning on staying for a while, among them **Xs4all** (as in 'access', not 'excess'; www.xs4all.nl), **Cistron** (www.cistron.nl) and **Chello** (www.chello.nl). Similarly, all

of the main global ISPs, such as AOL and Compuserve, have a remote presence in the city (contact your ISP before you leave for a local number). However, given that the city now has the largest cybercafé in the world – EasyEverything, with an extraordinary 650 terminals (*see below*) – it may not be necessary. Many of Amsterdam's hotels, too, have some sort of Internet access, whether dataports in the rooms or a terminal in the lobby.

Cybercafés

Cyber Café

Nieuwendijk 19, Old Centre: New Side (623 5146/http://cybercafe. euronet.nl). Tram 1, 2, 5, 13, 17, 20. **Open** 10am-1am Mon-Thur, Sun; 10am-3am Fri, Sat. **Rates** *f*3/20min. **Map** p306 C2.

EasyEverything

Reguliersbreestraat 22, Grachtengordel: East (320 6289/ www.easyeverything.com). Tram 16, 24, 25. **Open** 24hrs daily. **Rates** *f*2,50/unit. **Terminals** 650. **Map** p311 D/E4.

The amount of time one unit allows depends on how busy it is: it could be up to five or six hours. It's the biggest cybercafé in the world, at least until another opens in Times Square in October. A branch at Damrak 33) will open in Oct 2000.

Freeworld

Nieuwendijk 30, Old Centre: New Side (620 0902). Tram 1, 2, 5, 13, 17, 20. **Open** 10am-1am Mon-Thur, Sun; 10am-3am Fri, Sat. **Rates** *f*2,50/20min. **Map** p306 D2.

Legal & immigration

ACCESS

Plein 24, 2511 CS The Hague (070 346 2525). **Open** 9.30am-3.30pm Mon-Fri; closed Sat, Sun; The Administrative Committee to Coordinate English Speaking Services is a non-profit organisation, which provides assistance in English through a telephone information line, workshops and counselling.

Bureau Voor Rechtshulp

Spuistraat 10, Old Centre: New Side (626 4477). Tram 1, 2, 5. **Open** *Phone enquiries* 9am-5pm Mon-Fri. *By appointment* 9am-1pm Mon-Fri. **Map** p306 C3.

Qualified lawyers who give free legal advice on matters of tenancy, social security, immigration, insurance, consumer complaints and disputes with employers.

Legal Advice Line

(444 6333). **Open** 9pm-5pm Mon-Thur; closed Fri-Sun.
Free advice from student lawyers; a relaxed, friendly service. They deal mainly with civil law queries and problems, but will occasionally be able to help with minor criminal law matters. Most speak English.

Libraries

You'll need to present proof of residence in Amsterdam and ID if you want to join a library (*bibliotheek*) and borrow books. It costs *f*39,15 (23-64s) or *f*230,75 (18-23s, over-65s) per year and is free for under-18s. However, in the public libraries (*openbare bibliotheek*) you can read books, papers and magazines without membership or charge. For information on university libraries, *see page 288*.

American Institute

Plantage Muidergracht 12, Plantage (525 4380). Tram 7, 9/Metro Waterlooplein. **Open** 10am-4pm Mon, Wed, Fri; closed Tue, Thur, Sat, Sun. **Map** p312 G3.

British Council Education Centre

Oxford House, Nieuwizijds Voorburgwal 328L, Old Centre: New Side (421 7040/fax 421 7003). Tram 1, 2, 5, 13, 14, 17. **Open** *Telephone enquiries* 9.30am-5pm Mon-Thur; closed Fri-Sun. *In person* 1-5pm Tue, Wed; 1am-6pm Thur; closed Mon, Fri-Sun. **Map** p306 D3.

Centrale Bibliotheek

Prinsengracht 587, Grachtengordel: West (523 0900). Tram 1, 2, 5. **Open** 1-9pm Mon; 10am-9pm Tue-Thur; 10am-5pm Fri, Sat. *Oct-Apr* also 1-5pm Sun. **Map** p310 C4.
Anyone is welcome to use this, the main public library, for reference purposes. There is a variety of English-language books and newspapers and a small coffee bar.

Lost property

For the sake of insurance, report lost property to the police immediately; *see page*

286. If you lose your passport, inform your embassy or consulate as well. For anything lost at the Hoek van Holland ferry terminal or Schiphol Airport, contact the company you're travelling with. For lost credit cards, *see above* **Emergencies**.

Centraal Station

NS Lost Property Information, Stationsplein 15, Old Centre: New Side (557 8544). Tram 1, 2, 4, 5, 9, 13, 16, 17, 20, 24, 25. **Open** 5am-midnight daily. **Map** p306 D1.
Items found on trains are kept here for four days and then sent to NS Afdeling Verloren Voorwerpen, Tweede Daalsedijk 4, 3500 HA Utrecht (030 235 3923; open 2-4pm Mon-Fri; closed Sat, Sun).

GVB Lost Property

Prins Hendrikkade 108-114, Old Centre: New Side (460 5858). Tram 1, 2, 4, 5, 9, 13, 16, 17, 20, 24, 25. **Open** 9am-4.30pm Mon-Fri; closed Sat, Sun. **Map** p306 C1.
Where to head for items lost on a bus, metro or tram. If you're reporting a loss from the previous day, phone after 2pm to allow time for the property to be sorted.

Police Lost Property

Stephensonstraat 18, Zuid (559 3005). Tram 12/Metro Amstel station/14 bus. **Open** *In person* 9.30am-3.30pm Mon-Fri; closed Sat, Sun. *By phone* noon-3.30pm Mon-Fri; closed Sat, Sun.
For items lost in the streets or parks. Report any loss to the police station in the same district: they generally hold items for a day or so before sending them here for up to three months.

Media

Newspapers & magazines

De Telegraaf, a one-time collaborationist and still right-wing daily, is Holland's biggest-selling paper, and the nearest the country has to a tabloid press. *Het Parool* was the main underground wartime journal, but is now a hip, afternoon local rag; its sister morning paper, *De Volkskrant*, also enjoys a relatively young, progressive readership. *Trouw*, the other Amsterdam-

published national daily, is owned by Perscombinatie, the same company that owns *Het Parool* and *De Volkskrant*. For some socio-religious reason, Sunday papers have never taken off here.

There's not a great deal news-wise for Anglophones, save for the *Financieel Dagblaad*'s sole English page each day. The Amsterdam Tourist Board publish *Day by Day* (monthly, *f*2,50), a basic listings guide. However, *Shark*, a photocopied freesheet found in assorted bars and clubs, does an excellent job of picking up the slack with a fortnightly round-up of movies and music, as well as a supplement for gay and lesbian events, *Queer Fish*. It's online at www.underwateramsterdam.com.

Wherever the Dutch press is available, you can also expect to find a wide range of foreign magazines and newspapers (British papers are available here, but are expensive at around *f*4 for a daily and *f*7 for a Sunday paper). Particularly good selections can be found around Spui: **Athenaeum** (*see page 142*) is a browser's dream, and 100 metres away, **Waterstone's** (*see page 143*) has all the main UK magazines, as well as five floors of English books, cards and videos. The **American Book Center** (*see page 142*), round the corner, has four floors of US and British books, and its selections of New Age literature and American magazines are unrivalled.

Broadcast media

Until 1992, a unique system of airtime allocation and strictly limited commercialisation had stranded Dutch television in a state of creative torpor. Three state channels had their hours divided among a number of stations according to the numbers of 'members' each

Clear sited

If you're on the web (and if you're not, then you should be), log on and prepare your trip the modern way. Below is a list of five sites that might be useful.

www.amsterdam.nl
An accessible site with advice on living in, as well as visiting, Amsterdam. The searchable maps are terrific.

www.amsterdamhotspots.nl
An upbeat review-based site of, uh, Amsterdam's hotspots.

www.amsterdamlive.nl
Get a close look at the city's venues with the webcam, or make use of the excellent links. In Dutch only.

www.channels.nl
Takes you, virtually, through Amsterdam's streets with reviews of sights, hotels, restaurants and clubs.

www.visitamsterdam.nl
Factual and comprehensive (if a little drab) tourist guide.

---

channel had, a figure determined by sales of each channel's weekly TV guide. They were – and remain – worthy but, at times, a little dull, though the arty VPRO produces plenty of merit.

This arrangement began to crack when RTL4 started broadcasting commercial Dutch TV from Luxembourg. Reform produced a number of new stations in the latter part of the 1990s, including Veronica and SBS6 (both painfully commercial), TV10 (old repeats, such as *Black Adder*), RTL5 (series and films from the US), and the Music Factory (a Europop-heavy, Dutch-language MTV clone). The city currently has ten commercial stations, most of which are as short on viewers as they are on style, and about three times that number on cable, including non-commercial stations in German, French, Italian and Belgian, various awful local channels, and English-language multinationals such as CNN and MTV. The basic also includes BBC1 and BBC2,

so there's no need to miss out on *EastEnders*. The wall-to-wall porn is an urban myth, so don't expect any late-night thrills unless your hotel has the 'extended service', which usually also features film channels, Discovery, the Cartoon Network, Eurosport and others. Dutch radio is generally as bland as the TV.

Money

Until 2002, the unit of Dutch currency is the guilder (or occasionally, florin), variously abbreviated as *f*, fl or Hfl. Throughout this Guide, the abbreviation '*f*' is used.

The guilder is divided into 100 cents, abbreviated to ¢. Coins in use are 5¢, 10¢, 25¢, *f*1, *f*2,50 and *f*5. The 5¢ coin is copper; 10¢, 25¢, *f*1 and *f*2,50 coins are silver-coloured and the *f*5 coin is gold-coloured (it closely resembles the £1 coin). The 5¢ coin is also known as a *stuiver*, the 10¢ coin as a *dubbeltje*, 25¢ as a *kwartje* and the *f*2,50 coin is called a *rijksdaalder*. Notes come in denominations of *f*10,

*f*25, *f*50, *f*100, *f*250 and *f*1,000 . The *f*10 note is blue, *f*25 pink, *f*50 yellow, *f*100 brown, *f*250 purple and *f*1,000 green. Since the Dutch no longer have 1¢ or 2¢ coins, prices are rounded up or down to the nearest 5¢. Amsterdammers prefer to use cash for most transactions, though larger hotels, shops and most restaurants will accept some credit cards. Many will also accept travellers' cheques with ID.

In 2002, the single European currency will at long last come into full effect, having been introduced as a kind of 'virtual' currency in 1999, and the guilder will be abolished. More and more establishments are listing its prices in both guilders and euros, though throughout this guide, we have limited our listings to guilders only for reasons of consistency.

Banks

Banks and bureaux de change offer similar rates of exchange, but banks tend to charge less commission. Most banks are open from 9am to 5pm Monday to Friday, with the Postbank opening up on Saturday mornings. Dutch banks buy and sell foreign currency and exchange travellers' cheques and Eurocheques, but few give cash advances against credit cards. For a list of banks, *see page 275*, or consult the *Amsterdam Yellow Pages* under 'Banken'.

Bureaux de change

Bureaux de change can be found throughout the city centre, especially on Leidseplein, Damrak and Rokin. Those listed below offer reasonable rates, though they charge more commission than banks. Hotel and tourist bureau exchange facilities are generally more expensive.

American Express

Damrak 66, Old Side: New Side (504 8777). Tram 4, 9, 14, 16, 20, 24, 25. **Open** 9am-5pm Mon-Fri; 9am-noon Sat; closed Sun. **Map** p306 D2. A number of facilities here.

Change Express

Damrak 86, Old Centre: New Side (624 6681/624 6682). Tram 4, 9, 14, 16, 20, 24, 25. **Open** 8am-11pm daily. **Map** p306 D2.
Branch: Leidseplein 123, Grachtengordel: East (622 1425). **Open** 8am-11.30pm daily. **Map** p310 C5.

GWK

Centraal Station, Old Centre: New Side (627 2731). Tram 1, 2, 4, 5, 9, 13, 16, 17, 20, 24, 25. **Open** 7am-11pm daily. **Map** p306 D1.
Branches: Amsterdam Schiphol Airport (in the railway station; 653 5121). **Open** 24hrs daily.

Thomas Cook

Dam 23-25, Old Centre: New Side (625 0922). Tram 4, 9, 14, 16, 20, 24, 25. **Open** 9am-8pm daily. **Map** p306 D3.
Branches: Damrak 1-5, Old Centre, New Side (620 3236). **Open** 8am-8pm daily. **Map** p306 D2.
Leidseplein 31A, Grachtengordel: East (626 7000). **Open** 9am-7.30pm Mon-Sat; 10am-7.30pm Sun. **Map** p310 C5.
There's no charge for cashing Thomas Cook travellers' cheques.

Opening hours

For all our listings in this Guide we give full opening times, but as a general rule, shops are open from 1pm to 6pm on Monday; 9am to 6pm Tuesday to Friday, with some staying open until 9pm on Thursdays; and 9am to 5pm on Saturdays. Smaller, specialist shops tend to open at varying times; if in doubt phone first. For shops that are open late, *see page 158*.

The city's bars open at various times during the day and close around 1am throughout the week, except for Fridays and Saturdays, when they stay open until 2am or 3am. Restaurants are generally open in the evening from 5pm until 11pm (though some close as early as 9pm); many are closed on Sunday and Monday.

Police & security

The Dutch police are under no obligation to grant a phone call to those they detain – they can hold people for up to six hours for questioning if the alleged crime is not serious, 24 hours for major matters – but they'll phone the relevant consulate on behalf of a foreign detainee.

If you are a victim of theft or assault, report it to the nearest police station. In the case of a serious incident or an emergency, phone the emergency switchboard on 112 and ask for the police.

Hoofdbureau van Politie (Police Headquarters)

Elandsgracht 117, The Jordaan (559 9111). Tram 7, 10, 20. **Open** 24hrs daily. **Map** p310 C4.

Postal services

For post destined for outside Amsterdam, use the *overige bestemmingen* slot in letter boxes. The logo for the national postal service is *ptt post* (white letters on a red oblong). Most post offices – recognisable by their red and blue signs – are open 9am to 5pm, Monday to Friday. The postal information phoneline is 0800 0417 (open 8am-8pm Mon-Fri, 9am-1pm Sat, closed Sun). Housed in every post office is the Postbank, a money-changing facility.

It costs 80¢ to send a postcard from Amsterdam to anywhere in Europe (*f*1 to the USA) and *f*1 for letters weighing less than 20g. To send post elsewhere, prices vary according to weight and destination. Stamps (*postzegels*) can also be bought with postcards from tobacconists and souvenir shops.

Main Post Office

Singel 250, Old Centre: New Side (556 3311). Tram 1, 2, 5, 13, 14, 17, 20. **Open** 9am-6pm Mon-Wed, Fri; 9am-8pm Thur; 10am-1.30pm Sat; closed Sun. **Map** p306 C3.

In addition to usual services, facilities include phones, self-service faxes, directories, maps, stamp machines, counters where you can buy packaging for parcels and a counter for collectors' stamps and stationery (closes 4.30pm Mon-Fri).

Centraal Station Post Office

Oosterdokskade 3, Old Centre: Old Side (622 8272). Tram 1, 2, 4, 5, 9, 13, 16, 17, 20, 24, 25. **Open** 8.30am-9pm Mon-Fri; 9am-noon Sat; closed Sun. **Map** p307 E1.
Only this and the main post office (*see above*) deal with large parcels.

Post Restante

Post Restante, Hoofdpostkantoor, Singel 250, 1016 AB Amsterdam. **Map** p306 C3.
If you're not sure where you'll be staying in Amsterdam, people can send your post to the above address. You'll be able to collect it from the main post office (*see above*) with ID.

Telegrams

Telegrams can be sent from post offices for a basic charge of *f*23,50, plus 49¢ per word under 11 letters (including address and signature). Details are available on 0800 0409.

Rape & sexual abuse

De Eerstelijn

(613 0245/fax 613 3341). **Open** 10.30am-11pm Mon-Fri; 4-11pm Sat, Sun.
Formerly called TOSG, this helpline is for women who are the victims of rape, assault, sexual harassment or threats. The line is often busy.

Meldpunt Vrouwenopvang

(611 6022). **Open** 9.30-11pm Mon-Fri; 4-11pm Sat, Sun.
Women who are being abused will be referred to a safe house or safe address within Amsterdam.

Religion

Catholic

St John and St Ursula *Begijnhof 30, Old Centre: New Side (622 1918). Tram 1, 2, 4, 5, 16, 20, 24, 25.* **Open** 1-6pm Mon; 8.30am-6pm Tue-Sat; closed Sun. **Services** in Dutch and French; phone for details. **Map** p306 D3.

Dutch Reformed Church

Oude Kerk *Oudekerksplein 33, Old Centre: Red Light District (625 8284).* Tram *4, 9, 16, 20, 24, 25.* **Open** 11am-5pm Mon-Sat; 1-5pm Sun. **Services** in Dutch; 11am Sun. **Map** p306 D2.

Jewish

Liberal Jewish Community Amsterdam *Jacob Soetendorpstraat 8, Zuid (642 3562/office rabbinate 644 2619).* Tram *4.* **Open** 9am-3pm Mon-Fri. *Office rabbinate* 10am-3pm Mon-Thur. **Services** 8pm Fri; 10am Sat.
Orthodox Jewish Community Amsterdam *Postbus 7967, Van der Boechorststraat 26, Zuid (646 0046).* Bus *69, 169.* **Open** 9am-5pm Mon-Fri by appointment only.
Information on orthodox synagogues and Jewish facilities.

Muslim

THAIBA Islamic Cultural Centre *Kraaiennest 125, Zuid (698 2526).* Metro *Gaasperplas.*
Phone for details of prayer times and cultural activities.

Quaker

Religious Genootschap der Vrienden *Voissiusstraat 20, Museum Quarter (679 4238).* Tram *1, 2, 5.* **Open** 11am-4pm Tue; on other days call 070 363 2132. **Service** 10.30am Sun.

Reformed Church

English Reformed Church *Begijnhof 48, Old Centre: New Side (624 9665/minister Mr John Cowey 672 2288/www.ercadam.nl).* Tram *1, 2, 4, 5, 9, 16, 20, 24, 25.* **Open** May-Sept 2-4pm Mon-Fri; closed Sat, Sun and Oct-Apr. **Services** in English 10.30am Sun; Dutch 7pm Sun. **Map** p306 D3.
The main place of worship for Amsterdam's English-speaking community.

Salvation Army

National Headquarters *Oudezijds Armsteeg 13, Old Centre: Red Light District (520 8408).* Tram *4, 9, 16, 20, 24, 25.* **Open** 9am-5pm Mon-Fri; closed Sat, Sun. **Map** p306 D2.
Information on Salvation Army Citadels in Amsterdam.

Students

Amsterdam's two major universities are the UvA (Universiteit van Amsterdam), which currently has around 27,000 students, and the VU (Vrije Universiteit), with about half that. Many of the UvA buildings scattered across town are historic and listed (you can recognise them by their red and black plaques), whereas the VU has just one big building at de Boelelaan, in the south of Amsterdam.

Dutch higher education is divided in two sectors: Institutes of Higher Education (HBO) and universities. Only students between the ages of 18 and 27 are eligible for the four-year grant (or five years for technical studies courses). Students must pass at least half of their courses each year, otherwise they have to pay the grant back to the government.

Students are often entitled to discounts at shops, clubs, museums, attractions, cinemas and entertainment venues; presenting an ISIC card is usually enough.

Courses

A number of UvA departments offer international courses and programmes for postgraduates, graduates and undergraduates, all taught in English. Details are available from the Foreign Relations Office (Spui 25, 1012 SR Amsterdam). Most postgraduate institutes of the UvA also take foreign students.

Amsterdam Summer University

Felix Meritis Building, Keizersgracht 324, Grachtengordel: East (620 0225/www.amsu.edu). Tram *1, 2, 5.* **Courses** mid July-early Sept. **Map** p310 C4.
The ASU offers an annual summer programme of courses, workshops, training and seminars in the arts and sciences, plus international classes.

Crea

Turfdraagsterpad 17, Old Centre: Old Side (626 2189). Tram *4, 9, 14, 16, 20, 24, 25.* **Open** 10am-11pm Mon-Fri; 10am-5pm Sat; 11am-5pm Sun; closed July.
Inexpensive creative courses, lectures and performances, covering theatre, radio, video, media, dance, music, photography and fine art. Courses are not in English. Sunday hours may be extended during July.

Foreign Student Service (FSS)

Oranje Nassaulaan 5, Zuid (671 5915). Tram *2.* **Open** 9am-5pm Mon-Fri.
The FSS promotes the well-being of foreign students, providing personal assistance and general information on studying in the Netherlands. It also runs the International Student Insurance Service (ISIS) and organises social activities.

UvA Service & Information Centre

Binnengasthuisstraat 9, Old Centre: Old Side (525 8080). Tram *4, 9, 16, 20, 24, 25.* **Open** *In person* 10am-4pm Mon-Wed, Fri; 10am-7pm Thur; closed Sat, Sun. *Phone enquiries* 9am-5pm Mon-Fri. **Map** p306 D3.
Personal advice on studying and everything that goes with it. The documentation centre stocks all the information you need to find a course for you in the Netherlands or abroad.

VU Student Information

Office 444 7777/direct line 444 5000. **Open** 9am-4.30pm Mon-Fri.
This is the helpline for the Vrije Universiteit, and can provide help and advice on courses, studying and accommodation.

Student bookshops

Because English textbooks are widely used in Dutch colleges, they are sold everywhere, often cheaply. *See page 141.*

VU Boekhandel

De Boelelaan 1105, Zuid (644 4355). Tram *5/Metro 51.* **Open** 9am-7pm Mon-Fri; 10am-3.30pm Sat; closed Sun. **Credit** AmEx, MC, V.
The VU Academic Bookshop has a large selection of books relating to all sciences, plus a good and varied collection of novels, tourist guides and children's books.

Student unions

Student unions in the Netherlands tend to have a fairly low volume of members. However, the following are all excellent sources of help and advice.

AEGEE

Vendels straat 2, Grachtengordel: East (525 2496/aegee@mail.uva.nl). Tram *1, 2, 5.* **Open** 2-5pm Mon-Thur; closed Fri-Sun. **Map** p311 E4.

The Association des Etats Généraux des Etudiants de l'Europe basically organises seminars, workshops, summer courses and sporting events in Amsterdam and around 170 other European university cities.

ASVA-OBAS

Binnengasthuisstraat 9, Old Centre: Old Side (accommodation agency 623 8052). Tram 4, 9, 14, 16, 20, 24, 25. **Open** *July, Aug* 11am-4pm Mon-Fri; closed Sat, Sun. *Sep-Jun* 12.30-4pm Mon-Wed, Fri; 12.30-6pm Thur; closed Sat, Sun. **Map** p306 D3.
ASVA offers assistance to foreign students. Its accommodation agency can find you a room for about ƒ350 per month, charging a ƒ10 deposit. An accommodation lottery is held daily at 4pm and at 6pm on Thursdays. Anyone with an ASVA card (ƒ25 for a year) can enter.

SRVU

De Boelelaan 1183A, Zuid (444 9424). Tram 5/Metro 51. **Open** *Mid Aug-June* 12.30-3.30pm Mon-Fri; closed Sat, Sun. *July-mid Aug* irregular hours.
SRVU is the union for VU students. Its accommodation service can also help foreign students find a place to stay, and offer general advice. Membership is ƒ17,50 per year.

University libraries

Both libraries below cover many academic titles and also provide access to the Internet.

UvA Main Library

Singel 425, Old Centre: New Side (525 2301/information 525 2326). Tram 1, 2, 5. **Open** *Study* 9am-midnight Mon-Fri; 9.30am-5pm Sat; closed Sun. *Borrowing* 9.30am-5pm Mon, Wed, Fri; 9.30am-8pm Tue, Thur; 9.30am-1pm Sat; closed Sun; closed July-mid Aug. **Map** p310 D4.
To borrow books you need a UB (Universiteit Bibliotheek-University Library) card (ƒ40): foreign students can also get one if they're in Amsterdam for three months or more, though a passport, driving licence or ID card will be needed as ID. Cards can be issued for one day, one month or one year.

VU Main Library

De Boelelaan 1105, Zuid (444 5200). Tram 5/Metro 51. **Open** *Study* Sep-Jun 9am-9pm Mon-Thur; 9am-5pm Fri; closed Sat, Sun; July-Aug 9am-5pm Mon-Fri; closed Sat, Sun. *Borrowing* 10am-4pm Mon-Fri. **Membership** ƒ30 per year.
Not one big library, but several small ones. The books are spread over different floors, which can make

them hard to track down, and some sciences such as maths, chemistry and biology have their own library in a building next door. Membership is open to foreign students.

Telephones

All Amsterdam numbers within this book are listed without the city code, which is 020. To call Amsterdam from within Amsterdam, you don't need the code: just dial the seven-digit number. To call an Amsterdam number from elsewhere in the Netherlands, add 020 at the start of the listed number. Numbers in the Netherlands outside of Amsterdam are listed with their code in this Guide.

In addition to the standard city codes, three other types of numbers appear from time to time throughout this book. Public information numbers with the prefix 0800 are freephone numbers; those prefixed 0900 are charged at premium rates (50¢ a minute or more); and 06 numbers designate mobile phones. If you are in any doubt, phone directory enquiries (0900 8008).

For more information on phone codes, *see below.*

Making a call

Listen for the dialling tone (a low-pitched hum), insert a phonecard (look for the small red arrow to see which side up it should go) or money (a minimum of 50¢), dial the appropriate code (no code is required for calls within Amsterdam), then dial the number. A digital display on public phones shows the credit remaining, but only wholly unused coins are returned. Phoning from a hotel is pricey.

International calls

International calls can be made from all phone boxes. Off-peak rates apply 8pm to 8am Monday to Friday and all weekend. For more information on off-peak rates, phone international directory enquiries (0900 8418).

Telephone directories

Found in post offices (*see p286*). When phoning information services, taxis or train stations you may hear the recorded message, 'Er zijn nog drie [3]/twee [2]/een [1] wachtende(n) voor u.' This tells you how many people are ahead of you in the telephone queueing system.

Phone codes

From the Netherlands

Dial the following code, then the number:

To Australia: 00 61
To Irish Republic: 00 353
To UK: 00 44, plus number (drop first '0' from area code)
To USA: 00 1

To the Netherlands

Dial the relevant international access code listed below, then the Dutch country code 31, then the number; drop the first '0' of the area code, so for Amsterdam use 20 rather than 020. To call 06 (mobile) numbers from abroad, there is no city code: just drop the first '0' from the 06 andf dial the number as it appears. However, 0800 (freephone) and 0900 (premium rate) numbers cannot be reached from abroad.

From Australia: 00 11
From Irish Republic: 00
From UK: 00
From USA: 011

Within the Netherlands

National directory enquiries: 0900 8008
International directory enquiries: 0900 8418
Local operator: 0800 0101
International operator: 0800 0410

Mobile phones

Amsterdam's mobile network is run on a mix of the 900 and 1800 GSM bands, which means that all dual-band UK handsets should work in the city. However, always be sure to check with your telephone service provider before you leave for the Netherlands that they have an arrangement with a Dutch provider that will enable you to use their network while abroad. For phone users from the US, where there are countless different networks, the situation is more complicated: always contact your provider before departure.

Public phones

Public phone boxes are mainly glass with a green trim. There are also telephone poles all over the city, identifiable by their blue and green KPN Telecom logo. Most phones take phonecards rather than coins (those that do take coins take 25¢, ƒ1 and ƒ2,50 coins). Phonecards are available from post offices, the Amsterdam Tourist Board, stations and tobacconists, priced at ƒ10, ƒ25 and ƒ50. You can use credit cards in many phones.

Time

Amsterdam is one hour ahead of Greenwich Mean Time (GMT). All clocks on Central European Time (CET) now go back and forward on the same spring and autumn dates as GMT. For the speaking clock in Dutch, phone 0900 8002.

Tipping

Though a service charge will be included in hotel, taxi, bar, café and restaurant bills, most Amsterdammers generally round up the change to the nearest five guilders for large bills and to the nearest guilder for smaller ones, leaving the extra in small change rather than putting it on a credit card. In taxis, the most common tip is around ten per cent for short journeys.

Tourist information

For VVV, read Amsterdam Tourist Board. Though national tourist offices have maintained their old name, the visitor information service in Amsterdam is now known as the Amsterdam Tourist Board

There are three offices in Amsterdam, and staff in all three speak English.

Amsterdam Tourist Board

Stationsplein 10, Old Centre: New Side (0900 400 4040). Tram 1, 2, 4, 5, 9, 13, 16, 17, 20, 24, 25. **Open** 9am-5pm daily. **Map** p306 D1.
The main office of the Amsterdam Tourist Board is right outside Centraal Station. English-speaking staff can change money and provide details on transport, entertainment, exhibitions, and day-trips in the Netherlands. They also arrange hotel bookings for a fee of ƒ6, and excursions and car hire for free. There is a good range of brochures for sale detailing walks and cycling tours, as well as cassette tours, maps and, for ƒ2,50, a monthly listings magazine *Day by Day*. The premium-rate information line features an English-language service.
Branches: Leidseplein 1 (open 9am-5pm daily); Centraal Station (open 8am-8pm daily); Schiphol Airport (open 7am-10pm).

Visas

A valid passport is all that is required for a stay of up to three months in the Netherlands if you are an EU national or from the USA, Canada, Australia or New Zealand. If you are a national of any other country, apply for a tourist visa from your country of origin.

For stays of longer than three months, you need to apply in advance from your country of origin for a residents' permit (MVV visa), regardless of your country of origin (though it is generally harder to get one if you're not from one of the countries listed above). When you have a fixed address in the Netherlands, you need to get an application form from the **Bureau Vreemdelingenpolitie** (the Aliens' Police) and then submit yourself for interview.

Bureau Vreemdelingenpolitie

Johan Huizingalaan 757, Slotervaart (559 6213/6214). Tram 2/bus 19, 63. **Open** 8am-4.30pm Mon-Fri.

Washing & cleaning

A comprehensive list of launderettes (*wassalons*) can be found in the *Yellow Pages* (*Gouden Gids*).

Baths & showers

Stichting De Warme Waterstaal

Da Costakade 200, Oud West (612 5946). Tram 3, 7, 12, 17. **Open** noon-6.30pm Tue; noon-3.30pm Thur; 10am-4.30pm Sat; closed Mon, Wed, Sun. *Sauna* 2-10.30pm Mon, Tue 2.30-10.30pm Sun. **Rates** ƒ3 per shower; ƒ5 per bath. *Sauna* 2-6pm ƒ12; after 6pm ƒ15; Sun ƒ15. **Map** p309 B5.
Bring your own towel or rent one for ƒ1. Treat yourself to a massage or a sunbed session.

When to go

Climate

Amsterdam's climate is very changeable, and often wet and windy. January and February are coldest, with summer often humid. The average daytime temperatures are: January, February 5°C (41°F); March 8°C (47°F); April 12°C (54°F); May 16°C (61°F); June 19°C (66°F); July, August 21°C (69°F); September 18°C (64°F); October 14°C (57°F); November 9°C (48°F); December 6°C (42°F). If you understand Dutch, try the 24-hour recorded information weather line on 0900 8003.

Public holidays

Called 'Nationale Feestdagen' in Dutch, they are: New Year's Day; Good Friday; Easter Sunday and Monday; Koninginnedag (Queen's Day, 30 April; *see page 172*); Remembrance Day (4 May); Liberation Day (5 May); Ascension Day; Whit (Pentecost) Sunday and Monday; Christmas Day, and the day after Christmas.

Directory

Further Reading

Literature

Van Dantzig, Rudi
For a Lost Soldier
Autobiographical story set in the years following 1944.
De Moor, Margriet *First Grey, Then White, Then Blue*
Compelling story of perception, love and mortality.
Grunberg, Arnon
Blue Mondays
Philip Roth's *Goodbye Columbus* goes Dutch in this cathartic 1994 bestseller.
Joris, Lieve
Back to the Congo
Historical novel about Belgium and its ex-colony.
Krabbé, Tim *The Vanishing*
A man's search for his vanished lover. Twice made into a feature film.
Minco, Marga *Bitter Herbs*
Autobiographical masterpiece about a Jewish family falling apart during and after the war.
Morley, John David
The Anatomy Lesson
Novel about two very different American brothers growing up in Amsterdam.
Mulisch, Harry *The Assault*
A boy's perspective of the last war.
Multatuli *Max Havelaar or the Coffee Auctions of the Dutch Trading Company*
The story of a colonial officer and his clash with the corrupt government.
Nooteboom, Cees
The Following Story
An exploration of the differences between platonic and physical love.
Rubinstein, Renate
Take It or Leave It
Diary of one of the Netherlands' most renowned journalists and her battle against MS.
Welsh, Irvine
The Acid House
Short stories, one set – perhaps predictably – in Amsterdam's druggy underworld.

Van der Wetering, Janwillem
The Japanese Corpse
Marvellously off-the-wall police procedural set in Amsterdam. One of an excellent series.

Architecture

Fuchs, RH *Dutch Painting*
A comprehensive guide.
Groenendijk, Paul
Guide to Modern Architecture in Amsterdam
Exactly what the title suggests.
Kloos, Maarten (ed)
Amsterdam, An Architectural Lesson
Architects and town planners on the city.
Overy, Paul *De Stijl*
Amsterdam's modern art examined.
De Wit, Wim
The Amsterdam School: Dutch Expressionist Architecture
Early 20th-century architecture.

History

Andeweg, Rudy B, & Irwin, Galen A
Dutch Government & Politics
An introduction to Dutch politics that assumes no prior knowledge.
Boxer, CR
The Dutch Seaborne Empire
The Netherlands' wealth and where it went.
Burke, Peter
Venice & Amsterdam
A succinct comparative history of these two watery cities. Intriguing stuff.
Gies, Miep & Gold, Alison Leslie
Anne Frank Remembered
The story of the woman who helped the Frank family during the war.
Israel, Jonathan I
The Dutch Republic and the Hispanic World 1606-1661

How the Dutch Republic broke free.
Kussmann, EH
The Low Countries 1780-1940
Good background reading.
Mak, Geert *Amsterdam: A Brief Life of the City*
The history of the city told through the stories of its people, both acclaimed and plain. Terrific.
Parker, Geoffrey
The Thirty Years' War; The Dutch Revolt
The fate of the Netherlands and Spain in descriptive, analytical history.
Schama, Simon
The Embarassment of Riches
Lively, witty, social and cultural history of the Netherlands. His tour de force biography of sorts, *Rembrandt's Eyes*, is also worth a look.
Schetter, William Z
The Netherlands in Perspective
An essential book that goes beyond the usual stereotypes.

General interest

Blyth, Derek
Amsterdam Explored
Nine walks around the city.
Frank, Anne
The Diary of Anne Frank
The war-time diary of the young Anne Frank. Compulsively readable.
Herbert, Zbigniew
Still Life with a Bridle
The Polish poet and essayist meditates on the Golden Age.
Van Straaten, Peter
This Literary Life
Highly amusing collection of one of the Netherlands' most popular cartoonist's works.
Various *Dedalus Book of Dutch Fantasy*
Contemporary Dutch short stories.
Vossestein, Jacob
Dealing With the Dutch
Netherlanders explained in fascinating fashion.

Index

Advertisers' Index

Maps

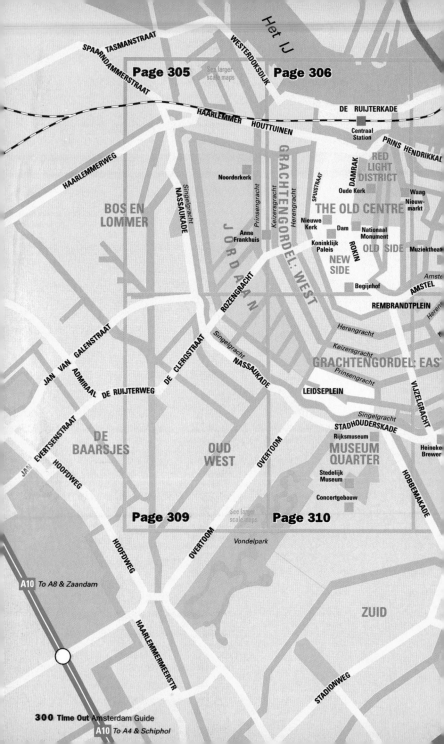

Het IJ

SPAARNDAMMERSTRAAT
TASMANSTRAAT
WESTERDOKSDIJK

Page 305

See larger scale maps

Page 306

DE RUIJTERKADE

HAARLEMMER HOUTTUINEN

Centraal
Station

PRINS HENDRIKKAD

HAARLEMMERWEG

Noorderkerk

Singelgracht
NASSAUKADE

Prinsengracht

GRACHTENGORDEL: WEST

SPUISTRAAT

DAMRAK

RED
LIGHT
DISTRICT

Oude Kerk

Waag

**BOS EN
LOMMER**

JORDAAN

Keizersgracht

Herengracht

Nieuwe
Kerk

THE OLD CENTRE

Nieuw-
markt

Anne
Frankhuis

Dam

Nationaal
Monument

OLD SIDE

Koninklijk
Paleis

NEW
SIDE

ROKIN

Muziektheat

Amste

ROZENGRACHT

Begijnhof

AMSTEL

REMBRANDTPLEIN

Singelgracht

Herengracht

Heren

JAN VAN GALENSTRAAT

NASSAUKADE

Keizersgracht

GRACHTENGORDEL: EAS

DE CLERQSTRAAT

ADMIRAAL DE RUIJTERWEG

Prinsengracht

JAN EVERTSENSTRAAT

LEIDSEPLEIN

VIJZELGRACHT

Singelgracht

STADHOUDERSKADE

**DE
BAARSJES**

HOOFDWEG

**OUD
WEST**

OVERTOOM

Rijksmuseum

**MUSEUM
QUARTER**

Heineke
Brewer

HOBBEMAKADE

Stedelijk
Museum

Concertgebouw

See larger
scale maps

Page 309

Page 310

OVERTOOM

Vondelpark

A10 To A8 & Zaandam

HAARLEMMERMEERSTR

ZUID

STADIONWEG

A10 To A4 & Schiphol

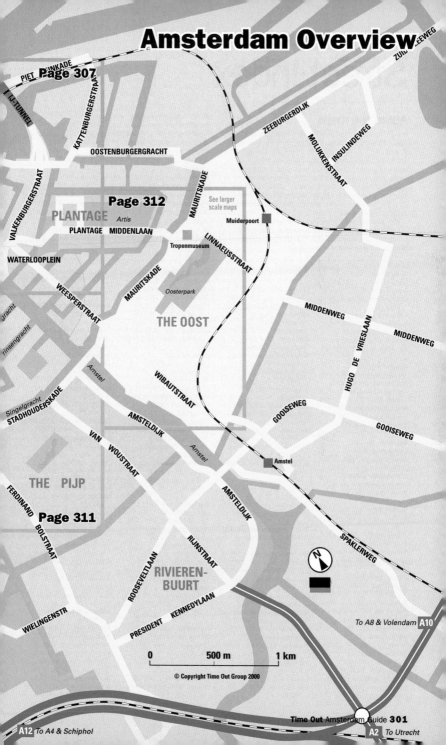

Amsterdam Overview

PIET HEINKADE

IJ TUNNEL

KATTENBURGERSTRAAT

OOSTENBURGERGRACHT

ZUIDERZEEWEG

ZEEBURGERDIJK

MOLUKKENSTRAAT

INSULINDEWEG

VALKENBURGERSTRAAT

MAURITSKADE

PLANTAGE

Artis

See larger
scale maps

Page 312

PLANTAGE MIDDENLAAN

Muiderpoort

WATERLOOPLEIN

Tropenmuseum

LINNAEUSSTRAAT

WEESPERSTRAAT

MAURITSKADE

Oosterpark

THE OOST

MIDDENWEG

MIDDENWEG

rinsengracht

Amstel

HUGO DE VRIESLAAN

WIBAUTSTRAAT

Singelgracht

STADHOUDERSKADE

AMSTELDIJK

VAN WOUSTRAAT

Amstel

GOOISEWEG

GOOISEWEG

Amstel

FERDINAND

THE PIJP

Page 311

AMSTELDIJK

SPAKLERWEG

BOLSTRAAT

RIJNSTRAAT

ROOSEVELTLAAN

**RIVIEREN-
BUURT**

N

WIELINGENSTR

PRESIDENT KENNEDYLAAN

To A8 & Volendam **A10**

0   500 m   1 km

© Copyright Time Out Group 2000

A12 *To A4 & Schiphol*

A2 *To Utrecht*

Street Index

About the maps

Due to the crowded layout of Amsterdam and the length of many of the street names, not all street names have been given on the map itself. However, all are alphabetised and referenced below. Where a street name has proven too long to fit on the map, it has instead been given a number and designated on the index with an asterisk and the number as it appears on the map. 'Begijnensteeg - p306 D3 *2', for example, means that Begijnensteeg can be found on page 311, grid reference D3, and is marked on the map not by its street name but by the number 2.

This index has been designed to tie in with other commercially available maps of Amsterdam, and certain principles of the Dutch language have been followed for reasons of consistency and ease of use:

● Where a street is named after a person – Albert Cuypstraat, for example – it is alphabetised by surname. Albert Cuypstraat, therefore, is listed under 'C'.
● Where a street takes a number as a prefix, it has been listed under the name of the street, rather than the number. 1e Bloemdwarsstraat, then, is alphabetised under 'B'.
● The following prefixes have been ignored for alphabetisation: Da, De, Den, 's, Sint (St), 't, Van, Van der. Where street names contain one of these prefixes, they have been alphabetised under the subsequent word. For example, Da Costakade can be found under 'C', and Van Breestraat is listed under 'B'.
● In Dutch, 'ij' is the same as 'y'. Streets containing 'ij' – Vijzelstraat, for example – have been alphabetised as if 'ij' was a 'y'.

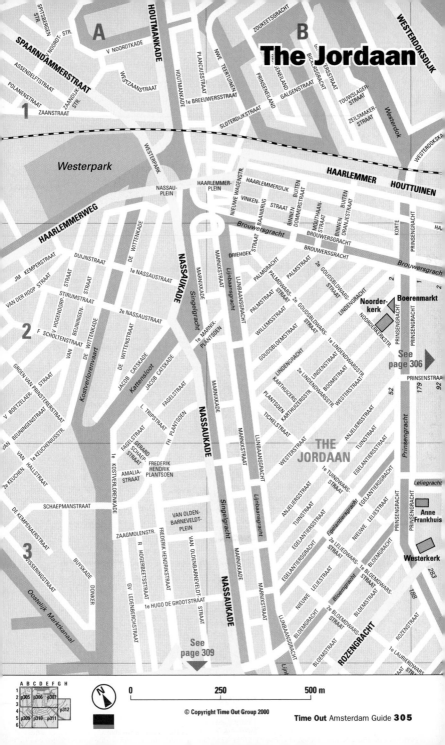

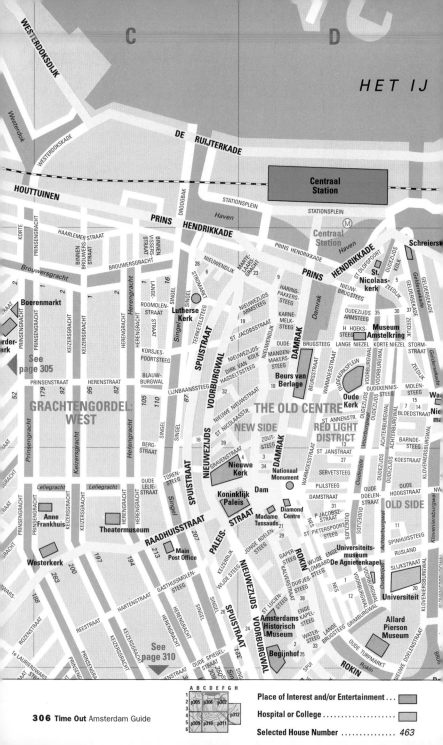

HET IJ

DE RUIJTERKADE

HOUTTUINEN

WESTERDOKSDIJK

Westerdok

WESTERDOKSKADE

STATIONSPLEIN

**Centraal
Station**

STATIONSPLEIN

PRINS
HENDRIKKADE

Haven

PRINS HENDRIKKADE

Ⓜ **Centraal
Station**

KORTE PRINSENGRACHT

HAARLEMER STRAAT

BINNEN
BROUWERS-
STRAAT

BINNEN
VISSERS-
STRAAT

BROUWERSGRACHT

Brouwersgracht

PRINSENGRACHT

PRINSENGRACHT

KEIZERSGRACHT

KEIZERSGRACHT

HERENGRACHT

HERENGRACHT

LANGE-
NIEUW-
STRAAT

ROOMOLEN-
STRAAT

SINGEL

16

NIEUWENDIJK

DROOGBAK

Haven

PRINS HENDRIKKADE

MARTE-
LAARS-
GRACHT

23

9

HARING-
PAKKERS-
STEEG

NIEUWEZIJDS
ARMSTEEG

Schreiers

St Nicolaaskerk

ST OLOFSPOORT

OUDEZIJDS
KOLK

5

GELDERSEKADE

ZEEDIJK

Boerenmarkt

2

1

2

**Luthers
Kerk**

TEERKETELSTEEG

SINGEL

ST JACOBSSTRAAT

KARNE-
MELK-
STEEG

H HOEKS-
STEEG

Damrak

OUDEZIJDS
ARMSTEEG

35

30

37

**Museum
Amstelkring**

See
page 305

KEIZERSGRACHT

PRINSENGRACHT

HERENGRACHT

KORSJES-
POORTSTEEG

BLAUW-
BURGWAL

LIJNBAANSSTEEG

NIEUWEZIJDS

NIEUW-
MANDEN-
MAKERS-
STEEG

DIRK VAN HASSELTSSTEEG

BRUGSTEEG

BEURSSTRAAT

WARMOESSTRAAT

LANGE NIEZEL

OUDEZIJDS VOORBURGWAL

OUDEKERKSPLEIN

KORTE NIEZEL

STORM-
STRAAT

ZEEDIJK

MOLEN-
STEEG

15

**Beurs van
Berlage**

18

**Oude
Kerk**

OUDEZIJDS VOORBURGWAL

OUDEKENNIS-
STEEG

ACHTERBURGWAL

ACHTERBURGWAL

BLOEDSTRAAT

Wa
ma

**GRACHTENGORDEL:
WEST**

179 92

95 82

PRINSENGRACHT

105

110

87

SINGEL

NIEUWE NIEUWSTRAAT

ST NICOLAASSTR.

32

BERG.
STRAAT

16

39

ZOUT-
STEEG

GRAVENSTRAAT

THE OLD CENTRE

NEW SIDE

DAMRAK

**RED LIGHT
DISTRICT**

13

ST ANNENSTR.

ST JANSTRAAT

27

BARNDE-
STEEG

KOESTRAAT

**Anne
Frankhuis**

KEIZERSGRACHT

PRINSENGRACHT

HERENGRACHT

Theatermuseum

Leliegracht

Leliegracht

OUDE
LELIE-
STRAAT

TOREN-
STEEG

SINGEL

4

34

3

**Nieuwe
Kerk**

**Nationaal
Monument**

DAMRAK

WARMOESSTRAAT

SERVETSTEEG

PIJLSTEEG

OUDEZIJDS

31

OUDE
DOELEN-
STRAAT

OLD SIDE

SPINHUISSTEEG

11

RUSLAND

NW
Nie
ma

Westerkerk

188

283

200

197

194

213

**Main
Post Office**

WIJDE STEEG

KEIZERSGRACHT

SINGEL

207

**Koninklijk
Paleis**

PALEIS-
STRAAT

RAADHUISSTRAAT

Dam

**Madame
Tussauds**

21

**Diamond
Centre**

DAMSTRAAT

NES

P JACOBSZ-
STRAAT

ST PIETERSPOORT
STEEG

29

**Universiteits-
museum
De Agnietenkapel**

1

OUDEZIJDS VOORBURGWAL

12

SLIJKSTRAAT

20

Universiteit

KLOVENIERSBURGWAL

ROZENSTRAAT

1e LAURIERDWARS

KEIZERSGRACHT

PRINSENGRACHT

HARTENSTRAAT

GASTHUISMOLEN-
STEEG

REESTRAAT

HERENGRACHT

See
page 310

OUDE SPIEGEL-
STRAAT

360

NIEUWEZIJDS VOORBURGWAL

SPUISTRAAT

WLIDE STEEG

KEIZERSGRACHT

JONGE ROELEN-
STEEG

GAPER-
STEEG

KALVERSTRAAT

WIJDE LOMBARD-
STEEG

DUIFJES-
STEEG

ENGE LOMBARD-
STRAAT

ROKIN

NES

LANGE
BRUGSTEEG

GRIMBURGWAL

**Allard
Pierson
Museum**

NIEUWE DOELENSTRAAT

ST LUCIEN-
STEEG

38

ENGE
KAPEL-
STEEG

**Amsterdams
Historisch
Museum**

24

WATER-
STEEG

33

OUDE TURFMARKT

Begijnhof

25

SPUI

ROKIN

Rokin

A	B	C	D	E	F	G	H
1							
2		p305	p306	p307			
3							
4		p309	p310	p311			
5							
6				p312			

Place of Interest and/or Entertainment . . . ▢

Hospital or College . . . . ▢

Selected House Number *463*

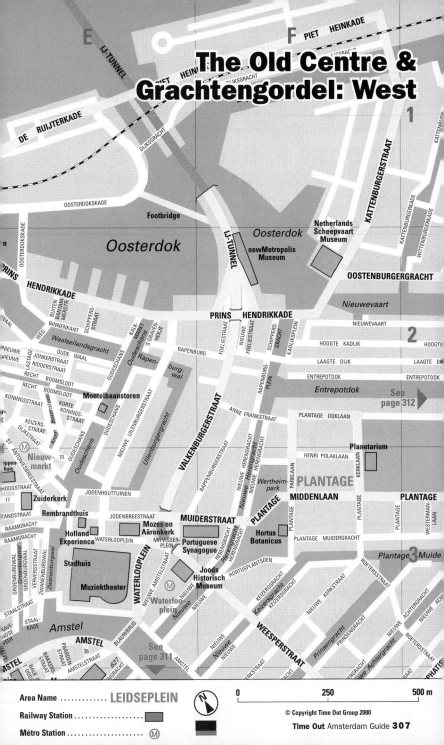

The Old Centre & Grachtengordel: West

PIET HEINKADE

1

DE RUIJTERKADE

OOSTERDOKSKADE

Footbridge

Oosterdok

IJ-TUNNEL

Oosterdok

Netherlands
Scheepvaart
Museum

KATTENBURGERSTRAAT

KATTENBURGERKADE

WITTENBURGERKADE

newMetropolis
Museum

OOSTENBURGERGRACHT

PRINS
HENDRIKKADE

BUITEN
BANTAM-
MEERSTR

BINNENKANT

SCHIPPERS-
STRAAT

PRINS HENDRIKKADE

Nieuwevaart

2

Waalseilandsgracht

OUDE WAAL

JONKERSTRAAT

RIDDERSTRAAT

BOOMSLOOT

BOOMSLOOT

KALK
MARKT

S GRAVEN-
HEKJE

RAPENBURG

FOELIESTRAAT

NIEUWE
FOELIESTRAAT

SCHIPPERS-
GRACHT

KADIJKSPLEIN

NIEUWEVAART

HOOGTE KADIJK

HOOGTE

NIEUWE

NIEUWE

LASTAGE

WEG

RECHT

KONINGSSTRAAT

KORTE
KONINGS-
STRAAT

Montelbaanstoren

OUDESCHANS

OUDESCHANS

NIEUWE UILENBURGERSTRAAT

Uilenburgergracht

RAPENburg-
wal

RAPENBURG
PLEIN

LAAGTE DIJK

LAAGTE D

ENTREPOTDOK

ENTREPOTDOK

Entrepotdok

See
page 312

KEIZERS-
STRAAT

DIJKSTRAAT

ANNE FRANKSTRAAT

PLANTAGE DOKLAAN

VALKENBURGERSTRAAT

RAPPENBURGERSTRAAT

NIEUWE Herengracht

NIEUWE Herengracht

Wertheim-
park

PARKLAAN

HENRI POLAKLAAN

KERKLAAN

Planetarium

Nieuw-
markt

ippen-
huis

St
ANTONIESBREESTRAAT

OUDESCHANS

10

PLANTAGE

PLANTAGE

HOOGSTRAAT

Zuiderkerk

JODENHOUTTUINEN

MIDDENLAAN

PLANTAGE

PLANTAGE

PLANTAGE

WESTERMAN-
LAAN

17

Rembrandthuis

JODENBREESTRAAT

MUIDERSTRAAT

PLANTAGE

ZANDSTRAAT

Holland
Experience

Mozes en
Aäronkerk

WATERLOOPLEIN

MR VISSER-
PLEIN

NIEUWE
Herengracht

Hortus
Botanicus

PLANTAGE MUIDERGRACHT

RAAMGRACHT

RAAMGRACHT

Portuguese
Synagogue

HERENGRACHT

HERENGRACHT

Plantage **3** Muide

Stadhuis

WATERLOOPLEIN

Joods
Historisch
Museum

HORTUSPLANTSOEN

ROETERSSTRAAT

GROENBURGWAL

GROENBURGWAL

VERVERSGRACHT

ZWANENBURGWAL

Muziektheater

NIEUWE AMSTELSTRAAT

KEIZERSGRACHT

KEIZERSGRACHT

NIEUWE KERKSTRAAT

NIEUWE ACHTERGRACHT

NIEUWE ACH

STAALSTRAAT

STAAL-
KADE

Amstel

Waterloo
plein

Nieuwe

Nieuwe

Prinsengracht

PRINSENGRACHT

NIEUWE ACHTERGRACHT

ROETERSSTRAAT

AMSTEL

36

BLAUWBRUG

See
page 311

WEESPERSTRAAT

HATIS

AMSTEL

PAARDEN
STRAAT

BAKKERS
STRAAT

AMSTELSTRAAT

627

Museum

AMSTEL

NIEUWE

NIEUWE

NIEUWE

Nieuwe Achtergracht

Legend

Area Name .... **LEIDSEPLEIN**

Railway Station ....

Métro Station .... Ⓜ

N

| 0 | 250 | 500 m |

© Copyright Time Out Group 2000

JAN VAN GALENSTRAAT

HUGO DE GROOTPLEIN

2e H DE GROOTSTR.

See page 305

ROZENGR

1e LAURIER
DWARS

2e LAURIERDWARS-
STRAAT

LAURIE

ROZENSTRAAT

Laurier
gracht

LAURIERGRACHT

HAZEN-

ELANDSSTR

3e H DE GROOTSTRAAT

H DE GROOTKADE

FREDERIK HENDRIKSTRAAT

Lijnbaansgracht

MARNIXSTRAAT

LIJNBAANSGRACHT

ELANDSSTRAAT

STRAA

ELANDSGRACHT

2e

3e LOOI
STR

KOP VAN JUT

Kostverlorenvaart

V HOUWENINGENSTRAAT

V REIGERSBERGENSTRAAT

4

KOP VAN JUT

Westelijk Marktkanaal

H de Grootgracht

BILDERDIJKPARK

DA COSTASTRAAT

DA COSTASTRAAT

DA COSTAKADE

NASSAUKADE

Singelgracht

Politie

GEUZENSTRAAT

GEUZENKADE

AV BERGEN
STRAAT

DE CLERCQSTRAAT

POTGIETERSTRAAT

KINKERSTRAAT

See page 310

NA

Da Costagracht

DA COSTASTRAAT

ADMIRAAL DE ZWIJGERLAAN

DE RUIJTERWEG

BILDERDIJKKADE

BILDERDIJKKADE

E WOLFFSTRAAT

A OEKENSTRAAT

KWAKERSSTR

BILDERDIJKSTRAAT

Bilderdijkgracht

KINKERSTRAAT

DA COSTAKADE

DA COSTAKADE

Jacob van Lennepkanaal

BOSBOOM

TOI

3e HELMF

SLATUINENWEG

TOLBURGSTRAAT

BAARSJESWEG

2e KOSTVERLORENKADE

SCHIMMELSTRAAT

BELLAMY-
PLEIN

BELLAMYSTRAAT

OUD WEST

BILDERDIJKKADE

BILDERDIJKKADE

TOLLENSSTRAAT

Polikliniek

2e

5

CHASSESTRAAT

V KINSBERGENSTR.

V SPEIJKSTRAAT

Kostverlorenvaart

J HANZENSTRAAT

WENSLAUERSTRAAT

BELLAMYSTRAAT

HASEBROEKSTRAAT

KINKERSTRAAT

N BEETSSTRAAT

SCHOOL-
MEESTERSTR

JACOB VAN LENNEPKADE

JACOB VAN LENNEPKADE

2e C HUYGENSSTRAAT

W GASTHUISPLEIN

A SPRENGLESTRAAT

WITTE DE WITHSTRAAT

ADMIRALENGRACHT

BAARSJESWEG

JAN PIETER HEIJESTRAAT

BORGERSTRAAT

JACOB VAN LENNEPSTRAAT

Jacob van Lennepkanaal

KANAALSTRAAT

N BEETSSTRAAT

WILHELMINASTRAAT

1e HELMERSSTRAAT

OVERTOOM

VONDELSTRAAT

6

BAARSJESWEG

KINKERSTRAAT

KOSTVERLORENKADE

LOOTSSTRAAT

JAN PIETER HEIJESTRAAT

BREDERODESTRAAT

1e HELMERSSTRAAT

OVERTOOM

G BRANDTSTR.

VONDELSTR.

POSTJESKADE

STUYVESANTSTRAAT

2e KOSTVERLORENKADE

JACOB VAN LENNEPKADE

JACOB VAN LENNEPKADE

KANAALSTRAAT

LOOTSSTRAAT

WILHELMINA
STR

A

B

A B C D E F G H
p305 p306 p307
p309 p310 p311 p312

N

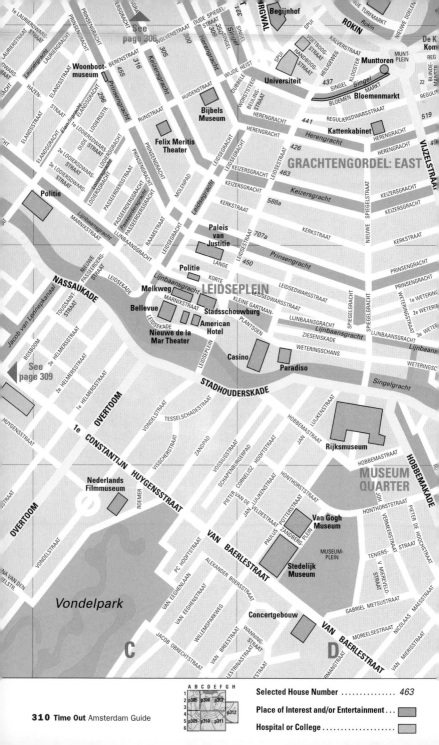

Selected House Number *463*

Place of Interest and/or Entertainment . . .

Hospital or College . . . .

Grachtengordel: East & beyond

See page 307

See page 312

Museum Willet-Holthuysen

REMBRANDTPLEIN

Magere Brug

Weesperplein

Koninklijk Theater Carré

Museum Van Loon

THE PIJP

Sarphatipark

Heineken Brewery

Area Name	....	LEIDSEPLEIN
Railway Station	....	
Métro Station	....	Ⓜ

0   250   500 m

© Copyright Time Out Group 2000

Time Out Amsterdam Guide **311**

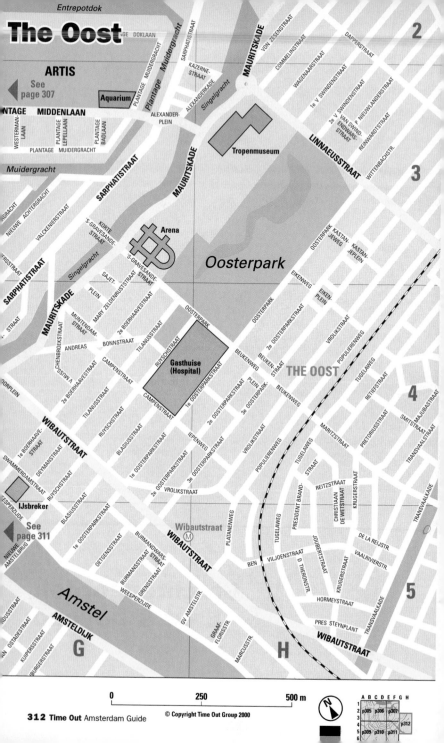

The Oost

Entrepotdok

ARTIS
See
page 307

Aquarium

MIDDENLAAN

Tropenmuseum

Oosterpark

Arena

Gasthuise
(Hospital)

THE OOST

Wibautstraat

IJsbreker

See
page 311

Amstel

© Copyright Time Out Group 2000

0   250   500 m

he Netherlands

0   25   50 km

Schiermonnikoog

Ameland

Borkum

Terschelling

Vlieland

WADDEN ISLANDS

Hoogebeintum
Dokkum

LEEUWARDEN

Uithuizermeeden
Uithuizen
Warffum   Spijk   **Bierum**
Kantens
Middlestum   Stedum   **Appingedam**
Loppersum

GRONINGEN   Garmerwolde

Harlingen
Grouw

Drachten

Veendam   **Winschoten**

Bellingwolde

Texel

Sneek   FRIESLAND
Terherne

Fochteloaërveen   **Assen**

Stadskanaal

Heeg

Heerenveen

DRENTHE

Den Helder

Sloten   **Lemmer**

Borger

Anna
Paulowna

Ellertsveld
Uffelter   Westerbork   Orvelte
Veen

Schagen   Opperdoes   Medemblick

IJSSELMEER

Steenwijk

Dwingeloose
Heide

Emmen

Broek-op-
Langedijk

Twisk   **Enkhuizen**

Emmeloord

Blokzijl
Wanneperveen   Giethoorn
Uffelte

Hoogeveen

Heiloo   **Alkmaar**

Hoorn

Urk

Meppel

Limmen   NOORD

HOLLAND   MARKERMEER

Vollenhove   Staphorst

Zwartsluis

Beverwijk   IJmuiden   **Pumerend**

Edam
Volendam

Lelystad

Ketelhaven

Kampen

ZWOLLE   Ommen

Kennemer
Duinen Nat.Pk.

Zaanstad

Oostvaarders-
Monnikendam-plassen
Broek in W.

Flevohof

Lemelerveld

Ootmarsum
Denekamp

HAARLEM   **AMSTERDAM**   FLEVOLAND

Hellendoorn

OVERIJSEL

Zandvoort

Muiden   **Almerestad**   **Harderwijk**

Raalte

Almelo   **Oldenzaal**

Vogelenzang   Bennebroek   Fort

Bussum

Deventer

Holterberg
81m

Hengelo

Lisse

Aalsmeer Vreeland-1
Laren   Bunschoten-
Spakenburg

1. Oud-Loosdrecht
2. Breukeleveen
3. Westbroek

Keukenhof   Hillegom

Noordwijk

Naarden
1
Hilversum

APELDOORN

ENSCHEDE

Katwijk   Rijnsburg

Soest
Soestdijk

Zutphen

Scheveningen

Oudaen

LEIDEN

Amersfoort

Hoge Veluwe
Nat. Park

ZUID

HOLLAND   **Alphen**

De Haar
Castle

UTRECHT

Austerlitz

DEN HAAG

Zoetermeer   **Gouda**

Oudewater

UTRECHT

Wijbij
Duurstede

Ede

GELDERLAND

Naaldwijk   **DELFT**

Hoek van Holland

Europoort

ROTTERDAM   Schoonhoven

Culemborg

Rhenen

Oosterbeek

ARNHEM   **Winterswijk**

Doetinchem

Vlaardingen
Voorne

Gorinchem

Tiel

Stellendam

Putten
Alblasserdam

NIJMEGEN

Schouwen
Brouwershaven

Goeree-
Overflakkee

DORDRECHT

De Biesbosch
Nat. Park

Oss

Oosterschelde

Delta Expo   **Zierikzee**

Noord
Beveland

Hoeksche-Waard

Geertruidenberg   Drunen

'S-HERTOGENBOSCH

Oudenbosch   **BREDA**

Oosterhout

Waalwijk

Uden

Overloon

Veere

Goes   Yerseke

Tholen

Roosendaal

Kaatsheuvel

TILBURG

NOORD - BRABANT

De Groote Peel
Nat. Reserve

Middelburg

Kapelle

**Bergen op
Zoom**

Nuenen   **Helmond**

Zoutelande

Kruiningen

Vlissingen

ZEELAND

EINDHOVEN

Venlo

Zeebrugge   Zeeuws - Vlaanderen

Terneuzen

**ANTWERPEN
ANVERS**

Weert   Thorn

LIMBURG

**BRUGGE
BRUGES**

Roermond

DEUTSCHLAND

**GENT
GAND**

Sittard

Geleen

Heerlen

B E L G I Q U E

Valkenburg

MAASTRICHT   Schin

AACHEN

NOORDZEE

© Copyright Time Out Group 2000

Amsterdam Transport

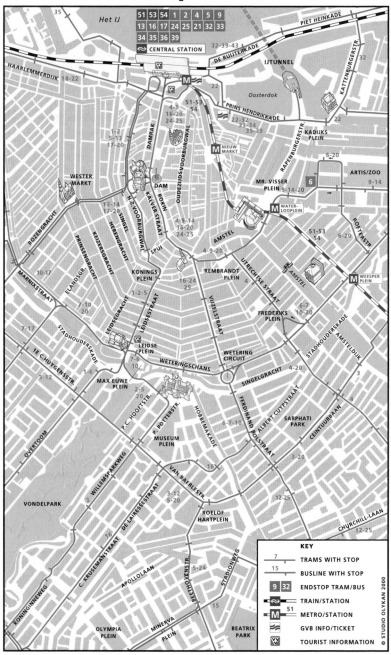

KEY

7	TRAMS WITH STOP
15	BUSLINE WITH STOP
9 32	ENDSTOP TRAM/BUS
M 51	TRAIN/STATION
M	METRO/STATION
	GVB INFO/TICKET
	TOURIST INFORMATION

© STUDIO OLYKAN 2000